Archaeology in Practice

**Edited by Jane Balme
and Alistair Paterson**

Archaeology
in Practice

A Student Guide to
Archaeological Analyses

Blackwell
Publishing

BLACKWELL PUBLISHING
350 Main Street, Malden, MA 02148-5020, USA
9600 Garsington Road, Oxford OX4 2DQ, UK
550 Swanston Street, Carlton, Victoria 3053, Australia

First published 2006 by Blackwell Publishing Ltd

1   2006

Library of Congress Cataloging-in-Publication Data

Archaeology in practice : a student guide to archaeological analyses / edited by Jane Balme
and Alistair Paterson.
   p. cm.
   Includes bibliographical references and index.
   ISBN-13: 978-0-631-23573-6 (hardback : alk. paper)
   ISBN-10: 0-631-23573-6 (hardback : alk. paper)
   ISBN-13: 978-0-631-23574-3 (pbk.: alk. paper)
   ISBN-10: 0-631-23574-4 (pbk. : alk. paper)   1. Archaeology—Methodology.   2.
Archaeology—Laboratory manuals.   I. Balme, Jane.   II. Paterson, Alistair 1968–

   CC75.A657 2006
   930.1—dc22

2005006163

A catalog record for this title is available from the British Library.

Set in 11/13.5pt Dante
by Graphicraft Limited, Hong Kong
Printed and bound in India
by Replika Press, PVT Ltd, India

For further information on
Blackwell Publishing, visit our website:
www.blackwellpublishing.com

Contents

5 Absolute Dating

Simon Holdaway

7 Residues and Usewear

Richard Fullagar

10   Plant Remains   296
Wendy Beck

11 Mollusks and Other Shells   316
Sandra Bowdler

12 Sediments   338
Gary Huckleberry

15 Producing the Record   410

Peter White

Index   426

Chapter Abstracts

Chapter 1 This chapter provides an introduction to the many ways and means by which both submarine and terrestrial landscapes may be explored for archaeological sites, and how these can be further examined and mapped using nondestructive techniques. Attention is given to aerial and satellite remote imaging, but the main emphasis is on ground-based and submarine geophysical methods. These are areas of highly significant recent development and they hold considerable potential in the future of cultural resource management.

Chapter 2 Archaeology's stakeholders are many and diverse, but we must learn to consult with them. Many believe that they own the past of their ancestors; that it is not a public heritage. The chapter briefly examines the history of archaeological interaction with stakeholders and epistemological issues that may block successful consultation. Consultation problems involve informed consent, competing claims, and notions of cultural property. Successful consultation involves building partnerships out of mutual respect.

Chapter 3 Rock-art is an evocative form of material evidence for past peoples. Rock-art takes many different forms around the world. Two primary forms result from their production either as engraving or by the use of pigment. Rock-art can be classified according to technique, form, motif, and size. The recording technique will depend on the site context. Effective field recording will require technical skills and training. The appropriate analysis of rock-art will depend on the questions asked by researchers, and might include spatial distribution analysis, information exchange and stylistic analyses, questions of gender, statistical techniques, dating techniques, and examination of change over time and space.

Chapter 4 Stratigraphy is the study of stratification; that is, the interpretation of layers that form the deposits of a site over time. This study of stratification is of crucial importance for understanding what happened at an archaeological site – in particular, the order in which events occurred. There are four main principles, drawn from Earth science disciplines, upon which the interpretation of stratigraphy is based, but the human element in the accumulation of archaeological sites makes the application of these principles especially difficult. Discussion of change over time within and between sites is usually done by creating analytical units that are formed by combining material from stratigraphic units.

The varieties of methods that archaeologists use to obtain age estimates for the materials that they analyze are outlined under the term "chronometry." Most of the major techniques are discussed, with a particular emphasis on radiocarbon. The chapter then reviews the range of assumptions involved in taking the resulting age estimates and developing these into archaeological chronologies. Case studies emphasize the need for archaeologists to relate the temporal scales at which deposits may be resolved to the nature of the inferences about past behavior that they subsequently draw.

Chapter 5

This chapter discusses a range of methodological issues and analytical techniques that offer modern alternatives to traditional typology of stone artifacts. This approach emphasizes the identification and description of variation and time-ordering in manufacturing activities and their effects on artifact form, selection for further modification, and discard. A range of issues are also discussed, including research design, classification, data management, sample size effects, statistics, fragmentation, sourcing, and other topics of relevance to current and prospective stone analysts.

Chapter 6

Usewear and residues can provide reliable indicators of how stone, bone, ceramic, and other artifacts were used in the past. In this chapter, procedures and methods are described for undertaking functional analysis, including introductory experiments and microscope equipment. The identification of organic residues requires knowledge of typical plant and animal structures, properties, and composition. Stone tools provide an example for discussing the main forms of usewear (scarring, striations, polish, and edge rounding), and the wear patterns that are diagnostic of particular tasks, such as sawing bone, cutting wood, and scraping hides. There is a focus on recent archaeological applications and methodological problems.

Chapter 7

After describing the geology and chemistry of clays and technology of ceramic production, suggestions are provided for excavating, cleaning, marking, and

Chapter 8

handling of ceramics, followed by discussion of sampling and quantitative analysis. Initiating an analytical program requires appropriate laboratory methods matched carefully with areas of ceramics research (technology studies, usewear studies, dating, identification of potters, and provenance studies). Also included are suggestions for further study, a table of analytical methods, and a ceramics examination report.

Chapter 9 The chapter stresses the importance of project planning and recovery procedures of animal bones. Consistency in sieving and sampling and full documentation of all on-site procedures are essential to ensure data quality. Recording protocols balance the need for an archive and the research aims of the project. We discuss the categories of data that form the majority of any zooarchaeological record, and exemplify the link between recording and analysis by reviewing bone quantification.

Chapter 10 Plant remains survive at archaeological sites more often than might be expected. This chapter briefly reviews the major areas of current research into macroscopic plant remains in archaeology. The first of these areas is the question of what plant remains can contribute to archaeology as a whole; the second is the problems associated with the identification and origin of plant remains; and the third is the available methods that can be effectively used to retrieve and analyze plant remains.

Chapter 11 This chapter describes the processes involved in analyzing a shell midden site, which is defined as an archaeological deposit that contains 50 percent or more by weight of shellfish remains, or one in which the principal visible constituent is shell. Problems in the identification of such sites are discussed, as are processes that may disturb them. Sampling issues are critical in midden analysis, and appropriate excavation techniques are canvassed. Some basic approaches to analyzing shell remains are described, and more complex techniques are mentioned.

Chapter 12 Although the focus in archaeology is on material culture, it is the sedimentary matrix containing the material culture that provides key contextual information such as chronology, site formation, and paleoenvironments essential for fully understanding human behavior. Some of the most common techniques used in laboratory sediment analysis are grain size, pH, organic matter, and phosphorous content. The selection of the particular analyses performed will depend on the nature of the samples, the research questions at hand, and, of course, cost. Granulometry was the main laboratory method used to understand the vulnerability of Hokokam canal systems in the American Southwest, while several techniques were used in combination to determine the age of Kennewick Man in Washington State, without recourse to destructive sampling of the skeleton.

Chapter 13

Basic principles used in cataloging artifacts common to historical archaeological sites are reviewed, together with some of the major categories of artifacts found at historical archaeological sites. These categories include domestic ceramics and glass, building materials, and, more briefly, clay tobacco pipes, beads and buttons, glass tools, firearms, and metal containers. Methods used by historical archaeologists for quantifying and analyzing artifact information are discussed, with specific reference to minimum vessel counts and mean dates, and a guide to the most important literature on historic artifacts is provided.

Chapter 14

A review of historical sources includes general guidelines for research preparation, selecting materials, and judging source credibility. A case study illustrates the use of documents at Braudel's three broad scales of history: long-term history, social time, and individual time. Relationships between documents and archaeological evidence are described as (i) identification, (ii) complement, (iii) hypothesis formation and testing, (iv) contradiction, (v) confronting myths, and (vi) creating context. An appeal is made for archaeological contributions to history.

Chapter 15

The starting points of writing are knowing what you want to say and who your audience is. Writing in the science structure – aims, background, methods, results, and conclusions – is suitable for most presentations, especially if you remember KISS (Keep It Simple, Stupid). All writing benefits from being read and critiqued by your friends and colleagues; writing well requires constant practice. When writing for publication, follow the instructions meticulously, use only clear and relevant illustrations, and get your references right.

Preface and Acknowledgments

This volume is intended for archaeology students who are learning how to analyze archaeological materials. For many years, we have been involved in teaching university courses in field and laboratory techniques in archaeology. Over a cup of coffee during one of these courses, we were bemoaning the fact that, although there are many books on field methods (especially excavation techniques), much less is available on archaeological analysis techniques beyond the introductory first-year archaeology level. What we wanted was a series of essays that showed students how different kinds of archaeological materials are used to answer research questions. In our experience, students are more likely to understand this link when they learn from archaeologists who are talking about their own research problems and how they solved them. It brings a sense of immediacy to the work that makes it much more fun for them to read. Thus, to remedy the problem of the lack of such materials for students to read, we decided to assemble a collection of essays by experts on archaeological analysis.

There is such a variety of archaeological evidence, and so many differences across time and space, that we could not possibly cover all material types in all places and all time periods. To make the book manageable, we have restricted ourselves to those topics that are usually covered in general university courses on archaeological analysis. To identify which topics to include, with the help of Blackwell Publishing, we sent out a questionnaire to university teachers of field and laboratory methods mainly in North America, the United Kingdom, and the Australia Pacific region, asking them which topics they would want included in a text for higher undergraduate/lower graduate students. The final selection of chapters for this book is a result of the respondents' feedback, for which we were very grateful.

Not surprisingly, given our original reasons for beginning this book, most of the topics suggested by our reviewers are about post-excavation analysis. Thus the 15 chapters that comprise this volume concentrate on what archaeologists do with the archaeological evidence, rather than on how to obtain the archaeological evidence in the field. "Finding sites" (Chapter 1) and "Rock-art" (Chapter 3) are the main exceptions to this. They have been included because, although neither the sites nor the art are brought back from the field for analysis, the records of both are. We were also keen to have a chapter on the ethical context of doing archaeology (Chapter 2, "Consulting stakeholders"), so that students are constantly aware of this important issue in all the work that they do. Most of the remaining chapters deal with particular types of evidence available to archaeologists. The final chapter on writing up the results is the important conclusion to any analysis in archaeology, and its usefulness to students will be self-evident.

When we originally imagined this book we thought that each chapter would include student exercises, but it seems from our respondents that teachers like to do their courses their own way. What they wanted instead was a series of essays that drew together the main areas of the subject matter and directed students to related further reading.

All of the authors who have contributed to this book are leading experts in their subject areas. Because the book is intended as a textbook, for the most part we selected contributors who have experience in teaching at university level. As a guide to the content of each chapter, we asked authors to think about what they would like their students to know about their particular topic in a university course on laboratory methods in archaeology. The remaining part of their brief was to make sure that they explained the main techniques of analysis, and used examples from their own work to demonstrate how some of those techniques are applied.

The resulting book of essays does not pretend to cover all aspects of all possible forms of analysis of the archaeological evidence discussed. To do so would have resulted in a book of insufficient depth for our target audience. We therefore had to make some decisions about what could and could not be included within each topic. Thus, for example, Chapter 6 is restricted to stone artifacts in prehistory, as this technology provides the major evidence for most of the human past and is an important aspect of most university courses. Rather than trying to include something on every historical period, we included a chapter on artifacts of the modern world (Chapter 13), as this topic was nominated by our respondents.

We have not attempted to provide case studies from every corner of the globe. As we have said above, our overall objective was to demonstrate the link between research question, analysis, and conclusion rather than produce a book on world archaeology. By and large, the methods by which archaeologists achieve their aims are global. To show the diverse applications of techniques, each chapter provides additional references to other work on the particular archaeological evidence that has been discussed. We expect that the book will be relevant to many archaeology students across the globe and that it will provide insight into the breadth of modern archaeology.

We would like to thank all of the people who have helped to bring this book to fruition. The contributors produced to schedule and responded promptly to our ongoing requests. We would also like to give thanks to the

Blackwell editors who guided us through, and especially to the many anonymous reviewers who responded to the Blackwell questionnaire and provided much advice on the content. We think that the final book has benefited from this advice. Each chapter can be read by students before a laboratory class, so that they know the context of the work that they are about to do in the laboratory. For students who are at the stage at which they are thinking about designing their own projects, the chapters in this book will be a guide to the possibilities from their evidence and the problems of which they need to be aware.

Jane Balme and Alistair Paterson

Notes on Contributors

Jane Balme is a Senior Lecturer in archaeology at the University of Western Australia. She has been teaching undergraduate and graduate students in Australian universities for 15 years. Areas of research and publication include the archaeology of hunter–gatherer societies (especially subsistence) and Australian Indigenous archaeology.

James Barrett teaches zooarchaeology and medieval archaeology at the University of York, UK. His interests include maritime economies and the historical ecology of peripheries – topics that converge in his present work on Viking Age and medieval Scotland.

Wendy Beck is an Associate Professor in Archaeology at the University of New England in New South Wales. Her recent research and teaching interests include hunter–gatherer subsistence, especially plant food resources, and Indigenous archaeology. Her publications include articles in *Economic Botany, Journal of Archaeological Science*, and *Australian Aboriginal Studies* and she co-edited the book *Plants in Australian Archaeology*.

Sandra Bowdler is Professor of Archaeology at the University of Western Australia. She has long been interested in coastal archaeology and hence midden analysis, having published an earlier paper of which this is a revised version ("Sieving seashells: midden analysis in Australian archaeology," in G. E. Connah (ed.), *Australian Archaeology: A Guide to Field Techniques*, 1983). She is also the author of *Hunter Hill, Hunter Island*, which describes her research in Tasmania, and numerous articles on her research at Shark Bay in Western Australia.

Chris Clarkson is a postdoctoral fellow in the School of Social Science, University of Queensland. He undertook doctoral research at the Australian National University on lithic technology and land use in northern Australia. Chris then took up a postdoctoral fellowship at the University of Cambridge, investigating modern human dispersals, and is continuing research into early human lithic technologies. Chris has co-edited a forthcoming book, *Rocking the Boat: New Approaches to Stone Artefact Reduction, Use and Classification in Australia*.

Andrew David is Head of Archaeological Science at English Heritage, UK. He has been responsible for geophysical survey for English Heritage for many years, and has particular interests in early prehistory and geophysical applications on British prehistoric sites.

Linda Ellis is Professor and Director of the Museum Studies Program at San Francisco State University. Her books include *Archaeological Method and Theory: An Encyclopedia*. Areas of research and publication include laboratory methods, museum professional practices, and archaeology of Eastern Europe. She conducts ongoing archaeological excavations and surveying in Romania.

Richard Fullagar is an Honorary Research Associate in Archaeology at the University of Sydney. With colleagues, he has recently published papers in *Science*, the *Journal of Human Evolution*, and *Antiquity* on early utilization of starchy plants from Africa, Papua New Guinea, and Australia. Current interests include initial colonization of Australia, megafaunal extinctions, and the history of plant food processing.

Simon Holdaway is an Associate Professor in the Department of Anthropology, University of Auckland. His research interests include the arid zone archaeology of Australia and he specializes in stone artifact analysis.

Gary Huckleberry is an Adjunct Associate Professor of Anthropology at Washington State University. His specialties are geoarchaeology and geomorphology, and he has published in several journals, including *American Antiquity*, the *Journal of Field Archaeology*, *Geology*, and *Quaternary Research*.

Susan Lawrence has taught historical archaeology since 1992, and has excavated a range of domestic and industrial sites in southeastern Australia. Her recent publications include *Dolly's Creek: Archaeology and History of a Victorian Goldfields Community* and *Archaeologies of the British*.

Barbara Little is an archeologist with the US National Park Service's National Center for Cultural Resources Archeology program in Washington, DC. She is the editor of *Heritage of Value, Archaeology of Renown: Reshaping Archaeological Assessment and Significance*, *Public Benefits of Archaeology*, and *Text-Aided Archaeology* and is co-author of *Assessing Site Significance: A Guide for Archaeologists and Historians*.

Jo McDonald is the managing director of an archaeological consulting company. She conducted her doctoral research on rock-art in the Sydney region and has written rock-art conservation plans and heritage management studies for the art of that region. She co-edited an Aura occasional publication on regional rock-art studies in Australia and Melanesia, and is published in *The Archaeology of Rock-Art* (C. Chippindale and P. Taçon, eds.), *Rock Art Research*, *Archaeology in Oceania*, and *Australian Archaeology*.

Sue O'Connor is a Senior Fellow in archaeology in the Research School of Pacific and Asian Studies, Australian National University. Her research interests in Australia and Island South East Asia are reflected in her publications and books *East of Wallace's Line: Studies of Past and Present Maritime Cultures of the Indo-Pacific Region* (with P. Veth) and *30,000 Years of Aboriginal Occupation, Kimberley, North West Australia.*

Terry O'Connor is Professor of Archaeological Science at the University of York, UK. His books include *The Archaeology of Animal Bones, Environmental Archaeology: Principles and Methods* (with J. G. Evans), and volumes in the Archaeology of York series.

Alistair Paterson is an archaeology lecturer at the University of Western Australia. He researches the archaeology of colonial Australia and culture contact. He has taught archaeological field and laboratory schools since 1999. He has published in *Australian Archaeology, Archaeology in Oceania,* and *Historical Archaeology,* and has contributed to the *Encyclopedia of Historical Archaeology* (C. E. Orser, ed.; Routledge, 2002).

Peter White is Reader in Archaeology at the University of Sydney. His books include *The Past is Human* and *A Prehistory of Australia, New Guinea and Sahul.* He has edited refereed journals such as *Archaeology in Oceania* all his professional life.

Larry J. Zimmerman is Professor of Anthropology and Museum Studies and Public Scholar of Native American Representation at Indiana University–Purdue University Indianapolis and the Eiteljorg Museum. He has served as Head of the Archaeology Department for the Minnesota Historical Society, Chair of American Indian and Native Studies at the University of Iowa, and Distinguished Regents Professor of Anthropology at the University of South Dakota. His research emphases include the Great Plains of the United States and Indigenous relationships with archaeology.

Andrew David

1
Finding Sites

Introduction

There are many ways in which the physical traces of past societies are made apparent and become a part of archaeological analysis. Of course, a multitude of structural remains obtrude themselves unmistakably above ground, where they are obvious for all to see and to study. Here, we will mainly concern ourselves with those remains that are concealed below ground or water level, or are only partially comprehensible at the surface. The discovery and analysis of such remains, either as sites or as part of the cultural fabric of the wider landscape, is fundamental to archaeology.

Early in the history of archaeology attention was drawn, naturally enough, to the highly visible remains of former societies and civilizations, for instance in the Mediterranean and East Asia and, later, in the Americas. Literary sources such as the Bible and the Homeric sagas encouraged the search for particular sites, and much else was revealed by simple exploration, observation, and – especially – by chance. The deliberate and systematic exploration of land-scapes for signs of past human activity as a discipline in its own right came of age following the realization, early in the twentieth century, that vertical and oblique aerial photographs could reveal an astonishing wealth of information about monuments and their settings. Most importantly, aerial exploration was seen to be able to identify new sites that were invisible or incomprehensible at the ground surface. This literal overview from the air allowed both the recognition of new sites and their interpretation within the wider physical and cultural landscape. At the time, the airborne camera was declared to be "as valuable to archaeology as that of the telescope has proved to astronomy" (Crawford 1923: 358).

Archaeological Prospection

This is the term that has lately been adopted to encompass all those methods by which past human activity can be located and characterized. Typically, these are presumed to include the nondestructive techniques of remote sensing, from the air, using optical and multispectral sensors, from the ground surface, or below the water, using geophysical techniques. Chemical and geochemical surveys are also included, as are the slightly more intrusive uses of coring, augering, or probing. Not least, of course, are the more traditional methods of surface observation and the mapping of artifact scatters and topographic variation. Nowadays, all of these methods can and do generate digital data that can be geo-referenced and hence presented, integrated, and analyzed through the medium of Geographic Information Systems (GIS). Such systems can themselves contribute to site location by helping to identify the factors that seem to influence recurrent patterns of behavior and then modeling or predicting the presence of sites unseen (Kvamme 1999).

Remote Sensing   In its broadest sense, remote sensing is defined as the imaging of phenomena from a distance (Shennan & Donoghue 1992). It thus includes photography and imaging from kites, aircraft, and satellites, and contrasts with ground-based or underwater remote sensing, which takes place at or below the Earth's surface.

Aerial photography   There are several ways in which archaeological features are made visible by aerial photography (Wilson 2000). Most familiar are crop marks, which – as Figure 1.1 shows – may be positive or negative. Positive marks occur in dry conditions, when the moisture and fertility of the soil in a buried ditch or pit (comprising an underlying archaeological feature) allows the crop above it to grow more vigorously than the surrounding crop, reproducing the plan of the feature as a pattern of differential crop growth. This growth results in a color difference, with the stronger crop, which is usually visible as a greener mark, surrounded by yellow, ripening crops. Negative marks occur when the

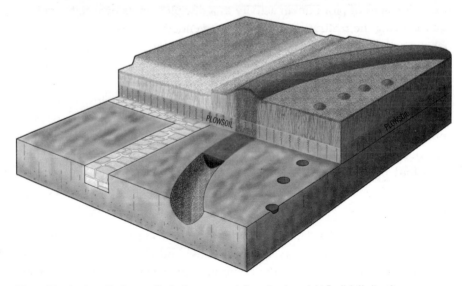

Figure 1.1   A schematic diagram illustrating crop mark formation (copyright English Heritage).

ANDREW DAVID

Figure 1.2 An aerial photograph showing crop marks that reveal traces of settlements, field systems, and burials, dating from the Neolithic to Iron Age: Foxley Farm, Eynsham, Oxfordshire, UK (copyright English Heritage).

underlying feature (a buried wall, for instance) restricts the crop growth, and thus the crops ripen sooner (as they have less water) and a yellow mark is visible in a green field. One of the main factors affecting the development of crop marks is therefore the moisture distribution in the soil. In turn, this is a function of the contrasting physical properties of the archaeological features and their surroundings. The generation and clarity of crop marks are thus influenced primarily by soil conditions and season, as well as the depth of the features (within the rooting zone of the crop), the nature of the overlying crop itself, its stage of growth, and the time and lighting conditions when photographs are taken. When all these conditions are favorable, the outcome is often dramatic, with the definition of remarkable detail (Figure 1.2). Crop marks are most commonly seen in cereal crops, but root and fodder crops are also susceptible, and marks have also been recorded in a diversity of other vegetation types, such as vines, sisal, lavender, maize, tea plantations, and paddy fields.

Aside from differential crop growth, the bare soil is itself capable of revealing significant variations that can resolve into archaeological patterning when viewed from aloft. For this to be the case, however, the soil usually has to be exposed by cultivation, and this means that the plow is already biting into the archaeological features and deposits. Some soils and substrates are more suited than others to the development of the color and tonal contrasts upon which recognition depends. In chalky areas, for instance, the red and brown marks of archaeological soils contrast clearly with the paler shades of up-cast chalk, and in such areas the traces of ancient field systems and plowed-down burial mounds are very distinctive. As in all aerial photography, weather conditions and timing are critical, as many types of mark are fleeting and ephemeral and may only be seen when a certain combination of conditions momentarily prevails. For example, the differential melting of a light frost in the early morning can briefly reveal and accentuate subtle patterning of a former garden (Keevil & Linford 1998).

Aerial images can also capture the patterns of archaeological sites that still survive as topographic features, but where the earthworks or structures are either too complex or too weakly defined to be easily comprehended at ground level. From the aerial perspective, seemingly jumbled earthworks can resolve themselves into a coherent plan; for instance, of a deserted village or town. The success of such viewing usually depends upon the favorable direction and angle of sunlight. Low-raking light casts shadows that can reveal even the most delicate variations in topography. Such details can also be picked out by variations in snowfall, waterlogging, or flooding. Differences in the health of vegetation can sometimes be accentuated when photographed with film that is sensitive to the near-infrared part of the spectrum (viewed either in monochrome or as "false color"), but black-and-white or color panchromatic film is usually preferred.

Once it is accepted that such a wealth of otherwise obscure detail can be made visible by aerial photography, there follows the need to interpret and analyze the resulting images – for instance, making necessary distinctions between genuine archaeological features and those that are natural or spurious. Stereoscopic interpretation of vertical photographic coverage allows landscape form to be better appreciated. However, most photographs are oblique views and these will require geometric correction, or rectification, before the archaeological features can be accurately mapped and correctly geo-referenced. Rectification is now easily achieved by computer and specifically dedicated programs are available (for instance, AirPhoto by Irwin Scollar (2002), and Aerial 5 by John Haigh (1998). Relevant websites are listed below, under "Resources."

Remote imaging   It is the reflection of visible light that allows images to be captured on aerial photographs taken from aircraft, as described, and now also from cameras orbiting the Earth on satellites. There are also reflections generated by electromagnetic radiation at wavelengths that are invisible to the naked eye (and to most film emulsions), and optical-electronic sensors mounted on either aircraft or satellites can digitally record these. Thermal energy emitted from the Earth's surface is also detectable. By contrast, active sensors operate by generating their own energy, which is transmitted to the ground; the signal that is received back is able to provide information on the form of the ground surface. RAdio Detection And Ranging (RADAR) and LIght Detection And Ranging (LIDAR) are good examples of active remote sensing systems. RADAR utilizes high-frequency (microwave) energy that has the advantage of being able to "see" through cloud and to operate during day or night. LIDAR operates as an airborne system in which a laser beam is scanned across the land surface to provide detailed topographic images. There is therefore a growing range of digital remote imaging techniques, all of which are capable of revealing, to varying degrees, archaeological information analogous and complementary to that obtained by conventional aerial photography. The growing sophistication and availability of these Earth observation and ground imaging techniques has been driven by military and other agendas, such as environmental monitoring, and archaeological discoveries have been almost incidental curiosities. Until quite recently, the imagery was expensive, difficult to obtain, and of poor spatial resolution for archaeological needs. Now, however, all this is changing and high-quality data are starting to become more accessible. Whilst conventional air photography as described above remains the preeminent means of reconnaissance, greater attention is being paid to these other forms of airborne remote sensing as their resolution and availability rapidly increase.

Mapping of the Earth's surface from space started in 1960, with the American CORONA spy satellite images. These were panoramic images, many of which have stereoscopic coverage, with ground resolutions of 2–9 m, depending on the camera system and orbit path of the satellite. The CORONA archive from 1960 to 1972 and part of the follow-on Lanyard archive have been declassified and are now commercially available. Higher-resolution photographs (1.5–2.0 m) are also available from Russian (e.g., KVR-1000) declassified satellite data that are now commercially available, although coverage is partial and of variable quality (Donoghue 2001; Fowler 2002). **High-altitude photography**

High-altitude panchromatic digital photography is a feature of the French SPOT5 (2.5 m), Indian IRS-1D (5 m), and American Landsat 7-ETM+ (15 m) satellites. More recently, civilian satellite sensors have offered resolutions that are better still (EROS-A, 1.8 m; IKONOS, 1.0 m; QuickBird, 0.61 m). Other high-resolution (military) systems are not normally available to the archaeological community. QuickBird data get close to 1:25,000 scale photography and has excellent radiometric resolution. While the best satellite photography is therefore now approaching that of conventional survey photography (mostly 0.3–0.5 m; Figure 1.3), its main advantage would seem to be in the overview

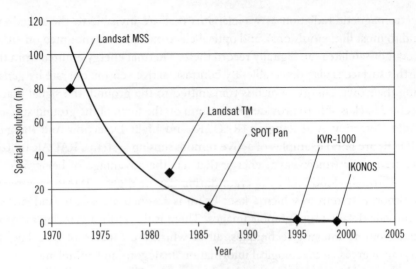

Figure 1.3 A diagram illustrating the rapid increase in ground resolution for commercially available digital satellite remote sensing imagery, 1972–2000 (courtesy of M. Fowler).

that it can provide, and for the assessment of areas of the world where base mapping or conventional aerial photographic coverage is limited, such as in the Middle East. An example of the latter application, using CORONA imagery, is the recognition of networks of Mesopotamian Early Bronze Age tracks in northeast Syria (Ur 2003). The reflective properties of large aggregations of artifact material, contrasting against those of their geological surroundings, probably account for the ability of CORONA imagery to be able to identify settlement remains (0.5–1.5 ha in size) elsewhere in Syria (Philip et al. 2002).

Multispectral
imaging

Multispectral sensors detect electromagnetic radiation in the visible, shortwave infrared, and middle infrared wavelengths (420–13,000 nanometers, or nm; 1 nm = 10^{-9} m). Sensors simultaneously record separate wavelength bands, and some of these have been shown to be especially responsive to vegetation growth, moisture, and temperature. Studies in England using an airborne scanner (Shennan & Donoghue 1992) have shown that crop marks are readily detectable in the near-infrared (760–900 nm) and that soil marks are well-defined at the wavelength range of red light (630–690 nm), with some features detectable in the thermal infrared band (8,000–12,000 nm). The near and shortwave infrared bands seem to be particularly sensitive to the effects of plant stress that are not normally visible to the naked eye (Powlesland et al. 1997; Donoghue 2001).

Whilst astronauts were able to see the Great Wall of China and the Great Pyramids during Earth orbital missions, it was not until the Landsat satellite program was established in 1972 that the Earth's surface was explored with a Thematic Mapper (TM) sensor in more detail, down to a ground resolution of 30 m. At this scale, it is possible to detect major features such as routes, canals,

ANDREW DAVID

and the distribution of archaeologically significant sediment bodies such as peats (Cox 1992). Sensors on current satellite platforms have a ground resolution typically of the order of 4 m, although a resolution of 2.44 m is claimed for the QuickBird satellite launched in October 2001. Clearly, there are limitations to the recognition of archaeological features below this size and so such imagery seems unlikely to supersede photography, but it has great potential for examining poorly mapped and relatively inaccessible areas of jungle and desert.

Multispectral sensors mounted on aircraft have resolutions down to 2 m, or less, still well below that of optical aerial photography, but nevertheless are now capable of imaging a wider range of features, at least some of which are not otherwise apparent (Powlesland et al. 1997). An example of an airborne imaging system is CASI (Compact Airborne Spectrographic Imager), which is in use by the English Environment Agency for the monitoring, classification, and assessment of natural and man-made influences on the landscape. This hyperspectral system has a ground resolution down to 1 m and can collect data from as many as 288 spectral bands within the visible and near infrared regions of the spectrum (430–900 nm). The benefits that such systems can bring to archaeological exploration have yet to be assessed in detail (Holden et al. 2002). It is at least certain that the massive coverage obtainable, together with the flexibility allowed by digital data processing (image processing and combination in GIS), provides a powerful complement to more conventional methods of exploration.

Thermal imaging

The differential melting of frost and snow on the bare ground surface, as captured in aerial photography, demonstrates that archaeological features exposed at the ground surface can have a different temperature to that of their surroundings. Whilst the growth of vegetation tends to even out such contrasts, it is possible that varying soil characteristics at depth can also be expressed at the surface (Donoghue 2001). As mentioned above, some temperature differences can be captured on film (near infrared panchromatic and false-color) but a wider range (visual – thermal infrared) can be recorded by multispectral sensors, mounted on aircraft. Thermal images can also be obtained by thermal infrared linescan (TIRLS). In both cases, there is good evidence to show that stressed vegetation reveals detectable thermal contrasts and that these can be related to buried archaeological features (Shell 2002). Perhaps the greatest potential for such imagery (which can reach ground resolutions down to about 3 cm) would appear to be an ability to detect features below vegetation such as pasture, where crop marks and soil marks are absent. This approach has so far seen limited application but may develop a wider role in such circumstances in future. In passing, it is worth noting that such thermal (and other remote sensing techniques) have applications in the study of the fabric of buildings (e.g., Brooke 1987). Sensitive thermal cameras, for instance, are capable of detecting temperature differences as small as 0.025°C (32°F), and can locate unseen features, such as plastered-over doorways, in building fabric.

Rather than passively measuring the reflections and emissions from the Earth's surface, radar actively generates its own energy and measures its reflection characteristics. Pulses of microwave radio energy are generated by an antenna and at the Earth's surface this energy is scattered, with some reflected back to the antenna. The characteristics of such echoes, and their backscatter, help to define the nature of the reflecting surface, and the return time of the pulses (at the speed of light) provides accurate information on the distance traveled.

In 1994 the Space Shuttle *Endeavour*, using Spaceborne Imaging Radar (SIR-C), helped (with multispectral data from Landsat and SPOT) to identify patterns that have subsequently been used to claim the discovery of the lost city of Ubar (El Baz 1997; Clapp 1999). The same mission also located and mapped an early course of the Great Wall of China, by detecting reflections from the badly degraded and partly concealed Sui Dynasty (CE 589–618) alignment in the sand dunes of the north-central China desert.

The SIR-C system is an example of Synthetic Aperture Radar (SAR). This represents a way of artificially synthesizing an extended antenna to increase resolution. SAR systems are also flown at lower altitudes on aircraft. In 1996, NASA's AIRSAR/TOPSAR system succeeded in imaging previously undocumented mounds and temples at Angkor, Cambodia. These features were shown most clearly by the radar interferometery technique, which combines two images to create a digital terrain model (DTM), allowing the topographic form of structures to be recognized. Airborne IFSAR methodology (Inteferometric Synthetic Aperture Radar) is now allowing large areas of the Earth's surface to be mapped in detail and at resolutions of increasing potential for archaeological purposes. For instance, seamless elevation data are now available for all of the United Kingdom to a vertical accuracy of 1.0 m or better (at about 5 m horizontal spacings). Similar coverage is in the process of being undertaken for the United States and elsewhere (www.intermap.com). Satellite-born SAR is set to achieve resolutions down to 3 m with the launch of the Canadian RADARSAT2, anticipated for late 2005.

Digital Terrain Models (or Digital Elevation Models, DEMs) of much higher resolution have for some years been achievable through the use of LIDAR devices mounted on aircraft (fixed wing and helicopter). Using dual-frequency GPS both on the aircraft and at a ground station, to provide accurate positional information, and onboard instrumentation to correct for aircraft movement, LIDAR data can be collected at rates of 30–40 km^2 per hour. Current systems can sample at horizontal resolutions of less than a meter (depending on flying height) with a vertical resolution of as little as ±5 cm. The principal applications are currently for environmental studies, but the archaeological potential is becoming better recognized (Holden et al. 2002). As for any DTM, the data can be manipulated – for instance, by vertical exaggeration and directional shading – to enhance subtle surface features. The topography can also be mounted as a layer in a GIS, allowing analytical comparison with other mapped data.

ANDREW DAVID

Once the archaeological background to an area has been assessed ("desktop" **Field Methods** survey), perhaps the most obvious means of finding new sites, or of further assessing a landscape, is by going out on foot and looking at the ground **Reconnaissance** surface. Strategies for doing this are very numerous, depending on individual **survey** project circumstances, and are often described generally as pedestrian survey, field-walking or walk-over survey, each involving walking over an area in order to observe, record, and map additional archaeological traces, structures, and landscape features.

One of the most persistent signatures in the landscape is scatters of artifacts or residues, which are visible on the ground surface where cultivation or erosion has exposed them. Systematic searching and the mapping of distributions of such material can identify foci of activity, which help to define settlement or industrial sites, as well as identifying the broader character of landscape usage. Lithic and ceramic artifacts, being relatively resistant to attrition, are amongst the commonest indicators of former activity in the landscape, and their recognition and mapping is a well-recognized means of site identification. The aims of surface artifact collection will vary widely, being dependent, for instance, on the scale of the area requiring study, its physical characteristics, and the particular prior knowledge available; very many permutations are possible (Wilkinson 2001). The total *intensive* coverage of an area is relatively unusual, and more often a sampling strategy is adopted that will allow a degree of reasonable assumption regarding the totality (Shennan 1997). Widely spaced reconnaissance transects may be walked across the landscape in *extensive* surveys or, more usually, a survey grid is established and a sample of this (random, systematic, or stratified random) examined in detail. Effort needs to be made to ensure that the many variables that can influence the recognition and recording of artifact scatters, such as the relative experience of fieldworkers and the degree of surface exposure, are minimized in order to eliminate biases. Within individual quadrats or transects, recovery may be total or sampled, and objects can either be collected and retained for later analysis or recorded *in situ*. Where the ground conditions are not suitable for artifact exposure (e.g., pasture), it may be necessary to employ a grid of test pits where soil is deliberately exposed and searched for artifacts (see below). In whatever case, a distribution map, or series of maps, is generated from which an archaeological interpretation can be made. Such surveys have, for instance, made major contributions to the recognition of early prehistoric societies prior to their ability to physically modify the landscape and create recognizable entities such as earthworks. Throughout most of the Pleistocene and into the Holocene, the most common evidence for a human presence has been the occurrence of lithic material (Chapter 6), often recognized for the first time during field survey of the ground surface.

With the adoption of settled lifestyles, agriculture, and an increasingly elabor- **Earthwork survey** ate and intensive use of the landscape, less reliance need be placed on artifact scatters alone, once the land is itself subjected to a range of both deliberate and incidental modifications. Whilst, say, the earthworks of a Maori *pa*, an American Indian burial or temple mound, or the accumulated settlement levels of a tell, are obvious enough, field survey has a role not only in defining such visible remains in detail, but also in recognizing associated and more subtle upstanding traces in the landscape. Read as a palimpsest, the land has imprinted upon it a huge range of more or less obvious physical traces of past activities. Whilst these may be viewed and interpreted remotely, as described above, new evidence is also accumulated by direct observation, such as during a "walk-over" survey (the generalized observation and recording of a variety of tell-tale signs), and, in much greater detail, by earthwork survey. Methods of earthwork investigation (Bowden 1999) rely both on traditional techniques of land survey and increasingly on digital recording, linked to both GIS and GPS. Together, earthwork survey, surface artifact collection, aerial survey, documentary, and historical analysis are all methods of enquiry that are mutually supportive and compatible, each contributing to the wider understanding of the whole.

Intrusive and semi-intrusive methods

Amongst the many methods of field survey, it is worth emphasizing the less obvious opportunities offered by semi-intrusive activities such as engineering and drainage works, or ditch or dyke cleaning. Observations of the latter, for instance in areas of wetland drainage, can reveal sites or structures that are otherwise difficult to see from the surface.

Observations such as these, and of surface traces, can be supplemented by coring or augering (both terms being taken here to refer to the extraction of undisturbed columns of deposit, using manual or motor-driven devices). Coring can identify dense aggregations of artifacts, structures, and anthropogenic soil horizons. It can provide important geoarchaeological information on the stratigraphy, genesis, and chronology of sediments, all of which can have a bearing on the location and interpretation of sites (Canti & Meddens 1998). Transects of cores can establish basin morphology and the sedimentary sequence of infilled lakes or valley bottoms. Identification and analysis of charcoal particles, burnt soil, and environmental indicators such as microflora and -fauna, can all help to define the presence and (sometimes) the character of anthropogenic influences in the locality.

Whilst coring can provide information at depth, it nonetheless samples only a small portion of a deposit. Larger samples at shallower sites can be obtained by test-pitting (e.g., shovel test-pitting), where small pits (of varying sizes and shapes, up to about 4 m^2) are excavated in detail to identify archaeological features and artifacts. Test pits can be arranged systematically, for instance on a grid across a site or a landscape, or they can be specifically targeted at features identified, for example, by aerial photography or geophysical survey. In the latter sense they provide "ground truth," verifying the predictions of other sources of investigation.

More extensive intrusive reconnaissance can be achieved by the excavation of "trial" or "evaluation" trenches, opened usually by machine (e.g., backhoe trenching). Although more costly and time-consuming, as well as destructive, machining is the most effective means of obtaining indisputable and direct information about buried archaeological remains – although that information will of course be limited by the sampling strategy adopted. Trial trenching (and coring or test-pitting) may be the only suitable means of locating artifact scatters or structural remains in built-up or urban "brownfield" areas, or other areas with a deep overburden. For rural areas, a recent pilot study modeled the predictions of sampling strategies to the results of subsequent total excavation, suggesting that, to provide an adequate archaeological assessment (for planning and site development purposes), trial trenching needs to be at a minimum of 3 percent of the study area, although this would be insufficient for sites with dispersed remains (Hey & Lacey 2001).

Further supplements to field survey include the use of metal detection and geochemical survey. Metal detection is an electromagnetic method (see below), and is an activity often unfortunately associated with treasure hunting rather than with dedicated archaeological reconnaissance. However, metal detectors can be a highly valuable source of archaeological information, and the survey and recording of metallic finds can lead to the discovery of important sites. Metal detectors are sophisticated instruments that are capable of discriminating against nonprecious metals, and with a depth of penetration that varies according to several factors, especially the size of the target: objects the size of large coins are detectable to a depth of only about 30 cm. Finds made with metal detectors are therefore usually limited to artifacts in the topsoil, often introduced into this zone by plowing. Many of these may be casual losses, but others might, for instance, be the remains of grave goods from disturbed cemeteries, or votive objects from religious sites or shrines. Knowledge of the distribution of Anglo-Saxon sites in East Anglia, England, has been greatly expanded by the reporting of finds of distinctive associated metalwork. In the county of Norfolk, England, metal detection has led to the discovery of 40 new Anglo-Saxon cemeteries. Deliberate deposits of coins have led to the discovery of associated settlements, as was the case in 1998–9 in Somerset, when the largest hoard of Roman silver coins yet found in England was shown to have been hidden within the room of a previously undiscovered villa building (Abdy et al. 2001). Finds of coins provide new and unique information on the political geography and trading of little understood periods, as in the Iron Age of England. Finds of gold and silver can reveal high-status burials and religious sites. A gold cup recently found in Kent, England, and shown to have come from a previously unidentified barrow mound, is one of a rare group of European finds of sophisticated Bronze Age grave goods.

Metal detection

Before moving on to geophysical methods, it is worth drawing attention to geochemical survey, although its uses as a means of site location have so far been very limited (Heron 2001). The principle is that both geochemical and biochemical residues or effects of human activities may persist in the soil, and can be mapped and interpreted in a similar way to artifact distributions. It is even possible that chemical signatures in the soil may, in some circumstances, be the only traces of certain types or periods of activity (Aston et al. 1998). However, this is unusual and geochemical survey is generally used as a supplement to other methods of site investigation.

The element most commonly believed to reflect the presence of former human activity is phosphorus, added to the soil through the decay of bodily tissue and excreta, waste, and ashes (Bethell & Máté 1989). Samples are taken from appropriate soils, from profiles, specific features, or on grids or transects across the area or horizon of investigation. Subsequent laboratory analysis determines the relative concentrations of inorganic, organic, or total phosphate, but there is little standardization of field or laboratory practice, and as yet only a poor understanding of the many variables that may affect the retention of phosphate in soil (Crowther 1997). The presumption is that concentrations of phosphate might help to indicate the presence of manure, livestock penning, middens, habitation sites, and burials. Whilst some studies have supported this generality (e.g., Craddock et al. 1985; Aston et al. 1998; Bethell & Smith 1989), others suggest a complexity of factors leading to relative enrichment/depletion (e.g., Entwhistle et al. 2000). Multi-element geochemical surveys, which examine the concentrations of a range of elements, remain an area in which future work has yet to demonstrate any wide benefits to site location. A similar case, but perhaps with more potential, is the mapping and analysis of biomarkers in soil (Evershed et al. 1997; Bull et al. 1999). Lipid biomolecules in particular have been shown to persist in soils, and their identification has been used to identify manure and cesspit features.

Ground-Based Remote Sensing: Geophysical Methods

Geophysical methods of subsurface detection have been in use in archaeology for over half a century, but in the past decade or so have seen considerable expansion in sophistication and application. Whilst the principles of geophysical detection have been recognized for a long time, and these remain unchanged, there have been significant advances in archaeologically dedicated instrumentation, digital recording, data analysis, and presentation. Previously the preserve of relatively few practitioners based in university departments and government agencies, geophysical techniques are now recognized as major contributors to heritage conservation, or cultural resource management (CRM). Correctly applied and in favorable circumstances, nondestructive geophysical methods have the ability to locate and define archaeological features, from the detailed scale of an individual posthole or palisade trench to entire settlement landscapes. Such sites can be economically mapped, interpreted, and protected and, where necessary, designs for more detailed and targeted intrusive excavation drawn up. In addition to the texts cited below, see Kvamme (2001) and Gaffney and Gater (2003).

Earth resistance survey is by far the most common method for investigating Electrical methods the electrical properties of soils. It depends largely on the fact that dissolved salts in moisture within the pore spaces of soil will conduct electricity. The mobility of the dissolved salt ions is generally determined by the fraction of the soil's pore space that is occupied by water; hence the degree of electrical conductivity will be proportional to the prevalence of moisture at the point of measurement. By convention in earth resistance survey it is electrical resistivity, the inverse of electrical conductivity, that is measured (conductivity is simply the reciprocal of resistivity and vice versa). Variation in earth resistance across an area of ground will therefore reflect variations in soil moisture and these, in turn, often relate to textural contrasts that have archaeological significance. Certain types of sediment or archaeological feature are more moisture-retentive than other types and demonstrate a lower electrical resistance. The fine-textured sediments in buried ditches and some pits, for example, are often damper than their immediate surroundings and manifest as low-resistance anomalies. It is just such moisture traps that allow taller and more lush plant growth, giving rise to crop marks (see above). Conversely, large pore spaces in coarser sediments and structures (such as walls), or in nonporous materials, tend to retain less moisture and give rise to reduced plant growth (parch marks) and high-resistance anomalies.

Earth resistance survey was first used in an archaeological context in 1946, to detect the ditches and pits of flattened and buried prehistoric monuments threatened by gravel extraction at Dorchester, England (Clark 1996: 12). Then, as now, a system of four electrodes was used, one current (C) pair setting up a field of potential gradient in the ground, which is sampled by a potential (P) pair of electrodes. The use of two pairs of electrodes overcomes problems of contact resistance and an alternating current (AC) avoids polarization in the measurement (P) electrodes. The response to buried features varies according to the geometric arrangement of the current and potential electrodes, or the probe configuration. For archaeological detection, the most commonly used configuration is the twin probe (or twin electrode), in which one CP pair is separated widely from the other. This has the practical advantage that many measurements may be made over an area with a single (mobile) pair of (CP) probes mounted together on a frame supporting the electronics. The second (remote) CP pair remains fixed at a distance from the survey area. This is the arrangement favored by the widely used Geoscan Research RM equipment.

As in most ground-based geophysical surveys, a grid is set out over the area under investigation to serve as the basis for detailed measurements. The grid units will vary depending upon the methodology to be used, but a grid of

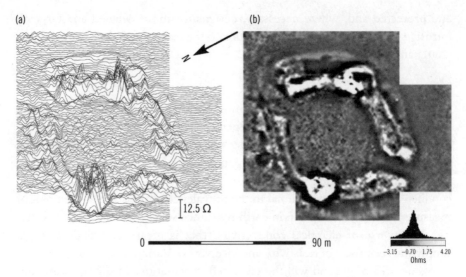

(a)   (b)

12.5 Ω

0 ▬▬▬▬▬▬▬▬▬▬ 90 m

−3.15 −0.70 1.75 4.20
Ohms

Figure 1.4 Earth resistance survey: images of data obtained over the site of a Roman amphitheater at Richborough, Kent, England: (a) a graphical trace plot; (b) a grayscale plot. Pale tones indicate high resistance, and show the outlines of the buried structure. Two entrances are visible – one at either end of the amphitheater – as well as a pair of additional opposed structures, which may be the foundations of towers and/or arched entrances (copyright English Heritage).

20 × 20 m or 30 × 30 m units is typical. Earth resistance measurements are then taken at regular intervals within each grid unit, building up a two-dimensional array of data in which patterns of anomalies can be recognized in computer generated plots or images (Figure 1.4).

The depth of detection of earth resistance surveys is primarily dependent upon the separation of the mobile electrodes. The wider this is, the greater is the penetration but also the greater is the volume of soil that is sampled – so definition, or resolution, declines significantly with depth. The choice of probe spacing is therefore a trade-off between the required feature definition and depth. In many instances, where the archaeological targets are within the topmost meter of the ground surface, a mobile probe spacing of 0.5 m is adequate and allows a compact arrangement for survey, with readings taken at 0.5 or 1.0 m intervals. The Geoscan system, with multiplexing, allows for multiple probe spacings, and programmable measurement sequences and configurations. For example, a survey can be conducted with three probes separated by 0.5 m on the mobile frame; this allows twin probe readings to be taken simultaneously at both 0.5 m spacing and at 1.0 m spacing, thereby creating both a shallower and a deeper data set for comparison and analysis. More elaborate arrangements are possible (see below and www. geoscan-research.co.uk). Very substantial features at greater depth would require wider probe separations, but detail is severely compromised.

The widening of electrode spacing to allow a greater depth of penetration can be used to generate electrical *pseudo-sections* of the ground, thereby providing approximate information on the vertical disposition and depth of

ANDREW DAVID

archaeological features (Griffiths & Barker 1994). At its simplest, termed *vertical electrical sounding*, measurements are made with a successively expanding electrode array over a single point, providing a single sequence of depth information at that point. The pseudo-section is built up from a sequence of such expanded measurements progressing along a survey transect across a site. Modern survey equipment allows many combinations of measurements to be taken using multiple arrays of electrodes along transects, and recent years have seen the increasing use of data inversion techniques to create true tomographic sections (Nöel 1992; Szymanski & Tsourlos 1993). Future advances should see the increasing use of such profiling methods linked to the computation of *depth slices*, in which the resulting data are used to create a series of two-dimensional images, or apparent horizontal "slices" through a site (see below). Such advances hold considerable promise, but for the time being it holds generally true that earth resistance sectioning is a method of detailed investigation rather than site reconnaissance (e.g., Kvamme 2003).

For some years, attempts have been made with varying success to deploy mobile electrode arrays to speed up data acquisition and the rate of ground coverage. Such arrays have not seen much use outside mainland Europe and commercial systems are not yet widely available (but see, e.g. www. iris-instruments.com). A recent encouraging development, though, has been the use of electrostatic electrodes that do not require ground contact to measure apparent resistivity; both electrostatic and ground-contacting electrodes can be towed in arrays that allow variable spacing and hence a capacity for providing depth information (Panissod et al. 1998). Electrostatic arrays are now commercially available and may make an increasing contribution to archaeological survey in the future.

Of the geophysical techniques available to archaeology, the greatest single contribution to site reconnaissance and characterization is probably made by the measurement of variations in soil magnetism, or magnetometry. The methods are relatively swift to apply, and a wide range of archaeological and natural features display recognizable magnetic enhancement, distinguishing them from their surrounding soil medium. Magnetic surveys now routinely cover areas of many hectares and coverage of several square kilometers mapping entire buried settlements and landscape can now be contemplated. As far as ground-based methods go, magnetometry provides the nearest approach to the scope and coverage of aerial photography, and the two sources of information can work together to considerable mutual advantage.

All soils possess a weak magnetic susceptibility. This means that when they are placed in a magnetic field (such as that of the Earth), certain of their constituent minerals become magnetized, thus locally increasing the ambient magnetic field. These magnetic minerals are inherited from the parent rock during pedogenesis and are usually more concentrated in the topsoil relative

Magnetic techniques

to the subsoil. Fortunately for archaeological detection, ordinary day-to-day human activities, associated with settlement and industry in particular, are capable of considerably enhancing the initial magnetic susceptibility of soils.

Anthropogenic magnetic enhancement is principally associated with burning and the resultant conversion of weakly magnetic oxides of iron such as hematite to the more magnetic form, magnetite (Tite & Mullins 1971; Clark 1996). The transition of other weakly magnetic minerals may also be equally important. Soils associated with settlement thus often contain a relative concentration of such enhanced material and it is usually the case (though not always) that these soils are consequently more magnetic than the underlying unaffected subsoil. Enhanced soils accumulate in features such as the pits and ditches that define so many archaeological sites and thereby generate a measurable local perturbation, or anomaly, in the Earth's magnetic field. Despite their enhancement, such anomalies are usually extremely weak, often within the range of 0.5–30 nT (nanotesla), a tiny fraction of the Earth's magnetic field (approximately 48,000 nT).

Apart from the acknowledged effects of burning, it is also apparent that there are pedological mechanisms of magnetic enhancement of soils (Weston 2002). One of these is the similar but much less intense "fermentation" effect of a periodic alternation between oxidizing (dry) and reducing (wet) conditions in soil, in which both soil bacteria and organic matter have a role (Weston 2002). A third and perhaps related factor is the relatively recent realization that certain species of soil bacteria, termed *magnetotactic* because they manufacture intracellular crystalline inclusions of magnetite or goethite, may be responsible for concentrating these magnetic particles in archaeological features. Magnetotactic bacteria have been identified in certain meadow soils, and the fills of ancient postholes can be enriched by concentrations of biogenic magnetite presumed to be the residue of the bacteria that once fed on the formerly decaying wood (Fassbinder et al. 1990; Fassbinder & Stanjek 1993).

As well as exhibiting magnetic susceptibility, certain types of magnetic minerals that occur naturally in soils and clays (such as titanomagnetites) are permanently magnetized, like a bar magnet, even in the absence of the Earth's field. However, within just a single crystal, several different regions (or magnetic domains) will be found, each magnetized in a different, randomly selected, direction. Thus, at a macroscopic level, the magnetic fields of all these microscopic randomly orientated bar magnets cancel each other out and the mineral appears not to be magnetized. Heating the mineral to a characteristic temperature known as the *Curie temperature*, typically in the range of 500–700°C (900–1,300°F), causes thermal energy to disrupt the crystal forces that maintain this magnetization and the domains become demagnetized. On cooling again, they re-magnetize and, preferentially, will all do so in the same direction: the prevailing direction of the Earth's magnetic field. The mineral thus acquires a permanent, measurable, thermoremanent magnetization that will persist even in the absence of the Earth's field. This process explains why, for instance, a fired brick or tile is magnetic with its own north and south poles, like a bar magnet. The same applies to intact fired structures such as kilns, furnaces, hearths, and corn-dryers, which can demonstrate magnetic fields of several hundreds of nanotesla (often in the range of 60–1,000 nT) in close proximity to the feature.

Magnetometers that are sensitive to the range of magnetic fields described above have been used in archaeological detection since the late 1950s (Clark 1996). Today, there are two main types in use: the fluxgate gradiometer and the alkali-vapor magnetometer. The former is typified by the Geoscan Research FM series, which is in use worldwide. Such instruments are usually made up of two fluxgate sensors separated vertically at either end of a rigid tube to which is attached an electronics box and carrying handle. Each sensor measures just the vertical component of the Earth's magnetic field: their exact mutual alignment, with the output of one subtracted from the other, is essential to reduce the effects of both instrument tilt and the diurnal variation of the Earth's magnetic field. Measuring the magnetic gradient, by subtracting the output of the upper sensor from that of the lower sensor, also has the effect of limiting detection to local magnetic features. The separation of the two sensors is set commonly at 0.5 m, but a 1.0 m separation is also in use, offering slightly improved sensitivity to anomalies at greater depth.

Alkali-vapor instruments operate on a different principle and measure the total Earth's field with much higher sensitivity. Some cesium-vapor type instruments, which are becoming widely used in archaeology, have a reported sensitivity of ± 10 pT (picotesla; 10 pT = 0.01 nT). The sensors may be arranged in vertical gradiometer configuration, as fluxgates are, or may be used separately to measure just the total field. In both cases, there has been a preference for mounting two or more sensors together on a wheeled frame, allowing an increased speed of ground coverage. Fluxgate detectors can also be mounted on carrying frames, allowing two or more pairs of sensors to be used together.

Detailed magnetometer surveys are conducted on a predetermined site grid. The instrument, carried singly or wheeled as a horizontal array of sensors, is moved across the grid, with the data being logged simultaneously for later downloading and processing. The sampling interval can be varied according to necessity, but for handheld instruments is usually at least 1.0×0.5 m, and two surveyors can cover about 2 ha per day. This rate can be improved if multiple sensors are used (such as in the Bartington Grad601 or Geoscan FM256 dual gradiometer systems), and wheeled arrays can cover the ground at a rate of up to 5 ha per day at a sampling interval of 0.5×0.125 m. The resulting data plots are usually in the form of graduated grayscale or color images in which patterns of anomalies can be visualized and interpreted.

As stated above, magnetically responsive features include pits, ditches, and structures such as kilns, hearths, and furnaces. In addition, at responsive sites, gullies, pit dwellings, and palisade trenches can be detected. Sensitive and detailed surveys can locate individual large postholes and, on occasion, graves.

Sites of industrial production can be highly magnetic owing to the quantities of thermoremanently magnetized material. Magnetic surveys can also detect structural remains associated with buildings: burnt foundations, or in-filled foundation trenches, may be magnetic or, conversely, the surviving structural material may be relatively nonmagnetic, giving rise to recognizable patterns of depleted magnetic strength contrasted against a surrounding more strongly magnetized medium. However, where there are no such patterns of contrasts, the presence of buildings may only be signaled by a generalized increase in magnetic activity, or "noise." This is created by responses to concentrations of bricks, tile, daub, or industrial debris, and may be used to infer the presence of associated structural remains. It is in these sorts of circumstances that it may well be desirable to turn to earth resistance survey as a complementary method with a generally better reputation for the discrimination of building foundations (Figure 1.5).

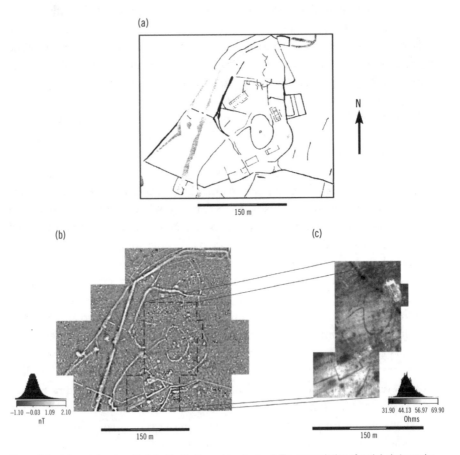

Figure 1.5 Integrated survey: Grateley South, Hampshire, England. The transcription of aerial photography (a) has revealed a variety of enclosures, ditches, and even the foundations of buildings. The magnetometer survey (b) has added considerable detail, especially related to the distribution of evidence for occupation (pits). Earth resistance survey (c) confirms and amplifies the evidence for building foundations and their relative state of preservation. Excavation has subsequently taken place on the basis of these findings.

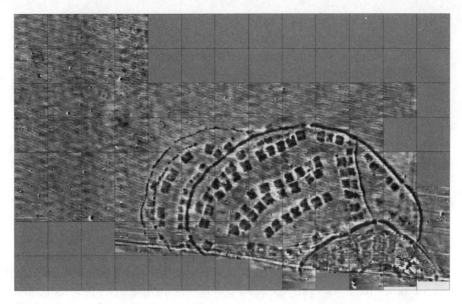

Figure 1.6 Magnetometer survey: an image of a Scythian settlement near Cicah, Siberia. Darker tones represent positive magnetic responses, and these reveal many newly discovered rectangular pits, which are the foundations of former buildings contained within ditched enclosures. Two burial sites (ring ditches with central grave pits) are visible near the limit of the survey (courtesy of J. Fassbinder and H. Becker, Bavarian State Department of Historic Monuments).

There are countless examples of the power of magnetic detection, illustrative both of the variety of features that can be detected as well as the increasing sensitivity and scale of coverage of such surveys. Many are figured in the proceedings of Archaeological Prospection conferences (Fassbinder & Irlinger 1999; Doneus et al. 2001b; Herbich 2003). Figure 1.6 illustrates the results of a cesium magnetometer survey over the site of a Scythian settlement (eighth to seventh centuries BCE) near Cicah, Siberia (Becker & Fassbinder 1999). During three days of fieldwork over 8 ha, a fortified settlement containing over one hundred sunken-featured buildings has been mapped, and seen to be divided into several phases by ditches and palisades, with gates or entrances in places; two burials with encircling ditches are apparent beyond the limits of the settlement. The better-defined magnetic anomalies are in plowed land, and represent features cut into underlying loess and infilled with magnetically enhanced topsoil (chernozem). These results illustrate the ability of such surveys both to identify wholly new components of sites and in this case to focus attention on the formerly neglected significance of fixed settlement within the otherwise nomadic existence of the Scythian peoples (Becker & Fassbinder 1999).

Despite their enormous potential, magnetometer surveys are disadvantaged by their extreme sensitivity to ferrous metals. Modern pipelines, other services, and ferrous litter in the soil can create anomalies that obliterate the more subtle responses to archaeological features. Fences, pylons, buildings, and vehicles are other examples of sources of unwanted interference, and surveys in built-up areas are therefore only very rarely to be recommended. Occasionally, ferrous responses can be identified as being of archaeological significance; for instance, if they indicate the presence of iron grave goods at burial sites.

The value and potential of magnetometry is also heavily dependent on the type of the local soil and geology. Most sedimentary and metamorphic solid geologies and their associated soils are suitable for survey and, for instance, soils over limestone often have high magnetic susceptibilities. More caution is necessary over igneous and drift geologies, as some igneous rocks (e.g., basalts) have very strong thermoremanence, which overwhelms all weaker responses, a problem that extends to secondary deposits that contain such material. Glacially derived sediments can be highly heterogeneous, whilst alluvial and colluvial deposits can bury features too deeply for detection – a significant problem for valleys, where archaeological activity can be intense but still difficult to detect. Deposits such as peats, sands, and other alluvia can be relatively nonmagnetic, blanketing and obscuring underlying features. Loess-derived soils, on the other hand, can provide ideal conditions for magnetic detection, and this has been a significant factor in the success of many surveys on the continental European mainland.

Topsoil magnetic susceptibility survey

Magnetometer survey can be highly responsive to specific archaeological features, delineating their spatial pattern very effectively. By contrast, measurements of topsoil magnetic susceptibility (MS), taken at regular intervals across a site or landscape, can reveal more generalized spatial fluctuations in magnetism that can often be used to provide clues about the presence of former settlement or industrial activity. This is possible because magnetically enhanced soils (see above) from buried archaeological features become exposed at or near the ground surface through agencies such as cultivation and bioturbation, and become detectable as areas of locally raised susceptibility values. Burnt soil, occupation soil (e.g., midden), comminuted ceramic material, or industrial debris (e.g., hammerscale) can all contribute to such increases. Specific features are rarely identifiable, but the areas of resulting high readings can be indicative of an underlying archaeological site deserving of more detailed investigation (especially by magnetometer survey). For this reason, topsoil magnetic susceptibility survey has sometimes been adopted as a means of reconnaissance and land-use interpretation (Clark 1996). Readings are made with a magnetic susceptibility meter (such as the Bartington MS series of instruments), either *in situ* (volume MS) or on samples removed from the site (mass-specific and volume MS). The sample interval will vary depending upon the objectives of the survey, but is usually quite broad – at 5 or 10 m, for example – allowing for rapid coverage. Slingram-type EM instruments (Scollar et al. 1990), which measure conductivity (utilizing the quadrature component of the received signal), also simultaneously measure the in-phase component, which responds to magnetic susceptibility. They thereby offer a valuable dual mode of

ANDREW DAVID

operation (e.g., Cole et al. 1995) – but, despite this, they have not been used much for MS surveys.

The results of magnetic susceptibility surveys have to be interpreted with caution, taking account of both natural (geological) effects as well as those of recent land use. Additionally, there are many types of site (e.g., burial sites, field systems) where magnetic enhancement will be absent or too slight to be discriminated from background values. Also, as magnetic susceptibility measurements (at least with Bartington-type instruments) will only relate to shallow depths (<10 cm), features or enhanced deposits below this level will not be detected (although MS sensors can be lowered down auger holes to obtain readings at depth).

This has already been encountered, above, in the references to conductivity measurement, metal detection, and magnetic susceptibility survey, all of which are EM methods, or rely on EM measurement. A further application of EM is in the use of ground-penetrating (or -probing) radar (GPR), which makes use of the fact that transmitted high-frequency electromagnetic energy is reflected back to a receiver by conducting objects. This was applied in the 1940s, when radar was first used to detect aircraft. In the 1960s, radio-echo sounding was used to probe polar ice, and its role in polar and glaciological studies has been much exploited ever since. A singular demonstration of the method in these conditions occurred in 1992, when a P-38 Lightning fighter plane, one of a squadron of six fighters and two B17 Flying Fortresses that ditched over Greenland in 1942, was pinpointed in the ice by radar, and recovered from a depth of 75 m (Hayes 1994). GPR now has very many areas of application in geology, engineering, environmental geophysics, and forensics. Its development and application in archaeology is explored in Bevan and Kenyon (1975), Vickers et al. (1976), Vaughan (1986), Conyers and Goodman (1997), Conyers (2004), and Nishimura (2001).

The principle of operation is similar to that of echo sounding (see below). A transmitter emits a pulse of microwave radio energy downward into the ground and a proportion of this is energy is reflected back from electrical interfaces in the ground to a receiver at the surface. The great potential of the technique relies on the fact that the average velocity of the outward and returning signals can be estimated and the two-way travel time therefore allows an estimate of depth to the reflection event, or target. Radar therefore offers the ability to map archaeological features both horizontally and vertically, in three dimensions. Initially, this potential was only realized by the construction of individual radar profiles, or *radargrams*, but these are difficult to interpret on their own. Recent advances, however, allow the simultaneous visualization of reflection amplitudes at the same two-way travel time from multiple profiles across a site, and it is this ability – referred to as "time-slicing" – that is revolutionizing the applications of GPR in archaeology today.

Electromagnetic (EM) detection: ground-penetrating radar

The physical factors that most affect the velocity of radio energy as it passes through the soil are the latter's electrical conductivity, its magnetic permeability, and its dielectric permittivity. The dielectric permittivity varies according to the composition, moisture content, bulk density, porosity, physical structure, and temperature of the soil, and the higher its value the slower is the velocity of the radar wave, reducing its penetration and reflection. High magnetic permeability and high conductivity also slow down EM wave propagation, and together these factors lead to the dissipation or attenuation of the signal. Energy transmission is most efficient through relatively dry and non-magnetic materials (e.g., dry sand) and is least efficient through wet conducting materials (e.g., wet clay), and there is no transmission through metal. The recognition of archaeologically significant features depends upon these being defined by sharply contrasting interfaces between their electrical and magnetic properties and those of their surroundings. Examples of such interfaces include soil/stone/brick and air (allowing voids such as caves, tunnels, chambers, and crypts to be detected), soil and stone (allowing the detection of structures such as walls and foundations), and soil and water (allowing detection of the water table). Archaeological sites are, of course, rarely composed of simple contrasts and are instead complex combinations of materials with differing properties, and of varying disposition, each of which will affect the passage of the signal differently. In many cases, therefore, the radar returns are highly complex and difficult to interpret.

Apart from the physical characteristics of the ground, the efficiency of the transmission of the radar wave, the depth to which it will penetrate, and the size of features that it will detect (its resolution) are also dependent on its frequency. Most GPR systems operate with a wide-bandwidth impulse around a center frequency in the range of 10–1,000 MHz (megahertz). As a general rule, the lower the frequency, the greater is the depth of penetration, but the associated increase in wavelength reduces resolution. Greater resolution can be achieved at higher frequencies but, conversely, penetration is shallower. Whilst low-frequency antennas (10–120 MHz) can penetrate up to 50 m in certain conditions, they are only capable of resolving large features. A 900 MHz antenna, on the other hand, has a maximum depth of penetration of only about a meter in typical soils, but can resolve features down to a few centimeters in size. In soils with high conductivity, energy loss through attenuation can limit penetration by signals of any wavelength to less than a meter. As was the case for electrical profiling (see above), there is therefore a trade-off between depth and resolution, and surveyors using GPR need to assess a number of factors before choosing a particular survey strategy or configuration. Most important will be the choice of the center frequency of the GPR antenna, and this will depend largely upon the dielectric permittivity of the ground and the size and expected depth of the archaeological targets.

The GPR antenna comprises the transmitter and receiver, either combined as a single device (*monostatic*) or separated (*bistatic*). Both types can be contained within a single box, or as two separate units, the size and arrangement being dependent on the frequency. High-frequency antennas are small and can be handheld and manipulated in small spaces, but size increases with lower frequencies and these need to be dragged across the ground or pulled by a vehicle. Other components of the system include the control unit, which generates the radar pulses, fiber-optic or copper coaxial cable, a battery, and a computer for setting parameters and displaying output.

To record a GPR profile, the antenna unit is pulled over the ground surface along a pre-surveyed transect line. As it goes it transmits pulses of energy into the ground, the returns from which are averaged and sampled at a preset time interval, allowing a horizontal sampling interval of a few centimeters. Transect spacing will depend upon the dimensions of the archaeological features that are being sought, but it is now usual to use an interval of 1 m or less where structural remains such as building foundations are anticipated. Successive narrowly spaced transects can then be used to build up a more detailed coverage. However, if the anticipated targets are larger and more extensive – as, for instance, in the case of buried topographic features such as paleochannels – then the transect spacing would be widened.

The antenna needs to be in close contact with the ground surface, both to prevent excessive reflections from the ground surface itself as well as "leakage" of the signal, which can introduce spurious reflections from nearby objects. The returning signals from within the ground are subject to a variety of factors, which need to be taken into account. One of these is the fact that the radar emits a cone-shaped beam that "illuminates" targets. The elliptical shape and size of the beam is influenced by the ground conditions, the direction of travel of the antenna, and its center frequency. Whilst reflections from a planar surface, such as a buried floor, are relatively uncomplicated, the undulations introduced by archaeological features result in multiple reflections that can confuse the true shape of the target. Also, as the radar pulse is cone-shaped, it "sees" a target before, during, and after the antenna travels over it, the result being that isolated or *point-source* targets are detected in the radargram as hyperbolas. Whilst this need not be problematic for large features, many point sources can create confusing noise or clutter. A further complication is that returning signals from increasing depths have decreasing strength, or amplitude, and may therefore be difficult to discriminate from shallower and higher-amplitude reflections. The application of *range gain* amplifies weaker returns to counteract this effect.

Other counteracting measures can be implemented by post-acquisition data processing. For instance, some types of background and instrument noise can be filtered out, whilst the distorting effects of the subsurface and point-source hyperbolas can be reduced by applying a suitable migration algorithm. At sites where there is significant topographic variation – for example, over a burial mound or other earthworks – it will be necessary to incorporate elevation data in order to correctly displace the radar data.

In order to take advantage of the ability of GPR to determine depth, it is essential to derive an estimate of the average signal velocity on site. There are several means of achieving this to varying levels of accuracy, the most reliable involving measurements to targets of known depth on site. If this is not possible, estimates can be achieved using the common midpoint (CMP) type of test (Conyers 2004). Whatever the accuracy of the determination, the resulting conversion of two-way travel time (in nanoseconds) to actual depth is an estimate only, and may require validation by direct observation or *ground-truthing* (e.g., trial pitting or coring).

It can therefore seem daunting to devise an optimum GPR strategy and interpret the results. However, a major advance has proved to be the use of amplitude time-slice presentation, which is a versatile means of maximizing the interpretative potential of such large and complex data sets (Goodman et al. 1995). Rather than attempting to interpret individual radar profiles, the time-slice method allows the data from multiple sets of successive profiles to be visualized together, allowing continuities of anomalous reflections to be recognized across a site. The profiles are first processed to maximize the display of significant reflections and then stacked together, interpolated if necessary, to create a three-dimensional volume of data; this can then be "sliced" horizontally by extracting the data from successive averaged "time windows" that allow two-dimensional viewing of different levels of the site. The data may need manipulation to compensate for the effects of topographic variation, and it is important to recollect that because of subsurface heterogeneities the radar velocities across a site will vary, so time-slices will always be an approximation of real depth. This aside, the ability to examine GPR data in a spatially extensive mode, as in the more familiar two-dimensional magnetic and earth resistance imagery, is very welcome. High- and low-amplitude anomalies that may be difficult to signify in single radar profiles can cohere into recognizable patterns that are easier to interpret as archaeological (or other) entities, and can also allow ready comparison with other geophysical imagery. A good demonstration of the method has been provided by GPR and magnetometer surveys over the site of Trajan's Villa, Italy, where extensive remains of ancillary structures, including a bathhouse, have been mapped (Piro et al. 2003). Figure 1.7 shows an example of time-slice data obtained over the site of a Roman building that has recently been discovered at Groundwell Ridge, Swindon, England. The building was first planned by earth resistance survey, but the use of GPR has significantly sharpened and added detail, as well as providing information on its changing structural integrity with depth.

The interpretation of GPR data can be further enhanced by viewing a rapid time-lapse sequence of time-slices using computer animation. This greatly helps the visualization of the disposition and preservation of subsurface structures as these change with depth. From this, it is only a small step to the virtual reconstruction of buried structures in three dimensions, as has been attempted, for example, at the Roman town of Carnuntum, Austria (Neubauer et al. 2002).

ANDREW DAVID

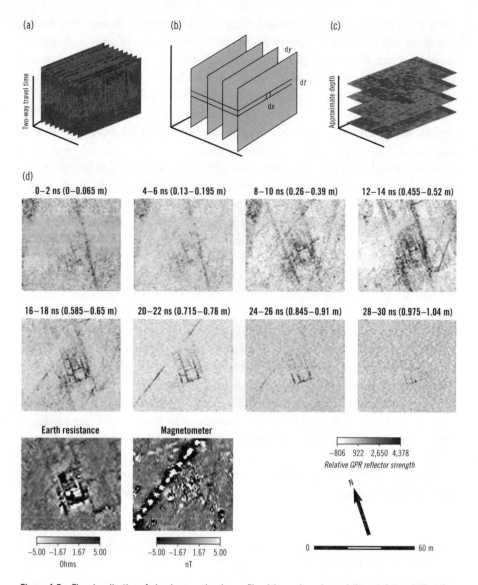

Figure 1.7 The visualization of closely spaced radar profiles (a) may be enhanced through interpolation of the average reflector strength into a series of individual cells (b) representing the entire subsurface volume. The dimension of each cell, $dx \times dy \times dt$, is determined through the summation of the average amplitude within a time window t between x traces along parallel profiles separated by a distance y. The resulting data may be displayed as a series of incremental amplitude time-slices (c) representing the horizontal variation of reflector strength at a particular two-way travel time from the ground surface. Where the average velocity of the radar wavefront can be estimated, an approximate depth may be suggested for each amplitude time-slice, resulting in a GPR data set (d) with depth information to complement the results from other geophysical techniques, such as earth resistance or magnetic survey.

The most powerful and most commonly applied methods of geophysical prospection in archaeology have now been touched upon. Other geophysical methods have less appeal for various reasons, largely because they are difficult and slow to use in the field and have a poor or overcomplicated response to

Other geophysical methods

most types of archaeological feature. Despite some promise, radiometric measurements fall into this category (Ruffell & Wilson 1998). Seismic and gravity survey are familiar techniques to geological studies, but have rather limited application at the scaled-down level of archaeological requirements. If their role in archaeological reconnaissance is therefore slight, there have nonetheless been occasions on which these methods have been used to help elucidate specific situations. For instance, microgravity survey has the potential advantage that it is not affected by electrical or magnetic interference, and has been shown to be able to detect cavities (Linford 1998), and to assist in the evaluation of the composition of large artificial mounds (Di Filippo et al. 2000). Seismic survey has had rather wider application, for instance, to locate tombs (e.g., Tsokas et al. 1995) and experimental burials (Hildebrand et al. 2002), and to help to confirm the presence of major features such as buried defensive ditches and canals. An example of the latter includes the apparent confirmation of the presence of the canal that was reputedly built, on the orders of Persian King Xerxes, across the Athos peninsula isthmus in Greece. Here, a high-resolution seismic reflection survey identified a feature over 25 m wide, with a depth estimated to be 14–15 m below the present ground surface (Jones et al. 2000), a finding confirmed by coring. Seismic tomographic sections of the feature have been constructed and, incorporating topographic data, full three-dimensional reconstruction of the canal becomes feasible. Seismic survey has also been used recently to map the buried topography of the now silted Lion Harbour of Miletus, Turkey, which is 20 m deep in places (Rabbel et al. 2001); for other examples, see also Ovenden-Wilson (1994), Goulty (2000), and Sambuelli and Deidda (2000). If seismic survey has otherwise contributed relatively little to archaeological site location on land so far, its potential and its role change dramatically when applied through water.

| Underwater geophysical techniques | The archaeological record, of course, extends under both fresh water and seawater, in the latter case opening up truly vast expanses of continental shelf and deeper waters to the need for exploration. Major changes in global ocean volume have occurred on at least five occasions over the past 500,000 years (Rohling et al. 1998), placing many coastlines up to 400 km further offshore than at present. The continental shelves therefore potentially include the remains of entire landscapes that were once accessible for human exploitation, settlement, and migration. Following Holocene marine transgressions, they have become the scenes of multitudes of wreckage, of seacraft, aircraft, and cargo, extending beyond onto the ocean floors. Inland seas and lakes similarly conceal and preserve a hugely important archaeological record, which has been appreciated since at least the nineteenth-century discovery of finely preserved prehistoric settlements in the Swiss and other European lakes. |

The intertidal zone is accessible to the same range of ground-based and remote sensing techniques that have already been described, subject to obvious physical constraints. For instance, aerial photography, walk-over, and historical cartography of the coastal zone can all be highly informative, but because of salinity and waterlogging, geophysical methods are usually limited to metal detection and magnetometry. Below water level, sites and artifacts may be located visually by divers or remotely operated vehicles (ROVs). There are severe limitations to both approaches, though – not least the depth to which divers can safely reach, and the problems of light penetration and scattering, which affect the efficiency of vision and photography. Searches are often initially directed by historical records of wrecks and submergence, but finds are frequently a matter of chance; for example, when artifacts are an incidental recovery of dredging, trawling, or engineering operations. Metal detectors can be used under water by divers who are investigating specific sites or their environs for artifacts.

For wider reconnaissance, marine magnetometers of proton precession, alkali-vapor, or Overhauser types, towed behind a vessel, are used to locate submerged objects (e.g., wrecks, cables, or unexploded ordnance) where there is a sufficient aggregation of iron debris to create a detectable anomaly. A good example of such an anomaly (25 nT) was recorded with an Overhauser instrument over the wreck of the French frigate *La Surveillante*, off Ireland (Quinn et al. 2002). However, such magnetic material is uncommon or absent on pre-medieval wrecks and, conversely, the method is unreliable where there is too much magnetic clutter on the seabed. Modern cesium magnetometers, such as the Geometrics G-880/1, offer a sensitivity of 0.02 nT at ten samples per second and may have a future role in the location of weakly magnetic targets such as early ceramic cargoes. Such instruments can be towed in pairs to increase coverage and, in gradiometer configuration, to help reduce noise. However, the spatial resolution of marine magnetic surveys will remain low compared to their terrestrial equivalents. Seismic methods have more to offer.

Water is fortunately a perfect medium for the transmission of seismic, or acoustic, energy, and consequently sonar (SOund Navigation And Ranging) techniques are highly appropriate for underwater reconnaissance and characterization. The seabed is a very distinct physical interface from which sonar pulses can be reflected and their two-way travel times measured and converted to an estimate of depth. Most sounding devices are therefore designed to map its topography at different levels of detail. Other sonar systems, using reflection data, are capable of penetrating the seabed to varying degrees and depths, providing information on subsurface structures and remains. Several varieties of sonar device are therefore capable of returning useful archaeological information, although this ability is secondary to a diverse range of primary commercial, engineering, and other applications.

At the most elementary level is the use of echo sounding, in which a transmitter and receiver (the transceiver, or transducer) is mounted on the hull of a survey vessel, providing a single bathymetric trace, or profile of depth to seabed, directly beneath the vessel. This, however, has rather limited archaeological application.

An enormous leap forward has occurred from the early 1990s onward, with the development of swath bathymetry techniques; in particular, the use of digital multibeam echo sounders, which have revolutionized the remote sensing of submerged surfaces. The new technology involves a multielement transducer, fixed to the survey vessel, or to a ROV, which is capable of scanning a swath of the underlying seabed (or lake bed), with many individual soundings of water depth for each sonar pulse. Automatic corrections are made for water characteristics, vessel movement, and positioning. The swath width is a multiple of the water depth, and successive widely spaced transects can rapidly provide extensive coverage of the seabed. A recent multibeam survey of the scuttled German fleet at Scapa Flow, Orkney, covered an area of 3.5 × 5.0 km in 4 days. The horizontal resolution for such systems is claimed to be as low as 6 mm and, even if this is exaggerated and cannot be achieved in shallow depths (less than 2 m), the amount of detail that is made visible is astonishing. Considerable post-acquisition data processing, involving spatial rectification and mosaicing, is necessary, but the resulting images produced by such systems can be of such clarity that an analogy with aerial photography over land is not too far-fetched. In much the same way as aerial photography, therefore, multibeam surveys can be used to recognize wrecks (Figure 1.8) and other artifacts and can provide views of their submarine landscape context. Interpolation is still required, but is not a significant problem at such high

Figure 1.8 A multibeam sonar image of the A1 submarine, built by Vickers in 1903, the first British-designed and -built submarine used by the Royal Navy. She sank in 1904, was recovered, but was then lost off Selsey Bill in 1911. The wreck was relocated in 1989 and surveyed in 2003 by Wessex Archaeology, for English Heritage.

ANDREW DAVID

(decimeter) resolutions – although noise introduced by turbulence may prejudice the clarity of fine detail. The geo-referenced digital elevation data can be mounted within a GIS for comparative analysis with other data sets; for instance, inshore multibeam data can be accurately mapped with adjacent onshore elevation data or aerial photographs. This is important because, for the purposes of reconnaissance, and also in terms of broader archaeological perception, the submarine landscape needs to be recognized as a seamless continuum with the dry land.

Swath equipment is expensive; however, side-scan sonar is cheaper and has been used since the early 1960s. In this case, a narrow fan-shaped sonar beam is generated to either side of a towed transducer and scanned at right angles to the path of the vessel, building up a swathe of reflection data to either side of the vessel track, to a horizontal distance of up to several hundred meters or more. Upstanding features such as wrecks provide reflections, whilst in their lee and in depressions there is a lack of response or acoustic "shadow" on the resulting image, the geometry of which allows estimates of relative depth to be calculated. Successive overlapping transects can build up a complete coverage and digital bathymetric models can be derived upon which other survey information can be draped.

Side-scan sonar is also now becoming available in multibeam format, and is thus a very powerful tool for seabed mapping and the location of submerged archaeological sites. It has high resolution and its ability to characterize seafloor surface texture is valuable, suggesting that both multibeam echo sounding and side-scan sonar can be profitably combined for comprehensive seabed characterization.

The systems so far described only detect features exposed on the seabed; even partially buried material is difficult to interpret. However, sonar techniques are also capable of penetrating below the seafloor (sub-bottom profiling) interrogating the underlying structure and disposition of sediments and rock, providing information that is much in demand for engineering projects and mineral extraction. These towed transmitters use higher-energy and lower-frequency signals than those discussed so far, and are termed *pingers*, *boomers*, or *sparkers*, depending upon the source and type of signal that is generated.

Sub-bottom profilers have rather limited potential for archaeological reconnaissance, although this will develop. Boomer devices, for instance, can provide useful information on underlying offshore geomorphological structures such as paleochannels and terraces, which, as on land, may allow predictive modeling of the location of archaeologically sensitive deposits. Rather than reconnaissance, however, these techniques offer greater potential for detailed investigations of sites already discovered by other means (e.g., Schurer & Linden 1984). More recently, higher-frequency sub-bottom profilers have been developed, and provide a good illustration of this potential. For example, in 1999 a 150 kHz (kilohertz) instrument used over an eighth-century BCE Phoenician wreck off the coast of Israel was able to image reflections from structure and cargo (amphorae) to a depth of about a meter below the seafloor. The transducer was mounted on a ROV that traversed the wreck site at a height of 3.5 m, with successive passes at 1.5 m intervals, located to an accuracy of about 5 cm by fixed local transponders (Ballard et al. 2002). Such devices, operated from ROVs, automated underwater vehicles (AUVs), or even on site by divers, can thus provide a series of closely spaced profiles that, with interpolation, offer the opportunity for the creation of data volumes suitable for time-slicing in the same way as GPR data (see above). The survey methodology is demanding, though, and coverage is consequently limited (< 100 × 100 m).

Another form of sub-bottom profiling instrument with growing potential for archaeological site analysis is the *chirp*. This is a high-resolution, swept-frequency device, frequency modulated (FM) in the range 0.4–24 kHz, but typically 1–12 kHz. It has a vertical resolution down to 10 cm and penetration to depths of 20–30 m through fine-grained unconsolidated sediments, and can be used in shallow water depths of less than 2.5 m. Experiments with chirps have shown that they are capable of imaging both wreck sites and submerged landscapes (Quinn et al. 1997, 1998). It has also been shown that chirp data are capable of distinguishing between archaeological material types with differing reflection coefficients, and providing data on grain size and hence sediment characteristics. A new generation of chirp instruments also aims to optimize penetration and resolution, with wider bandwidth and energy input, to enable improved imaging within coarser sediments. A further refinement, which requires highly accurate positioning of the source and receiver, linked to complex post-acquisition processing (3-D data migration), will be the development of chirp systems that record three-dimensional volumes of subsurface data, rather than single linear profiles.

The Future Role and Development of Archaeological Prospecting

The finding of sites purely for research or for the sake of discovery alone, whilst still an important motive, is now secondary to the needs of cultural resource management. Although some archaeological sites and historic monuments have received legal protection since the nineteenth century, the choice of these was limited and the majority of archaeological remains are at the mercy of new housing and infrastructural development, mineral extraction, agriculture, dewatering, natural effects, and pillage. Archaeological sites are also in the uniquely difficult position whereby detailed knowledge about them is achieved by the destructive process of excavation itself.

Concern for the protection of the historic environment has increased. At a global level, the number of cultural properties designated as World Heritage Sites by Unesco exceeds 600. The 1992 Valetta Convention on the Protection of the Archaeological Heritage states the need to ensure that "non-destructive methods of investigation are applied whenever possible" (Article 3). At a national level, governments in many countries are tightening the planning controls that allow the protection of archaeological remains – with the inevitable consequence that such remains need first to be properly identified before their protection can be managed – and it is this requirement that has driven the development of archaeological prospection high up the archaeological agenda.

This new emphasis has contributed to a rapid development in the applications of methods of prospection, especially in the case of ground-based geophysical methods. In the case of larger-scale reconnaissance, aerial photography remains the quintessential method, but other forms of aerial and satellite remote sensing are breaking new barriers now that image resolutions are narrowing down to levels appropriate to the scale of archaeological detection. The main potential of these latter methods will probably be in the study of less well-understood and accessible areas of the world, and in the detailed monitoring of change to heritage sites and landscapes as part of the CRM process.

Recent advances are allowing ground-based geophysical investigations to be applied with greatly increased speed and sophistication. Although earth resistance surveys are still mostly conducted using manual insertion of electrodes, the mechanical automation of this process is increasingly in use, as is electrical profiling; electrostatic arrays seem to offer very promising benefits but await widespread trials. Magnetometer survey, which is responsive to such a wide variety of buried remains, is rapidly increasing both in sensitivity and in the rate of ground coverage – with the result that more weakly defined (and therefore sometimes more deeply buried) and smaller features can be detected over wider areas than formerly. Furthermore, research is beginning to demonstrate that analysis of magnetic data can also provide information on target shape and depth. Magnetic modeling (Scollar 1969), based upon magnetic survey data, has already been used to recreate the three-dimensional morphology of buried ditches, allowing first attempts at virtual reconstruction of the former appearance of sites (e.g., Doneus et al. 2001a). Advances in instrumentation, such as the development of a triple-axis magnetometer, may also allow enhanced target characterization (Kamei et al. 1992; Nishimura 2001). Such developments, though only tentatively realized at present, extend the potential of magnetic survey data well beyond mere reconnaissance into the realm of highly detailed site characterization.

A prerequisite for such detailed characterization, and perhaps the main direction in which archaeological prospection is now advancing, is three-dimensional reconstruction, both on land and below the seabed. Recent emphasis has been on the use of GPR now that large data volumes can be collected and processed with relative ease, allowing both time-slicing (see above) and more complete three-dimensional visualization (Leckebusch et al. 2001). In the field, an area where there may be room for future development is the adaptation of cross-hole tomographic techniques to the detection and characterization of archaeological targets, especially using GPR, but also seismic methods (Reynolds 1997). Such methods are perhaps unlikely to be applied widely in archaeology except in highly specific investigations, such as the definition of buried geomorphological features (e.g., sinks and paleochannels), large voids, or the structural nature of large artificial mounds (e.g., tells, middens, and burial mounds).

There still remain intractable circumstances in which archaeological prospection is and will remain difficult. Perhaps most problematic are built-up or urban areas, where geophysical methods are at a disadvantage unless there are specific circumstances where the presence of a site or structure can be anticipated and where physical conditions allow the methods (e.g., GPR) to be viable. In most circumstances, the location of archaeological sites in urban conditions depends on accumulated historical knowledge and the records of previous archaeological finds and observations. Where geophysical applications are constrained, there is then often little alternative but to resort to invasive methods such as trial trenching, test-pitting, or coring.

Problems also occur where there is overlying material such as river alluvium, marine sediments, blown sand, or peat. Archaeological features are often only detectable in any acceptable detail at shallow depths, and there are entire categories of archaeological feature and materials that are difficult or impossible to detect when concealed, even near the surface. Small features with poor physical contrasts, such as stake holes, postholes, and even graves, are often indistinguishable from their surroundings, as are many organic structures within waterlogged deposits: buried traces of early prehistoric sites, identified only as concentrations of worked lithic material, are undetectable except by excavation.

Prospecting over areas of deep overburden using geophysical methods can be very time-consuming for relatively little payback, potentially overlooking highly significant remains. In these less than ideal circumstances, it may only be feasible to attempt to locate sites from proxy information and inferences. One approach, for instance, might be to use a geophysical method such as GPR and/or conductivity measurement in conjunction with coring and environmental analysis (e.g., palynology), to arrive at a crude topography of a buried landscape, with a reconstruction of its environmental character, to allow the predictive modeling of site location using GIS. Such predictive modeling has received much attention since the 1980s and, in the absence of more direct information on site location, can provide information useful to CRM. There are of course limits to which environmental determinism can be expected to dictate site location, and future modeling will have to increase the incorporation of social and other factors (Kvamme 1999).

In many circumstances where ground conditions are difficult, or where the underlying archaeological targets are elusive for some reason, it will be necessary to integrate several methods of investigation in the expectation that their separate strengths will be complementary. Archaeologists and curators of the historic environment now have at their disposal a diverse array of highly potent and developing methods of nondestructive site discovery and investigation, at many scales and combinations of application. In making use of these methods, they provide a crucial contribution to the wider aims of archaeological analysis and conservation.

Acknowledgments

I am very grateful to Bob Bewley, Justin Dix, Danny Donoghue, Paul Linford, and Neil Linford, who have helped by reading and improving upon portions of the text – although they cannot of course be blamed for any errors that remain. For assistance with the provision of figures, I am especially grateful to Bob Bewley, Helmut Becker, Jorg Fassbinder, Martin Fowler, Neil Linford, Louise Martin, and Wessex Archaeology.

Resources

Some journals of interest are the *Journal of Archaeological Science*, the *Journal of Field Archaeology*, *Archaeological Prospection* (www3.interscience.wiley.com), and *Archaeometry*.

There are numerous satellite and remote sensing links, such as:

- www.nasa.gov/home/index.html
- http://earthobservatory.nasa.gov/
- http://landsat.gsfc.nasa.gov/
- AIRSAR/TOPSAR: http://airsar.jpl.nasa.gov/
- RADARSAT2: www.radarsolutions.dera.gov.uk
- SIR missions – http://southport.jpl.nasa.gov/sir-c/
- aerial photographs – http://wings.buffalo.edu/anthropology/BASP/

A searchable directory of images, visualizations, and animations of the Earth, and images from past and present satellite missions, can be found at http://visibleearth.nasa.gov/

A range of satellite images is available from www.spotimage.fr

Examples of the value of MS survey and the technique can be found at www.archaeotechnics.co.uk/magsus.htm and www.cast.uark.edu/~kkvamme/geop/geop.htm

Since 1995, biannual conferences on archaeological prospection have been held: papers from the Second International Conference on Archaeological Prospection were published in *Archaeological Prospection*, 7(4) (2000). The abstracts of the conferences held in 1999, 2001, and 2003 have been published by the host institutions, most recently as Herbich (2003).

The International Society for Archaeological Prospection (ISAP) was established in 2003. More information on this, as well as comprehensive links to archaeological prospection resources can be found at www.bradford.ac.uk/acad/archsci/subject/archpros.htm

Unesco and the Valetta Convention: http://portal.unesco.org/

References Abdy, R., Brunning, R. A. and Webster, C. J. 2001: The discovery of a Roman villa at Shapwick and its Severan coin hoard of 9238 silver *denarii. Journal of Roman Archaeology*, 14, 358–72.

Aston, M. A., Martin, M. H. and Jackson, A. W. 1998: The potential for heavy metal soil analysis on low status archaeological sites at Shapwick, Somerset. *Antiquity*, 72, 838–47.

Ballard, R. D., Stager, L. E., Master, D. et al. 2002: Iron Age shipwrecks in deep water off Ashkelon, Israel. *American Journal of Archaeology*, 106(2), 151–68.

Becker, H. and Fassbinder, J. W. E. 1999 Magnetometry of a Scythian settlement in Siberia near Cicah in the Baraba Steppe 1999. In J. W. E. Fassbinder and W. E. Erlinger (eds.), *Archaeological Prospection, Third International Conference on Archaeological Prospection*. Munich: Bayerisches Landesamt, für Denkmalpflege, 168–72.

Bethell, I. H. and Smith, J. U. 1989: Trace element analysis of an inhumation from Sutton Hoo, using inductively coupled plasma emission spectrometry: an evaluation of the technique applied to analysis of organic residues. *Journal of Archaeological Science*, 16, 47–55.

Bethell, P. H. and Máté, I. 1989: The use of soil phosphate analysis in archaeology: a critique. In J. Henderson (ed.), *Scientific Analysis in Archaeology*. Monograph 19. Oxford: Oxford University Committee for Archaeology, 1–29.

Bevan, B. and Kenyon, J. 1975: Ground penetrating radar for historical archaeology. *MASCA Newsletter*, 11(2), 2–7.

Bowden, M. 1999: *Unravelling the Landscape*. Stroud: Tempus.

Brooke, C. J. 1987: Ground-based remote sensing for archaeological information recovery in historic buildings. *International Journal of Remote Sensing*, 8(7), 1039–48.

Bull, I. D., Simpson, I. A., van Bergen, P. F. and Evershed, R. P. 1999: Muck 'n' molecules: organic geochemical methods for detecting ancient manuring. *Antiquity*, 73, 86–96.

Canti, M. G. and Meddens, F. M. 1998: Mechanical coring as an aid to archaeological projects. *Journal of Field Archaeology*, 25, 97–105.

Clapp, N. 1999: *Road to Ubar: Finding the Atlantis of the Sands*. USA: Mariner Books.

Clark, A. J. 1996: *Seeing Beneath the Soil*, 2nd edn. London: Batsford.

Cole, M. A., Linford, N. T., Payne, A. W. and Linford, P. K. 1995: Soil magnetic susceptibility measurements and their application to archaeological site investigation. In J. Beavis and K. Barker (eds.), *Science and Site: Evaluation and Conservation*. Occasional Paper 1. Bournemouth: Bournemouth University School of Conservation Sciences, 144–62.

Conyers, L. B. 2004: *Ground-Penetrating Radar for Archaeology*. Walnut Creek, CA: AltaMira Press.

—— and Goodman, D. 1997: *Ground-Penetrating Radar: An Introduction for Archaeologists*. Walnut Creek, CA: AltaMira Press.

Cox, C. 1992: Satellite imagery, aerial photography and wetland archaeology – an interim report on an application of remote sensing to wetland archaeology: the pilot study in Cumbria, England. *World Archaeology*, 24, 249–67.

Craddock, P. T., Gurney, D., Pryor, F. and Hughes, M. J. 1985: The application of phosphate analysis to the location and interpretation of archaeological sites. *Archaeological Journal*, 142, 361–76.

Crawford, O. G. S. 1923: Air survey and archaeology. *Geographical Journal*, May, 324–66.

Crowther, J. 1997: Soil phosphate surveys: critical approaches to sampling, analysis and interpretation. *Archaeological Prospection*, 4, 93–102.

Di Filippo, M., Ruspandini, T. and Toro, B. 2000: The role of gravity surveys in archaeology. In M. Pasquinucci and F. Trément (eds.), *Non-Destructive Techniques Applied to*

Landscape Archaeology. Archaeology of Mediterranean Landscapes, 4. Oxford: Oxbow Books, 148–54.

Doneus, M., Eder-Hinterleitner, A. and Neubauer, W. 2001a: Archaeological prospection in Austria. In M. Doneus, A. Eder-Hinterleitner and W. Neubauer (eds.), *Archaeological Prospection: Fourth International Conference on Archaeological Prospection.* Vienna: Austrian Academy of Sciences, 11–33.

——, —— and —— (eds.) 2001b: *Archaeological Prospection: Fourth International Conference on Archaeological Prospection.* Vienna: Austrian Academy of Sciences.

Donoghue, D. N. M. 2001: Remote sensing. In D. R. Brothwell and A. M. Pollard (eds.), *Handbook of Archaeological Sciences.* Chichester: John Wiley, 555–63.

El Baz, F. 1997: Space age archaeology. *Scientific American,* August, 40–5.

Entwhistle, J. A., Abrahams, P. W. and Dodgshon, R. A. 2000: The geoarchaeological significance and spatial variability of a range of physical and chemical properties from a former habitation site, Isle of Skye. *Journal of Archaeological Science,* 27, 287–303.

Evershed, R. P., Bethell, P. H., Reynolds, P. J. and Walsh, N. J. 1997: 5β-Stigmastanol and related 5β-stanols as bio-markers of manuring: analysis of modern experimental material and assessment of the archaeological potential. *Journal of Archaeological Science,* 24, 485–95.

Fassbinder, J. W. E. and Irlinger, W. E. (eds.) 1999: *Archaeological Prospection, Third International Conference on Archaeological Prospection.* Munich: Bayerisches Landesamt, für Denkmalpflege 108.

—— and Stanjek, H. 1993: Occurrence of bacterial magnetite in soils from archaeological soils. *Archaeologia Polona,* 31, 117–28.

——, —— and Vali, H. 1990: Occurrence of magnetic bacteria in soil. *Nature,* 343, 161–3.

Fowler, M. J. 2002: Satellite remote sensing and archaeology: a comparative study of satellite imagery of the environs of Figsbury Ring, Wiltshire. *Archaeological Prospection,* 9, 55–70.

Gaffney, C. and Gater, J. 2003: *Revealing the Buried Past: Geophysical Survey Techniques in Archaeology.* Stroud: Tempus.

Goodman, D., Nishimura, Y. and Rogers, J. D. 1995: GPR time-slices in archaeological prospection. *Archaeological Prospection,* 2, 85–9.

Goulty, N. R. 2000: Seismic refraction surveying. In L. Ellis (ed.), *Archaeological Method and Theory: An Encyclopedia.* New York: Garland, 544–7.

Griffiths, D. H. and Barker, R. D. 1994: Electrical imaging in archaeology. *Journal of Archaeological Science,* 21, 153–8.

Haigh, J. G. B. 1998: Rectification of aerial images under Microsoft Windows. *Archaeological Computing Newsletter,* 51, 12–20.

Hayes, D. 1994: *The Lost Squadron: A True Story.* New York: Hyperion.

Herbich, T. (ed.) 2003: *Archaeological Prospection.* Theme issue, *Archaeologia Polona,* 41. Warsaw: Institute of Archaeology and Ethnology, Polish Academy of Sciences.

Heron, C. 2001: Geochemical prospecting. In D. R. Brothwell and A. M. Pollard (eds.), *Handbook of Archaeological Sciences.* Chichester: John Wiley, 565–73.

Hey, G. and Lacey, M. 2001: *Evaluation of Archaeological Decision-Making Processes and Sampling Strategies.* Oxford: Oxford Archaeological Unit.

Hildebrand, J. A., Wiggins, S. M., Henkart, P. C. and Conyers, L. B. 2002: Comparison of seismic reflection and Ground-Penetrating Radar imaging at the Controlled Archaeological Test Site, Champaign, Illinois. *Archaeological Prospection,* 9, 9–22.

Holden, N., Horne, P. and Bewley, R. 2002: High resolution digital airborne mapping and archaeology. In R. Bewley and W. Raczklowski (eds.), *Aerial Archaeology: Developing*

Future Practice. NATO Science Series I: Life and Behavioural Sciences, vol. 337. Amsterdam: IOS Press, 173–80.

Jones, R. E., Isserlin, B. S. J., Karastathis, V. K. et al. 2000: Exploration of the Canal of Xerxes, northern Greece: the role of geophysical and other techniques. *Archaeological Prospection*, 7, 147–70.

Kamei, H., Nishimura, Y., Komatsu, M. and Saito, M. 1992: A new instrument: a three-component fluxgate gradiometer. Abstract, 28th International Symposium on Archaeometry, Los Angeles, 1992, 171.

Keevil, G. D. and Linford, N. T. 1998: Landscape with gardens: aerial, topographical and geophysical survey at Hampstead Marshall, Berkshire. In P. Pattison (ed.), *There by Design: Field Archaeology in Parks and Gardens*. Swindon: Royal Commission on the Historical Monuments of England, 13–22.

Kvamme, K. L. 1999: Recent directions and developments in geographical information systems. *Journal of Archaeological Research*, 7, 153–201.

—— 2001: Current practices in archaeogeophysics: magnetics, resistivity, conductivity and ground-penetrating radar. In P. Goldberg, V. Holliday and R. Ferring (eds.), *Earth Sciences and Archaeology*. New York: Kluwer/Plenum Press, 353–84.

—— 2003: Multidimensional prospecting in North American Great Plains village sites. *Archaeological Prospection*, 10, 131–42.

Leckebusch, J., Peikert, R. and Hauser, M. 2001: Advances in 3D visualisation of georadar data. In M. Doneus, A. Eder-Hinterleitner and W. Neubauer (eds.), *Archaeological Prospection: Fourth International Conference on Archaeological Prospection*. Vienna: Austrian Academy of Sciences, 143–4.

Linford, N. T. 1998: Geophysical survey at Boden Vean, Cornwall, including an assessment of the microgravity technique for the location of suspected archaeological void features. *Archaeometry*, 40, 187–216.

Neubauer, W., Eder-Hinterleitner, A., Seren, S. and Melichar, P., 2002: Georadar in the Roman civil town Carnuntum, Austria: an approach for archaeological interpretation of GPR data. *Archaeological Prospection*, 9, 135–56.

Nishimura, Y. 2001: Geophysical prospection in archaeology. In D. R. Brothwell and A. M. Pollard (eds.), *Handbook of Archaeological Sciences*. Chichester: John Wiley, 543–53.

Nöel, M. 1992: Multi-electrode resistivity tomography for imaging archaeology. In P. Spoerry (ed.), *Geoprospection in the Archaeological Landscape*. Oxbow Monograph 18. Oxford: Oxbow Books, 89–99.

Ovenden-Wilson, S. M. 1994: Application of seismic refraction to archaeological prospecting. *Archaeological Prospection*, 1, 53–63.

Panissod, C., Dabas, M., Florsch, N. et al. 1998: Archaeological prospecting using electric and electrostatic mobile arrays. *Archaeological Prospection*, 5, 239–52.

Philip, G., Donoghue, D., Beck, A. and Galiatsatos, N., 2002: CORONA satellite photography: an archaeological application from the Middle East. *Antiquity*, 76, 109–18.

Piro, S., Goodman, D. and Nishimura, Y. 2003: The study and characterization of Emperor Traiano's Villa (Altopiani di Arcinazzo, Roma) using high resolution integrated geophysical surveys. *Archaeological Prospection*, 10, 1–25.

Powlesland, D., Lyall, J. and Donoghue, D. N. M. 1997: Enhancing the record through remote sensing. The application and integration of multi-sensor, non-invasive remote sensing techniques for the enhancement of the Sites and Monuments Record. Heslerton Parish Project, N. Yorkshire, England. *Internet Archaeology* 2. Electronic document: http://intarch.ac.uk/journal/issue2/pld_toc.html, accessed December 3, 2003.

Quinn, R., Adams, J. R., Bull, J. M. and Dix, J. K. 1998: A high resolution geophysical investigation of the *Invincible* wreck site: east Solent. *The International Journal of Nautical Archaeology and Underwater Exploration*, 27(3), 126–38.

——, Bull, J. M., Dix, J. K. and Adams, J. R. 1997: The *Mary Rose* site – geophysical evidence for palaeo-scour marks. *The International Journal of Nautical Archaeology and Underwater Exploration*, 26(1), 3–16.

——, Breen, C., Forsythe, W., Barton, K., Rooney, S. and O'Hara, D. 2002: Integrated geophysical surveys of the French frigate *La Surveillante* (1797), Bantry Bay, Co. Cork, Ireland. *Journal of Archaeological Science*, 29, 413–22.

Rabbel, W., Stuempel, H. and Woelz, S. 2001: The ancient Lion Harbour of Miletus: geophysical investigations. In M. Doneus, A. Eder-Hinterleitner and W. Neubauer (eds.), *Archaeological Prospection: Fourth International Conference on Archaeological Prospection*. Vienna: Austrian Academy of Sciences, 162–3.

Reynolds, J. M. 1997: *An Introduction to Applied and Environmental Geophysics*. Chichester: John Wiley.

Rohling, E. J., Fenton, M., Jorissen, F. J., Bertrand, P., Ganssen, G. and Caulet, J. P. 1998: Magnitudes of sea-level lowstands of the past 500,000 years. *Nature*, 394, 162–5.

Ruffell, A. and Wilson, J. 1998: Near-surface investigation of ground chemistry using radio-metric measurements and spectral gamma-ray data. *Archaeological Prospection*, 5, 203–15.

Sambuelli, L. and Deidda, G. P. 2000: Seismic methods. In M. Pasquinucci and F. Trément (eds.), *Non-Destructive Techniques Applied to Landscape Archaeology*. Archaeology of Mediterranean Landscapes 4. Oxford: Oxbow Books, 136–47.

Schurer, P. J. and Linden, R. H. 1984: Results of a sub-bottom acoustic survey in the search for the Tonquin. *The International Journal of Nautical Archaeology and Underwater Exploration*, 13(4), 303–9.

Scollar, I. 1969: A program for the simulation of magnetic anomalies of archaeological origin in a computer. *Prospezione Archeologiche*, 4, 59–83.

—— 2002: Making things look vertical. In R. Bewley and W. Raczklowski (eds.), *Aerial Archaeology: Developing Future Practice*. NATO Science Series I: Life and Behavioural Sciences, vol. 337. Amsterdam: IOS Press, 166–72.

——, Tabbagh, A., Hesse, A. and Herzog, I. 1990: *Archaeological Prospecting and Remote Sensing*. Cambridge: Cambridge University Press.

Shell, C. 2002: Airborne high-resolution digital, visible, infra-red and thermal sensing for archaeology. In R. Bewley and W. Raczklowski (eds.), *Aerial Archaeology: Developing Future Practice*. NATO Science Series I: Life and Behavioural Sciences, vol. 337. Amsterdam: IOS Press, 181–95.

Shennan, I. 1997: *Quantifying Archaeology*, 2nd edn. Edinburgh: Edinburgh University Press.

—— and Donoghue, D. N. M. 1992: Remote sensing in archaeological research. In A. M. Pollard (ed.), *New Developments in Archaeological Science*. Proceedings of the British Academy 77, 223–32.

Szymanski, J. E. and Tsourlos, P. 1993: The resistive tomography technique for archaeology: an introduction and review. *Archaeologia Polona*, 31, 5–32.

Tite, M. S. and Mullins, C. 1971: Enhancement of the magnetic susceptibility of soils on archaeological sites. *Archaeometry*, 13, 209–19.

Tsokas, G. N., Papazachos, C. B., Vafidis, A., Loukoyiannakis, M. Z., Vargemezis, G. and Tzimeas, K. 1995: The detection of monumental tombs buried in tumuli by seismic refraction. *Geophysics*, 60, 1735–42.

Ur, J. 2003: CORONA satellite photography and ancient road networks: a northern Mesopotamian case study. *Antiquity*, 77, 102–15.

Vaughan, C. J. 1986: Ground-penetrating radar surveys used in archaeological investigations. *Geophysics*, 51, 595–604.

Vickers, R. S., Dolphin, L. T. and Johnson, D. 1976: Archaeological investigations at Chaco Canyon using subsurface radar. In T. R. Lyons (ed.), *Remote Sensing Experiments in Cultural Resource Studies*. Albuquerque: Chaco Center, USDI–NPS, and the University of New Mexico, 81–101.

Weston, D. G. 2002: Soil and susceptibility: aspects of thermally induced magnetism within the dynamic pedological system. *Archaeological Prospection*, 9, 207–15.

Wilkinson, T. J. 2001: Surface collection techniques in field archaeology: theory and practice. In D. R. Brothwell and A. M. Pollard (eds.), *Handbook of Archaeological Sciences*. Chichester: John Wiley, 529–41.

Wilson, D. R. 2000: *Air Photo Interpretation for Archaeologists*, 2nd edn. Stroud: Tempus.

Larry J. Zimmerman

2
Consulting Stakeholders

Introduction

Many archaeologists now fully understand that the past has many stakeholders; in fact, some may even recognize that there are several pasts, all of them capable of explicating a particular set of material remains that an archaeologist might find. Recognition by archaeologists of the rights of these stakeholders and the complexities of the past has taken decades, with no small amount of contention. Pressure for such recognition came primarily from Indigenous people, but also from other descendent communities, starting with demands for the return of human skeletal remains and sacred objects. In the process, their distrust of archaeology and the pasts that it generates became abundantly clear. Out of this contention came demands for consultation with descendent community members. Some of these demands became part of governmental law and regulation. As archaeology has entered the new century, many archaeologists have begun to consider consultation with stakeholders to be a regular part of their work.

This chapter will present a simplified, and to a degree personal, "history" of archaeological interaction with stakeholders to illustrate these changing views of archaeologists toward stakeholders. The chapter will explore some core theoretical and practical aspects of consultation; that is, direct interaction by archaeologists with other stakeholders. The chapter may not be what you expect. Unlike some aspects of archaeological methods, it cannot be a set of techniques to apply in standard ways or to typical situations. It is not intended to be a primer. To provide a "cookbook" for consultation actually would be irresponsible and misleading because, even within the same culture, descendent communities can be extremely diverse. Please heed this warning: approaches that work for consulting with one group may bring disaster with another.

Still, several underlying epistemological (that is, "how we know what we know") issues and some practical matters seem to appear with regularity. The practical considerations discussed here will also include some of the primary consultation laws, regulations, or policies in the United States, Canada, and Australia, along with a discussion of how consultation works (or doesn't work). Throughout, brief examples will illustrate key points.

What and Who is an Archaeological Stakeholder?

Most of us have a basic notion of what an archaeological stakeholder might be – an individual or group with an interest or "stake" in some aspect of the archaeological record. However, there can be substantially greater complexity, as many practicing archaeologists will tell you. There are concerns with possession of, or rights to, some "property" that is contested, property that will be "turned over" to the winner of the contest. Each stakeholder has resources to be committed to the contest and what negotiators call *salience*, the level of commitment the stakeholder has in pursuing this issue over other issues, "a measure of their preparedness to focus on the issue when it comes up, even if it means putting aside some other issue" (Decision Insights, n.d.). Thus, the archaeological record can have multiple stakeholders, all of them contending for archaeological property, whether for artifacts or for control of the very nature of the past and how stories about it get told. To the contest they bring varied resources and salience that range from low levels, at which they do little more than announce that they are stakeholders, to intense contention that might include strong rhetoric, legal action, or even violence.

Stakeholders are varied, with archaeologists themselves being an important group. Many archaeologists have seen themselves as scientific, and therefore objective, parties to these issues, aloof from the politics of the past. By the early 1980s, however, there was clearly a disciplinary stake in the past, as some scholars saw the repatriation issue as a threat to their access to human remains, grave goods, sacred objects, and data generated from them. Levels of salience increased dramatically, as did the resources put to the contest, when some archaeologists went so far as to go to court to stake their claims (e.g., the Kennewick skeleton in the USA – for two views of this case, see Thomas 2001; Chatters 2001; see also the discussion in Chapter 12 of this book). Indigenous people also have become important stakeholders, with many seeing their very identities at stake in the stories that archaeologists create about Indigenous pasts (Zimmerman 2001a). For specific statements by Indigenous peoples, see Forsman (1997: 109), Langford (1983), Tsosie (1997: 66), several papers in Layton (1989), and especially Bielawski (1989).

To see Indigenous people and archaeologists as the major stakeholders would be a vast oversimplification. Members of other, non-Indigenous, descendent communities also have a stake in pasts that they see as being inherited from their ancestors. Sometimes, descendent communities can even be comprised of members of ethnic communities that are part of the dominant society. Contested pasts are sometimes violent, as in the case of the destruction of the Babri Mosque in Ayodhya, India (Romey 2004). There are stakeholder groups beyond those who have a direct cultural or genetic affiliation to a particular contested past. Passions are equally felt, for example, over Greek demands for the return of Elgin/Parthenon Marbles (*Guardian Unlimited* 2004). Some groups, archaeologists among them, even tend to think of the past as a public heritage where everyone has a stake. As a case in point, people from many parts of the world showed great concern about possible damage to

LARRY J. ZIMMERMAN

archaeological sites from warfare in Iraq and looting of Iraqi museums and sites (Garen 2004).

Private citizens have a stake, particularly when it comes to artifacts. In several countries, most notably the USA, artifacts found on privately held land are usually considered to be the landowner's property (the rare exception being human remains). Even antiquities dealers, collectors, and looters are stakeholders, some making their living directly from acquisition and sales of antiquities. However, public monies from citizen-paid taxes pay for most archaeological research. Government required and paid for cultural and heritage resources management activities make up the vast majority of all archaeology in several countries. Thus, project managers and government agencies comprise a substantial group of stakeholders who make demands about how the archaeology gets done and what happens to materials recovered. Museums and other educational organizations also may have concerns about what happens to archaeological artifacts, as well as interpretations of them.

In short, the stakeholders to the past can be many and varied in agenda, resources, and salience, attributes that must be considered when archaeologists interact with them. Simple, general guidelines for consultation with stakeholders don't work, so all interaction with stakeholders needs to be carefully planned. Archaeologists come to consultation with relatively little experience, but archaeology has had a history relevant to the issue that can be helpful.

Archaeological experience with other stakeholders has been relatively limited until recent decades, particularly as Indigenous stakeholders turned increasing resources and salience to concerns about repatriation. Still, archaeologists have actually had more experience with stakeholders than might be imagined. For the most part, we have not been so foolish as to think that stakeholders know nothing of their own pasts, and we have sometimes sought out their knowledge to answer our questions. However, our connections to some stakeholders have been more accidental than anything else. Because there are no simple formulas for working with stakeholder groups, personal and professional experiences in learning how to do it can be instructional.

A Brief History of Interaction between Archaeologists and Other Stakeholders

Many archaeologists have actually used stakeholders as workers on projects, and some stakeholders have become rather skilled archaeological field technicians. Even in the days of antiquarianism, scholars often used members of local communities to assist with excavation, as Carter did at the excavation of Tutankhamun (Orr 2002) or as in Heinrich Schliemann's use of 200 workers at Troy (Traill 1997). Even though they receive bare mention in field notes or reports, locals usually provided the heavy labor, but some facilitated interaction with political entities, translated, and handled day-to-day operations.

Learning to work with stakeholders: a personal journey

This is common practice in lots of places. My own experiences in this vein may be typical.

My first experience with stakeholders as workers came as an undergraduate in the Valley of Mexico. The professor in charge of the project paid local *campesino* men (i.e., mostly "peasant" farmers) to work as the primary laborers on our excavations. Many had worked on archaeological excavations near Teotihuacan for 20 years or more and were vastly more experienced field technicians than I was. I rarely considered the fact that they were working on their own heritage and the impact that might have on them, but that changed when we took two of our workers to Mexico City. These men had never gone to Mexico City and apparently knew little detail about their own past. We spent part of the day in the Museum of Anthropology. After a few hours, a friend and I happened to find one worker, Alejandro, standing in front of the massive Aztec calendar stone, tears rolling down his cheeks. When we asked him if there was something wrong, this dear man responded: "I never realized how great my people once were." From that, I learned the emotional power of the past upon individuals.

By the time in 1978 when I completed work on the Crow Creek Massacre site in central South Dakota, on the Crow Creek (Sioux) Reservation, I understood the value of using local, descendent community labor (for details about the excavation, see Zimmerman and Whitten 1980). As we worked on the skeletal remains of nearly 500 individuals, the Sioux residents became concerned about the spiritual dangers to their people (the massacre victims were from a culture ancestral to the Arikara, sworn enemies of the Sioux). They were very protective of these remains, even though they were from their enemies. Local rumors also had us throwing skulls around, placing sunglasses on them, and putting cigarettes in their mouths. To stop the rumors, we hired several tribal members to become part of our excavation team. They could go back home at night to tell their parents and friends that we had acted respectfully. We also brought a holy man to the site to carry out ceremonies, and he found that the *wanagi*, the sometimes malevolent spirits who guard graves, were gone, so that what we were doing posed no dangers. This solved most problems with local interaction.

Interestingly, I later found out that one of my professors had done the same thing when he worked on the Crow Creek Reservation two decades before me. Hiring local workers who are stakeholders to the past being studied is nothing new, but archaeological attitudes toward those workers are changing and can be important. We cannot afford to think that these people are in any way removed from the archaeology. Even if they are not descended from the culture that left the remains, they might feel some level of concern or attachment to the material.

By 1988, Doug McDonald, a student on my field school, came to me with a question: Would I mind if two elders from his tribe spent a few days with us in the field and classroom? As it turned out, he was Northern Cheyenne, a Plains

Indian group now from Montana. I agreed, and in a few days Bill Tall Bull and Ted Rising Sun arrived. After spending a few days listening and talking with each student, they came to me with a proposition. They said they had been suspicious of archaeologists, but liked what they heard and saw at the field school. They asked if they might come to my house and if a few of the students could be invited too. When everyone came that night, they began to tell stories of the recent history of their people, especially Chief Dull Knife's daring escape from Indian Territories, fighting a running battle with soldiers over 1,300 miles. All of this was well documented, including the breakout, early in the winter of 1879, of Dull Knife's people from incarceration at Fort Robinson, Nebraska, where they had been held without food, water, or heating. The story had us in tears. They then told us a story about the escape from the fort that differed from historical accounts, a story that showed Dull Knife to be the hero and brilliant tactician that he was. At that point, they asked us if we could help them to use archaeology to prove their story, so that the story of the victors would no longer degrade the qualities of their culture hero. With them, we devised a method to determine whether it was possible that Dull Knife indeed used the daring tactics told in their oral tradition (for details, see McDonald et al. 1991). With spiritual guidance, we used metal detectors and small excavations to show that their story was indeed feasible. In our minds, we had proved nothing; in theirs, a culture hero was vindicated. For the students, who had been chosen for their respectful attitudes, the experience was life changing. It was no less for me, and professionally it was my first planned partnership with stakeholders and it changed my approach for the rest of my career.

In 1999, after a career of mostly accidental experience in working with stakeholders, I began to understand that I should begin to teach students about the complexities and rewards of collaboration. A colleague, John Doershuk, and I put together an archaeological field school aimed directly at addressing the concerns of American Indians about archaeology. We determined that interaction with stakeholders should be an almost daily part of instruction. We taught traditional field methods, certainly, but evenings were often spent listening to American Indian speakers or watching videos in which Indian worries about archaeology were prominently featured. To advise on curriculum, we set up a national board of Indian advisors, all of whom had substantial experience in archaeology or were themselves professional archaeologists. Some visited the excavations during the day, spending time interacting with students. We frequently took field trips, often to nearby reservations, where we met with a wide range of Indian people. All of this had two core lessons for our students: that Indian people are contemporary, not just from the past, and that what archaeologists do affects their lives. By the second and third years of the school, the subject of our investigations was the interaction of Indians and whites on the frontier in northeastern Iowa, and we looked at both white and Indian settlements. What made this especially fruitful was that the area had not only Indian descendants who had concerns, but whites descended from settlers of the period. Students got to work with the two groups and had to deal with the concerns of both. We did entrance and exit video interviews with students and could see how much their attitudes about archaeology had changed. For some, it was an epiphany. They understood for the first time the power and complexity of the past.

My own journey is not so dissimilar from that of archaeology. Our first collaborations were accidental, but in recent years many archaeologists have understood the need to consider the concerns of other stakeholders.

<table>
<tr><td>Learning to work with stakeholders: a discipline's journey</td><td>By the mid-1950s, an interdisciplinary effort to promote ethnohistory appeared, developed mostly by scholars of American Indian history and anthropology, who recognized that history was being written from a Western point of view, relying mostly on printed documents. Growing out of their research on American Indian land claims cases, they decided that Indian views needed to be incorporated so as to dissipate a one-sided, Eurocolonial past (for an explanation and history of the approach, see Axtell 1982; for an example of a good, recent application, see Helm 2000). Ethnohistory tries to understand human behavior through a mix of written documents, oral tradition, and material culture, and it is now being applied comparatively in many places in the world. However, the research questions and methods are mostly those of the scholars, not of the people whose past is being studied.</td></tr>
</table>

Archaeologists have concluded, following notions of uniformitarianism, that to understand the past, we often need to look to the present. Archaeologists began to seek analogies between the behaviors of living peoples and those of people from the past. This became something of a specialty in archaeology by the mid-1960s, and was often labeled *ethnoarchaeology*: it was pioneered by Gould (1968, 1971) in Australia, and by Yellen (1977), among the !Kung San in Africa, to mention just two examples. In essence, archaeologists undertake ethnology of living peoples, often making observations about material culture, site formation, and meaning on the basis of their observations and discussions with the groups that they study. For an excellent overview of the approach as it is now used, and for a wide range of applications worldwide, see Nicholas David and Carol Kramer's (2001) *Ethnoarchaeology in Action*. As with ethnohistory, however, the research designs are mostly those of the scholars, who may study elements of a culture that are of little importance to the culture being studied, and in that sense may exclude stakeholders from core elements of the research process.

Ethnohistory and ethnoarchaeology have proven to be fruitful approaches *for archaeology*, but from the perspective of stakeholders being studied, the center of gravity for the scholarship still resides with the archaeologists, not the stakeholders. In that sense, many stakeholders still see such approaches as just another version of scientific colonialism. Nevertheless, these approaches

LARRY J. ZIMMERMAN

recognize that stakeholders do know something about their own pasts, and in that sense show respect for the knowledge stakeholders possess. Working with "locals" also provided a level of experience that would become useful in the 1980s and onward. Initial archaeological responses to the repatriation and reburial issues, however, were a real step backward.

Starting in the late 1960s, but mostly in the 1980s, issues surrounding repatriation and reburial brought archaeologists face-to-face with the fact that archaeologists were also stakeholders, not just aloof observers. When Indigenous people began to demand the return of remains and sacred objects, many archaeologists felt threatened, believing that their "investments" in collections and their access to certain information would be restricted, going so far as to contend that Indigenous claims violated their academic freedom to conduct research on anything they chose to – for a good example of this, see Mulvaney (1991) and Bowdler's (1992) response. Some went so far as to claim that archaeology was the only valid way to know the past and that the past would be "lost" with repatriation (for an example, see Meighan 1985). Initially, local, state, and provincial governments responded to the demands, but by 1989 the first national laws started to appear in the USA. The *National Museum of the American Indian Act* (1989) covered remains in the Smithsonian Institution and the *Native American Graves Protection and Repatriation Act* (1990), commonly know as NAGPRA, required inventory of all Native American human remains, grave goods, and sacred objects, notification to possible genetic or cultural descendants, and repatriation where possible for all federal agencies and any organization that received federal funds or permits (almost all university or government museums and archaeological research facilities). Important in the law was a demand that these agencies also consult with tribes whenever construction projects might disturb graves; consultation also appeared in a number of other laws relating to religious freedom and environmental protection.

In Australia, Canada, and elsewhere, the demands of Indigenous people for return of ancestral remains were no less powerful, but there was perhaps less movement toward passage of sweeping legislation. In the early 1970s in Australia, there was an outcry over the treatment of the remains of Truganini, who was unfortunately labeled the "last Tasmanian." By 1974, the Advisory Committee for Prehistory and Human Biology of the Australian Institute of Aboriginal Studies (now the Australian Institute for Aboriginal and Torres Strait Islander Studies, or AIATSIS) had advised that Truganini's remains be reburied. Her remains were cremated and her ashes scattered in 1976. By 1984, Victoria amended its *Archaeological and Aboriginal Relics Preservation Act* so that remains could be returned to communities. In 1984, the *Federal Aboriginal and Torres Strait Islander Protection Act* was passed, with a special section (Victorian Provisions Part IIA – now *The Aboriginal and Torres Strait Islander Protection Amendment Act* 1987). Because the Victorians would not recognize ownership, Tasmania soon followed, also in 1984, not in their heritage legislation, but in the *Museums (Aboriginal Remains) Act*, which allows return of remains in the museum (Jane Balme, personal communication, June 3, 2003). By 1987, AIATSIS had drafted a policy that recognized Aboriginal ownership of remains but also suggested that the remains were a valuable source of information about the past. Federal law recognizes Aboriginal ownership pre-1778 and that Aboriginal councils should control such materials (for a summary, see Sinclair 2003). The *Commonwealth Native Title Act* (1993) has caused the commonwealth and states to look at questions of title in law that may have implications for archaeology or cultural property, although not specifically about them. All state and territory government departments responsible for Acts protecting Aboriginal sites have policies that require consent from Aboriginal communities before permits for excavation are given. Consent is also required before any permits are given for destruction/collection or other disturbance of Aboriginal sites associated with development (Jane Balme, personal communication, June 3, 2003). However, some feel that these measures are not specific enough to demand reburial or consultation, and the system seems to operate mostly on the basis of moral grounds and political pressure (Claire Smith, personal communication, May 30, 2003).

Canada's path is similar to that of the USA. Some early confrontations, such as that in 1976–7 over the Grimsby burial ground (Kenyon 1982), were well publicized, but there has never been law or policy beyond that of the provinces. The *Ontario Cemeteries Act* (1990), for example, notes that disposition of human remains is to be negotiated between the landowner and a designated representative for the deceased, usually from the First Nation nearest the discovery; the archaeologist has no direct role. Alberta has a *First Nations Sacred Ceremonial Objects Repatriation Act* limited to the Alberta Museum, but questions about the ability of First Nations communities to file claims with other institutions remain (Ferris 2003). Parks Canada (2000) has published an excellent summary of the way in which federal and provincial laws interact regarding archaeological heritage. Hanna (2003) provides an excellent summary of Canada's path in the repatriation issues. As with Australia, moral grounds and political pressure are the primary reasons for consultation in most cases.

Although legislation has been variable, the sense of professional obligation to work with stakeholders, especially on matters of repatriation, has grown and, to a degree, has been made part of professional ethics codes. Efforts to develop professional ethics codes started in the late 1960s with an attempt to ask the Society for American Archaeology (SAA) for a policy to guide its members on such matters (Johnson 1973), but there was no real push until the 1980s. The SAA tried to push through what was essentially an anti-repatriation policy in 1982, which was resisted by Native Americans and some members (Zimmerman 1989a). Four years later the SAA did pass a policy, which has guided its responses to NAGPRA and, most recently, the Kennewick Case. The policy "encourages close and effective communication between scholars engaged in the study of human remains and the communities that may have biological or cultural affinities to those remains" (Society for American Archaeology n.d. a). No policy demanded professional consultation with stakeholders until the World Archaeological Congress (WAC), following on the Vermillion Accord on Human Remains, enacted its First Code of Ethics (Members' Obligations to Indigenous Peoples) in 1990 (Zimmerman & Bruguier 1994). The WAC code clearly states that the ownership of cultural materials and information about Indigenous peoples rests with Indigenous people themselves, and that WAC members are obligated to engage those whose heritage is being studied, at all stages of an investigation. The Canadian Archaeological Association (2002) and the Australian Archaeological Association (2004) have passed similar codes. The Register of Professional Archaeologists (n.d., then the Society of Professional Archaeologists) in the USA stated in its Code of Conduct notes that its members should "be sensitive to, and respect the legitimate concerns of, groups whose culture histories are the subjects of archaeological investigations." The SAA was slower to develop ethical principles and has never made interaction with Indigenous peoples a primary focus. Adopted in 1996, the SAA (n.d. b) Principles of Archaeological Ethics acknowledge accountability to the public and "a commitment to make every reasonable effort, in good faith, to consult actively with affected group(s)."

The problem with these ethical codes is that they tell what you are obliged to do, but provide little guidance as to how to do it. This is where things get difficult. The problems start at fundamental levels, even in terms of differences between how the past is known to archaeologists and stakeholders.

Differing Ways of Knowing the Past

To understand that there can be different ways of knowing the past may be difficult for archaeologists who are intensely focused on knowing the past through material remains and their contexts. Any other way seems less powerful, and most archaeologists are fully aware of the problems associated with oral history, written documentation, and lore. Archaeology as a science is a well-buttressed worldview for archaeology's practitioners. If archaeology can be called a profession, then knowing the past the way we do, through excavation, analysis, and scientific interpretation, is what we profess. The problem is that most nonarchaeologists don't know the past this way.

True or valid?

For many people, the past is a "received" wisdom, given to them by elders, religious and political leaders, kinspeople, or other knowledgeable authorities. This wisdom is laden with meaning that supports personal and cultural identity. Knowledge that contradicts it, no matter the source, is viewed skeptically at best and as threatening and heretical at worst. In order to interact successfully with stakeholders, archaeologists must understand this. For some stakeholders, especially Indigenous people, the matter is critical, as Deloria's (1995) stunning attack on archaeology makes abundantly clear. For them to accept contradictory, archaeologically derived information, they must reject their own pasts and thus reject their own identity. Their version of their past is "true." This poses a problem for archaeologists who actually seek validity, not truth.

Validity and truth are difficult, closely related concepts, used too loosely by most archaeologists, and most stakeholders use the terms almost interchangeably. Validity is authority based on arguments, proofs, and assertions, or something that is well founded, in accordance with known "facts," and agreeing with a standard. In other words, it follows rules outlined from the start. Scientists assess validity, not truth. Truth is a function of belief and is absolute. Most stakeholders "are seekers of truth, not validity. Archaeological validity will have meaning and utility only insofar as it coincides with their truths" (Zimmerman 2001b). Both groups have ways of knowing that provide valid answers to questions, but scientists should understand that truth is ever elusive, and by definition scientists suppose that they can only reach an approximation of a truth. In other words, archaeologists never "prove" anything, only that some explanations of the past are more or less feasible than others.

How can there be different versions of the same past?

What this means is that there can literally be different pasts; that is, several true versions that account for the same set of events and material remains. People string together a selection of "facts" that provide meaning or explanation (cf., Davidson 1995: 3). This should not be too difficult to understand. Witnesses to an event often differ in accounts of the event because of their perceptive abilities, their locations, intervening factors, their culturally determined biases (for want of a better word), and even how questions are asked (Loftus 1996). An important cultural bias involves how people understand and perceive time and the past. In brief, not all people see time as archaeologists do (for discussions with numerous examples, see Zimmerman 1987, 1989b; for elaboration on the very complex nature of time and its impacts on perceptions of the "other," see Fabian 1983). Archaeologists, as part of a Western, literate tradition, have their perceptions of time patterned by the written word; that is, for them time operates in a linear sequence – A leads to B leads to C, and so forth. This is especially true for sciences that demand linearity so that others can replicate experimental models. Oral tradition peoples tend to see time in a more circular, cyclical, or spiral way. The key is not chronology but regularity of events. For literate people, the emphasis is on the past and future, with the present being only a fleeting moment. They seek precedents from the past that will influence events in the future (for example, consider the common statement that one who is ignorant of the past need not hope to make the future great – or, as archaeologists sometimes claim, they are saving the past for the future). For oral people, the present receives the emphasis. The constancy of events is crucial and important. This doesn't mean that oral people don't understand the notion of calendrical time; rather, they emphasize a different aspect of the passage of time. Similarly, literate people also understand cyclical time. They can see the regularities of nature, but they don't emphasize them except in the most general ways (for a more complete description, see Ong 1982).

For archaeology, an emphasis on linear time produces a past that is compartmentalized into chronologies using periods, phases, traditions, and other linguistic labels (see Chapters 4 and 5). Archaeological approaches demand detailed attention to the passage of time. Oral tradition peoples, including most Indigenous peoples, tend to emphasize the present. With a cyclical view of time, the past, present, and future are essentially the same in terms of the important events. Nature is unchanging, although the actors and minor elements may differ slightly. Thus, the present receives the emphasis. Cycles that have been completed form the past, but the past and future are always "out there," not distant, but immanent.

These differences are often crucial when archaeologists communicate with Indigenous stakeholders. Archaeologists consider the past to be lost unless archaeology gets done, whereas oral tradition peoples consider the past always to be present, often alive, but on another plane. If archaeologists say that the past is lost, it is like saying that the people themselves have no past, and thus, no present (or future). Like the past, they too are gone. For Indigenous people, who are often threatened with extinction or assimilation, this is a powerful message (for a more complete discussion, see Zimmerman 1989b).

For most Indigenous people, but also for other stakeholders, information about the past is contained in oral tradition. Oral tradition is usually a set of stories that contain information about a people's origin, movements, interactions with the world around them, and, as much as anything else, teachings to help people live their lives. Thus, they are usually not historical documents, although they may contain historical elements. Most archaeologists are very suspicious of oral tradition as an accurate representation of a people's past (for a discussion of issues, see Mason 2000). Still, with a proper understanding of how oral tradition is formed and of its limits, it can potentially provide useful chronological information (see Echo-Hawk 2000).

To gain a more complete understanding of an event or history, the best approach may be to gather a wide range of accounts and determine where overlap occurs. The points of overlap may be a closer approximation of the truth than any single account might offer. In other words, rather than relying solely on archaeological methods, understanding how a people "processes" – that is, constructs, utilizes, and values – its own past may provide insights beyond those offered by analysis of artifacts or documents. To acquire these insights should be enough of a reason to consult with stakeholders, but showing respect for stakeholders' versions of their past may actually allow outsiders to gain greater access than usual to certain sources of information and to places where archaeologists often are not allowed.

General Thoughts about How to Consult with Stakeholders

Showing respect for stakeholders and pasts that they claim as their own is perhaps the key element in successful consultation. After all, if as an archaeologist you view the past as a public heritage, the past is at least as much a heritage of any stakeholder as it is yours. This requires a certain amount of humility, recognition that your way of knowing is not the only reasonable way of understanding the past. If you openly advocate, as some have (cf., Mason 1997: 3), that archaeology's job is to challenge their view of the past, any hope for good relations with stakeholders is probably lost.

On the other hand, if you happen to believe that a particular group has a greater stake in a past than you do, then stakeholders probably are due substantial deference. The simplest rule is one of the oldest: act toward them as you would like them to act toward you. What this means at the very least is that you must communicate with them about what you are doing and, if possible, you might work toward developing partnerships with them.

How can you develop partnerships? The simplest approach is to ask them *how* they wish for you to consult with them. This surprisingly straightforward approach can work very well, but in a few cases, groups may be suspicious when you are so open. On a recent project to assess the cultural affiliation of Effigy Mounds National Monument for the United States National Park Service, a colleague and I asked exactly that. One of the tribes with which we dealt expressed shock and suspicion. No one had ever bothered to ask permission to do research on the tribe, let alone how they wanted to be consulted with. They had no protocols to handle our request, and so had to develop them. Don't be surprised if stakeholders react in this way. Some have never had the opportunity to develop a partnership with a group of which they are fundamentally suspicious. Allow time to build trust.

You can't build a solid trust if you act out of fear, or just because of a legal or ethical requirement to consult. Partnerships work best if the partners genuinely believe the arrangements to be of mutual benefit. My experience has been that once trust is built and the stakeholders see that you are treating them as equals, they tend to open up to you. Access increased dramatically once they understood that I truly respected their rights and their concerns. In fact, what we discovered was that in many ways we could be natural allies for protecting heritage sites. They began to understand that archaeology offers a powerful set of tools and a way of seeing the past that they could put to good use. I began to understand that the past is vastly more complex than I had realized.

Specific Issues and Concerns

With partnerships and trust, many problems can be solved readily. However, there are a number of specific issues to consider as you work toward partnership. The first, and perhaps most insidious, is that archaeological consultation almost always involves groups with different levels of power.

As Watkins (2001b) explores, archaeological consultation is rarely a meeting of equals. The status and power of each party determine the effectiveness of their consultation. For the most part, it is fair to say that with most stakeholder groups, archaeologists will come to negotiations with the most power. Archaeologists are usually members of the dominant society and have research money to spend. This is especially the case if stakeholders are Indigenous. Where the stakeholder is part of a dominant society group, controls funding, or is of a higher status than most academics, the relationships change. Even when there is differential power or status, roles can shift during negotiations. Legal demands for consultation, especially with Indigenous people, may well have altered the power relationships in some countries. In the USA, American Indians have substantially more say in what happens on their lands, and some federal and state agencies now deal with tribal bodies on a government-to-government basis.

Be aware of the differences and understand that stakeholders probably have less to gain from us than we from them. That alone should help to generate humility in dealing with stakeholders.

Differential power levels

Part of the complexity of the past derives from the fact that the past is multivocal. Not just groups of stakeholders, but individuals within a group might have a particular perspective or make a claim to a past (cf., Colley 2002: chs. 4 & 5). When you deal with stakeholders, the most difficult problems relate to claims made by multiple groups or individuals. Are some claims less legitimate than others? What if there are apparently equally compelling cases to be made for more than one group? These matters can pitch archaeologists into difficult situations. Where the stakeholder group is small, as in the case with some Indigenous groups, there may be few problems. If a stakeholder group is large, however, it may have competing factions. For example, one might have thought that Orser's (Singleton & Orser 2003: 146–9) work on early nineteenth century rural life in Ballykilcline in County Roscommon, Ireland, just preceding the Irish Potato Famine, would be relatively free of controversy, but exactly the opposite was true. The Potato Famine caused one of the major diasporas in human history, with immigrants leaving Ireland for many places. As Orser's work developed, he had not only to contend with concerns of local residents descended from families who stayed in Ireland, but also with descendants of immigrant families, especially in North America. The latter often saw themselves as emotionally attached to the site, even though they had never visited Ireland. They wanted a say in Orser's work.

Whose versions of the past should have priority? Competing interests are not uncommon, and by siding with one group over another, you may shut yourself off from valuable information. Even within a relatively small group of American Indians within the metropolitan Minneapolis – Saint Paul, Minnesota, area, the Minnesota Historical Society (MHS) has to deal with contention

Competing claims

between two groups who make claim to the past of their tribe. MHS tries to stay neutral, but tends to fall back on the legal recognition by the federal government of one group and not the other. Still, certain programs within MHS go out of their way to treat the concerns of the other group respectfully and work with them on the interpretation of one MHS historic site near the unrecognized group's primary residence.

There are no easy answers to the dilemma of competing claims. The best advice is to treat all claimants respectfully, openly, and honestly, and you will usually succeed in being able to maintain communications. Try to let the groups work out problems themselves. Sometimes you can't stay in the middle, so if you decide that you must accept one claim over another, be prepared to deal with the consequences.

Informed consent
Informed consent is letting people know the nature of your work, how it will be accomplished, what its results might be, and how those results might be used, and then asking permission to carry out your research with them. Archaeology is usually not seen to be as dangerous as some medical or psychological research but, as discussed above, the past can have powerful influences on people. Therefore, you should feel obligated to obtain informed consent, and in some cases, you may have legal requirements to do so imposed by law or regulation. Some universities or agencies have institutional review boards to examine your research plan and methods for acquiring consent.

But how do you really know if people really understand what you are doing and its implications? Do you even understand the implications of your research for their lives? There are no easy answers to these questions, partly because you don't know what you might find and how people will react to it. If you happen to find something that contradicts their view of their past, how can you begin to know its possible impacts? Again, you must act from respect and humility.

If you value the people and their pasts, then you will have no wish to bring them harm. Certainly, most archaeologists would say that they would not want their work to bring harm to anyone and that it would be unlikely to do so. But how do they know for sure? For example, in the case of repatriation many archaeologists assumed for generations that Indigenous people didn't care what happened to the remains of ancestors, when exactly the opposite was true. Likewise, claiming that you are an objective scientist and that the results of research are not your problem simply will not do. A better approach might be to assume that your research could cause harm, and then work with the stakeholders to ensure that harm never comes.

When pasts conflict
Developing a partnership and trust is only a beginning. Dealing with a group of stakeholders is an ongoing process. You can assume that contacting them at

the beginning of a project will be adequate. Opinions and attitudes change. A wise person will realize that problems will always crop up. One of the most difficult problems will occur when the past that you construct as an archaeologist is substantially different from the past in which the stakeholder believes and has an investment in identity. In fact, this problem is almost inevitable. The best approach is to make the stakeholder aware of the limitations of your findings from the start; after all, we usually deal with fragmentary evidence. Our stories are hypotheses, not truths. Realizing this, as part of consultation, before research starts, negotiate what is to happen when just such a conflict arises. Are you to be limited in what you say? To whom can you release your findings? Would they rather you not publish your findings at all? For most scholars, any one of these may seem to be a violation of your academic freedom, but remember that you have asked permission to study the past of these people. If you choose to go against their wishes, you will certainly alienate them, and you will do archaeology no service. However, if you have discussed what will happen up front, there may be no problem at all.

One of the best approaches from the start is to make clear that the past is complicated and that the story told by archaeology is but one version. You can say that their story is important to you (and hopefully it really is) and true for them, and that the story that archaeology tells is one hypothesis, not the only story.

Good Examples of Consultation with Stakeholders

There probably are a thousand pieces of advice to give on how to deal with stakeholders. You can gain many tips from reading good ethnographic field methods volumes: see *The Ethnographer's Toolkit* series (Schensul & LeCompte 1999) as one example. You might also pay attention to the detailed ethics codes of groups such as the American Anthropological Association (www.aaanet.org/committees/ethics/ethics.htm). For archaeology, the number of examples of good partnerships between stakeholders and archaeologists is growing. Some have been collected into volumes that will be worth reading. In them, you will see that successful work with stakeholders can be fruitful, though sometimes difficult.

Among the best volumes is a collection of case studies from Canada, *At a Crossroads: Archaeology and First Peoples in Canada* (Nicholas & Andrews 1997). Twenty papers detail a range of projects from dealing with uses of traditional knowledge to how to present Indigenous history in museums. The paper by Thomas Andrews and John Zoe (a Dogbrib tribal member) on archaeology and Dogrib cultural landscapes is a discussion of almost ideal partnership, where both the Dogrib and archaeology worked to profound mutual benefit. Also from Canada, Neal Putt provides simple but compelling stories from the Ojibwe, Cree, and Metis of Manitoba in a volume entitled *Place where the Spirit Lives: Stories for the Archaeology and History of Manitoba* (1991), that combines archaeology and First Peoples' stories. For Australia, *Archaeologists and Aborigines*

Working Together (Davidson et al. 1995) has 19 brief case studies, many of them emphasizing connections to place. Also of interest are the number of interviews with Aborigines in the volumes and the fact that many papers are jointly authored by archaeologists and Aborigines. *After Captain Cook: The Archaeology of the Recent Indigenous Past in Australia* (Harrison & Williamson 2002), is primarily historical archaeology, with many of the papers combining Indigenous knowledge and archaeological method. Another extremely useful, highly recommended volume of advice and case studies from Australia is *Uncovering Australia: Archaeology, Indigenous People, and the Public* (Colley 2002). In the USA, there are numerous case studies, but the best collection is a series of papers reprinted from the Working Together column (www.saa.org/publications/saabulletin/) of the Society for American Archaeology *Bulletin* (now *The Archaeological Record*), entitled *Working Together: Native Americans and Archaeologists* (Dongoske et al. 2000). AltaMira Press is sponsoring a new series entitled "Indigenous Archaeologies." The first book in this series is *Indigenous Archaeology: American Indian Values and Scientific Practice* (2001a) by Joe Watkins, a Choctaw archaeologist. Several more volumes are in preparation. Another useful book is *Tribal Cultural Resource Management: The Full Circle to Stewardship* (Stapp & Burney 2002), which explores a wide range of issues regarding tribal control of archaeological and historical resources, with an excellent chapter on consultation.

There are many more useful case studies, and the number is growing as archaeologists come to realize that working with consultants can be beneficial. There remains one delicate issue to consider, which in many ways underlies the entire issue of consultation: Who owns the past?

Why Consult with Stakeholders? The Past as Cultural and Intellectual Property

If you concur with many archaeologists that archaeological sites are a public heritage and that archaeologists are its primary stewards, then the information that archaeologists generate from archaeological research is also "owned" by no single group. Given this view, there is no real reason to work with stakeholders.

Some archaeologists question these views. Given the opportunity to critique the Society for American Archaeology's proposed ethical principles, Zimmerman (1995: 65) openly criticized the idea of archaeologists as the primary stewards of the past, noting that such a position was self-declared and open to question from nonarchaeologists with legitimate interests in the past. Asch (1997: 271) examined assumptions of underlying title in Canada and concluded that it is "the First Nations – not Canada and/or the provinces – that are presumed to have ownership and jurisdiction over at least the cultural property that comes from their own cultures and from their own history." Issues of cultural and intellectual property are complicated. At the heart may be differing interpretations of traditional cultural notions of property and, in some places, those of English common law. But there is also common sense.

Why should archaeological rights to the past take precedence over those of the people whose ancestors lived that past and whose traditions revere and sustain it over millennia? Such an opinion seems foolish. Archaeologists in the USA believed that human remains were a public heritage, but with NAGPRA discovered that failure to pay attention to contention over such matters could result in the imposition of law that substantially changed relationships with Native Americans.

Wouldn't it be better to understand that working with stakeholders is actually a reasonable interpretation of what a public heritage is and what accountability to our publics actually means? As Stapp and Burney (2002: 123) note: "It's the legal thing to do, it's a good thing to do, and it's the right thing to do." Perhaps it is also the smart thing to learn how to do.

Acknowledgments

This chapter results from discussions with many people over many years. I owe so many more than I can name, but several directly provided material or ideas for this paper or I benefited from useful discussion with them: Robert Cruz, Bill Green, Jan Hammil, Hirini Matunga, Steve Dasovich, John Doershuk, Tom King, Dawn Makes Strong Move, Randy McGuire, George Nicholas, Maria Pearson, Neal Putt, Tristine Smart, Claire Smith, Joe Watkins, Colin Pardoe, Martin Wobst, Alison Wylie, and Karen Zimmerman. George Nicholas provided material on Canada. Michael Westaway, Jane Balme, and Claire Smith provided material used in the discussion of Australia. I would especially like to thank Alistair Paterson and Jane Balme for the opportunity to write this chapter, but especially for their gracious and extreme patience.

References

Asch, M. 1997: Cultural property and the question of underlying title. In G. Nicholas and T. Andrews (eds.), *At a Crossroads: Archaeology and First Peoples in Canada*. Burnaby, BC: Archaeology Press, 266–71.

Australian Archaeological Association 2004: Code of Ethics of the Australian Archaeological Association (Members' Obligations to Australian Aboriginal and Torres Strait Islander People). Electronic document: www.australianarchaeologicalassociation.com.au/

Axtell, J. 1982: *The European and the Indian: Essays in the Ethnohistory of Colonial North America*. Oxford: Oxford University Press.

Bielawski, E. 1989: Archaeology and Inuit culture. In R. Layton (ed.), *Conflict in the Archaeology of Living Traditions*. London: Unwin Hyman, 228–36.

Bowdler, S. 1992: Unquiet slumbers: the return of the Kow Swamp burials. *Antiquity*, 66, 103–6.

Canadian Archaeological Association 2002: Statement of Principles for Ethical Conduct Pertaining to Aboriginal Peoples. Electronic document: www.canadianarchaeology.com/ethical.lasso

Chatters, J. C. 2001: *Ancient Encounters: Kennewick Man and the First Americans*. New York: Simon & Schuster.

Colley, S. 2002: *Uncovering Australia: Archaeology, Indigenous People, and the Public*. Washington, DC: Smithsonian Institution Press.

David, N. and Kramer, C. 2001: *Ethnoarchaeology in Action*. Cambridge: Cambridge University Press.

Davidson, I. 1995: Introduction. In I. Davidson, C. Lovell-Jones and R. Bancroft (eds.), *Archaeologists and Aborigines Working Together*. Armidale, NSW: University of New England Press, 3–5.

——, Lovell-Jones, C. and Bancroft, R. (eds.) 1995: *Archaeologists and Aborigines Working Together*. Armidale, NSW: University of New England Press.

Deloria, V. 1995: *Red Earth, White Lies: Native Americans and the Myth of Scientific Fact*. New York: Scribner.

Decision Insights n.d.: The Science of Negotiation and Politics. Electronic document: www.diiusa.com/salience.html

Dongoske, K., Aldenderfer, M. and Doehner, K. (eds.) 2000: *Working Together: Native Americans and Archaeologists*. Washington, DC: Society for American Archaeology.

Echo-Hawk, R. 2000: Ancient history in the New World: integrating oral traditions and the archaeological record. *American Antiquity*, 65(2), 267–90.

Fabian, J. 1983: *Time and the Other*. New York: Columbia University Press.

Ferris, N. 2003: Between Colonial and Indigenous archaeologists: legal and extra-legal ownership of the archaeological past in North America. *Canadian Journal of Archaeology*, 27(2), 154–90.

Forsman, L. 1997: Straddling the current: a view from the bridge over clear salt water. In N. Swidler, K. Dongoske, R. Anyon and A. Downer (eds.), *Native Americans and Archaeologists: Stepping Stones to Common Ground*. Walnut Creek, CA: AltaMira Press, 105–11.

Garen, M. 2004: The war within a war. *Archaeology*, 57(4), 28–31.

Gould, R. A. 1968: Living archaeology: the Ngatatjara of Western Australia. *Southwestern Journal of Anthropology*, 24, 101–22.

—— 1971: The archaeologist as ethnographer: a case from the Western Desert of Australia. *World Archaeology*, 2, 143–77.

Guardian Unlimited 2004: Special Report: The Parthenon Marbles. Electronic document: www.guardian.co.uk/parthenon/0,12119,184528,00.html

Hanna, M. G. 2003: Old bones, new reality: a review of issues and guidelines pertaining to repatriation. *Canadian Journal of Archaeology*, 27(2), 234–57.

Harrison, R. and Williamson, C. (eds.) 2002: *After Captain Cook: The Archaeology of the Recent Indigenous Past in Australia*. Archaeological Methods Series, vol. 8. Sydney: University of Sydney.

Helm, J. 2000: *The People of Denendeh: Ethnohistory of the Indians of Canada's Northwest Territories*. Iowa City: University of Iowa Press.

Johnson, E. 1973: Professional responsibilities and the American Indian. *American Antiquity*, 38(2), 129–30.

Kenyon, W. 1982: *The Grimsby Site: A Historic Neutral Cemetery*. Toronto: Royal Ontario Museum.

Langford, R. 1983: Our heritage – your playground. *Australian Archaeology*, 16, 1–6.

Layton, R. (ed.) 1989: *Conflict in the Archaeology of Living Traditions*. London: Unwin Hyman.

Loftus, E. 1996: *Eyewitness Testimony*. Cambridge: Harvard University Press.

Mason, R. J. 1997: Letter to the editor. *Society for American Archaeology Bulletin*, 15(1), 3.

—— 2000: Archaeology and Native American oral tradition. *American Antiquity*, 65(2), 239–66.

McDonald, J. D., Zimmerman, L. J., Tall Bull, W. and Rising Sun, T. 1991: The Cheyenne outbreak of 1879: using archaeology to document Northern Cheyenne oral history. In R. Paynter and R. McGuire (eds.), *The Archaeology of Inequality*. Oxford: Blackwell, 64–78.

Meighan, C. 1985: Archaeology and anthropological ethics. *Anthropology Newsletter*, 26(9), 20.

Mulvaney, D. J. 1991: Past regained, future lost: the Kow Swamp Pleistocene burials. *Antiquity*, 65, 12–21.

Nicholas, G. and Andrews, T. (eds.) 1997: *At a Crossroads: Archaeology and First Peoples in Canada*. Burnaby, BC: Archaeology Press.

Ong, W. J. 1982: *Orality and Literacy: The Technologizing of the Word*. London: Methuen.

Orr, D. 2002: A. C. Mace's Account of the Opening of the Burial Chamber of Tutankhamun on February 16, 1923. Electronic document: www.ashmol.ox.ac.uk/gri/4maceope.html

Parks Canada 2002: *Unearthing the Law: Archaeological Legislation on Lands in Canada*. Hull, Quebec: Parks Canada.

Putt, N. 1991: *Place where the Spirit Lives: Stories for the Archaeology and History of Manitoba*. Winnipeg, MB: Pemmican Publications.

Register of Professional Archaeologists n.d.: Code of Conduct. Electronic document: www.rpanet.org/conduct.htm

Romey, K. 2004: Flashpoint Ayodhya. *Archaeology*, 57(4), 49–55.

Schensul, J. J. and LeCompte, M. D. (eds.) 1999: *The Ethnographer's Toolkit* (vols 1–7). Walnut Creek, CA: AltaMira Press.

Sinclair, A. 2003: Issues in the Reburial of Human Remains. Electronic document: pcwww.liv.ac.uk/~sinclair/ALGY399_Site/reburial.html

Singleton, T. A. and Orser, C. E. 2003: Descendant communities: linking people in the present to the past. In L. J. Zimmerman, K. D. Vitelli and J. Hollowell-Zimmer (eds.), *Ethical Issues in Archaeology*. Walnut Creek, CA: AltaMira Press, 143–52.

Society for American Archaeology n.d. a: Statement Concerning the Treatment of Human Remains. Electronic document: www.saa.org/repatriation/repat_policy.html

—— n.d. b: Principles of Archaeological Ethics. Electronic document: www.saa.org/Aboutsaa/Ethics/prethic.html

Stapp, D. C. and Burney, M. S. 2002: *Tribal Cultural Resource Management: The Full Circle to Stewardship*. Walnut Creek, CA: AltaMira Press.

Thomas, D. H. 2001: *Skull Wars: Kennewick Man, Archaeology, and the Battle for Native American Identity*. New York: Basic Books.

Traill, D. 1997: *Schliemann of Troy: Treasure and Deceit*. New York: St Martin's Press.

Tsosie, R. 1997: Indigenous rights and archaeology. In N. Swidler, K. Dongoske, R. Anyon and A. Downer (eds.), *Native Americans and Archaeologists: Stepping Stones to Common Ground*. Walnut Creek, CA: AltaMira Press, 64–76.

Watkins, J. 2001a: *Indigenous Archaeology: American Indian Values and Scientific Practice*. Walnut Creek, CA: AltaMira Press.

—— 2001b: "The powers that be": power, role, and interaction in the consultation process. Paper presented at the 2001 Annual Meeting of the Society for American Archaeology, New Orleans, LA. Electronic document: www.uiowa.edu/~ainsp/saa2001/watkins.html

Yellen, J. E. 1977: *Archaeological Approaches to the Present*. New York: Academic Press.

Zimmerman, L. J. 1987: The impact of the concept of time on the concept of archaeology. *The Archaeological Review from Cambridge*, 6(1), 42–50.

—— 1989a: Made radical by my own: an archaeologist learns to understand reburial. In R. Layton (ed.), *Conflict in the Archaeology of Living Traditions*. London: Unwin Hyman, 60–7.

—— 1989b: Human bones as symbols of power: Native American views of "grave-robbing" archaeologists. In R. Layton (ed.), *Conflict in the Archaeology of Living Traditions*. London: Unwin Hyman, 211–16.

—— 1995: Regaining our nerve: ethics, values, and the transformation of archaeology. In M. J. Lynott and A. Wylie (eds.), *Ethics in American Archaeology: Challenges for the 1990s*. Washington, DC: Society for American Archaeology, 64–7.

—— 2001a: Usurping Native American voice. In T. Bray (ed.), *The Future of the Past: Archaeologists, Native Americans, and Repatriation*. New York: Garland, 169–84.

—— 2001b: Processing the pasts: interacting with descendent communities. Paper presented at the 2001 Annual Meeting of the Society for American Archaeology, New Orleans, LA. Electronic document: www.uiowa.edu/~ainsp/saa2001/ljz.html

—— and Bruguier, L. R. 1994: Indigenous peoples and the World Archaeological Congress Code of Ethics. *Public Archaeology Review*, 2(1), 5–8.

—— and Whitten, R. 1980: Mass grave at Crow Creek in South Dakota reveals how Indians massacred Indians in 14th century attack. *Smithsonian*, 11(6), 100–9.

3
Rock-Art

What is Rock-Art?

Every culture on Earth produces visual art as an expression of its creative self. This can take many forms – including body decoration (painting, tattooing, cicatrizing), decoration of habitations or items of material culture, such as men's houses in Papua New Guinea, funeral poles made by the Tiwi people of northern Australia, stone sculpture (such as those found on Easter Island), earth sculptures such as chalk horses in the United Kingdom and bora ceremonial grounds (southeastern Australia), as well as individual artistic expressions (clothing, bark paintings, oil paintings or water colors, and modern graffiti). It is known that the earliest *Homo sapiens sapiens* produced mobiliary art (e.g., portable sculptures including the "Venus figurines") and that rock-art surfaces have been dated to at least 30,000 years (Clottes et al. 1995; O'Connor 1995). The appearance of rock-art at this time (along with various other cultural accoutrements such as personal adornment and music) happened in Africa, Australia, Europe, and India. The evolution of shared symbolic systems is argued as representing the development of a human cognitive capacity (e.g., Davis 1986; Davidson & Noble 1989). For many Indigenous cultures around the world, the only surviving record of their earliest artistic endeavors is rock-art. Here, I am following the hyphenated convention of "rock-art" – as opposed to "rock art." The logic of this convention is to formalize (or "portmanteau") the concept of art produced on the rock medium (Chippindale & Taçon 1998a).

There are practically no rock-art traditions that continue into the present, and very few rock-art regions around the world have been described adequately in ethnographic or ethnohistorical records. In a few remote areas in Australia today, rock-art is occasionally produced by Aboriginal people (Morwood 2002) but in most areas, rock-art production ceased at – or shortly after – contact with European settler groups (Chaloupka 1993; Frederick 2000). Very rarely do we have informed knowledge about the *meaning* of rock-art. Even in Africa, where an intricate picture of San mythology and spiritual practice has allowed for an extremely complex interpretation of the Bushman art (Lewis-Williams 1981; Solomon 1998), the San knowledge came from Bushmen who were geographically distant from the rock-art in question and did not themselves have a rock-art tradition.

How is Rock-Art Made? Rock-art is defined as human-made marks on natural immovable rock surfaces – boulders, cliff lines, shelters, caves, and platforms. For rock surfaces to be suitable for the production of art, they need to be relatively smooth and homogenously textured. The hardness of the rock will often determine the technique used to produce art. Very hard surfaces are often only painted or drawn upon, although engraved motifs do occur on such "canvases." Soft matrices, such as mud or limestone, will provide the opportunity for a very different range of techniques to be applied, such as finger "fluting" (Bednarik 1986), abrading, and scratching. Rock-art takes two primary forms:

1 Rock engravings (*petroglyphs*), where the pattern/image is one of relief. The images were produced by removing material from the rock surface. Techniques are variously described as abrading, engraving, incising, pecking, battering, gouging, scratching, and etching.
2 Rock paintings, prints, stencils, or drawings (*pictographs*), where pigment or other materials (e.g., beeswax/resin) have been added to the rock surface.

There are a number of techniques that can be used to distinguish between modes of rock-art production. These are usually included in any classification system used for rock-art analysis.

Classification The classification or typology (based on taxonomic principles) is the system by which rock-art researchers "order" their assemblages and attempt to make sense of them. A typology describes the range of phenomena present in any rock-art assemblage and categorizes these in a consistent (and repeatable) fashion, so that the variation within the assemblage can be organized and described. While early structuralists (such as Shapiro 1953) might have considered that "Style" is an emic characteristic, whereby art producers and cultures knowingly produce "categories" or "types" that can be discerned subsequently by researchers, most researchers recognize that taxa used in the formulation of assemblage classification (i.e., for quantitative analyses) are mostly etic in nature, having reality only to the classifier or taxonomer.

It is important to realize that any typology imposed on a rock-art assemblage reveals as much about the researcher as it does about the rock-art assemblage! Most researchers endeavor to achieve a classificatory system that reflects the likely cultural reality (see the case study), while recognizing that the intentions of the artist cannot be discerned (see the discussion below about motifs).

Classification systems usually use a multi-trait (and sometimes -tiered) approach that allows for the description of each individual figure in any assemblage according to technique, form, motifs, and other characteristics (see, e.g., Maynard 1979). Classification plays a primary role in any structural analysis of rock-art, particularly where the researcher is attempting to demonstrate selectivity on the part of the artist(s), be it choice of motif (subject), technique, or

JO MCDONALD

placement in an art system (i.e., within a rockshelter or broader landscape). Structural analyses (see below) can apply to figurative and nonfigurative assemblages. Spatial, temporal, economic, and ideological frameworks are a few of the underpinning explanatory devices that can be applied to the interpretation of rock-art assemblages in this manner.

Technique is the technical aspect of the art's production. Engraved motifs are generally made by the following mechanical actions, which are identifiable because of the profile of the engraved line/motif. These techniques can be generally grouped as follows: Technique

- *Friction* (abraded, grooved, rubbed, or scratched).
- *Percussion* (pecked, pitted, or pounded). Clegg (1983) defined the methods of direct and indirect percussion as the distinguishing feature between pounding and pecking, respectively.
- *Rotation* (drilled).

Pigment art (referred to as pictographs in the American literature) can also be described according to the technique(s) used in its production. Delineated (or depictive) motifs consist of those that have been applied in wet pigment (painted) or dry (drawn). When wet pigment is used, ochers are usually ground up and mixed with water (and sometimes organic binders) before being applied to the wall. The result is a relatively even color on the rock. Dry pigment is applied as with a crayon and the resultant effect depends on the evenness of the rock surface being decorated. Uneven surfaces often create a streaky effect, with the pigment adhering only to the knobby protruding surfaces of the rock. Other materials (e.g., beeswax) are occasionally applied to create pictures. This material is generally chewed and molded into small evenly sized balls before being applied to the wall (see Nelson 2000). The result with all delineated motifs is a depiction of the artist's rendering, comprised of lines and/or solid areas that contain inherent stylistic information (cf., Forge 1991). Stenciling, however, creates mechanically reproduced motifs. In this instance, the object (e.g., hand, boomerang, or shield) is held onto the wall of a shelter and pigment either blown around it or applied wet on it. The effect is a negative (or positive) image of the actual object.

Form is a term that is often used to describe the visual organization of the component parts of any motif (other words that are used in a similar context are "composition," "design," "pattern," or "treatment"). Form characteristics can be used to describe any motifs, regardless of technique. Many classification systems will use very detailed hierarchical classification to describe the range of potential variation in an assemblage (see, e.g., Maynard 1979; Sognnes 1998; Form

Wilson 1998; Ross 2002). For instance, a motif type that resembles a rainforest shield (Brayshaw 1990), with parallel line and dot decoration, could be described as a continuous line/which encloses space/with interior infill/of scattered marked and concentric/geometric/bands (after Maynard 1977). The formal descriptions based on these possible permutations are often lengthy and unwieldy, but multivariate analysis (see below) happily deals with such variation and complex description.

Motif   Motif describes the shape that any particular figure takes. In most rock-art assemblages there is a finite range of shapes present and most researchers find it convenient to give these shapes names. In figurative assemblages, descriptions are given that describe these shapes, such as "man," "man with headdress," "woman," and "snake." In nonfigurative assemblages, geometric terms are often used (such as "circle," "chevron," "grid," and "diamond"), as are the terms "simple nonfigurative" and "complex nonfigurative" (e.g., Clegg 1987). A motif is a recurrent visual image with a requisite set of component traits. Clear definitions should be made that ensure that distinguishing between motif types is a repeatable process in which value judgments are minimized.

Size   Size (or scale) is also often recorded as a characteristic of an assemblage. Precise measurements can be made but relative scale is also sometimes relevant. In some assemblages – for example, Sydney Basin (see McDonald 1991, 2000a) – the engraved motifs can be life size, including whale engravings that are 10–13 m long! In other assemblages – for example, the Cobar Pediplain in eastern Australia – the human figures are much smaller than life size (McCarthy 1976). Although both of these simple figurative assemblages occur in southeastern Australia, they are in distinctly different *style regions*. The size of their respective motifs is one of the distinguishing characteristics.

Character   Character is one way of describing the unique characteristics of the motifs in any particular rock-art style. In most style regions, the character of the motifs is consistently created using a relatively narrow range of traits. Sackett (1990: 33) described this as "stochastic variation" which, crudely put, means "knowing that there are various ways to skin a cat but choosing to use only one or a few of these!"

How is Rock-Art Recorded?   The methods used to record rock-art should reflect the research questions and/or goals of the recording exercise (Chippindale 2001; Loendorf 2001). Very detailed recording work is required when conservation works are intended, such as installing a silicone drip-line to avert water flow from painted panels, or if the site is to be destroyed by development. Other less rigorous types of recording can be employed if the analysis being undertaken is at a regional scale and the aim of the research is to investigate broad-scaled stylistic variation. Site managers whose role it is to protect sites need to know accurately where a site is located and what it contains. A "complete" record of a site through photogrammetric recordings (Ogilby & Rivett 1985) is rarely achieved. Most researchers aim to accurately record what rock-art is present at a site, how the different motifs and/or panels relate to each other, and the relationship of the art to other natural features; for example, whether it is on the edge of a platform/shelter, close to the drip-line or other rock-art sites/panels. There are various basic techniques or methods that are used either individually or in combination. For most rock-art recording exercises, these include:

- photography (digital still, digital video and still)
- mechanical reproduction (drawing to scale and sketching)
- tracing (using clear plastic/polythene)
- counting (using a predetermined taxonomy/classification – see above), and
- enhancement of the image to assist in any or all of the above.

- *Basic equipment* – camera (SLR/digital), lenses (macro, wide angle, 50 mm, telephoto), film (black and white/color/transparency), memory card, tripod, flash, and scale.   Photography

Photography is the most practical and economical way to record rock-art and one that has the lowest impact on the art being recorded. The disadvantages of this technique arise from the vagaries of field conditions generally, such as the poor lighting in dark caves, art with low contrast between background and motifs, art in difficult positions on the wall, such as in crevices, and so on. Lighting is usually the critical issue and most rock-art recorders have found that viewing (and photographing) art at different times of the day is helpful. Many people photograph engravings at night, when they can control the lighting conditions (see Figure 3.1). The use of reflectors, such as space blankets and large plastic mirrors, is another way of enhancing faint images and improving the possibility of recording and photographing art that is difficult to see.

The use of filters on camera lenses can also assist in embellishing and/or controlling for certain lighting conditions. Blue and red filters can control for red and blue wavelengths (respectively) in daylight, often improving the ambient light conditions. Green and blue filters will improve color saturation in red pigments. Polarizing filters cut down the glare from shiny rock surfaces.

Use of flash photography, including oblique or side-light approaches (Loendorf 2001), is another way of improving lighting conditions either on engraved motifs or on faint pigment art. Flash meters can take the guesswork out of this technique. It is important to note that when using different types of

Figure 3.1 A photograph of an engraved macropod, boomerangs, and a ship at Devil's Rock, Maroota. The motifs were photographed at night, using oblique lighting (photograph by J. McDonald).

Figure 3.2 A digital photograph of pigment art with control points for later electronic stitching of the images (Whale Cave, Cordeaux catchment; photograph by J. McDonald).

lenses, distortion of the outer portions of the image is a danger with anything but a 50 mm lens. This is especially so when a series of overlapping images are shot in the field to produce a collage of a large motif and/or panel. If, for instance, a wide-angle lens is used, an accurate overlap is unlikely to be achieved because of the distortion at the edges of the overlapping prints. When using a digital camera, it is also a good idea to affix control points to the rock surface to allow for the later electronic "stitching" of the digital images (Figure 3.2).

In some instances (particularly with petroglyphs), people use stereo-photographs of sites to aid in the interpretation of motifs (e.g., Clegg 1983). This technique can be achieved quite easily by taking two photographs of any particular motif from the one position, but with knees bent first to the right and then to the left. The resultant photographs can be viewed as stereo-pairs. A similar result is achieved on horizontal engraving platforms using a monopod – a length of rod (with horizontal balance) 2–3 m long, atop which a camera is affixed. By methodically moving across an engraved panel (Figure 3.3), this

Figure 3.3   John Clegg using a camera affixed to a monopod to photograph large horizontal engravings (John Clegg, with permission).

technique can be used to produce a photographic collage of the panel. A 55 mm lens should be used to reduce distortion.

A scale is a vital component of any photograph being taken for recording purposes. This allows the image to be reduced, printed, and accurately reproduced later. The International Federation of Rock Art Organizations provides its members with a scale with both metric measure and color scale capacity. Color scales have a dual purpose, both of allowing comparison with pigment colors in the art and as a vital archival record from which changes over time to the image (on film) can be assessed.

Drawing and sketching

- *Basic equipment* – graph paper (various scales) and blank paper, tape measures (hand-held and longer), pencils, rubbers/erasers.

Site plans, sections, and drawings can be drawn to scale (Figure 3.4) or can be sketched/drawn in a manner that aids in the interpretation of more accurate methods (tracings and photography). Most researchers produce a sketch plan (often on their standard site recording form) that shows the location of the art within the site, its compass orientation, the relationship of the art to other archaeological features, the relationship between panels in complex sites, and any other pertinent details (Figure 3.5). Often, sketches are made of significant figures to aid in the subsequent interpretation of photography. Control points for photography are usually indicated on site sketch plans, as might be the locations of traced motifs/panels. These types of information assist in producing the composite record of the site.

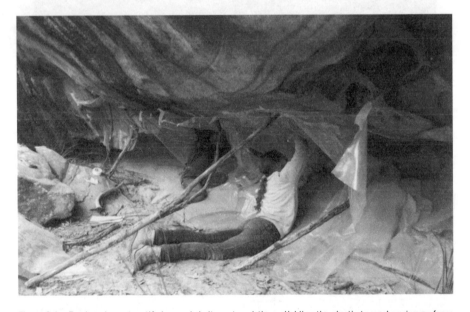

Figure 3.4 Tracing pigment motifs in a rockshelter onto polythene. Holding the plastic to overhanging surfaces often requires the assistance of various props, to say nothing of flexibility! (Photograph by J. McDonald.)

JO MCDONALD

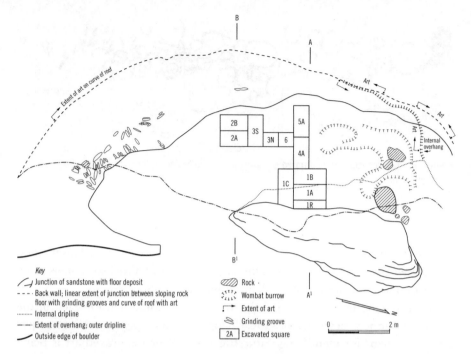

Figure 3.5 A site plan of Yengo Rockshelter, showing the locations of the art panels.

- *Basic equipment* – clear plastic medium (rolls of 2 m wide builder's plastic, or smaller pieces of more expensive acetate from artists' suppliers), permanent marker pens (in a range of colors and thicknesses), masking tape/reusable adhesive, scissors, alcohol spirits (to remove mistakes), and chalk to outline the edges of the engravings to aid in their tracing. As chalk can damage engravings (particularly those on friable surfaces), in most places a permit from the relevant regulatory authority is required for the use of chalk.

Tracing is a method that results in a 1:1 record of the art being recorded. A tracing is produced by placing clear polythene (or acetate or other translucent materials) directly onto the rock surface and by drawing directly onto this material an accurate representation of the underlying art (Figure 3.4). It is a very successful technique on engravings that are faint (and/or complex) and with complex pigment assemblages. In the latter case, separate layers for each color can be traced as a way of disentangling the art.

As with all techniques, tracing can produce a variety of outcomes, ranging from incredibly detailed and accurate (where every individual piece of pigment residue on a surface is recorded) to relatively accurate (where only the outside edge of a motif is traced). The degree of accuracy that is required will depend on the purpose of the recording. Indeed, the degree of accuracy will affect the time that it takes to complete this type of recording, which is

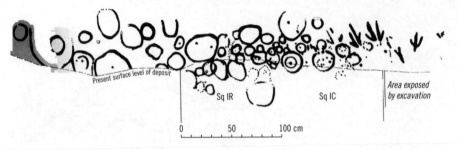

Figure 3.6 A scaled reduction of a traced engraving panel on a boulder at the front of Yengo Rockshelter (see Figure 3.5).

perhaps the most time-consuming kind that many researchers use. This method also allows the recorder to document natural features on rock-art panels (such as edges, natural cracks, and exfoliation; see Figure 3.6).

When tracing pigment art, it helps to have a colored pen for each of the colors of pigment being traced. Most people use blue pens for white ochers and green pens for identifying natural features. When engraved art is being traced, most people use black for the engravings and colored pens for natural features.

As engravings provide good archival data, recorders should remember to provide on the tracing the following information: site identification (region, site name/number), name of recorder, date, orientation of panel (down, up, or north – if horizontal), and the relationship to other tracings in the site/ recording project.

The plastic should be attached to the rock in a manner that avoids attaching adherents such as masking tape to any pigment from the art panel.

Drawbacks to using this technique arise from the vagaries of field conditions. It is extremely difficult to affix the polythene to vertical or overhanging surfaces, particularly those with lichens or loose surface sediments, which makes it difficult to achieve a completely immovable positioning of the plastic medium (Figure 3.4). In extreme heat polythene will stretch (and sometimes tear), making the traced motif positions inaccurate. Lighting conditions need to be optimal. The use of large pieces of polythene will make close inspection of faint art on the underlying rock surface very difficult. It is recommended that pieces of polythene used should be no larger than 2 × 2 m: there are significant difficulties in photographing (and reducing) larger pieces accurately.

When tracings are photographically reduced, it is important to attach a scale such as a meter rule (smaller, if the art is smaller) and to photograph this with the art to ensure that subsequent records are printed to scale. It is also a good idea to photograph the art with an even backlight (Figure 3.7) to ensure that the image produced is evenly illuminated.

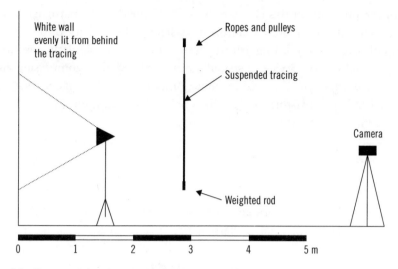

Figure 3.7 The suggested equipment setup for photographing tracings.

The quickest method of recording rock-art in the field is often to count the motifs present. This requires the presence of an existing classificatory system (or taxonomy) and a recording form that allows for this type of information to be summarized. Such a technique is usually used in conjunction with (at least) photography and sketching. When counting the motifs, the basic information for each individual motif, including color, technique, and size as well as comments relating to unusual or significant features, is also usually recorded. During a regional management study of the Sydney Basin rock-art assemblages, a total of 525 shelter art sites and 634 engraving sites were recorded in this fashion, with up to four shelter art sites being recorded in any one day (McDonald 1991).

Most of the questions that are asked of rock-art assemblages can be summarized as follows:

- What does it mean?
- When was it made?
- Who made it?
- What can it tell us about the people who made it?

The way in which most researchers approach the majority of rock-art as a series of archaeological data questions is through style. There is an extensive literature on the definition of style (Shapiro 1953; Sackett 1982, 1990; Wiessner 1984, 1989, 1990; Schaafsma 1985; Layton 2001). It is assumed that style is meaningful to its own culture; that is, to the makers of the art. Thus style has an emic value, not just an etic one (see the discussion regarding classification).

For the purposes of this chapter, "style" is defined as the particular way of doing or producing material culture that signals the activity of a particular group of people who distinguish themselves from other similarly constituted groups (Deetz 1965). Style is a spatially restricted and all-encompassing visual system that expresses the cultural unity of its makers (Schaafsma 1985: 246; and see Conkey & Hastorf 1990). Style is nonverbal communication that negotiates identity (Wiessner 1990: 107).

Rock-art researchers use a variety of methods to address the questions identified above.

Informed methods This method relies on information or a source of insight passed on directly or indirectly from the original makers or participants in the rock-art tradition. Ethnographic analogy falls into this category and has been used (with varying success) in a number of different contexts (Hodder 1982; Smith 1992; Solomon 1998). Examples of where informed methods have been used successfully to explore and interpret rock-art include Lewis-Williams (1981), Lewis-Williams and Dowson (1988), Layton (1989, 1992), Utemara and Vinnecombe (1992), Whitley (1992), York et al. (1993), and Vinnecombe and Mowaljarlai (1995).

There are a number of pitfalls of which researchers attempting to use ethnographic analogy need to be mindful. Cross-cultural comparison is not always achievable. The extrapolation of ethnographic information on symbolism can often only be justified in terms of human universals (Layton 1992), and assembled ethnographic material will be framed in terms of its collector's worldview and can suffer from clumsy cultural translation.

Formal (or structural) methods When we have no "inside" knowledge about the nature of a rock-art assemblage, we need to use formal methods to discern and interpret patterning. For this approach, the relationship of motifs to each other, inter- and intra-site patterning, landscape location, and other archaeological contextual information are used. An art assemblage is then interpreted according to the inherent patterning within it, in much the same manner as the interpretation of other archaeological assemblages. *Semiotics* (the science of signs) is an important structuralist approach that assumes that the imagery made was generated from a set of underlying cultural premises that are structured like language (Lorblanchet 1977; Conkey 1990, 2001; Tilley 1991). *Analogy* is one aspect of this approach. This comes into play when the results of one's analysis is interpreted and relationships and patterns perceived are explained according to what is known of another rock-art assemblage or cultural explanation (for a range of examples, see Lewis-Williams & Loubser 1981; Morwood 1987; Lee 1992). The comments above about the dangers of ethnographic analogy are relevant to such analogies.

Throughout the world, rock-art styles may be localized or widespread. The spatial distribution for rock-art regions is often determined by the suitability of available rock but, equally, environmental and cultural factors appear to have played a part. An example of a spatial analysis is the investigation of the distribution of Venus figurines across Paleolithic Europe between 33,000 and 29,000 years ago (Gamble 1982). This was interpreted in terms of open social networks operating in severe climatic conditions (although for a contrary interpretation, see Soffer 1987). Explorations of regional stylistic trends throughout Europe, which have been explained in a variety of ways, are further examples of spatial analyses (Conkey 1980, 1987; Bahn 1982; Jochim 1983). While in Australia the classification of a very old, pan-continental rock-art style across Australia (known as the *Panaramitee*: Davidson 1937; Maynard 1977) and subsequent more recent regionalization (Lewis 1988; McDonald 1998; Taçon 2001) with localized, presumably more territorial, style areas being developed reveals how structural patterns in rock-art assemblages have been demonstrated and explained.

Spatial distribution analysis

By studying where rock-art occurs in the landscape, researchers investigate how topography conditions the choices made by artists in their use of landscape. These types of studies are based on the premise that cultural choices are being made in the selection of place for use by artists, that rock-art will occur in a patterned way within the landscape (and in relation to other cultural remains), and that indeed the cultural landscape can provide an explanatory mechanism for how many rock-art systems may have functioned (see, e.g., Bradley 1989; David & Wilson 2002). The placement of art in the dark deep limestone caves of Paleolithic Europe has long been interpreted as indicating the nonsecular nature of this art's production. This has recently been restated in terms of the topographic placement of motifs being indicative of shamanistic visions (Clottes & Lewis-Williams 1998). Bradley (1989) and Dronfield (1995) offer similar interpretations for the placement of art in the tombs of megalithic Britain and Ireland. The work of Hartley and Vawser (1998) on the Colorado Plateau is another example. Here, the placement of rock-art was seen as a vital part of the land-use strategy, marking residential and storage locales and access routes to them. The ruggedness of the landscape – and the constraints that this placed on human mobility – provided a perfect opportunity to investigate the inside/outside (emic/etic) social dichotomy and the role that rock-art may have played in mediating this dichotomy (McDonald 2000b).

The notion of style as social strategy is based on the seminal paper by Wobst (1977), in which he proposes general principles for stylistic expression in terms of social communication processes. The major function of stylistic behavior is seen as linking members of a community who are not in constant verbal contact with each other, making their interaction more predictable and less stressful.

Information exchange and stylistic heterogeneity

This general theoretical approach has been applied to style in living societies to explain the degree of competition between groups over resources (Hodder 1978, 1979). It has also been developed to explore the maintenance of personal and social identity distinctions (Wiessner 1984, 1989, 1990). In an archaeological context, this approach has been applied to relate degrees of stylistic heterogeneity to the nature of prehistoric social networks. The European Upper Paleolithic provided a focus for this type of analysis most famously with the widespread distribution of Venus figurines discussed above. Specific applications have also been made on hunter–gatherer art in Australia (Lewis 1988; David & Cole 1990; McDonald 1998, 1999), on pastoral rock-art in Africa (Brandt & Carder 1989), and in the canyon country of Colorado (Hartley & Vawser 1998).

Gendered behavior and art

Most classificatory systems dealing with figurative rock-art assemblages engender – or at least interpret the gender of – the human figures (i.e., male, female, indeterminate anthropomorph). It is occasionally possible to determine the sex of animals either by association or by particular characteristics (e.g., a kangaroo with a joey in its pouch is obviously female).

Art has been interpreted in various countries around the world to engender those participating in the production (or viewing) of rock-art. The presence of women in rock-art production has been inferred by the identification of babies' hand stencils amongst a range of hand sizes (McDonald 1995). Stylistic variation and information messaging differences between art assemblages in demonstrably open versus closed social situations has also been achieved by having engendered the audiences in the various social contexts: occupation sites and art sites in economic zones around the foreshore are argued to be in open social contexts, where the entire population can be assumed to be an audience. Art sites that are secluded or removed from the general economic realms are assumed to have a more restricted audience (McDonald 2000a). The subject has been theorized (Gero & Conkey 1991). Interpretations of rock-art's meaning are often engendered in a dualistic way – that is, in terms of the art's production and/or meaning having male or female associations (e.g., Helskog 1995; Parkington 1996; Dowson 1998; Solomon 1998; Whitley 1998) – again on the basis of the presence of motifs or themes that are interpreted to have this type of significance.

Statistical techniques

A range of multivariate techniques are used by rock-art analysts to compare variables (motifs) and/or objects (usually sites) in large data sets. These techniques are particularly useful in regional analyses where a large number of sites are used (e.g., McDonald 1998; Wilson 1998). There are a number of techniques generally used, including Cluster Analysis, Principal Components Analysis, Discriminant Function Analysis, and Correspondence Analysis. The appropriateness of the technique must be determined by the analysis – often in consultation with a friendly statistician. Useful texts include Bolviken et al. (1982) and Clegg (1990). It is important that the results of these analyses are recognized in terms of statistical significance. The relationship of the results to cultural significance or culturally determined outcomes needs to be determined by appropriately focused research design.

The investigation of changing patterns of rock-art production over time is another quest for the structural analyst. Changing uses in symbolic behavior over time are thought to reflect broader social changes (e.g., Conkey 1978; Gamble 1983; Chen Zhao Fu 1992; Walsh 1994; Yates et al. 1994). In various style regions of Australia, changing social networks and the development of increased territoriality have been explored though stylistic shifts in art assemblages (Morwood 1980, 2002; McDonald 1998). In the Sydney region, a three-phase art sequence was defined. The sequence was based on superimposition analysis (see below) – 189 instances at 65 rockshelters. The first phase of the art sequence (Figure 3.6) was defined as containing an early regional variant of the Panaramitee style (Figure 3.8) – an ancient pan-continental Australian style of art, dominated by engraved tracks and circle motifs (Maynard 1979), which is usually heavily weathered and patinated. Confirmation of this art tradition's age comes from Accelerator Mass Spectrometry (AMS) (on desert varnish) and oxalate crust dating (Dragovich 1986; Nobbs & Dorn 1993; but see Watchman 1992), which places its initial production from at least 30,000 years ago. The regional variant in the Sydney Basin was dated to a minimum of 4,000 years BP (before present). This was replaced by an early pigment phase, dominated by red paintings and hand stencils. The most recent art phase (dated to the past 1,600 years) is dominated by a regionally distinctive range of figurative motifs (mostly macropods and a variety of human figures). This third phase is seen to coincide with major population increase and amplified signaling behavior stimulated by the increase pressures of interaction. The study used a combination of AMS direct dates and relative dating techniques (portrayal of dateable objects – contact items, such as ships and metal axes – excavation of dateable art materials, or excavation of buried art panels) to support the superimposition analysis and structural changes in assemblage content. This analysis is an example of how the advent of AMS (and other chronometric dating techniques) has assisted relative dating techniques to provide an absolute chronology and cultural context for rock-art analysis.

Diachronic change

Because rock-art images rarely occur in dated archaeological contexts, reliable determination of the age of rock-art assemblages has always posed a major challenge for rock-art studies. It is only recently, with the advent of AMS on very small organic samples (e.g., charcoal and plant fibers) and other advances

Dating art

Figure 3.8 An example of Panaramitee-style engravings with tracks, circles, and geometric graphics: Ewaninga, Northern Territory (photograph by J. McDonald).

in chronometric techniques (see below) that the reliable dating of rock-art has been achieved (see Chapter 5). Direct dating programs combined with conventional archaeological investigations have demonstrated that rock-art was produced from at least 40,000 years ago in Australia (O'Connor 1995) and from 32,000 years ago in Europe (Clottes et al. 1995), and for at least 25,000 years in Africa (Wendt 1976). In most rock-art assemblages, organic (carbon-based) materials occur in only minute quantities. This causes not only difficulties in terms of the measurement (dating) of samples from the art but ethical dilemmas in terms of collection, since this is an inherently destructive process. In the absence of direct chronological control, a number of relative dating approaches have been developed by which the relative ages of rock-art images could be inferred. Relative dating techniques use a range of methods to infer the relative age(s) of motifs within any rock-art assemblage. The following examples are given to describe the main types of evidence used in these approaches.

The technique used to engrave rock surfaces involves the puncturing of the weathered outer skin of the rock to expose a lighter- and/or different-colored interior stone matrix. The effect of a newly pecked engraving is a stark contrast between the art and the rock upon which it has been placed. Over time, this contrast is reduced by patination (oxidation and weathering) of the surface, and the engraving eventually returns to the original color of the rock. If certain motifs or styles appear older on the basis of differences in the relative amount of weathering, a generalized chronology can be developed (see, e.g., Lorblanchet 1992).

Differential weathering and patination

Many rock surfaces develop a varnish (which can be chronometrically dated – see below), but the examination of the differential development over time of varnish formation provides another relative dating opportunity. In his study of the Coso Range petroglyphs in California, Whitley (1994) determined that there were three phases of art production. The most recent of these (that with the least varnish development) was found to include an item of material culture (a bow), which was only introduced to the region in the past 1,500 years. Subsequent chronometric analysis confirmed that the most recent period of art production dated to this time frame (Whitley et al. 1999).

This type of technique includes both available access to images and the differential distribution of motifs within and between art locations. A variety of changing environmental conditions has meant that certain art panels can only have been produced under certain conditions. Changing sea levels and the sealing of caves create time capsules that allow for relatively firm chronometric control when used in conjunction with detailed climatic data. For instance, the changing sea levels in Scandinavia have meant that art assumed to have been created adjacent to the sea is now distant from it (Helskog 1999), while the sealing of Cosquer Cave (in France) by rising sea levels (10,000 years ago) meant that its recent discovery was only able to be made by a scuba diver (Clottes & Courtin 1993, 1996)! The relative position of datable archaeological deposit below and/or encroaching on rock-art panels can also be used to deduce the relative age of art production (e.g., Mulloy 1958; Butzer et al. 1979; Rosenfeld et al. 1981; Sundstom 1990; McDonald 1998).

Chronology from spatial analysis

Chronologies may also be derived from a spatial analysis of episodic art production across style regions, based on the recognition that at many rock-art sites, specific techniques, motifs, and colors tend to cluster together (e.g., Morwood 1980). This approach is only useful in regions where there is an extensive corpus of recorded material and where superimpositioning analysis is also possible as a means of seriating the trends observed in isolated art episodes. Such an approach requires the application of an appropriate multivariate technique.

Superimposition analysis Occasionally, an art motif or assemblage will be painted or engraved over another. The principle of superimposition analysis is that the overlapping motif must be younger than any underlying motif. While this sounds simple, there are a number of factors that complicate this type of analysis. With pigment art, some colors adhere well to rock surfaces (e.g., red ochers – hematite) while others are more precarious (e.g., white pipe clay – kaolinite). Some colors are more intense and (visually) penetrate through overlying pigments. Some overlapping motifs will have been deliberately positioned for cultural or aesthetic reasons (Lewis-Williams 1974; Leroi-Gourhan 1976; Wellman 1979) but are contemporaneous in their production. With engraved motifs there are also interpretive difficulties that arise from differential weathering, consistent patination, and different depths and/or techniques of engraving.

Because of the inherent difficulties often encountered in this technique, researchers rarely use the approach in isolation. Rather, a combined approach that also involves differential weathering and stylistic analyses is preferred. Despite the difficulties, this technique has been used extensively in many countries to sequence rock-art traditions (Cox & Stasack 1970; Anati 1976; McCarthy 1976; Sundstom 1990; Chaloupka 1993; Chippindale & Taçon 1998b; Morwood 2002).

Stylistic dating Rock-art researchers identify chronologically meaningful "styles" within any regional rock-art assemblage by analyzing distinctive traits – such as color, motif range, formal attributes, and recurring associations (for motif preferences in the Sydney region over time, see Figure 3.9). Archaeologists often expend considerable effort organizing images into relevant taxonomic units (see above). This process, in association with (usually rare) superimpositioning evidence, can be used to work out the relative ages of paintings or engravings in an area (Butzer et al. 1979; McCarthy 1988; Sundstom 1990; Cole et al. 1995; Chippindale & Taçon 1998b; McDonald 1998). It is only through the development of regional stylistic chronology that absolute dating can be applied in a meaningful fashion (Rosenfeld & Smith 1997); that is, by identifying and dating culturally significant variations in style (i.e., indicative of different cultural groups or changing patterns of art production). Keyser (2001: 131) notes that with the advent of more accurate chronometric control many relative chronologies, while likely to provide reliable regional sequences and stylistic traditions, have been found to seriously underestimate the overall time span represented (e.g., Sundstom 1990; Tratebas 1993).

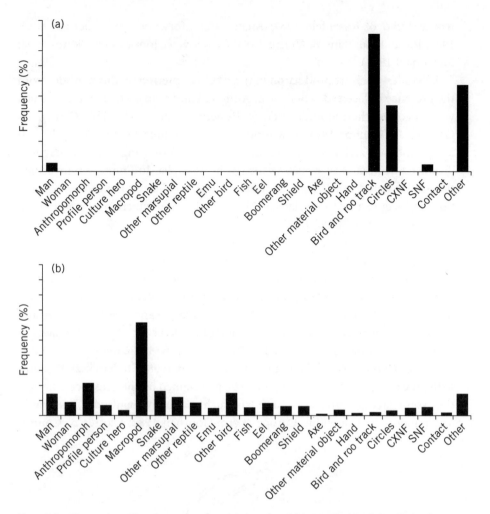

Figure 3.9 Changes in motif preference over time: (a) phase 1 and (b) phase 3 of the Sydney Region Art Sequence (McDonald 1994: fig. 7.2).

In various places around the world, artists created the same motifs or designs on rock-art panels and portable object. The Caves of Altimira and El Castillo (Conkey 1980) contain a related assemblage of (excavated) engraved Solutrean deer scapulae, which can be also identified amongst the rock-art in these caves. The European Paleolithic is best known for this type of relative dating and the resultant analyses (e.g., Conkey 1980; Gamble 1982; Jochim 1983; Begouen & Clottes 1985; Bahn & Vertut 1988; Clottes & Courtin 1996).

Association of dated portable art

There are often situations in which rock-art panels are found partially buried by, or decorated slabs of rock are found within, occupation deposit. Conventional dating of the archaeological deposit will provide a relative date for the art's production. In these cases, the art will be older than the sediments that bury it. Such instances have been documented in most countries around the

Association with dated archaeological deposit or art materials

world (Ucko & Rosenfeld 1967; Anati 1976; Morwood 1980; Kiernan et al. 1983; Prous 1986; Bahn & Vertut 1988; Cosgrove & Jones 1989; Clottes 1994; McDonald 1998).

The oldest rock-art production in the world is inferred by this method, from the presence of facetted ochers in an Arnhem Land sand body dated to c.60,000 years ago by thermoluminescence (Roberts et al. 1993). The Carpenters Gap site (O'Connor 1995) is a more reliable example of this method: with a conventional archaeological investigation demonstrating that rock-art was produced from at least 40,000 years ago in Australia. In France, an investigation of decorated panels with associated dateable ocherous material in occupation deposits resulted in a date of 21,650 BP for the depiction of a red bovid (Clottes & Courtin 1996: 165).

Portrayal of datable subject matter   The historical, archaeological, and paleoenvironmental record can often be used to chronologically interpret rock-art. The depiction of motifs or events that have historic definition, such as the arrival of settler animals and artifacts (boats, horses, carts, rifles) into an Indigenous landscape (see Figures 3.1 and 3.10), allow for relatively accurate pinning of the later (or often last) phases of a rock-art tradition (Cox & Stasack 1970; Vinnicombe 1976; Keyser 1987, 2001; Brandt & Carder 1989; Chaloupka 1993; Klassen 1998; Frederick 2000). Similarly, the antiquity of assemblages can be ascertained by the presence amongst the assemblage of now extinct animals, such as woolly mammoth, great auk, and reindeer in Paleolithic Europe (Leroi-Gourhan 1982; Clottes & Courtin

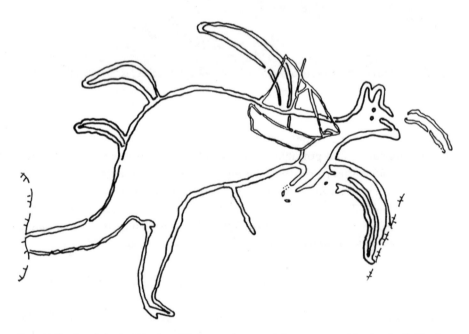

Figure 3.10   A scaled reduced tracing of the engraved macropod, boomerangs, and (post-contact) ship at Devil's Rock, Maroota, in Sydney.

JO MCDONALD

1996), crocodiles and hippopotamus in the Sahara Desert (Anati 1993), Tasmanian tigers on the Australian mainland (Lewis 1977), and extinct megafauna in ancient engraved kangaroo tracks (McDonald 1993).

Direct (or absolute) dating

Rock-art dating using an assortment of "new" scientific (chronometric) techniques is still in its adolescence (Keyser 2001), mainly as a result of the relative newness of the techniques and the lack of theorizing about the applicability of these techniques to art assemblages generally (see McDonald et al. 1990; Bednarik 1994, 1996; Hyman & Rowe 1997; Rosenfeld & Smith 1997; Beck et al. 1998).

Direct dating techniques involve the collection and dating of small samples from art (e.g., pigment, charcoal, and beeswax) or from crusts and/or deposits overlaying (or underlying) art motifs (e.g., oxalate crusts, desert varnish, and mud-wasp nests). Accelerator Mass Spectrometry (AMS) is the most widely used technique, because it requires much smaller samples ($\sim$ 0.0005 g versus 5 g) than conventional radiocarbon (see Rowe 2001). AMS counts the number of radiocarbon (^{14}C) molecules (as a ratio to carbon) in any organic material. The main difference between this and conventional radiocarbon dating is that AMS counts the actual ^{14}C atoms – as opposed to the number of atoms that decay over a given time period (for a detailed discussion of the techniques, see Chapter 5).

Charcoal is the most common archaeological material used for dating and although there are certain identified caveats, such as potential contamination and the old wood and fossil charcoal problems (i.e., whereby freshly felled trees are not the source of the charcoal used for the art production: Schiffer 1986; Bednarik 1996), the techniques for dating it are reliable and well tested (Rowe 2001).

Researchers have experimented with a number of other materials and techniques. These have included plasma-chemical extraction of organic carbon from inorganic pigments (Hyman & Rowe 1997), fibers found in paints (Watchman & Cole 1993), beeswax (Nelson 2000), blood residues (Loy et al. 1990; although see Nelson 1993; Gillespie 1997), oxalate crusts (Watchman 1993) and optically stimulated luminescence dating (OSL) of mud wasp nests over or beneath rock-art (Roberts et al. 1997).

Focused dating programs have resulted in firm chronological control on a variety of art styles from a number of countries. This technique, however, is still in its infancy. As Rowe (2001: 148) points out, in the order of only about 100 radiocarbon dates have so far been published. France has a number of well-dated sites (Valladas et al. 1992; Clottes & Courtin 1996), while most other countries have as yet just a smattering of tantalizing (but not necessarily reliable) dated evidence. In Australia, charcoal, beeswax, oxalate crusts, Bradshaw figures, and plant fibers in paint have been dated (McDonald et al. 1990; Watchman et al. 1997; David et al. 1999; Nelson 2000). In Africa, despite one of the earliest attempts at this technique (Van der Merwe et al. 1987) there have been few (published) successful attempts (Lewis-Williams 1998). In the United States there have been a number of dating exercises that have resulted in the dating of charcoal and red (iron oxide) drawings (Chaffee et al. 1994; Ilger et al. 1995; Hyman et al. 1999; Whitely 2000).

Case Study
The Depiction of Species in Macropod Track Engravings

This case study describes the use of formal methods to investigate stylistic variation within a very old engraved assemblage of the Panaramitee style (see under "Diachronic change" above). There is no ethnographic information about the site analyzed and in many parts of Australia Aboriginal people describe the Panaramitee art form (Figure 3.8) as being "from the Dreamtime."

The case study reported here describes the investigation of variability in an engraved motif type (for a detailed description, see McDonald 1993). The art assemblage consisted of macropod (kangaroo and wallaby family) tracks from Sturt's Meadows (New South Wales). This is a Panaramitee engraving site in the Australian semiarid zone, with over 20,000 individual engraved motifs (Clegg 1987). The site stretches over an area of approximately 2 × 1 km. The engravings occur on a smooth, Precambrian mudstone.

The predominant motifs at this site are macropod tracks, but these vary in appearance across the site. The aim of this analysis was to discover whether macropod species differentiation accounted for any of the variability in the engraved macropod track assemblage; that is, whether the tracks of different species of kangaroos can be recognized in this art body. As Aboriginal hunters learn from childhood how to recognize animal tracks and to decipher them accurately, it was felt that such a cause of variation in the macropod track engravings was highly probable. Further, it was thought that this investigation could result in a credible cultural classification of the tracks in the art assemblage. Animal identification in Australian Aboriginal art has been a longstanding quest, mostly to establish the antiquity of Aboriginal art (Basedow 1904; Hale 1926).

The analysis consisted of two experiments. One of these involved the zoological specimens and the other the engraving assemblage. The zoological experiment investigated macropodid taxonomy and pes (foot) morphology. This was done to establish whether different kangaroos had different-shaped feet and, if so, to find out what characteristics were significant in distinguishing between species. The archaeological experiment analyzed patterning within the engraved macropod track assemblage. The overriding assumption for this analysis, which focused on one subsite, was that attribute analysis of animal depictions would reveal (archaeological) patterns that could be interpreted culturally. A more specific assumption was that those engravings that look like animal tracks were intended to be representations of animal tracks. In other words, the engraved motifs were assumed to be naturalistic, possessing explicit visual resemblance.

The combined experimental designs were formulated in the hope that this would allow various cultural questions to be asked of the engraved assemblage. Was any particular preference indicated by the depiction of kangaroo species? What is the likely economic or cultural significance of such an artistic partiality? Were there environmental changes indicated in changing preferences over time?

The zoological experiment

The zoological experiment was undertaken to discover whether it was possible to distinguish between the feet and footprints of the macropod species known to have been in the semi arid zone over the past 4,000–10,000 years. The pes of a macropod has four digits (Figure 3.11). Several of these digits are syndactylous (enclosed in one skin, with both claws protruding). Their function is primarily grooming. The largest and main supporting

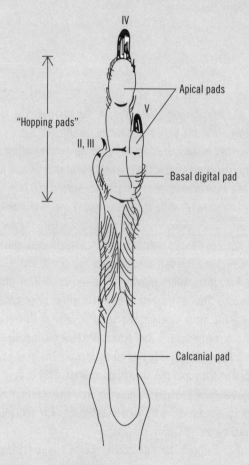

Figure 3.11 A posterior view of a typical macropod pes.

digit is the fourth, with balance being provided by second-largest digit (the fifth). There are various external characteristics that differ markedly according to different environmental zones. For instance, the length of the fourth toe claw is short on rock-dwellers but long on grass/sand-dwellers.

The species of relevance in this analysis are the eastern and western gray kangaroos (*Macropus giganteus, M. fuliginosus*), the red kangaroo (*Macropus rufus*), the euro (*Macropus robustus*), and the yellow-footed rock wallaby (*Petrogale xanthopus*). These species are thought to have inhabited the Sturt's Meadows area throughout (at least) the Holocene.

Mounted specimens (of 43 extant and extinct macropod species) from the Australian and Macleay Museums' mammal collections were used for the analysis. Sixteen variables were recorded, 11 metrical and five assorted variables on ordinal scales. These described the variation observable and included measurements such as length and breadth of various foot parts, as well as degrees of hairiness and separateness of the pads. Only for the red kangaroo, which exhibits marked sexual dimorphism (Dawson 1977), were a male and female included in the sample.

The results

Principal Components Analysis (PCA) was used for this analysis. PCA is designed to reveal the effect of particular variables used in the analysis. The results of the PCA revealed that almost all of the variables counted contributed equally to the variability within the sample. That is, each was equally good at discriminating between different species and genera. The results indicated a separation of the relevant macropod species. Cluster Analysis was also used to demonstrate this separation. The red kangaroos and the euros clustered cohesively; while the yellow-footed rock wallaby was the closest of the other key species (this species clustered most closely with the six other rock wallabies). There was internal species cohesion within the euro/red cluster. This analysis indicated that sexual dimorphism (i.e., size) does not create shape differences within species. The gray kangaroos, while showing a marked correlation with each other, are distanced from the other Sturt's Meadows species. The grays' closest statistical neighbors are an amorphous group, none of which is present in western New South Wales.

On the basis of pes morphology, it was determined that the macropod species likely to be found at Sturt's Meadows fall into two broad groups. The gray kangaroos form one group, and the rock wallaby and red kangaroos another. This finding formed a springboard for the archaeological analysis. Before this was undertaken, however, the normal range of variation in macropod tracks was investigated. Any one species will produce vastly different tracks under differing conditions.

The best published authority for this information is Triggs (1985), who states that when tracking an animal, the following seven categories of information can be obtained:

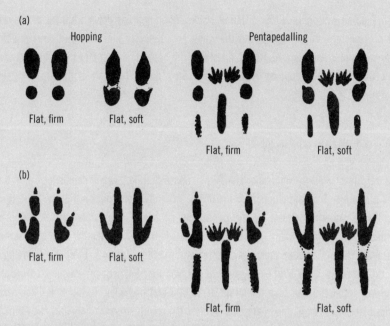

(a)

Hopping   Pentapedalling

Flat, firm   Flat, soft

Flat, firm   Flat, soft

(b)

Flat, firm   Flat, soft

Flat, firm   Flat, soft

Figure 3.12 Variations in gait for two species in different surface conditions: (a) *Macropus robustus*; (b) *M. fuliginosus*.

species, approximate size (age), gait, speed, surface, terrain, and (sometimes) sex. All of these categories can affect the resulting track imprint and therefore all required investigation for this analysis. They are briefly summarized here.

Any species can move by any number of gaits (Figure 3.12). The most popularly recognized gait of the kangaroo is bipedal hopping ("leaping" and "bounding"). This gait involves only the distal pesal pads. The heel (calcanial pad) does not touch the ground; nor does the tail (used here only for balance). When browsing ("punting"), kangaroos move either quadrapedally or pentapedally. In the former, both manus (hands) and pes are involved. Pentapedally, the tail is also employed, resulting in five imprints per track. Depending on the speed, these gaits can include either the entire foot or only the "hopping pads" (Figure 3.11). The final variation of imprint is sitting, and here the entire length of the pes is involved, as is the tail, but not the hands.

Every type of gait is affected by speed, numerous configurations being possible. At high speed, the imprint is usually deepest around the distal fourth toe area, while the fifth toe is not visible. The distance between imprints becomes greater as an animal speeds up.

The hardness and consistency of the surface directly affect the shape of the track imprint (Figure 3.12): the softer the soil matrix, the more of the foot is incorporated into the track. A loosely packed matrix such as dry beach/desert sand is not at all conducive to clear print outlines, but then neither is rock or any other extremely hard surface. With terrain, the factor of slope is introduced. Hopping up, down, or around a hill on one stable matrix will produce four different tracks. When hopping down a hill the prints will not only become further apart, but the whole foot tends to move forward, creating the impression of greater length. Uphill, often only the imprint of the tip of the fourth toe and claw will be visible. Hopping around and down a slope, the pair of imprints will not be parallel.

The archaeological experiment

The subsite chosen for this experiment was "South Saddle," which consists of nine flat rock platforms. The engravings here are dense and indicate a great antiquity. As well as significant superimposition, on the peripheries of these great slabs, the remains of earlier surfaces are evident. These are badly eroded and fragmented from the fresher surfaces. The surfaces of these fragments contain older, deeply patinated, engravings. All the surfaces have a thick layer of desert varnish. Subsequent calcium carbonate analysis dated the site to a minimum of 10,000 BP (Dragovich 1986). It is likely that artistic activities took place here over several thousands of years and that the earliest phases of art production occurred much earlier than this (e.g., Nobbs & Dorn 1993).

A total of 233 macropod track allomorphs were recorded from South Saddle. Polythene tracing and photography was used to record these motifs in the field. These were subsequently measured and subject to quantitative analysis in the laboratory. A roughly symmetrical pair of imprints counted as a single track. Single imprints, pairs of "bars," incomplete motifs, and combination tracks indicating complex gaits (e.g., pentapedals) were excluded from the analysis. The final analysis was thus made on a sample of 204 "hopping" track allomorphs. These 204 motifs were classified into 23 "varieties" or types on morphological criteria (Figure 3.13a). This classification was based purely on shape characteristics (i.e., not size). Quantitative analysis involved the measurement of 19 variables (see McDonald 1993: fig. 6). The sample was subjected to PCA. A detailed description of the data treatment, methods, and results can be found elsewhere (McDonald 1993). Each track allomorph was treated individually – with the classification assigned to each track not included as a variable. The aims of the analysis were to determine whether:

1   It would reveal clusters of morphologically similar tracks that could be interpreted in terms of the two species groups that were distinguished in the zoological experiment.
2   The track allomorphs outside the modern range of variation (e.g., possible extinct megafauna depictions) would also cluster distinctively.

Visually, the species-specific trait that discriminates between the engraved "species" is the separation between the fourth toe and the basal digital pad, and the length of the fifth toe. It was contended that the rounder track engravings consisting of two or more parts represent the euro/red kangaroo species, while single-entity engravings represent

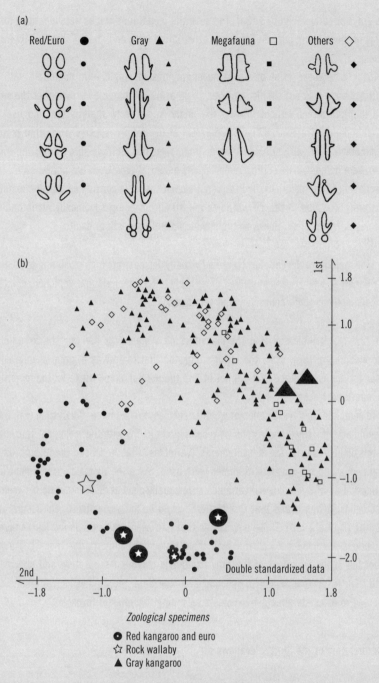

Figure 3.13 (a) Seventeen of the 23 artifact (motif) types identified at South Saddle site, ordered into species: red kangaroo/euro, gray kangaroo, megafauna, and others. (b) The bivariate graph for component scores (PCA) shows how the engraved motif types cluster around zoological macropod pes types.

the gray kangaroos (Figure 3.13a). The potential megafauna tracks were identified on the basis of these being outside the range of variation (size and shape) observed on extant species.

Clear differences exist between the engravings of single form compared with the multiple ones. It is not simple, however, to measure comparable variables for the single and multiple forms without biasing the analysis. An early analysis that did use this variable demonstrated conclusive separation of the defined species. To further test the assemblage then, all variables that distinguished the multiple forms from the single form were deleted. This editing removed any potential bias from the analysis but, as a consequence, the results of the PCA were inconclusive. It is considered that the resultant clustering was due to the 19 variables measured not being specifically attributable to species differentiation. However, there were several interesting results:

1   The majority of the varieties classified visually demonstrate high clustering tendencies.
2   Variety A, which was considered most likely to be a megafaunal depiction, clustered distinctively (both cohesively and separately).

The first result indicated that the classification system was dividing the assemblage into meaningful taxa, while the latter suggested that there was a group of engravings amongst the assemblage that did not fit into the normal shape range for the majority of the engraved tracks.

To complete the investigation of whether species was a source of variation within this assemblage, the track allomorphs were compared directly with the zoological specimens. In this final analysis, six measurements (variables) that had been made both on the engravings and the museum examples were used. Since the zoological experiment indicated that all of the zoological variables were equally good at discriminating between the macropods, it was hoped that this analysis would be more conclusive. The results were exciting (Figure 3.13b). Those engravings that had been predicted as red kangaroo/euro depictions were found to cluster with their zoological counterparts. Those engravings predicted to be depictions of the gray kangaroos clustered separately, and specifically with their respective zoological specimens. At the time, the archaeological results contributed to a debate amongst zoologists regarding macropodid taxonomy.

Interpretation of the Sturt's Meadows art

This research demonstrated that some of the observed variation in the ancient engraved assemblage at Sturt's Meadows can be explained in terms of macropod species differentiation. As well as addressing this specific question of variability, the project formulated a method for interpreting general variability within an assemblage. It was discovered that the classification of macropods on the basis of pes morphology divides the family into two groups that can be observed both zoologically and archaeologically. Such a strong correlation between nature and the archaeology indicated that culturally meaningful questions could be asked of the assemblage; namely, the presence and distribution of particular species and their importance to the artisans who produced them. At other Panaramitee sites across Australia, it should be possible to draw similar conclusions involving the local macropod species.

As well as interpretations relating to economic or cultural significance, the recognition of megafaunal depictions was also a significant outcome. Engravings outside the acceptable modern range of variation (based on shape, not size) within the macropod track assemblage may well be interpreted as such following appropriate analysis, without incurring the usual range of criticisms based on size/style (e.g., Davidson 1937; McCarthy 1979). This case study is given as an example of how a research question and assumptions can be addressed by formal methods using systematic and quantified analysis.

Conclusion

This chapter has attempted to identify why people investigate rock-art and some of the approaches that are used to achieve this end. Rock-art provides an insight into the human condition – a glimpse of humanity's response to its environment, its people, and its realities. It reveals artistry. It often reveals a sense of humor. By grappling with its meaning, archaeologists strive to understand more about human complexity than can often be achieved by studying other forms of archaeological evidence.

Resources

There are a number of rock-art associations around the world, of which interested practitioners are members. These associations produce journals and other publications on the subject of rock-art research.

Key associations and journals

- *The International Federation of Rock Art Organizations (IFRAO)*. IFRAO is a federation of national and regional organizations promoting the study of paleoart and cognitive archaeology globally. Their website (www.ifrao.com/home/ifrao/web/brepols.html) provides link information to the numerous federated members – 36 in all at the time of writing this chapter.

The rock-art research associations with the largest memberships are listed below:

- *American Rock Art Research Association (ARARA)*. Contact details: Box 210026, Tucson, AZ 85721 0026, USA. Telephone: (888) 668 0052. Fax: (888) 668 0052. Email: LaPintura@earthlink.net. Official newsletter: *La Pintura*. Journal: *American Indian Rock Art*: www.arara.org

- *Australian Rock Art Research Association, Inc. (AURA)*. Contact details: Robert Bednarik (Editor), P.O. Box 216, Caulfied South, Victoria, 3162, Australia. Telephone and fax: 613 9523 0549. Email: auranet@optusnet.com.au. Journal: *Rock Art Research*: http://mc2.vicnet.net.au/home/aura/web/index.html
- *Association pour le Rayonnement de l'Art Pariétal Européen (ARAPE)*. Contact: Jean Clottes, 11, rue du Fourcat, 09000 Foix, France. Email: j.clottes@wanadoo.fr

For a more complete listing of relevant associations, see www.cesmap.it/ifrao/ifrao.htm/

Further reading

The following recent key texts summarize the field of rock-art research:

Chippindale, C. and Taçon, P. S. C. (eds.) 1998: *The Archaeology of Rock-Art*. Cambridge: Cambridge University Press.

David, B. and Wilson, M. (eds.) 2002: *Inscribed Landscapes*. Honolulu: University of Hawaii Press.

Helskog, K. 2001: *Theoretical Perspectives in Rock Art Research*. Oslo: Novus Forlag.

Morwood, M. J. 2002: *Visions from the Past: The Archaeology of Australian Aboriginal Art*. Crows Nest, NSW: Allen and Unwin.

Whitley, D. S. (ed.) 2001: *Handbook of Rock Art Research*. Walnut Creek, CA: AltaMira Press.

References

Anati, E. 1976: *Evolution and Style in Camunian Rock Art*. Archivi, 6. Edizioni del Centro Camuno di Studi Preistorica: Capo di Ponte, Italy.

—— 1993: *World Rock Art: the Primordial Language*. Studi Camuni, 12. Edizioni del Centro: Capo di Ponte, Italy.

Bahn, P. G. 1982: Inter-site and interregional links during the upper Palaeolithic: the Pyrean evidence. *The Oxford Journal of Archaeology*, 1, 247–68.

—— and Vertut, J. 1988: *Images of the Ice Age*. Leicester: Windward.

Basedow, H. 1904: Anthropological notes made on the South Australian Government North-west Prospecting Expedition 1903. *Transactions of the Royal Society of South Australia*, 28, 12–53.

Beck, W., Donohue, D. J., Jull, A. J. T. et al. 1998: Ambiguities in direct dating of rock surfaces using radiocarbon measures. *Science*, 280, 2132–5.

Bednarik, R. 1986: Cave use by Australian Pleistocene Man. *Proceedings of the University of Bristol Speleological Society*, 17(3), 227–45.

—— 1994: Conceptual pitfalls in dating of Palaeolithic rock art. *Préhistoire Anthropologie Méditerrannées*, 3, 95–102.

—— 1996: Only time will tell: a review of the methodology of Direct Rock Art Dating. *Archaeometry*, 38, 1–13.

Begouen, R. and Clottes, J. 1985: L'art mobilier des Magdaleniens. *Archaeologia*, 207, November, 40–9.

Bolviken, E., Helskog, E. and Helskog, H. 1982: Correspondence analysis: an alternative to principal components. *World Archaeology*, 14(1), 41–60.

Bradley, R. 1989: Deaths and entrances: a contextual analysis of megalithic art. *Current Anthropology*, 39, 68–75.

Brandt, S. A. and Carder, N. 1989: Pastoral rock art in the Horn of Africa: making sense of udder chaos. *World Archaeology*, 19(2), 194–213.

Brayshaw, H. C. 1990: *Well Beaten Paths: Aborigines of the Herbert Burdekin District, North Queensland: An Anthropological and Archaeological Study.* Townsville: James Cook University.

Butzer, K. W., Fock, G. J., Scott, L. and Stuckenrath, R. 1979: Dating and context of rock engravings in southern Africa. *Science*, 203(4386), 1201–14.

Chaffee, S. D., Hyman, M., Rowe, M. W., Coulman, N., Schroedl, A. and Hogue, K. 1994: Radiocarbon dates on the All American Man. *American Antiquity*, 59, 769–81.

Chaloupka, G. 1993: *Journey in Time: The World's Longest Continuing Art Tradition.* Chatswood: Reed.

Chen Zhao Fu 1992: Discovery of rock art in China. In M. Lorblanchet (ed.), *Rock Art in the Old World.* India: Indira Gandhi National Centre for the Arts, 361–71.

Chippindale, C. 2001: Studying ancient pictures as pictures. In D. S. Whitley (ed.), *Handbook of Rock Art Research.* Walnut Creek, CA: AltaMira Press, 247–72.

—— and Taçon, P. S. C. (eds.) 1998a: *The Archaeology of Rock-Art.* Cambridge: Cambridge University Press.

—— and —— 1998b: The many ways of dating Arnhem Land rock-art, northern Australia. In C. Chippindale and P. S. C. Taçon (eds.), *The Archaeology of Rock-Art.* Cambridge: Cambridge University Press, 90–111.

Clegg, F. 1990: *Simple Statistics: A Course Book for the Social Sciences.* Cambridge: Cambridge University Press.

Clegg, J. K. 1983: Recording prehistoric art. In G. Connah (ed.), *Australian Field Archaeology: A Guide to Techniques*, 3rd edn. Canberra: Australian Institute of Aboriginal Studies, 87–108.

—— 1987: Style and tradition at Sturt's Meadows. *World Archaeology*, 19(2), 236–55.

Clottes, J. 1994: Dates directes pour les peintures paléolithiques. *Bulletin de la Société Préhistorique Française de l'Ariège*, 91, 51–70.

—— and Courtin, J. 1993: Dating a new painted cave: the Cosquer Cave, Marseille, France. In J. Steinbring, J. A. Watchman, P. Faulstich, and P. S. C. Taçon (eds.), *Time and Space: Dating and Spatial Consideration in Rock Art Research.* Occasional AURA Publication, 8. Melbourne: Archaeological Publications, 22–31.

—— and —— 1996: *The Cave Beneath the Sea: Palaeolithic Images at Cosquer.* New York: Harry N. Abrahams.

—— and Lewis-Williams, J. D. 1998: *The Shamans of Prehistory: Trance and Magic in the Painted Caves.* New York: Harry N. Abrahams.

——, Chauvet, J. M., Bruel-Deschampes, E. et al., 1995: Radiocarbon dates for the Chauvet-Pont-d'Arc Cave. *International Newsletter of Rock Art*, 11, 1–2.

Cole, N. A., Watchman, A. and Morwood, M. J. 1995: Chronology of Laura rock art. In M. J. Morwood and D. R. Hobbs (eds.), *Quinkan Prehistory: The Archaeology of Aboriginal Art in S.E. Cape York Peninsula.* Tempus, 3. St Lucia: Anthropology Museum, University of Queensland, 147–60.

Conkey, M. W. 1978: Style and information in cultural evolution: towards a predictive model for the Palaeolithic. In C. L. Redman, M. J. Berman, E. V. Curtvin et al. (eds.), *Social Archaeology: Beyond Subsistence and Dating.* New York: Academic Press, 61–85.

—— 1980: The identification of hunter–gatherer aggregation sites – the case of Altimira. *Current Anthropology*, 21(5), 609–30.

—— 1987: Interpretative problems in hunter–gatherer regional studies: some thoughts on the European Upper Palaeolithic. In O. Soffer (ed.), *The Pleistocene Old World: Regional Perspectives.* New York: Plenum Press, 63–77.

—— 1990: Experimenting with style in archaeology: some historical and theoretical issues. In M. Conkey and C. Hastorf (eds.), *The Uses of Style in Archaeology*. New Directions in Archaeology. Cambridge: Cambridge University Press, 5–17.

—— 2001: Structural and semiotic approaches. In D. S. Whitley (ed.), *Handbook of Rock Art Research*. Walnut Creek, CA: AltaMira Press, 273–310.

—— and Hastorf, C. A. 1990: Introduction. In M. W. Conkey and C. A. Hastorf (eds.), *The Uses of Style in Archaeology*. New Directions in Archaeology. Cambridge: Cambridge University Press, 1–4.

Cosgrove, R. and Jones, R. 1989: Judds Cavern: a subterranean Aboriginal painting site, southern Tasmania. *Rock Art Research*, 6(2), 96–104.

Cox, J. H. and Stasack, E. 1970: *Hawaiian Petroglyphs*. Bernice P. Bishop Museum Special Publication no. 60. Honolulu: Bernice P. Bishop Museum.

David, B. and Cole, N. 1990: Rock art and inter-regional interaction in northeast Australian prehistory. *Antiquity*, 64, 788–806.

—— and Wilson, M. (eds.) 2002: *Inscribed Landscapes*. Honolulu: University of Hawaii Press.

——, Armitage, R. A., Hyman, M., Rowe, M. W. and Lawson, E. 1999: How old is North Queensland rock-art? A review of the evidence, with new AMS determinations. *Archaeology in Oceania*, 34, 103–20.

Davidson, D. S. 1937: *A Preliminary Consideration of Aboriginal Australian Decorative Art*. Memoirs of the American Philosophical Society, vol. 9. Philadelphia: American Philosophical Society.

Davidson, I. and Noble, W. 1989: The archaeology of perception: traces of depiction and language. *Current Anthropology*, 30(2), 125–55.

Davis, W. 1986: The origins of image making. *Current Anthropology*, 27, 193–215.

Dawson, T. J. 1977: Kangaroos. *Scientific American*, August, 78–89.

Deetz, J. 1965: *The Dynamics of Stylistic Change in Arikara Ceramics*. Illinois Studies in Anthropology 4. Urbana: University of Illinois Press.

Dowson, T. A. 1998: Rain in Bushmen beliefs, politics and history: the rock art of rain-making in the south-eastern mountains, southern Africa. In C. Chippindale and P. Taçon (eds.), *The Archaeology of Rock-Art*. Cambridge: Cambridge University Press, 73–89.

Dragovich, D. 1986: Minimum age of some desert varnish near Broken Hill, NSW. *Search*, 17(5–6), May/June, 149–50.

Dronfield, J. 1995: Subjective vision and the source of Irish megalithic art. *Antiquity*, 69, 539–49.

Forge, A. 1991: Hand stencils: rock art or not art. In P. Bahn and A. Rosenfeld (eds.), *Rock Art and Prehistory: Papers Presented to Symposium G of the AURA Congress, Darwin 1988*. Oxbow Monograph, 10. Oxford: Oxbow Books, 39–44.

Frederick, U. 2000: Keeping the land alive: changing social contexts of landscape and rock art production. In R. Torrence and A. Clarke (eds.), *The Archaeology of Difference: Negotiating Cross-Cultural Engagements in Oceania*. London: Routledge, 300–30.

Gamble, C. S. 1982: Interaction and alliance in Palaeolithic society. *Man*, 17(1), 92–107.

—— 1983: Culture and society in the Upper Palaeolithic of Europe. In G. Bailey (ed.), *Hunter–Gatherer Economy in Prehistory: A European Perspective*. Cambridge: Cambridge University Press, 201–11.

Gero, J. and Conkey, M. (eds.) 1991: *Engendering Archaeology*. Oxford: Blackwell.

Gillespie, R. 1997: On human blood, rock art and calcium oxalate: further studies on organic carbon content and radiocarbon age of materials relating to Australian Rock Art. *Antiquity*, 71, 430–7.

Hale, H. M. 1926: Aboriginal rock carvings in South Australia. *The South Australian Naturalist*, 8(1), 12.

Hartley, R. J. and Vawser, A. W. 1998: Spatial behavior and learning in the prehistoric environment of the Colorado Drainage (south-eastern Utah), western North America. In C. Chippindale and P. S. C. Taçon (eds.), *The Archaeology of Rock-Art*. Cambridge: Cambridge University Press, 185–211.

Helskog, K. 1995: Maleness and femaleness in the sky and underworld – and in between. In K. Helskog and B. Olsen (eds.), *Perceiving Rock Art: Social and Political Perspectives*. Oslo: The Institute of Comparative Research in Human Culture, 247–66.

—— 1999: The Shore connection: cognitive landscapes and communication with rock carvings in northernmost Europe. *Norwegian Archaeological Review*, 32(2), 73–94.

—— 2001: *Theoretical Perspectives in Rock Art Research*. Oslo: Novus Forlag.

Hodder, I. R. 1978: The maintenance of group identities in the Baringo district, West Kenya. In D. Green, C. Haselgrove and M. Spriggs (eds.), *Social Organization and Settlement*. BAR International Series, 47(i). Oxford: British Archaeological Reports, 47–74.

—— 1979: Economic and social stress and material culture patterning. *American Antiquity*, 44(3), 446–54.

—— 1982: *Symbols in Action: Ethnoarchaeological Studies of Material Culture*. Cambridge: Cambridge University Press.

Hyman, M. and Rowe, M. W. 1997: Plasma-chemical extraction and AMS dating of rock paintings. In S. M. Freers (ed.), *American Indian Rock Art*, vol. 23. San Miguel: American Rock Art Research Association, 1–9.

——, Sutherland, K., Armitage, R. A., Southon, J. R. and Rowe, M. W. 1999: Radiocarbon analyses of Hueco Tanks Rock Paintings. *Rock Art Research*, 16, 75–88.

Ilger, W. A., Dauvois, M., Hyman, M. et al. 1995: Datation radiocarbone de deux figures parietales de la Grotte du Portel (Commune de Loubens, Ariège). *Préhistoire Ariègeoise*, 50, 231–6.

Jochim, M. A. 1983: Palaeolithic cave art in ecological perspective. In G. Bailey (ed.), *Hunter–Gatherer Economy in Prehistory: A European Perspective*. Advances in Archaeological Method and Theory. Cambridge: Cambridge University Press, 212–19.

Keyser, J. D. 1987: Lexicon for historic Plains Indian rock art: increasing interpretive potential. *Plains Anthropologist*, 32(115), 43–71.

—— 2001: Relative dating methods. In D. S. Whitley (ed.), *Handbook of Rock Art Research*. Walnut Creek, CA: AltaMira Press, 116–38.

Kiernan, K., Jones, R. and Ranson, D., 1983: New evidence from Fraser Cave for glacial man in southwest Tasmania. *Nature*, 301, 28–32.

Klassen, M. A., 1998: Icon and narrative in transition: contact period rock-art at Writing-on-Stone, southern Alberta, Canada. In C. Chippindale and P. Taçon (eds.), *The Archaeology of Rock-Art*. Cambridge: Cambridge University Press, 42–72.

Layton, R. 1989: The political use of Australian Aboriginal body painting and its archaeological implications. In I. Hodder (ed.), *The Meanings of Things: Material Culture and Symbolic Expression*. London: Unwin Hyman, 1–11.

—— 1992: The role of ethnography in the study of Australian rock art. In M. J. Morwood and D. R. Hobbs (eds.), *Rock Art and Ethnography*. Occasional AURA Publication no. 5. Melbourne: Australian Rock Art Research Association, 7–9.

—— 2001: Ethnographic study and symbolic analysis. In D. S. Whitley (ed.), *Handbook of Rock Art Research*. Walnut Creek, CA: AltaMira Press, 311–31.

Lee, G. 1992: *Rock Art of Easter Island: Symbols of Power, Prayers to the Gods*. Monumenta Archaeologica, 17. Los Angeles: The Institute of Archaeology, University of California.

Leroi-Gourhan, A. 1976: The evolution of Palaeolithic art. In B. Fagan (ed.), *From Avenues to Antiquity: Readings from* Scientific American. San Francisco: W. H. Freeman, 55–65.

—— 1982: *The Dawn of European Art: An Introduction to Palaeolithic Cave Painting*, trans. S. Champion. Cambridge: Cambridge University Press.

Lewis, D. 1977: More striped designs in Arnhem Land rock paintings. *Archaeology and Physical Anthropology in Oceania*, 12(2), 140–5.

—— 1988: *The Rock Paintings of Arnhem Land, Australia: Social, Ecological and Material Culture Change in the Post-Glacial Period*. BAR International Series, 415. Oxford: British Archaeological Reports.

Lewis-Williams, J. D. 1974: Superimpositioning in a sample of rock paintings from the Barkly East District. *South African Archaeological Bulletin*, 29, 93–103.

—— 1981: *Believing and Seeing: Symbolic Meanings in Southern San Rock Paintings*. London: Academic Press.

—— 1998: Current South African rock art research: a brief history and review. *International Newsletter on Rock Art*, 20, 12–22.

—— and Dowson, T. 1988: The signs of all times: entoptic phenomena in Upper Palaeolithic rock art. *Current Anthropology*, 29(2), 201–45.

—— and Loubser, J. H. N. 1981: Deceptive appearances: a critique of South African rock art studies. *Advances in World Archaeology*, 5, 253–89.

Loendorf, L. 2001: Rock art recording. In D. S. Whitley (ed.), *Handbook of Rock Art Research*. Walnut Creek, CA: AltaMira Press, 55–79.

Lorblanchet, M. 1977: From naturalism to abstraction in European prehistoric rock art. In P. J. Ucko (ed.), *Form in Indigenous Art*. Canberra: Australian Institute of Aboriginal Studies, 44–56.

—— 1992: The rock engravings of Gum Tree Valley and Skew Valley, Dampier, Western Australia. Chronology and function of sites. In J. J. McDonald and I. Haskovek (eds.), *State of the Art: Regional Rock Art Studies in Australia and Melanesia*. AURA Publication no. 6. Melbourne: Australian Rock Art Research Association, 39–59.

Loy, T. H., Jones, R., Nelson, D. E. et al. 1990: Accelerator radiocarbon dating of human blood proteins in pigments from Late Pleistocene art sites in Australia. *Antiquity*, 64, 110–16.

McCarthy, F. D. 1976: *Rock Art of the Cobar Pediplain in Central Western New South Wales*. Australian Institute of Aboriginal Studies Regional Research and Studies, 7. Canberra: Australian Institute of Aboriginal Studies.

—— 1979: *Australian Aboriginal Rock Art*, 4th edn. Sydney: Australian Museum.

—— 1988: Rock art sequences: a matter of clarification (with comments by Clegg, David, Franklin, McDonald, Maynard, Moore, Morwood, Rosenfeld and Bednarik: with author's reply). *Rock Art Research*, 5(1), 16–42.

McDonald, J. J. 1991: Archaeology and art in the Sydney region: context and theory in the analysis of a dual medium style. In P. Bahn and A. Rosenfeld (eds.), *Rock Art and Prehistory: Papers Presented to Symposium G of the AURA Congress, Darwin 1988*. Oxbow Monograph, 10. Oxford: Oxbow Books, 78–85.

—— 1993: The depiction of species in macropod track engravings at an Aboriginal art site in western New South Wales. *Records of the Australian Museum, Supplement*, 17, 105–16.

—— 1995: Looking for a woman's touch: indications of gender in shelter sites in the Sydney Basin. In J. Balme and W. Beck (eds.), *Gendered Archaeology: The Second Australian Women in Archaeology Conference*. Canberra: ANH Publications, Australian National University, 92–6.

—— 1998: Shelter rock art in the Sydney Basin – a space–time continuum: exploring different influences on stylistic change. In C. Chippindale and P. Taçon (eds.), *The Archaeology of Rock-Art*. Cambridge: Cambridge University Press, 319–35.

—— 1999: Bedrock notions and isochrestic choice: evidence for localized stylistic patterning in the engravings of the Sydney region. *Archaeology in Oceania*, 34(3), 145–60.

—— 2000a: Beyond hook, line and dillybag: gender, economics and information exchange in prehistoric Sydney. In M. Casey, D. Donlon, J. Hope and S. Welfare (eds.), *Redefining Archaeology: Feminist Perspectives*. Canberra: ANH Publications, Australian National University, 96–104.

—— 2000b: Media and social context: influences on information exchange networks in prehistoric Sydney. *Australian Archaeology*, 51, 54–63.

——, Officer, K. C., Donahue, D., Jull, T., Head, J. and Ford, B. 1990: Investigating AMS: dating prehistoric rock art in the Sydney Sandstone Basin, NSW. *Rock Art Research*, 7(2), 83–92.

Maynard, L. 1977: Classification and terminology in Australian rock art. In P. J. Ucko (ed.), *Form in Indigenous Art*. Canberra: Australian Institute of Aboriginal Studies, 385–402.

—— 1979: The archaeology of Australian Aboriginal art. In S. M. Mead (ed.), *Exploring the Visual Art of Oceania*. Honolulu: University Press of Hawaii, 83–110.

Morwood, M. J. 1980: Time, space and prehistoric art: a principal components analysis. *Archaeology and Physical Anthropology in Oceania*, 15(2), 98–109.

—— 1987: The archaeology of social complexity in south-eastern Queensland. *Proceedings of the Prehistoric Society*, 53, 337–50.

—— 2002: *Visions from the Past: The Archaeology of Australian Aboriginal Art*. Crows Nest, NSW: Allen and Unwin.

Mulloy, W. 1958: *Preliminary Historical Outline for the Northwestern Plains*. University of Wyoming Publications 22(1). Laramie: University of Wyoming.

Nelson, D. E. 1993: Second thoughts on a rock art date. *Antiquity*, 67, 893–5.

—— (ed.) 2000: *The Beeswax Art of Northern Australia*. Burnaby, BC: Simon Fraser University.

Nobbs, M. and Dorn, R. I. 1993: New surface exposure ages for petroglyphs from the Olary Province, South Australia. *Archaeology in Oceania*, 28, 18–39.

O'Connor, S. 1995: Carpenters Gap Rockshelter I: 400,000 years of Aboriginal occupation in the Napier Ranges, Kimberley, WA. *Australian Archaeology*, 40, 58–9.

Ogilby, C. and Rivett, L. J. 1985: *Handbook of Heritage Photogrammetry*. Special Australian Heritage Publication Series, 5. Canberra: Australian Government Publishing Service.

Parkington, J. 1996: What is an eland? N!ao and the politics of age and sex in the paintings of the Western Cape. In P. Skotnes (ed.), *Miscast: Negotiating the Presence of the Bushmen*. Cape Town: University of Cape Town Press, 281–9.

Prous, A. 1986: L'archéologie au Brésil: 300 siècles d'occupation humaine. *L'Anthropologie*, 90(2), 257–306.

Roberts, R., Jones, R. and Smith, M. A., 1993: Optical dating at Deaf Adder Gorge, Northern Territory, indicates human occupation between 53,000 and 60,000 years ago. *Australian Archaeology*, 37, 58.

——, Walsh, G. L., Murray, A. et al. 1997: Luminescence dating of rock art and past environments using mud-wasp nests in Northern Australia. *Nature*, 387, 696–9.

Rosenfeld, A. and Smith, C. E. 1997: Recent developments in radiocarbon and stylistic methods of dating rock art. *Antiquity*, 71, 405–11.

——, Horton, D. and Winter, J. 1981: *Early Man in North Queensland*. Terra Australis 6. Canberra: Department of Prehistory, Research School of Pacific Studies, Australian National University.

Ross, J. 2002: Rocking the boundaries, scratching the surface: an analysis of the relationship between paintings and engravings in the Australian central arid zone. In S. Ulm, C. Westcott, J. Reid et al. (eds.), *Barriers, Borders, Boundaries: Proceedings of the 2001 Australian Archaeological Association Annual Conference*. Tempus, 7. St Lucia: Anthropology Museum, University of Queensland, 83–91.

Rowe, M. M. 2001: Dating by AMS radiocarbon analysis. In D. S. Whitley (ed.), *Handbook of Rock Art Research*. Walnut Creek, CA: AltaMira Press, 139–66.

Sackett, J. R. 1982: Approaches to style in lithic archaeology. *Journal of Anthropological Archaeology*, 1, 59–112.

—— 1990: Style and ethnicity in archaeology: the case for isochrestism. In M. Conkey and C. Hastorf (eds.), *The Uses of Style in Archaeology*. New Directions in Archaeology. Cambridge: Cambridge University Press, 32–43.

Schaafsma, P. 1985: Form, content and function: theory and method in North American rock art studies. In M. B. Schiffer (ed.), *Advances in Archaeological Method and Theory*, vol. 8. New York: Academic Press, 237–77.

Schiffer, M. B. 1986: Radiocarbon dating and the "old wood" problem: the case of Hohokam chronology. *Journal of Archaeological Science*, 13, 13–30.

Shapiro, M. 1953: Style. In A. L. Kroeber (ed.), *Anthropology Today*. Chicago: The University of Chicago Press, 287–312.

Smith, C. E. 1992: The use of ethnography in interpreting rock art: a comparative study of Arnhem Land and the Western Desert of Australia. In M. Morwood and D. Hobbs (eds.), *Rock Art and Ethnography*. Occasional AURA Publication no. 5. Melbourne: Australian Rock Art Research Association, 39–45.

Soffer, O. 1987: Upper Palaeolithic connubia, refugia, and the archaeological record from eastern Europe. In O. Soffer (ed.), *The Pleistocene Old World: Regional Perspectives*. New York: Plenum Press, 333–48.

Sognnes, K. 1998: Symbols in a changing world: rock art and the transition from hunting to farming in mid-Norway. In C. Chippindale and P. Taçon (eds.), *The Archaeology of Rock-Art*. Cambridge: Cambridge University Press, 146–62.

Solomon, A. 1998: Ethnography and method in southern African rock-art research. In C. Chippindale and P. Taçon (eds.), *The Archaeology of Rock-Art*. Cambridge: Cambridge University Press, 268–84.

Sundstrom, L. 1990: *Rock Art of the Southern Black Hill: A Contextual Approach*. New York: Garland.

Taçon, P. S. C. 2001: Australia. In D. S. Whitley (ed.), *Handbook of Rock Art Research*. Walnut Creek, CA: AltaMira Press, 531–75.

Tilley, C. 1991: *Material Culture and Text: The Art of Ambiguity*. London: Routledge.

Tratebas, A. M. 1993: Stylistic chronology versus absolute dates for early hunting style rock art on the North American Plains. In M. Lorblanchet and P. Bahn (eds.), *Rock Art Studies: The Post Stylistic Era or Where Do We Go From Here?* Oxbow Monograph, 35. Oxford: Oxbow Books, 163–78.

Triggs, B. 1985: *Mammal Tracks and Signs: A Field Guide for South-Eastern Australia*. Melbourne: Oxford University Press.

Ucko, P. and Rosenfeld, A. 1967: *Palaeolithic Cave Art*. London: Weidenfeld and Nicholson.

Utemara, D., with Vinnicombe, P., 1992: North-west Kimberley belief systems. In M. J. Morwood and D. R. Hobbs (eds.), *Rock Art and Ethnography*. Occasional AURA Publication no. 5. Melbourne: Australian Rock Art Research Association, 24–6.

Valladas, H., Cachier, H., Maurice, P. et al., 1992: Direct radiocarbon dates of prehistoric paintings at the Altimira, El Castilo and Niaux Caves. *Nature*, 357, 68–70.

Van der Merwe, N. J., Sealy, J. and Yates, R. 1987: First accelerator carbon-14 date for pigment from a rock painting. *South African Journal of Science*, 83, 56–7.

Vinnicombe, P. 1976: *People of the Eland*. Pietermaritzburg: University of Natal Press.

—— and Mowaljarlai, D. 1995: That rock is a cloud: concepts associated with rock images in the Kimberley region of Australia. In K. Helskog and B. Olsen (eds.), *Perceiving Rock Art: Social and Political Perspectives*. Oslo: The Institute of Comparative Research in Human Culture, 228–46.

Walsh, G. L. 1994: *Bradshaws: Ancient Rock Paintings of North-West Australia*. Carouge-Geneva: The Bradshaw Foundation.

Watchman, A. 1992: Doubtful dates for Karolta engravings. *Journal of the Australian Institute of Aboriginal and Torres Strait Islander Studies*, 1, 51–5.

—— 1993: Perspectives and potentials for absolute dating rock paintings. *Antiquity*, 67, 58–65.

—— and Cole, N. 1993: Accelerator radiocarbon dating of plant fibre binders in rock paintings from northeast Australia. *Antiquity*, 67, 355–8.

——, Walsh, G. L., Morwood, M. J. and Tuniz, C. 1997: AMS radiocarbon age estimates for early rock paintings in the Kimberley, NW Australia: preliminary results. *Rock Art Research*, 14, 18–26.

Wellman, K. 1979: A quantitative analysis of superimpositions in the rock art of Coso Range, California. *American Antiquity*, 44, 546–56.

Wendt, W. E. 1976: "Art mobilier" from the Apollo II Cave, South West Africa: Africa's oldest dated work of art. *South African Archaeological Bulletin*, 31, 5–11.

Whitley, D. S. 1992: Shamanism and rock art in far western North America. *Cambridge Archaeological Journal*, 2, 89–113.

—— 1994: By the hunter, for the gatherer: art, social relations and subsistence change in the prehistoric Great Basin. *World Archaeology*, 25, 356–73.

—— 1998: Finding rain in the desert: landscape, gender and far western North American rock art. In C. Chippindale and P. Taçon (eds.), *The Archaeology of Rock-Art*. Cambridge: Cambridge University Press, 11–29.

—— 2000: *The Art of the Shamans: Rock Art of California*. Salt Lake City: University of Utah Press.

—— (ed.) 2001: *Handbook of Rock Art Research*. Walnut Creek, CA: AltaMira Press.

——, Simon, J. M. and Dorn, R. I. 1999: The vision quest in the Great Basin. *American Indian Rock Art*, 25, 1–31.

Wiessner, P. 1984: Reconsidering the behavioral basis for style: a case study among the Kalahari San. *Journal of Anthropological Archaeology*, 3, 190–234.

—— 1989: Style and changing relations between individual and society. In I. Hodder (ed.), *The Meanings of Things: Material Culture and Symbolic Expression*. London: Unwin Hyman, 56–63.

—— 1990: Is there a unity to style? In M. Conkey and C. Hastorf (eds.), *The Uses of Style in Archaeology*. New Directions in Archaeology. Cambridge: Cambridge University Press, 105–12.

Wilson, M. 1998: Pacific rock art and cultural genesis: a multivariate exploration. In C. Chippindale and P. Taçon (eds.), *The Archaeology of Rock-Art*. Cambridge: Cambridge University Press, 163–84.

Wobst, H. M. 1977: Stylistic behavior and information exchange. In C. E. Cleland (ed.), *For the Director: Research Essays in Honor of James B. Griffin*. Anthropological Papers, Museum of Anthropology, University of Michigan, no. 61. Ann Arbor: Museum of Anthropology, University of Michigan, 317–42.

Yates, R., Parkington, J. and Manhire, A. 1994: Rock painting and history in the south-western Cape. In T. A. Dowson and J. D. Lewis-Williams (eds.), *Contested Images: Diversity in Southern African Rock Art Research*. Johannesburg: Witwatersrand University Press, 29–60.

York, A., Daly, R. and Arnett, C. 1993: *They Write Their Dreams on the Rock Forever: Rock Writings in the Stein River Valley of British Columbia*. Vancouver: Talonbooks.

Jane Balme and Alistair Paterson

4
Stratigraphy

Introduction

The interpretation of site stratigraphy is of crucial importance for understanding what happened at an archaeological site. It is the starting point for developing time sequences at the site and determining the relative ages of artifacts within the site. In conjunction with other analyses, such as sediment analyses (Chapter 12) and an absolute dating program (Chapter 5), stratigraphy can provide information about the environment at the time of deposition and the relative lengths of time over which different cultural events occurred.

It is not our intention here to teach you how to excavate, as there are many excellent textbooks on this subject (see "Further reading" below). However, it is important that as much stratigraphic information as possible is extracted during excavation and that laboratory analyses are designed to take advantage of that information. In this chapter we will instead concentrate on why archaeologists study stratigraphy, how different stratigraphic layers occur in archaeological sites, how information about stratification is extracted from archaeological sites, how stratification is interpreted to create a framework for a relative chronology of cultural remains within sites, and how that interpretation is used by archaeologists to create analytical units. The main case studies that we have referred to here (Devil's Lair and Sos Höyük) are the two sites at which we first learned the principles of stratigraphy and their application in the interpretation of archaeological sites.

What is Stratigraphy?

Stratigraphy is the study of stratification; that is, the interpretation of horizontal layers that form the deposits of a site over time. In archaeological sites, stratigraphic layers may consist of a variety of materials. They may be composed entirely of natural deposits such as sediments accumulated by, for example, wind deposition. They may consist entirely of cultural material, such as shell in a shell midden or building material, or they may consist of a combination of natural and cultural materials.

Why do Archaeologists Study Stratification?

The main reason why archaeologists study stratification is to understand the history of a site or sites. Of primary importance is the interpretation of the order in which events occurred at a site and the relative ages of artifacts and features found. Knowledge of these is crucial for decisions about analytical units for comparison of archaeological remains across time and space. The study of stratification within sites allows archaeological materials from the same relative time period to be grouped together for further analysis.

Interpretation of layers in archaeological sites can also be used to reconstruct the natural shape of landscapes at both fine and broad scales. The shape of the natural landscape can influence people's choice of the location for particular activities, such as using sheltered areas for campsites. At a fine level, the shape of the landscape affects the distribution of sites, as artifacts gather in depressions and are trampled in areas that are more likely to be traversed (Nielsen 1991). Stratigraphy also helps in the identification of modifications of the broader landscape by humans, such as those associated with agricultural practices (for agriculture in New Guinea, for example, see Denham 2003).

Like most archaeological interpretation, the interpretation of stratification is stronger when multiple lines of evidence are used. For example, the argument for the timing of plant domestication in New Guinea mentioned above is stronger when combined with other lines of evidence (Denham et al. 2003). In combination with other kinds of evidence such as sediment analysis and analyses of botanical remains, stratigraphy is used to identify environmental change over time (Chapter 12) and to understand and explain other kinds of variation in the archaeological record. For example, the fact that shell middens are only present in some horizons represented by the 35,000 or so years of human occupation of sand dunes surrounding inland lakes in western New South Wales has more to do with changes in the rate of deposition of sediments (that protect and preserve the middens) than with changes in shellfish consumption over time (Balme & Hope 1990).

How do Different Layers Occur in Archaeological Sites?

Deposition of sediments occurs through such processes as wind and water action and glacier transportation, as well as through volcanic action. These processes do not usually occur continuously and, when they do occur, the rates of deposition may vary. So, for example, in an area in which sand dunes accumulate, a period of strong winds will deposit a thick layer of sand on the dunes, whereas a period of gentler wind will deposit only a thin layer of sand on the dune. In addition, the source of the sediments can vary between different episodes of deposition. Different-colored sediments may also be caused by changes in chemical composition over time. Oxidation of iron-rich particles, for example, may cause some sediments to become red. Or, if sediments are exposed without additional deposition for enough time to allow vegetation to grow, soils may form and the vegetation mixed with the sediment may give it a rich, dark appearance. Over time, a series of layers build up that in section

JANE BALME AND ALISTAIR PATERSON

appear as separate horizons of different colors or different-sized particles. It is important to be aware that because the layers are deposited in different ways, the thickness of the layers is not necessarily a guide to the time that they took to accumulate.

Some of these points are illustrated in the south section of Devil's Lair, a small limestone cave (Figure 4.1) that is important for providing the oldest evidence for human occupation in southwest Australia. In this section, most of the thin layers are orange or brown sands (Figure 4.2). These sands have been deposited by water flow and probably derive from the same source. Periods in which there has been no deposition from this source are represented by bands of consolidated flowstone that forms when water flowing through the limestone of the cave walls dissolves calcium carbonate that, once deposited on the cave surface, becomes hard and crystalline. The thick layer "30 lower part" is much darker than the other layers because it contains much organic material. It appears to have been deposited relatively quickly, and was probably associated with the formation of a new cave entrance. The large pieces of rubble in the layers below this indicate deposition by water flowing at a much greater velocity than those above.

At times when humans occupy the area, they leave behind artifacts or other cultural debris that become incorporated with the surface sediments deposited at that time. At times when few sediments are deposited, or when humans create a lot of rubbish, some layers in the "layer cake" may be distinguished because they are composed entirely of cultural material. There are some kinds of sites that are composed almost entirely of layer upon layer of cultural material. Tells are an obvious example of such sites (e.g., Miller Rosen 1986). In some situations (particularly shell accumulations) it can be difficult to identify whether or not the material was deposited through natural or cultural agency (see, e.g., Henderson et al. 2002).

Interpretation of the stratification to infer the chronology of the site is based on a set of principles that summarize the implications of the way in which layers form. The principles of stratigraphy used by archaeologists draw on those developed within the discipline of geology. There are some archaeologists who believe that the discipline of archaeology requires its own stratigraphic theory. Harris is principal amongst these. His main argument is that the contribution of humans to site formation is quite unlike any natural site formation processes, and therefore geological laws cannot cover all of the circumstances that we require. The fact that many cultural layers, such as walls, are horizontal rather than vertical is one example of this. Harris' Laws of archaeological stratigraphy, detailed in Harris (1979, 1989), are nevertheless based on the geological laws, with modifications for the goals of archaeology. The need for separate stratigraphic theory is continuously debated (see, e.g., Farrand 1984; Stein 1987).

Principles (or laws) of stratigraphy

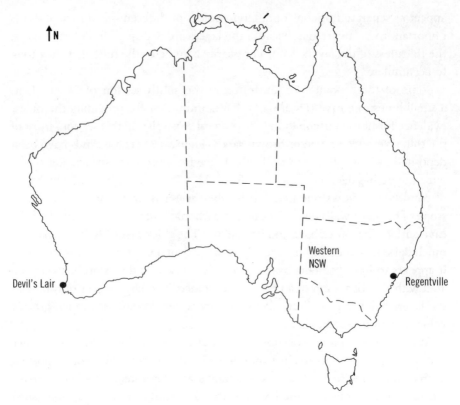

Figure 4.1 The locations of Devil's Lair, Regentville, and western New South Wales, Australia, showing places referred to in the text.

For now, we just want to draw your attention to the four main principles of stratigraphy used by archaeologists. Once you know how deposits form, perhaps these laws seem like common sense, but when you are faced with confusing stratification in an archaeological section it is useful to remind yourself of these principles when you are trying to interpret the sequence. Whether the stratigraphic layers are thick and represent long time periods, such as at some of the early hominid sites in East Africa, or very thin layers in rockshelters, the principles of deposition and interpretation of the stratigraphy are the same:

1 The *Law of Superposition*. This refers to the layer cake effect described above. Simply, it states, provided that there has been no subsequent disturbance, deeper stratigraphic layers are older than those overlying them.
2 The *Law of Association* states that, provided that there has been no disturbance, materials in the same stratigraphic layer are associated with each other. However, because some stratigraphic layers represent vastly greater time periods than others, the usefulness of this law varies.
3 The *Law of Horizontal Deposition* states that any layer deposited in an unconsolidated form will tend toward the horizontal. This means that strata found tilted lie over the contours of previous basins. Of course, the

JANE BALME AND ALISTAIR PATERSON

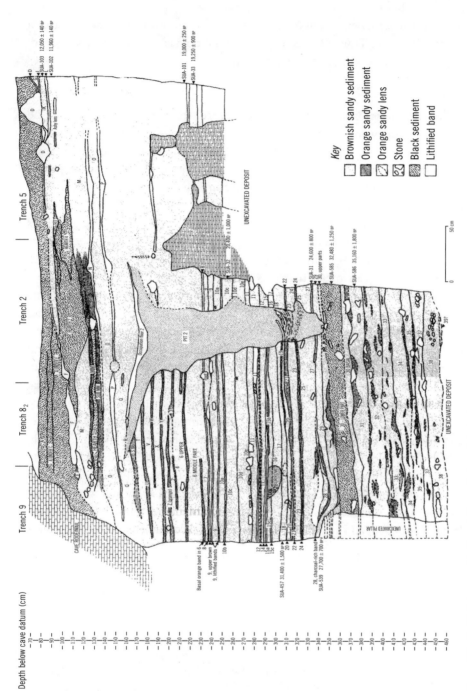

Figure 4.2 Devil's Lair: a section through the south face of the main excavation (adapted from Balme et al. 1978).

shape of stratigraphic layers composed of cultural material will not necessarily be horizontal but, rather, will be determined by the people who made them.

4 The *Law of Original Continuity* states that a natural deposit will end in a feather edge. Thus if the edge of a stratigraphic layer is not feather edged, its original extent has been destroyed.

Sources of disturbance

Following these laws, the interpretation of the stratification should be very straightforward. However, nothing is ever quite so simple and the reason for this lies in the importance of the phrase in the first two of these laws, "provided that there has been no disturbance." The stratigraphic succession in almost all archaeological sites has been disturbed. The sources of disturbance can be either natural or cultural.

Between periods of deposition, sediments often erode. The same processes that cause deposition cause erosion (often exacerbated though other agents such as animal scuffage) and sediments are scoured, mixed, and redeposited elsewhere. This can mean that it is possible to have materials side by side that are of different ages. Sometimes, such disturbance is recognizable as cuts through layers. Figure 4.3 shows a section through a sand dune bordering an inland lake in western New South Wales, Australia (Figure 4.1). In this sequence, the Buntigoola, Kinchega, and Packer are the oldest sediments and do not contain archaeological remains. The Tandou unit is an ancient soil in which extinct fauna remains have been found and, although archaeological remains dating to about 30,000 BP have been found on its surface, none have been found unequivocally within the soil sediments. The sediments lying above, and therefore younger than the Tandou unit, form the Bootingee unit, in which archaeological remains have also been recovered (Balme & Hope 1990; Balme 1995). However, either before or during the time in which the Bootingee sands were deposited, the lake side of the dune eroded away and was replaced by Bootingee sands. This means that the sediments of a much more recent layer (Bootingee) and any archaeological material contained in those sediments

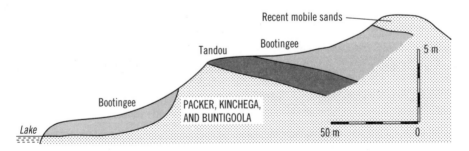

Figure 4.3 A section through a sand dune bordering an inland lake in western New South Wales, Australia (adapted from Balme 1995).

JANE BALME AND ALISTAIR PATERSON

are younger than those lying alongside them. The same effect of layers along-side each other is also produced through tectonic movement, where slippage along a fault line can result in horizontal layers of vastly different ages lying alongside each other. It is this kind of slippage that created the rift valley in East Africa, so that old layers containing fossils, including early hominid fossils, are exposed in the valley.

When deposition occurs on sediments from which erosion has removed the surface, or on which there has been no deposition for some time, the boundary between the old and new sediments is referred to as an unconformity. These are often represented as wavy lines in section drawings.

Disturbance may also occur through chemical processes such as leaching (although these are not so likely to change the horizontal layering within the deposit). Shrinking and expansion of sediments caused by water retention or freezing of sediments may allow artifacts to fall down cracks, so that they are no longer in their original position. Bioturbation refers to biological pro-cesses that disturb the site. These may be caused by animals or by plants. Small animals such as worms that burrow cause sediments to become compacted, and burrowing animals that live at various times throughout the history of the site dig into layers that were laid down before they occupied the area. While digging, they will excavate materials from lower layers and kick them onto the surface from which they are digging. Once the animal no longer uses the burrow, sediments from the surface from which the burrow was dug will fill it. This means that artifacts excavated from the surface from which the burrow was dug may not be associated (Law 2 above) because they may derive from layers deeper in the site. The burrow should be visible in section, because the fill sediments will be the same as those on the surface from which it was dug rather than the surrounding sediments. Plant roots growing at a site also mix sedimentary layers. Again, the presence of tree roots in the past may be indicated by remnant dark organic matter.

When humans occupy places they also affect the horizontal layering by adding cultural materials, by clearing behaviors that remove cultural materials and sediments, and through deliberate modification of the surface, such as building foundations and digging wells, privies, trash pits, and graves. One such action is the pit dug into the Devil's Lair site from layer Q (Figure 4.2), which is between two dates of about 12,000 and 19,000 BP. The fill of the pit clearly cuts through older deposits down to layer 30, which was originally dated to about 30,500 BP (Balme et al. 1978), but has recently been re-dated using the ABOX-SC method to about 45,500 BP (Turney et al. 2001). The consequence for establishing a relative chronology is that artifacts found in layer Q deposits are very likely to not be associated. Mixing of objects be-tween layers in the deposits can happen simply through human trampling of the site (see, e.g., Nielsen 1991).

Therefore, placing the various stratigraphic layers and disturbance features into their chronological order involves the use of the laws of stratigraphy and recognition of when and how disturbances to the site took place in relation to the deposition of sediments. This is not always an easy task. At a landscape level where erosion has exposed the section, it begins with examination and recording of the exposed sections. For excavated sites, boundaries between many stratigraphic layers and features are discovered during excavation.

Excavation and Stratigraphy

Recognizing boundaries between layers and features is clearly the best way to ensure that all materials that were deposited together (from the same stratigraphic layer) are kept separately. This is the reason why archaeologists try to excavate by stratigraphic units. That is, whenever an excavator notices a change in color or texture of the sediments, he or she begins a new excavation unit (i.e., all bags containing the material in which the evcavator has been digging are closed off and material in the new sediments are bagged separately). The bags are all labeled clearly to show which excavation unit they derive from. Where possible, features such as hearths and pits are excavated separately, since their fill will be composed of sediments that are different from, and probably of a different age to, the surrounding sediments.

However, digging by stratigraphic unit is not always possible because of the difficulties of identifying separate layers that are very similar in color and/or texture. Excavation is then usually carried out in arbitrary levels of equal depth. Because the depth of these arbitrary units is recorded during excavation, it is often possible to assign artifacts within them to stratigraphic units whose divisions are identified either after excavation has exposed the profile or – if the divisions are based on micromorphology of the sediments (see Chapter 12) – in the laboratory.

Arbitrary excavation units are also usually used when stratigraphic layers are very thick. If the absence of distinct layering can be established to be the result of long-term deposition from a single source, it can be assumed that the deepest artifacts even within a single stratigraphic unit are the oldest. This is hard to control for, so shallow artificial layers allow comparative analysis and ordering of artifacts after excavation.

It is common for archaeologists to excavate in artificial units, sometimes even when there are clearly demarked stratigraphic layers. The justification for this might be that it is quicker to use artificial units, or that unskilled excavators may not identify differences between stratigraphic units. The technique is often justified in terms of their ability to correlate the measured depths of the artificial units with natural stratigraphy once the section drawings are made. However, the technique assumes horizontal deposition, which – as has been shown – is not always true for archaeological sites. Perhaps more importantly, much resolution is lost if an arbitrary unit cuts through more than one stratigraphic unit. This can mean that occupation surfaces (and directly associated material) are missed.

JANE BALME AND ALISTAIR PATERSON

Whether or not all of the stratigraphic layers can be identified during excavation and all of the artifacts for each layer are kept separate, the sequence has to be recorded to ensure that layers and features that are of similar time periods can be grouped for later analysis. It is often not possible to identify the relationships between layers and features during excavation. In particular, when you are working across large areas, and not all layers are represented in each part of the landscape, it is only possible to establish a chronology for the area by recording and cross-referencing the various stratigraphic successions in each location.

Recording Stratification

When working at a landscape scale, such as at the East African sites, where long-term erosion has exposed the stratigraphic layers in the valley walls, the first steps in interpretation begin with recording the stratigraphic layers across the landscape, trying to match up sequences. In the case of Hadar, in Ethiopia, where many early hominid fossils have been found, the study area is so large and the stratigraphy is very complicated, mainly because many stratigraphic units do not extend over the whole area. The task of establishing a regional sequence required the use of other techniques, including different kinds of absolute dating methods and the use of biostratigraphy to sort out the relative ages of layers. Establishing a sequence has occupied geologists, paleontologists, and various kinds of absolute dating experts for great amounts of time (for a history of the development of the stratigraphic sequence for the Lucy site, see Johanson & Edey 1981). As each new season of work begins in the area and new stratigraphic horizons are found, these have to be fitted into the sequence developed previously.

At a smaller scale, the stratigraphic succession is first exposed during excavation. Observations about stratigraphic differences occur during excavation as changes in sediments and structures are noticed. It is at this stage that interpretation begins. Records of stratigraphic differences are recorded in stratigraphic section drawings and by taking photographs. The drawings are scale drawings of the layers seen in trench walls. They are usually drawn after several layers have been exposed, at the end of a field season or during a break in the digging of the trench or feature.

For these drawings, the boundaries of each layer, or layer interface, are measured and drawn onto graph paper. The sections are annotated so that the color and texture of each layer is described in everyday language (as, for example, in Figure 4.2) and is usually also determined with the aid of a Munsell color chart and the texture determined by feel; for example, "clayey" or "sandy" (see Chapter 12). Intrusions and larger inclusions, such as stones or pottery exposed in the section, are described and included in the drawing. The distinction between natural and cultural inclusions may not be clear at the time of excavation (for example, fish bones in a fluvial deposit related to a site could be naturally deposited through river action or food remains). The objective is to record the stratigraphy in as much detail as possible, so that the drawing can be used as a tool for establishing the chronology of the site and for analysis of cultural materials.

Although the features and layers are measured and recorded, it is important to realize that these drawings are nevertheless interpretations of the stratigraphic layering. The recorders document their interpretation of what they see in the profile. In addition, distinctions between layers are inevitably simplified and the lines only approximately represent features and strata.

The records of the stratification in the section drawings, along with other information from the sediments, are then interpreted by using the laws of stratigraphy, and by being aware of the possible disturbance processes, to build up a chronology of the order in which the layers and features were created. In the Devil's Lair example (Figure 4.2), where most of the natural layers extended across the whole site, the Law of Superposition is applicable because there is clearly little disturbance (with the exception of the large pit). The discontinuous waves of orange sand near the base of the deposit represent sediment sorting caused by the greater velocity of the water that deposited it than in the layers further up the deposit. The ordering of events at this site is pretty straightforward, as the Law of Superposition says that the oldest material will be the deepest. Thus the pit belongs to the same period as layer Q.

It is not always possible to identify all kinds of disturbance from field observations and sediment analyses. Downward movement of small artifacts caused by trampling or compaction may not be obvious. One solution is to try refitting artifacts or bones from different layers. Both of these approaches are time-consuming, but they have yielded good results on the vertical distances that artifacts travel through the stratigraphic layers (for examples, see Cziesla et al. 1990; Morrow 1996).

The Harris Matrix: interpreting the spatial record

When there are many pits and features at a site, it becomes a bit more complicated to describe the order of events and determine which features and stratigraphic layers represent the same time period. It is for this reason that Harris developed a system for visually representing stratigraphic relationships. The system, known as the Harris Matrix, was first published in Harris (1975), and in an expanded version in Harris (1979). It was initially developed by Harris for complex sites in urban Britain, and it gained currency in the United States especially after being used at Colonial Williamsburg (Brown & Muraca 1993).

The system uses the concept of the interface (Harris 1989: 54–68) to describe boundaries (or surfaces) between layers and features. Interfaces may be the surfaces of strata equivalent to the geological "bedding plane," which Harris refers to as "layer interfaces," or surfaces formed by the destruction of existing strata (equivalent to the geological term "unconformity"), which he refers to as "feature interfaces." Layer interfaces may be horizontal – that is, deposited

JANE BALME AND ALISTAIR PATERSON

in a horizontal state – or vertical structures such as walls. Feature interfaces may also be horizontal, in which case they mark the level to which upstanding structures, such as walls, have been destroyed. Vertical feature interfaces involve the removal of strata such as pits and ditches. Harris also uses the term "period interface" to describe all of the layer and feature interfaces that were ground surfaces at the same time.

The matrix represents each feature, layer, or interface as a box and the relationship between each as a line. Boxes in the same vertical line are placed in sequential order with the oldest layer, feature, or interface placed at the bottom. When the stratigraphic relationship between features is not known – for example, because they are separated by a wall – they are shown as a separate branch. The strength of this approach is that clear categories can be shown for interfaces between surfaces, and all features that are the result of human activity can be placed within the sequence. Because of this, the Harris Matrix is very widely used by archaeologists around the world. Harris maintains a website (www.harrismatrix.com/) that includes references about the development of the matrix and links to computer programs that can be used to construct Harris Matrices (see also Harris 1989; Greene 1996: 68).

Figure 4.4 is a very simple example of a Harris Matrix constructed to describe the stratigraphic sequence recovered during the excavation of a drain. The drain once led from Regentville, a grand mansion built in New South Wales, Australia, by Sir John Jamison in about 1824 (Figure 4.1). Over the past 20 years or so, archaeological investigations of the remains of the mansion and associated features have been carried out under the direction of Judy Birmingham and Andrew Wilson (University of Sydney; see http://acl.arts.usyd.edu.au/projects/ourprojects/regentville/).

A cross-section of the drain is shown in Figure 4.4a. The different features, layers, and interfaces have been given numbers, which were allocated during excavation. The numbering system is used for the whole of the Regentville project. In other words, the number 191 allocated to the surface layer of this drain indicates that it was the 191st unit to be recorded in the Regentville project.

The hatched area in the section drawing is bedrock. The first activity in the construction of the drain was the excavation into the bedrock in c.1824–6 (according to colonial records, the area was not occupied prior to this date). According to Harris' definition, this is a vertical feature interface and in Figure 4.4a it is labeled 270. The next part of the construction was the placement of a large sandstone boulder cap over the drain cavity (271) and the remaining part of the excavation was filled with rubble and chips (269). The drain was the void beneath this wall. From the time of the original excavation of the bedrock until some time before the 1960s, when the site was cleared, the drain filled with sediments. Some of this fill may have occurred while the sandstone drain cover was built and some certainly occurred after. The fill is shown in Figure 4.4a and has two parts: the deeper sediments are labeled 273 and those above it (and therefore younger) are labeled 272. The hatched line between

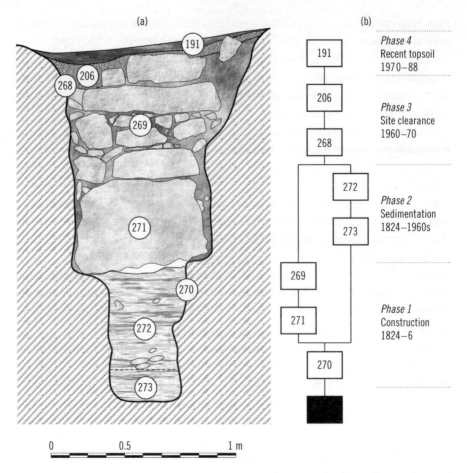

Figure 4.4 A section of the Main Drain (a) at the historic site of Regentville and the Harris Matrix (b) (adapted with permission from Andrew Wilson and Judy Birmingham).

the two units separates them: however, this barrier is slightly arbitrary, as the main difference between the fills has been established from differences between the artifacts. Early nineteenth-century artifacts were found in the deeper sediments and later nineteenth-century artifacts were found in the upper deposits. When the site was cleared in the 1960s, the drain structure was truncated and 268 marks the horizontal feature interface caused by the cut. The sediments that were subsequently deposited are labeled 206 and recent topsoil placed on the site is labeled 191.

The Harris Matrix given in Figure 4.4b shows these relationships, with the number for each layer or feature written in a box and lines drawn between the boxes to show the sequence. The black box at the base represents the base rock or "geological past." The cut is the basal archaeological feature. There are then two branches. We know that the sandstone construction was built in c.1824–6. We are not sure when the sedimentation began, but it may have begun at the same time as the wall construction and it appears to have been filled by the time the site was cleared. In the Harris Matrix these layers are

JANE BALME AND ALISTAIR PATERSON

shown further up the diagram because the sedimentation process was much longer than the drain construction process.

Another related technique that Harris has used to show the relationships between units is his "single-context plans" (Harris 1989; Pearson & Williams 1993). These are horizontal plans of stratigraphic units with all of their composite features and interfaces. The point of producing the plans as well as the sections is that not all layers, features, and interfaces are cut by the excavation sections, and so stratigraphic information is missing from section drawings (Brown & Harris 1993: 3–4). If, for example, we had selected our trench at Devil's Lair 30 cm further to the west, we would not have exposed its section in the trench wall (Figure 4.2). The pit profile would therefore not have appeared in the section drawings.

Figure 4.4b shows the four phases into which the excavators placed the stratigraphic information for the Regentville drain. In this example, the phases are used simply to describe the sequence of events. When the research aims include questions about changes in human behavior through time at the site, or between sites across space, decisions will almost certainly need to be made about how to group the archaeological evidence to form analytical units (or phases) for analysis.

Creating Analytical Units

Stratigraphy is the starting point for the creation of analytical units. Decisions about how to group the site material into time periods depend on your research question (which dictates the desired chronological resolution) and the quality of the stratification (which dictates the possible resolution). Other sources of chronological evidence may also be helpful in refining the resolution. If there are few artifacts at the site, a large number of stratigraphic units may need to be combined to create an analytical unit simply so that the sample sizes can be made large enough for comparisons. Obviously, much time resolution is lost if this becomes necessary.

Some research questions are about short-term events. For example, you might be interested in types of grave goods of a particular person buried in the Middle Bronze Age at Sos Höyük (see below). Because this short-term event is stratigraphically readily recognizable, all you have to do is describe the goods associated with the skeleton. Interpretation of the activities associated with the pit at Devil's Lair (Figure 4.2) is more difficult, because we know that the surface at the top of the pit has been contaminated with material from beneath (we never have worked out the purpose of this pit).

Investigation of these single activities might tell us about something specific that happened thousands of years ago, but it doesn't allow discussion about change over time and space. To answer these questions, you will need to group material from different stratigraphic units. If the stratigraphic units are fine and represent short-term time scales, it may be possible to characterize change at a very fine resolution. On the other hand, thick stratigraphic units (or thin ones that have accumulated very slowly) will only allow coarse resolution. It may, of course, be possible to subdivide undifferentiated thicker units with the help of absolute dating techniques.

For example, in the Devil's Lair sequence shown in Figure 4.2 you could look at change in artifact form by comparing artifacts from each of the very fine stratigraphic units represented in the part of the deposit on the left of the section. Because the sequence is well dated and sedimentation was reasonably uniform, analysis of change over time at a fine resolution is possible. The only difficulty here is to ensure that the sample sizes in each unit are sufficiently high to make the comparisons meaningful. To the right of the deposit, where the stratigraphic resolution is low, the artifacts would need to be treated as one assemblage representing the time period of 12,000–19,000 BP.

The main point to be aware of here is that the character of the change recorded will vary depending on how you group the material. This is explained very well, with examples, in Frankel (1988). Comparisons at a fine resolution will make changes over time at a site appear very gradual, whereas changes based on a coarser resolution will make changes appear more dramatic. However, while fine-resolution comparison will show trends in change, it will not necessarily be better because short-term events may create "noise" that obscures major changes.

A related issue is the need to choose a scale that is appropriate for the scale of the processes that you are investigating. This is discussed in some detail in Chapter 5 under "Time perspectivism," with the example of Bone Cave.

Case Study
Sos Höyük

Archaeological excavations at the multi-period mound site of Sos Höyük, in eastern Turkey, reveal a site with a complicated stratigraphy. It provides a good example of how the stratigraphic succession is used in combination with other kinds of archaeological evidence to understand the behaviors of people at sites and the chronological sequences. The results of the work at Sos Höyük so far are reported in Sagona et al. (1995, 1996, 1997, 1998), Sagona (2000), and Sagona and Sagona (2000).

The site of Sos Höyük is in the northeastern highlands of Turkey, on the natural routes between Anatolia, the Transcaucasus/Iranian region, and the Upper Euphrates Basin (Figure 4.5). For over a century, archaeologists have studied the evidence for human settlement and activities in these regions. Sos Höyük, a place where a community has existed on a small hill overlooking the Çökender Stream for thousands of years, is one of many sites studied by archaeologists. The earliest occupation of the site was around

JANE BALME AND ALISTAIR PATERSON

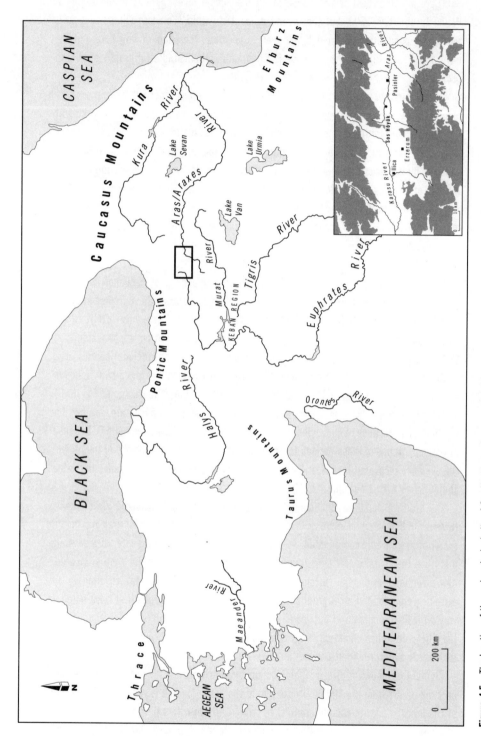

Figure 4.5 The location of the archaeological site of Sos Höyük, northeastern Anatolia (adapted with permission from Sagona 2000: 347, fig. 1).

3500 BCE and the most recent period of archaeological investigations is the Medieval Period to about AD 1200, but the mound is located within a modern village and so it represents occupation of about 5,500 years. Over time, the people living here and the natural forces acting on the site have left behind a complicated stratigraphy of human occupation.

Excavations began at Sos Höyük in 1994 and, as at many other substantial archaeological sites (the mound covers an area of about 640 m^2), the archaeologists working at Sos Höyük have returned annually to continue their excavations. Finds include houses and other built structures, ceramics, lithic artifacts, human burials, and animal bone, as well as small amounts of metal and other objects. Excavations at this site form part of a wider archaeological project of which the aims are, in part, to explore social structure and settlement patterns. At Sos Höyük one of the excavation aims is to identify chronological change and explore contacts with other cultures. As more and more evidence has been revealed, the sequence of the human use of the site has become clearer, but it is by no means complete and continues to be added to and refined each year.

As in many areas in the world, the Anatolian archaeological sequence has been divided into cultural periods associated with calendar years. Those represented at Sos Höyük are listed in Figure 4.6a. Those at the bottom of the sequence – that is, the Late Chalcolithic, and the Bronze and Iron Age ages – are based on regional trends in technology, while later phases at the site are defined by dominant regional polities. It is worth mentioning that while terms such as "Early Bronze Age" indicate regional trends in metallurgy, the amount of metal is actually very small. The Early Bronze Age at Sos Höyük is almost entirely a lithic and bone industry. The technological phases are retained for the Near East because of convenience (everyone knows the general time period). Because of the general use of these periods for the interpretation of the archaeology of the region, the evidence recovered from Sos Höyük needed to be placed into this sequence to enable comparisons with other sites.

The starting point for producing the chronology of occupation is the stratigraphy. However, 5,500 years of more or less continuous occupation in a small area has made the stratigraphy very complicated. As successive groups occupied the site, they severely disturbed the remains left by earlier occupants. Pits and burial shafts were excavated, new structures were built on old, and material was reused. This has resulted in an extremely complicated stratigraphy with many discontinuous horizons that have made it very difficult to understand the sequence for the whole site. Establishing a sequence for the whole site relies on establishing chronologies for many small areas and fitting them together to build a bigger picture.

Figure 4.6b shows a stratigraphic section through trench M16. In this cross-section only the period from the Middle Bronze Age to the early Iron Age is represented. The age of the lowest deposits was determined by recognizing that this part of the deposit was a grave. The grave lies beneath some plaster layers and was clearly intrusive and deliberately filled and capped with stone rubble that can also be seen in the section. The

JANE BALME AND ALISTAIR PATERSON

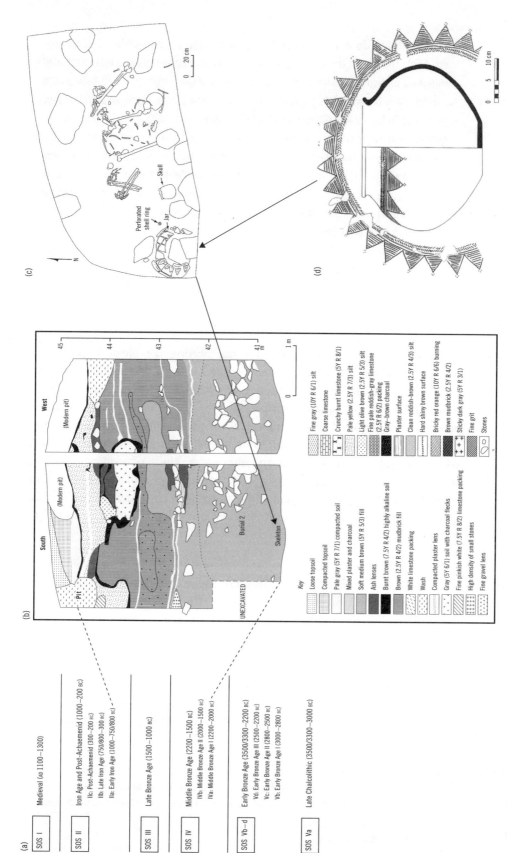

(a)

Figure 4.6 Sos Höyük. (a) The sequence of ages at the site. (b) A section showing the Middle Bronze Age to the Early Iron Age IIa in Trench M16 c/d, south and west sections. (c) A burial shown in section. (d) A ceramic vessel to date the associated burial. (Adapted with permission from Antonio Sagona.)

grave is about 1.75 m deep and at its base was a partly disarticulated skeleton (Figure 4.6c). The age of the burial could be determined from the grave goods associated with it, in particular an incised black burnished jar (Figure 4.6d) that had been placed directly above the body. This jar is of a type found in the Trialeti region in Georgia, dated to the Middle Bronze Age (Sagona et al. 1997: pl. 8; Sagona 2000: 337). In this case, the stratigraphic evidence could be used to identify the association between objects that provided a date for both the burial and cultural affiliations in the region. Another burial from the same period was found with a pot that was similar to, but not exactly the same as, grave goods in the Trialeti burials (Sagona 2000: 336–7). In this case, the age of the burial could be confirmed with the help of a radiocarbon date.

Ceramics have been very useful at Sos Höyük for providing dates for the stratigraphic sequence, because the style change over time in the region is well established. For the Post-Achaemenid and Medieval Periods, other kinds of artifacts can be used to pin down the age.

Conclusion   Stratigraphy is the starting point for interpreting the chronological order of events and artifacts at a stratified site, and it is the basis of the analytical units used to discuss the human activities at the site. However, a firm understanding of the geological principles and of the effects of site formation processes are required to disentangle all of the events that have produced the stratification at the site. When there has been much disturbance, or when layers are not continuous over the site, other kinds of evidence, such as an absolute dating program, biological evidence, and artifact seriation, may be needed to help put the layers and features into chronological order. Like most archaeological analyses, multiple kinds of evidence lead to the strongest conclusions.

Acknowledgments   We thank Associate Professor Antonio Sagona (Centre for Classics and Archaeology, The University of Melbourne) for his assistance with the case study of Sos Höyük, and Ben Marwick (Archaeology, University of Western Australia) for his comments.

Resources   The Harris Matrix is described at www.harrismatrix.com/, which includes a comprehensive related publications list. There are also links to computer programs to construct Harris Matrices (see also Harris 1989; Greene 1996: 68).

Further reading   Barker, P. 1982: *Techniques of Archaeological Excavation*. London: B. T. Batsford.

Excavation   —— 1986: *Understanding Archaeological Excavation*. New York: St Martin's Press.

Dancey, W. S. 1981: *Archaeological Field Methods: An Introduction*. Minneapolis: Burgess.

Dever, W. G. and Lance, H. D. (eds.) 1978: *A Manual of Field Excavation: Handbook for Field Archaeologists*. Cincinnati: Hebrew Union College.

Hester, T. R., Feder, K. L. and Shafer, H. J. 1997: *Field Methods in Archaeology*. Mountain View, CA: Mayfield.

Hodder, I. 1999: *The Archaeological Process: An Introduction*. Oxford: Blackwell.

Jeske, R. J. and Charles, D. K. (eds.) 2003: *Theory, Method, and Practice in Modern Archaeology*. Westport, CT: Praeger.

Joukowsky, M. 1980: *A Complete Manual of Field Archaeology: Tools and Techniques of Field Work for Archaeologists*. Englewood Cliffs, NJ: Prentice-Hall.

Rice, P. C. 1998: *Doing Archaeology: A Hands-On Laboratory Manual*. Mountain View, CA: Mayfield.

Roskams, S. 2001: *Excavation*. Cambridge: Cambridge University Press.

The following texts includes articles about the interpretation of stratigraphic record at a variety of scales:

Stratigraphy and formation processes

Boggs, S. 1995: *Principles of Sedimentology and Stratigraphy*. Englewood Cliffs, NJ: Prentice-Hall.

Goldberg, P., Nash, D. T. and Petraglia, M. D. (eds.) 1993: *Formation Processes in Archaeological Context*. Madison, WI: Prehistory Press.

Schiffer, M. B. 1996: *Formation Processes of the Archaeological Record*, 2nd edn. Salt Lake City: University of Utah Press.

References

Balme, J. 1995: 30,000 years of fishery in western New South Wales. *Archaeology in Oceania*, 30, 1–21.

—— and Hope, J. 1990: Radiocarbon dates from midden sites in the Lower Darling River area of western New South Wales. *Archaeology in Oceania*, 25, 85–101.

——, Merrilees, D. and Porter, J. 1978: Late Quaternary mammal remains spanning about 30,000 years, from excavations in Devil's Lair, Western Australia. *Journal of the Royal Society of Western Australia*, 6, 33–65.

Brown, G. J. and Muraca, D. F. 1993: Phasing stratigraphic sequences at Colonial Williamsburg. In E. C. Harris, M. R. Brown III and G. J. Brown (eds.), *Practices of Archaeological Stratigraphy*. London: Academic Press, 155–66.

Brown, M. R. III and Harris, E. C. 1993: Introduction. In E. C. Harris, M. R. Brown III and G. J. Brown (eds.), *Practices of Archaeological Stratigraphy*. London: Academic Press, 1–6.

Cziesla, E., Eickhoff, S., Arts, N. and Winter, D. (eds.) 1990: *The Big Puzzle International Symposium on Refitting Stone Artifacts*. Studies in Modern Archaeology I. Bonn: Holos-Verlag.

Denham, T. 2003: Archaeological evidence for mid-Holocene agriculture in the interior of Papua New Guinea: a critical review. *Archaeology in Oceania*, 38, 159–76.

Denham, T. P., Haberle, S. G., Lentfer, C. et al. 2003: Origins of agriculture at Kuk Swamp in the Highlands of New Guinea, *Science*, 301, 189–93.

Farrand, W. 1984: Stratigraphic classification: living with the law. *Quarterly Review of Archaeology*, 5(1), 1–5.

Frankel, D. 1988: Characterising change in prehistoric sequences: a view from Australia. *Archaeology in Oceania*, 23, 41–8.

Greene, K. 1996: *Archaeology: An Introduction*, 3rd edn. Philadelphia: University of Pennsylvania Press.

Harris, E. C. 1975: The stratigraphic sequence: a question of time. *World Archaeology*, 7, 109–21.

—— 1979: The laws of archaeological stratigraphy. *World Archaeology*, 11, 111–17.

—— 1989: *Principles of Archaeological Stratigraphy*, 2nd edn. London: Academic Press.

Henderson, W. G., Anderson, L. C. and McGimsey, C. R. 2002: Distinguishing natural and archaeological deposits: stratigraphy, taxonomy, and taphonomy of Holocene shell-rich accumulations from the Louisiana chenier plain. *Palaios*, 17, 192–205.

Johanson, D. C. and Edey, M. A. 1981: *Lucy: The Beginnings of Humankind*. London: Granada.

Miller Rosen, A. 1986: *Cities of Clay: The Geoarchaeology of Tells*. Chicago: The University of Chicago Press.

Morrow, T. M. 1996: Lithic refitting and archaeological site formation processes: a case study from the Twin Dutch site, Greene County, Illinois. In G. H. Odell (ed.), *Stone Tools: Theoretical Insights into Human Prehistory*. New York: Plenum Press, 345–73.

Nielsen, A. E. 1991: Trampling the archaeological record: an experimental study. *American Antiquity*, 56(3), 483–503.

Pearson, N. and Williams, T. 1993: Single-context planning: its role in on-site recording procedures and in post-excavation analysis at York. In E. C. Harris, M. R. Brown III and G. J. Brown (eds.), *Practices of Archaeological Stratigraphy*. London: Academic Press, 89–103.

Sagona, A. G. 2000: Sos Höyük and the Erzurum region in late prehistory: a provisional chronology for northeast Anatolia. In C. Marro and H. Hauptmann (eds.), *Chronologies des pays du Caucase et de l'Euphrate aux IVe–IIIe millenaires: actes du colloque d'Istanbul, 16–19 décembre 1998*. Acta anatoli ca XI. Paris: Institut français d'études anatoliennes d'Istanbul & de Boccard, 329–73.

—— and Sagona, C. 2000: Excavations at Sos Höyük, 1998 to 2000: fifth preliminary report. *Ancient Near Eastern Studies*, 37, 56–127.

——, —— and Özkorucklu, H. 1995: Excavations at Sos Höyük, 1994: first preliminary report. *Anatolian Studies*, 45, 193–218.

——, Erkmen, M., Sagona, C. and Howells, S. 1997: Excavations at Sos Höyük, 1996: third preliminary report. *Anatolica*, 23, 181–226.

——, ——, —— and Thomas, I., 1996: Excavations at Sos Höyük, 1995: second preliminary report. *Anatolian Studies*, 46, 327–48.

——, ——, ——, McNiven, I. and Howells, S., 1998: Excavations at Sos Höyük, 1997: fourth preliminary report. *Anatolica*, 24, 31–64.

Stein, J. 1987: Deposits for archaeologists. *Advances in Archaeological Methods and Theory*, 11, 337–93.

Turney, C. S. M., Bird, M. I., Fifield, L. K. et al. 2001: Early human occupation at Devil's Lair, southwestern Australia 50,000 years ago. *Quaternary Research*, 55, 3–13.

Simon Holdaway

5
Absolute Dating

Introduction

Most discussions of dating in archaeology spend a great deal of time dealing with the physics of dating, the principles and practice of measuring time-dependent radioactive decay, radiogenic processes, or some other mechanism by which an age estimate may be determined. A variety of authors refer to this as *chronometry* and differentiate it from the tasks involved in constructing a relationship between the age estimate and its archaeological significance (e.g., Dean 1978; Ramenofsky 1998; O'Brien & Lyman 2000). In this chapter you will find a great deal of discussion of the problems involved in establishing the archaeological significance of age estimates and rather less on chronometry, although some of the more common techniques used by archaeologists who work in a number of different places in the world are described in the next section. For those interested in details of the different methods that are available, a large amount of material exists in print (e.g., Taylor & Aitken 1997; Brothwell & Pollard 2001), and on the Internet (e.g., Higham 1999).

Rather than concentrate on chronometry alone, this chapter reviews some of the problems faced by archaeologists who attempt to "date" their sites (both the term and the concept of "dating" are critiqued below). This is done in four stages, using – where applicable – examples drawn from my own research in Australia. First, some chronometric methods are reviewed, with the aim of demonstrating just what it is that archaeologists have to consider when they begin to construct a chronology using one or more of the variety of methods currently on offer. As suggested, the emphasis is less on the mechanics of the various techniques and more on the nature of the assumptions that must be made and inferences that can be drawn. Secondly, the discussion moves to problems of interpretation. What issues are involved when archaeologists have to associate an age estimate with a set of artifacts that are not directly datable? Problems of interpretation are also encountered when archaeologists are forced to deal with deposits that span different periods of time. Age estimates may sometimes indicate the year or decade during which a site was occupied, while at other times the temporal resolution will be measured in millennia. Differences in time resolution such as this impact on the nature of the interpretations that can be drawn from the archaeological record. Those familiar with the paleontological literature first drew problems such as these to the attention of archaeologists, and some of the concepts and terms drawn from paleontology are useful for archaeologists to consider. This leads into the third topic, a more general discussion of the archaeological theory of time, particularly the need to consider processes operating at multiple temporal scales when evaluating the archaeological record. This is termed *time perspectivism*, a complicated sounding name, but one that is now well established in the literature. Finally, I illustrate how you might go about dealing with some of the problems of interpretation encountered when constructing a chronology through examples drawn from my own fieldwork in Australia, dealing first with the definition of multiple scales of temporal enquiry at Bone Cave, a Pleistocene site in the southwest of Tasmania, and then with the late Holocene archaeology of western New South Wales where, with Patricia Fanning, I have directed a research project during the past few years.

Chronometry   Why make a distinction between *chronology* and *chronometry*? The answer largely reflects different areas of expertise and differences in research interests. Using radiocarbon dating as an example (Taylor 1997, 2001), researchers have either become involved in assessing the impact of deviations from the primary assumptions upon which the method is based or, alternatively, they have concentrated on the results of the dating process and the nature of the behavioral inferences that can be drawn from these results about the past. One of the clearest examples of such a divergence concerns efforts to estimate the age of some ancient archaeological sites with radiocarbon, where one group of researchers has emphasized the need to overcome problems of sample contamination (e.g., Chappell et al. 1996) while another group has emphasized the difficulties involved in correlating age estimates from charcoal samples with the location of artifacts (e.g., O'Connell & Allen 1998). We begin with the issues raised by the first group of researchers and return to the second group below.

The reasons why archaeologists are able to "date" a site, deposit, or artifact with radiocarbon begin in the upper atmosphere, when atomic nuclei are hit by cosmic rays, split apart, and then collide with other nuclei. If one of these particles (a neutron) happens to hit a passing nitrogen nucleus, the nitrogen nucleus changes to carbon, but to a special form of carbon with 14 atomic particles rather than the normal 12. This form of carbon, called carbon 14 – and hence the term carbon 14 (or ^{14}C) dating – is unstable and begins to decay immediately. The decay process continues to occur over several thousand years. Carbon 14 occurs throughout the biosphere and so is metabolized in the same way as carbon 12, being constantly replaced in living organisms.

However, when an organism dies, no new carbon is added, so the amount of carbon 14 will start to decrease according to the rate of decay. Archaeologists excavate things abandoned by people in the past and if these things are organic (i.e., contain carbon) they can often be "dated" by the radiocarbon method using this process of carbon 14 decay. Higham (1999) lists 27 materials (including such things as shell, leather, peat, and coprolites, as well as the more common charcoal) containing carbon in some form of which the age is regularly determined with radiocarbon. As he comments, the great advantage of radiocarbon is the range of materials that can be used to obtain uniform age estimates throughout the world.

Every 5,730 years, the amount of carbon 14 in the abandoned material will halve (hence the term *half-life*). Because the half-life is known, it is possible to calculate the time elapsed since an organism died on the basis of the amount of carbon 14 remaining in the sample. The half-life value is some 1.03 percent greater than the value originally proposed by the Libby, who calculated the half-life as 5,568 ± 30 years. This rate is known as the *Libby half-life* and is still used by radiocarbon dating laboratories, the difference between the new and old rates being incorporated into the conversion process in which radiocarbon ages are changed into calendar ages (see discussion below) (Higham 1999).

Of the three most common naturally occurring isotopes of carbon, carbon 14 accounts for only 0.0000000001 percent (Higham 1999), so there is very little carbon 14 in a modern sample, let alone one that is several thousand years old. This means that samples of organic material for dating must meet certain minimum weights (Table 5.1).

It is also important for archaeologists to remove possible carbon contaminants, since age estimates will be obtained for any organic material. Higham (1999) notes a range of common contaminants ranging from cigarette ash (so don't smoke!) to paper from packing materials (foil is a useful material with which to package samples). Samples from the heat-retainer hearths excavated in western New South Wales, Australia, discussed in the second case study

Table 5.1 Sample size requirements as dry weights (from Waikato Radiocarbon Dating Laboratory 2002, with permission).

Material	Radiometric samples		AMS samples
	Ideal weight[a]	Minimum weight	
Wood	8–12 g	1.0 g	10 mg
Charcoal	8–12 g	1.0 g	10 mg
Carbonates	35 g	5.0 g	30 mg
Peat[b]	–	5–10 g	0.5 g
Bone[b]	100–200 g	20–80 g	0.5 g
Lake sediment[b]	30–100 g	10–20 g	1 g

[a] This is the minimum weight to avoid dilution
[b] Ranges reflect varying carbon content (weights approximate)

Figure 5.1 A sample from the excavation of a heat-retainer hearth before pretreatment. Rootlets, pieces of wood, and other organic contaminants are removed from the charcoal by hand.

below are typically filled with root hairs, pieces of wood, lumps of soil (Figure 5.1), and even the occasional dead ant! This material is carefully separated from the charcoal to be submitted to the laboratory. Another source of contamination comes from humic acids (from decayed plant matter). These may be adsorbed onto the surface of the sample material, particularly charcoal, so the exteriors of lumps of charcoal are often carved down with a scalpel blade. Cleaning the sample in this way is termed the *physical pretreatment*, and is differentiated from the *chemical pretreatment* usually undertaken by the dating laboratory. The latter involves the use of acid and base washes to remove inorganic carbonates and humic acids.

Once treated, a sample provided to a radiocarbon laboratory will be analyzed in one of two ways. Following the first method – the *beta-counting method* – the sample will be converted into a gas, or sometimes into another form, weighed, and then placed in a machine that is shielded from outside sources of radiation. Over a set period of time, some carbon 14 will radioactively decay by ejecting an atomic particle and changing back to nitrogen. The machine counts the number of times that this occurs and the number of disintegrations that take place over a set period of time is used to calculate the amount of carbon 14 remaining in the sample. When combined with the known rate of decay given by the half-life, this measurement can be used to calculate an estimate of the time elapsed since the organism that provided the sample died. Following the second method, termed *Accelerator Mass Spectrometry* (AMS), the proportion of carbon 14 in the sample is measured directly rather than through radioactive decay. Carbon atoms are converted into ions (charged atoms) and their mass measured by the application of magnetic and electric fields (Higham 1999). AMS permits the dating of very small samples (30 μg – 3 mg of carbon; see Table 5.1, and note that 1 μg = 10^{-6} g), well below those possible with the beta-counting method, so careful sample preparation is critical to minimize the chance of contamination. AMS dating is more expensive than the *beta-counting method* and so it is usually reserved for small samples that cannot be dated using the former methods.

Radiocarbon is only one of a number of techniques employed by archaeologists and other researchers interested in the Quaternary. Table 5.2 lists dating methods grouped together on the basis of shared assumptions, mechanisms, and applications (following Coleman et al. 1987). Descriptions of a number of these techniques as used in archaeology can be found in a volume of papers

Table 5.2 Dating methods grouped by shared assumptions, mechanisms and applications (from Colman et al. 1987).

Dating method groups	Description and examples
Sidereal methods (calendar or annual)	Calendar dates or count annual events; e.g., dendrochronology, varve chronologies, historical records
Isotopic methods	Change in isotopic composition due to radioactive decay; e.g., radiocarbon, potassium argon
Radiogenic methods	Cumulative nonisotopic effects of radioactive decay; e.g., crystal damage and electron energy trap methods (fission-track, OSL, thermoluminescence)
Chemical and biological methods	Measure some time-dependent chemical or biological processes; e.g., AAR, obsidian hydration
Geomorphic methods	Measure the results of complex interrelated time-dependent geomorphic processes; e.g., chemical and biological processes, soil profile development and progressive landscape modification
Correlation methods	Establish age equivalence using time-independent properties; e.g., tephrachronology, paleomagnetism

edited by Taylor and Aitken (1997) as well as more recent books on archaeological science (e.g., Brothwell & Pollard 2001; Goldberg et al. 2001).

Sidereal methods

Historical records and dendrochronology provide the best temporal resolution of any of the techniques, often allowing age estimates with a resolution of a single year. Dendrochronology is based on the annual rings of wood laid down by climatically sensitive trees beneath the bark (Dean 1997; Kuniholm 2001). Patterns of growth rings are matched between trees, and the rings used to count back in years from a known date. In some cases, very precise age estimates are possible. In the European Alps, for instance, it is sometimes possible to assign Neolithic lake settlement structures to the year (Billamboz 1996) and a similar level of precision is possible for some pueblo sites in the southwest of the United States (Dean et al. 1978).

Isotopic methods

At the other extreme from sidereal methods are a number of isotopic methods, useful for periods in excess of one million years (expressed as 1 m.y.a.), which have a resolution of 10,000–100,000 years (often expressed as 10–100 ka) (Blackwell & Schwarcz 1993). These methods are based on changes in the isotopic composition of a range of elements found in different materials, along the lines of radiocarbon dating described above. For truly ancient sites, with ages of 1–5 m.y.a., and which contain volcanic deposits, $^{40}Ar/^{39}Ar$ dating methods have proved useful (Rink 2001). The technique works by using a mass spectrometer to measure the amount of the two argon isotopes directly. The amount of ^{40}Ar originally in the sample is estimated by determining the amounts of various potassium (K) isotopes in the sample, one of which, ^{40}K, is the parent of ^{40}Ar. With a long half-life, the technique has formed the basis for age determinations for early hominin sites in Africa (e.g., Walter et al. 1991) and elsewhere.

For more recent periods, the radioactive decay of uranium 234 (^{234}U) into thorium (^{230}Th) provides a means of dating calcite. The technique, termed *U-series dating*, works because uranium is soluble and thorium is not; therefore uranium is present when calcite is precipitated but thorium is not. Thorium will gradually accumulate through time as ^{234}U decays, and this provides a technique with a range from 1,000 to 500,000 BP. U-series dating may also be used to date teeth (enamel, dentine, and cementum) and even eggshell, but because the uranium isotope may absorb onto the teeth at any time after burial, the technique gives only a minimum age (applications are described in Schwarcz & Blackwell 1991).

Radiogenic methods

Coleman et al. (1987) differentiate isotopic methods from radiogenic methods, where change occurs not through isotopic decay but through the accumulation of changes due to the presence of natural radiation. Four radiogenic techniques are commonly used: *thermoluminescence* (TL), *Optically Stimulated Luminescence* (OSL), *Electron Spin Resonance* (ESR), and *fission-track*. The availability of radiogenic methods has increased dramatically over the past 20 years and these changes have proved particularly useful for providing age estimates beyond the limits of radiocarbon. Good examples come from Australia, where thermoluminescence and OSL are both commonly used radiogenic techniques to provide age estimates for some of the earliest sites on the continent (e.g., Roberts 1997 and discussion below), and from the Levant and Europe, where thermoluminescence provides age estimates for sites connected with the arrival of modern humans (e.g., Valladas et al. 1988; Mercier et al. 1991).

Both thermoluminescence and OSL work by measuring the light emitted when a sample is heated to over 250°C (480°F); hence the name *thermoluminescence* (Aitken 1997; Grün 2001). The light comes from the release of trapped electrons that are held in the crystal structure of quartz, feldspar, and calcite when these minerals are heated. Over time, electrons in a sample become trapped as the result of exposure to natural radiation. For thermoluminescence, the radiogenic clock is "set" by a heating event at some point in the past that was sufficient to remove all the electrons from the trapping sites. This allows the calculation of an age estimate for the period since this heating event occurred. The calculation is made by dividing the thermoluminescence signal by the product of a measure of the rate of exposure to natural radiation and the sensitivity of the sample to the uptake of this radiation (Aitken 1997).

Thermoluminescence is best known as a technique applied to gain age estimates from pottery, where the firing process sets the clock, but the technique is now also routinely applied to obtain age estimates from burnt chert or flint artifacts (Valladas et al. 1988; Mercier et al. 1991), particularly from Paleolithic sites.

Optically Stimulated Luminescence works in a similar manner to thermoluminescence, except that it is light, rather than heat, that causes the trapped electrons to be released. As discussed below, OSL is often used to obtain age estimates for the sediments that surround archaeological deposits.

Electron Spin Resonance uses the same electrons, trapped in what are termed *paramagnetic centers*, that form the basis for OSL and TL, but measures them directly by applying microwave energy. The amount of microwave energy absorbed by the sample is proportional to the number of centers, and therefore to the age of the sample (Grün 2001). The main application to archaeology is seen in age estimates for tooth enamel and the technique has proved useful for obtaining ages ranging from a few thousand years to more than a million years (Rink 1997). One of the problems experienced when obtaining age estimates from teeth is uptake of uranium, which complicates the natural radiation dose and therefore the number of paramagnetic centers (Grün 2001). For this reason, U-series determinations and ESR are often conducted together (e.g., Grün et al. 1998).

One final radiogenic technique needs to be mentioned. Fission-track dating also makes use of structural changes in minerals as a result of exposure to natural radiation through time, but the results of the radiation exposure are measured optically. Minerals that naturally contain high amounts of uranium and thorium impurities accumulate zones of damage called *tracks* due to natural radioactive decay. This damage can be measured optically with a microscope, since the fission tracks are of the order of 0.02 mm in length (Rink 2001). Archaeological applications generally involve age estimates for volcanic materials, as discussed by Wagner and Van den Haute (1992).

Chemical and biological methods

Chemical and biological techniques are not based on radioactive systems at all, but instead use a variety of other time-dependent processes. *Amino Acid Racemization* (AAR), for instance, is based on a change in the orientation of amino acids detectable in polarized light. Through time, the predominantly *left* (L) version (isomer) transforms to the *right* (D) isomer in a process that is temperature dependent. If paleotemperature can be controlled for, the ratio of the D to L forms can be used to provide an age estimate for a sample, as long as the results are calibrated against a second age estimation technique (Hare et al. 1997; Dincauze 2000: 102). Johnson and Miller (1997) review archaeological examples noting that after an initial period of controversy, the technique is now used successfully with avian eggshell, mollusk shell, teeth, and bone over age ranges that extend beyond the limit of radiocarbon.

Chemical changes also form the basis for *obsidian hydration dating*, a technique that is based on the rate of absorption of water into freshly fractured obsidian surfaces. Results vary considerably according to temperature, and this has led to much debate about the effectiveness of the rate of hydration through time. In New Zealand, the combination of abundant obsidian outcrops, a relatively short period of time since human colonization, and difficulties in interpreting radiocarbon age estimates have led to the development of the technique (e.g., Ambrose 2001), but large numbers of age estimates are also available from archaeological sites in Mesoamerica. Here, Freter (1993) differentiates between results where obsidian hydration is used directly to obtain age estimates for artifacts and studies where the technique is used to place artifacts in chronological order rather than establish actual age estimates. This latter technique has found application in the Great Basin of the USA, where obsidian artifacts occur in surface deposits that are otherwise difficult to age (e.g., Beck & Jones 1994).

Geomorphic methods

Geomorphic methods of dating rely on a range of time-dependent processes. A well-known application of this technique is at Lake Mungo in Australia, where Bowler (Bowler & Price 1998) defined a series of stratigraphic layers representing episodes of lake filling and emptying to which age estimates were

SIMON HOLDAWAY

assigned. Bowler was able to relate the stratigraphic position of archaeological deposits to the sequence of layers, and through this means assign age estimates.

Correlation methods are sometimes used to provide age estimates for archaeological materials. *Tephrachronology* uses the stratigraphic position of volcanic ash deposits, where an estimate is available for the date of the eruption to provide either the starting point (the *terminus post quem*) or the ending point (the *terminus ante quem*) for artifacts that are deposited above or below the ash layer. The technique forms the basis for the early hominin chronologies from East Africa, but has also proved useful in obtaining age estimates for more recent records. In the Bismarck Archipelago in the western Pacific, for instance, a series of eruptions bracket archaeological deposits, permitting age estimates to be obtained (e.g., Machida et al. 1996).

Limits on Chronometric Techniques

Maximum limits

The selection of which method to apply depends partly on the context, particularly which materials are available, but also on the upper and lower limits of the ages that can be determined using each of the techniques. For the isotopic methods, including radiocarbon, the maximum age that can be obtained is limited largely by the half-life of the element that decays. Using radiocarbon as the example, the reason for the maximum limit can be displayed graphically (Figure 5.2). As the proportion of radiocarbon compared to its decay product decreases, the decay curve in Figure 5.2 asymptotically approaches a flat line. After this point, there is no change in the relative abundance of carbon 14. An age estimate (expressed as half-lives in Figure 5.2) is read from the decay curve at the point of intersection with the relative proportion of carbon 14. As described by Blackwell and Schwarz (1993), the maximum age occurs when the error associated with the age estimate intersects with zero. Around this point, when the abundance of the radioactive element is low, the signal-to-noise ratio decreases, leading to an exponential increase in errors. The signal refers to the relative proportion of radiocarbon, while the noise reflects contamination of the machines used to measure radiocarbon. This noise means that even a sample that contains no radiocarbon will give a positive reading. Also important is contamination of the sample itself. Even minute amounts of modern carbon in an ancient sample will drastically alter the age estimate. For instance, the addition of just 1 percent of modern carbon to a sample that is 50,000 years old will produce an apparent age of 35,000 BP.

Contamination of radiocarbon samples has proved to be of great significance in dating archaeological sites at the limits of the radiocarbon technique. The estimation of the age of the earliest sites in Australia provides one of the best examples discussed in the world literature. A number of years ago, Allen (1989) noted that radiocarbon determinations obtained by archaeologists, which had steadily increased in age since the first Pleistocene-aged determination obtained by Mulvaney (Mulvaney & Joyce 1965), had reached a plateau, with no determinations attaining ages older than 40,000 BP. The radiocarbon record

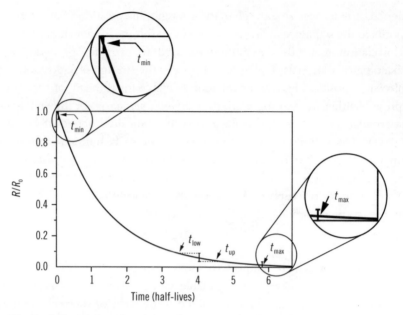

Figure 5.2 The limits of radiometric techniques for age estimation, displayed as a radiometric decay curve. The radioactive isotope ratio R/R_0 decreases through time. Precision is shown by the vertical bar and the t_{low} and t_{up} age estimates. The maximum and minimum ranges are indicated when the error bars strike the 0 and 1.0 values on the y-axis, respectively (modified from Blackwell and Schwarcz 1993).

appeared to be at odds with age estimates obtained from diagenic techniques (e.g., thermoluminescence) from sites in the Northern Territory (Roberts et al. 1990a). A variety of explanations were put forward to explain the discrepancy (e.g., Bowdler 1990; Hiscock 1990; Roberts et al. 1990b,c; Allen 1994; Roberts et al. 1994; Allen & Holdaway 1995); however, discussion quickly turned to the problem of sample contamination (e.g., Chappell et al. 1996; Roberts 1997). Recently, special techniques have been developed to pretreat samples in an effort to remove contaminants. Only through the application of these techniques have age estimates in excess of 40,000 BP been achieved for early Australian archaeological sites (e.g., Fifield et al. 2001; Turney et al. 2001), although in some cases even these rigorous treatments are not sufficient to remove all contaminants and the radiocarbon age estimates appear too young in comparison to ages obtained using other techniques (e.g., Bird et al. 2002).

This limit on radiocarbon imposed by the contamination of radiocarbon samples is better understood as a reflection of the resolution of radiocarbon age estimation rather than as the "problem" of sample contamination. Faced with this limitation, archaeologists have increasingly turned to radiogenic techniques. As discussed above, the techniques are now applied to burnt flint or chert artifacts in Europe and the Levant, which are thought to be older than the limit of radiocarbon dating. However, it is in Australia where these techniques have provided some of the most dramatic results. Here, thermoluminescence and OSL have been used to provide age estimates from the lowest

SIMON HOLDAWAY

layers in sites thought to date the earliest human entry into the continent (e.g., Roberts et al. 1990a; Roberts 1997). In some cases, the diagenic techniques have provided results significantly older than for samples aged with radiocarbon.

As with radiocarbon dating, contamination can sometimes pose problems for radiogenic techniques as illustrated by age estimates for the Australian site of Jinmium (Fullagar et al. 1996). At this site, incomplete optical bleaching of some sand grains produced age estimates well in excess of the likely age of the associated artifacts (Roberts et al. 1998, 1999). In effect, the OSL samples used from Jinmium contained quartz grains from the rockshelter itself, as well as those from sands exposed on the surface at the time artifacts were deposited at the site. Waters et al. (1997) and Gibbons (1997) discuss another example based on a controversial set of age estimates from Siberia.

At the other end of the scale, the minimum limit for radiocarbon and other isotopic techniques is set when the error associated with the relative proportion of the radioactive element cannot be differentiated from one (Figure 5.2). This is simply the reverse of the signal-to-noise problem encountered at the maximum limit of any given technique. In this case, however, the errors are such that the change in the relative amount of radiocarbon cannot be differentiated from the natural levels in living organisms. **Minimum limits**

For radiocarbon, three factors contribute to the size of the error for recent samples and so contribute to the minimum limit for the technique (Taylor 1997). First, since the seventeenth century there has been considerable variability in the natural levels of radiocarbon production in the atmosphere due to changes in solar radiation. In fact, this is just part of a much wider problem connected with changes in the production of radiocarbon in the past. Changing the amount of radiocarbon available when an organism was alive will change the age estimates after its death, since the age is calculated by measuring the amount of radiocarbon left in the sample relative to the amount that existed at the moment of death.

Variation in the natural production of radiocarbon proved to be a problem when the technique was first developed, but was solved by matching radiocarbon ages with those obtained from tree rings (Taylor 1997). As discussed above, counting tree rings (dendrochronology) back from the outermost layer provides a sidereal (solar) chronology. What is more, the wood laid down each year can be used to obtain radiocarbon ages. Therefore, in principle, calibration simply involves correlating the radiocarbon age of a tree ring with its sidereal age (Higham 1999). However, for some periods, atmospheric concentrations of radiocarbon have varied so much that several possible sidereal ages correlate with one radiocarbon age estimate (an illustration of this is provided in the second case study below). This is the case after the seventeenth century, limiting the utility of radiocarbon for recent periods. The need to calibrate radiocarbon determinations into ages in sidereal years also explains why some age estimates are presented in "radiocarbon years" and some in "calibrated years." Computer programs such as OxCal v. 3.8 (Bronk Ramsey 2002) are available that automatically provide one and two standard deviation ranges for calibrated age estimates as well as graphical output. The term *radiocarbon years* therefore refers to an age estimate that is uncorrected for variation in the natural production of radiocarbon, while *calibrated* age estimates incorporate an estimate of this effect.

The second factor that affects recent samples is attributable to burning of fossil fuels since the nineteenth century, which has released a large amount of "ancient" carbon (i.e., carbon that has no radioactivity) into the atmosphere. Organisms absorbing this carbon have a reduced relative proportion of radiocarbon at the point of death, which means that their radiocarbon ages will appear too old.

The final factor that affects recent samples relates to atmospheric tests of nuclear bombs during the twentieth century. This greatly increased the available levels of radiocarbon in the atmosphere, hence making samples appear too old. The complex interplay between these three factors means that, in general, it is not possible to assign ages to materials that are less than 300 years old using radiocarbon.

It is important to mention one other set of corrections that sometimes must be applied. As in the case of fossil fuels, these corrections make adjustments for what are termed *apparent ages*, a correction needed when, in life, an organism accessed a carbon reservoir that was relatively depleted in carbon 14. The most common archaeological example concerns the oceans, where the apparent age is caused by the delay in the exchange between atmospheric CO_2 and dissolved bicarbonates. At times, the apparent age caused by this delay in exchange can be of the order of centuries. Tables of corrections are available for the world's oceans (for more details, see Higham 1999).

Limits on radiogenic techniques
Just as there are maximum and minimum limits to isotopic dating techniques, so similar limits exist for radiogenic techniques (Table 5.2). These techniques are based on measurement of the degree of physical damage in solids caused by natural radiation. The maximum limit is imposed by a saturation point, after which additional radiation exposure is not recorded. In part, this depends on the nature of the material being dated, but it also depends on the environmental radiation rate. Like radiocarbon dating, the minimum limits are determined by signal-to-noise levels (Blackwell & Schwarcz 1993).

Precision
Signal-to-noise levels place limits on the age ranges over which techniques may be used, but within these limits techniques vary in the precision with which age estimates may be obtained. Using the radiocarbon technique as an example, the precision of an age estimate reflects the nature of carbon

SIMON HOLDAWAY

14 decay. Although this decay is continuous, it is also spontaneous. The rate of decay can be measured, but each decay event can only be predicted statistically, not precisely. Over time, the distribution of decay events forms a normal curve spread around the average. It is this distribution that is one source for the estimate of the standard error associated with an average radiocarbon age determination (indicated by the "±" term). Another source of error comes from the laboratory multiplier, effectively a measure of the laboratory reproducibility of radiocarbon age estimates. This multiplier is applied by many laboratories to the calculated standard error based on the distribution of decay events (Higham 1999). Typically for a radiocarbon estimate, the calculated standard error will span several decades and means that the true radiocarbon age estimate will fall within the range formed by subtracting and adding the error from the mean, 68 percent of the time (the proportion increases to 95 percent if two standard errors are subtracted and added). The precision of radiocarbon age estimates as measured by the standard error means that events that occurred in the past that were separated by a few days, months, or years, or in some cases decades or centuries, will not be distinguishable from one another. Note that this does not mean that radiocarbon age estimates are inaccurate. Accuracy refers to whether the age estimate is a true estimate of the death of the carbon-bearing organism. A radiocarbon age estimate with a standard error of ± 500 years may be accurate even though, with this size of error, it may not be very precise.

Radiocarbon provides an estimate of the age at death of the organism, but it is up to the archaeologist to relate this process to constructing a chronology of past human behavior. This process may seem simple but, as a number of authors have pointed out (e.g., Dean 1978; Ramenofsky 1998), this simplicity is an illusion. Imagine, for instance, concentrations of charcoal derived from a hearth buried within a stratigraphic layer in a cave site such as those excavated at the front of the Bone Cave (Figure 5.3), one of a series of rockshelter sites excavated in Tasmania with age estimates ranging back to older than 30,000 BP (Allen 1996). These sites are important because they represent a Southern Hemisphere equivalent to the European Upper Paleolithic, and provide archaeologists with the opportunity to compare and contrast the archaeological records of modern humans who occupied glacial environments at opposite ends of the globe (e.g., Holdaway & Cosgrove 1997).

From Age Estimates to Chronology

At Bone Cave, concentrations of charcoal were identified toward the front of the cave. Within the same layer are scattered a number of stone artifacts and bones from animals. Using a sample from the concentrations of charcoal, an archaeologist may obtain a radiocarbon determination to "date" hearth construction and, by extension, the stone artifacts and animal bones. In fact, use of the term *date* in contexts such as these has been much criticized, since the word implies a specific moment in time and, as discussed above, age

Figure 5.3 Concentrations of charcoal from hearths as seen in the section at Bone Cave (Allen 1996: pl. 6, reproduced with permission).

estimates using radiogenic techniques such as radiocarbon return means and associated standard errors, not fixed dates (Coleman et al. 1987). The preferred term is *age* or *age estimate* (as used throughout this chapter), because these terms convey the uncertainty connected with age estimation while the term *date* does not.

Archaeologists are able to obtain an estimate for the age of a hearth using the radiocarbon technique, but the age that is provided (assuming no contamination problem) does not relate to the construction of the hearth but to the death of the carbon-based organism (i.e., the plant) that provided the wood that was burned to form the charcoal that was "dated." The archaeologist must ensure that these two events are not separated by too great a period of time. Determining both the type of plant and the nature of the wood (heart wood or twigs) that was burnt in the hearth will give an indication of the length of time likely to have elapsed between the death of the organism and the construction of the hearth. Clearly dating the heartwood of a long-lived species will lead to a considerable age difference. The problem is common in some regions of the world (e.g., New Zealand and the Northwest region of the USA), where long-lived tree species are found and where driftwood was a common source of fuel in the past.

Assuming that there is no major discrepancy between the age of the death event estimated with radiocarbon and the age of the hearth construction, the archaeologist may argue that because the hearth is located within a layer that also contains a number of stone artifacts and animal bones, the age of these artifacts and faunal materials may be inferred through association with the age estimate of the hearth. This process is referred to as *cross-dating* (Ramenofsky 1998). As Spaulding (1960) discussed many years ago, cross-dating involves a series of archaeological inferences, since age estimates refer to events rather than things. In other words, it is the attributes of the artifacts and their spatial distribution that form the basis for inference about the association of the age estimate obtained by radiocarbon and the archaeological materials. Such an inference might be possible if the characteristics of the sediment in which the artifacts are deposited suggest deposition over a relatively short period of time (e.g., Stein 2001; see also Chapter 12 of this book). They may, for instance, derive from the flooding of a stream (e.g., Stern et al. 2002). Additionally, the state of the artifacts may suggest that exposure on the surface before burial was of a relatively short duration. For instance, archaeologists have used changes in the nature of bone to suggest relatively short periods of exposure (e.g., Potts 1986; Holliday et al. 1999; but see Lyman & Fox 1989). Finally, refitting stone artifacts may indicate that the artifacts within the layer were manufactured at one time, because flakes can be placed back onto a core, suggesting that they were knapped together during a single event (e.g., Villa 1982). If all these lines of evidence converge, it may be possible for the archaeologist to infer that the age estimate for the death of the plant burnt to form the charcoal in the hearth forms a reasonable estimate of the age of the hearth, and of the abandonment of the artifacts and animal bones deposited in the same layer as the hearth. However, the more various lines of evidence diverge, the greater is the temporal separation between the dated event and the other events that make up the artifact assemblage.

It should be clear from this example that "dating" of a "site" is not something that actually occurs in archaeology. But even if the phrase is rewritten to read "obtaining an age estimate for a group of archaeological materials thought to derive from a contemporary set of events discovered in one part of a site," it involves a series of inferences that extend well beyond those related to obtaining a radiocarbon determination. Instead, "dating" involves a complex set of inferences derived from a wide array of archaeological methodologies.

Temporal Resolution and Behavioral Variation

In the example of the Bone Cave hearth, the archaeologist was able to infer that the radiocarbon age estimate and the hearth manufacture, along with artifact and faunal deposition, were nearly contemporaneous. However, even in this example, "contemporaneous" is a relative term. For some purposes, differences in the amount of time represented by sediment deposition and estimates of the time that it took for the burial of faunal material to occur, based on the state of preservation, may become important. Even when items are found together within a single stratigraphic context, the archaeologist may be interested in developing measures that indicate, at least in a relative sense, the amount of time represented by different behaviors. As Ramenofsky (1998) emphasizes, construction of a chronology is as dependent on the nature of the research question being posed as any other archaeological investigation. The units used to build a chronology and how close the age estimates must be to be treated as deriving from different depositional events depend on the research goals (e.g., Fletcher 1992). There are no universal or superior chronologies; nor are there chronological units that existed in the past, waiting to be discovered by archaeologists. Time is a continuum that takes different forms depending on the scale at which it is observed. At the scale of the universe, time is warped, while Earth time appears to be linear (Hawking 1998). Therefore, the perception of time depends on the location of the observer and the scale at which this individual is considering time. On the basis of this observation, Ramenofsky (1998) argues that archaeologists are not in the business of discovering time. Because time is a continuum, archaeologists impose their own conceptual units, breaking the continuity that is time into a series of arbitrary packages that reflect their interests in inferring the outcomes from past actions. In this sense, units of time cannot be discovered because there is nothing to discover (see the discussion of time in Chapter 2).

Fidelity and resolution

Paleontologists have dealt with many of the same issues faced by archaeologists when considering geological fossil deposits (Stern 1994). Like archaeologists, they recognize that the way in which time is packaged has more to do with the nature of the research question than it has to the discovery of something from the past. For instance, *fidelity* and *resolution* are two terms developed by paleontologists to describe the fossil record (Behrensmeyer et al. 2000). Fidelity refers to how faithfully the fossil record captures biological information, while resolution refers to the sharpness of the record in a temporal sense, the finest temporal or spatial unit into which the fossils may be placed. These concepts may be rewritten in archaeological terms.

SIMON HOLDAWAY

Imagine a site at which several lines of evidence point to short occupation duration with a limited number of activities. For many years, the classic portrayal of such a site has been the Meer site in Belgium (Cahen et al. 1979). At this site, a combination of technological, refitting, and usewear studies all suggest that the stone artifacts were deposited together during a short period. The site provides high time and space resolution but has low fidelity. We know what went on at the Meer site in great detail; the high time resolution and refitting tells us where those activities occurred – hence the high spatial resolution. But fidelity is low, because the site can tell us little about the full range of activities undertaken by the people who manufactured, used, and abandoned the artifacts. We know nothing about what occurred at other places in the landscape at different times.

Sites such as Meer are of little use if we are interested in studying behavioral variability, because we will learn nothing about the set of different behaviors that occurred outside the time-slice that we are viewing. Other sites used by the same or related groups of people might contain artifacts relating to quite different types of behaviors. If we want to learn about behavioral variability, we have to wait around (i.e., allow time to pass) so that these behaviors can occur at locations at which artifacts are preserved (i.e., archaeological sites). To study variability in an archaeological sense, we do not always want sites such as Pompeii, where life stopped in an instant in time; rather, we want sites where much behavior has accumulated through time, so that we can see the accumulated variability. Discussion of this idea formed part of a famous debate between Binford (1981) and Schiffer (1985) (discussed by Murray 1999; see also Knapp 1992; Smith 1992).

The alternative to thinking about Meer is to consider an assemblage that represents a very large number of behavioral events, with material deposited over an extended period of time. Depending on the location of the assemblage, a wide range of activities may have taken place, leading to the deposition of many types of artifacts. Such a site will have low temporal resolution, because so many events that may not be separable are mixed together. But the fidelity will be high, because a high proportion of all the activities that occurred within a landscape are represented in the assemblage. This follows from the reasoning that, over time, many people will eventually visit the point in the landscape represented by the site under study. In this sense, the spatial resolution will also be high, not in the same way as at the Meer site discussed above, but in the sense that the artifact assemblage will represent a good example of all the artifacts that have been used within the landscape that surrounds the site.

Sites with low temporal resolution but high fidelity are referred to as *time averaged* (Stern 1993, 1994). In paleontology, time averaging (the term was first introduced by Walker & Bambach 1971) refers to the difference in rates of

Time averaging

population turnover of individual taxa versus the rate of sedimentation (Behrensmeyer et al. 2000). Because rates of sedimentation at many fossil locations are relatively slow, the fossil remains of many organisms that did not live together in contemporaneous populations will accumulate together within a single geological bed (the equivalent of a single archaeological site). Thus time-averaged assemblages group together organisms that may never have functioned together in a living community but provide a good idea of the range of organisms that have existed through time in an environment. The application of the concept to archaeology uses a similar definition.

As Stern (1994) comments, the sedimentary processes that lead to the formation of archaeological sites vary in magnitude and frequency, just as they do for paleontological sites. The rates at which artifacts are deposited also vary depending on a range of factors, including the functions for which the artifacts were created, the way they were disposed of, and the degree of curation (Wandsnider 1996). This means that, depending on the mode and rate of accumulation of sediment, and the mode and rate of artifact accumulation, artifact assemblages may include a variety of objects deposited at different times that were never used together for the same purposes (e.g., that never formed functionally related "toolkits").

Stern (1993, 1994) uses time averaging as the basis for a critique of conceptual models for inferring behavior from the earliest African Paleolithic sites. As she points out, models based on ethnographic or ecological theory effectively ignore the time-averaged nature of many artifact assemblages, because they ignore the time it took for assemblages to accumulate (more will be said on this subject below).

There are two things to consider when assessing the time averaging of an archaeological deposit. First, there is the time span represented by the sediment layer in which artifacts are found. Secondly, there is the time span represented by the artifacts themselves: paleontologists refer to these as the *scope* and *micro-stratigraphic acuity*, respectively (Schindel 1982). It is not hard to imagine a layer represented in a site that took several centuries or even millennia to accumulate. Bone Cave again provides good examples. Here, a series of radiocarbon age estimates indicate that accumulation occurred at various times from as early as 29,000 BP through to the end of the Pleistocene. It is possible to calculate the rate of sedimentation for one of the excavated squares in the cave by plotting the depth against age in radiocarbon years (Figure 5.4). This gives a value of 145 radiocarbon years per centimeter of deposit as an estimate for the rate of sedimentation in this square over the whole occupation of the cave. This rate can in turn be used to provide an estimate of the rate of artifact accumulation. Bone Cave was excavated in 2.5 cm deep excavation units and it is a simple matter to total the number of artifacts in each of these 55 excavation units for one of the squares ($n = 3,187$) and use this number to provide the estimate of the rate of artifact deposition per year. The result suggests that on average 0.16 artifacts from the largest

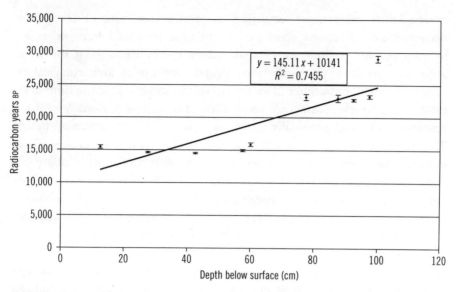

Figure 5.4 The sedimentation rate for Square C, Bone Cave, southwest Tasmania, calculated by plotting radiocarbon age against depth. The linear regression line and associated equation indicate an average deposition rate of 1 cm of deposit every 145 radiocarbon years. The R^2 statistic indicates that 74 percent of the variance is accounted for by the regression line (however, see the text for further discussion).

sieve fraction with a maximum length of 7 mm or greater were deposited each year over the length of the occupation. The Tasmanian sites contain some of the richest Pleistocene artifact assemblages in Australia, so while this rate may appear to be low, it is in fact much higher than that calculated at other Pleistocene Australian sites. O'Connor, for instance, reports rates of only 0.046–0.099 artifacts per year for Koolan Shelter 2 (O'Connor 1999: 36). Nevertheless, the rate at Bone Cave suggests that it took a little over 6 years to deposit a single artifact, a rate that is far below the number of artifacts that ethnographic studies would suggest were normally deposited by small groups of hunter–gatherers over time (e.g., Hayden 1979). The discrepancy reflects the action of time averaging. As Stern (1994) points out, there is little reason to assume continuous rates of sedimentation in archaeological sites. In fact, studies of cave sites indicate that a variety of factors (including human occupation) will lead to changes in the mode and frequency of sediment accumulation (e.g., Stein 2001).

It is also clear that rates of artifact accumulation vary. Calculating an overall rate of artifact deposition assumes that humans behaved in highly uniform ways in the past. In fact, the opposite is likely to be true, both in a short-term behavioral sense (people undertook a variety of tasks at more or less the same time) and in a longer-term processual sense. Empirically, in many instances it may be better to model rates of artifact accumulation not as a straight line but as a sigmoid curve (Shennan 1988: 154). This is because of a phenomenon termed *autocorrelation*. At many archaeological sites, there is a greater probability of sequential occupations occurring in groups (i.e., sets of occupations occurring over relatively short periods of time separated from other sets by long periods of time) rather than spaced evenly throughout the whole sequence (Holdaway & Porch 1996). People who use an archaeological site at one time will, more often than not, return to this site at some time in the future, because even as people move around to exploit seasonally available resources, they will eventually return to a place that they inhabited before. This means that occupations will tend to form clusters that are closely related in time. Eventually, however, a region may be abandoned or the utility of a particular site may decline. The site will then be abandoned, often for long periods of time. As periods of use and abandonment alternate, archaeological materials will tend to form clusters separated by sterile or near-sterile deposits. Such sequences are not well modeled by straight lines.

At Bone Cave, there is stratigraphic evidence to back up a nonlinear trend. A nearly sterile layer separates radiocarbon age estimates that indicate occupation around 15,000–17,000 BP and another group of estimates that indicate occupation around 24,000–29,000 BP (all age estimates are in radiocarbon years). Clearly there is a significant gap in deposition at Bone Cave, one that is made obvious by the large number of radiocarbon determinations that were acquired for the site. As an aside, imagine the difficulty faced by an archaeologist who, in the absence of the sterile layer, obtained only a small number of radiocarbon determinations for a site such as Bone Cave. Selecting three or four determinations and plotting these against depth makes the rate of sedimentation appear much more linear (Figure 5.5).

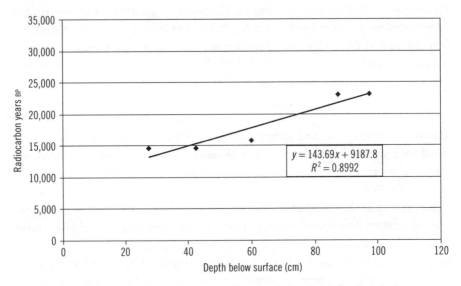

Figure 5.5 Selected radiocarbon determinations from Bone Cave Square C plotted against depth versus the full suite of determinations. The R^2 statistic is higher for the linear regression based on these five radiocarbon determinations than it is for the ten determinations that were actually obtained (Figure 5.4). The example illustrates how a small number of determinations can mask nonlinear trends.

Geologists refer to the presence of gaps in the sequence, the proportion of a time interval that is represented by actual sedimentation versus the actual duration of sedimentation in a section, as the *stratigraphic completeness* of a deposit (Stern 1994). If this concept were ignored, the difference between the maximum and minimum radiocarbon determinations at Bone Cave would indicate a period of occupation spanning 15,000 radiocarbon years. But when the concept is applied, the gaps indicated by the stratigraphic record combined with the distribution of radiocarbon determinations throughout the deposit suggest age estimates for the actual occupation of the cave that span much shorter periods of time. Actual periods of artifact deposition are liable to be shorter still. At one extreme, periods as short as a few days each could easily account for the number of artifacts represented in one of the Bone Cave squares. In effect, this would mean that during the majority of the time represented by the archaeological record, nothing happened that resulted in the deposition of artifacts.

Figure 5.6 shows two plots of the number of artifacts per radiocarbon year for one square at Bone Cave. In Figure 5.6a, the rate of accumulation and the number of artifacts per excavation unit have been used to provide a plot of the number of artifacts deposited per year as though occupation at the site were continuous. In Figure 5.6b, the rate of accumulation has been recalculated taking into account the distribution of radiocarbon determinations that suggest significant temporal gaps in the record. In Figure 5.6b, three separate deposition rates are used to display the number of artifacts deposited per year at the site. The result is two plots that give quite different impressions of the nature of deposition at Bone Cave and thereby suggest quite different behavioral interpretations for the cave. Clearly, our procedures can have a dramatic effect on the way we think about modeling behavior in the past. A number of archaeologists have considered this topic under the heading of "time perspectivism."

Different types of processes operate at different time scales, so if archaeologists are going to be able to study these processes they must be willing to alter the time scale at which they investigate the archaeological record. This simple notion is termed *time perspectivism* (Bailey 1983). The operation of the concept is easiest to see in the Earth sciences, where the subjects considered range widely in temporal scale (Bailey 1983, 1987). At one extreme, it may take millions of years for some processes such as continental drift to occur, while at the other end of the temporal scale, changes in the course of drainage lines found in arid regions can happen in a matter of a few hours during rain events. Clearly, investigators interested in these two different types of phenomena have to view their data at radically different temporal scales or else their research endeavors would become ridiculous.

Multiple Scales of Time

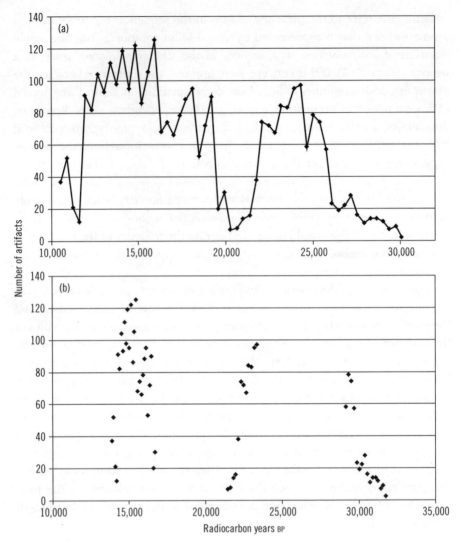

Figure 5.6 Two views of the rate of artifact deposition in one square from Bone Cave. In (a), the average rate of deposition for the whole site combined with the number of artifacts per excavation unit provides one view of the differing rate of artifact deposition. In (b), the long temporal gaps in the sequence of radiocarbon determinations are incorporated, suggesting three quite different periods of artifact deposition.

Bailey and others who have written on time perspectivism in archaeology (e.g., Fletcher 1992; Stern 1994; Murray 1999) argue that just as in the Earth sciences, explanations of past behavior must be tailored to the temporal scale of the phenomena being studied. Stern (1993) for instance, has criticized attempts by archaeologists interested in the earliest African Paleolithic sites, because the models that they use to interpret the distributions of artifacts and animal bones that they find are largely derived from ecological theory or ethnographic observations. Both bodies of theory are founded on short-term observations, yet the artifact and faunal assemblages that these theories are being used to interpret come from time-averaged deposits where the *scope* (to use Schindel's [1982] term, introduced above) is measured in tens of thousands of years or more. Stern questions whether it is useful to mix temporal scales in this way.

Bailey (1987) likened the problem that Stern subsequently raised to a scientist using an instrument like the Hubble telescope not to study the distant universe, but instead pointing it toward Earth to demonstrate that, from the point of view of a person standing on the ground, the Earth appears to be flat. The procedure appears silly because the Hubble telescope was not designed to look at phenomena at the scale of a person standing on Earth.

Archaeologists interested in time perspectivism suggest that besides the short time scale processes that we experience as part of our daily lives, and which form the basis for the processes recorded in many ethnographies, there are other processes operating at larger scales over longer periods of time to which attention should be paid. If inferences are drawn only on the basis of analyses that focus on the operation of short-term processes, then these longer-term processes are liable to remain unanalyzed.

While discussing time, Ramenofsky (1998) makes the point that the units in which time is measured must be closely related to the nature of the question being posed by the archaeologist. The outcome of this position – and a time perspective view of the archaeological record – is that there is not one time, but many times; or, as Bailey (1983) corrects himself after making this statement, not one way of representing time, but many ways in which time may be represented. The need to talk of ways of representing time rather than time itself occurs because time cannot be measured directly, but is assessed in terms of a series of processes. This means that archaeologists may usefully group their artifacts into a number of different temporal units, depending on the scale of the processes that they are interested in studying.

Examples of how this may be done are provided in two case studies. In the first, a number of potential temporal scales are discussed that are useful for answering different research questions at the stratified Tasmanian Pleistocene cave site of Bone Cave, which was introduced at the start of this chapter. The second example discusses a quite different form of archaeological record. Stud Creek, in the arid zone of western New South Wales, Australia, contains no stratigraphy in the conventional sense at all. Rather, artifacts and the remains of hearths are distributed across an eroded surface, providing evidence of occupation by Indigenous Australians during the past 2,000 years. The research summarized here indicates how geoarchaeological techniques may be used to construct a chronology even when the archaeological record is deflated onto a single surface.

As discussed above, Bone Cave is interesting because it is one of a number of cave sites in Tasmania that preserve a record of late Pleistocene human occupation, the Southern Hemisphere equivalent of the European Upper Paleolithic. During the late Pleistocene, low sea levels meant that Tasmania was joined to mainland Australia, forming the continent known as Sahul.

Depending on the scale at which the record at Bone Cave is analyzed, a range of different research questions may be addressed. Four of these have proved useful in formulating different types of questions.

To place Bone Cave into a regional context, the temporal scale needs to be adjusted so that comparisons may be made with other Tasmanian cave sites, including those on what are today islands between Tasmania and the mainland, since during the Pleistocene these islands were hills distributed across an ancient land bridge.

Figure 5.7 provides a graph on which many radiocarbon determinations from Tasmanian cave sites are displayed together (the methods used are described elsewhere – see Holdaway & Porch 1995, 1996; see also Housley et al. 1997). The plot effectively sums the number of radiocarbon age estimates and plots this sum radiocarbon year by radiocarbon year (many of the age determinations fall outside the current limits of

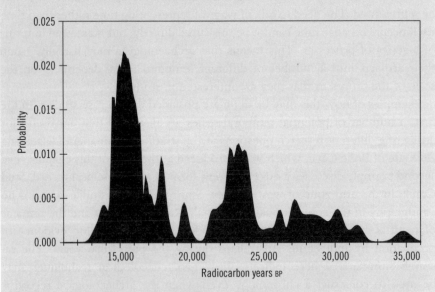

Figure 5.7   An area plot, showing the probability of a particular year having one or more radiocarbon age estimates based on a moving average of Pleistocene radiocarbon determinations from Tasmanian cave sites (modified from Holdaway & Porch 1995).

calibration programs). Moving through time along the *x*-axis, the plot fluctuates up and down, indicating that there are times when more deposits have radiocarbon age estimates than at others. Fluctuations occur every few thousand years and markedly increase in amplitude after the Late Glacial Maximum (approximately 18,000 BP).

The pattern illustrated in Figure 5.7 suggests two sets of research questions. First, the results may indicate that deposition in the sites was not continuous over the late Pleistocene. This may reflect times either when the sites were not occupied and/or when the conditions for preservation were poor over some or all of Tasmania. Secondly, there is a possible correlation between the fluctuating numbers of radiocarbon determinations and a series of long-term environmental changes documented at a Tasmanian swamp site (Pulbeena Swamp) that has a particularly good record of past environments, including periods of wetter and drier climate (Holdaway & Porch 1995). If this correlation does not reflect differential preservation of deposits, then it may reflect long-term adjustments in the way people used the ancient Tasmanian landscape. Individuals inhabiting the southern extreme of Sahul could not have perceived the climatic variations indicated at sites such as Pulbeena, so this is not a case of individuals reacting to climatic changes. Rather, looking at the pattern created by multiple radiocarbon determinations at this scale reflects the long-term outcome of a large number of distinct individual behaviors.

To discover what adjustments people made to the changing environment, it is necessary to shift from a global to a local scale. If the radiocarbon determinations are considered on a site-by-site basis, it becomes apparent that most of the artifacts found at the sites come from deposits associated with radiocarbon determinations that overlap. This is illustrated in Figure 5.8 by the deposits at Bone Cave. Despite the long sequence at this site, most of the artifactual material was deposited during four periods of occupation indicated by artifact-rich deposits, for which a number of radiocarbon determinations

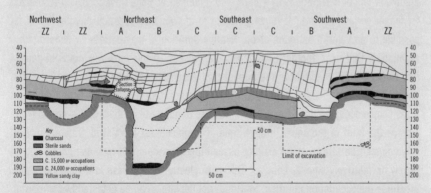

Figure 5.8 A stratigraphic diagram from Bone Cave, Tasmania, showing layers covered by groups of radiocarbon determinations. Most of the deposit belongs to periods with age estimates ~ 15,000 BP and ~ 24,000 BP. Two shorter periods of occupation indicted by the radiocarbon results are not shown (from Holdaway 2004: fig. 1.4).

have returned results that overlap. Although the duration of these periods cannot be determined precisely, they appear to be relatively short compared to the overall time for which the site was available for use. Thus, at this scale one of the research questions becomes why Bone Cave and its neighbors fell out of use between periods of occupation and whether these periods of disuse correlate between sites. Correlation of occupation and disuse between sites may indicate the operation of long-term regional processes perhaps related to changes in the regional environment.

By looking at the nature of the artifacts from each of the four periods suggested by the radiocarbon determinations, changes in the way Bone Cave itself was used through time may be investigated. One of the interesting patterns to emerge from an analysis of the stone artifacts from Bone Cave is that the relative proportions of different raw materials obtained locally versus those brought to the site change through time (Holdaway 2000, 2004). This suggests changes in the mobility of people who occupied the site at different times throughout its 15,000-year history, since more mobile people had more access to nonlocal raw material sources. There is a change represented at the site, with relatively more sedentism after the Late Glacial Maximum than before (approximately 18,000 BP). However, differences in mobility are not the same as, and in fact may be independent of, the changes that led to the formation of four discrete periods of occupation indicated by the radiocarbon determinations from Bone Cave, since each is apparent at a different chronological scale.

The fourth chronological scale is used to investigate the duration of occupation at Bone Cave after the Late Glacial Maximum. A series of radiocarbon determinations indicate that deposits belonging to this period were formed around 15,000 BP, but do not indicate how long it took for the deposits to build up. Radiocarbon determinations indicate that occupations at 15,000 BP were spread over several centuries, but give no indication of the length of these individual occupations. Were they fleeting visits by small groups, or longer occupations by groups who remained at Bone Cave to exploit resources for longer periods of time? It is not possible to answer this question directly, but it is possible to provide an estimate of the relative duration of occupations by constructing an analysis that uses another time-dependent process, in this case raw material depletion through time, to estimate the impact that occupation had on resources. A greater impact would imply longer occupation duration rather than a series of fleeting visits.

As people occupied Bone Cave, they made use of quartzite cobbles that even today lie outside the front of the cave. Through time, if large cobbles are flaked preferentially (a very common pattern in stone artifact assemblages), people will increasingly be forced to rely on relatively smaller cobbles. The more clearly this process is documented, the greater is the occupation duration. Raw material depletion can be detected by comparing the size of quartzite flakes with the proportion of the flakes that retain cortex.

At Bone Cave, the 15,000 BP assemblage flake size diminishes through time, just as the proportion of cortical flakes increases. On the basis of the relative increase in the cobble surface area to volume ratio as cobble size decreases, this result suggests that cobble size diminished through time, and therefore occupation was sufficiently prolonged to have a detectable effect on raw material availability (Holdaway 2000, 2004). As more sites are analyzed, the application of similar measures will help to build a richer view of the chronology of ancient Tasmanian occupation – not simply when sites were occupied, but also for how long, as reflected in the impact on resources.

There is no one "correct" scale at which to analyze the artifacts from Bone Cave; nor is there one "correct" interpretation of the radiocarbon chronology for the site. Depending on the nature of the research questions asked, time can be understood in different ways. For some questions, long-term correlations with regional paleoenvironmental records are of interest. For these types of questions, age estimates for general trends in the occupation of many sites are needed. For other questions, radiocarbon determinations merely indicate how artifacts may be grouped together. Changes that indicate raw material depletion, and therefore occupation duration, are seen within deposits producing radiocarbon determinations that overlap. As Ramenofsky (1998) contends, scale of analysis depends very much on what questions are asked.

Case Study 2

Time Perspectivism in Practice, Stud Creek, Western New South Wales

Conventional archaeological sites consist of artifacts buried in layers of sediment. These layers often provide the means by which artifacts are grouped for analysis and associated with age estimates obtained from datable materials. But what about artifacts left lying on surfaces? These surface sites dominate the archaeology of many regions of the world, particularly in arid areas where sedimentation processes do not lead to burial. Even if features that retain datable material (such as the hearths discussed in this example) exist on these surfaces, how can age estimates for these features be applied to the artifacts found lying next to them?

Part of the answer to these questions requires that we stop thinking of age determinations as simply a sequence of dates and start thinking about searching for patterns among groups of age estimates, much as we seek for patterns in assemblages of artifacts. We also need to broaden our understanding of stratigraphy and what it means to develop a chronology for an archaeological site.

In western New South Wales, on the edge of the Australian arid zone, stone artifacts and associated heat-retainer hearths dominate the archaeological record (Holdaway et al. 1998, 2000). The heat-retainer hearths, once constructed as shallow stone-lined pits, in which a fire was lit to heat the stones, are today exposed as concentrations of heat-fractured stones and fragments of charcoal resting on the modern surface. Surrounding these are many thousands of stone artifacts.

The artifacts and hearths are exposed today as lag deposits because of erosion of the sediments into which they were originally incorporated. Much of this erosion occurred in the 150 years following the introduction of sheep grazing by European pastoralists (Fanning 1999), with the result that artifacts and hearths representing occupations that differ in age today are found mixed together on a single surface.

This archaeological record may appear to lack stratigraphy, since it is exposed on the surface. But if we step back a bit and look at the record from a landscape perspective, it is not hard to see that the surface deposit itself rests on a sedimentary layer. Therefore, in this sense, the surface forms a stratigraphic layer. Understanding the chronology of this surface will begin to tell us something about the age of the artifacts, since in the absence of processes that have transported them from older deposits, they cannot be older than the age of the surface on which they rest (although they could be considerably younger). The age of the surface on which they rest therefore gives the *terminus ante quem* for the artifacts.

Geomorphological history

Like many archaeological projects, at Stud Creek much effort was expended on determining the geomorphological history of the deposit on which the artifacts rested. Surface deposits were mapped into a Geographic Information System (GIS) with units defined on the basis of their depositional or erosional history (Fanning & Holdaway 2002). A 3-m deep trench and smaller bank sections were excavated adjacent to the present-day stream channel to provide a sedimentary history of the valley (Fanning & Holdaway 2001). These excavations allowed the definition of a series of sedimentary units with age estimates determined by OSL and radiocarbon.

Two sedimentary units are of interest here, the first representing remains of a former floodplain that existed prior to European occupation and the second a series of deposits resulting from stable pools of water. An OSL age estimate of 2,040 ± 100 BP (OxL 1050) was obtained from the first sedimentary unit. In reporting OSL determinations such as this, age estimates are given in sidereal years before present. The OxL number that appears after the age estimate refers to the laboratory where the estimate was obtained (the Oxford Luminescence Laboratory (RLAHA 2003) and the individual determination number). At Stud Creek, many of the artifacts currently resting on the surface adjacent to the modern stream channel are scattered across this sedimentary unit.

Below this layer, a gravelly, sandy mud was laid down by a series of relatively stable pools. Six radiocarbon age estimates for this unit provide calibrated ages around 5,000 BP (Fanning 1999; Fanning & Holdaway 2001). The results of the radiocarbon

Table 5.3 (a) Radiocarbon and (b) selected OSL determinations from valley fill sediments in the catchment of Stud Creek. NZA, Rafter Radiocarbon Laboratory, New Zealand (AMS); OxL, University of Oxford Luminescence Dating Laboratory, United Kingdom (OSL); Wk, University of Waikato Radiocarbon Dating Laboratory, New Zealand (radiometric). Note that the OSL determinations are given as before AD 2000, while the radiocarbon determinations are given as before AD 1950. From Fanning and Holdaway (2001).

(a) Radiocarbon determinations

Unit	$\delta^{13}C$	% Modern	^{14}C BP	Depth (m)	Laboratory no.
GSC	-23.2 ± 0.2	58.8 ± 0.4	$4,221 \pm 58$	0.48	NZA8957
	-25.9 ± 0.2	57.9 ± 0.5	$4,340 \pm 64$	0.27	NZA8958
	-25.8 ± 0.2	59.1 ± 1.3	$4,220 \pm 180$	0.50	Wk5326
	-26.6 ± 0.2	58.0 ± 0.6	$4,380 \pm 80$	0.29	Wk5327
	-25.4 ± 0.2	57.4 ± 0.4	$4,460 \pm 60$	0.38	Wk5325
	-27.9 ± 0.2	56.4 ± 0.7	$4,600 \pm 100$	0.18	Wk5328
RSG	-25.4 ± 0.2	47.5 ± 0.4	$5,939 \pm 60$	1.73	NZA8959
	-26.1 ± 0.2	21.2 ± 0.2	$12,452 \pm 68$	1.48	NZA8960

(b) OSL determinations

Unit	OSL yB2k	Depth (m)	Sample code
PEM	192 ± 23	0.35	OxL1051
	$1,220 \pm 50$	0.38	OxL1054
PRE	$2,040 \pm 100$	0.47	OxL1050
GSC	$7,640 \pm 380$	0.92	OxL1057

determinations are presented in Table 5.3 and the calibration plots of the ages are given in Figure 5.9 (generated using the OxCal software discussed above).

Table 5.3 provides a variety of different types of information needed when reporting radiocarbon determinations such as those from Stud Creek (Higham 1999). The laboratory code number is a unique identifier for the radiocarbon sample. Laboratories each have a letter code and number their samples sequentially. The conventional radiocarbon age is given using the original Libby half-life (rather than the more recent half-life, as discussed above) and referenced to one of a number of standards that give the modern level for radiocarbon activity. The age estimate is given in radiocarbon years before present, where present is taken as AD 1950 (the decade closest to when Libby discovered radiocarbon). The percent modern refers to the proportion of carbon 14 remaining in the sample relative to the standard. Finally, $\delta^{13}C$ measures fluctuation in the isotopic ratios as a result of certain natural processes (e.g., photosynthesis). These processes change the relative proportions of carbon 13 and 14 relative to carbon 12. The term $\delta^{13}C$ represents the parts per mille difference between the carbon 13 content of the sample and that of a standard used by the laboratories. Laboratories generally correct radiocarbon

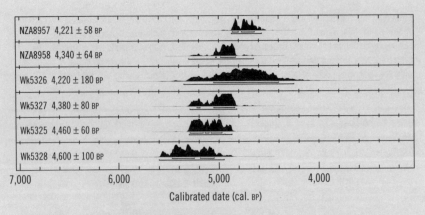

Figure 5.9 A multiplot for radiocarbon determinations from the GSC unit, Stud Creek, produced using OxCal v. 3.8 (Bronk Ramsey 2002).

age estimates for isotopic fractionation relative to this standard, reporting what are described as normalized estimates (Higham 1999).

The nature of the calibration process is well illustrated by the radiocarbon determination Wk5328 (as for the OSL determination given above, "Wk" stands for the radiocarbon laboratory that supplied the determinations, in this case the University of Waikato Radiocarbon Dating Laboratory in New Zealand) (Figure 5.10). In this figure, the wavy line that runs diagonally across the graph represents the calibration curve, while the normal curve on the left represents the probability distribution of the radiocarbon age estimate centered on 4,600 BP. The calibration is given by the area plot at the bottom of the figure, a graph that represents the probability of true age falling within any one calendar year. The higher this area graph, the greater is the probability that the true age is represented by a particular calendar year. Because the calibration curve has a number of oscillations in this time period, there are several points at which the probability plot for the radiocarbon determination strikes the calibration curve. This is the reason for the rather mountainous looking calibration area graph below the calibration line. In fact, for this age estimate, the probability that the true age falls within one standard deviation from the mean radiocarbon age produces two calibrated age ranges: one accounting for about 44 percent of the probability for the range 5,740–5,250 BP and a second accounting for 25 percent of the probability for the range 5,190–5,050 BP. Clearly, this is a more complex picture than is apparent from the radiocarbon age estimate itself.

Two of the determinations listed in Table 5.3 have NZA prefixes in front of their laboratory numbers. The "NZ" refers to the Rafter Laboratory in Wellington, New Zealand, while the "A" indicates that the age estimate was obtained by AMS.

Figure 5.9 shows the calibration plots for the four conventional radiocarbon age estimates and the two ages determined by AMS plotted on the same graph. The effect of variations in the calibration curve for this time period is clearly visible in the spread of

SIMON HOLDAWAY

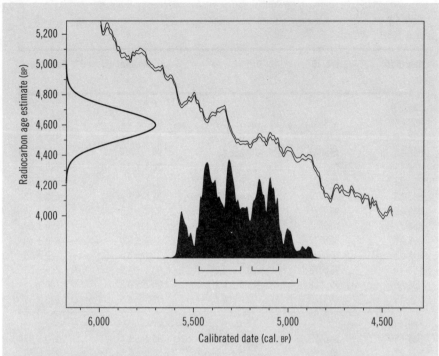

Figure 5.10 An OxCal calibation plot for radiocarbon determination Wk5328, redrawn from OxCal v. 3.8 output (Bronk Ramsey 2002).

the probability area plots for the calibrated age ranges. However, it is also clear that there is relatively good agreement among the six determinations. All fall immediately before or after 5,000 BP. The age estimates suggest that Stud Creek was characterized by a series of relatively stable pools during the mid-Holocene, after which there was a period of erosion until around 2,000 BP (Fanning & Holdaway 2001).

Combining the results from both techniques suggests that the sediments into which the stone artifacts at Stud Creek were deposited, and from which they have been lagged, are certainly no older than 5,000–6,000 BP, and probably a lot younger, perhaps as young as 2,000 BP. This provides the terminal age for the Stud Creek archaeological deposits. Despite the lack of stratigraphy in a conventional sense at Stud Creek, taking a landscape perspective and applying what are termed geoarchaeological techniques provides an initial estimate of the age of the surface archaeological record.

Heat-retainer hearths

Table 5.4 gives the radiocarbon age estimates for 28 heat-retainer hearths excavated at Stud Creek. The oldest age estimate, Wk6630, has a calibrated age expressed as two ranges at two standard deviations: 1,690–1,650 BP (4.5 percent probability) and 1,630–1,400 BP (90.9 percent probability). Both of these ranges are more recent than the

Table 5.4 Radiocarbon determinations from heat-retainer hearths, Stud Creek (modified from Holdaway et al. 2002).

Hearth ID	Lab. ID	$\delta^{13}C$	% Modern	Result (BP)
Phase θ1				
H98-75	Wk6632	−23.1 ± 0.2	97.3 ± 0.6	220 ± 55
H98-16	Wk6621	−23.6 ± 0.2	95.4 ± 0.6	380 ± 50
H98-46	Wk6625	−23.2 ± 0.2	94.5 ± 1.4	450 ± 120
H98-13	Wk5332	−23.3 ± 0.2	94.3 ± 0.6	470 ± 50
H98-12	Wk5127	−22.0 ± 0.2	93.1 ± 0.6	580 ± 60
H98-59	Wk6627	−24.1 ±] 0.2	92.5 ± 1.4	630 ± 130
H98-11	Wk5125	−22.6 ± 0.2	92.2 ± 0.5	660 ± 50
H98-71	Wk6631	−23.4 ± 0.2	92.1 ± 0.6	660 ± 50
H98-21	Wk5330	−23.6 ± 0.2	91.8 ± 0.5	690 ± 50
H98-32	Wk6624	−24.0 ± 0.2	91.4 ± 0.6	720 ± 55
H98-4	Wk6038	−23.0 ± 0.2	93.1 ± 4.9	790 ± 50
H98-60	Wk6628	−23.3 ± 0.2	90.7 ± 0.8	790 ± 75
H98-15	Wk5329	−22.0 ± 0.2	90.3 ± 0.5	820 ± 50
Phase θ2				
H98-65	Wk6629	−23.3 ± 0.2	86.4 ± 1.4	1,170 ± 130
H98-28	Wk5124	−22.8 ± 0.2	86.0 ± 0.5	1,210 ± 50
H98-22	Wk5122	−22.5 ± 0.2	85.5 ± 0.4	1,260 ± 40
H98-25	Wk5126	−23.2 ± 0.2	85.5 ± 0.6	1,260 ± 60
H98-19	Wk6622	−22.7 ± 0.2	85.2 ± 0.6	1,280 ± 60
H98-10	Wk6036	−23.2 ± 0.2	85.2 ± 0.4	1,290 ± 50
H98-20	Wk5331	−23.2 ± 0.2	85.1 ± 0.5	1,300 ± 50
H98-30	Wk6037	−23.4 ± 0.2	84.9 ± 0.5	1,310 ± 60
H98-54	Wk6626	−23.0 ± 0.2	84.8 ± 1.5	1,330 ± 150
H98-23	Wk6623	−22.6 ± 0.2	84.5 ± 0.8	1,350 ± 75
H98-8	Wk6620	−23.6 ± 0.2	84.1 ± 0.7	1,390 ± 70
H98-27	Wk5123	−23.6 ± 0.2	83.9 ± 0.5	1,410 ± 50
H98-2	Wk6039	−22.9 ± 0.2	83.6 ± 0.6	1,440 ± 60
H98-9	Wk6035	−22.5 ± 0.2	83.4 ± 0.5	1,460 ± 50
H98-66	Wk6630	−23.6 ± −0.2	81.7 ± −0.5	1,630 ± 50

OSL-based estimate for the age of the valley floor on which the hearths and artifacts rest (i.e., more recent than 2,000 BP).

There are two ways to think about the results of these hearth age estimations. At one level of interpretation, they provide an indication of when Indigenous Australians occupied Stud Creek, a sequence that spans the past 1,700 years or so. Interpreted in a different way, the hearth age estimates provide an opportunity to search for pattern in long-term human behavior in ways similar to those discussed for Bone Cave. Placing the hearth age estimates in sequence shows that they fall into two groups, one before and one after 1,000 BP, indicated as Phase 1 and Phase 2 in Table 5.4. Between these phases there appears to be a gap when no hearths were constructed (or at least none have survived).

Both the existence and duration of the gap in hearth construction can be assessed statistically using a technique called *sample-based Bayesian inference* (Holdaway et al. 2002) that is increasingly being applied to the analysis of age estimates. Bayesian inference owes its origin to the work of Thomas Bayes in the eighteenth century; however, its application to archaeological problems is comparatively recent. The technique allows information coming from different sources to be combined, evaluated statistically and integrated into the interpretation process. Buck (2001) provides a good introduction to Bayesian analysis and details of the application to the Stud Creek hearths are provided in Holdaway et al. (2002).

Applying a Bayesian analysis, we can supplement the probability plots for the calibrated determinations produced by programs such as OxCal with a probability plot that provides an estimate of the duration for the gap between the two phases of hearth age estimates (Figure 5.11). Figure 5.11 was produced using the Datelab v. 1.2 software, which performs radiocarbon age calibration and allows Bayesian analysis (Nicholls & Jones 1998; Jones & Nicholls 2002). The software was also used to provide probability plots for the beginning and ending of each of the two phases of hearth construction (Figure 5.12).

Figure 5.11 suggests a duration for the gap in hearth construction in the range 320–460 calibrated years at 68 percent probability and 200–500 calibrated years at 95 percent probability (i.e., one and two standard deviations, respectively). Both before and after this gap, hearths were constructed every few decades and the combined probability plot for the hearths in each phase gives an indication of the duration of hearth construction.

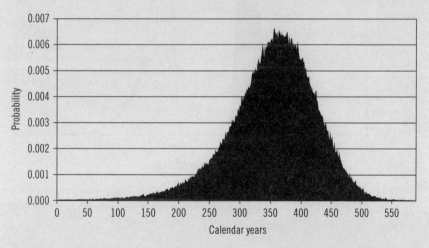

Figure 5.11 The probability distribution (read as the area beneath the plot) of the length in calendar years for the hiatus between the two phases of hearth construction at Stud Creek (from Holdaway et al. 2002).

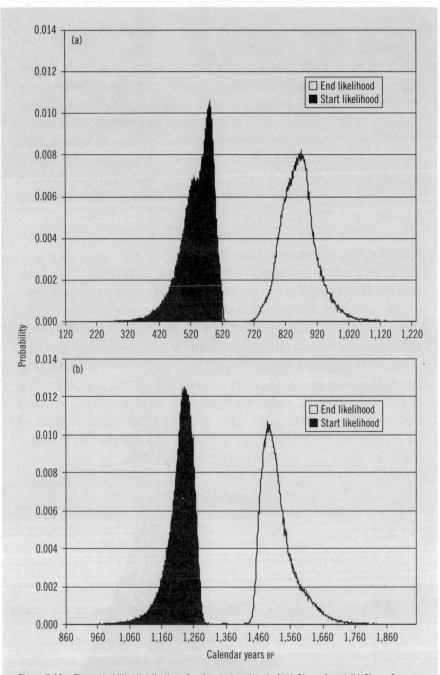

Figure 5.12 The probability distributions for the start and end of (a) Phase 1 and (b) Phase 3 hearth construction at Stud Creek, in calibrated years BP (from Holdaway et al. 2002).

Stud Creek chronology

Combining the hearth chronology with the results of the sediment history study discussed above allows a number of inferences to be drawn. First, if the results of the heat-retainer hearth chronology were viewed alone, it might be tempting to conclude that human occupation of Stud Creek began only within the past 1,500 years. This pattern might then be correlated with paleoenvironmental evidence that suggests a period of drier climate from ~4,000 BP to 1,500 BP, together with studies that suggest that people moved to better-watered areas during such times. However, such an interpretation would ignore the sediment history documented at Stud Creek. It is clear that in the Stud Creek valley at least, the lack of archaeological evidence older than 2,000 BP is likely to reflect increased erosion that would have destroyed older archaeological deposits rather than a lack of human occupation (Holdaway et al. 2002).

Secondly, placing the Stud Creek hearth chronology within a wider context indicates that the hiatus in hearth construction correlates with a worldwide period of climatic variability indicated by paleoenvironmental records from other parts of Australia, and known as the *Medieval Warm Period* (Holdaway et al. 2002). As is the situation at Bone Cave, changing the scale of analysis produces correlations that suggest new types of research questions.

Thirdly, the chronology for Stud Creek has important implications for the way in which the stone artifact assemblages associated with the hearths should be interpreted. Although the hearths do not provide age estimates of the stone artifacts directly, the spatial association of both strongly suggests that the artifacts were deposited over a number of occupations, and that these occupations occurred through time in a clear temporal pattern. Most archaeologists would expect discontinuous occupation by groups of hunter–gatherers as they moved from location to location in a seasonal round. In the Australian arid zone, such movement is often reconstructed in relation to the availability of water. However, the Stud Creek chronology suggests something more than this. The hearths in the two phases of occupation do not cluster together tightly; rather, they are more or less uniformly distributed during each of the phases. This suggests intermittent use of the valley rather than occupation as part of a regular cycle measured in years. During the gap in hearth construction, this pattern changed substantially enough for no hearths to be constructed for some centuries. Hearth reconstruction then started again, returning to the pattern of intermittent hearth construction until the historical period.

Given this chronology, it would be wrong to consider the stone artifact assemblages as the material record of a single set of functions, the equivalent of toolkits deposited by people who used Stud Creek in the same way through time. Nor would it be correct to interpret the assemblages as the result of a single settlement pattern (Holdaway et al. 2000, 2004). Instead, the hearth chronology suggests at least three separate patterns, represented by Phases 1 and 2 and the gap. The stone artifact assemblages therefore most likely form a time-averaged record, incorporating variability produced as a result of a number of differing occupations, and so must be analyzed accordingly.

Conclusion   As illustrated both by the case studies described here and virtually any other archaeological report, time is a key dimension in archaeology and the ability to obtain age estimates for events in the past has revolutionized the discipline. A wide range of chronometric techniques is now available, applicable to many materials and able to provide age estimates that span all two million years of the archaeological record. There is now a wealth of resources describing these techniques, only a small sample of which is cited in this chapter. Yet despite the wealth of material dealing with the mechanics of obtaining an age estimate, the literature dealing with the method and theory behind the formation of archaeological chronologies is rather less developed. Understanding the bases on which chronometric techniques are founded is certainly a key to their successful application. As is clear from the experience of obtaining age estimates for some of the earliest archaeological sites, there are limits to all of the techniques, and only some of the problems will be solved by better technologies. But, as should also be clear from the discussion and examples provided here, many of the problems involved in "dating" archaeological sites are problems of archaeological inference rather than dating technology. Time is an elusive quarry that cannot be observed directly. Therefore, archaeologists must be at their most resourceful when attempting to investigate temporality.

In the past, some archaeologists have sought to determine "the chronology for a site," but clearly such an approach will provide only a very limited understanding of the past. The past can be viewed at a variety of scales and in doing so, a variety of inferences may be drawn concerning behavior in the past – inferences, moreover, that will not necessarily build into a neat ordered picture of past ways of life. In dealing with dating, archaeologists must therefore rise to a challenge that is every bit as theoretical as it is methodological. As a discipline, we have access to an increasingly sophisticated array of procedures for considering time. The challenge that we face is to understand more fully how to integrate the results from these procedures with explanations of cause and effect in the past that ensure we are pointing the archaeological telescope in the correct direction.

Acknowledgments   This chapter was written while I was an Honorary Research Fellow at the Department of Anthropology, University of Washington, Seattle. Martin Jones, Thegn Ladefoged, Julie Stein, Peter Sheppard, and LuAnn Wandsnider, as well as the editors, read earlier drafts of this chapter and provided useful comments. Seline McNamee drew the figures and Tim Mackerel took the photographs.

Further reading   There are a number of books that bring together specialists who write about different chronometric techniques: see Taylor and Aitken (1997), Brothwell and Pollard (2001), and Goldberg et al. (2001). Dincauze (2000) provides details of a number of techniques in a textbook on environmental archaeology. Articles in journals that review the application of specific techniques may supplement these sources: see, for example, Roberts (1997) on TL/OSL, Rink (1997) on ESR, Schwarcz (1989) on U-series dating, and Johnson and Miller (1997) on AAR. Blackwell and Schwarcz (1993) provide a good general treatment of chronometric methods. In addition, there is now a growing body of information on the Internet. Higham (1999) is a particularly useful site for radiocarbon, with links to a range of other useful sites including radiocarbon laboratories, most of which also have their own websites. The OxCal (Bronk Ramsey 2002) site provides a good discussion of calibration. Godfrey-Smith (2001) has useful information on OSL, TL, and ESR, as does RLAHA (2003).

Rather less is written on the theory of time and archaeology. The classic sources include Bailey (1983) and Binford (1981). Murray (1999) discusses Bailey's time perspectivism in a book that that includes a number of papers on time and archaeology. Ramenofsky (1998) and, more recently, Holdaway and Wandsnider (2005) deal with issues of scale. Stern (1994) discusses paleontological approaches to time from an archaeological perspective, while Behrensmeyer et al. (2000) reviews the paleontological literature itself.

Holdaway et al. (2004) provides a detailed discussion of the Stud Creek evidence, while Allen (1996) provides details of the Bone Cave excavation in a book with papers on a number of other Tasmanian Pleistocene sites.

References

Aitken, M. J. 1997: Luminescence dating. In R. E. Taylor and M. J. Aitken (eds.), *Chronometric Dating in Archaeology*. New York: Plenum Press, 183–216.

Allen, J. 1989: When did humans first colonize Australia? *Search*, 20(5), 149–55.

—— 1994: Radiocarbon determinations, luminescence dating and Australian archaeology. *Antiquity*, 68(259), 339–43.

—— 1996: Bone Cave. In J. Allen (ed.), *Report of the Southern Forests Archaeological Project*, vol. 1, *Site Descriptions, Stratigraphies and Chronologies*. Melbourne: School of Archaeology, La Trobe University, 91–121.

—— and Holdaway, S. 1995: The contamination of Pleistocene radiocarbon determinations in Australia. *Antiquity*, 69(262), 101–12.

Ambrose, W. R. 2001: Obsidian hydration dating. In D. R. Brothwell and A. M. Pollard (eds.), *Handbook of Archaeological Sciences*. Chichester: John Wiley, 81–92.

Bailey, G. N. 1983: Concepts of time in Quaternary prehistory. *Annual Review of Anthropology*, 12, 165–92.

—— 1987: Breaking the time barrier. *Archaeological Review from Cambridge*, 6, 5–20.

Beck, C. and Jones, G. T. 1994: Dating surface assemblages using obsidian hydration. In C. Beck (ed.), *Dating in Surface and Exposed Contexts*. Albuquerque: University of New Mexico Press, 47–76.

Behrensmeyer, A., Kidwell, S. and Gastaldo, R. 2000: Taphonomy and paleobiology. *Paleobiology*, 26(4), 103–47.

Billamboz, A. 1996: Tree-rings and pile-dwellings in southern Germany: following in the footsteps of Bruno Huber. In J. S. Dean, D. M. Meko and T. W. Swetnam (eds.), *Tree Ring, Environment and Humanity*. Tucson: University of Arizona, 471–83.

Binford, L. R. 1981: Behavioral archaeology and the "Pompeii Premise," *Journal of Anthropological Research*, 37(3), 195–208.

Bird, M. I., Turney, C. S. M., Fifield, L. K. et al. 2002: Radiocarbon analysis of the early archaeological site of Nauwalabila I, Arnhem Land, Australia: implications for sample suitability and stratigraphic integrity. *Quaternary Science Reviews*, 21(8–9), 1061–75.

Blackwell, B. A. and Schwarcz, H. P. 1993: Archaeochronology and scale. In J. K. Stein and A. R. Linse (eds.), *Effects of Scale on Archaeological and Geoscientific Perspectives*. Boulder: The Geological Society of America Special Paper, 39–58.

Bowdler, S. 1990: 50,000 year-old site in Australia – is it really that old? *Australian Archaeology*, 32, 93.

Bowler, J. M. and Price, D. M. 1998: Luminescence dates and stratigraphic analyses at Lake Mungo: review and new perspectives. *Archaeology in Oceania*, 33, 156–68.

Bronk Ramsey, C. 2002: OxCal v. 3.8. Electronic document: www.rlaha.ox.ac.uk. Accessed January 2004.

Brothwell, D. R. and Pollard, A. M. (eds.) 2001: *Handbook of Archaeological Sciences*. Chichester: John Wiley.

Buck, C. E. 2001: Applications of the Bayesian statistical paradigm. In D. R. Brothwell and A. M. Pollard (eds.), *Handbook of Archaeological Sciences*. Chichester: John Wiley, 695–702.

Cahen, D., Keeley, L. H. and Van Noten, F. 1979: Stone tools, toolkits, and human behavior in prehistory. *Current Anthropology*, 20, 661–83.

Chappell, J., Head, J. and Magee, J. 1996: Beyond the radiocarbon limit in Australian archaeology and quaternary research. *Antiquity*, 70(269), 543–52.

Coleman, S. M., Pierce, K. L. and Birkeland, P. W. 1987: Suggested terminology for quaternary dating methods. *Quaternary Research*, 28, 314–19.

Dean, J. S. 1978: Independent dating in archaeological analysis. *Advances in Archaeological Method and Theory*, 1, 223–55.

—— 1997: Dendrochronology. In R. E. Taylor and M. J. Aitken (eds.), *Chronometric Dating in Archaeology*. New York: Plenum Press, 31–64.

——, Lindsay, A. J. and Robinson, W. J. 1978: Prehistoric settlement in Long House Valley, northeastern Arizona. In R. C. Euler and G. J. Gummerman (eds.), *Investigations of the Southwestern Anthropological Research Group: An Experiment in Archaeological Cooperation*. Flagstaff: Museum of Northern Arizona, 25–44.

Dincauze, D. F. 2000: *Environmental Archaeology: Principles and Practice*. Cambridge: Cambridge University Press.

Fanning, P. C. 1999: Recent landscape history in arid western New South Wales, Australia: a model for regional change. *Geomorphology*, 29, 191–209.

—— and Holdaway, S. 2001: Temporal limits to the archaeological record in arid Western NSW, Australia: lessons from OSL and radiocarbon dating of hearths and sediments. In M. Jones and P. Sheppard (eds.), *Australasian Connections and New Directions: Proceedings of the 7th Australasian Archaeometry Conference*. Research in Anthropology and Linguistics 5, Department of Anthropology, University of Auckland, 85–104.

—— and —— 2002: Using geospatial technologies to understand prehistoric human/landscape interaction in arid Australia. *Arid Lands Newsletter* 51. Electronic document: http://ag.arizona.edu/OALS/ALN/aln51/fanning.html. Accessed January 2004.

Fifield, L. K., Bird, M. I., Turney, C. S. M., Hausladen, P. A., Santos, G. M. and di Tada, M. L. 2001: Radiocarbon dating of the human occupation of Australia prior to 40 ka B.P. – successes and pitfalls. *Radiocarbon*, 43(2B), 1139–45.

Fletcher, R. 1992: Time perspectivism, *Annales*, and the potential of archaeology. In A. B. Knapp (ed.), *Archaeology*, Annales, *and Ethnohistory*. Cambridge: Cambridge University Press, 35–50.

Freter, A. 1993: Obsidian-hydration dating: its past, present, and future applications in Mesoamerica. *Ancient Mesoamerica*, 4, 285–303.

Fullagar, R. L. K., Price, D. M. and Head, L. M. 1996: Early human occupation of northern Australia: archaeology and thermoluminescence dating of Jinmium rock-shelter, Northern Territory. *Antiquity*, 70(270), 751–73.

Gibbons, A. 1997: Doubts over spectacular dates. *Science*, 278, 220–2.

Godfrey-Smith, D. I. 2001: Thermally and Optically Stimulated Luminescence. Electronic document: http://is.dal.ca/~digs/t-intro.htm. Accessed January 2004.

Goldberg, P., Holliday, V. and Ferring, R. 2001: *Earth Sciences and Archaeology*. New York: Kluwer Academic/Plenum Press.

Grün, R. 2001: Trapped charge dating (ESR, TL, OSL). In D. R. Brothwell and A. M. Pollard (eds.), *Handbook of Archaeological Sciences*. Chichester: John Wiley, 47–62.

——, Huang, P. H., Huang, W. et al. 1998: ESR and U-series analysis of teeth from palaeoanthropological site of Hexian, Anhui Province, China. *Journal of Human Evolution*, 34, 555–64.

Hare, P. E., Von Endt, D. W. and Kokis, J. E. 1997: Protein and amino acid diagenesis dating. In R. E. Taylor and M. J. Aitken (eds.), *Chronometric Dating in Archaeology*. New York: Plenum Press, 261–96.

Hawking, S. W. 1998: *A Brief History of Time*. London: Bantam Press.

Hayden, B. 1979: *Palaeolithic Reflections*. Canberra: Australian Institute of Aboriginal Studies.

Higham, T. 1999: Radiocarbon WEB-info. Electronic document: www.c14dating.com. Accessed January 2004.

Hiscock, P. 1990: How old are the artefacts in Malakunanja II? *Archaeology in Oceania*, 25(3), 122–4.

Holdaway, S. J. 2000: Economic approaches to stone artefact raw material variation. In A. Anderson and T. Murray (eds.), *Australian Archaeologist. Collected Papers in Honour of Jim Allen*. Canberra: Centre for Archaeological Research, The Australian National University, 217–30.

—— 2004: *Continuity and Change*. Melbourne: Archaeology Program, School of Historical European Studies, La Trobe University.

—— and Cosgrove, R. 1997: The archaeological attributes of behaviour: difference or variability? *Endeavour*, 21, 67–71.

—— and Porch, N. 1995: Cyclical patterns in the Pleistocene human occupation of southwest Tasmania. *Archaeology in Oceania*, 30, 74–82.

—— and —— 1996: Dates as data: an alternative approach to the construction of chronologies for Pleistocene sites in southwest Tasmania. In J. Allen (ed.), *Report of the Southern Forest Project*, vol. 1. Melbourne: School of Archaeology, La Trobe University, 251–75.

—— and Wandsnider, L. 2005: Temporal scales and archaeological landscapes from the Eastern Desert of Australia and intermontane North America. In G. Lock and B. Molyneaux (eds.), *Confronting Scale in Archaeology: Issues of Theory and Practice*. London: Kluwer, in press.

——, Fanning, P. C. and Witter, D. C. 2000: Prehistoric Aboriginal occupation of the Rangelands: interpreting the surface archaeological record of far western New South Wales, Australia. *Rangeland Journal*, 22(1), 44–57.

——, Shiner, J. and Fanning, P. 2004: Hunter–gatherers and the archaeology of discard behavior: an analysis of surface stone artifacts from Sturt National Park, western New South Wales, Australia. *Asian Perspectives*, 43(1), 34–72.

——, Fanning, P., Witter, D., Jones, M., Nicholls, G. and Shiner, J. 2002: Variability in the chronology of late Holocene Aboriginal occupation on the arid margin of southeastern Australia. *Journal of Archaeological Science*, 29, 351–63.

——, Witter, D., Fanning, P. et al. 1998: New approaches to open site spatial archaeology in Sturt National Park, New South Wales, Australia. *Archaeology of Oceania*, 33, 1–19.

Holliday, V. T., Johnson, E. and Stafford, T. W. Jr. 1999: AMS radiocarbon dating of the type Plainview and Firstview (Paleoindian) assemblages: the agony and the ecstasy. *American Antiquity*, 64(3), 444–54.

Housley, R. A., Gamble, C. S., Street, M. and Pettitt, P. 1997: Radiocarbon evidence for the lateglacial human recolonisation of northern Europe. *Proceedings of the Prehistoric Society*, 63, 25–54.

Johnson, B. J. and Miller, G. H. 1997: Archaeological applications of amino acid racemization. *Archaeometry*, 39, 265–87.

Jones, M. and Nicholls, G. 2002: New radiocarbon calibration software. *Radiocarbon*, 44(3), 663–74.

Knapp, A. B. 1992: Archaeology and *Annales*: time, space, and change. In A. B. Knapp (ed.), *Archaeology*, Annales, *and Ethnohistory*. Cambridge: Cambridge University Press, 1–21.

Kuniholm, P. I. 2001: Dendrochronology and other applications of tree-ring studies in archaeology. In D. R. Brothwell and A. M. Pollard (eds.), *Handbook of Archaeological Sciences*. Chichester: John Wiley, 35–46.

Lyman, R. L. and Fox, G. L. 1989: A critical-evaluation of bone weathering as an indication of bone assemblage formation. *Journal of Archaeological Science*, 16(3), 293–317.

Machida, H., Blong, R. J., Specht, J. et al. 1996: Holocene explosive eruptions of Witori and Dakataua caldera volcanoes in west New Britain, Papua New Guinea. *Quaternary International*, 34–6, 65–78.

Mercier, N., Valladas, H., Joron, J. L., Reyes, J. L., Lévêque, F. and Vandermeersch, B. 1991: Thermoluminescence dating of the late Neanderthal remains from Saint-Césaire. *Nature*, 351, 737–9.

Mulvaney, D. J. and Joyce, E. B. 1965: Archaeological and geomorphological investigations on Mt. Moffatt Station, Queensland, Australia. *Proceedings of the Prehistoric Society*, 31, 147–212.

Murray, T. 1999: A return to the "Pompeii Premise." In T. Murray (ed.), *Time and Archaeology*. London: Routledge, 8–27.

Nicholls, G. K. and Jones, M. 1998: Radiocarbon dating with temporal order constraints. Technical report, Mathematics Department, Auckland University, New Zealand, no. 407. Electronic document: www.math.auckland.ac.nz. Accessed January 2004.

O'Brien, M. and Lyman, R. L. 2000: *Seriation, Stratigraphy and Index Fossils: The Backbone of Archaeological Dating*. New York: Kluwer Academic/Plenum Press.

O'Connell, J. F. and Allen, J. 1998: When did humans first arrive in Greater Australia and why is it important to know? *Evolutionary Anthropology*, 6(4), 132–46.

O'Connor, S. 1999: 30,000 *Years of Aboriginal Occupation: Kimberley, North West Australia*. Terra Australis 14. Canberra: ANH Publications and the Centre for Archaeological Research, The Australian National University.

Potts, R. B. 1986: Temporal span of bone accumulations at Olduvai Gorge and implications for early hominid foraging behavior. *Paleobiology*, 12, 25–31.

Ramenofsky, A. F. 1998: The illusion of time. In A. F. Ramenofsky and A. Steffen (eds.), *Unit Issues in Archaeology*. Salt Lake City: University of Utah Press, 74–84.

SIMON HOLDAWAY

RLAHA 2003: Luminescence Dating Laboratory. Electronic document: www.rlaha.ox.ac.uk. Accessed January 2004.

Rink, W. J. 1997: Electron spin resonance (ESR) dating and ESR applications in Quaternary science and archaeometry. *Radiation Measurements*, 27, 975–1025.

—— 2001: Beyond ^{14}C dating. In P. Goldberg, V. T. Holliday and R. Ferring (eds.), *Earth Sciences and Archaeology*. New York: Kluwer Academic/Plenum Press, 385–417.

Roberts, R. G. 1997: Luminescence dating in archaeology: from origins to optical. *Radiation Measurements*, 27(5–6), 819–92.

——, Jones, R. and Smith, M. A. 1994: Beyond the radiocarbon barrier in Australian prehistory. *Antiquity*, 68, 611–6.

——, Smith, M. A. and Jones, R. 1990a: Stratigraphy and the statistics at Malakunanja II: reply to Hiscock. *Archaeology in Oceania*, 25(3), 125–9.

——, —— and —— 1990b: Thermoluminescence dating of a 50,000 year old human occupation in northern Australia. *Nature*, 345, 153–6.

——, —— and —— 1990c: Early dates at Malakunanja II: a reply to Bowdler. *Australian Archaeology*, 31, 94–7.

——, Galbraith, R. F., Olley, J. M., Yoshida, H. and Laslett, G. 1999: Optical dating of single and multiple grains of quartz from Jinmium rock shelter, northern Australia: part II, results and implications. *Archaeometry*, 41, 365–95.

——, Bird, M., Olley, J. et al. 1998: Optical and radiocarbon dating at Jinmium rock shelter in northern Australia. *Nature*, 393(6683), 358–62.

Schiffer, M. B. 1985: Is there a "Pompeii Premise" in archaeology? *Journal of Anthropological Research*, 41, 18–41.

Schindel, D. E. 1982: Resolution analysis: a new approach to the gaps in the fossil record. *Paleobiology*, 8(4), 340–53.

Schwarcz, H. P. 1989: Uranium series dating of Quaternary deposits. *Quaternary International*, 1, 7–17.

—— and Blackwell, B. A. 1991: Archaeological applications. In M. Ivanovich and R. S. Harmon (eds.), *Uranium Series Disequilibrium Applications to Environmental Problems*. Oxford: Oxford University Press, 512–52.

Shennan, S. 1988: *Quantifying Archaeology*. Edinburgh: Edinburgh University Press.

Smith, M. E. 1992: Braudel's temporal rhythms and chronology theory in archaeology. In A. B. Knapp (ed.), *Archaeology*, Annales, *and Ethnohistory*. Cambridge: Cambridge University Press, 23–33.

Spaulding, A. C. 1960: The dimensions of archaeology. In G. E. Dole and R. L. Carneiro (eds.), *Essays in the Science of Culture in Honor of Leslie A. White*. New York: Thomas Y. Crowell, 437–56.

Stein, J. K. 2001: Archaeological sediments in cultural environments. In J. K. Stein and W. R. Farrand (eds.), *Sediments in Archaeological Context*. Salt Lake City: University of Utah Press, 1–28.

Stern, N. 1993: The structure of the lower Pleistocene archaeological record. *Current Anthropology*, 34(3), 201–25.

—— 1994: The implications of time-averaging for reconstructing the land-use patterns of early tool-using hominids. *Journal of Human Evolution*, 27, 89–105.

——, Porch, N. and McDougall, I. 2002: FxJj43: a window into a 1.5-million-year-old palaeolandscape in the Okote Member of the Koobi Fora Formation, northern Kenya. *Geoarchaeology: An International Journal*, 17, 349–92.

Taylor, R. E. 1997: Radiocarbon dating. In R. E. Taylor and M. J. Aitken (eds.), *Chronometric Dating in Archaeology*. New York and London: Plenum Press, 65–96.

—— 2001: Radiocarbon dating. In D. R. Brothwell and A. M. Pollard (eds.), *Handbook of Archaeological Sciences*. Chichester: John Wiley, 23–34.

—— and Aitken, M. J. (eds.) 1997: *Chronometric Dating in Archaeology*. New York: Plenum Press.

Turney, C. S. M., Bird, M. I., Fifield, L. K. et al. 2001: Early human occupation at Devil's Lair, southwestern Australia 50,000 years ago. *Quaternary Research*, 55(1), 3–13.

Valladas, H., Reyes, J. L., Joron, J. L., Valladas, G., Bar-Yosef, O. and B. Vandermeersch, B. 1988: Thermoluminescence dating of Mousterian "proto-Cro-Magnon" remains from Israel and the origin of modern man. *Nature*, 331, 614–16.

Villa, P. 1982: Conjoinable pieces and site formation processes. *American Antiquity*, 47, 276–90.

Wagner, G. A. and Van den Haute, P. 1992: *Fission-Track Dating*. Dordrecht: Kluwer Academic.

Waikato Radiocarbon Dating Laboratory 2002: Electronic document: www.radiocarbondating.com. Accessed January 2004.

Walker, K. R. and Bambach, R. K. 1971: The significance of fossil assemblages from fine-grained sediments: time-averaged communities. *Geological Society of America Abstracts with Programs*, 3, 783–4.

Walter, R. C., Manega, P. C., Hay, R. L., Drake, R. E. and Curtis, G. H. 1991: Laser-fusion $^{40}Ar/^{39}Ar$ dating of Bed I, Olduvai Gorge, Tanzania. *Nature*, 354, 145–9.

Wandsnider, L. 1996: Describing and comparing archaeological spatial structures. *Journal of Archaeological Method and Theory*, 3(4), 319–84.

Waters, M. R., Forman, S. L. and Pierson, J. M. 1997: Diring Yiriakh: a lower Paleolithic site in central Siberia. *Science*, 275, 1281–4.

Chris Clarkson and Sue O'Connor

6

An Introduction to Stone Artifact Analysis

Introduction

Perhaps the best place to begin this chapter is by stating what it is not. This chapter is not a "cookbook" of methods and techniques for aspiring stone analysts confronted with an assemblage of stone artifacts for the first time, or those seeking to bolster their work with the latest literature or new techniques. Nor is it an exhaustive overview of analysis conducted over the past few decades that details their strengths and weaknesses, and points to major theoretical stumbling blocks or methodological advancements. Readers in search of such critical reviews are directed to Odell (2000, 2001b) for a global perspective (but with a North American focus), Dibble (1995) for a view of emerging continental schools of thought, and Hiscock and Clarkson (2000) for a review of pressing issues in Australian lithic studies. Rather, this chapter aims to arm the student of lithic technology with a set of principles to guide the construction of their research design, alert them to the philosophical underpinnings of various kinds of stone analysis, point to simple but frequently overlooked issues of data management, provide an overview of some common laboratory techniques, and provide case studies and suggested readings that offer insight into both the process of actually doing stone analysis and drawing meaningful conclusions from the results. It takes a "question and answer" format, in the hope that some frequently asked questions might be addressed in a straightforward manner.

An overview

Why study stone artifacts?

There are a number of very good reasons why archaeologists study stone artifacts. Primary among them is the fact that stone artifacts are usually the most durable and often numerous remains of past human activities, and in many cases constitute the only surviving trace of people that lived hundreds, thousands, and even millions of years ago (in the case of our recent hominid ancestors). Because they survive under conditions that typically destroy most other human creations and castoffs, stone artifacts are ubiquitous in the landscape.

A second reason for studying stone artifacts is that for most of human history stone tools played a vital role in our day-to-day survival, in shaping the physical world to our various needs, and even in signifying to others our identity and place in the world. They therefore constitute a vast and invaluable record of the enormous diversity of strategies people have devised to make a living, solve common problems, communicate, and to live and compete with one another. As this chapter deals exclusively with methodological issues and laboratory techniques, it offers little discussion of the sorts of theoretical frameworks that might adopt these techniques in addressing the "big questions" in archaeology. The potential for lithic analysis to engage with disciplinary theory, however, now seems far more practicable than at any time in the past.

For instance, a great deal of thought has been given to the place of technology as an integral aspect of cultural variability, adaptation, and change (Lemonnier 1986; Pfaffenberger 1992; Bleed 1997; Schiffer & Skibo 1997), the social and evolutionary mechanisms giving rise to technological innovation (van der Leeuw & Torrence 1989; Bamforth and Bleed 1997), the behavioral and physical factors governing variability in both individual artifacts (such as fracture mechanics and the effects of reduction intensity) (Dibble & Whittaker 1981; Cotterell & Kamminga 1987; Dibble & Pelcin 1995; Pelcin 1997a, 1998; Shott et al. 2000; Macgregor 2005) and whole assemblages (such as patterns of artifact procurement, transport, use and discard) (Binford 1979; Shott 1989; Torrence 1989; Nelson 1991; Kuhn 1995), the symbolic role of stone in communicating social, political, and ideological relationships or differences (Ingold 1990; Sinclair 1995; Wurz 1999; Harrison 2002), the role of social agency in stone artifact manufacture and use (Dobres 2000; Sinclair 2000), the technological signatures of various mechanisms of trade and exchange (see, among many more, Renfrew et al. 1968; Ericson & Earle 1982; Zeitlin 1982; Torrence 1986; Peterson et al. 1997; Torrence & Summerhayes 1997; Specht 2002), as well as stone artifacts as markers of gender (Gero 1991; Sassaman 1992; Dobres 1995; Walthall & Holley 1997). Most recently, archaeologists have begun to explore technological variability using formal optimality models drawn from evolutionary ecology (Bright et al. 2002; Brantingham 2003; Ugan et al. 2003). Many of these studies are moving toward the development of new theoretical approaches for explaining assemblage variation.

What are stone artifacts?   A stone artifact is any piece of rock modified by human behavior, whether intentionally or unintentionally. Although this definition could properly be applied to extreme and even ridiculous cases, such as humanly modified landscapes, aqueducts, or open cut mines, it is most often used to signify portable, chipped, ground, or pecked stone objects created by a single or small group of individuals, and usually in the context of hunter–gatherer, pastoralist, early agricultural, or other nonindustrialized societies.

CHRIS CLARKSON AND SUE O'CONNOR

Most people are familiar with the simplest form of stone artifact manufacture commonly portrayed in depictions of our early ancestors banging two rocks together. While this is, generally speaking, the way most stone artifacts were made, there is nothing simple about controlling the process to the degree that allows artifacts of specific shapes to be accurately and repeatedly produced from a block of stone, as was achieved by prehistoric artisans with sometimes startling finesse. The symmetry and regularity of some of the highest known forms of flintknapping can be astounding, as seen for instance in the fluted Folsom points of north American Paleo-Indians, the Solutrean points of Upper Paleolithic Europe, the flint daggers of the Danish Neolithic, the Gerzian ripple-flaked knives of Late Stone Age Egypt, or the obsidian eccentrics and polyhedral blades of Mayan and Aztec artisans (Figure 6.1).

In reality though, most stoneworking tended to be far less sophisticated than these examples suggest (in terms of the precision and investment of labor), and literally involved the striking of flakes of varying shapes and sizes from a block of stone (a core), using a stone pebble (a hammerstone), or some hard object (an indentor) such as a piece of bone, antler, or hard wood. Removing a flake from a block of stone creates a positive scar or ventral surface, on the flake, and leaves behind a negative flake scar on the core. The opposite side to the ventral surface on the resulting flake is called the dorsal surface.

Cores are artifacts that possess only negative flake scars. Flakes that have had other flakes removed from their surfaces after they were struck from the core are called retouched flakes. Because flakes can be removed from the dorsal surface of a flake before or after it is struck from a core, the term "retouched flake" is reserved only for artifacts that show clear signs of flakes having been detached after the creation of the ventral surface, and hence scars must either derive from or modify the ventral surface in some way to be treated as retouch. The term "nucleus" will be used in the following discussion to refer to any body from which flakes have been removed, whether flakes or cores.

The process of fracture propagation that underlies flaked stone artifact manufacture is complex, and the effects of various core morphologies on the fracture path are not well understood, even by engineers. Yet it is the fracture path that ultimately determines the morphology of flakes and cores, and archaeologists have therefore begun to try to understand this process. Due to the complexity of this subject, readers are directed to a number of papers that provide detailed overviews of fracture mechanics for archaeologists (Cotterell & Kamminga 1977, 1987; Phagan 1985), as well as more narrowly focused experimental investigations (Dibble & Whittaker 1981; Phagan 1985; Dibble & Pelcin 1995; Dibble 1997; Pelcin 1997a,c, 1998; Shott et al. 2000; Macgregor 2005). Without delving into the details, it is possible to briefly describe some of the main principles and the most common fracture features that result.

First of all, only a limited number of stone types are well suited to making flaked stone artifacts, and these generally possess three qualities: they are elastic,

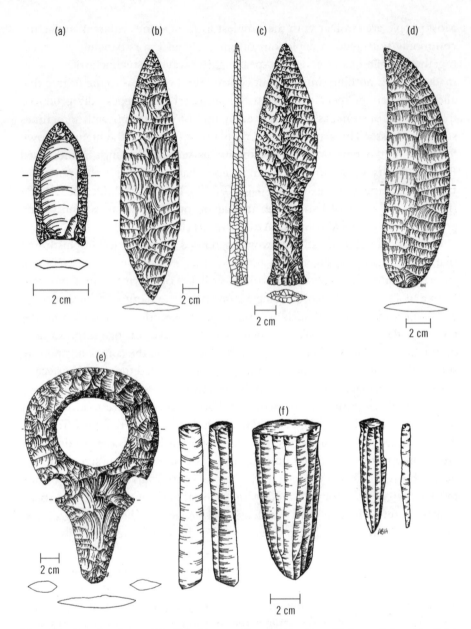

Figure 6.1 Examples of some of the highest known achievements in stone artifact manufacture: (a) a fluted Folsom point; (b) an Upper Paleolithic Solutrean point; (c) a Danish Neolithic flint dagger; (d) a Late Stone Age Egyptian Gerzian ripple-flaked knife; (e) a Mayan chert eccentric; (f) Aztec obsidian pressure blades and cores (from Whittaker 1994, copyright © 1994, by permission of the University of Texas Press).

in that they will temporarily deform when force is applied to them; they are brittle, in the sense that they will fracture if the applied force exceeds the capacity of the material to deform elastically; and they are isotropic, meaning they are equally susceptible to fracture in any direction and will not preferentially fracture along particular planes.

CHRIS CLARKSON AND SUE O'CONNOR

Cryptocrystalline or amorphous silicates (such as chert, chalcedony, and flint), monocrystalline or microcrystalline silicates (crystal quartz and "milky" quartz), acrystalline silicates (such as glass and obsidian) and some larger-grained and less homogeneous materials such as silcrete and quartzite all possess these qualities to varying degrees and are commonly employed in flaked stone artifact manufacture (Cotterell & Kamminga 1987; Kooyman 2000).

In most forms of flaking, force is directed into the platform (i.e., any surface receiving force) of a nucleus with an indentor (any object imparting force to a nucleus) using one of four techniques: striking the nucleus at high velocity with either a hard indentor such as a hammerstone (hard hammer percussion) or a soft indentor such as a piece of wood, bone or antler (soft hammer percussion); slowly applying pressure through a process called dynamic loading (pressure flaking); striking a positioned punch (indirect percussion); or applying compressive force by placing the nucleus on an anvil and striking it from above (the bipolar technique) (Cotterell & Kamminga 1987; Kooyman 2000).

Skilled flintknappers observe that in most flaking, force is generally directed into the nucleus using both an inward and outward motion (Crabtree 1972a; Whittaker 1994), creating both "opening" and "shearing" stresses in the nucleus (Figure 6.2a). Fracture occurs when stresses within the nucleus reach a critical threshold and break the molecular bonds that hold the nucleus together. The most common form of fracture is known as conchoidal fracture, which begins from preexisting flaws in the surface of the nucleus close to the point of impact and creates what is known as a Hertzian cone, as illustrated in Figure 6.2b. The Hertzian cone propagates in a circle around the contact area and expands down into the nucleus in a cone shape at an angle that is partly dependent on the angle of the applied force. If the nucleus is struck close to the edge, only a partial cone will be visible on the flake (Figure 6.2b). Whether or not a fracture will continue to propagate through the core once a cone is formed (i.e., rather than just leaving an incipient cone in the nucleus), depends on whether the force of the blow is sufficient to accelerate and overcome the inertia of the material that is to be removed. Once fracture is initiated, a number of counteracting stresses created by the magnitude and direction of force (tensile, bending, and compressive stresses) will influence the path that it then takes through the core. In conchoidal fracture, the path will typically first head into the core before diving back toward the free face, creating the bulb of force, and then stabilizing on a path that is more or less parallel to the free surface.

Conchoidal flakes (i.e., those with Hertzian initiations) often retain a ring crack at the point of force application (PFA), and an *eraillure scar* just below the point of percussion on the bulb of force (Figure 6.3). Undulations in the fracture path also often leave compression waves on the ventral surface of flakes. Fissures radiating out from the point of percussion are also often found on the ventral surfaces of flakes, but are most often seen on fine-grained materials.

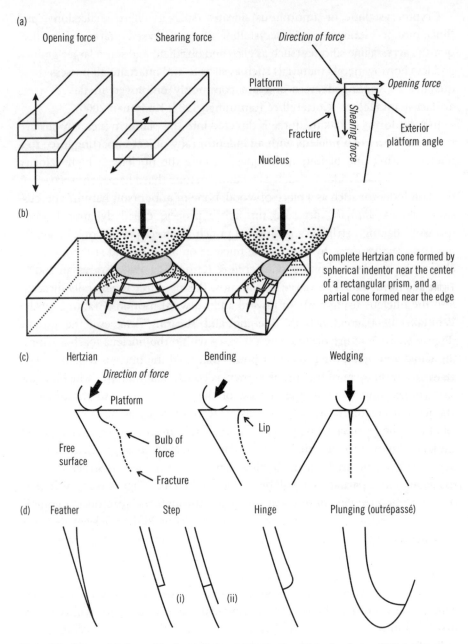

Figure 6.2 Types and features of fracture initiation and termination: (a) fracture forces; (b) Hertzian cones; (c) fracture initiations; (d) termination types (after Cotterell & Kamminga 1987; Andrefsky 1995).

Force eventually exits the nucleus either gradually and at a low angle, creating a feather termination, or more rapidly and at around 90 degrees, creating a step or hinge termination (Figure 6.2d). Not all fractures follow this path, however, and the fracture path sometimes travels away from the free surface and exits on the other side of the nucleus, creating a plunging or *outrépassé* termination (Figure 6.2d). Pelcin's (1997c: 1111) controlled experiments have

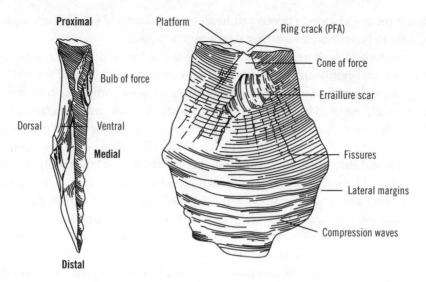

Figure 6.3 Fracture features often found on the ventral and dorsal faces of a conchoidal flake (reproduced courtesy of the Trustees of the British Museum).

shown that when all other variables are held constant, increasing platform thickness will produce regular changes in termination type from feather through to hinge terminations, as the force becomes insufficient to run the length of the free face. The direction of force is also often implicated as a determinant of either hinge or step terminations, but this proposition has not been tested under controlled circumstances. Others have suggested that thick platforms and inward-directed force are more likely to produce outrépassé terminations, given sufficient force to initiate a fracture (Crabtree 1968; Phagan 1985: 237, 243).

Less commonly, fracture will initiate behind the point of percussion, creating a bending initiation, which dives rapidly toward the free face without forming a Hertzian cone, and leaves a pronounced "lip" on the ventral edge of the platform (Figure 6.2c). Bending initiations are most commonly formed on nuclei with low angled platforms and have a fracture surface that often resembles a diffuse bulb, even though no bulb is present (Cotterell & Kamminga 1987: 689). Although it has long been thought that bending initiations are typically produced by soft hammer and pressure flaking, Pelcin (1997c: 1111) found that bending initiations were repeatedly created on cores with low platform angles when blows were placed relatively far in from the edge, suggesting that their frequent association with soft hammer and pressure flaking is more likely a factor of the common use of these techniques in knapping cores with low platform angles (e.g., bifaces) than it is of either force or indentor type. Pelcin (1997b) was also able to show that soft hammer flakes were on average longer and thinner than hard hammer flakes, and that this technique was therefore better suited to bifacial thinning than hard hammer percussion.

Hence the association between soft hammer/pressure and bending initiations is likely to be coincidental rather than causally linked.

Compression fractures created by bidirectional forces produce a wedging initiation that results in flattish fracture surfaces without a bulb of force (Figure 6.2b; and see Cotterell & Kamminga 1987). Because compression fractures are typically initiated by particles driven into existing percussion cracks, flakes created through this process often exhibit battered or crushed platforms with cascading step scars on the platform edge (Cotterell & Kamminga 1987). Bipolar cores and flakes that have been rested on an anvil most commonly display this form of initiation. Because the anvil on which the nucleus is supported can also act like a hammerstone, bipolar flakes can at times exhibit platform and initiation features at both ends, such as crushing, dual bulbs of force, and bidirectional compression waves. When nuclei are stabilized on an anvil, problems of inertia – or the probability of a blow moving the core rather than detaching a flake – can be dramatically reduced. This technique is therefore ideally suited to working very small cores (Hiscock 1982).

Recent controlled fracture experiments have revealed that the closer the Hertzian cone is to the edge of the nucleus, and the lower the external platform angle (EPA), the less material needs to be accelerated away from the core, and hence the less force will be required to initiate a fracture (Speth 1974, 1981; Dibble & Whittaker 1981; Dibble & Pelcin 1995; Pelcin 1997a–c). The more these variables are reduced, however, the smaller the resulting flake will be. This relationship is illustrated in Figure 6.4a, and can be seen to be a simple result of changing core geometry. Alternatively, increasing platform

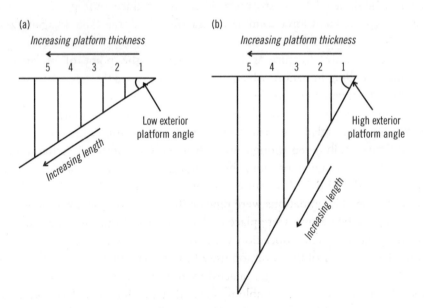

Figure 6.4 The effects of increasing or decreasing platform angle and platform thickness: (a) low exterior platform angle; (b) high exterior platform angle.

CHRIS CLARKSON AND SUE O'CONNOR

angle and striking further from the edge requires greater force input to initiate a fracture, but also results in larger flakes (Figure 6.4b). Increasing force input by too much can result in longitudinal splitting of the flake or crushing of the platform edge. At some point, increasing EPA and/or platform angle will reach a threshold at which the amount of force required to detach a flake will exceed the inertia of the nucleus itself, and will result in moving the nucleus rather than detaching a flake (Phagan 1985: 247). At this point, force requirements can be reduced by decreasing EPA, platform thickness or both, or by stabilizing the core on an anvil.

Most recently, Macgregor's (2005) experiments have demonstrated that removing some of the mass of the free face (such as might occur through overhang removal, for instance) allows a blow to be placed further from the platform edge (given the same amount of force) than would have been possible were it not removed (thereby detaching a larger flake). Furthermore, Macgregor found that the morphology of the free face directly affected the morphology of the resulting flakes. His experiments demonstrated that features such as large preexisting step or hinge terminations on the free face will decrease the viable platform area at which fractures can be successfully initiated. In the case of preexisting step and hinge fractures, more force and the placement of blows further into the nucleus was required to successfully remove a preexisting step or hinge termination without adding another one. It can be expected then that as more step and hinge terminations build up on the dorsal surface, it will become increasingly difficult to remove them from the free face, as the viable platform area will become too small and the amount of force required too excessive to strike off a flake without shattering the platform, adding new step terminations, splitting the flake longitudinally, creating an outrépassé termination, or failing to initiate a flake altogether. A recent study by Pelcin (1997a) also demonstrated that varying the shape of the free face morphology affected the dimensions of the resulting flakes. His findings confirm the observations of flintknappers that setting up ridges running the length of the core face aids the production of longer, thinner, and more parallel-sided flakes (Crabtree 1972a: 31; Whittaker 1994: 106).

Thus, a number of trade-offs exist between the interdependent variables of platform size, platform angle, core inertia, force input, and nucleus morphology that knappers must manipulate to gain control over the fracture path and to extend the reduction of raw materials. A large number of strategies were employed in the past to modify force variables, rectify problematic morphologies, and prevent prematurely damaging the nucleus. Some of these strategies are listed in Table 6.1. These focus on variables that are under the direct control of the knapper and tend to be visible archaeologically. As should be apparent by now, fracture mechanics plays a preeminent role in shaping each individual artifact. It is important to keep this in mind when inferring the meaning of variation in flake and core form. While different forms could be interpreted as having stylistic or functional meaning,

Table 6.1 Common problems, solutions, and negative effects of various stoneworking procedures.

Problem	Strategy	Positive effect	Negative effect	Reference(s)
High platform angles (excessive force requirements)	Faceting	Reduces EPA and force requirements by removing flakes from the platform surface	Reduces control over the fracture path by complicating the platform morphology	Dibble and Whittaker (1981), Phagan (1985: 237), Dibble and Pelcin (1995)
	Decrease platform area of intended flake	Reduces force requirements by reducing the amount of mass that must be accelerated	May result in smaller flakes; if blow is placed too close to the edge, the platform may shatter	
	Core rotation	Creates a new platform with lower angles	Reduces the size, mass, and inertia of the nucleus	
Low platform angles (decreased flake size and increased platform crushing)	Overhang removal	Increases platform angle and strength; allows blows to be placed further in from the edge, creating larger flakes	May create step or hinge terminations to the free face	Phagan (1985: 237)
	Increase platform thickness of intended flake	Reduces chances of platform crushing and results in bigger (heavier) flakes	Increases force requirements, removes mass more quickly from the nucleus, increases platform angle by removing more material from the platform end of the nucleus	Speth (1974, 1981), Dibble and Whittaker (1981), Dibble and Pelcin (1995), Pelcin (1997a–c)
Low nucleus inertia	Decrease platform area of intended flake	Reduces force input requirements by reducing the amount of mass that must be accelerated	May result in smaller flakes; if blow is placed too close to the edge, the platform may shatter	Dibble and Whittaker (1981), Phagan (1985: 237), Dibble and Pelcin (1995)
	Faceting	Reduces EPA and force requirements by removing flakes from the platform surface	Reduces control over the fracture path by complicating the platform morphology	

	Stabilize core	Increases the inertia of the nucleus by supporting it against a larger object	Less control over force delivery	Phagan (1985: 247)
	Bipolar technique	Increases the inertia of the nucleus by resting it on an anvil and imparting a compressive force	May shatter the nucleus through excessive force	Hiscock (1982, 1996), Cotterell & Kamminga (1987)
	Increase speed of force input	By increasing the speed of force input (e.g., by using a faster swing and/or lighter indentor, or a longer indentor that enables greater leverage from the wrist), force can be imparted to the nucleus faster than its inertia can be overcome through movement	Harder to initiate fracture	Phagan (1985: 247)
Insufficient platform friction	Grinding and/or faceting	Increases the coefficient of friction and creates micro-flaws in the surface		Speth (1972: 38), Phagan (1985)
Poor free face morphology	Increase platform thickness of intended flake, platform angle, and force input	Removes projections, irregularities or preexisting step or hinge terminations from the free face by removing larger, thicker flakes	Flake may terminate abruptly if insufficient force; excessive force may result in a plunging termination or shattering the flake	Macgregor (2005)
	Position blow to left or right	Removes problematic features gradually	Flake may terminate abruptly if insufficient force to overcome the irregularity; excessive force may result in a plunging termination or shattering the flake	
	Rotate nucleus	Projections, irregularities, or preexisting step or hinge terminations are removed from the free face from the opposite end	Can increase curvature of the free face, resulting in more curved flakes; new platforms can encounter irregularities left by knapping from previous platforms	Macgregor (2005)

Table 6.1 (cont'd)

Problem	Strategy	Positive effect	Negative effect	Reference(s)
Flakes have insufficient cutting edge for weight	Soft hammer technique	Results in thinner bulbs, and hence thinner flakes, creating higher cutting edge to weight ratios	Thinner flakes will have a greater chance of transverse snapping due to "end shock"	Crabtree (1968, 1972b: 60), Kobayashi (1985), Pelcin (1997b)
	Increase platform thickness of intended flake relative to thickness	Produces a higher cutting edge to weight ratio while minimizing increases in platform angle	Greater chance of longitudinally splitting the flake	Dibble (1997)
	Setup arises on core face	Produces longer, thinner flakes with a higher cutting edge to weight ratio	Increases the probability of transverse breaks due to "end shock"	Crabtree (1968, 1972b), Phagan (1985), Pelcin (1997a), Andrefsky (1998), Kooyman (2000)
No replacement raw material	Extend reduction of nucleus	Use several of the strategies listed above, such as core rotation, stabilization or bipolar working, preparing the platform (faceting and overhang removal), changing the indentor type (e.g., soft hammer), and adjusting the platform size (increasing or decreasing platform the thickness and width)	As above	

they might just as well relate to the methods employed in working various raw materials, to create flakes of different shapes, to prolong reduction, or to overcome certain difficulties.

Pecking and grinding are quite different manufacturing processes to flaking. Pecking involves either dislodging grains or small pieces of material from the surface of a nucleus, or creating small and intersecting impact pits (incipient cones of force) over the surface of the nucleus until a specific shape is attained (Crabtree 1972a). Grinding, either on or with an abrasive material, likewise gradually wears away the surface of an artifact and usually results in the formation of many parallel striations (sometimes microscopic) aligned in the direction of the grinding motion that may blur preexisting fracture features or polish high points on the surface of the artifact.

Above all, the recognition of fracture features and the various techniques employed by past knappers to rectify problems or improve their control over the fracture path requires experience. Replicative flintknapping also provides a rapid way of improving your identification skills by generating large numbers of flakes and cores showing a range of features created using known techniques. Flintknapping can also provide a means of generating hypotheses about how an assemblage might have been created, although analogical arguments of this kind do not provide tests in themselves of the various procedures used in the past. Only the archaeological record itself can provide such tests (e.g., refitting and attribute analysis; Schindler et al. 1984: 176).

How do you recognize different techniques?

It is often difficult to develop consistent sets of criteria to reliably identify specific procedures, as the case of soft hammer percussion discussed above demonstrates, but fortunately the recognition of some of the most common techniques is quite straightforward. A list of some of the commonly employed features used to identify various techniques, compiled from the observations of archaeologists and flintknappers, is presented in Table 6.2 (see, among many others, Crabtree 1972a; Cotterell & Kamminga 1987; Ahler 1989; Hayden & Hutchings 1989; Whittaker 1994), although such features should be used with extreme caution. Entire assemblages should also provide a better "feel" for the use of dominant techniques than should individual specimens (Kooyman 2000: 78).

According to replicative flintknappers (Crabtree 1972a; Newcomer 1975; Whittaker 1994), hard hammer techniques more frequently produce pronounced bulbs of force, compression waves and ring cracks, and expanding flake margins, whereas soft hammer technique produces more diffuse bulbs, flatter fracture surfaces, and narrower flakes. These observations are borne out to some degree by controlled experiments (Cotterell & Kamminga 1987: 686; Pelcin 1997b), although it is difficult to know how well controlled observations translate to archaeological assemblages in which a wide range of variables have presumably varied freely (Dibble 1997: 151). Studies of replicative flintknapping debitage, or the by-products of flaking, have produced arguments

Table 6.2 A list of features and their supposed frequency in various forms of stone artifact manufacture.

Feature	Flaking				Abrasion: ground implement	Pecking: pecked implement
	Hard hammer flake	Soft hammer flake	Pressure flake	Bipolar flake		
Platform	Tend to large size and triangular	Variable size, tend to plano-convex	Small			
Bulb of force	Pronounced	Diffuse	Diffuse	Flat/pronounced	N/A	N/A
Compression waves	Pronounced and closely spaced	Subdued and widely spaced	Subdued and widely spaced	None/pronounced	N/A	N/A
Bulbar fissures	May be present	Rare	May be present			
Erraillure scar	Common (95%)/shallow	Less common/shallow	Rare/deep	Absent	N/A	N/A
Ring crack	Common (60–80%)	Rare (5–10%)	Rare	Absent	N/A	N/A
Bending Initiation	Rare (<1%)	Common (20–60%)	Common			
Shape	Variable	Thin and expanding	Thin and parallel	Parallel	Variable	Variable
Platform scarring	Variable	Facetted/crushed	Facetted	Crushed	N/A	N/A
Ventral curvature	Variable	Pronounced	Pronounced	Flat	N/A	N/A
Thickness	Thicker than soft hammer	Thinner than hard hammer	Much smaller			
Termination	Variable	Tend to feather	Variable	Crushed	N/A	N/A
Striations	N/A		Platform	Absent	Present	N/A
Impact pitting	N/A	Absent	Absent	Platform	Absent	Present

both for and against feasible identification of soft hammer working in archaeological assemblages (Mewhinney 1964; Touhy 1987).

Pressure techniques can sometimes be quite distinctive and recognizable on retouched implements (Akerman & Bindon 1995). Likewise, some analysts believe they can recognize the flakes produced during pressure flaking from a combination of size, thinness, bending initiations, high ventral curvature, and a complex platform and dorsal morphology. As flintknappers point out, however, these same features can be created by percussion flaking, and cannot be considered diagnostic of any one technique in and of themselves (Touhy 1987; Whittaker 1994).

Bipolar flaking also presents difficulties for consistent identification (Jeske & Lurie 1992). Crushing of the platform edge, together with a flattish fracture surface and a battered distal end are the usual criteria employed in identifying bipolar flakes, although not all flakes removed from bipolar cores possess these features (Cotterell & Kamminga 1987), and some possess platform features at both ends, or crushing in addition to fully formed Hertzian initiations. Negative scars can sometimes also appear on the ventral surfaces of bipolar flakes, directed from either end as a result of the crushing blow. Bipolar flakes also are not easily separated from bipolar cores, but the presence of a single flat scar on one face may serve as a guide, whereas bipolar cores may tend to exhibit a number of scars on all faces.

The identification of stoneworking techniques such as overhang removal, faceting, core rotation, retouching, and burination is generally more straightforward. Figure 6.5 illustrates the characteristics of overhang removal and faceting. Overhang removal can be identified by the presence of a series of

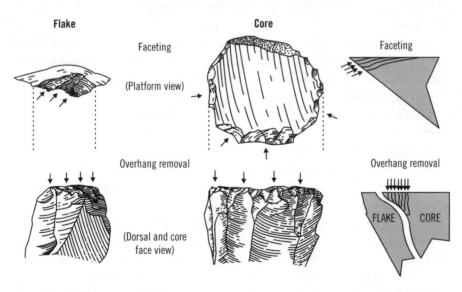

Figure 6.5 Platform features indicative of various preparatory techniques (arrows indicate the location of blows).

smallish scars initiated from the platform surface onto the dorsal surface of flakes or the face of cores. Overhang removal is performed by rubbing or gently tapping the edge of the core to remove the lip remaining after previous flake removals. Faceting looks much like overhang removal, but is oriented in the reverse direction, with smallish flake scars initiated from the dorsal surface onto the platform surface of cores and flakes. There is no real size cutoff between overhang removal or faceting flakes and other dorsal flake scars, and most analysts either employ an arbitrary cutoff (we use 15 mm), or simply use their intuition. Attempts have also been made to identify the distinctive features of overhang removal and faceting flakes so that they may be identified in archaeological assemblages (Newcomer & Karlin 1987).

Core rotation is identified simply by the presence of a number of platforms on cores, or by the existence of truncated flake scars that originate from a point at which a platform no longer exists. Core rotation can also be detected by the presence of redirecting flakes that preserve old platform edges on their dorsal surfaces at different orientations to the current platform (Figure 6.6a). Not every rotation of a core will result in a redirecting flake, and many rotations simply result in striking cortical flakes or flakes with complex platform morphologies (see "How do you measure flake reduction?"). Some of the potential uses of these three stoneworking techniques are listed in Table 6.1.

Retouching is also easily identified if flake scars can clearly be seen to initiate from or modify the ventral surface (Figure 6.6c), but in cases where flaking is initiated from the dorsal surface without clearly modifying the ventral surface, it is often hard to be sure whether it is retouch or preexisting dorsal scars that are present. A classic case of this problem occurs in Australia, where redirection flakes with old steep platform edges on their dorsal surfaces are misidentified as backing retouch. The key to the proper identification of retouch therefore is to locate the actual point of initiation of scars in order to determine whether they were formed before or after the creation of the ventral face. Lateral spalling of the margins, or burination, is another form of retouching that can be misidentified as preexisting dorsal scarring or old platforms (Figure 6.6b).

Bifacial reduction is recognized on cores and flakes as flaking that is directed from either side of the platform edge or lateral margin (Figure 6.6e). Modern flintknappers have identified a set of criteria that they believe can be used to consistently recognize the debris resulting from reduction of bifacial cores and bifacially retouched flakes. These include the high prevalence of bending initiations, pronounced curvature along the percussion axis, low platform angles, faceted and or ground platforms, and complex dorsal scar patterns that remove a portion of the opposite margin (Bordes 1972; Crabtree 1972a,b; Touhy 1987; Patterson 1990; Whittaker 1994: 196). Once again, it is unclear what proportion of bifacial debitage displays some or all of these features.

A large number of recent studies have employed a range of techniques, such as mass and attribute analysis on replicated debitage (Patterson & Sollberger

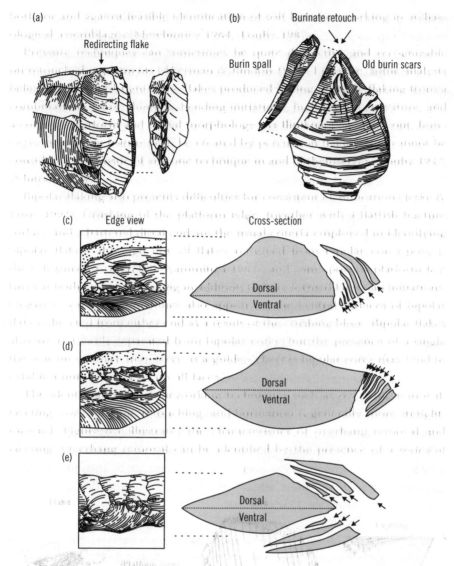

Figure 6.6 Various reduction techniques and forms of retouch: (a) platform redirection; (b) burination; (c) dorsal retouch; (d) ventral retouch; (e) bifacial retouch.

1978; Patterson 1982, 1990; Stahle & Dunn 1984; Ahler 1989; Odell 1989; Shott 1996; Austin 1997; Steffen et al. 1998), breakage patterns (Sullivan & Rozen 1985; Baulmer & Downum 1989; Prentiss & Romanski 1989), or a combination of these (Morrow 1997a; Bradbury 1998), to try to differentiate the various techniques used to create archaeological assemblages (such as hard and soft hammer, pressure, bifacial reduction, and core versus flake reduction), but with varying degrees of success (Prentiss & Romanski 1989; Shott 1994; Prentiss 1998; Bradbury & Carr 1999).

A final technique discussed here is heat treatment. Although the manner in which heat treatment works is still not well understood, this technique often results in improvement of the strength (Purdy & Brooks 1971) and flaking properties of stone (Crabtree & Butler 1964). Heat treatment is often discussed in the technological literature, but discrimination between deliberate and accidental thermal alteration is almost impossible, and requires careful attention to the context of heat application and the range of assemblage elements affected. When properly executed, thermal alteration can cause fine-grained materials to acquire a "greasy luster" or change color. Alteration to the homogeneity of the stone can also be seen directly via electron microscopy when samples of the same stone with and without heating are compared (Purdy & Brooks 1971; Flenniken & White 1983). Excessive or rapid heating and cooling can result in the formation of pot lid scarring, crenated fractures, crazing, spalling, and color alteration, but the presence of these features does not necessarily imply that heating was unintended.

Analyzing Stone Artifacts

Research design

What are you trying to find out?

The first step in any analysis should be to determine what it is that you are trying to find out, and what analytical techniques will provide the answers. We use the word "should" because no project can ever anticipate the full range of possibilities that will eventuate, and as new problems may spring up in the course of the analysis, these may require a different set of techniques or even the development of novel methods.

How do you build your questions?

The questions can come from many sources; they may spring from the imagination fully formed, or coalesce gradually as you digest the disciplinary literature and analyze its strengths and weaknesses. Good questions stand to shed new light on important issues in archaeology and can be answered through empirical research (i.e., stone artifact analysis) that can be undertaken within the time frame available (Odell 2001a).

Are some analyses more meaningful than others?

This depends entirely on whether a good match exists between the questions that you are setting out to answer and the methods and data used to address them. Beyond this, there is no "right" way to analyze stone that will guarantee more meaningful results. The philosophical position that is taken, however, often leads us to choose various forms of analysis over others for the particular advantages that they offer. The following section on classification provides an example of one such situation in which our underlying ontological positions, or "views of reality," may influence the sorts of data we collect and the types of classifications we employ.

Classifying an assemblage of stone artifacts

Why classify?

Classification in archaeology, as in all fields, really only serves two purposes. The first is to structure our observations into a limited set of groupings that can be said to be alike in a defined way. Grouping our observations in this way allows our results to be compared, contrasted, and explained. The second purpose is to provide a set of terminological conventions, usually a set of

CHRIS CLARKSON AND SUE O'CONNOR

named groupings or "classes," that allows us to communicate about the world in a simplified and understandable fashion (Lyman et al. 1997: 15).

There are three basic rules on which successful classifications are based. The first is that classifications should be based on sets of variables whose importance and means of combination is somehow determined from a body of theory. The second is that there must be recognizable similarities and differences between the phenomena being observed in relation to the variables on which the classification is based (Hill & Evans 1972; Dunnell 1986; Bailey 1994: 232). The third rule is that the classification must be exhaustive, or in other words, it must encompass all of the observed variation. Many classifications fail on these three counts, and particularly in the case of exhaustiveness. For instance, many classifications adopt the use of "miscellaneous" categories in which to place specimens that do not meet any of the classificatory criteria, rather than revising the classification to include unique objects. Obviously, the variables employed in a classification, as well as their means of combination, are of prime importance in determining its utility for a particular research design, its comparability to alternative systems, its sensitivity to variation, and its sufficiency as an exhaustive and unambiguous description of variation.

Are there rules of classification?

There are numerous forms of classification, ranging from *ad hoc* folk classification to systematic forms, and a potentially infinite range of variables upon which to base any system of division. We can usefully distinguish three elements of classification, all of which find their way into lithic classification to some degree.

What are the different types of classification?

A first principle relates to the criteria used to assign objects to a particular class, and it is possible to differentiate between monothetic and polythetic class construction. In monothetic class construction, objects belong to a certain class only if they possess all of the specified attributes (or properties) that define that class (see Figure 6.8 below). The implication of this type of classification is that an object can be assigned to a particular class according to the presence of any single attribute, because it is assumed that if it possesses one, it must possess them all.

Polythetic classification, on the other hand, is better suited to dealing with variation in that it requires that an artifact possess only one or more of the total number of defining properties to belong to a class, and that no artifacts possess all of them. The implication of this form of classification is that a single property does not always provide an accurate basis on which to assign an artifact to its proper class, and classification must instead take into account the total combination of attributes and their overall weighting in the system. Polythetic classifications require explicit definition of each defining property, so that different analysts do not accidentally produce different classifications.

To give an example of the kinds of classes that each system might produce, as well as the ways in which properties can be combined to form distinct

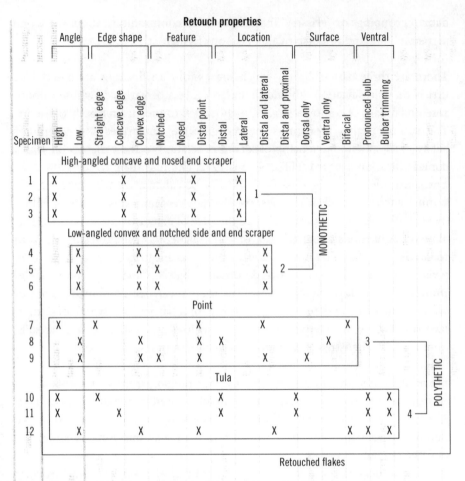

Figure 6.7 An illustration of some typical classifying variables and their means of combination under monothetic or polythetic classification.

classes, two monothetic and two polythetic classes are shown in Figure 6.7. The first three specimens are assigned to the monothetic class "High-angled concave and nosed-end scrapers," on the basis that all members possess high edge angles, concave edges, nosed projections, and distal retouch. In this system, the presence of any one of those features will identify the artifact as belonging to that class, as they are mutually exclusive and do not occur in any other monothetically defined class. The second class is also a monothetic class with a different set of attributes that are also held in common by all its members. In contrast, the next two classes are constructed using a polythetic system in which not all properties are held in common by all members, although at least one property is held in common by all (e.g., a distal point for Points, and both pronounced bulbs and dorsal bulbar trimming for Tulas).

Each system has its own strengths and weaknesses. For instance, monothetic classifications are simple and straightforward to design and implement, but suffer difficulties when dealing with variation and complexity. It must be

CHRIS CLARKSON AND SUE O'CONNOR

acknowledged that monothetic classes are also high-level abstractions in the sense that they impose rigid boundaries around phenomena that may in fact form a continuum. Polythetic classifications are better able to deal with variation, but may embody too much flexibility. Unless the various defining properties are rigorously defined and weighted, there is great potential for each researcher to come up with a different set of assignments.

A second principle of classification is that objects can either belong exclusively to a certain class and no other, or they can belong to many classes, sometimes with a "membership weighting." This division again determines how variation is dealt with. Exclusivity means that variation is suppressed to fit unique objects into a limited set of classes, as is the case for Classes 1 and 2 in Figure 6.7. Alternatively, overlapping classifications mean that variation is allowed expression, and that unique objects are recognized for their potential to fit into any number of classes, depending on which attributes are given prominence in the classificatory scheme. For example, Classes 3 and 4 in Figure 6.7 share features in common with specimens found in other classes, and we could theoretically assign them to all of the classes with which they overlap – if we were to find this useful for some purpose. By placing a weighting on specific variables, however, it would be equally possible to narrow the range of classes into which they fit. Tinkering with the choice and weighting of variables allows the degree of overlap between each type to be expanded or narrowed.

A third principle centers on whether classes have some sort of structure imposed on them, such as a hierarchical arrangement of the sort seen in Linnean biological classification. Unordered classifications impose no precedence or structure and treat each class is as though it is "on the same level." In stone artifact classification, hierarchical classification is best seen in classifications that attempt to order each stage of the reduction process in terms of the chronological sequence in which it takes place (Hiscock 2005). For instance, all of the specimens in Figure 6.7 also belong to the higher-order grouping "Retouched Flakes." Andrefsky (1998: 65) provides an example of the way in which either monothetic and polythetic methods could be used in the construction of a hierarchical classificatory system.

Classifications can be undertaken by manually allocating objects to a class using a set of variables whose importance is deduced from theory, or using statistical techniques that find clusters within the data. It has sometimes been claimed that these techniques can provide an objective means of "discovering" natural types (Spaulding 1953), but as Dunnell (1971) points out, while statistical techniques may indeed derive attribute clusters from empirical data that are of utility for certain problems, they cannot discover types with an independent reality, as the robustness of class divisions ultimately rests on the value and weighting of the attributes employed. Statistical types are therefore always constructed at some level.

What are the different methods of classification?

Choosing between classificatory systems is not straightforward, but depends on the sorts of data that you want to collect and the types of questions being addressed. Our underlying views of reality may also sway our decision to use one form of classification over another, as these tend to favor a certain depictions of the world over another.

Most classifications in use today are built around one or other of two alternative views of the world that have important consequences for the way things are classified. The first was discussed at least as long ago as Plato's time and is today called "essentialism." This idea holds that the world is divided into real, discontinuous, and immutable "kinds." This notion underlies most typological constructions, which hold that artifacts, particularly retouched implements and certain types of flakes and cores, can be separated into discrete and mutually exclusive kinds (Dunnell 1986; Dibble 1995; O'Brien 1996; Lyman et al. 1997; Hiscock 2002b, 2005). In the context of stone artifact manufacture, essential forms are often thought of as "mental templates," or combinations of traits that are favored by the maker. Variation is seen as a consequence of the imperfect realization of the conceptually perfect form, and is usually attributed to differences in raw material properties or individual skill levels (Dunnell 1986). In practice, individual artifacts are usually assigned through comparison with the "type specimens," or sets of artifacts that exemplify the ideal forms for each class. The essentialist metaphysic lends itself to the use of mutually exclusive, unordered, monothetic classes of the sort typically employed in most typologies.

An alternative view of reality is called "materialism," and holds that all phenomena are unique, often arranged as continuums, and that "kinds" are illusory and imposed on reality rather than extracted from it. Materialist classifications therefore set out to find ways of depicting variation as well as central tendency, and treat observational units as units of measurement rather than real kinds. In archaeological classification, the materialist metaphysic has been particularly embraced by evolutionary and processual schools. The processual school has argued the position that there is no natural, single, or "best" typology and no inherent meanings to be discovered in an assemblage of artifacts (Hill & Evans 1972). Rather, the meaning imposed on archaeological phenomena derives from *a priori* problems, hypotheses, and other interests (Hill & Evans 1972: 252). Hence processualists encourage the selection of attributes that are derived from the discipline's problems and that will lead to classifications that are useful in addressing those problems. Evolutionary archaeologists make the additional claim that most phenomena are in a state of constant change (as in cultural phenomena and artifacts themselves), and that classifications may be enhanced by somehow factoring time, distance, and/or historical relatedness into their formulations (Lyman & O'Brien 2000). This can be clearly seen, for instance, in the changes that take place in the form of an artifact as reduction continues (Dibble 1995; Hiscock & Attenbrow 2002, 2003; Clarkson 2005).

CHRIS CLARKSON AND SUE O'CONNOR

By this stage, we hope we have convinced you that classification requires some thought, that no classification is "real" or fixed, and that it is most useful if approached as a tool for measurement, description, and problem-solving. Important points as far as stone artifacts are concerned are that different levels of classification can exist, that the same artifacts can be assigned to different classes according to the weighting and combination of variables used, and that all classifications will create a certain level of abstraction and ambiguity, but that this can be reduced by being explicit about the choice of variables and the weightings given to each. This also increases the ease with which each classification can be replicated by other researchers (Andrefsky 1998: 62). Building your own problem-oriented classifications therefore requires attention to these factors. Once they have been dealt with, however, virtually any set of groupings based on a potentially infinite range of variables is conceivable.

How do you build your own classification?

Another approach that we would advocate in classifying stone artifacts is that some categories should always remain exclusive, whereas others might be allowed to overlap, as in the case of the three chronologically separate and mutually exclusive categories of cores, flakes, and retouched flakes. Classifications that set out to describe and order manufacturing processes and/or products should generally seek to keep these classes distinct. Unfortunately, many classifications blur these classes, and draw an initial division within assemblages between "tools" and "debitage" (e.g., Andrefsky 1998). "Tools" are all those artifacts believed to represent the intended "end-products" of the process, while "debitage" constitutes all the waste left over from tool production, use, and maintenance (Dibble 1995; Hiscock 2005). These divisions are based on propositions that cannot be verified empirically, and it is therefore safest when building classifications to start with basic observational categories, and if other higher-level categories are required, to build on them as required.

The selection of variables to record and measure in an analysis is clearly one of the most important decisions that you will make. As Hiscock and Clarkson (2000) state:

Choosing attribute: to record and measure

What attributes should you choose?

> . . . the most crucial consideration must be the analytical power of the attribute and its relevance to the questions posed . . . [T]he application of a single standardized method of analysis, including the use of a standard set of attributes, is not an appropriate response because different observations will be needed for each new question and in each archaeological context. However, for any particular question there may be a number of relevant attributes, and it is valuable to also consider the power of equally relevant variables.

Our advice for choosing the most powerful attributes is to read widely within the technological literature and identify attributes that help address the questions you have posed. Compiling a table of justifications and references to successful uses of each attribute can also provide a useful starting point, as in Table 6.1. Phagan (1985) provides a fairly extensive list of attributes (and some justification for each) commonly employed in the analysis of flakes and cores, as does Clarkson and David (1995). Attributes relevant to the recording of retouch are detailed by Hiscock and Attenbrow (2002, 2003, 2005), Clarkson (2002a, 2005), Hiscock and Clarkson (2005), and Dibble (1995).

What is a "basic" analysis?

In the broader scheme of things, a basic analysis, if such a thing could be said to exist, would probably try to incorporate some description (whether quantitative or qualitative) of the size, shape, level of reduction, raw material, and technological and typological category for each artifact in an assemblage, in the hope that the broadest range of questions possible might be addressed. It may be possible to cover each of these aspects and yet still record only a small number of variables. As stated above, it will be the power of each attribute to address each criterion that will determine how streamlined the analysis can be.

Managing data

How should you record your attributes?

Because laboratory analysis is slow and painstaking, there is a good argument to be made for reducing data handling time by entering information straight into the computer as it is gathered. Although some archaeologists still prefer to use spreadsheets, there is no doubt that a database provides a far superior means of entering, storing, and retrieving data about individual specimens. Computer data entry may not be practical in some field situations, where the use of recording forms may still be the most suitable option.

When do you need to use statistics and what statistics are most useful?

Statistics are typically used in stone analysis to provide a means of seeking independent confirmation that the patterns observed in the data are not simply a result of the vagaries of sampling (i.e., random effects), small sample size, or the result of a complex interaction of several variables that makes the important variables or patterns difficult to determine.

It is difficult to advise what statistics should be used to analyze the data, as each question and analysis lends itself to different techniques and tests. Nevertheless, several tests tend to be used over and again in lithic analysis. These include chi-square tests, t-tests, Spearman's rho, and regression analysis. These are all basic techniques for working with the kinds of data that archaeologists use in lithic analysis. A good introduction to all of these techniques, as well as a demystification of concepts such as *significance* and *sampling*, and useful suggestions for identifying and working with skewed populations (which most lithic assemblages tend to be), is provided for archaeologists by Drennan (1996). These basic tests are all that is typically needed to make comparisons between assemblages, confirm ordering in the data, and determine whether a relationship between two variables is strong and significant.

Statisticians can be helpful in identifying the techniques that best address your questions, and in navigating and interpreting the complex world of multivariate statistics, but you should be capable of performing most simple tests yourself with the help of statistics software.

As stoneworking is a reductive technology, the measurement of the degree to which this process has progressed often forms the basis of many modern analyses. Quantifying the extent of reduction allows estimations to be made of the amount of time and energy invested in the production of an artifact, the level of departure of the observed form from its original form, the amount of material likely to have been created as a product of the process, and the position in the sequence at which changes in manufacturing strategies took place and their likely effects on artifact morphology. At a higher interpretive level, many archaeologists see measures of reduction as critical to the testing of behavioral models that hypothesize the place of stone artifacts in broader systems of time budgeting, mobility, and land use. Consequently, measures of reduction have come to be associated, at least implicitly, with discussions of risk, cost, and efficiency in past technological systems (Bleed 2001). These discussions build on the assumption that the differential distribution of sequential steps and stages through space and time will reflect aspects of planning, land use, ecology, and settlement and subsistence patterns affecting people's daily lives (Nelson 1991; Kuhn 1995). Measures of reduction are consequently fast becoming a central component of lithic analysis, and also form the basis of the European *chaîne opératoire* approach (Leroi-Gourhan 1964; Meignen 1988; Roebroeks et al. 1988; Geneste 1990). This approach places emphasis on the technical "choices" that people make during lithic reduction between a variety of possible solutions and the context of these decisions within broader cultural values and social relations (Lemonnier 1986; Dobres 2000).

Both fracture mechanics and basic engineering principles would suggest that striking more and more mass from a core will affect its size and geometry, which will have direct consequences for the nature of force input, the viability of different reduction strategies, and the size and morphology of the flakes produced over the sequence. We can speculate, for instance, that the gradual reduction of cores will result in more flake scars and less cortex, that continued use of a platform will result in a decrease in platform size, and that as more mass is struck from a core, the size of the core and resulting flakes might also decrease. If cores are rotated during this process to create fresh platforms once old ones become damaged or unproductive, cores should begin to preserve signs of former flaking on the platform surfaces as well as indications of the existence of old platforms.

To provide an example of the sorts of procedures that can be used to track morphological changes and the use of different technological strategies over the sequence of core reduction, a number of variables are plotted against increasing numbers of core rotations in Figure 6.8. These changes are

Measuring extent of reduction

Why measure reduction?

How do you measure core reduction?

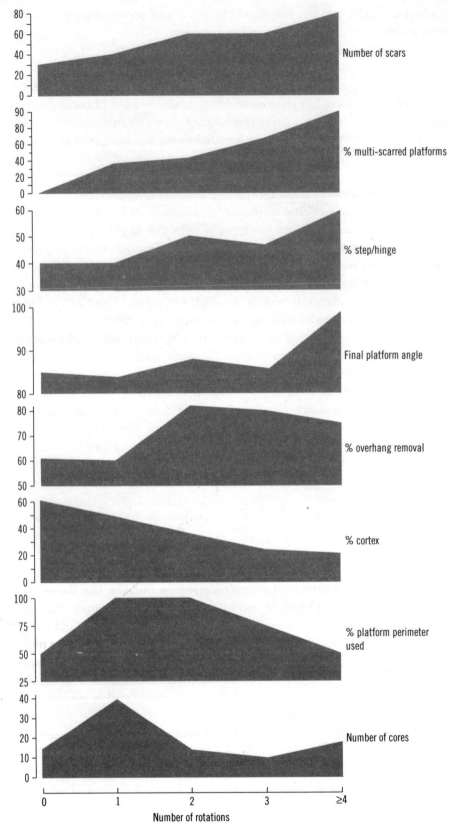

Figure 6.8 Changes in core morphology over the sequence of reduction.

documented from a set of 87 small, locally occurring, river-rounded chert cobbles found at a site near Wollongong on the southern coast of New South Wales, Australia. This diagram shows that many core characteristics show an increase over the sequence of reduction, while others decrease.

For instance, as might be expected, the number of scars found on cores increases with each rotation, as does the percentage of platforms that have more than one conchoidal scar (resulting from former use as a core face). The percentage of scars found on the core showing step and hinge terminations also increases as core rotation proceeds, as does the external angle of the last platform used on the core. Overhang removal increases early on and remains high throughout the remainder of the reduction sequence. Overhang removal was presumably used to strengthen the platform to better receive the forceful blows required to remove flakes from small cores with increasingly high-angled platform edges. In contrast, cortex diminishes at a fairly consistent rate throughout the sequence, indicating that similar amounts of material were likely removed from each platform with each rotation. The used portion of the platform edge first increases and then decreases, as irregularities left on the core face and platform by previous rotations reduce the usable platform perimeter. The number of cores from each stage of reduction also clearly indicates that most cores were abandoned in early stages of reduction, although a small proportion continued into later stages of reduction, by which time cores were heavily rotated and generally lacking cortex, or were subjected to bipolar reduction.

Changes in core morphology over the reduction sequence are illustrated as a reduction flowchart in Figure 6.9, which depicts a number of the ways of flaking small spherical nodules followed at the site. While archaeologists have sometimes used this type of chart to illustrate normative reduction sequences through which most forms are argued to pass, this chart ascribes frequencies to each stage in each sequence as determined from the assemblage itself. Reduction begins with a single flake removed from a cortical platform. In the left-hand sequence (Sequence 1), new platforms are always created from the previous flaked surface via 90 degree core rotations. In the middle sequence (Sequence 2), new platforms are always created from cortical surfaces. In the right-hand sequence (Sequence 3), a single large scar is removed from each surface, which then becomes the platform for the next single large flake removal. Also illustrated in Figure 6.9 are late-stage rotated and bipolar cores with and without cortex, which represent the very end stages of all sequences.

From this diagram, it can be seen that Sequence 1 was most commonly followed at the site, but that Sequences 2 and 3 also formed common alternatives. The mapping of reduction sequences in this way allows variation as well as the central tendency to be explored, and also demonstrates that core reduction was a highly variable process, with knappers responding to the results of each successful or unsuccessful blow in a flexible fashion, in which the options

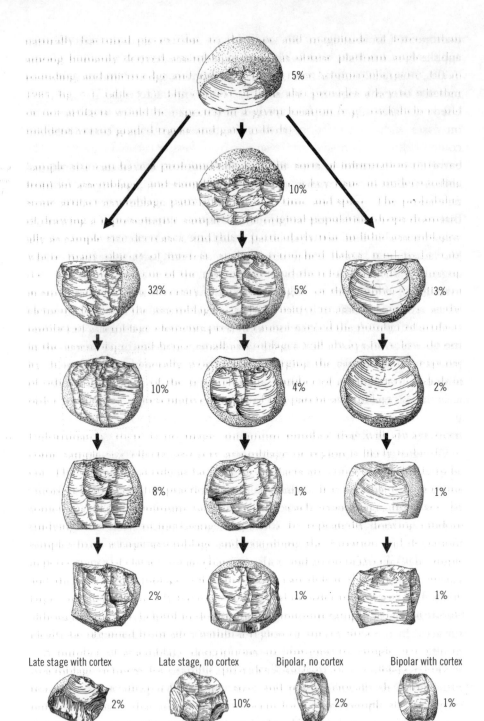

Figure 6.9 The reduction flowchart and the frequencies with which various core reduction sequences were employed at Sandon Point.

CHRIS CLARKSON AND SUE O'CONNOR

for rotation, discard, or strategy switching (such as to bipolar reduction) were appraised at various points along the way.

   This simple case study indicates that a number of variables are likely to be useful measures of reduction intensity, at least for this type of core reduction. Used in combination, these attributes would provide a reasonably sound basis on which to infer the level of reduction reached by any individual core. This could be done by dividing the continuum into a number of intervals (such as early, medium, and late), or by using a continuous ranking system. Assigning each core its own degree of reduction then allows the intensity of core reduction to be traced across space and time. It should be kept in mind, however, that different forms of reduction might well require the use of different variables than those employed here.

Lithic analysts employ various means of assigning flakes from archaeological assemblages into reduction stages, but most of these tend to involve comparison of archaeological specimens with experimentally produced assemblages. To avoid this analogical approach, our case study ranks flake reduction according to simple and universal changes in flake morphology that are deduced from the analysis of changing core morphology presented above, as reflected in dorsal and platform scar morphology. This type of analysis is called diacritical analysis (Sellet 1993), and aids in the construction of hypothetical reduction models. In this case, diacritical analysis allows changes in flake morphology to be examined for Sequence 1 of the pebble core reduction sequence illustrated in Figure 6.9.

   The reduction process can be modeled by examining stages in flake scar superimposition on the platform and dorsal surfaces of flakes and the stages of decortication present. Nine stages of flake production can be envisaged. As in Figure 6.9, the first phase involves the creation of an initial flake scar on the core to serve as a platform for the next stage of reduction. This results in the production of Stage 1 flakes that possess primary cortex (i.e., 100 percent) on all surfaces. The second stage involves the rotation of the core through 90 degrees, so that flakes can be struck from the first scar. These Stage 2 flakes will possess a single conchoidal scar on the platform and primary cortex on the dorsal surface. Stage 3 flakes result from continued reduction of this second face, and will have single conchoidal platforms but only secondary cortex (<100 percent) remaining on the dorsal surface. Stage 4 flakes result from the final stages of reduction on this face, and will possess the same type of platform, but will have no cortex remaining on the dorsal surface (tertiary cortex). At some point, reduction is likely to end on this second face as nonfeather terminations increase, or platforms become unproductive due to high platform angles. This will either result in discarding the core, or the formation of another platform by rotating the core again. Redirection flakes, or flakes that remove the edge of an old platform, are sometimes created by this process, and these are here labeled Stage 5 flakes. At this early stage of reduction,

How do you measure flake reduction?

redirection flakes should preserve cortex on one or more of their surfaces (and this is the criteria used for determining Stage 5 redirection flakes). The process of reduction then begins anew on the third face, with cortical flakes with multiple scarred platforms (as a result of striking from previously flaked surfaces) produced first (Stage 6), followed by flakes with secondary cortex (Stage 7), and then by flakes with no cortex (Stage 8). Once this face also begins to encounter difficulties for further reduction, the core may be discarded or rotated again, and another redirection flake may be produced. As cores enter increasingly later stages of reduction, cortex is likely to have been entirely removed from all surfaces, and hence redirection flakes from this stage would show no cortex on their surfaces. These flakes are assigned to Stage 9 (or 3 to N rotations). Although not included in this hypothetical reduction model, another option for knappers is to switch to the use of a bipolar reduction technique once cores become too small to continue freehand percussion, and this was frequently undertaken at the site.

Figure 6.10 maps out the sorts of changes in flake characteristics that accompany each of the stages of Sequence 1 reduction as deduced from dorsal and platform scar patterns. Interestingly, these changes are largely cyclical, with the gradual increases or decreases in characteristics taking place throughout the first phase of flake removals (Stages 2–4) often repeated in the second phase (Stages 6–8). The basic series of changes is as follows: flakes are at first rather squat but become increasingly elongate toward the end of each phase as parallel ridges become more common, platform area decreases, platform preparation becomes common, the proportion of nonfeather terminations increases, and the size of flakes measured by width and thickness decreases (weight does not show a sequential decrease due to differences in initial nodule size).

Redirecting flakes stand out in terms of their larger size and their apparent nonconformity to the trends otherwise seen for most characteristics. This is not surprising, since striking off old platforms often requires delivering large amounts of force to the core from a sub-optimal platform. Hence, striking off old platforms is unlike other forms of flaking, and the resulting flakes are often distinctive. The last line shows the frequency with which flakes at each stage of reduction are found in the assemblage, and indicates that the greatest proportion of flakes belong to early stages of reduction. This is consistent with the pattern seen for cores, which were rarely taken into later stages of reduction.

How can you explore blank selection? Archaeologists are often interested in the process of blank selection – or the selection of a subset of flakes from the total population produced at a site – in which prehistoric knappers selected appropriate flakes for further use, retouching, and transport away from the site. Blank selection is of interest as it has the potential to inform us about design considerations (such as tool performance, reliability/maintainability, suitability to prehension and hafting, and multifunctionality), a range of environmental and cultural constraints

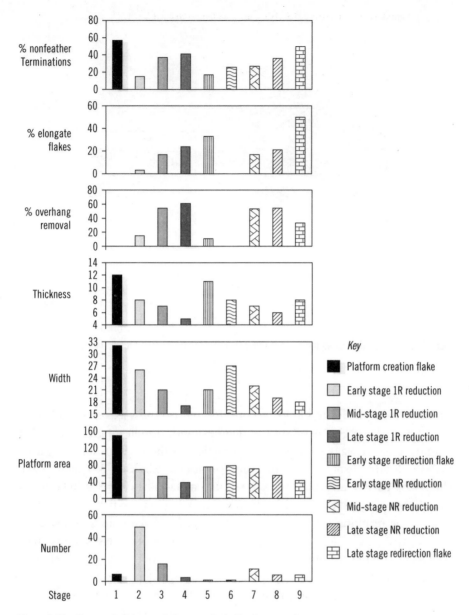

Figure 6.10 Changes in flake morphology over Reduction Sequence 1.

(functional, material, technological, socioeconomic, and ideological; Hayden et al. 1996), and the level of standardization in the production system, both in terms of overall flake production and selection from the larger pool of flake variation.

An example of one approach to examining the pool of variation in flake forms produced at the same site near Wollongong, and the range of blank shapes selected for various forms of retouching, is shown in Figure 6.11. Here, two measures of flake shape are plotted against one another to illustrate the

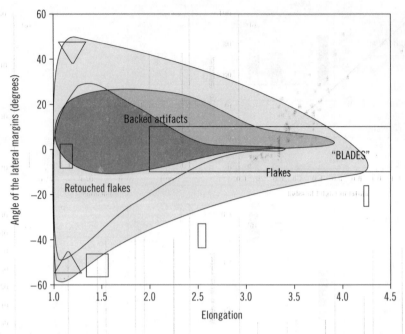

Figure 6.11 A graph illustrating the range of variation in flake shape employed in different forms of retouching.

spread of flake shapes found at the site. Plotted on the y-axis is the angle of the retouched margins expressed in degrees, with 0 indicating parallel-sided margins, positive values indicating contraction of the margins, and negative values indicating expansion of the lateral margins (Clarkson & David 1995). The x-axis plots elongation (length/width), with values ranging from very squat flakes (i.e., values of 1) through to extremely elongate flakes (i.e., values of 4.5). The resulting graph shows a wide spread of flake shapes produced at the site, with the majority proving to be squat flakes of widely varying marginal angles that likely derive from earlier stages of core reduction (see above).

Retouched flakes clearly represent a much smaller subset of the total range of flake shapes, while backed artifacts (large and small symmetrics and asymmetrics) (Hiscock 2002a) make up an even narrower range still. Overall, retouched and backed flake shapes mirror the broader pattern of squat flakes with variable marginal angles produced at the site, although backed artifacts tend more frequently to be parallel-sided with contracting margins. The graph also indicates that flake production and blank selection were far from standardized, suggesting that few design considerations affected the types of blanks chosen for further modification. The greater constriction of variation seen in backed artifacts, however, points to tighter constraints on the design of these implements than was the case for retouched artifacts more generally, and these may be related to hafting requirements, functional efficiency, potential for multifunctionality, or all of these factors.

CHRIS CLARKSON AND SUE O'CONNOR

Retouched flakes are most commonly the subject of detailed lithic analysis, but until recently few techniques existed to measure the amount of time and labor invested in their production. More recently, a number of measures have been proposed and tested that offer a means of measuring reduction for a number of different forms of retouching (Kuhn 1990; Clarkson 2002b; Hiscock & Clarkson 2005).

The *Index of Invasiveness*, for instance, provides a measure of retouch coverage over both the dorsal and ventral surfaces of an artifact that is suited to measuring unifacial and bifacial retouch (Clarkson 2002b). It is best suited to the measurement of artifacts that tend to become more invasively retouched over the sequence of reduction. The Index of Invasiveness calculates intensity of retouch as a value between 0 and 1 by estimating the extent of retouching around the perimeter of a flake as well as the degree to which it encroaches onto the dorsal and ventral surfaces (for procedures, see Clarkson 2002b).

Another measure, the *Geometric Index of Unifacial Reduction* (GIUR), was developed by Kuhn (1990) and calculates edge attrition as the ratio of the height of retouch to the maximum thickness of the flake. This technique is designed for the measurement of unifacial retouch, as the name suggests, but is also best suited to the measurement of steep and marginal retouch. Again, a score of 0 indicates no retouch, while a score of 1 indicates that retouch height is equal to flake thickness. Used in conjunction, these two techniques are capable of describing almost any form of retouching, and of quantifying the degree to which retouch in steep and marginal or acute and invasive.

Although retouched flakes (commonly termed "scrapers") have often been treated as stylistically irregular artifacts shaped simply to meet immediate needs (Hayden 1979; White & O'Connell 1982), recent studies (Clarkson 2002a, 2005; Hiscock & Attenbrow 2002, 2003, 2005) have demonstrated that this group of implements can display marked internal consistency when examined in light of increasing retouch intensity, with a regular series of changes noted to the shape, extent, and type of retouch found on their margins as retouch increases. These changes can be depicted using a number of indices of retouch extent, shape, and type. These are the percentage of the perimeter of an artifact that is retouched, the curvature of the retouched edge, the angle of retouch, and the invasiveness of retouch.

The percentage perimeter of retouch is calculated by dividing length of retouch by the perimeter of the flake. The angle of the retouched edge is calculated as the mean of several edge angle measurements taken at regular intervals along the retouched edge. Edge curvature is measured by dividing the maximum diameter of retouch by the total depth of retouch (Clarkson 2002a). Negative results indicate concave edges, while positive ones indicate convex edges.

An example of the power of these measures of flake reduction is illustrated in Figure 6.12 by plotting the morphological changes that occur in a population of 128 retouched flakes from the same site near Wollongong as retouching

How do you measure retouch?

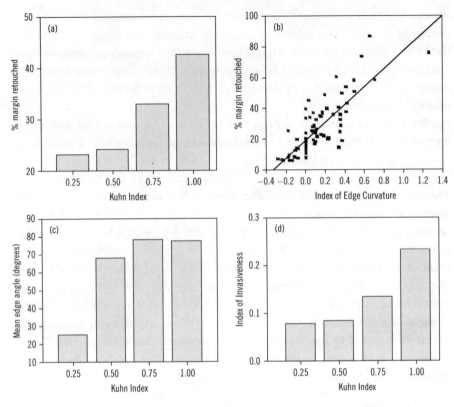

Figure 6.12 Changes in flake morphology as retouching increases: (a) the percentage of the margin retouched; (b) the edge curvature; (c) the mean retouched edge angle; (d) the Index of Invasiveness.

increases. Figure 6.12a, for instance, indicates that retouching usually starts out covering only a short section of the lateral margins, but as Kuhn's GIUR index increases, eventually extends to cover around 50 percent of the margin. As retouch spreads around the margin, the curvature of the edge also changes, as shown in Figure 6.12b. Retouch usually starts out slightly concave, but then straightens out before finally becoming quite convex. Similarly, Figures 6.12c and 6.12d indicate that retouch generally starts out quite low-angled and marginal, but ends up steep and more invasive. This sequence of changes accounts for much of the variation in retouched flake morphology, and underlies the differences in form that have sometimes been formalized as elaborate scraper typologies (such as that of McCarthy et al. 1946).

Much like the situation for cores argued above, once these changes in flake form are documented and the reduction sequence understood, individual artifacts can be assigned their positions in a particular reduction sequence. An understanding of reduction sequences also enables the construction of classifications that divide the continuum in sensible places, rather than jumbling together artifacts on the basis of features that are disconnected from the mechanisms actually creating that variation. The resulting classes could be treated as

CHRIS CLARKSON AND SUE O'CONNOR

measurement units (in this case of intensity of reduction) that expressed temporal and historical relationships (in this case departure from an original form), thereby meeting some of the expectations of materialist classificatory systems.

Other studies have also explored stage and continuum models in artifact reduction, and some of these employ quite different measures of reduction intensity to those employed here (Barton 1988; Gordon 1993; Marcy 1993; Neeley & Barton 1994; Dibble 1995; Holdaway et al. 1996; Morrow 1997b; Yvorra 2000; Lamb 2005; Law 2005).

Dealing with difficult assemblages

What if most of your artifacts are broken or damaged?

This can be a big problem for any analyst working on assemblages that have been subjected to intense heating and trampling, extensive reduction and use, or some other post-depositional process. However, even broken and damaged artifacts can preserve information relevant to the reconstruction of the overall manufacturing system, and assemblage attrition can also reveal much about site formation, disturbance, and occupational intensity (Flenniken & Haggarty 1979; Mallouf 1982; Hall & Love 1985; Hiscock 1985; Jung 1992).

Figure 6.13 illustrates a range of fragment types that are commonly found in flaked stone assemblages. Different kinds of technological information can be recovered from each fragment type. For instance, transversely broken fragments such as proximal pieces preserve information about the platform surface, the presence and type of platform preparation, and the platform angle, while distal pieces preserve information about the flake termination type. Medial pieces can be informative about the cross-section of the flake, while all of these fragments may reveal something of the original width and thickness of the flake, its dorsal scar morphology, or the presence, type, and amount of cortex. Longitudinally split flakes may preserve original length and thickness as well as some features of the platform and termination. Once transverse and longitudinal fractures occur together on the same artifact, however, information loss increases dramatically. Surface fragments and flaked pieces often yield little technological information at all. Combining the relevant information from each type of fragment with that gained from complete flakes may be a useful way of increasing the number of observations if assemblages are highly fragmented, especially for categories that suffer high breakage rates and may be underrepresented in the assemblage (such as very thin artifacts or retouched flakes). The recovery of information from broken artifacts is often a necessary means of increasing sample size (see "What if you only have a small number of stone artifacts?").

One problem that results from fragmentation can be to accurately determine how much flaking took place at a site. In cases where, for instance, an assemblage contains only a few heavy artifacts, or where post-depositional processes such as burning and trampling have caused severe artifact fragmentation, simple measures such as weight or number of artifacts can be unreliable. Hiscock (2002b) has recently explored this problem and suggested some

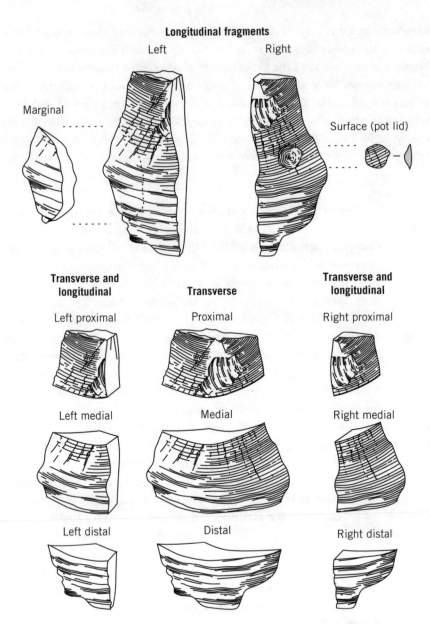

Figure 6.13 An illustration of the range of flake fragment types found in many assemblages.

counting procedures that may assist in the quantification of numbers of flaking events and in assessing the effects of breakage and weathering. Hiscock's technique allows a number of different indices to be calculated, including the Minimum Number of Flakes (MNF) present in an assemblage. This is derived by dividing the assemblage into raw material types and then adding the number of complete flakes of each raw material to whichever is the greater number of proximal or distal fragments, the greater number of left or right fragments, and the greater number of left or right proximal or distal fragments. MNF, or

CHRIS CLARKSON AND SUE O'CONNOR

better still MNA (i.e., Minimum Number of Artifacts, including both flakes and cores), provides a superior means of assessing and comparing the intensity of flaking within or between sites than weight of raw numbers. Shott (2000) also offers various techniques (MNT, ETE, and TIE) for estimating the original number of artifacts in an assemblage.

To determine how serious a problem fragmentation is, a number of simple techniques exist that provide quantitative assessments of artifact fragmentation. The simplest index is calculated by dividing the number of broken fragments and flaked pieces by the number of complete artifacts. A more sophisticated measure of fragmentation is obtained by dividing the number of broken fragments and flaked pieces by Hiscock's (2002b) MNF or MNA statistics. A measure of information loss, on the other hand, can be calculated by dividing the total number of fragments from which little or no technological information can be derived (such as surface fragments, marginal fragments, flaked pieces, and longitudinally and transversely broken fragments) by those that provide a great deal more technological information (such as proximal, medial, distal, right, and left fragments). These two techniques can be particularly useful in assessing the severity of attritional processes and their effects on the information potential of a site.

This dilemma is quite common in archaeology and was central to the long-running naturefact/artifact debate, in which claims were made for very old but dubious artifacts (Schnurrenberger & Bryan 1985; Peacock 1991). Pseudo-artifacts (often called *eoliths* or *geofacts*) can result from a host of natural processes, such as "natural soil movements, glaciation, wave action, high velocity water movement, gravity (such as alluvial fans or steep inclines), rapid temperature changes, internal pressure (such as starch fractures and pot lids), exfoliation, tectonic movements, diastrophism, solifluction, foot trampling, and other unintentional activity caused by nature" (Crabtree 1972b: 78). As well as the difficulties faced in differentiating natural fractures from artifacts, certain types of stone, such as vein quartz, fracture in such a way that identification of artifacts becomes difficult. Weathering of artifact surfaces can also have severe effects on assemblages and can obscure or obliterate the diagnostic features of stone artifacts (Hiscock 2002b: 251).

In cases in which natural fracture is common, or stone type or weathering renders artifacts difficult to distinguish from nonartifactual rocks, it may be helpful to try to determine the presence or absence of the fracture features identified above for each specimen, as well as those for grinding or pecking. Peacock's (1991) analysis of natural and artifactual stone assemblages found many of these features to be reliable indicators of human manufacture. The compilation of lists of fracture features for each piece will enable the ranking of specimens in degrees of certainty (i.e., number of features present), with the aim of rejecting those lower in the rank order and accepting those higher up. Additionally, certain fracture features tend to occur more commonly among

What should you do if you can't tell artifacts from natural rocks?

naturally fractured pieces (due to the type and magnitude of forces) than among humanly derived assemblages (such as obtuse platform angles, edge rounding, and micro-edge and -ridge fracturing) (see Schnurrenberger & Bryan 1985, fig. 5.1, table 5.1). The context of finds also provides a key to whether or not artifacts would be expected in a given location (e.g., rockshelters and middens versus graded tracks and garden beds).

What if you only have a small number of stone artifacts? Sample size can have a profound effect on the sorts of information retrieved from an assemblage, and sampling is therefore a key issue in understanding stone artifact assemblage patterning through time and space. The probability of drawing a representative sample of the original population drops dramatically as sample size decreases, and this is particularly true in lithic assemblages, where many objects of interest, such as retouched flakes, tend to be rare (i.e., less than 5 percent of the assemblage) and therefore unlikely to turn up in small samples. The diversity of an assemblage – or the number of different elements found in the assemblage – is also sensitive to assemblage size, as the number of assemblage elements present cannot exceed the number of artifacts in the assemblage, and hence small assemblages will always have low diversity. It is therefore generally worthwhile enlarging the sample at the expense of other components of the research (e.g., number of attributes recorded) in order to obtain a representative sample of the parent assemblage.

How can you overcome sample size effects? Unfortunately, there is no magic minimum number that will always overcome sample size effects, as every assemblage or region is likely to be different. The only general rule as far as stone artifacts are concerned is likely to be "more is better" (within practical limits, of course). It is possible to determine something like a minimum sample size for each assemblage, however, by studying the effects of increasing sample size by repeatedly drawing random samples from a large assemblage and examining the variation and deviations in percentages of classes, mean characteristics, and so on between each sample and the parent assemblage. Of course, this can defeat the purpose, since a large sample must already have been collected in order to perform such a test, although it may be helpful in determining minimum sample sizes that should ideally be obtained from sites within a region or survey area.

A number of assemblage descriptions are immune to sample size effects. Assemblage richness, for example, provides a measure of assemblage composition that is not affected by sample size, and mathematically determines the number of classes that are expected to occur for a given sample size (Leonard & Jones 1989). Assemblage richness is calculated by dividing assemblage diversity, however measured (e.g., raw materials, or classes), by sample size. Differences in assemblage richness between populations can be determined by plotting diversity against sample size (using a scatterplot) and comparing the gradients of slope for each population (higher gradients mean richer assemblages). Richness therefore provides a more robust comparative measure of assemblage

CHRIS CLARKSON AND SUE O'CONNOR

complexity than does diversity. Assemblage richness also has real interpretive applications. For instance, archaeologists often interpret differences in the richness of raw materials and assemblage elements as a reflection of the range and diversity of activities carried out at a site (Binford 1979; Shott 1989).

Theoretically, it is possible to determine how large a sample is needed before all classes recognized in an analysis will be present in an assemblage (or even a number of each class), by increasing sample size until the line of best fit flattens out, such that further increases in assemblage size no longer yield new classes. Obviously, the number of classes used in the analysis will affect the point at which this takes place. Such a technique could be used, say, to identify the ideal sample size to be recovered from a site threatened with destruction.

Archaeology increasingly draws on specialist information from fields outside of its own core knowledge and practice, and the incorporation of such technical analyses (usually involving measurement), particularly from the physical sciences – often called archaeometry – can play a vital role in stone artifact analyses. Common examples of applications include the use of geochemical or elemental analyses to identify stone types, their age, origins, and alterations to the composition of artifacts due to time, weathering, and heat.

> When do you need specialist archaeometric analyses?

While the range of materials used to make stone artifacts often tends to be fairly limited (depending on local geology), the ability to differentiate reliably between materials depends on a combination of expertise and experience, and archaeologists should solicit the help of geologists for identification of all but the most common types. A useful first step in identifying the range of raw materials in an assemblage is to consult a geological map of the region. Unfortunately, geological maps are rarely drawn at the scale that archaeologists desire, and usually do not pinpoint small sources of flakable stone. A second step might involve sorting artifacts into broad material categories (based on texture, grain size, and color). Without significant experience in stone identification, a next step would be to take a sample of the various types to a geologist for identification. Once materials have been identified, it is often useful to know the original size in which they were available and their shape and original cortex, as this may influence the types of reduction strategies used. Often, archaeologists tackle these questions by looking for cores at earlier stages of reduction, to determine the size, shape, and nature of cortex for each raw material type.

> Determining the type and flaking properties of stone
>
> *How do you identify different raw material types?*

The ethnographic literature often points to a range of cultural factors that determined the types of stones selected to make various implements, and these were often strongly influenced by associations with ancestral beings, totemic affiliations, or powerful substances (Gould 1968; Jones & White 1988; Taçon 1991). In the absence of information about social and ritual value,

> *How do you determine whether it is good- or poor-quality stone?*

however, archaeologists often look to observable measures of the properties of stone that might have influenced the choices of prehistoric knappers. These might help to quantify the ease with which stone fractures, how well it holds its fracture path, its suitability for particular functions, or its durability. The quality of raw materials has also been given prominence in modeling raw material selection in times and places where greater demands are placed on toolkit performance (Goodyear 1989). Materials testing laboratories offer a number of tests that can be useful in determining how suited certain materials are to conchoidal fracture. These include tests of tensile strength, compressive strength, elasticity, and hardness.

Sourcing stone artifacts

Why is sourcing important?

Sources of stone with good flaking qualities are not evenly distributed in the landscape and were often so highly valued that they were exchanged over many hundreds of miles. Sourcing stone artifacts from archaeological sites can therefore provide insights into past exchange networks or interaction spheres, changes in territoriality, or changing access to stone resources.

How do you find out which source an artifact came from?

Sourcing analysis is to some extent a misnomer because, as Shackley (1998b: 261) points out, "nothing is ever really 'sourced'. The best we can do is provide a probable fit to known source data." How good this fit is will depend on how good the source data are, which in turn will rely on the location and sampling of potential sources. If no source localities have been mapped or sampled, archaeologists may have to do the field source sampling of geological outcrops themselves. Luedtke (1992) and Shackley (1998b: 262) outline useful hierarchical procedural guidelines for the archaeologist embarking on an artifact sourcing study.

In the past, sourcing proceeded by visual inspection and comparison of stone artifacts and samples of stone from potential sources, either in the form of hand specimens or using microscopic characterization of the structure and texture of ground thin sections mounted on slides. Today, archaeologists routinely use chemical composition analyses such as *X-ray fluorescence spectrometry* (XRF), *neutron activation analysis* (NAA or INAA), *inductively coupled plasma–atomic emission spectrometry* (ICP–AES), and *proton-induced X-ray – proton-induced gamma ray emission* (PIXE/PIGME). Quantitative statistical analyses are then used to determine the best fit from the results of each analysis. While in some respects this eliminates qualitative assessments and allows vast numbers of specimens to be analyzed, sourcing studies will still only be as good as the field sampling that underpins them.

What is an adequate sample?

In order to have confidence in the match of artifact to source, it is necessary to have an adequate sample of reference material from potential source locations as well as an adequate sample of the artifacts from the archaeological assemblage with which to compare against the reference material. In theory, the

CHRIS CLARKSON AND SUE O'CONNOR

more homogeneous the material, the smaller is the sample size that should be necessary to be confident that a representative sample has been obtained. Conversely, the greater the heterogeneity of a geological outcrop, the larger is the sample size required to obtain an accurate representation of its variability. While obsidian is relatively homogeneous, cherts and other secondary siliceous sediments can be extremely heterogeneous even within a single small outcrop. When undertaking field sampling, it is also necessary to keep in mind that secondary depositional contexts (such as stream beds and moraines) may have been equally important sources of stone as primary geological sources (such as quarries), and that to ignore them in field sampling can result in serious misassignments (Shackley 1998a: 6). These in turn may result in major interpretive errors where stone from an archaeological site is argued to have been traded or exchanged when in fact the raw material could have been derived from a secondary source close to the site.

Conclusion

Material culture, technology, and technological strategies were vital in the operation of all cultural and social processes in the past. For much of human history, stone artifacts constitute a large part of the record of what humans accomplished, how they behaved, and how they interacted with one another. Happily, archaeology now seems set on investing a great deal more effort into rethinking and advancing lithic studies. Many old and current debates require the development of new analytical frameworks for their resolution and these are also likely to be aided by new advances in archaeometry. New practitioners in lithic studies will witness and take part in the development of new applications that will engage with disciplinary theory to an unprecedented degree. This chapter has attempted to provide a glimpse of the range of approaches employed in the subject today, and a baseline from which you may begin to explore the diversity of stone artifact analysis for yourselves.

Acknowledgments

The authors would like to thank Brit Asmussen for early comments on the structure of this chapter, Peter Hiscock, Sophie Collins, and Oliver Macgregor for their helpful advice on later drafts, and Wal Ambrose for advice on recent advances in archaeometry. Navin Officer Heritage Consultants are thanked for access to the assemblages used in our case studies.

References

Ahler, S. A. 1989: Mass analysis of flaking debris: studying the forest rather than the trees. In D. O. Henry and G. H. Odell (eds.), *Alternative Approaches to Lithic Analysis*. Archaeological Papers of the American Anthropological Association, 1, 85–118.

Akerman, K. and Bindon, P. 1995: Dentate and related stone biface points from northern Australia. *The Beagle*, 12, 89–99.

Andrefsky, W. 1998: *Lithics – Macroscopic Approaches to Analysis*. Cambridge: Cambridge University Press.

Austin, R. J. 1997: Technological characterization of lithic waste-flake assemblages: multivariate analysis of experimental and archaeological data. *Lithic Technology*, 24, 53–68.

Bailey, K. D. 1994: *Typologies and Taxonomies: An Introduction to Classification Techniques*. California: Sage.

Bamforth, D. B. and Bleed, P. 1997: Technology, flaked stone technology, and risk. In C. M. Barton and G. A. Clark (eds.), *Rediscovering Darwin: Evolutionary Theory in Archaeology*. Archaeological Papers of the American Anthropological Association, no. 7. Washington, DC: American Anthropological Association, 109–40.

Barton, C. M. 1988: *Lithic Variability and Middle Paleolithic Behavior: New Evidence from the Iberian Peninsula*. BAR International Series, S408. Oxford: British Archaeological Reports.

Baulmer, M. F. and Downum, C. E. 1989: Between micro and macro: a study in the interpretation of small-sized lithic debitage. In D. S. Amick and R. P. Mauldin (eds.), *Experiments in Lithic Technology*. Oxford: British Archaeological Reports, 110–16.

Binford, L. R. 1979: Organizational and formation processes: looking at curated technologies. *Journal of Anthropological Research*, 35, 255–73.

Bleed, P. 1997: Content as variability, result as selection: toward a behavioral definition of technology. In G. A. Clark and C. M. Barton (eds.), *Rediscovering Darwin: Evolutionary Theory in Archaeology*. Archaeological Papers of the American Anthropological Association, no. 7. Washington, DC: American Anthropological Association, 95–104.

—— 2001: Trees or chains, links or branches: conceptual alternatives for consideration of stone tool production and other sequential activities. *Journal of Archaeological Method and Theory*, 8(1), 101–27.

Bordes, F. 1972: *A Tale of Two Caves*. New York: Harper and Row.

Bradbury, A. P. 1998: The examination of lithic artifacts from an Early Archaic assemblage: strengthening inferences through multiple lines of evidence. *Midcontinental Journal of Archaeology*, 23, 263–88.

—— and Carr, P. J. 1999: Examining stage and continuum models of flake debris analysis: an experimental approach. *Journal of Archaeological Science*, 26, 105–16.

Brantingham, P. J. 2003: A neutral model of stone raw material procurement. *American Antiquity*, 68(3), 487–509.

Bright, J., Ugan, A. and Hunskar, L. 2002: The effect of handling time on subsistence technology. *World Archaeology*, 34(1), 164–81.

Clarkson, C. 2002a: Holocene scraper reduction, technological organization and landuse at Ingaladdi Rockshelter, Northern Australia. *Archaeology in Oceania*, 37(2), 79–86.

—— 2002b: An index of invasiveness for the measurement of unifacial and bifacial retouch: a theoretical, experimental and archaeological verification. *Journal of Archaeological Science*, 29, 65–75.

—— 2005: Tenuous types: "scraper" reduction continuums in Wardaman Country, northern Australia. In C. Clarkson and L. Lamb (eds.), *Rocking the Boat: New Approaches to Stone Artifact Reduction, Use and Classification in Australia*. British Archaeological Reports International Monograph Series. Oxford: Archaeopress, forthcoming.

—— and David, B. 1995: The antiquity of blades and points revisited: investigating the emergence of systematic blade production south-west of Arnhem Land, northern Australia. *The Artefact*, 18, 22–44.

Cotterell, B. and Kamminga, J. 1977: The mechanics of flaking. In B. Hayden (ed.), *Lithic Use-Wear Analysis*. New York: Academic Press, 97–112.

—— and —— 1987: The formation of flakes. *American Antiquity*, 52(4), 675–708.

Crabtree, D. E. 1968: Mesoamerican polyhedral cores and prismatic blades. *American Antiquity*, 33, 446–78.

—— 1972a: The cone fracture principle and the manufacture of lithic materials. *Tebiwa*, 15, 29–42.

—— 1972b: *An Introduction to Flintworking*. Occasional Papers of the Idaho State University Museum. Idaho: Idaho State University Museum.

—— and Butler, B. R. 1964: Notes on experiments in flintknapping: 1. Heat treatment of silica materials. *Tebiwa*, 7(1), 1–6.

Dibble, H. 1995: Middle Paleolithic scraper reduction: background, clarification, and review of evidence to date. *Journal of Archaeological Method and Theory*, 2(4), 299–368.

—— 1997: Platform variability and flake morphology: a comparison of experimental and archaeological data and implications for interpreting prehistoric lithic technological strategies. *Lithic Technology*, 22(2), 150–70.

—— and Pelcin, A. 1995: The effect of hammer mass and velocity on flake mass. *Journal of Archaeological Science*, 22, 429–39.

—— and Whittaker, J. 1981: New experimental evidence on the relation between percussion flaking and flake variation. *Journal of Archaeological Science*, 6, 283–96.

Dobres, M.-A. 1995: Gender and prehistoric technology. *World Archaeology*, 27(1), 25–49.

—— 2000: *Technology and Social Agency*. Oxford: Blackwell.

Drennan, R. D. 1996: *Statistics for Archaeologists: A Commonsense Approach*. New York: Plenum Press.

Dunnell, R. C. 1971: *Systematics in Prehistory*. New York: The Free Press.

—— 1986: Methodological issues in Americanist artifact classification. In M. B. Schiffer (ed.), *Advances in Archaeological Method and Theory*. New York: Academic Press, 35–99.

Ericson, J. E. and Earle, T. K. 1982: *Contexts for Prehistoric Exchange*. New York: Academic Press.

Flenniken, J. J. and Haggarty, J. 1979: Trampling as an agency in the formation of edge damage: an experiment in lithic technology. *Northwest Anthropological Research Notes*, 13, 208–14.

—— and White, J. P. 1983: Heat treatment of siliceous rocks and its implications for Australian prehistory. *Australian Aboriginal Studies*, 1983(1), 43–8.

Geneste, J. M. 1990: Dévelopment des systèmes de production lithique au cours de Paléolithique moyen en Aquitaine septentrionale. In C. Farizy (ed.), *Paléolithique moyen recent et Paléolithique supérieur ancien en Europe*. Nemours: Mémoirs de Musée d'Ile de France 3, 203–14.

Gero, J. M. 1991: Genderlithics: women's roles in stone tool production. In J. M. Gero (ed.), *Engendering Archaeology: Women in Prehistory*. Oxford: Blackwell, 163–93.

Goodyear, A. C. 1989: A hypothesis for the use of crypto-crystalline raw materials among Paleoindian groups of North America. In C. G. Ellis and J. C. Lothrop (eds.), *Eastern Paleoindian Lithic Resource Use*. Boulder, CO: Westview Press, 1–9.

Gordon, D. 1993: Mousterian tool selection, reduction, and discard at Ghar, Israel. *Journal of Field Archaeology*, 20(2), 205–18.

Gould, R. A. 1968: Chipping stones in the outback. *Natural History*, 77(2), 42–8.

Hall, J. and Love, W. 1985: Prickly Bush, a site with backed blades on the Brisbane River: a pilot study towards the measurement of site "disturbance." *Queensland Archaeological Research*, 2, 71–81.

Harrison, R. 2002: Archaeology and the colonial encounter, Kimberley spearpoints, cultural identity and masculinity in the north of Australia. *Journal of Social Archaeology*, 2(3), 352–77.

Hayden, B. 1979: *Paleolithic Reflections: Lithic Technology and Ethnographic Excavations among Australian Aborigines*. Canberra: Australian Institute of Aboriginal Studies.

—— and Hutchings, W. K. 1989: Whither the billet flake? In D. S. Amick and R. P. Mauldin (eds.), *Experiments in Lithic Technology*. Oxford: British Archaeological Reports, 235–57.

——, Franco, N. and Spafford, J. 1996: Evaluating lithic strategies and design criteria. In G. H. Odell (ed.), *Stone Tools: Theoretical Insights into Human Prehistory*. New York: Plenum Press, 9–50.

Hill, J. N. and Evans, R. K. 1972: A model for classification and typology. In D. L. Clarke (ed.), *Models in Archaeology*. London: Methuen, 231–74.

Hiscock, P. 1982: A technological analysis of quartz assemblages from the south coast. In S. Bowdler (ed.), *Coastal Archaeology in Eastern Australia*. Canberra: Department of Prehistory, Research School of Pacific and Asian Studies, Australian National University, 32–45.

—— 1985: The need for a taphonomic perspective in stone artefact analysis. *Queensland Archaeological Research*, 2, 82–95.

—— 1996: Mobility and technology in the Kakadu coastal wetlands. *Bulletin of the Indo-Pacific Prehistory Association*, 15, 151–7.

—— 2002a: Pattern and context in the Holocene proliferation of backed artefacts in Australia. In R. G. Elston and S. L. Kuhn (eds.), *Thinking Small: Global Perspectives on Microlithization*. Archaeological Papers of the American Anthropological Association (AP3A) no. 12, 163–77.

—— 2002b: Quantifying the size of artefact assemblages. *Journal of Archaeological Science*, 29(3), 251–8.

—— 2005: Looking the other way: a materialist/technological approach to classifying tools and implements, cores and retouched flakes, with examples from Australia. In S. McPherron and J. Lindley (eds.), *Tools or Cores? The Identification and Study of Alternative Core Technology in Lithic Assemblages*. Pennsylvania: University of Pennsylvania Museum, forthcoming.

—— and Attenbrow, V. 2002: Early Australian implement variation: a reduction model. *Journal of Archaeological Science*, 30(2), 239–49.

—— and —— 2003: Morphological and reduction continuums in eastern Australia: measurement and implications at Capertee 3. *Tempus*, 7, 167–74.

—— and —— 2005: Reduction continuums and tool use. In C. Clarkson and L. Lamb (eds.), *Rocking the Boat: Recent Australian Approaches to Lithic Reduction, Use and Classification*. British Archaeological Reports International Monograph Series. Oxford: Archaeopress, forthcoming.

—— and Clarkson, C. 2000: Analysing Australian stone artefacts: an agenda for the twenty first century. *Australian Archaeology*, 50(1), 98–108.

—— and —— 2005: Measuring artefact reduction – an examination of Kuhn's Geometric Index of Reduction. In C. Clarkson and L. Lamb (eds.), *Rocking the Boat: Recent Australian Approaches to Lithic Reduction, Use and Classification*. British Archaeological Reports International Monograph Series. Oxford: Archaeopress, forthcoming.

Holdaway, S., McPherron, S. and Roth, B. 1996: Notched tool reuse and raw material availability in French Middle Paleolithic sites. *American Antiquity*, 61, 377–87.

Ingold, T. 1990: Society, nature and the concept of technology. *Archaeological Review from Cambridge*, 9, 5–17.

Jeske, R. J. and Lurie, R. 1992: The archaeological visibility of bipolar technology: an example from the Koster site. *Midcontinental Journal of Archaeology*, 18, 131–60.

Jones, R. and White, N. 1988: Point blank: stone tool manufacture at the Ngilipitji Quarry, Arnhem Land, 1981. In R. Jones (ed.), *Archaeology with Ethnography: An Australian*

Perspective. Canberra: Department of Prehistory, Research School of Pacific Studies, Australian National University, 51–87.

Jung, S. 1992: Trample damage of stone flakes as an index of occupation intensity: a case study from Magnificent Gallery. *Queensland Archaeological Research*, 9, 26–8.

Kobayashi, H. 1985: The accidental breakage of backed blades. *Lithic Technology*, 14, 16–25.

Kooyman, B. P. 2000: *Understanding Stone Tools and Archaeological Sites*. Calgary: University of Calgary Press and University of New Mexico Press.

Kuhn, S. 1990: A geometric index of reduction for unifacial stone tools. *Journal of Archaeological Science*, 17, 585–93.

Kuhn, S. L. 1995: *Mousterian Lithic Technology*. Princeton: Princeton University Press.

Lamb, L. 2005: Backed and forth: an assessment of typological categories and technological continuums. A case study from the Whitsunday Islands, Central Queensland Coast. In C. Clarkson and L. Lamb (eds.), *Rocking the Boat: Recent Australian Approaches to Lithic Reduction, Use and Classification*. British Archaeological Reports International Monograph Series. Oxford: Archaeopress, forthcoming.

Law, W. B. 2005: Stone artefact reduction, mobility, and arid zone settlement models: a case study from Puritjarra Rockshelter. In C. Clarkson and L. Lamb (eds.), *Rocking the Boat: Recent Australian Approaches to Lithic Reduction, Use and Classification*. British Archaeological Reports International Monograph Series. Oxford: Archaeopress, forthcoming.

Lemonnier, P. 1986: The study of material culture today: toward an anthropology of technical systems. *Journal of Anthropological Archaeology*, 5, 147–86.

Leroi-Gourhan, A. 1964: *Le geste et la parole 1: technique et langage*. Paris: Albin Michal.

Leonard, R. D. and Jones, G. T. (eds.) 1989: *Quantifying Diversity in Archaeology*. Cambridge: Cambridge University Press.

Luedtke, B. E. 1992: *An Archaeologist's Guide to Chert and Flint*. Archaeological Research Tools, no. 7. Los Angeles: Institute of Archaeology, University of California.

Lyman, R. L. and O'Brien, M. J. 2000: Measuring and explaining change in artifact variation with clade-diversity diagrams. *Journal of Anthropological Archaeology*, 19, 39–74.

——, —— and Dunnel, R. C. 1997: *The Rise and Fall of Culture History*. New York: Plenum Press.

McCarthy, F. D., Brammell, E. and Noone, H. V. V. 1946: The stone implements of Australia. *Memoirs of the Australian Museum*, 9, 1–94.

Macgregor, O. 2005: Abrupt terminations and stone artefact reduction potential. In C. Clarkson and L. Lamb (eds.), *Rocking the Boat: Recent Australian Approaches to Lithic Reduction, Use and Classification*. British Archaeological Reports International Monograph Series. Oxford: Archaeopress, forthcoming.

Mallouf, R. J. 1982: An analysis of plow-damaged chert artifacts: the Brookeen Creek cache (41H186), Hill County, Texas. *Journal of Field Archaeology*, 9(1), 79–98.

Marcy, J. L. 1993: Aperçu sur les stratégies de producion des raclois du niveau. In *Riencourt-lès-Bapaume (Pas-de-Calais): un gisement du Paléolithique moyen*, dirigé par Alain Tuffreau. Éditions de la Maison des Sciences de l'Homme, coll. Documents d'Archéologie Française, no. 37, 87–94.

Meignen, L. 1988: Variabilité technologique au proche orient: l'exemple de Kebara. In J. P. Rigaud (ed.), *L'homme de Néandertal*. Liège: Université de Liège, 87–95.

Mewhinney, H. 1964: A skeptic views the billet flake. *American Antiquity*, 30, 203–5.

Morrow, T. A. 1997a: A chip off the old block: alternative approaches to debitage analysis. *Lithic Technology*, 22, 51–69.

—— 1997b: End scraper morphology and use-life: an approach for studying Paleoindian lithic technology and mobility. *Lithic Technology*, 22(1), 51–69.

Neeley, M. P. and Barton, C. M. 1994: A new approach to interpreting late Pleistocene microlith industries in southwest Asia. *Antiquity*, 68, 275–88.

Nelson, M. C. 1991: The study of technological organization. *Archaeological Method and Theory*, 3, 57–100.

Newcomer, M. H. 1975: "Punch technique" and Upper Paleolithic blades. In E. H. Swanson (ed.), *Lithic Technology: Making and Using Stone Tools*. The Hague: Mouton, 97–102.

—— and Karlin, C. 1987: Flint chips from Pincevent. In G. D. G. Sieveking and M. H. Newcomer (eds.), *The Human Uses of Flint and Chert: Proceedings of the Fourth International Flint Symposium, Held at Brighton Polytechnic, 10–15 April 1983*. Cambridge: Cambridge University Press, 33–6.

O'Brien, M. J. 1996: Evolutionary archaeology: an introduction. In M. J. O'Brien (ed.), *Evolutionary Archaeology: Theory and Application*. Salt Lake City: University of Utah Press, 1–15.

Odell, G. H. 1989: Experiments in lithic reduction. In D. S. Amick and R. P. Mauldin (eds.), *Experiments in Lithic Technology*. BAR International Series, 528. Oxford: British Archaeological Reports, 163–98.

—— 2000: Stone tool research at the end of the millennium: procurement and technology. *Journal of Archaeological Research*, 8(4), 269–331.

—— 2001a: Research questions R us. *American Antiquity*, 66(4), 679–85.

—— 2001b: Stone tool research at the end of the millennium: classification, function and behavior. *Journal of Archaeological Research*, 9(1), 45–100.

Patterson, L. W. 1982: Replication and classification of large sized lithic debitage. *Lithic Technology*, 11, 50–8.

—— 1990: Characteristics of bifacial-reduction flake-size distribution. *American Antiquity*, 55, 550–8.

—— and Sollberger, J. B. 1978: Replication and classification of small size lithic debitage. *Plains Anthropologist*, 23, 103–12.

Peacock, E. 1991: Distinguishing between artifacts and geofacts: a test case from Eastern England. *Journal of Field Archaeology*, 18(3), 345–61.

Pelcin, A. 1997a: The effect of core surface morphology on flake attributes: evidence from a controlled experiment. *Journal of Archaeological Science*, 24, 749–56.

—— 1997b: The effect of indentor type on flake attributes: evidence from a controlled experiment. *Journal of Archaeological Science*, 24, 613–21.

—— 1997c: The formation of flakes: the role of platform thickness and exterior platform angle in the production of flake initiations and terminations. *Journal of Archaeological Science*, 24, 1107–13.

—— 1998: The threshold effect of platform width: a reply to Davis and Shea. *Journal of Archaeological Science*, 25, 615–20.

Peterson, J., Mitchell, D. R. and Shackley, M. S. 1997: The social and economic contexts of lithic procurement: obsidian from Classic-period Hohokam sites. *American Antiquity*, 62, 231–59.

Pfaffenberger, B. 1992: Social anthropology of technology. *Annual Review of Anthropology*, 21, 491–516.

Phagan, C. J. 1985: Lithic technology: flake analysis. In R. MacNeish, A. Nelken-Terner, C. J. Phagan and R. Vierra (eds.), *Prehistory of the Ayacucho Basin, Peru*. Michigan: The University of Michigan Press, 233–81.

Prentiss, W. C. 1998: The reliability and validity of a lithic debitage typology: implications for archaeological interpretation. *American Antiquity*, 63(4), 635–50.

—— and Romanski, E. J. 1989: Experimental evaluation of Sullivan and Rosen's debitage typology. In D. S. Amick and R. P. Mauldin (eds.), *Experiments in Lithic Technology*. Oxford: British Archaeological Reports, 89–99.

Purdy, B. A. and Brooks, H. K. 1971: Thermal alteration of silica materials: an archaeological approach. *Science*, 173, 322–5.

Renfrew, C., Dixon, J. E. and Cann, J. R. 1968: Further analysis of Near Eastern obsidians. *Proceedings of the Prehistoric Society*, 34, 319–31.

Roebroeks, W., Kolen, J. and Rensink, E. 1988: Planning depth, anticipation and the organization of technology: the "archaic natives" meet Eve's descendants. *Helinium*, 28, 17–34.

Sassaman, K. E. 1992: Lithic technology and the hunter-gatherer sexual division of labor. *North American Archaeologist*, 13, 249–62.

Schiffer, M. B. and Skibo, J. M. 1997: The explanation of artifact variability. *American Antiquity*, 62, 27–50.

Schindler, D. L., Hatch, J. W., Hay, C. A. and Bradt, R. C. 1984: Thermal alteration of Bald Eagle jasper. *American Antiquity*, 49(1), 173–7.

Schnurrenberger, D. and Bryan, A. L. 1985: A contribution to the study of the naturefact/artifact controversy. In M. G. Plew, J. C. Woods and M. G. Pavesic (eds.), *Stone Tools Analysis: Essays in Honor of Don E. Crabtree*. Albuquerque: University of New Mexico, 133–59.

Sellet, F. 1993: *Chaîne opératoire*; the concept and its applications. *Lithic Technology*, 18(1), 106–12.

Shackley, M. S. 1998a: Current issues and future directions in archaeological volcanic glass studies. In M. S. Shackley (ed.), *Archaeological Obsidian Studies: Method and Theory*. New York: Plenum Press, 1–14.

—— 1998b: Gamma rays, X-rays and stone tools: some recent advances in archaeological geochemistry. *Journal of Archaeological Science*, 25, 259–70.

Shott, M. J. 1989: On tool-class use lives and the formation of archaeological assemblages. *American Antiquity*, 54, 9–30.

—— 1994: Size and form in the analysis of flake debris: review of recent approaches. *Journal of Archaeological Method and Theory*, 1, 69–110.

—— 1996: Stage versus continuum models in the debris assemblage from production of a fluted biface. *Lithic Technology*, 21(1), 6–22.

—— 2000: The quantification problem in stone-tool assemblages. *American Antiquity*, 65(4), 725–38.

——, Bradbury, A. P., Carr, P. J. and Odell, H. O. 2000: Flake size from platform attributes: predictive and empirical approaches. *Journal of Archaeological Science*, 27, 877–94.

Sinclair, A. 1995: The technique as symbol in late glacial Europe. *World Archaeology*, 27(1), 50–62.

—— 2000: Constellations of knowledge: human agency and material affordance in lithic technology. In M.-A. Dobres and J. Robb (eds.), *Agency in Archaeology*. London: Routledge, 197–212.

Spaulding, W. G. 1953: Statistical techniques for the discovery of artifact types. *American Antiquity*, 18, 305–13.

Specht, J. 2002: Obsidian, colonising and exchange. In S. Bedford, C. Sand and D. Burley (eds.), *Fifty Years in the Field. Essays in Honour and Celebration of Richard Shutler Jr's Archaeological Career*. Monograph 25. Auckland: New Zealand Archaeological Association, 37–50.

Speth, J. D. 1972: Mechanical basis of percussion flaking. *American Antiquity*, 37, 34–60.

—— 1974: Experimental investigations of hard-hammer percussion flaking. *Tebiwa*, 17, 7–36.

—— 1981: The role of platform angle and core size in hard-hammer percussion flaking. *Lithic Technology*, 10(1), 16–21.

Stahle, D. W. and Dunn, J. E. 1984: An analysis and application of the size distribution of waste flakes from the manufacture of bifacial stone tools. *World Archaeology*, 14, 84–97.

Steffen, A., Skinner, E. J. and Ainsworth, P. W. 1998: A view to the core: technological units and debitage analysis. In A. Ramenofsky and A. Steffen (eds.), *Unit Issues in Archaeology*. Salt Lake City: University of Utah Press, 131–46.

Sullivan, A. P. and Rozen, K. C. 1985: Debitage analysis and archaeological interpretation. *American Antiquity*, 50, 755–79.

Taçon, P. S. C. 1991: The power of stone: symbolic aspects of stone use and tool development in western Arnhem Land, Australia. *Antiquity*, 65, 192–207.

Torrence, R. 1986: *Production and Exchange of Stone Tools: Prehistoric Obsidian in the Aegean*. Cambridge: Cambridge University Press.

—— 1989: Re-tooling: towards a behavioral theory of stone tools. In R. Torrence (ed.), *Time, Energy and Stone Tools*. Cambridge: Cambridge University Press, 57–66.

—— and Summerhayes, G. 1997: Sociality and the short distance trader: Inter-regional obsidian exchange in the Willaumez Peninsula region, Papua New Guinea. *Archaeology in Oceania*, 32(1), 74–8.

Touhy, D. R. 1987: A comparison of pressure and percussion debitage from a Crabtree obsidian stoneworking demonstration. *Tebiwa*, 23, 23–30.

Ugan, A., Bright, J. and Rogers, A. 2003: When is technology worth the trouble? *Journal of Archaeological Science*, 30, 1315–29.

van der Leeuw, S. E. and Torrence, R. 1989: *What's New? A Closer Look at the Process of Innovation*. London: Unwin Hyman.

Walthall, J. A. and Holley, G. R. 1997: Mobility and hunter–gatherer toolkit design: analysis of a Dalton lithic cache. *Southeastern Archaeology*, 16, 152–62.

White, J. P. and O'Connell, J. F. 1982: *A Prehistory of Australia, New Guinea and Sahul*. Sydney: Academic Press.

Whittaker, J. 1994: *Flintknapping: Making and Understanding Stone Tools*. Austin: University of Texas Press.

Wurz, S. 1999: The Howiesons Poort backed artefacts from Klaises River: an argument for symbolic behavior. *South African Archaeological Bulletin*, 169, 38–50.

Yvorra, P. 2000: *Exploitation de l'analyse quantitative des retouches pour la caractérisation des industries lithiques du Moustérien: application au faciès Quina de la vallée du Rhône*. BAR International Series, no. 869. Oxford: British Archaeological Reports.

Zeitlin, R. N. 1982: Toward a more comprehensive model of interregional commodity distribution: political variables and prehistoric obsidian procurement in Mesoamerica. *American Antiquity*, 47, 260–75.

Richard Fullagar

7
Residues and Usewear

Introduction

The form or shape of an artifact can tell us only so much about how it functioned in the past. In this chapter, we look at microscopic observations and other techniques that archaeologists employ to determine the function of things. Our primary interest is in the context and use of tools, but this is rarely an end in itself. Tools can potentially tell us about subsistence history, plant food preparation, craft production, weaponry, and other technologies. The determination of function is a fundamental step, but context is always important. Whether or not they are actually used for cooking or storage, ceramic pots or bronze jars can have stylized forms, decoration, and a ceremonial purpose. Intention may be difficult to reconstruct, but it is also an important element of functional analysis. Not even stone tools function in a world devoid of social meaning (Edmonds 1995), but with a handle on function we can better understand other influences on artifact variability (such as personal, stylistic, and other constraints).

Implements are not only identified by signs of utilization, but sometimes by observed use, ethnography, patterned production, purposeful shape, or design (see Kamminga 1985). Nor do they have to be actually made by people (as implied by the Latin root of the word "artifact"). A stick thrown at a dog is a kind of artifact. Ethnographic studies show that some manufactured tools have no purposeful or planned shape, and sustain no clear macroscopic traces of use, despite intensive work (White & Thomas 1972; Hayden 1977). The by-products of implement manufacture (stone axe production, for example) can also be used as expedient tools (Burton 1989).

The best way to reconstruct the function of prehistoric implements is to study traces on the tool surfaces themselves. Examples in this chapter come from the study of stone artifacts and pottery, because they have been studied extensively. Similar methods are employed to interpret functional traces on other types of artifact, such as cut marks on human and other bones (e.g., Potts & Shipman 1981), manufacturing marks on wood chips (e.g., Coutts 1977), or cracks on seeds (Beck et al. 1988).

In this chapter we consider two main functional traces: *residues* and *usewear*. *Residues* refer to materials that are transferred and adhere to an artifact (Briuer 1976; Evershed et al. 1992; Loy 1994; Pollard & Heron 1996). Of particular interest is the transfer of residues during use, but some residues are unrelated to use, and reflect incidental contact, burial processes, or even modern contaminants (Fankhauser 1993a). Certain residues can survive on artifacts for millions of years, and the techniques of residue analysis are broadly applicable to all archaeological objects, although methods of extraction may differ.

Usewear (or "use-wear") refers to the wear on the edges and surfaces of an implement (Hayden 1979a). *Microwear* sometimes refers to an approach that employs microscopes usually at high magnification, and especially (but not exclusively) to observe and interpret polishes on stone tools (see below). *Traceology* is a term that may refer to study of any traces (whether residues or surface alterations) but usually in the context of tool use, and can be synonymous with microwear (see Vaughan & Hopert 1982–3; Plisson et al. 1988). All of these terms refer to surface modifications during use, hafting, handling, and storage (see Hayden 1979a). Some forms of usewear may incorporate or absorb residues within surface layers, providing a mixture of additive residue and usewear traces. The general principles of usewear analysis are applicable to all material classes (including artifacts made of wood, bone, stone, and metal), but specific methods and interpretive rules have been developed for particular raw materials.

Functional Analysis

There are distinctive types of usewear and residues, and in some instances a single trace on its own may be diagnostic of tool use, but the most robust approach to functional analysis is to systematically document all the main forms of usewear and residues on any one artifact.

It is important to emphasize that some traces are not related to use. Imagine the life history of an arrowhead from the time the stone was quarried, through production, use, breakage, recycling, discard, and burial. Many organic and inorganic compounds are transferred to tool surfaces, although the finished arrow may be set aside for exchange, and never actually used as a functional weapon (Akerman et al. 2002). Additionally, conditions of poor preservation can prevent survival of residues, and weathering can distort or remove usewear. Which artifacts in an assemblage warrant a closer look, and how many should be analyzed? The answer depends on the archaeological questions, but at least three levels of analysis are common:

- determining the function of a particular tool or tool type
- assessing site function and the range of activities undertaken at particular places
- evaluating theory and archaeological explanations of cultural change and stability.

RICHARD FULLAGAR

Tool function may indicate important aspects of human behavior in the context of evolution or prehistory. For example, certain classes of implement, such as the early nut-cracking stones identified by Goren-Inbar et al. (2002), may be indicative of surprisingly sophisticated food-processing techniques. A similar kind of question might be the function of pottery vessels (Evershed & Tuross 1996): Were they used for cooking or decorative display? It is possible to determine what food was cooked by analyzing residues adhering to pots (e.g., Patrick et al. 1985; Hurst et al. 2002) and prehistoric oven stones (Fankhauser 1993b, 1994), or from the abrasive wear on pottery (Reid & Young 2000)?

The comparison of lithic assemblages within a region permits reconstruction of on-site activities and evaluation of settlement models through time. Some studies, such as Jensen (1994), focus on particular resources – in this case plant working in eastern European sites. Odell (1995) integrated functional analyses in the Illinois Valley, United States, with hypotheses about economizing behaviors, symbolizing behavior, and site usage. For example, he evaluated predicted responses to curation and mobility by analyzing traces indicative of *holding* (manual prehension) or *hafting* (Odell 1996). In West New Britain, Papua New Guinea, Fullagar (1992) identified a trend toward more diverse on-site activities with more plant food processing. Similar regional studies have been undertaken in many parts of the world (see Sinha & Glover 1984; Rots & Vermeersch 2000; Dockall 2001; Nami 2001; Dendarsky 2002; Lammers-Keijsers 2002).

Usewear and residue studies can provide a test for theory. For example, Backwell and d'Errico (2001) showed that usewear on bone points is consistent with digging out a meal of grass-eating termites and could better account for the dietary carbon ratios in early hominid bones, previously thought to indicate high meat diet and male provisioning (O'Connell et al. 2002). Similarly, Fullagar and Field (1997) argued that 30,000-year-old seed-grinders from the Australian arid zone margins were consistent with theoretical predictions of Edwards and O'Connell (1995), relating dietary shifts to climatic change and resource availability.

Methodology, Experiments, and Procedures

Usewear and residue analysis aims to be an experimental science that draws on controlled experiments, replicative experiments, and ethnography to reconstruct prehistoric tasks. Experiments with known variables determine the typical patterns that form the basis of archaeological interpretation. An advantage of this approach is that the techniques depend upon a set of safe uniformities rather than problematic ethnographic analogies (Salmon 1982: 80). However, it remains difficult (and undesirable) to avoid ethnographic information when structuring experiments and interpreting residues and usewear.

Semenov (1964) undertook the first large systematic experimental study of stone tools to interpret archaeological artifacts, and advocated follow-up experiments to replicate how particular tools were used. During the 1970s and early 1980s, important doctoral studies (including Odell 1979; Anderson 1980; Keeley 1980; Kamminga 1982; Vaughan 1985; Beyries 1987) and an international conference (Hayden 1979a) revitalized interest in the field. Experimental data sets have been specifically compiled for less common stone materials, including obsidian (Hurcombe 1992), basalt (Richards 1988), and quartz (Knutsson 1988).

Experiments provide a useful first step for students, and can be designed to gain familiarity with particular tool materials, prehistoric resources, and microscopes (see below). For example, proposed research on coastal middens may prompt experiments on likely tool use in the past: fish processing, bone and shell working, and the use of available timbers. Experimental tools should be first examined microscopically at low magnification. This preliminary work familiarizes researchers with microscopes, tool materials, wear patterns, and residues. Experimental observations are vital because residues and usewear associated with particular tasks may not be adequately described in the literature.

---

1   What to look for first? Which microscope? Should the artifacts be cleaned of loose dirt? When a collection arrives in the laboratory, it is useful to scan each object in a systematic way.

2   Examine the artifact macroscopically, and scan or sketch the ventral and dorsal sides in pencil. Note raw material and cross-section.

3   Examine with a stereomicroscope at ×10–×50 magnifications, with external oblique light. Adjust the sketch, and note aspects of preservation, sediment, and other adhering material.

4   Document used edges, edge shapes, forms of residues (note resin, films, plant tissue, hairs, and other visible structures) and usewear (note scarring types, striations, edge rounding, polish, smoothing, and beveling).

5   Determine whether the artifact needs cleaning in order to see edges more clearly.

6   Clean loosely adhering sediment by: gently rubbing inside plastic bags; brushing; or, if necessary, by partial immersion of specific edges in disposable nylon containers (weighing boats), half-filled with distilled water – the container may be floated in a sonic bath for about 30 seconds. Some residues are likely to remain intact on the tool, but what has been removed can then be stored in small, capped tubes.

7   The residue can then be removed from the tubes by pipette, and delivered to glass slides for transmitted-light microscopy.

8   Residues (particles, films, and structures) can also be observed and documented at high magnifications.

9   Note the distribution of residues and usewear. Check edges and inner surfaces.

10 Residues from particular locations can be removed by pipette. The extracted residue can be analyzed in a variety of ways (see below) or simply mounted on a glass slide for more detailed study.

11 Document the residues on microscope slides.

12 The artifact edges may need further cleaning. Various solutions of alcohol, acids, and bases have been suggested for routine removal of organic and inorganic traces that may obscure observations of the tool surface.

13 The tool edges and surfaces can then be studied under an incident-light compound microscope at magnifications up to ×1000.

14 Document usewear (scarring types, striations, edge rounding, polish, smoothing, or beveling) and check for hafting or holding wear.

Figure 7.1   A procedure for looking at stone tools.

RICHARD FULLAGAR

A common second step is to consider and develop appropriate collection and handling procedures for particular archaeological materials. The artifacts to be analyzed may have been excavated without any plan for functional analysis, or artifacts may have been carefully recovered in the field, bagged

---

USEWEAR AND RESIDUE ANALYSIS

BASIC DESCRIPTION
Site name: field name   **Institutional site code:**

Museum catalog number: unique ID for museum artifact

M number: unique ID for archaeological artifact   **Label details:**

Location of collection: artifacts are stored

Experiment: unique ID for experimental artifact notes

Recorder: name of analyst   **Date:**

Photographs: refer to film catalog and to frames as per sketch

Raw material: stone type, color   **Cortex:** in %

Technological class: flake, core   **Reduction stage:** if identified

Morphological type: recognized type – e.g., backed blade, elouera

Manufacture damage: platform preparation   **Other damage:** e.g., break

Weight: **Length:**   **Width:**   **Thickness:**

Microscopes used and magnifications: e.g., stereo, metallographic, transmitted light, scanning electron microscope

RESIDUES
Color: **Structures:**   **Striations:**

Extent: **Material worked:** interpretation (e.g., plant tissue)   **Confidence:** three levels (e.g., high)

Tests: for starch, hemoglobin, cellulose, etc.

POLISH AND ABRASIVE SMOOTHING
Stage: **Texture:**   **Extent:**   **Pitting:**

Striations: **Material worked:** interpretation

Confidence: three levels   **Location** (see sketch): bifacial?

NOTES: compare unaltered surfaces, edge stability, etc.

Figure 7.2   A sample of a usewear and residue recording sheet.

FRACTURES/SCAR TYPES

Indicate frequency and size estimates. Note bending initiations.

Bending:	**Step:**
Feather:	**Cleft:**
Hinge:	**Bipolar:**

RETOUCH
Extent: Location: Range of scar sizes:

STRIATIONS
Extent: Orientation: **Morphology:** shape and cross-section

Length: Width: Depth:

ROUNDING
Extent: indicate degree of rounding

BEVELING
Extent:

EDGE SHAPE sketch three views; indicate straight, irregular, concave, and convex edges

Plan view: End view: Cross-sectional view:

UTILIZED EDGE LENGTH:

MODE OF USE: transverse/perpendicular   **DEGREE OF USE:**

HAFTING: indicate evidence   **USE BREAKAGE:**
HOLDING:

USED: four levels – unused, possible use, probable use, definite use

SKETCH: dorsal and bulbar surfaces; indicate location of use traces and photographs

Figure 7.2   *(cont'd)*

individually, and all made ready for the microscope. Ethno-archaeological collections have also been targeted for analysis (Miller 1979; Fullagar et al. 1999 [1992]). After undertaking introductory experiments and selecting appropriate archaeological collections, the next step is often to develop a standard analytical procedure (Figure 7.1) and recording sheet (Figure 7.2). This is important because it ensures that artifacts are recorded in a comparable way.

It is usual to look for residues first, because they are more susceptible than usewear to degradation or loss from inappropriate handling, washing, or brushing (Figure 7.1). It is best to begin with macroscopic and low-magnification observations under a microscope with an external light source (see the next section, "Microscopes"). Next, residues are observed under an incident-light microscope with high magnification, before removing samples for transmitted-light microscopy. Particles can be removed with forceps or needles or, if a small part of the artifact surface is being sampled, an aqueous solution may be removed with a variable pipette. Using disposable nylon tips, distilled water is drawn into the pipette and 10–20 µl (microliters; 1 µl = 10^{-6} l) are delivered to the area for sampling. The water is ejected to the area of interest, agitated with the pipette tip, and left for about 1 minute. The residue solution is then drawn back into the pipette and ejected directly onto a microscope slide or into clean tubes for later processing. If a larger area is to be sampled, parts of an artifact can be immersed in a distilled water-filled container (small nylon weighing "boats" are ideal) floated in a sonic cleaner for a short time. The residue solution can be stored in clean, capped vials for later analysis or concentration by separation in heavy liquids and centrifugation. Methods have been adapted for starch extraction from pollen and phytolith analysis (e.g., Kealhofer et al. 1999).

To prepare residue samples for transmitted-light microscopy, a 10-µl aliquot of residue solution is applied by pipette to a clean microscope slide. The solution is left to air dry and a cover slip is then lowered in place. For temporary mounts, the air-dried sample is mounted with a cover slip and sealed with drops of nail varnish at each of the four corners. A 10-µl aliquot of distilled water is then delivered by pipette to an edge of the cover slip, and the water is drawn below the cover slip by capillary reaction. Water in temporary mounts will evaporate, but another 10 µl of water can be delivered to re-hydrate the sample. Temporary mounts are easily stored (although a small amount of sample may be lost with each re-hydration), and are particularly useful if reagents (e.g., specific dyes, washes) are needed to highlight specific residues such as starch or lignin. Permanent mounts can be prepared by use of a commercially available mounting medium (Permount™, Euparol™, or DePeX™) or other readily available products (e.g., glycerin, silicon oil, Canada Balsam™, or Karo™). The residue will not be clearly visible if its refractive index is the same as the mounting medium.

Microscopes

Three kinds of light microscope are commonly used for routine study of usewear and residues: a stereomicroscope with an external light source; a compound incident-light microscope (e.g., a metallographic microscope) for reflected light viewing of opaque specimens (e.g., tool edges); and a compound transmitted-light microscope for viewing specimens mounted on glass slides (see Bradbury 1984). Compound microscopes can resolve microns (1 µm = 10^{-6} m).

A range of camera attachments is available and a choice is usually made between film and digital photography. Digital camera systems are better for handling a large number of items because images can be stored in a computer database, where observations and other records can also be documented and easily retrieved. However, film remains perfectly adequate for recording a relatively small number of images.

Under stereomicroscopes, artifacts can be handled (with clean, starch-free gloves if residues are to be recovered and contamination minimized) or set on a stage. Standard fiber-optic cold light sources permit good visibility at low magnifications (up to ×100), and objects are visible in a three-dimensional view. These microscopes are excellent for observing usewear, and some lithic analysts prefer the use of these instruments because a large number of artifacts can be analyzed rapidly, with good success at identifying tool function (see Odell & Odell-Vereecken 1980). An external point source of incident light at a low angle is particularly useful for observing smoothing, shallow edge scarring, and striations.

At magnifications typical of stereomicroscopes (up to about ×100), residue traces may also be located and described. It may be possible to see hafting resin, animal hair, cellular plant tissue, and other materials, but specific residue identifications usually demand further testing, higher magnifications, and optical techniques available with transmitted-light microscopes or SEM (scanning electron microscopes).

Reflected-light compound microscopes are the main instrument of microwear analysts who focus on *micropolish*, a term that refers to a combination of smoothing and other surface alterations that has resulted from utilization. Sometimes, usewear, including striations, edge scarring, and edge rounding is only visible at high magnifications (commonly at ×200 to ×500) that are not normally available under stereomicroscopes. Sometimes, large forms of usewear are only visible at low magnification with oblique light. Different lens and incident-light systems permit *brightfield* view (a central column of light passing through the vertical illumination system of lenses) and *darkfield* view (the central part of the light column is obscured so that light shines on the object from a low angle). Darkfield illumination is very useful for observing three-dimensional relief of shallow scars, striations, and surface features. Different lenses are available to enhance image contrast and to observe particular optical properties (polarization and phase contrast) of the objects.

Transmitted-light microscopes are used for examining translucent residues that are removed from artifact surfaces, and then mounted on glass microscope slides. Compound transmitted-light microscopes permit high magnifications (×50 to ×1,000), and have dedicated filters and attachments for revealing subtle variations in the light properties of particular materials. For example, Nomarski phase contrast or DIC (Differential Interference Contrast) lenses permit clear images of material boundaries and particle surfaces at high magnification. See, for example, the images of starch granules under DIC that clearly show surface features (Figure 7.3).

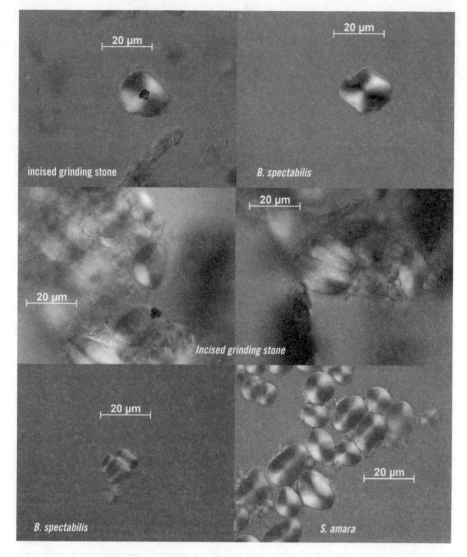

Figure 7.3 Starch granules under a transmitted-light microscope with DIC (courtesy of Corinne Barlow, Jirrbal Community, Ravenshoe, North Queensland, and Judith Field, Archaeology, University of Sydney).

Electron microscopes can resolve nanometers (1 nm = 10^{-9} m) and under special instrumentation can even discriminate atomic structure. Electron microscopes include both transmission electron microscopes (TEM) and scanning electron microscopes (SEM). The SEM provides excellent surface images of usewear and diagnostic surface structures on pollen grains, phytoliths, and other tiny particles. The SEM can show clear relief on highly polished surfaces (e.g., Kamminga 1977, 1982; Knutsson 1988; Sussman 1988) and residues (e.g., Jahren et al. 1997). A disadvantage of most electron microscopes is that samples usually need special preparation (carbon or gold coating) and must be placed inside a vacuum chamber, making it very difficult to view live or wet organic specimens. However, larger organic material including fresh specimens can be viewed in an environmental SEM (Robertson 1996).

The SEM has an added advantage over light microscopy because particular electron beams can cause a specimen to emit a variety of sub-atomic particles, including electrons and X-rays with distinctive energies that are indicative of atomic number. Energy Dispersion Spectroscopy (EDS, also called EDAX) is a common feature of modern SEMs. It is possible to map the elemental composition of very small areas or particles using the SEM. Ion Beam Analysis (IBM) has been used in a similar way to map tool residues (Christensen et al. 1992).

Artifact Cleaning

Cleaning of artifact surfaces is considered vital by some researchers who want to observe tool surfaces and need to remove materials unrelated to use. These contaminants include sediment from excavation trenches, dust from museum shelves, plant and animal materials, and also handling traces from lipids to sunscreen. An added problem is the need to ensure that all tools are handled and processed in a standardized way during analysis. Microwear analysts suggest brushing, washing, sonic cleaning, and a variety of chemicals and procedures to dissolve and remove contaminants. Although Keeley (1980) utilized solutions of sodium hydroxide (NaOH) and hydrochloric acid (HCl) for a standard time, these chemicals may destroy residues and even alter certain stone surfaces, including use-polished surfaces (e.g., Kamminga 1980; van Gijn 1990).

When these cleaning procedures were first recommended, many microwear and usewear analysts did not consider that any organic residues from use could survive for long periods of time. However, tool residues have been documented in a wide range of environmental conditions, and material removed from tool surfaces should be recovered for identification, and not just washed down the sink. Cleaning and handling should be minimized, and artifacts should be examined microscopically prior to cleaning for residues such as phytoliths, starch granules, and other distinctive structures.

Plant Residues Found on Artifacts

All plants are composed of cells variously comprised of cellulose, hemicelluloses, lignin, water-soluble sugar amino acids and aliphatic acids, ether- and alcohol-soluble constituents (e.g., resins), and proteins (e.g., Esau 1965). These compounds can be characterized biochemically (e.g., Fox et al. 1995), but distinct tissues, cells, and other structures are often visible microscopically on artifacts or in aqueous extractions from tool surfaces (Shafer & Holloway 1979). Cellulose fibers are ribbon-like and appear brighter under cross-polarized light. As residues on stone tools, the ends often appear cut or shattered. Different kinds of particles and fibers can be characterized by their refractive properties.

Textbooks on biological science and plant anatomy (e.g., Esau 1965; Murray 1965; Gould et al. 1996) describe plant cells, tissues, and organs, and several structures that can occur as archaeological tool residues, including starch granules, phytoliths, hairs (or *trichomes*), sclereids, tracheids, crystals (e.g., raphides), and xylem (the main constituent of wood). Silica in some plants, notably grasses (Esau 1965), can form cells that become microfossils with distinctive cellular features that survive long periods of time, and are diagnostic of plant taxa (e.g., Bowdery 1989; Pearsall & Piperno 1993). Charred plant fragments can be identified with comparative reference collections that document cell structures (e.g., Hather 1994; Thompson 1994; Smith et al. 1995).

Starch is common in many plants, particularly food plants like tubers and seeds (Esau 1965). Starch commonly occurs as granules composed of amylose and amylopectin in discrete layers, giving distinctive optical properties. Starch granules have been studied for over a century (e.g., Schleiden 1849; Reichert 1913), but only recently has their archaeological and paleoecological potential been investigated in prehistoric plant remains (Ugent 1981 et al.) and on tool surfaces (e.g., Briuer 1976; Shafer & Holloway 1979; Loy 1994; Fullagar 1998; Piperno & Holst 1998; Kealhofer et al. 1999; Piperno et al. 2000). **Starch**

Starch granules (Figure 7.3) provide energy storage for many plants, and most are less than 50 μm in maximum dimension. Surface features of starch granules should therefore be viewed under transmitted light at ×200 magnification or higher. With transmitted-light and incident-light microscopes, starch granules show a distinct dark "extinction cross" under cross-polarized light, caused by their crystalline properties. Unlike the fixed extinction cross in some crystalline particles, the extinction cross of starch granules will rotate when the polarizing filter is rotated. Under plain brightfield illumination, features (e.g., facets) may be visible that indicate how granules have formed.

Starch granules are best viewed under DIC (or brightfield with the condenser closed down) to see surface features. A growth center or hilum is often visible, and (for some species) with surrounding concentric lighter and darker layers, indicating the chemical structure of the starch compounds. The granule size, shape, hilum, surface features, concentric growth rings, and the nature of the extinction cross can indicate plant taxa, sometimes at the species level.

Starch is sensitive to particular stains such as iodine potassium iodide (IKI), which causes compounds in starch to change color from white to shades of blue, purple, and black (Hall et al. 1989; Loy 1994).

Raphides are needle-like crystalline structures made of calcium oxalate that function to defend some plants against predation (Esau 1965). They are very abundant in some plants, such as rhubarb and aroid root crops (e.g., taro), and these plants must be cooked or otherwise processed before human **Raphides** consumption, because they can be unpalatable and sometimes poisonous (Sakai 1979). Raphides, usually with other plant tissue, may adhere to food processing and storage implements (Shafer & Holloway 1979; Loy 1994). Raphides from temperate woody plants have also been noted on tools (P. Anderson, personal communication, 1980). Raphides can be hundreds of microns in length, and are visible under higher magnifications with reflected and transmitted light. Size, shape, and cross-section appear to be typical of particular plants and may enable identification.

Phytoliths   Plants produce tiny siliceous particles (usually less than 50 μm) called phytoliths that have precipitated to form exotic shapes within cells, or filled cells entirely to take on that characteristic shape. Phytoliths survive well archaeologically and have high potential for reconstructing past vegetation (from sediment samples) and resource utilization (from tool-edge samples). Phytoliths have been identified as residues on artifacts (see Shafer & Holloway 1979; Bowdery 1989) and have even been identified on archaeological tools from open sites in high rainfall regions of the equatorial tropics (e.g., Fullagar 1993).

Phytoliths can be diagnostic of plants, sometimes at the species level. Silica is common in many plants and some, such as grasses, have high levels with over 10 percent dry weight. Many trees produce silica, and the amorphous (noncrystalline) silica (usually less than 0.5 percent dry weight) can also act as a polishing agent on siliceous stone tools (Fullagar 1991). But they also produce thin sheets of connected cells, often 200 μm in length, which often survive in dry climates on storage structures and tool surfaces, such as querns associated with cereal cultivation (Anderson 1999; Procopiou & Treuil 2002).

Phytoliths are difficult to observe and quantify while still attached to tool surfaces under reflected light, and must be removed and processed to recover and isolate all particles (Kealhofer et al. 1999). Phytoliths can also be viewed under SEM (see Hart & Wallis 2003).

Resin, gums, waxes, and other exudates   Many plants secrete distinctive resins, gums, waxes, oils, toxins, and other compounds that have been chemically identified in archaeological contexts, and associated with tool function, often as fixatives or hafting media. Resins can sometimes be observed on stone artifact surfaces as hafting traces that are visible macroscopically. Resins observed microscopically can appear like small smooth droplets or have a mud-cracked appearance, often with plant and other tissue (sometimes distinctive starch granules) embedded in the matrix. A wide range of biochemical analyses is available for characterizing archaeological resins and other exudates with modern reference specimens (e.g., Bowden & Reynolds 1982; Fankhauser 1994; Fox et al. 1995; Pollard & Heron 1996; Edwards et al. 1997).

RICHARD FULLAGAR

Animal tissues such as blood, bone, muscle, lipids, fats, collagen, and shells do have distinctive cellular structures, but they may not be easily visible without biochemical staining. Nevertheless, a number of animal tissues do have distinct microscopically visible structures, and some are discussed below. Sometimes, tissue preservation can be exceptional, as in distinctive muscle fibers from the Iceman (the late Neolithic human found frozen in the Alps; Rollo et al. 2002).

Unless deeply pigmented, keratin (the molecule forming hair, feather, horn, hoof, beak, and claw) has a pale blue birefringence in cross-polarized light. Animal hair has a microscopic cuticular scale pattern that may survive on ethnographic and archaeological artifacts (Figure 7.4; and see Fullagar et al. 1999 [1992]). These features are visible at magnifications above about ×200. The surface scale features, cross-section, and internal structures (air pockets or medulla) of some animal hairs can be distinctive of species. Similarly, feathers include microscopic features such as barbs and barbules that have distinctive morphologies diagnostic of taxa (see Robertson 2002 and references therein). Atlases are available for identifying feathers and the hair of some animal species (e.g., Brunner & Coman 1974), and additional reference microscope slides can easily be prepared.

Like hair, fish scale fragments (that are visible microscopically) can have distinctive features, such as growth rings, that may be distinctive of taxa.

Blood is a connective tissue with several visibly distinct structures, including red and white blood cells. Mature mammalian red cells do not have a nucleus, and size can be an indicator of taxa (Andrew 1965). Under darkfield nonpolarized light, thick blood films (> 20 μm thickness) grade from maroon black to light red to pale straw yellow to no color in very thin deposits (T. Loy, personal communication, 2003).

Red cells, or erythrocytes, are well documented on archaeological and experimental artifacts and are sometimes remarkably intact (e.g., Loy 1983, 1993). A variety of other techniques (biochemical reaction, immuno-assay, isoelectric focusing, hemoglobin crystallization, and DNA) have provided indications if not secure determinations of taxa (Hyland et al. 1990; Heron et al. 1991; Kooyman et al. 1992; Newman et al. 1993; Petraglia et al. 1996; Loy & Dixon 1998). Some studies have questioned the sensitivity and ability of particular techniques to confirm or determine species of origin (Gurfinkel & Franklin 1988; Smith & Wilson 1992; Fiedel 1996; Garling 1998). DNA analysis holds great potential for species identification (Loy 1993: 44–63; Fullagar et al. 1996; Tuross et al. 1996; Loy & Dixon 1998; Smit et al. 1998; Shanks et al. 2001; Rollo et al. 2002).

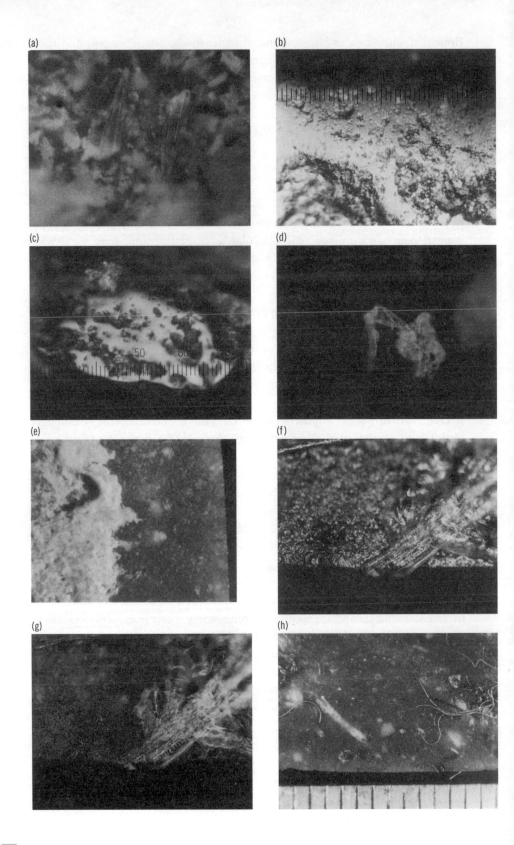

RICHARD FULLAGAR

Bone is a connective tissue hardened by minerals, principally calcium, carbonate, and phosphate (Murray 1965; Gould et al. 1996). Collagen is an important organic constituent that provides some elasticity. Bone is covered by a tough fibrous membrane (periosteum) that needs to be removed before carving or breaking the bone cleanly. Bone cells are not normally visible in granular or smeared residues on stone tool edges. Bone fragments can be visible as fine white-translucent grains, often smeared on to the tool edge, and shavings, sometimes twisted. Unlike cellulose, collagen usually has little birefringence with a dull appearance under crossed and plane polarized light. The secondary mineral vivianite (shades of blue to apple green) often accompanies fatty bone residues (T. Loy, personal communication, 2003). Bone residues have been identified on stone tools that have usewear, tool design, and archaeological context all consistent with working bone (e.g., Fullagar 1988). Bone residues can also be characterized by elemental composition (e.g., Christensen et al. 1992; Jahren et al. 1997).

Shell is secreted by the mantle of mollusks (Gould et al. 1996) and mostly comprises calcium carbonate and other minerals including aragonite that can be distinguished by staining and infrared spectroscopy. The multicolored nacre on the inside of many mollusk shells can survive as a distinctive residue visible microscopically on stone tools used to process shell (Kamminga comment in Hayden 1979a: 287; Kamminga 1982: 53; Allen et al. 1997; Attenbrow et al. 1998).

Functional analysis of stone tools draws on several sources of evidence including properties of the raw material, manufacture or design characteristics, tool-use experiments, ethnography, residues, and usewear. The history and development of lithic usewear has been reviewed by several researchers (e.g., Hayden & Kamminga 1979; Yerkes & Kardulias 1993), and despite earlier debate on appropriate magnification and the suitability of different optical microscope techniques, stereoscopic and compound microscope systems are now commonly used (for the magnification range, see "Microscopes" above).

The main forms of usewear on stone artifacts are scarring, striations, polish, and edge rounding (see Hayden 1979a; Kamminga 1982). *Bevels* (a form of

Figure 7.4 (*opposite*)   Experimental residues and usewear on experimental flint tools: note the lighter polished areas and edge rounding in (b) and (c). (a) Conical silica particles on a mortar used to grind wild rice, *Oryza* sp.; DF (0.3 mm). (b) Usewear on a tool used to scrape bamboo, *Bambusa* sp.; BF (0.3 mm). (c) Usewear on a tool used to slice reeds, *Phragmites australis*; BF (0.3 mm). (d) Collagen fibers on a tool used to scrape kangaroo, *Macropus* sp., skin; BF (0.3 mm). (e) Fleshy tissue on a tool used to scrape possum, *Trichosurus vulpecula*, skin; BF (4 cm). (f) Skin, hair, and blood on a tool used to skin a possum, *Trichosurus vulpecula*; BF (0.2 mm). (g) The same view as in (f); DF (0.2 mm). (h) Skin and hair on a tool used to skin a kangaroo, *Macropus* sp.; SM (14 mm). BF, brightfield incident light; DF, darkfield incident light; SM, stereomicroscope (width of field in mm).

edge rounding) constitute a less common form of usewear on some tool edges. Patterning in these five forms of usewear is determined in part by tool material, edge morphology, and duration of use in addition to the mode of use (e.g., sawing, scraping, chopping, and drilling) and the nature of the material worked (e.g., wood, bone, stone, shell, and skin). Nevertheless, there are regularities despite the complexity of variables. Directionality of striations, for example, tends to be aligned with mode of use, although the morphology and frequency of striations varies considerably. On the other hand, particular variables can greatly affect usewear patterns. For example, abrasive particles will affect the frequency and type of striations (Cotterell & Kamminga 1990: 152–3).

Tool-edge morphology also affects scarring. Low angled cross-sections, for example, will sustain high numbers of bending scars when used to cut or scrape any reasonably dense material. Softer stone tool materials, such as obsidian, will sustain greater degrees of usewear than harder stone tool materials such as quartz. Despite these complications, certain patterns of usewear on particular tool materials can be highly diagnostic of processing specific materials (e.g., bone sawing, skin scraping, and grass cutting).

Scarring or edge fracturing

Scarring is usually recorded according to fracture initiation, termination types, general size, and shape. Kamminga (1982) provides a detailed recording system, with measurements of particular scar types based on principles of fracture mechanics. Scar types are classified according to the types of initiation, propagation, and termination of the fracture (Figure 7.5; see also Cotterell et al. 1985; Cotterell & Kamminga 1990). Key determinants important for usewear are the amount of applied force and the nature of tool impact (e.g., pressure versus inelastic percussion). At the moment of fracture initiation, bending forces, wedging forces, or Hertzian forces each produce a distinctive type of flake, depending in part on the shape of the tool edge or core (Figure 7.6d).

Scarring on stone tool edges during use is very common, and patterns vary with the amount and direction of force applied. However, the kind of stone and the shape of cutting edges have a major effect on the nature of the scars. Consequently, extensive experiments with different edge shapes are required.

Striations

Striations can be classified according to their morphology in cross-section and plan view (Lawn & Marshall 1979; Kamminga 1982). Some striations, called *sleeks*, appear to have a smooth cross-section that seems to be a plastic deformation of the surface. Other striations, called *furrows*, appear to rip the surface and have jagged margins. Important variables are whether the abrasive particles are fixed, loose, sharp, or blunt. In plan view, striations produced by fixed abrasives tend to be continuous, whereas loose abrasive particles will produce a discontinuous alignment of cracks or pits, sometimes with a fern-like appearance if the particles are blunt (Cotterell & Kamminga 1990: 152–3). Abrasive

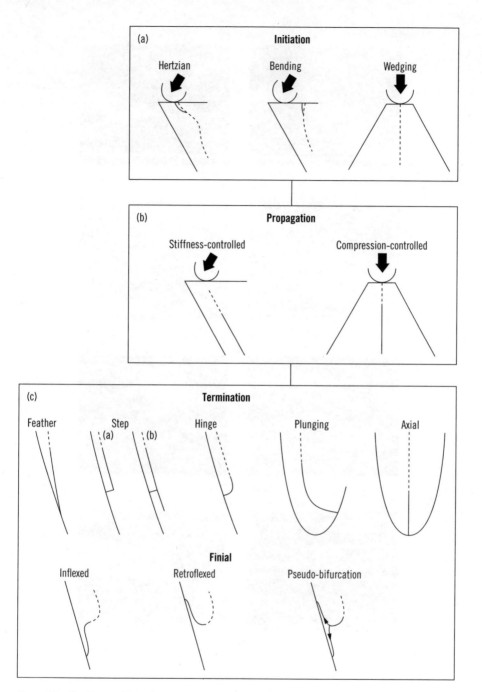

Figure 7.5 The phases of flake formation (after Cotterell & Kamminga 1990: 134, by permission of the author).

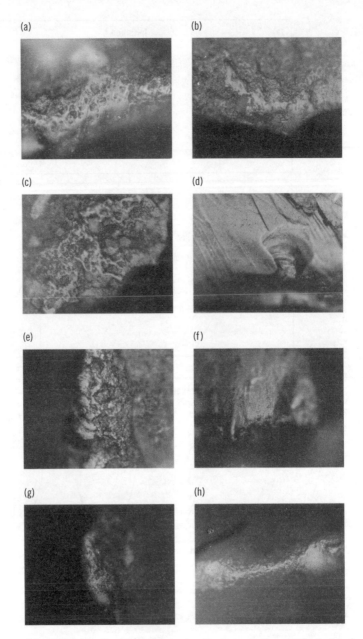

(a)

(b)

(c)

(d)

(e)

(f)

(g)

(h)

Figure 7.6 Experimental polishes on stone artifacts after 45 minutes (Fullagar 1991). Each image is under brightfield incident light, and the width of field is 0.3 mm. Note the lighter polished areas and edge rounding. (a) Usewear on a flint tool used to scrape light-density wood (*Dacrydium franklinii*). (b) Usewear on a quartz tool used to scrape light-density wood (*Dacrydium franklinii*). (c) Usewear on a flint tool used to scrape bamboo (*Bambusa* sp.). (d) Usewear on a quartz tool used to scrape bamboo (*Bambusa* sp.). Note the feather-terminated scar and fracture stress lines (not striations from use). (e) Usewear on a flint tool used to scrape cow (*Bos taurus*) bone. (f) Usewear on a quartz tool used to scrape cow (*Bos taurus*) bone. (g) Usewear on a flint tool used to scrape tanned seal (*Arctocephalus pusillus*) skin. (h) Usewear on a quartz tool used to scrape tanned seal (*Arctocephalus pusillus*) skin.

RICHARD FULLAGAR

particles are important in the context of usewear on stone tools, because some originate from the local environment (a sandy beach for example), some derive from the materials being processed, and others result from the tool surface that breaks up during use.

Keeley (1980) promoted analysis of polishes and polish distributions on the edges of flint tools, arguing that reasonably distinct patterns were diagnostic of materials worked. While the distinctive gloss from cutting cereal grasses had long been recognized on sickle blades, it became common for microwear analysts to refer in shorthand to "meat polish," "bone polish," "plant polish," and "hide polish" – even though other forms of wear such as scarring, edge rounding, and striations were considered significant in interpreting "polish" patterns. Extensive investigation demonstrates that micropolish (in conjunction with other forms of usewear) is a good indicator of function, especially on fine-grained flints and cherts (Yerkes & Kardulias 1993).

Polish

Scholars have been arguing for many years about the nature of use-polish, and the significance of various mechanisms involved in its formation (see articles in Hayden 1979a). Some scholars have been skeptical that polish can be employed as a diagnostic indicator of worked material unless the formation processes are properly understood (Kamminga 1982; Grace et al. 1985; Grace 1996). Argument still revolves around whether polishes (including silica polish) are residues, gel layers, additive, reductive, chemical, mechanical, or some combination (for a recent study with references, see Kaminska-Szymczak 2002). Patricia Anderson (personal communication, 2003), working with a team of tribologists, argues that the polish on threshing sledge blades is a deposit. However, surface leveling through abrasive smoothing is undoubtedly important in many tool-use situations, as indicated by the common co-occurrence of polish with edge rounding. Grasses and many timbers have naturally occurring amorphous silica in the form of tiny particles that act as polishing agents, hastening very smooth polish formation at a molecular level on stone tools (Figures 7.5 and 7.6). In my view, the molecular polishing theory is applicable to a wide variety of siliceous stone tools (Fullagar 1991).

Rounding of tool edges is an attrition process, associated with abrasive smoothing and polish development. Not all utilized edges display edge rounding and it is not just dense material like hardwoods that can cause edge rounding. Flint flakes can sustain massive and distinctive edge rounding, often with extensive striations, when used for hide scraping (e.g., Fig. 7.6; Hayden 1979b; Keeley 1980). Different conditions can have a marked effect. For example, marsupial skins do not require extensive scraping or softening because they have only a thin protein film lining the cutaneous layer, making wear on skin scraping tools more difficult to identify (Kamminga 1982). On the other hand, the

Edge rounding

presence of sand and other grit in the local environment can greatly increase the extent of edge rounding.

Beveling   Beveling is a form of asymmetric edge rounding where pressure on the tool edge is uneven (Kamminga 1982). A beveled or flat surface can also form after sustained contact with a flat hard surface. Such conditions are common with particular tasks. For example, *beveled pounders* (for processing plant food in eastern Australia) sustain marked beveling when used to process bracken fern rhizomes for their starch (Kamminga 1981).

Post-depositional damage   It may be difficult to distinguish usewear from damage caused by post-depositional processes such as trampling by humans, movement within archaeological sediments, or exposure to animal and other traffic, unless fresh fracture scars are clearly visible (e.g., Knudson 1979; Hiscock 1985, 2002; Moss 1997: 197; McBrearty et al. 1998). Kamminga (1982: 9) found experimentally that, contrary to expectations, acute edges are not more likely to suffer fracture, and also noted that a significant number of archaeological stone artifacts in museum collections lacked any recent damage.

Hafting traces   Stone artifacts with hafting resin attached have been found in many archaeological contexts, but recent studies have focused on wear traces from hafting that include polish and "bright spots" (e.g., Keeley 1982; Odell 1996; Rots 2002). Recent experiments indicate that wear from contact with worked materials can be distinguished from microwear traces typical of hafting and manual prehension, on the basis of polish distribution and "bright spot" frequency (Rots et al. 2001). Hafting polish is also influenced by the kind of materials worked and the amount of fine particles or dust available, and also produced, during use – for example, processing of bone, antler, and schist always created fine particles that influenced wear development (Rots et al. 2001: 136).

Conclusion   A key aim of this chapter has been to introduce techniques of usewear and residue analyses that can be undertaken by archaeologists. A range of chemical and other analyses may require specialist expertise in other fields. Stone artifacts have provided the most common case study, although the techniques have application to materials other than stone.

    The past 40 years have witnessed an extraordinary increase in knowledge of usewear and residues on stone artifacts. A deficiency has been in the field of controlled tool-use experiments designed to evaluate the importance of specific variables in wear formation and residue accretion. More replicative experiments are needed to evaluate how particular residues change with different tasks.

    RICHARD FULLAGAR

Applications to whole assemblages have been relatively rare, and only recently have researchers recognized traces of use on unmodified stone flakes that have no macroscopic design features indicating that they were tools.

A second deficiency has been the lack of experimental study of nonlithic tools such as wood, shell, and bone. These are common tool materials represented in museum collections, if not in the archaeological record, and interpretations of site function based on lithic analysis alone could misrepresent the range of tasks undertaken.

Although earlier studies focused on particular forms of usewear, in part to evaluate formation processes, archaeological applications now tend to embrace a wider range of techniques. The study of organic and inorganic residues is growing rapidly, and a major task is to develop appropriate comparative reference collections for the identification of certain residue types (e.g., starch granules, resins, and minerals).

Acknowledgments

I thank the editors and my colleagues for helpful advice in preparing this chapter. Judith Field provided microscope images and much discussion. For comments and proof-reading, I thank Patricia Anderson, Daniel Davenport, Joe Dortch, Judith Field, Johan Kamminga, Tom Loy, George Odell, and Michael Slack.

Resources

Computer software

- WAVES (van den Dries 1998). This is a very useful teaching resource on CD.
- FAST (Grace 1993).

Websites

- www.earth.arts.gla.ac.uk/Activities/Activities.htm
- www.ansoc.uq.edu.au/courses/2003/semester1/arca2010/index.shtml
- www.bradford.ac.uk/archsci/
- http://wings.buffalo.edu/anthropology/Lithics/index2.html
- http://archweb.leidenuniv.nl/fa/english/archaeologicalsciences.html
- www.hf.uio.no/iakk/roger/lithic/bar/bar1.html (online version of Grace 1989)

Journals

- *Ancient Biomolecules*
- *Archaeometry*
- *Journal of Archaeological Science*
- *Lithic Technology*

Chemistry, forensic science, genetics, and microscopy

Chemistry, forensic science, and other science departments within universities have access to sophisticated techniques for identifying organic and inorganic tissue. These techniques include chemical stains specific to protein, lignin, cellulose, and other tissue (for early archaeological applications, see Briuer

1976). For the determination of molecular structure and elemental composition, there are many spectroscopic and other techniques (see Pollard & Heron 1996). DNA analysis is a specialized technique that now requires only small samples of tissue to determine base pair sequences indicative of taxonomic groupings, sex, and (in some cases) individual identity.

The McCrone Institute (www.mcri.org/) publishes a particle atlas with microscopic optical properties of many materials.

Microscope units within universities usually have courses to familiarize students with a range of techniques and instruments, including optical and electron microscopes. Microscope companies also run special courses for particular applications, such as identification of fibers or minerals.

The Archaeological Science Laboratory, School of Social Science, at the University of Queensland has a digital database of experimental and archaeological residue types that is currently being developed on DVD and for website access. For further information, contact Tom Loy (email: t.loy@imb.uq.edu.au).

Further reading

Anderson, P., Beyries, S., Otte, M. and Plisson, H. (eds.) 1993: *Traces et fonction: les gestes retrouvés. Colloque Internationale de Liège 8, 9, 10 décembre, 1990*, 2 vols. Editions ERAUL 50. Liège: ERAUL.

Beyries, S. (ed.) 1988: *Industries lithiques: tracéologie et technologie*, 2 vols. BAR International Series, 411. Oxford: British Archaeological Reports.

Dominguez-Rodrigo, M., Serrallonga, J., Juan-Tresserras, J., Alcala, L. and Luque, L. 2001: Woodworking activities by early humans: a plant residue analysis on Acheulian stone tools from Peninj (Tanzania). *Journal of Human Evolution*, 40, 289–99.

Maniatis, Y. and Tsirtsoni, Z. 2002: Characterization of a black residue in a decorated Neolithic pot from Dikili Tash, Greece: an unexpected result. *Archaeometry*, 44, 229–39.

References

Akerman, K., Fullagar, R. and van Gijn, A. L. 2002: Weapons and Wunan: production, function and exchange of spear points from the Kimberley, northwestern Australia. *Australian Aboriginal Studies*, 2002(1), 13–42.

Allen, J. A., Holdaway, S. and Fullagar, R. 1997: Identifying specialisation, production and exchange in the archaeological record: the case of shell bead manufacture on Motupore Island, Papua. *Archaeology in Oceania*, 32, 13–38.

Anderson, P. 1980: A testimony of prehistoric tasks: diagnostic residues on stone tool working edges. *World Archaeology*, 12(1), 181–94.

—— 1999: Experimental cultivation, harvest and threshing of wild cereals. In P. Anderson (ed.), *Prehistory of Agriculture: New Experimental and Ethnographic Approaches*. UCLA Institute of Archaeology Monograph, 40, Los Angeles: UCLA, 118–44.

Andrew, W. 1965: *Comparative Hematology*. New York: Grune and Stratton.

Attenbrow, V., Fullagar, R. and Szpak, C. 1998: Reassessing the chronology and function of stone files in southeastern Australia and implications for the manufacture of shell fish-hooks. In R. Fullagar (ed.), *A Closer Look: Recent Studies of Australian Stone Tools*. Sydney University Archaeological Methods Series, 6. Sydney: Archaeological Computing Laboratory, School of Archaeology, University of Sydney, 127–48.

Backwell, L. R. and d'Errico, F. 2001: Evidence of termite foraging by Swartkrans early hominids. *Proceedings of the National Academy of Sciences of the United States of America*, 98(4), 1358–63.

Beck, W., Fullagar, R. and White, N. 1988: Archaeology from ethnography: the Aboriginal use of cycad as an example. In B. Meehan and R. Jones (eds.), *Archaeology with Ethnography: an Australian Perspective*. Canberra: Australian National University, 137–47.

Beyries, S. 1987: *Variabilité de l'industrie lithique au Mousterien*. BAR International Series, 328. Oxford: British Archaeological Reports.

Bowden, B. F. and Reynolds, B. 1982: The chromatographic analysis of ethnographic resins. *Australian Institute of Aboriginal Studies Newsletter*, 17, 41–3.

Bowdery, D. 1989: Phytolith analysis: introduction and applications. In W. Beck, A. Clarke and L. Head (eds.), *Plants in Australian Archaeology*. Tempus, 1. St Lucia: Anthropology Museum, University of Queensland, 161–96.

Bradbury, S. 1984: *An Introduction to the Optical Microscope*. Royal Microscopical Society: Oxford University Press.

Briuer, F. L. 1976: New clues to stone tool function: plant and animal residues. *American Antiquity*, 41(4), 478–84.

Brunner, H. and Coman, B. J. 1974: *The Identification of Mammal Hair*. Melbourne: Inkata Press.

Burton, J. 1989: Repeng and the salt makers: "ecological trade" and axe production in the Papua New Guinea Highlands. *Man*, 24, 255–72.

Christensen, M., Walter, Ph. and Menu, M. 1992: Usewear characterisation of prehistoric flints with IBA. *Nuclear Instruments and Methods in Physics Research. Section B: Beam Interactions with Materials and Atoms*, 64(1–4), 488–93.

Cotterell, B. and Kamminga, J. 1990: *Mechanics of Pre-Industrial Technology*. Cambridge: Cambridge University Press.

——, —— and Dickson, F. P. 1985: The essential mechanics of conchoidal flaking. *International Journal of Fracture*, 29, 205–21.

Coutts, P. J. F. 1977: Green timber and Polynesian adzes and axes: an experimental approach. In R. V. S. Wright (ed.), *Stone Tools as Cultural Markers: Change, Evolution and Complexity*. Canberra: Australian Institute of Aboriginal Studies, 67–82.

Dendarsky, M. 2002: Recent lithic research in Austria. *Lithic Technology*, 27(1), 7–11.

Dockall, J. E. 2001: A perspective on research trends in Pacific lithic studies. *Lithic Technology*, 26(1), 4–15.

Edmonds, M. 1995: *Stone Tools and Society*. London: Batsford.

Edwards, D. A. and O'Connell, J. F. 1995: Broad spectrum diets in arid Australia. *Antiquity*, 69, 769–83.

Edwards, H. G. M., Sibley, M. G. and Heron, C. 1997: FT–Raman spectroscopic study of organic residues from 2300-year-old Vietnamese burial jars. *Spectrochimica Acta Part A: Molecular and Biomolecular Spectroscopy*, 53(13), 2373–82.

Esau, K. 1965: *Plant Anatomy*. New York: John Wiley.

Evershed, R. P. and Tuross, N. 1996: Proteinaceous material from potsherds and associated soils. *Journal of Archaeological Science*, 23, 429–36.

——, Heron, C., Charters, S. and Goad, L. J. 1992: The survival of food residues: new methods of analysis, interpretation and application. In A. M. Pollard (ed.), *New Developments in Archaeological Science*. Oxford: Oxford University Press, 187–208.

Fankhauser, B. 1993a: Are your fingerprints destined to become part of prehistory? In M. Spriggs, D. Yen, W. Ambrose, R. Jones, A. Thorne and A. Andrews (eds.), *A Community of Culture: The People and Prehistory of the Pacific*. Occasional Papers in Prehistory, 21.

Canberra: Department of Prehistory, Research School of Pacific Studies, Australian National University, 49–55.

—— 1993b: Residue analysis in Maori ovens. In B. L. Fankhauser and J. R. Bird (eds.), *Archaeometry: Current Australasian Research*. Occasional Papers in Prehistory, 22. Canberra: Department of Prehistory, Research School of Pacific Studies, Australian National University, 13–20.

—— 1994: Protein and lipid analysis of food residues. In J. Hather (ed.), *Tropical Archaeobotany. Applications and New Developments*. One World Archaeology, 22. London: Routledge, 227–50.

Fiedel, S. 1996: Blood from stones? Some methodological and interpretive problems in blood residue analysis. *Journal of Archaeological Science*, 23(1), 139–47.

Fox, A., Heron, C. and Sutton, M. 1995: Characterization of natural products on native American archaeological and ethnographic materials from the Great Basin Region, U.S.A.: a preliminary study. *Archaeometry*, 37, 365–75.

Fullagar, R. 1988: Recent developments in Australian use-wear and residue studies. In S. Beyries (ed.), *Industries lithiques: tracéologie et technologie*. BAR International Series, 411. Oxford: British Archaeological Reports, 133–45.

—— 1991: The role of silica in polish formation. *Journal of Archaeological Science*, 18, 1–25.

—— 1992: Lithically Lapita. Functional analysis of flaked stone assemblages from West New Britain Province, Papua New Guinea. In J.-C. Galipaud (ed.), *Poterie Lapita et peuplement. Actes du Colloque Lapita, Noumea, janvier*. Noumea: ORSTOM, 135–43.

—— 1993: Taphonomy and tool-use: a role for phytoliths in use-wear and residue analysis. In B. Fankhauser and R. Bird (eds.), *Archaeometry: Current Australasian Research*. Occasional Papers in Prehistory, 22. Canberra: Department of Prehistory, Research School of Pacific Studies, Australian National University, 21–7.

—— (ed.) 1998: *A Closer Look: Recent Studies of Australian Stone Tools*. Sydney University Archaeological Methods Series, 6. Sydney: Archaeological Computing Laboratory, School of Archaeology, University of Sydney.

—— and Field, J. 1997: Pleistocene seed grinding implements from the Australian arid zone. *Antiquity*, 71, 300–7.

——, Furby, J. and Hardy, B. 1996: Residues on stone artefacts: state of a scientific art. *Antiquity*, 70, 740–5.

——, Meehan, B. and Jones, R. 1999 [1992]: Residue analysis of ethnographic plant-working and other tools from northern Australia. In P. Anderson (ed.), *Prehistory of Agriculture: New Experimental and Ethnographic Approaches*. UCLA Institute of Archaeology Monograph, 40. Los Angeles: Institute of Archaeology, UCLA, 15–23.

Garling, S. 1998: Megafauna on the menu? Haemoglobin crystallisation of blood residues from stone artefacts at Cuddie Springs. In R. Fullagar (ed.), *A Closer Look: Recent Studies of Australian Stone Tools*. Sydney University Archaeological Methods Series, 6. Sydney: Archaeological Computing Laboratory, School of Archaeology, University of Sydney, 29–48.

Goren-Inbar, N., Gonen, S., Melamed, Y. and Kislev, M. 2002: Nuts, nut cracking, and pitted stone at Gesher Benot Ya'aqov, Israel. *Proceedings of the National Academy of Sciences of the United States of America*, 99(4), 2455–60.

Gould, J. L. and Keeton, W. T., with Grant Gould, C. 1996: *Biological Science*, 6th edn. New York: W.W. Norton.

Grace, R. 1989: *Interpreting the Function of Stone Tools: The Quantification and Computerisation of Microwear Analysis*. BAR International Series, 474. Oxford: British Archaeological Reports.

—— 1993: The use of expert systems in lithic analysis. In P. Anderson, S. Beyries, M. Otte and H. Plisson (eds.), *Traces et fonction: les gestes retrouves. Colloque Internationale de Liège 8, 9, 10 decembre, 1990*, vol. 2. Editions ERAUL 50. Liège: ERAUL, 389–400.

—— 1996: Use-wear analysis: the state of the art. *Archaeometry*, 38, 209–29.

——, Graham, I. and Newcomer, M. 1985: The quantification of microwear polishes. *World Archaeology*, 17(1), 112–19.

Gurfinkel, D. and Franklin, U. 1988: A study of the feasibility of detecting blood residues on artefacts. *Journal of Archaeological Science*, 15, 83–97.

Hall, J., Higgins, S. and Fullagar, R. 1989: Plant residues on stone tools. In W. Beck, A. Clarke and L. Head (eds.), *Plants in Australian Archaeology*. Tempus, 1. St Lucia: Anthropology Museum, University of Queensland, 136–60.

Hart, D. M. and Wallis, L. A. (eds.) 2003: *Phytolith and Starch Research in the Australian–Pacific–Asian Regions: The State of the Art*. Terra Australis, 19. Canberra: Pandanus Books.

Hather, J. 1994: The identification of charred root and tuber crops from archaeological sites in the Pacific. In J. Hather (ed.), *Tropical Archaeobotany. Applications and New Developments*. One World Archaeology, 22. London: Routledge, 51–64.

Hayden, B. 1977: Stone tool functions in the Western Desert. In R. V. S. Wright (ed.), *Stone Tools as Cultural Markers: Change, Evolution and Complexity*. Canberra: Australian Institute of Aboriginal Studies, 179–88.

—— (ed.) 1979a: *Lithic Use-Wear Analysis*. London: Academic Press.

—— 1979b: Snap, shatter, and superfractures: use-wear of stone skin scrapers. In B. Hayden (ed.), *Lithic Use-Wear Analysis*. London: Academic Press, 207–29.

—— and Kamminga, J. 1979: An introduction to use-wear: the first CLUW. In B. Hayden (ed.), *Lithic Use-Wear Analysis*. London: Academic Press, 1–13.

Heron, C., Evershed, R., Goad, L. and Denham, V. 1991: New approaches to the analysis of organic residues from archaeological remains. In P. Budd, B. Chapman, R. Janway and B. Ottaway (eds.), *Archaeological Sciences 1989*. Oxbow Monographs, 9. Oxford: Oxbow Books, 332–9.

Hiscock, P. 1985: The need for a taphonomic perspective in stone artefact analysis. *Queensland Archaeological Research*, 2, 82–95.

—— 2002: Quantifying the size of artefact assemblages. *Journal of Archaeological Science*, 29, 251–8.

Hurcombe, L. 1992: *Use Wear Analysis and Obsidian: Theory, Experiments and Results*. Sheffield Archaeological Monographs, 4. University of Sheffield/J. R. Collis.

Hurst, W., Tarka, S. Jr, Powis, T., Valdez, F. Jr and Hester, T. 2002: Cacao usage by the earliest Maya civilization. *Nature*, 418, 289–90.

Hyland, D., Tersak, J., Adovasio, J. and Siegel, M. 1990: Identification of the species of origin of residual blood on lithic material. *American Antiquity*, 55, 104–12.

Jahren, A. H., Toth, N., Schick, K., Clark, J. D. and Amundson, R. G. 1997: Determining stone tool use: chemical and morphological analyses of residues on experimentally manufactured stone tools. *Journal of Archaeological Science*, 24, 245–50.

Jensen, H. J. 1994: *Flint Tools and Plant Working*. Aarhus: Aarhus University Press.

Kaminska-Szymczak, J. 2002: Cutting Graminae tools and "sickle gloss" formation. *Lithic Technology*, 27(2), 111–51.

Kamminga, J. 1977: A functional study of use-polished elouras. In R. V. S. Wright (ed.), *Stone Tools as Cultural Markers: Change, Evolution and Complexity*. Canberra: Australian Institute of Aboriginal Studies, 205–12.

—— 1980: Analysing stone tools. Review of experimental determination of stone tool use. *Science*, 210, 58–9.

—— 1981: The beveled pounder: an Aboriginal stone tool type from southeast Queensland. *Proceedings of the Royal Society of Queensland*, 92, 31–5.

—— 1982: *Over the Edge*. Occasional Papers in Anthropology, 12. University of Queensland: Anthropological Museum.

—— 1985: The Pirri graver. *Australian Aboriginal Studies*, 1985/2, 2–25.

Kealhofer, L., Torrence, R. and Fullagar, R. 1999: Integrating phytoliths within use-wear/residue studies of stone tools. *Journal of Archaeological Science*, 26, 527–46.

Keeley, L. H. 1980: *Experimental Determination of Stone Tool Uses: A Microwear Analysis*. Chicago: The University of Chicago Press.

—— 1982: Hafting and retooling: effects on the archaeological record. *American Antiquity*, 47(4), 798–809.

Knudson, R. 1979: Inference and imposition in lithic analysis. In B. Hayden (ed.), *Lithic Use-Wear Analysis*. London: Academic Press, 269–81.

Knutsson, K. 1988: *Patterns of Tool Use: Scanning Electron Microscopy of Experimental Quartz Tools*. Uppsala: Societas Archaeologica Upsaliensis.

Kooyman, B., Newman, M. and Ceri, H. 1992: Verifying the reliability of blood residue analysis on archaeological tools. *Journal of Archaeological Science*, 19, 265–9.

Lammers-Keijsers, Y. 2002: Lithic studies in Dutch archaeology. *Lithic Technology*, 27(2), 89–92.

Lawn, B. R. and Marshall, D. B. 1979: Mechanisms of microcontact in fracture in brittle solids. In B. Hayden (ed.), *Lithic Use-Wear Analysis*. London: Academic Press, 63–82.

Loy, T. H. 1983: Prehistoric blood residues: detection on tool surfaces and identification of species of origin. *Science*, 220, 1269–71.

—— 1993: The artefact as site: an example of the biomolecular analysis of organic residues on prehistoric stone tools. *World Archaeology*, 25, 44–63.

—— 1994: Methods in the analysis of starch residues on prehistoric stone tools. In J. Hather (ed.), *Tropical Archaeobotany. Applications and New Developments*. One World Archaeology, 22. London: Routledge, 86–114.

—— and Dixon, J. 1998: Blood residues on fluted points from Eastern Beringia. *American Antiquity*, 63(1), 21–46.

McBrearty, S., Bishop, L., Plummer, T., Duwar, R. and Conard, N. 1998: Tools underfoot: human trampling as an agent of lithic artefact edge modification. *American Antiquity*, 63, 108–29.

Miller, T. 1979: Stonework of the Xeta Indians of Brazil. In B. Hayden (ed.), *Lithic Use-Wear Analysis*. London: Academic Press, 401–7.

Moss, E. H. 1997: Lithic use-wear analysis. In G. Bailey (ed.), *Klithi: Paleolithic Settlement and Quaternary Landscapes in Northwest Greece*, vol. 1: *Excavation and Intra-Site Analysis at Klithi*. Cambridge: McDonald Institute for Archaeological Research, 193–205.

Murray, P. 1965: *Biology: An Introduction to Medical and Other Studies*. London: Macmillan.

Nami, H. G. 2001: Current trends in lithic technology in Argentina. *Lithic Technology*, 26(2), 94–104.

Newman, M., Yohe, R., Ceri, H. and Sutton, M. 1993: Immunological protein residue on nonlithic archaeological remains. *Journal of Archaeological Science*, 20, 93–100.

O'Connell, J. F., Hawkes, K., Lupo, K. D. and Blurton Jones, N. G. 2002: Male strategies and Plio-Pleistocene archaeology. *Journal of Human Evolution*, 43, 831–72.

Odell, G. H. 1979: A new improved system for the retrieval of functional information from microscopic observations of chipped stone tools. In B. Hayden (ed.), *Lithic Use-Wear Analysis*. London: Academic Press, 329–44.

—— 1995: *Stone Tools and Mobility in the Illinois Valley: From Hunting–Gathering Camps to Agricultural Villages*. Ann Arbor: International Monographs in Prehistory.

—— 1996: Economizing behavior and the concept of "curation." In G. H. Odell (ed.), *Stone Tools: Theoretical Insights into Human Prehistory*. Interdisciplinary Contributions to Archaeology. New York: Plenum Press, 51–80.

—— and Odell-Vereecken, F. 1980: Verifying the reliability of lithic use-wear determinations by "blind tests": low power approach. *Journal of Field Archaeology*, 7, 87–120.

Patrick, M., de Konig, A. and Smith, A. 1985: Gas chromatographic analysis of fatty acids in food residues from ceramics found in the Southwestern Cape, South Africa. *Archaeometry*, 27, 231–6.

Pearsall, D. and Piperno, D. (eds.) 1993: *Current Research in Phytolith Analysis: Applications in Archaeology and Paleoecology*. MASCA Research Papers in Science and Archaeology, 10. Philadelphia: MASCA, University of Philadelphia.

Petraglia, M., Knepper, D., Glumac, P., Newman, M. and Sussman, C. 1996: Immunological and microwear analysis of chipped-stone artifacts from Piedmont contexts. *American Antiquity*, 61(1), 127–35.

Piperno, D. R. and Holst, I. 1998: The presence of starch grains on prehistoric stone tools from the Humid Neotropics: indications of early tuber use and agriculture in Panama. *Journal of Archaeological Science*, 25, 765–76.

——, Ranere, A. J., Holst, J. and Hansell, P. 2000: Starch grains reveal early root crop horticulture in the Panamanian tropical rainforest. *Nature*, 407, 894–7.

Plisson, H., Giria, E. I. and Tchistiakov, D. A. 1988: Quelques termes Russes de technologie, tracéologie et typologie lithique. In S. Beyries (ed.), *Industries lithiques: tracéologie et technologie*. BAR International Series, 411. Oxford: British Archaeological Reports, 169–72.

Pollard, A. M. and Heron, C. 1996: *Archeological Chemistry*. Washington, DC: Royal Society of Chemistry.

Potts, R. and Shipman, P. 1981: Cutmarks made by stone tools on bones from Olduvai Gorge. *Nature*, 291, 577–80.

Procopiou, H. and Treuil, R. (eds.) 2002: *Moudre et broyer. L'interprétation fonctionnelle de l'outillage de mouture et de broyage dans la Préhistoire et l'Antiquité*, 2 vols. Paris: CTHS.

Reichert, E. T. 1913: *The Differentiation and Specificity of Starches in Relation to Genera, Species, etc.* London: Chapman.

Reid, A. and Young, R. 2000: Pottery abrasion and the preparation of African grains. *Antiquity*, 72, 101–11.

Richards, T. H. 1988: *Microwear Patterns on Experimental Basalt Tools*. BAR International Series, 460. Oxford: British Archaeological Reports.

Robertson, G. 1996: An application of environmental scanning electron microscopy and image analysis to starch grain differentiation. In S. Ulm, I. Lilley and A. Ross (eds.), *Australian Archaeology '95. Proceedings of the Australian Archaeological Association Annual Conference*. Tempus, 6. St Lucia: Anthropology Museum, University of Queensland, 169–82.

—— 2002: Birds of a feather stick: feather residues on stone artifacts from Deep Creek Shelter, New South Wales. In S. Ulm, C. Westcott, J. Reid et al. (eds.), *Barriers, Borders, Boundaries: Proceedings of the 2001 Australian Archaeological Association Annual Conference*. Tempus, 7. St Lucia: Anthropology Museum, University of Queensland, 175–82.

Rollo, F., Ubaidi, M., Ermini, L. and Marota, I. 2002: Ötzi's last meals: DNA analysis of the intestinal content of the Neolithic glacier mummy from the Alps. *Proceedings of the National Academy of Sciences of the United States of America*, 99(20), 12,594–9.

Rots, V. 2002: Bright spots and the question of hafting. *Anthropologica et Praehistorica*, 113, 61–71.

—— and Vermeersch, P. M. 2000: Lithics in Belgium. Some current research trends. *Lithic Technology*, 25(2), 76–9.

——, Pirnay, L., Pirson, P., Baudoux, O. and Vermeersch, M. 2001: Experimental hafting traces. Identification and characteristics. *Notae Praehistorica*, 21, 129–37.

Sakai, W. S. 1979: Aroid root crops, aridity and raphides. *Tropical Foods*, 1, 265–78.

Salmon, M. H. 1982: *Philosophy and Archaeology*. New York: Academic Press.

Schleiden, M. J. 1849: *Principles of Scientific Botany*, trans. E. Lankester. London: Longman.

Semenov, S. A. 1964: *Prehistoric Technology*, trans. M. W. Thompson. London: Cory, Adams and McKay.

Shafer, H. and Holloway, R. 1979: Organic residue analysis in determining stone tool function. In B. Hayden (ed.), *Lithic Use-Wear Analysis*. London: Academic Press, 385–99.

Shanks, O. C., Bonnichsen, R., Vella, A. T. and Ream, W. 2001: Recovery of protein and DNA trapped in stone tool microcracks. *Journal of Archaeological Science*, 28, 965–72.

Sinha, P. and Glover, I. 1984: Changes in stone tool-use in Southeast Asia 10,000 years ago: a microwear analysis of flakes with gloss from Leang Burung 2 and Ulu Leang 1 caves, Sulawesi, Indonesia. *Modern Quaternary Research in Southeast Asia*, 8, 137–64.

Smit, Z., Petru, S., Grime, G. et al. 1998: Usewear-induced deposition on prehistoric flint tools. *Nuclear Instruments and Methods in Physics Research. Section B: Beam Interactions with Materials and Atoms*, 140(1–2), 209–16.

Smith, M. A., Vellen, L. and Pask, J. 1995: Vegetation history from archaeological charcoals in Central Australia: the Late Quaternary record from Puritjarra rock shelter. *Vegetation History and Archaeobotany*, 4, 171–7.

Smith, P. R. and Wilson, M. T. 1992: Blood residues on ancient tool surfaces: a cautionary note. *Journal of Archaeological Science*, 19, 237–41.

Sussman, C. 1988: *A Microscopic Analysis of Use-Wear and Polish Formation on Experimental Quartz Tools*. BAR International Series, 395. Oxford: British Archaeological Reports.

Thompson, G. 1994: Wood charcoal from tropical sites: a contribution to methodology and interpretation. In J. Hather (ed.), *Tropical Archaeobotany. Applications and New Developments*. One World Archaeology, 22. London: Routledge, 86–114.

Tuross, N., Barnes, I. and Potts, R. 1996: Protein identification of blood residues on experimental stone tools. *Journal of Archaeological Science*, 23, 289–96.

Ugent, D., Pozorski, S. and Pozorski, T. 1981: Prehistoric remains of the sweet potato from the Casma Valley of Peru. *Phytologia*, 49, 401–15.

van den Dries, M. H. 1998: *Archaeology and the Application of Artificial Intelligence*. Archaeological Studies Leiden University 1, Leiden: Faculty of Archaeology, University of Leiden.

van Gijn, A. L. 1990: *The Wear and Tear of Flint: Principles of Functional Analysis Applied to Dutch Neolithic Assemblages*. Analecta Praehistorica Leidensia, 22. Leiden: University of Leiden.

Vaughan, P. C. 1985: *Use-Wear Analysis of Flaked Stone Tools*. Tucson: University of Arizona Press.

—— and Hopert, S. 1982–3: Suggestions for a list of basic terms in microwear analysis. *Early Man News: Newsletter for Human Palecology*, 7/8, 81–9.

White, J. P. and Thomas, D. H. 1972: What mean these stones? In D. L. Clarke (ed.), *Models in Archaeology*. London: Methuen, 275–308.

Yerkes, R. W. and Kardulias, P. N. 1993: Recent developments in the analysis of lithic artifacts. *Journal of World Prehistory*, 1(2), 89–119.

Linda Ellis

8
Ceramics

Introduction

As much as we today take for granted porcelain teacups, glass food condiment jars, plastic storage bowls, stainless steel cookware, or aluminum beer cans, it is easy to forget that the uses to which these materials are put represent a constant struggle for survival throughout ancient times: How do you consume food beyond the very time and place of hunting/gathering? How do you manage to drink away from the actual source of water and make sure that fluids are available when you need them? How do you survive when there is no food or water readily available for weeks or months during winter or drought? The underlying issue in all of these questions is the need for a system of sanitary containerization. But containerization goes beyond the biological requirement of providing nutrition and the need remains with us. The present-day carrier industry is eager to declare (as did ancient Greek sea traders) how well they package, protect, and transport our food and nonperishable goods. Both a bank's safe deposit box and a purposely buried ceramic pot containing hundreds of Roman coins, respectively, adequately protect valuables for future needs. While we never really think about it, containerization has always been a major part of human existence, and this is why pottery at archaeological sites speaks volumes on social, religious, economic, and even political behavior.

Of course, other materials were used as containers in prehistory – leather, basketry, wood, stone, and metals – and ceramics never completely replaced, nor was replaced by, any of these technologies. But while these materials are still very useful, they have a number of inherent limitations. Leather, basketry, and wood are organic materials that may themselves become infested and are neither completely waterproof nor heat tolerant. The making of stone bowls was common in prehistory, but this was arduous work and the resulting product was also difficult to handle and transport, and was thus best reserved for heavy and specialized operations such as grinding and milling. Until the Iron Age, metals were rare and expensive, and most bronze containers were restricted to those in the sociopolitical or religious hierarchies who could afford such luxuries. Clay and its fired end product, ceramics, are another matter entirely. The raw material is ubiquitous across the Earth, easy to procure and handle, and pliable into any desired shape. Ceramics are heat tolerant beyond the cooking temperature range, unattractive to pests, waterproof, sanitary and easy to clean, nonbiodegradable yet recyclable, sufficiently sturdy and lightweight to transport goods overseas, and both cheap enough to make at home and sufficiently elegant to serve an emperor. As with other materials, there are drawbacks: ceramic production does require fuel and pottery can fracture easily. However, the fuel can be as cheap as cattle dung and broken pots can easily be replaced and recycled.

In antiquity, besides containerization and food service, clay quickly became a building material for the manufacture of hearths and ovens in the home, bricks to create architecture, pipes to supply hot and cold water, and tiles to make pavements. Ceramics took on artistic, playful, or religious roles to make statuary, models and toys, and ritual altars. Fired clay is still used as an industrial material in the manufacture of other ceramics and products of other pyrotechnologies: as casting molds and cores in the production of elaborate metallic castings; as recycled material for future ceramics; and for the construction of kilns to fire pottery, to fuse glass, or to liquefy metals. Once human beings discovered the properties of raw and fired clay, the uses to which this material was put were multifarious and new uses are continuously being developed even today, from storage of nuclear waste to the manufacture of jet engine parts. Therefore, wherever humans have discovered the properties of fired clay, the products of this pyrotechnology are usually the most ubiquitous of archaeological finds encountered. Archaeologists have exploited this abundant material and focused considerable attention on the analysis of ceramics to further understand human cultural development.

This chapter can only suffice as an introduction to the study of archaeological ceramics. Anyone who is beginning ceramic studies should refer to the works by Shepard (1956), Rye (1981), Rice (1984, 1987), Arnold (1985), and Orton et al. (1993), which, taken together, will provide an excellent and comprehensive foundation. Before collecting samples and undertaking any kind of laboratory analysis, the student of archaeology should become familiar with the specialized terminology (in italics), the geology and chemistry of clays, and the technology of ceramic production. This chapter encourages you to think long-term about the excavating and handling of archaeological ceramics in the field, preserving the integrity of ceramics for prospective analyses, ensuring longevity of ceramics as a future archaeological resource, and even examining your own career development in ceramic studies.

What is a "Ceramic"?   Ceramic is best viewed as a transitional material, as a product of pyrotechnology lying on a solid–liquid continuum, between clay and glass. The term *ceramic* is usually applied to those objects or features made of clay and subsequently heat-treated so that the final product is durable and retains its shape when exposed to water. *Pottery* is a more specialized term, under the rubric of ceramics, and refers to containers for the preparation, consumption, and storage of food and liquid, or for the storage of other nonconsumable objects or materials. But in order to understand the manufacture and use of ceramics, you must first understand the raw, beginning product, "clay" (Ellis 2000a).

Geologically speaking, *clay* is a sedimentary rock formed from the products of erosion of other rocks, predominantly feldspars, but also granite, micas, other silicates, or volcanic formations. Clay is differentiated from other pedological materials (such as soils, silt, and sand) by extremely small particle sizes, less than 0.002 mm in diameter, which accounts for much of the observed behavior of clays when water is added (i.e., plasticity and colloidal suspension). Clays are classified either as *primary* (or *residual*) clays that formed at or near the parent rock, or *secondary* (*transported*) clays, formed from products of erosion, which were transported to various distances by weather systems, water currents, or glacial movement.

During the formation processes of primary and secondary deposits, the weathered sediments undergo both mechanical and chemical alterations, which result in the formation of clay minerals. A *mineral* is defined as a naturally occurring substance, with a known chemical composition, whose atoms are arranged in a regular geometric array (*crystallinity*). The chemical composition and atomic arrangement of clay minerals can be quite complex, but essentially are based on a unit of SiO_4 – one silicon atom surrounded by four oxygen atoms, arranged in a tetrahedral pattern. Characteristic of most clay minerals is that many silica tetrahedra are joined together into a network by sharing corner oxygen atoms, to form extensive sheets. These silicate sheets are then intercalated with layers of hydroxyl (OH) groups (i.e., chemically combined water) together with one or more additional elements (e.g., aluminum, magnesium, potassium, sodium, calcium, or iron), which derive from the weathered source rock. Two important issues derive from the chemistry of clays: (1) It is this variable composition, derived from the original parent rock, which has produced more than a dozen different clay minerals commonly found in nature. (2) Visible only under an electron microscope, these very delicate silicate sheets tend to form hexagonal-shaped platelets that measure half a micron or less. As will be described later, these platelets are the key to understanding all the unique aspects and behavior associated with clays and ceramics.

As part of the depositional process, clays also have natural inclusions (not to be confused with *temper*, defined below), which derive from the formation history of the clay deposit. Some of these inclusions (e.g., fragments of minerals and rocks, and microfossils) can affect the thermal behavior of clay but also allow us to identify sources of clays. Pure, white clays are not common and, therefore, most clays are naturally stained with iron oxides from the parent rock, and/or picked up during transport, and eventually determining the range of colors in fired clay.

For *clay* to become *ceramic*, heating has to be sufficient, in terms of both duration and intensity, to force the atoms in clay minerals to dissociate from their rigid crystalline arrangement. Once a certain temperature level (depending on the chemical composition of clay) has been reached during firing, the perimeters of the hexagonal clay platelets begin to melt into glass (liquid), which means that the atoms in this location are in an unpredictable (noncrystalline) arrangement. Meanwhile, the interior of the platelet remains crystalline (solid). In the course of firing pottery, there is an increased development of glass, as melting progresses inward toward the center of the platelet. As heating continues, the glass phase is extended further (*vitrification*), the result being a densification and shrinkage of the clay into a permanent, irreversible shape (e.g., the fired pot). If fired correctly, this partial formation of glass cements the clay particles together (*sintering* in ceramic terminology) and is responsible for producing a solid and potentially watertight object. If the heating process were to continue unabated at high temperatures, the clay platelets would completely melt into a glassy substance, too much liquid phase would not retain the potter's desired shape, and the end product would be a deformed and unusable mass (*slumping*). Hence, as stated earlier, a ceramic lies on the continuum between clay mineral (solid) and glass (liquid), retaining many of the visual and tactile characteristics of clay combined with the rigidity of glass.

Not all objects, features, structures, or materials made from clays should be classified as ceramics, however. Usually, clay products that have been *sun baked* (e.g., adobe, sun-dried brick) are insufficiently heated to cause a change in crystallinity and thus are technically dried clay and not ceramic. While the dense and compacted mass of sun-baked clay is still exceptionally durable for architecture in an arid environment, this building material will eventually be dissolved by rainfall if not protected by a plaster facing or otherwise maintained.

How is Pottery Made?

There are three required steps in the manufacture of pottery or other ceramics (i.e., clay preparation, object formation, and firing), with additional steps if the object is to be decorated either before or after firing.

Clay preparation

After raw clay is quarried and transported to the work site, it will usually need to be sorted and cleaned to remove vegetal and animal matter or other unwanted geological debris. Normally, raw clay has to be pulverized to provide a more even consistency, and to allow rapid and even absorption of water. If the finished product requires a certain fineness (a small particle-size range), then the clay may have to be refined by mixing it into a water suspension in a settling tank, or even a series of settling basins, in order to separate the finer fractions.

LINDA ELLIS

After cleaning and refining, the clay is then prepared for working. Different clays have vastly different mechanical behaviors (e.g., workability, absorption capability, shrinkage, and firing characteristics) based on the chemistry of each clay mineral. For this reason, potters often mix clays on the basis of their properties and availability. It is very important for both archaeologists and students to keep in mind that clays may have been mixed, and this can affect chemical analyses used to determine the provenance of the pottery.

When water is added to clay, it lubricates and interlocks the clay platelets, and the resulting plasticity allows the potter to form the object and the clay to retain that shape. However, added water will evaporate and the object will shrink during the drying and firing phases. To prevent excessive shrinkage and stress cracks, potters add *temper* to the cleaned clay. Temper may consist of any particulate or pulverized material that (ideally) is noncombustible, nonplastic, and nonhygroscopic; yet, in point of fact, potters will try anything at least once (e.g., sand, shell, rock, recycled ceramics, bone, gravel, volcanic glass, and even vegetal material). However, the natural inclusions in the clay, which may or may not be visible, can also serve the same purposes as temper, if they are present in sufficient quantities.

Ancient ceramics were produced completely by hand, with the assistance of rotary motion, and/or with molds. Clay pots may be made by the *pinch-pot* method (pinching and sculpting the clay into the desired form), the *coil method* (alignment of successive coils of clay, with each coil smoothed and joined to the one above and below), the *paddle-and-anvil method* (beating the exterior clay surface with a paddle while holding an anvil on the interior surface, both implements usually being made of wood), or any combination thereof. Pottery was also produced with the assistance of rotary motion, from a simple platen on a pivot, which is turned by hand or with a stick, to the more complicated fast-wheel (or *kick-wheel*). The fast-wheel consists of a circular turntable for the working of the clay, at the waist level of a seated potter who is able to use his or her feet to kick (i.e., spin) a lower, horizontal wheel – the turntable and the wheel are joined by a rod of wood or iron. Ceramic objects, especially bricks, can also be made with the use of molds, into which wet clay can be pressed, and then allowed to dry and shrink away from the mold to allow easy removal.

Object formation

The potter has a choice as to whether to decorate the finished object either before or after firing. Decorative surface treatment before firing takes advantage of the plasticity and absorptive properties of clay while still "leather-hard." A tremendous variety of decorative techniques were used in ancient times, including modifying the clay surface by *incising*, *excising* (gouging of clay to produce a design in sculptural relief), *impressing* (e.g., using shells, a

Pre-fire decoration

cord-wrapped stick, or fingernails), *clay appliqué*, or *inlay* work (for instance, filling incisions/excisions with powdered mineral colorants).

The surface of the unfired object may also be decorated by using a *slip*, which is a suspension of clay in water, plus an optional colorant (such as finely powdered iron-, manganese-, or calcium-based minerals). A slip is not a *glaze* (see below) and occasionally these two terms are used incorrectly in the archaeological literature. After a slip is applied, then it is usual practice to rub the surface of the slip (*burnishing*) with a smooth tool (e.g., polished bone or stone) or with a piece of leather. Burnishing has the effect of aligning the clay platelets in the slip, which increases its durability and also enhances surface reflectivity. Any of the above decorative techniques can and have been used in combination.

Firing   When the clay objects have been allowed to dry thoroughly, they can be fired. The firing of clay not only irreversibly changes its fundamental chemistry and crystallinity, but may also change the color of the final product. Pottery may be fired in simple pits dug into the ground; on the ground surface under a mound of fuel; or in single-, double-, or multi-chambered kilns, which themselves may be constructed out of compacted clay or brick. If firing in a simple pit, at the ground surface, or in a single-chamber kiln, the fuel and the objects to be fired (the *charge*) are placed together for the combustion process. In double- or multi-chambered kilns, the fuel can be kept separate in its own chamber (*fire box*); the heat then either travels up or down, depending on the design of the kiln, to fire the objects in another chamber.

The success of a firing and the quality of the ceramic products are ascertained by how effectively the potter achieves and controls the temperature of the fire and the surrounding gases (*atmosphere*). Combustion produces a mixture of gases including oxygen, carbon monoxide, carbon dioxide, sulfur compounds, and water vapor. However, depending on how the charge and fuel are arranged in the pit or in the kiln, a potter tries to control both the composition and flow of the gases to ensure an even firing. Unless the raw clay was originally white, natural iron oxides in the clay will render a permanent color depending on the firing atmosphere. If the potter desires a ceramic in the orange/pink/red range, then the surrounding gases will have to be oxygen-rich (an *oxidizing atmosphere*); that is, with a good input and circulation of air during firing. If the potter wants a brown/black/gray ceramic body, then the input airflow must be controlled to produce a *reducing atmosphere* that is rich in carbon monoxide. Any miscalculations in the firing process can result in serious surface imperfections.

Post-fire treatment   It can be more difficult or complicated to decorate a ceramic after firing, because the clay particles have now lost their original properties. At this point, the surface cannot be sculpted and any colorant has to be bonded to the surface in some way, using organic-based adhesives (e.g., tars, resins, gums, or proteins), the fresco process, or glass technology (i.e., glazes). *Glazes* are commonly formulations of finely powdered glass, quartz sand, or quartz-bearing rock, with or without added metal oxides as colorants or opacifiers, mixed with water and painted onto the ceramic surface. The object is then fired for a second time in order to melt the quartz-bearing base material or re-melt the powdered glass. The potter may apply several types of glazes (sometimes referred to as *enamels*) simultaneously, or even sequentially with multiple firings, provided that each overglaze melts at a temperature lower than the previous application. Glazes may be made from other, nonsiliceous materials, such as by throwing salt onto the pot during the firing.

In my 25 years of experience, I have yet to visit an archaeological excavation or storage facility where mistakes in the handling and processing of ceramic materials have not been made. My observations are based on being involved in, and teaching about – locally and internationally – all three facets of the archaeological process: conducting archaeological excavations, doing laboratory analytical studies of both my own and others' excavated ceramics, and working in the museum field. Therefore, what follows are a few easily implemented suggestions for the handling and treatment of finds at archaeological sites to help you (or scientists with whom you may collaborate in the future) to avoid problems when conducting laboratory analyses of ceramics.

Handling of Ceramics During and After Excavation

The combined effects of object handling at the site (excavating, cleaning, marking, and repairing) and long-term storage cause perhaps the greatest damage to ceramics and the potential to impact negatively the results of laboratory-based analyses. Unfortunately, a number of practices in field archaeology are propagated from one generation of archaeologists to the next, partly because we teach what we ourselves learned and partly because there is rarely enough time to include preventive conservation methods in typical, one-semester field methods courses (for more details, see Sease 1994). Moreover, two more serious problems are (1) the failure to think long-term on future research needs and (2) the tendency for archaeologists to neglect ceramic collections once the fieldwork and report-writing are over. The languishing of archaeological materials in (usually) poor packaging and storage conditions has been termed the *curation crisis*, and is especially prevalent in repositories designated for the collections of salvage and rescue archaeology (*cultural resources management* in North America). We do not know what future methods of analysis will be developed or refined for archaeological applications; nor do we know the future directions of archaeology as a discipline, or even if we will be able to continue the practice of archaeology in certain areas of the world as a result of repatriation legislation. Existing collections in storage may prove to be invaluable to future generations of archaeologists (cf., Cantwell et al. 1981).

Therefore, simple preventive conservation methods used at the time of excavation will ensure that (1) the integrity of samples will be maintained for future laboratory work, (2) samples will survive for new areas of archaeological research, and (3) samples will be available if archaeological excavations are limited or precluded.

Careful excavating

In the process of excavation, a lot of valuable information can be inadvertently destroyed or discarded with the back fill. Both seasoned archaeologists and their students should resist the temptation to "see" the surface of decorated pottery and sherds by scraping off soil or encrustations with the trowel or other abrasive tools. Tool marks and scratches are particularly damaging to fragile decorative slips and, since slips can be highly diluted by the potter, laboratory techniques may require as much slip as is on the entire surface of the sherd for analysis of the colorant. If a whole vessel, or a significant part of the base of a pot, is excavated, you should seriously consider *not* emptying out the soil contents. Retaining the soil inside the pot can allow you to analyze the residues for information about the original contents of the vessel. Retaining soil immediately surrounding the exterior of the vessel will also allow more precise dating of the ceramic using the thermoluminescence method. Attentiveness during the excavation of pottery manufacturing sites might also yield some of the raw materials used to decorate pottery – for example, lumps of hematite-, limonite-, or manganese-based minerals – which would otherwise easily be thrown out by a shovel.

Cleaning ceramics

On-site cleaning of sherds destined for laboratory analysis should be minimal and the least invasive. If time allows, soaking sherds in water to remove loose soil is the least damaging method for any future physicochemical and petrographic studies. After washing, pottery should be dried in the shade and packed only when thoroughly dried to avoid mold growth. Hard brushes can be quite abrasive to fragile slips and should be avoided on painted pottery. At many sites, however, ceramics are encrusted with hard, calcareous deposits (phosphates, sulfates, or carbonates), which are impossible to remove without the use of chemicals. Many archaeologists clean such encrusted pottery at the site, using baths of hydrochloric acid (HCl) diluted in water. Personally, I never use HCl on my excavations, first and foremost for the safety of students in the field. Secondly, HCl destroys certain information and negatively affects subsequent laboratory analysis by chemically altering white slips (with possibly calcium-based minerals added by the potter) and by dissolving calcium-based tempering materials and natural inclusions that are important for identifying the clay source (e.g., crushed shell, calcite, or microfossils). Thirdly, such strong acid baths have more harmful, long-term effects on the ceramic fabric once in museum storage. HCl can produce a powdery surface, even on well-fired sherds (900–1000°C range), which can be gently rubbed to remove the slip and other usable information. The dilemma for the archaeologist is that so much pottery is found, with usually no one else to take care of it, that some kind of bulk and rapid cleaning has to be done in the field. Therefore, if no local museum can assist with cleaning the pottery, citric acid is a milder alternative to HCl. The field team should first decide whether the pottery needs to be cleaned right away and, if so, experiment with a few heavily encrusted sherds, documenting different concentrations of citric acid and logging the time needed for the desired results, before subjecting all ceramics to the same treatment. But, *most importantly*, always reserve a representative sample collection of sherds that have *not* been cleaned at all, for subsequent laboratory analysis. (I have a policy of not accepting sherds cleaned with HCl for analysis, unless the archaeologist can supply uncleaned sherds as controls.) Even if no ceramic studies have been planned by the site director, and even if you are unsure whether analysis will ever be done, someone in the future may need this uncleaned pottery for analytical study – the dirt has been attached to the sherds for hundreds or thousands of years, and a little longer will not do any more harm.

The marking of artifacts with locational and inventorying information, while absolutely necessary, is a *cause célèbre* in archaeology, primarily because of the stubbornness of many archaeologists who continue to use inappropriate materials, such as nail varnish and white correction fluid. These highly improper products, which are still used as base coatings upon which to write information onto the object, are neither chemically stable nor permanent; and, when (not if) they peel off, both the critical provenance information and the topmost surface of a prehistoric ceramic will disappear. A conservation-safe varnish (such as Acryloid B-72) as a sealant and nonwaterproof black India ink or Pelikan white ink should be used for writing information on pottery. Moreover, thinking first about the placement of the written information on the object is also important if you anticipate removing a sample for laboratory analysis: I myself have had to saw through inventory numbers to make a viable thin section from ceramics excavated by other archaeologists. Marking ceramics

Ceramic materials should be repaired by a museum professional, not by an archaeologist. A particularly tragic, but not uncommon, event will illustrate the problems for laboratory analysis. While I happened to be visiting colleagues in the conservation laboratory of a museum, a highly regarded and experienced archaeologist brought in a large and unique ceramic altar dating to the Early Neolithic (sixth millennium BCE). It was found in the ground, already broken into several major sections, and also had traces of red decoration. The archaeologist was so enthralled and unrestrained in his curiosity that Repairing ceramics he had tried to piece together the sections in the field. But first, he had decided to clean the altar in HCl acid baths so that he could see the extent of the surface decoration; then he used huge amounts of commercially available white emulsion glue, which is more suitable for repairing paper products than ceramics. The results were disastrous. Since the ceramics of this early period were not well fired (~600–700°C), the acid baths had dissolved much of the red paint that was visible. Secondly, the inappropriate adhesive could not hold the fragments together; but, in trying to remove the sheer volume of dried glue, friable edges of the altar broke off. So, he finally did what he should have done at the very beginning (only now with an unholy mess in cardboard boxes): bring in the altar pieces to polite, but unamused, chemists and conservators in the museum's analytical laboratory. But, sadly, much valuable information had already been irretrievably lost.

| Initiating an Analytical Program for Ceramics | The study of any archaeological material usually begins with a question from which hypotheses are formulated, research designs developed, and samples selected, together with analytical methods appropriate to the problem. While the focus of this chapter is on laboratory analysis, it should be emphasized here that, first and foremost, the behavioral component of ceramic production must always be the aim of ceramic studies. The research program and objectives are always grounded firmly within the context of archaeological and anthropological theory, a subject that is beyond the scope of this chapter (see Arnold 1985). |

Chemical analysis for the sake of chemical analysis – as the segregated "appendix of numbers" to the site report that was so prevalent in archaeological publishing up to 20 years ago and is still occasionally seen – should no longer be considered in archaeological research. The objective in any analytical program is to reveal and better understand human behavior in the past, by whichever means that may be achieved. In this section of the chapter, issues concerning laboratory analysis of ceramics are outlined.

| Prefatory issues before undertaking an analytical program | If the research design necessitates the use of microscopy and/or physicochemical methods of analysis to answer questions or verify hypotheses about the ceramics under study, then you should first evaluate whether you, the research program, and the artifact samples are adequately prepared. Furthermore, decisions need to be made on the available resources, the expendability of the samples, and the kinds of results desired. |

First, is the proposed analysis of ceramics hypothesis-driven? If not, then not only may valuable time and resources be wasted, but unique archaeological material may be destroyed as an unavoidable part of the laboratory technique. It is not uncommon for both novice and seasoned archaeologist to ask a specialist to analyze a collection in the hope that the data will "speak" to the archaeologist, or that the analytical method will reveal inner secrets that can be exploited in thesis or dissertation research, a future publication, or a conference paper. (I once received a package of ceramics from a prominent archaeologist with a handwritten note, "Please analyze.") It is true that, oftentimes in the process of analyzing a collection, new ideas, unanticipated results, or different approaches can and do change the direction of research. Rarely is research purely deductive, and inductive reasoning is nearly always part of the intellectual process. Furthermore, specialists from other disciplines, such as chemistry, biology, physics, or geology, may not be able to make cogent decisions about approaching an archaeological problem (such as selection of the best analytical method, sample types, and sample size) if no well thought out basis for analysis has been formulated by the archaeologist.

Secondly, the archaeologist needs to evaluate which specialists from other disciplines should be consulted and what the archaeologist her- or himself can learn and do within a reasonable time frame. While not discussed often enough, this is a decision that is particularly critical for all students in archaeology to take seriously, since it may influence the career path of the individual to a large extent. If, as an undergraduate student, you anticipate entering a doctoral program in archaeology, once accepted into a PhD track you will be required to indicate a specialized area of research, as well as to decide what additional analytical skills or avenues for collaboration will be needed to undertake that research. In the case of ceramic studies, and depending on the nature and needs of the research, you may have to decide whether you should undertake some coursework in petrography, sedimentary geology, materials science, physicochemical methods of analysis, or dating methods. It should be emphasized this is not a requirement, but part of a larger career decision-making process. Unfortunately, most students of archaeology do not have enough basic education at the university level in the sciences, and this issue can be easily overlooked when archaeologists advise their students. Collaboration with colleagues outside of archaeology may be needed, because that is where the expertise resides; however, in order to make the collaboration more meaningful (i.e., to be able to ask the right questions of specialists and understand the significance of the results) and to develop a more competent research profile, those of you who are entering archaeology as a profession should try to strengthen your academic background in a relevant specialized field (e.g., geology and/or materials science for ceramic studies).

Much archaeological literature abounds on proper sampling strategies and quantitative analysis of archaeological finds (see Orton et al. 1993: 166ff., with cited publications by Orton, who has written extensively on this topic, especially for ceramics). However, the ability to subject ceramic objects and their laboratory analysis to quantitative treatment needs to be approached with great caution. The longstanding controversy over quantification of pottery

Quantitative analysis of ceramics

(and, in fact, of all archaeological materials) begins at the excavation and field collection phase. Statistical treatment of a group of objects or data implies that the total population is known – an impossible task in archaeology, because we only see a residual component of what formerly existed in the past. Other basic issues are as follows: How much of the site was excavated? How were the excavated areas chosen and sampled? How was the site excavated (which can be anywhere on a continuum from salvage or "bulldozer" archaeology, at one extreme, to fine screening of all soil excavated, at the other)? Furthermore, how do you interpret fragments from a single object that end up in different archaeological contexts at the site? Just as importantly, these biases in quantification will, unavoidably, be transmitted throughout the "chain of research" to all subsequent laboratory analyses – a point that is often ignored. You should not be nihilistic about quantitative studies of ceramics – quite the contrary – but the results cannot conform to the rigorous standards of scientific *accuracy* and *precision*; that is, respectively, the veracity of the information and the ability to reproduce the same results if the analysis is conducted by someone else. Therefore, results of quantitative analysis should not be solely relied upon as a final data set, but rather be considered useful guidelines whose conclusions should be corroborated by other kinds of studies.

For archaeologists, though, there are serious questions that can only be answered by employing some quantification method: How much pottery is there? How much pottery is local versus nonlocal (foreign)? Do some sites in the region have more pottery than others, and why? How long was the site occupied and how does it relate chronologically with other sites in the region? Therefore, quantification methods are necessary for (1) seriation (to ascertain the temporal distribution of categories of ceramics), (2) intra-site analysis (to identify spatial distributions of ceramic types, to determine the utilitarian functions of ceramics or social aspects of ceramic production, such as kinship patterns and social stratification), and (3) inter-site analysis (to identify regional distribution patterns and economic relations among sites).

Quantification of ceramics has followed four basic approaches. First, *sherd count* involves simply counting all individual sherds from each excavation unit and calculating the percentage of sherds according to local typologies. The obvious flaws here are that (1) individual fragments do not necessarily represent a unique vessel and (2) different ceramic types will have different degrees of *brokenness* (i.e., the more fragile the fabric, the greater is the number of fragments). Therefore, attempts are usually made to match sherds together to reflect the total vessel count more accurately. You can even provide two calculations – counting sherds before and after repair attempts – to provide a maximum and minimum number of vessels, but you can never be sure and inevitably the total vessel estimation will be too high. Ceramic fragmentation patterns are a major issue and are different for each object on the basis of its manufacture, size, shape, density, and mass, together with taphonomic

LINDA ELLIS

processes such as the manner of disposal, human behavior around refuse areas, and exposure to weather.

Sherd weight again is concerned with calculating percentages of sherds according to their classified types, but on the basis of their weight. This method may correct for one of the problems of sherd counting by taking into consideration the differential breakage patterns as a result of mass and density. Sherd weight counts may also be corrected by measuring wall thickness and dividing sherds accordingly into groups, weighing each of those groups separately, and treating the results mathematically to estimate the number of whole vessels (Hulthén 1974; but for other possible manipulations of sherd weight data, see Rice 1987: 290 ff.). However, ultimately, heavier pots will always be overrepresented.

Calculating the *number of vessels represented* (i.e., identifying and counting actual vessels) also has significant difficulties, because of both *brokenness* and *completeness*. Orton (1985) introduced the idea of *completeness*: the proportion of the original vessel that is present in the archaeological assemblage. The problem here is that ceramics with low completeness and a high degree of brokenness will, again, be overrepresented (the same problem as in the sherd count method). But, more importantly, the same vessel can have different degrees of brokenness and completeness depending on the nature of its use, discard, and depositional history. Assemblage calculations will therefore be biased but, worse, assemblages from different contexts at the same or different sites cannot be compared, even when analyzing a single pottery type. Furthermore, when dealing with ceramics produced on an industrial scale (e.g., in the Roman period), mass production techniques may thwart efforts to determine the uniqueness of individual ceramics.

Calculation of the *estimated vessel equivalents* (*EVE*) avoids the problem of having to sort and match sherds from the same vessel in order to reproduce actual numbers of vessels but, furthermore, acknowledges that our calculations can only be *estimates*. For this method, one distinctive part of the pot must be selected – for example, a rim or handle, but usually the former depending on the type of pottery and what survives – to represent that part of the whole pot. This procedure is analogous to the quantification of archeofaunal assemblages in which a distinctive bone, with a good survival rate and unique to the anatomy of the species, is used to count the minimum number of individual animals (see Chapter 9). Yet again, potential problems include underestimating the number of vessels, because sherds from the body of the pot – as opposed to the rim, base, or handle – are usually an overwhelming majority in an assemblage.

Ceramics have highly variable fragmentation patterns, based on their shape, density, size, and use–discard–depositional histories. Therefore, quantification methods for ceramics cannot mimic successfully those designed for other, especially biologically derived, materials such as faunal remains (e.g., the MNI concept). While every archaeologist has an opinion, the fact of the matter is that no one has really come up with a reliable system for quantifying ceramic assemblages that can yield reproducible results across different types of sites, cultures, time periods, technologies, and taphonomic processes (although Orton is an intrepid and clear exponent on the theoretical and mathematical issues). Among existing quantification methods, sherd weight and EVE, or permutations thereof, are the more reliable and should still be done, but with careful documentation of the procedures. The quantification of archaeological ceramics is a field that is definitely in need of continuing refinement.

Sampling for laboratory analysis

Ceramic manufacturing processes introduce further complications to quantitative analysis that are unknown to other types of archaeological remains. The transference of inherent errors in statistical results from the field through to the laboratory stage of research is unavoidable when examining products of *pyrotechnology*. The manufacture of ceramics, glass, and metals changes the original composition of the raw material, as opposed to the manufacture of objects by *subtractive technology* (rocks, flint, obsidian, and bone), which does not modify chemistry. When we examine the definition of ceramics, the nature of the raw clay, and the production techniques of potters, as purposefully detailed above, it is immediately apparent that many assumptions and presumptions have to be made, and a lot of uncomfortable issues ignored, for statistical studies and sampling strategies to work. Clay deposits are an open system in nature and the geochemistry within a single clay bed is subject to the vagaries of the lithosphere–atmosphere interface. Furthermore, all potters mix, match, and change their clay sources as well as tempering and painting materials, and may deviate, unnoticed and undetected, from other aspects of ceramic production technology.

Sampling strategies and subsequent quantitative studies can also be affected by the more pragmatic issue of availability of ceramics for laboratory analysis; the process of negotiation can be an interesting education in and of itself. It should be relatively easy to obtain ceramic samples, but this can be complicated by a number of factors: whether they are coming directly from the field or are housed and already inventoried by a museum; whether the analyst and the prospective samples reside in the same country or in different countries; and whether permission to take samples can be given by the archaeologist on site or by a government bureaucrat. Laboratory studies requiring whole vessels are rarely undertaken except for special purposes such as TL dating, or to determine their authenticity if they have circulated on the art market. Whole vessels deriving from current excavations have value as objects for public exhibition and are thus typically sent to museums for immediate conservation treatment and inventorying. However, and fortunately, fragmentary archaeological ceramics are plentiful and have little display value. Therefore, for most ceramic studies, sherds should be sufficient, and this should be emphasized in the course of your negotiations.

LINDA ELLIS

Given all of the foregoing, the selection of ceramic samples for laboratory work (e.g., microscopy or physicochemical analysis) will depend on the nature of the research problem and the analytical methods chosen. However, you should take into consideration the following basic guidelines for any *intra-site* study. For diachronic ceramic studies, representative samples should be taken from each chronological period, so that production variations through time can be documented. If the pottery has surface decoration (slip, glaze, incisions, excisions, or inlay), samples from each "type" or "ware" should be selected. Also, undecorated ceramics should not be ignored, as happens quite often. If there are ceramics with different uses (e.g., fine ware, cooking ware, or storage vessels), samples from each category should be analyzed for technological variation in connection with the intended use. If ceramic variation is to be studied *vis-à-vis* location within the site (i.e., variations in ceramic inventories from different types of burials or from different residences), then samples need to be carefully analyzed from each context. For *inter-site* study, in addition, representative samples need to be selected from each site, provided that there is chronological control. In order to identify the origin of "foreign" or otherwise intrusive ceramics, raw clay samples will have to be taken in addition to all of the preceding suggestions (more below). Another level of sampling will be needed on the sherds themselves if point-by-point elemental composition (e.g., electron microprobe analysis of glazes) or TL dating of individual grains is to be conducted. Depending on the complexity of the research program, this may add up to a lot of samples, and – together with museum personnel, the site director and/or the analyst – you will need to discuss available resources and costs (e.g., funding, equipment time, and sample preparation time): hence an additional constraint and factor for quantitative studies.

Before any work is done on ceramics, the student, supervising archaeologist, and any specialists should consult with each other as to the need for any specialized analytical investigations – such as dating methods, physicochemical methods of compositional analysis, or other kinds of testing – which are appropriate to answer the specific archaeological and anthropological questions. When analytical methods are under consideration, you should proceed from the most simple (e.g., optical microscopy) to the most complex avenues of investigation (e.g., nuclear methods of chemical analysis). It is imperative to plan laboratory analyses at the outset to determine financial requirements, to ascertain the student's role in such work, and, most importantly, to discuss all the implications for irreplaceable ceramic samples. Resources need to be identified and evaluated: What are the available laboratories, equipment, and expertise available at your own university, at other universities, or at major museums in the region? Are the samples expendable for destructive analysis (e.g., petrography), or must the analysis be less invasive or even nondestructive? If they are expendable, or if only a small amount of powder can be removed,

How to begin analysis and select an appropriate analytical method are the sherds or whole objects sufficiently durable to undergo sample extraction (e.g., sawing, grinding, or drilling)? For compositional studies, will quantitative results be necessary, or will semiquantitative or qualitative results be sufficient to answer the research questions?

Once a laboratory plan for analytical work has been agreed upon, and before work begins on ceramics, all safety and legal issues must be observed. First, the object is photographed showing different angles or interior/exterior, front/back surfaces, with both color and measuring scales (cf., Dorrell 1989). Secondly, ceramic objects should always be studied on a clean, safe, padded table; carried in a sturdy and padded tray or box to and from storage; and stored in secure and padded trays or boxes on nonslip shelves or (preferably) in cabinets. Thirdly, the student or analyst should remove all jewelry on hands and wrists when working with ceramics, remove other damaging materials (inks and pens), use only fabric (never metallic!) tape measures, use metallic profile gauges only if absolutely necessary (with a protective plastic sheet interface), and refrain from eating and drinking near archaeological objects. Fourthly, for legal and practical reasons, anyone handling ceramics, especially those inventoried by museums, must document any surface defects, fragile or damaged decoration, broken or missing appendages, or structural damage already present on the object. A condensed template for an "Object Condition and Examination Report," which can be simplified for sherds, is given in Figure 8.1, to help you develop a systematic pattern of observation and basic documentation.

In order to establish a foundation of knowledge, it is important to examine, with consistency, all phases in the production process as outlined earlier: clay preparation, vessel formation, firing process, and pre- or post-fire decorative techniques (if any). Visual inspection of cleaned objects should cover, in a consistent manner, all surfaces: top to bottom, front to rear, exterior to interior, appendages, and associated parts (handles, legs, supports, and lids). Examination should begin with the naked eye and progress to increasing levels of magnification using a stereomicroscope in the ×10–×60 range. Basic information on surface treatment, control over firing conditions (atmosphere), and kind and quantity of temper can usually be obtained at this level. On expendable sherds, a small chip can be snapped off, making a clean break, to examine the sherd in cross-section. The presence of a *core* (a darker/reduced interior sandwiched between lighter or oxidized exterior and interior surfaces), for instance, indicates the extent and duration of firing.

Once microscopic examination has been accomplished, the next phase of ceramic analysis will depend on the nature of the research program and must be tailored to the needs of the hypotheses or issues under investigation. A multitude of methods of physical examination from chemistry, physics, and materials science engineering exist and have been applied to the study of ceramics and other archaeological materials. The general avenue of inquiry – for example, dating, provenance, firing temperature determination, and use/

Object Condition & Examination Report for Ceramics

Institutional location of object: _____
Museum Accession No.: _____ Field Inventory No.: _____
Site & geographic location: _____
Archaeological context: _____
Cultural affiliation: _____
Chronological period/date: _____
Dimensions: ___|_____|_____|_____|_____|_____|
  [Metric unit ___ length   width/depth   height   max/min circumference   rim diameter   base diameter]

DESCRIPTION and CONDITION of CERAMIC

Type of object: ( ) vessel: _____ ( ) sculpture: _____
( ) architectural element: _____ ( ) other: _____
Auxiliary parts: ( ) handle(s) _____ ( ) leg(s): _____ ( ) lid/other cover: _____
( ) stand(s): _____ ( ) other: _____

Manufacture: ( ) hand built: _____ ( ) wheelmade _____ ( ) molded
Other production details: _____
Temper: _____
Firing: ( ) oxidized ( ) reduced ( ) mixed/uneven ( ) core: _____
Other firing details: _____
Color(s) of fired clay: _____
                    [indicate location, extent, and Munsell values]

Condition of ceramic body {note size/extent and location of problem}:
( ) Cracks _____
( ) Chipping _____
( ) Abrasion/spalling _____
( ) Scratches _____
( ) Weathering/erosion _____
( ) Exterior accretions/stains: _____
    ( ) Calcareous deposits ( ) crystallized salts ( ) organic materials/residues ( ) soil retained for analysis
( ) Interior accretions/stains: _____
    ( ) Calcareous deposits ( ) crystallized salts ( ) organic materials/residues ( ) contents retained for analysis
( ) Fire damage _____
    ( ) Fire clouds ( ) Slumping ( ) Cooking ( ) Secondary firing ( ) Other _____
( ) Missing/damaged parts: _____
( ) Previous repairs: _____
( ) Cleaned, materials used: _____

DESCRIPTION & CONDITION of SURFACE FINISH or DECORATION

Description: ( ) impressed ( ) stamped ( ) incised ( ) excised ( ) molded relief ( ) appliqué ( ) faience
( ) slip(s) ( ) glaze(s) ( ) inlay _____ ( ) other _____
Color(s) of slip/glaze: _____
Location of decoration: _____
Other details: _____

Condition of decoration {note size/extent and location of problem}:
( ) Scratches _____
( ) Abrasions _____
( ) Erosion/weathering _____
( ) Spalling _____
( ) Crazing _____
( ) Missing surface area _____
( ) Previous restorations: _____

Examined by {print}: _____ date: _____

Figure 8.1 An object condition and examination report for ceramics.

wear – will dictate which methods will be appropriate. The final selection of the most appropriate method(s) is made in consultation with specialists and in relation to the quality of the samples and available resources. The basic details of the most commonly used analytical methods are outlined in Table 8.1. The

Table 8.1 Laboratory methods of analysis for ceramic studies (for details of analytical methods, see Rice 1987; Ellis 2000c).

Analytical method	Acronym.	Type/focus of analysis	Materials analyzed	Research applications
Petrography		Microscopy of ceramic thin sections; magnification range: ×50—×400	Ceramic body, temper, slip, glaze	Manufacturing methods, temper characterization, geological sourcing of clay inclusions or temper
Electron microscopy: *Scanning electron microscopy* *Transmission electron microscopy*	SEM TEM	High magnification (×50K—×300K) microscopy of microstructure of fired clay, temper, inclusions, applied decoration	Ceramic body, temper, slip, glaze	Manufacturing methods, temper characterization, firing temperature determinations, structural and chemical characterization studies when used with electron microprobe
X-ray fluorescence	XRF	Elemental composition [chemical "fingerprinting"]	Source clays, ceramic body, slip, glaze	Provenance of pottery by matching to clay sources, manufacturing methods, compositional analysis of slips and glazes
Nuclear activation methods: *Neutron activation analysis* *Fast neutron activation analysis* *Proton activation analysis* *Proton-induced X-ray emission*	NAA FNAA PAA PIXE	Elemental composition [chemical "fingerprinting"]	Source clays, ceramic body	Provenance of pottery by matching to clay sources
X-ray diffraction	XRD	Determination of crystallographic structure of minerals	Raw clay, fired clay, slip	Identification of high-temperature clay minerals and slip colorants
Mössbauer spectroscopy		Crystallographic environment of ^{57}Fe isotope	Fired clay	Firing temperature and atmosphere of iron-rich clays; provenance
Thermoluminescence	TL	Ionizing radiation dosimetry since last firing	Fired clay, mineral grains	Dating of ceramics
Archaeomagnetic dating		Thermoremanent magnetism of iron grains since last firing	Fired clay	Dating of *in situ* fired clay structures (e.g., kilns)
Thermal analysis: *Differential thermal analysis* *Thermogravimetric analysis* *Thermal expansion analysis*	DTA TGA	Observation of thermal behavior of clay during controlled reheating experiments	Fired clay	Determination of original firing temperatures
Xeroradiography		X-ray photography of object	Whole object or any part thereof	Manufacturing and construction methods; identification of forgeries and restorations; analysis of particulate inclusions

limitations of this chapter cannot permit extensive discussion, and the reader is referred to the available literature for the underlying principles and applications of each individual method (cf., for descriptions by specialists in each field, Ellis 2000c). What follows are some guidelines for how to approach more detailed laboratory analysis.

Here, we will examine questions that are important for the understanding of human behavior with some concrete examples from recent research. It cannot be emphasized enough that analysis of ceramics, as with any other archaeological material, must be preceded by research questions. The examples of published research mentioned below are neither representative nor comprehensive of the discipline, but were selected from different areas of the world and from different time periods to give you a starting point in visualizing the variety of possible avenues of investigation relating to ceramics.

Areas of Ceramics Research and their Analytical Approaches

One of the first questions usually asked of pottery is "How was it made?" Oftentimes, this issue is addressed right at the beginning of archaeological work in a region as part of the process of creating ceramic typologies, since the archaeologist uses technology as well as ceramic form and decoration to differentiate pottery in time and space. However, the study of ceramic manufacturing methods can provide information on a far wider range of subjects beyond temporal and spatial distribution patterns, as was exemplified through the work of Frederick Matson (1965) – and his coining of the term *ceramic ecology* is still respected today. Furthermore, over the past 20 years, the field of *ceramic ethnoarchaeology* has demonstrated to archaeologists that the immeasurable variety of human behavior from living pottery traditions can inform the interpretation of analytical data from the laboratory (Longacre 1992; Nicholas & Kramer 2001). A new area for ceramic studies is the close examination of how technological skills are taught and learned, how information is distributed, and how knowledge is preserved or changed over time (Minar & Crown 2001). This research draws from the fields of developmental psychology, neurophysiology, and cognitive theory, and thus is beyond the scope of this chapter, but is nevertheless important for students' attention because behavioral studies can test longstanding assumptions based on archaeological and laboratory data.

Pottery-making can be evaluated as part of a larger "learning curve" about materials and their processing technology: Ascertaining the firing temperatures attained and the control over firing atmosphere will indicate how well the craftsperson understood empirically the chemical and physical changes that would take place during each phase of ceramic production. Furthermore, how ancient potters developed expertise to discover and evaluate the quality of available natural resources (e.g., different types of clays and tempers, selection

Technology studies

of appropriate fuels) can reveal a remarkable "ethnoscientific" understanding about geological resources, pyrotechnology, and the landscape. Research on the characterization of the clay through its natural inclusions (identification of rocks, minerals, and fossils) and a more precise analysis of temper can only be made from examining thin sections (0.03 mm) of ceramics using a *transmitted light* (or *petrographic*) microscope with magnifications in the range of ×50–×400. Making and analyzing thin sections is a method of examination developed within geology, which can, and should, be learned well by archaeology students interested in ceramic studies and is described in detail elsewhere (Ellis 2000b). This is a destructive laboratory technique, requiring a clean section of the ceramic to be sawn off, and should only be done on expendable sherds after they are photographed and drawn. The section can reveal much information about ceramic manufacturing methods, the interface between ceramic and applied decoration, as well as the most important details of temper and natural inclusions.

For technological investigations, petrographic analysis will yield most information required by archaeologists. More specific avenues of investigation include determinations of ceramic firing temperatures and compositional analysis of the slips, glazes, and fabrics. Scanning electron microscopy and Mössbauer spectroscopy can be used to determine the firing temperature of ceramics. X-ray diffraction, which identifies specific minerals, can be used to identify pigments in slips as well as high-temperature phases of minerals as a result of firing. Electron probe microanalysis, X-ray fluorescence analysis, and inductively coupled plasma–atomic emission spectrometry (ICP–AES) each analyze elemental composition of pigments and fabrics, depending on the needs of the research program (for descriptions of these methods, see Ellis 2000c).

Usewear studies of ceramics

The question "What was it used for?" may have interesting implications for dietary and medical studies of ancient populations. The technological quality of ceramics provides information on the possible uses for which the objects were made: different firing temperatures and the type and quantity of temper can determine whether a ware is more appropriate for cooking food and liquids or for food consumption and storage. Determining the use(s) to which ceramics – primarily vessels for the cooking, consumption, or transportation of food, oil, and wine – were put involves two separate avenues of investigation: indirect analysis of the contents of uncleaned pottery versus direct analysis of the ceramic surface. Analysis of the soil and residues of recently excavated pottery requires consultation with specialists in the field of organic chemistry to identify proteins, fats, oils, carbohydrates, and other complex organic molecules deriving from foods and beverages and the technical literature abounds on this topic (see any volume of the *Journal of Archaeological Science*). The direct analysis of the surface of artifacts for traces of the patterns of use or wear, while a major area of archaeological research on stone tools for over 40 years,

LINDA ELLIS

is still an underrepresented avenue of research in ceramic studies that students can exploit (see the study of abrasion patterns on pottery from Africa by Reid & Young 2000; see also Chapter 7).

For dating of ceramic materials, you will need to ascertain whether *direct investigation* (analysis of the ceramic itself) is necessary or if *indirect investigation* (analysis of material in association with the ceramics) will be sufficient. For archaeologists, carbon 14 dating of organic materials is the preferred dating method (see Chapter 5). If ceramic vessels are found reasonably intact, and not cleaned out at the time of excavation, much organic material is potentially available for ^{14}C dating. For direct dating of the ceramic itself, thermoluminescence (TL) dating can be used on movable objects such as pottery versus archaeomagnetic dating for *in situ* features consisting of fired clay (e.g., structures, hearths, or kilns) (cf., for details of dating methods by specialists, Ellis 2000c). For archaeomagnetic dating of buried, fired structures, a hand-sized specimen has to be cut out, with current magnetic north and sample orientation carefully indicated. However, TL dating can be expensive and is usually only undertaken on ceramic objects in museum collections with no archaeological context (for interesting applications, see Fleming 1975). Fortunately, the laboratory technique for thermoluminescence dating has been considerably refined so that dating can be done on individual grains taken unobtrusively from a valuable museum object. However, in a field situation, it also helps to have a sample of the soil surrounding an object to ascertain environmental radiation dosage to obtain a more precise date.

Dating of ceramics

The question "Who made the ceramics?" has remained alluring in archaeology because, with rare exceptions, we are not as fortunate as historians to have written records of named individuals. Archaeologists, however, have remained undaunted, and research to identify potters has been undertaken with success on a number of levels. The most extensive research in this area has been conducted in the southwestern United States, where Native Americans have produced numerous ceramic art traditions in prehistory. The painted pottery in Arizona has allowed archaeologists to identify individual potters by their techniques (Van Keuren 1999). At the next social level, the reflection of kinship structure and residence patterns, through analysis of pottery production, has been studied successfully over the past four decades, from the "ceramic sociology" of the 1960s to the behavioral archaeology of today (for an excellent history and thorough bibliography of this research, see Longacre 2000; also, for the northeastern USA, see Brumbach 1984–5). In order to identify individual potters, it is usually necessary to document very carefully the brushstroke patterns in painting, the development and spread of all artistic motifs, and patterns in the types and quantities of temper, as well as techniques

Identifying the potters

of vessel formation and firing. These kinds of studies, however, can reveal who learns and makes pottery, how the information is passed from one generation to the next, and how pottery reflects both kinship systems and residence patterns.

Another area of identification in ceramic studies is cultural affiliation of archaeological remains. There are two procedures, which should not be confused: using ceramics to designate "archaeological cultures" versus identifying ethnolinguistic groups through pottery. The naming of "cultures" on the basis of ceramic typology is a shorthand strategy to assist the archaeologist in establishing relative chronologies and understanding geographical distributions of archaeological materials from periods with no historical documentation, and does not reflect any emic or etic ethnic reality. The identification of ceramics with historically known ethnolinguistic groups is more suitable to areas where some written evidence can provide corroboration (Dever 1995). Unfortunately, archaeological research on ethnicity can become politically exploited by national governments; however, in my own research, following ceramic form from pre- to post-Roman periods, analyzing the socioeconomic differences of ceramics in children's burials, and documenting technological traditions through petrography can produce a more three-dimensional image of multi-ethnic interaction zones in times of hegemonic colonization (Ellis 1998).

Sourcing of ceramics
The investigation of *provenance* (also *provenience*), or *sourcing*, of ceramics has been a major field of inquiry throughout the history of archaeology because of the potentially wide distribution of ceramics or their contents. The archaeologist, however, must be careful to separate issues of research interest – to understand exchange systems in local, down-the-line, or long-distance trade networks; to match local ceramics to geological sources of clays; to verify whether pottery was made locally or to trace ceramics to archaeological sites outside the region; to identify interactions among populations at various levels of organization (inter-village, inter-city, and inter-ethnic); to identify distributional patterns of mass-produced ceramics from major manufacturing centers – to name a few avenues of such research. Two very different and successful studies, which should be read by students, also use provenance analysis as a way of solving other archaeological issues. Eerkens et al. (2002) undertook the tracing of (frequently neglected!) undecorated ceramics produced by mobile hunter–gatherers – a population not usually associated with ceramic production. Grave et al. (2000) traced industrially produced ceramics to specific kiln operations; their laboratory analyses were also able to detect changes in chemistry and firing over many years as a response to fluctuations in international markets for Asian products. At sites with obviously intrusive (nonlocal) pottery, the behavioral question becomes: Was the pot traded or were the contents traded? The trade in luxury Greek pottery versus Greek (and later Roman) amphorae for commercial trade in wine and olive oil are obvious examples, but most

other situations are not so clear and may need chemical analysis to determine the motive for the exchange. A further, hypothetical complication is that the pot may have been traded before being used a second time to trade contents, or vice versa. Such reuse and recycling of ceramic materials merits closer analysis in archaeology (and would be good fodder for student work, not to mention a few doctoral dissertations), the results of which could be quite revealing.

For some studies, overall ceramic style and petrographic analysis are adequate to determine the site of manufacture if sufficient research on ceramics exists for the region. In order to match pottery to geological clay sources, multiple samples will have to be taken from each known clay bed within walking distance of the potters' residences and chemically matched to examples of each type of ceramic ware. The farther away the ceramics are transported from their site of manufacture, the more difficult it is to trace their original clay sources because of the sheer quantity of clay beds in any region, unless there are unique aspects of technology and style that set them apart. When dealing with situations of long-distance trading, or to identify origins of ceramics with no archaeological context (e.g., pots that have circulated on the art market), the best that can be hoped for is to identify the most likely area of origin on the basis of stylistic attributes, to examine ceramics from all contemporaneous sites in that region, and to determine whether the geological sourcing of clays is practicable and affordable.

To match ceramics with clay sources, physicochemical "fingerprinting" methods of analysis are necessary to determine the chemical composition of the ceramics and clays. At this point, you need to appreciate the differences between major elements, minor elements, and trace elements, and the importance of quantitative, semiquantitative, and qualitative results. Clays have many elements in common – for example, silicon, aluminum, iron, or potassium – and the relatively high percentages of these major and minor elements will not assist in distinguishing among the various clay sources. Therefore, the trace amounts of rare elements need to be quantified to distinguish one clay source from another, and hence semiquantitative and qualitative results are not sufficient. Such analyses can be done using a wide array of methods based on the interaction of energy (e.g., radiation) with matter and further differentiated by what part of the atom is being targeted: X-ray fluorescence targets the inner shell of electrons; nuclear activation methods target the nucleus of the atom. In these examples, the radiation forces the atoms of the sample to produce secondary radiation, of an energy and wavelength unique to that element, which can then be detected and identified as belonging to that element (cf., for descriptions of available methods, Ellis 2000c). However, a warning before using such physicochemical methods of analysis: if the pottery was tempered with crushed sherds (*grog*), the recycled sherds may come from completely different ceramic traditions (skewing chemical analyses if the sherd temper is not carefully separated from the clay matrix); other types of temper may also have similar effects (Cogswell et al. 1998).

Besides the general texts recommended in the introduction, the reader will find the following journals useful for current research on archaeological ceramics: *Archaeometry* and the *Journal of Archaeological Science* publish technical articles on applications of existing and newly developed physicochemical methods of analysis. Journals focusing on archaeological method and theory (e.g., *Journal of Archaeological Method and Theory, Journal of Anthropological Archaeology,* and *Journal of Field Archaeology*) as well as national archaeological journals – such as *American Antiquity* (New World archaeology), the *American Journal of Archaeology* (archaeology of the circum-Mediterranean and the Near East), and *Antiquity* in the United Kingdom (covering archaeology worldwide) – regularly publish research articles relating to ceramic studies. For ceramic studies in the Pacific region, the following journals are pertinent: *Australian Archaeology, New Zealand Journal of Archaeology, Archaeology in Oceania, Journal of the Polynesian Society, Bulletin of the Indo-Pacific Prehistory Association,* and *Journal de la Société des océanistes.*

Students are also encouraged to become familiar with professional associations that focus exclusively on ceramic studies and publish their own technical journals – for example, the American Ceramics Society, the Canadian Ceramics Society, the European Ceramic Society, the Australasian Ceramic Society, the Ceramic Arts Association of Western Australia, the Ceramics Society (UK), and the Tiles and Architectural Ceramics Society (UK), as well as ceramics societies in other countries, that publish in their respective languages (e.g., Germany, France, Spain, and Japan). Other associations of interest are the Society for Archaeological Sciences and national and regional associations of archaeology and anthropology, all of which provide networking opportunities for students interested in archaeological ceramics studies.

References Arnold, D. E. 1985: *Ceramic Theory and Cultural Process.* Cambridge: Cambridge University Press.

Brumbach, H. J. 1984–5: Ceramic analysis and the investigation of matrilocality at the Smith Mohawk village site. *North American Archaeologist,* 6, 341–55.

Cantwell, A. M., Griffin, J. B. and Rothschild, N. A. (eds.) 1981: *The Research Potential of Anthropological Museum Collections.* Annals of the New York Academy of Sciences, vol. 376. New York: New York Academy of Sciences.

Cogswell, J. W., Neff, H. and Glascock, M. D. 1998: Analysis of shell-tempered pottery replicates: implications for provenance studies. *American Antiquity,* 63, 63–72.

Dever, W. G. 1995: Ceramics, ethnicity, and the question of Israel's origins. *Biblical Archaeologist,* 58(4), 200–13.

Dorrell, P. G. 1989: *Photography in Archaeology and Conservation.* Cambridge: Cambridge University Press.

Eerkens, J. W., Neff, H. and Glascock, M. D. 2002: Ceramic production among small-scale and mobile hunters and gatherers: a case study from the southwestern Great Basin. *Journal of Anthropological Archaeology,* 21, 200–29.

Ellis, L. 1998: Terra deserta: population, politics, and the [de]colonization of Dacia. *World Archaeology,* 30(2), 220–37.

—— 2000a: Clays and ceramics, characterization. In L. Ellis (ed.), *Archaeological Method and Theory: An Encyclopedia*. New York: Garland, 105–10.

—— 2000b: Petrography. In L. Ellis (ed.), *Archaeological Method and Theory: An Encyclopedia*. New York: Garland, 458–62.

—— (ed.) 2000c: *Archaeological Method and Theory: An Encyclopedia*. New York: Garland.

Fleming, S. J. 1975: *Authenticity in Art*. London: Institute of Physics.

Grave, P., Barbetti, M. and Hotchkis, M. 2000: The stoneware kilns of Sisatchanalai and early modern Thailand. *Journal of Field Archaeology*, 27(2), 169–82.

Hulthén, B. 1974: *On Documentation of Pottery*. Acta Archaeologica Lundensia, 3. Bonn: R. Habelt.

Longacre, W. A. 1992: *Ceramic Ethnoarchaeology*. Tucson: University of Arizona Press.

—— 2000: Exploring prehistoric social and political organization in the American Southwest. *Journal of Anthropological Research*, 56(3), 287–300.

Matson, F. R. 1965: Ceramic ecology: an approach to the study of early cultures of the Near East. In F. R. Matson (ed.), *Ceramics and Man*. Viking Fund Publications in Anthropology, 41. New York: Wenner-Gren Foundation for Anthropological Research, 203–17.

Minar, C. J. and Crown, P. L. 2001: Learning and craft production: an introduction. *Journal of Anthropological Research*, 57(4), 369–80.

Nicholas, D. and Kramer, C. 2001: *Ethnoarchaeology in Action*. Cambridge: Cambridge University Press.

Orton, C. 1985: Two useful parameters for pottery research. In E. Webb (ed.), *Computer Applications in Archaeology*. London: University of London, Institute of Archaeology, 114–20.

——, Tyers, P. and Vince, A. 1993: *Pottery in Archaeology*. Cambridge: Cambridge University Press.

Reid, A. and Young, R. 2000: Pottery abrasion and the preparation of African grains. *Antiquity*, 74(283), 101–11.

Rice, P. M. (ed.) 1984: *Pots and Potters: Current Approaches in Ceramic Archaeology*. Monograph 24. Los Angeles: Institute of Archaeology, University of California.

—— 1987: *Pottery Analysis: A Sourcebook*. Chicago: University of Chicago Press.

Rye, O. S. 1981: *Pottery Technology: Principles and Reconstruction*. Manuals on Archaeology, 4. Washington, DC: Taraxacum.

Sease, C. 1994: *A Conservation Manual for the Field Archaeologist*, 3rd edn. Archaeological Research Tools, vol. 4. Los Angeles: UCLA Institute of Archaeology Press.

Shepard, A. O. 1956: *Ceramics for the Archaeologist*. Washington, DC: Carnegie Institution of Washington.

Van Keuren, S. 1999: *Ceramic Design Structure and the Organization of Cibola White Ware Production in the Grasshopper Region, Arizona*. Arizona State Museum Archaeological Series, 191. Tucson: University of Arizona.

Terry O'Connor and James Barrett

9
Animal Bones

Introduction

This chapter reviews the field and laboratory techniques that are particular to the investigation of animal bones, from planning the investigation through to the point at which we have a recorded data set, ready for analysis and interpretation. The archaeological and paleobiological interpretation of animal bone assemblages lies beyond the remit of this chapter, but has been well covered in sources such as Reitz and Wing (1999) and O'Connor (2000).

Any archaeological project can be described as having five phases: planning, fieldwork, assessment of potential for analysis, analysis, and dissemination. The confidence that we have in our disseminated interpretation will depend upon the quality of the data analyzed, which in turn will depend upon the care and consistency with which the field and laboratory methods have been applied. However, there is not a single "right" way to recover and record animal bones, as every archaeological project offers unique opportunities and poses distinctive challenges. On site and in the laboratory, it is important to have a repertoire of practical techniques, and to understand their respective strengths and weaknesses. The most important thing for any field or laboratory researcher to know is when and why a particular procedure might be appropriate, and to be both confident and realistic about the quality of the raw material and the data acquired from its study. This chapter draws on published research and the authors' own experience to give an overview that will help such project-specific decisions to be made. As an example throughout this chapter, we use the excavation of a Viking Age to post-medieval settlement at Quoygrew (Barrett et al. 1998, 2001b; Barrett 2002). Located on Westray, in the archipelago of Orkney off the northernmost coast of Britain, Quoygrew is a good example of a field project in which animal bone recovery has been a high, but not exclusive, priority and in which constraints of time and location have required pragmatic decisions to be made.

The aims of a scholarly investigation should direct and inform the investigative methods, not the other way around. The first step in any animal bone research is therefore to stop and think. Why do we want to recover and study these bones? What do we hope to find out? Sometimes a published animal bone report gives the impression that the bones were studied only because they were dug up in the first place. That is not a good starting point for productive research!

The questions that drive the investigation will range from the purely zoogeographical (What was the early Holocene vertebrate fauna of this region?) to the more obviously archaeological (Was there a marked disparity in access to resources amongst these people?). In either case, the link from the research question to the data required in order to address that question needs to be thought through with care. The explicitly archaeological questions will require close attention to context, and to the analysis of material in small excavation units, whereas zoogeographical questions are often less context-sensitive but might impose more requirement for precise taxonomic identification. In the latter case, we might spend a lot of time identifying a small proportion of some difficult fragmented material to particular antelope species, requiring only that the specimens are satisfactorily well dated. In the former case, on the other hand, we might be satisfied with a division into size classes of artiodactyl, but require precise contextual information for each specimen.

Of course, we cannot predict every question that some present or future researcher might seek to answer using our data. We can, however, plan those that the research project in hand will address and adapt our working methods to give the optimal data set for our own needs, while also recording and disseminating the kinds of data that might reasonably be required by others to conduct meaningful comparative analyses. When students ask "What is the best way to recover and analyze these bones?", the answer "It depends what you are trying to find out" is infuriatingly pedantic, but nonetheless true.

Once the objectives of your research are established, the most critical aspect of project planning is to formulate appropriate and realistic sampling and recovery designs. To begin with some definitions, recovery involves the retrieval of bone specimens from a designated body of sediment, whereas sampling entails the choice of where recovery will be practiced within a site or archaeological landscape. Both must be consistent to achieve comparability within the project, but flexible enough to cope with unanticipated discoveries. Samples should represent the site as a whole: across space, through time, and between different feature types. Recovery methods should ensure that the bones you ultimately identify can be related to the bones in the original sediment excavated. Sampling and recovery decisions always have cost implications in terms of time and money. These need to be addressed at the initial planning stage if your goals are ultimately to be met.

The recovery of bones from the ground is a contentious business. It would be hopelessly unrealistic to say that we should seek to recover every fragment of bone from every excavation unit. Unless the bones are exceptionally well preserved and unusually complete, the deposit will contain a range of bone fragment sizes down to particles the size of sand grains. Clearly, it would be unreasonable to attempt the recovery of such small fragments. Below a certain size, a bone fragment ceases to be an informative specimen and becomes a sediment particle: it becomes, in Lyman's useful phrase, "analytically absent" (Lyman 1984). What we seek to do, therefore, is to recover every bone fragment above a certain size. That size limit is set by an informed but pragmatic compromise between what is required to achieve your research objectives (that is, the need to recover an assemblage that can convey as much information as possible) and the availability of personnel and resources on site.

In the early days of field archaeology, bone fragments and "finds" of all kinds were noticed during excavation, picked out of the excavated sediment, and put aside for subsequent study. This process of *hand* (or *trench*) collection still goes on, and it has been criticized by many researchers for imposing an unknown and uncontrollable degree of recovery bias (e.g., Clason & Prummel 1977; Stewart 1991; O'Connor 2001a). Experiments such as those carried out by Payne (1975) and by Levitan (1982) show that a specimen less than about 20 mm in length will probably be missed by hand-collection in most circumstances. We might, in some circumstances, be satisfied with that level of size-sorting of the recovered sample, but the real problem with hand-collection is that it is both inconsistent and uncontrollable. The same excavator working on the same sediment unit on different days might show quite marked variation in quality of recovery. Two samples of hand-collected bones can therefore only be compared with great caution, as any apparent differences between them might have arisen through recovery bias, and not because of inherent differences in the original deposits.

For these reasons, it is usual to recover bone samples by some form of *screening* (or *sieving*) of a sample of excavated sediments. Even if the screen mesh is relatively coarse, screening is much more consistent than hand-collection, and intra-site or inter-site assemblages using the same recovery method can be compared with greater confidence. The question then becomes how to choose what sediment to sieve – how to sample.

Entire books have been written on the subject of sampling strategies, and the ideal strategy for any excavation will depend upon the research aims and a series of logistic considerations. A useful review of the subject is given by Orton (2000; see also Peacock 1978; Wing & Quitmyer 1985; Shaffer & Sanchez 1994; Banning 2002). Ideally, all excavated sediment would be screened on a mesh fine enough to retain all potentially identifiable bone specimens, and a few excavations come close to meeting this ideal. In the many cases where 100 percent screening is not possible, however, sampling decisions have to be made. The purpose of sampling is to provide a representative selection of bone from your "sampling universe," typically a site or wider archaeological landscape. It was once fashionable to achieve this by randomly designating volumes of sediment for screening, often using a site grid as a sampling frame (e.g., Peacock 1978). Given the importance of retaining stratigraphic and other contextual information, however, it is now more common to follow systematic and/or judgmental sampling strategies.

Judgmental sampling is used when it is possible to rank different categories of deposit, concentrating the screening effort on those considered the most likely to yield useful quantities of bone and most likely to contribute to understanding the archaeology of the site. You must be careful in these instances, however, to sieve some control samples from superficially unproductive contexts. This procedure ensures (and allows you to document) that erroneous field perceptions were not perpetuated by a failure to test them.

Systematic sampling entails screening some sediment from a range of deposits across the site. If 100 percent screening is not practicable, then each (or every other, or every third, etc.) excavation unit might be sampled by taking a certain proportion, or a specified number of buckets (of known weight and volume, to allow standardization of any resulting data as specimens per liter of sediment). How big should such a sample be? That seemingly innocuous question is almost unanswerable, as it depends upon research aims, bone fragment concentration in the sediment, the nature of the sediment matrix, the mesh size, the time available for sorting the sieve residues, and probably more besides. We return to the question of sample size below, having first discussed some of the factors concerned. Sample size (the number of individual buckets or bags of sediment you sieve) and sample fraction (the proportion of the total sediment sieved) are inevitably influenced by recovery methods. The finer and more labor intensive the level of recovery, the fewer samples you are likely to take and vice versa.

For the moment, the most important general point is to consider *validity*. It is essential that the zooarchaeologist knows exactly what the sample of bones represents; for example, that these are all the bones retained by a 2 mm mesh from 30 l (liters) of unit 1001, nothing having been removed or added. If unit 1001 was laterally extensive, it will be important to know whether the sample was derived from the whole of that unit, or from a particular point or points within it. In the latter case, which other samples represent other parts of the extensive unit? Good sample documentation on site can greatly enhance the quality of the information that can be derived from bone samples: conversely, poor documentation can render a large, well-preserved sample completely useless. Similarly, the greater the degree of consistency in taking, documenting, and processing samples for screening, the greater is the validity of those samples and the confidence of the analyst. In comparison with tasks such as surveying or cataloging artifacts, taking and screening sediment samples can seem arduous and dull, and the quality of the on-site documentation can suffer as a consequence of that perception. As with many on-site tasks, the care and enthusiasm with which sampling is carried out can be substantially enhanced by ensuring that all those involved understand the whole process and the desired outcomes, and by feeding back initial results and observations at the earliest possible opportunity. The greatest danger to successful sampling and recovery of faunal remains is inconsistent execution of a planned strategy (in fact or in recording) due to field stresses, inadequate staff briefing, and contingent developments. This often results from lack of communication, but also from people taking well-intentioned, but misinformed, strategic decisions. There is thus a great need for an on-site specialist to keep an oversight of the process, and to advise in the case of unexpected deposits or when the bulldozers arrive.

What of screening techniques and equipment? At its simplest, sediment screening can consist of shoveling excavated sediment onto a mesh. The fraction finer than the mesh size falls through, and the coarse fraction remains on the mesh to be sorted through for bones and other "finds." Such a process is suitable for fine, disaggregated sediments, and may allow sediment to be screened almost as fast as it is excavated in an arid, sandy environment. Where sediments are more cohesive, perhaps because of clay or organic matter content, the sample will require some treatment in order for it to disaggregate. The simplest means of disaggregation is to spray water over the sample, in order to break down any "clods" of sediment, and to encourage the fine fraction to wash through the mesh. This is simple enough, but causes logistic problems on sites remote from piped water (though a freshwater stream can be used), and on sites in a cold climate. Most excavation personnel retain enough *joie de vivre* to enjoy spraying water around, but after the first 3–4 hours, or in cold weather, the enthusiasm and care with which screening is undertaken may begin to decline, and screening teams should be rotated, relieved (and if necessary revived) at regular intervals (Figure 9.1).

A diversity of devices has been developed to allow the water-screening of sediments (e.g., Williams 1973; Kenward et al. 1980; Jones 1983). Most were originally developed for the bulk recovery of charred seeds and wood charcoal, and those that emphasize recovery by flotation are not always well suited to the recovery of bones. In the simplest sieving tanks, the sample is placed on a mesh lining in a volume of water, with a throughput of flowing water to assist disaggregation, and to encourage floating materials over a weir into a suspended sieve or mesh bag. Dense particles smaller than the mesh on which the sample sits will drop to the bottom of the tank; dense, larger particles will remain on the mesh and will be progressively cleaned by the flowing water. Bone fragments will mostly remain in the dense fraction on the mesh. When separation of the fractions appears to be complete, the mesh can be removed, and the residue on it allowed to dry. In hot climates, drying may have to be inhibited, to prevent rapid desiccation leading to significant cracking of the bones. Conversely, cool, humid climates may necessitate further inventiveness in order to achieve drying in anything less than days. Faced with the challenge of drying samples in the Orkney climate (a by-word for cool humidity, even by British standards), the Quoygrew project has a fine contraption made out

TERRY O'CONNOR AND JAMES BARRETT

Figure 9.1 (a) Wet sieving at Quoygrew. (b) Flotation at Quoygrew.

of a rack of catering trays, a domestic room heater, and plenty of polythene sheeting. The stackable shallow wooden crates in which fruit is commonly packed – or any similar, easily available packaging – can be put to good use to enable the drying of residues.

Bones recovered by hand-collection will generally also require some form of washing. On many sites, this is accomplished by scrubbing at the bones with redundant (one hopes) toothbrushes, in a bowl of increasingly muddy water. Traditional though it is, this procedure cannot be recommended, as it is slow, haphazard, and likely to cause damage to fragile specimens. Hand-collected bones can be washed both quickly and satisfactorily by passing them through whatever water-screening procedure is in use on the site. A gentle spray of water from a hose is likely to do less superficial damage than fingers and toothbrushes. Even suspending the bones in a mesh bag in a nearby stream may be preferable, though seawater should be avoided unless the bones can be rinsed in fresh water before drying. As with residues from water screening, washed bones should be dried with some care, and certainly not in bright sunshine.

Whatever the screening technique employed on- or off-site, the choice of mesh size generally proves to be a fine balance between theory and practicality. To start at one extreme, the use of a mesh aperture coarser than 2 mm will, in most parts of the world, lead to the loss of some potentially identifiable fish, herpetile, and small mammal bones (Stewart 1991; O'Connor 2001a). In theory, then, all archaeological deposits should be screened through a 2 mm mesh. In reality, a 2 mm mesh typically retains not only numerous minute bone fragments, but even more numerous fragments of stone, ceramic, charcoal, and whatever else constitutes the excavation unit. At sites where the underlying geology is a coarse sand or sandstone, most of the sample matrix may be retained by the mesh. For a small, well-endowed field project, where storage space and labor to process the samples are in ample supply, that degree of retention may be feasible, even desirable. However, in most circumstances we will have to trim the recovery strategy. One option is to raise the mesh size to a point at which the larger-bodied taxa – whether cattle, llama, or macropod – can be satisfactorily recovered from most excavation units, relying on the fine-screening of a small proportion of the excavated material to give a useful subsample of the smallest taxa. Our own experience from projects in York, United Kingdom, indicates that analytically useful recovery of medium- to large-bodied ungulates can be achieved with a mesh as coarse as 10 mm (e.g., O'Connor 1991). Of course, that is only marginally "better" than hand-collection: indeed, a sharp-eyed excavator will recover small bones that would pass through a 10 mm mesh. However, even such coarse screening is more consistent than hand-collection, and gives bone samples that are reliably comparable.

Field projects with different aims, in different biomes, will adjust their screening strategies accordingly. The general recommendation that we would make is to combine two scales of screening. One should be fine enough to retain virtually every bone fragment likely to be identifiable below the level of zoological Class, and the other coarse enough to give satisfactory and consistent recovery of the larger-bodied taxa that are likely to have been the most economically significant. For European Holocene sites, meshes of 2 mm and 10 mm respectively will serve the purpose. An intermediate mesh size is of less utility unless your specific research questions demand it. A 5 mm mesh, for example, will give poor recovery of fish and rodent bones, whilst retaining more than is analytically necessary of the larger mammals.

If our suggestions regarding screening seem a little cavalier (". . . more than is analytically necessary . . ."?), it is because the material retained by a mesh of whatever aperture has to be sorted, and this is often the critical part of the whole process. A 30 kg sediment sample screened through a 2 mm mesh in pursuit of every last fish bone may leave a residue of 10 kg or more, which has to be sorted through, clast by clast. The sample required 10 minutes to take on site; maybe 2 hours to wash through the mesh; then, after drying, 2–3 days to sort. It may be that the material is of such importance as to justify the time. All too often, however, field projects build up a serious sorting backlog because this stage is not thought about and roughly quantified in advance. If sorting becomes a time-constrained chore, the care with which it is undertaken will quickly decline, and the quality of the samples available for analysis will be compromised. It is simply not possible to make quantified recommendations with regard to sorting – the variables are too many – other than to urge that this essential part of the process must be planned and discussed when the sampling strategy is set up (Figure 9.2).

It may seem strange that the question of sample size has been left until this point, as it is often the first question to be addressed on site. However, it is a question that can only be satisfactorily answered by considering the aims of the project and the practicalities of screening and sorting. The general answer to the questions "How many samples should I take?" and "How big should

Figure 9.2 Sorting shell midden samples.

each sediment sample be?" is "Numerous and big enough to yield a bone assemblage of sufficient quantity to give enough data to answer the proposed analytical questions." That, in turn, will depend upon the concentration of bones in the excavated deposits, the screening strategy, and the practicalities of sorting. For fine-screening, individual samples of sediment of 10–25 liters per analytical unit may be sufficient, whilst 50 liters or more may be more appropriate for coarse screening. The site itself may impose practical restrictions: one answer to the question "How big a sample?" could be "How much can you safely carry?" The use of standard containers, such as reusable nesting tubs with snap-on lids, can save much headache and ease the process of recording the weight and volume of your sample. As we have already said, replicated sampling of extensive deposits may be more adaptable and practicable than taking a single, very large sample. It is also more desirable from a statistical point of view. Many small samples (a large sample size) can provide more information than a single large sample (a large sample fraction).

One of the most important aspects of recovery is the need to take "whole earth" samples. All sediment and bones from a designated sampling unit need to be kept together for one treatment or another. A classic error is to hand-collect bones from an entire layer, and then screen a subsample of the remaining sediment. In this case the small bones will be missing from the hand-collected material, the large bones will be missing from the sieved sample, and there will be no way to recombine the data. Fragile objects or groups of articulated bone may need to be kept physically separate (see below), but the sample number can be included with their label to allow recombination of the data.

Turning to our case study, one goal of the Quoygrew excavation was to disentangle diachronic trends in the economic importance of marine resources (see Barrett et al. 1999, 2001a) from changes in refuse disposal practices. Put simply, we wanted to know whether large fish middens appeared in Viking Age and medieval Orkney because fish became more important or because people began to discard most of their fish bone in one place and most of their mammal bone in another. It was therefore necessary to establish a sampling design that would retain both spatial and chronological information – and a recovery design that would yield both fine recovery of fish bone (ideally a small mesh) and a large sample of mammal bone (ideally a large sample size).

The project began with the use of auger survey, geophysical survey, and topographic survey to map the distribution of midden and other settlement deposits across the settlement (Barrett et al. 1998, 2001b; Barrett 2002). Judgmentally placed excavation units were then opened over three areas: a large coastal fish midden, a large inland midden less dominated by fish bone (known as a "farm mound" in Scottish archaeology), and a nearby dwelling with its smaller associated accumulations of refuse. Within each area, deposits were sampled in one of three ways depending on whether they were interpreted as midden, house floor, or "sterile" layers.

Figure 9.3 Sampling house floors at Quoygrew.

Midden layers were divided into a 1-m grid, with four 10-liter samples usually taken from each alternate square in a "checkerboard" fashion as the size and shape of the stratum allowed. Two of these samples were treated as flotation samples, with 1 mm mesh used to retain the small fish bones of the heavy fraction and 0.5 mm mesh used to recover the floating botanical material. The two additional samples, intended mainly for the controlled recovery of mammal bone, were washed through a 4 mm mesh. In retrospect, however, a 10 mm mesh would have been adequate for the latter samples and saved a lot of time during the subsequent sorting process.

House floors were divided into contiguous 1-m squares, each of which was subdivided into four 0.5-m quadrants. Within each stratigraphic layer (most of which were only a few centimeters thick) one 10-liter sample was taken from each meter square for recovery of small bones and seeds using flotation. A 0.5-liter sample was then taken from each 0.5-m quadrant for possible analysis of spatial patterning at a finer resolution (Figure 9.3). Finally, a small number of flotation samples were taken from superficially "sterile" contexts. This procedure allowed us to document areas of the site that did not contain significant amounts of bone or other finds.

In all cases, the sediment was collected in stackable 10-liter plastic tubs with lids. Sample numbers were allocated from a single register to prevent double labeling. The register and the labels each recorded the site code, the context number, the sample number, the grid square (where relevant), the date, and the excavator. The analysis of this material is not yet complete. Nevertheless, it is already clear that we will be able to make convincing arguments regarding the spatial and chronological distribution of the fish and mammal bone from Quoygrew.

Look Before You Dig – On-Site Observation

Although it is conventional to think of animal bone research as beginning with a pile of bones on the bench, there is a great deal of useful observation that can be made on site, when the bones are first encountered during excavation. We study bones as the consequences of human activities or as zoological fossils, but they are also sediment clasts, the distribution of which might convey some information about the deposits in which they occur. A better understanding of deposit formation might, in turn, enhance or modify our interpretation of the bones.

The first, and most obvious, point to consider is the presence and absence of bones in different excavation units. Exceptionally, a site might have substantial concentrations of bone fragments in some units and none in others, a circumstance that immediately raises questions about the deposition and transformation of the units in question. Although such an uneven distribution ought to be evident from the excavation records, it is only on site that we can ask whether the apparent absence of bones in some units is a consequence of deposition or of differential preservation. That question might lead us to, for example, the fine-screening of some apparently bone-free deposits to check for minute fragments of degraded bone or the collection of soil micromorphology samples to test for bone decomposition products (Simpson et al. 2000). Even if the distribution of bone fragments is less markedly uneven, the concentration might visibly differ between, or even within, closely adjacent excavation units. If the bones are distributed very evenly across a number of units, we might try to compare that with the distribution of another similarly sized clast, such as pottery or lithics. If all such clasts seem to be rather homogeneously distributed, there could have been significant reworking and "homogenization" of the deposits, a possibility that can be further investigated when the bones are recorded. Some lines of enquiry can only be pursued on site. For example, what is the orientation of the bone specimens? Do they lie flat (suggesting deposition on an exposed surface followed by burial and little disturbance) or at diverse angles (implying rapid deposition as a single dump or considerable bioturbation)?

Concentrated patches of bone fragments deserve close attention on site. Do they show any consistency of alignment, or sorting by size? Either attribute might indicate deposition or subsequent reworking by a transport medium such as flowing water (Wolff 1973). Are there air-filled voids between some of the bones? Although this is encountered quite rarely, it is a good indication of a primary deposit with minimal reworking, as such voids are unlikely to persist if a group of bones is moved or disturbed after deposition. It is sometimes

TERRY O'CONNOR AND JAMES BARRETT

apparent that the sediment in spaces between bones in a dense accumulation differs in texture from that around the accumulation. This, too, might indicate a primary deposit in which fine sediment has washed into the voids between bone fragments (e.g., Lauwerier 2002). Some dense concentrations will show a degree of anatomical articulation, showing that the bones were deposited close together because they were all incorporated in all or part of a single animal. The presence of articulations can be crucial to the interpretation of a bone deposit, but can easily be overlooked on site, particularly if the excavation team is unfamiliar with basic vertebrate anatomy. Often, it is enough to remind excavators of the possibility that groups of articulated bones might occur. When encountered, or even suspected, articulations should be kept together, bagging the bones together and labeling so as to make it quite clear that they constitute one suspected articulation from a specified excavation unit (include the sample number if from a volume of sediment intended for screening). Some comment on the presence of articulations should be made in the excavation records, and a photograph might subsequently prove to be helpful.

Articulated groups of fish bones are of particular relevance at Quoygrew. Some of the fish bones in Viking Age and medieval middens at the site are groups of vertebrae, still in anatomical articulation. Their presence indicates that there has been no post-depositional movement of the material, and that it is an *in situ*, primary deposit, giving us precise information about the spatial distribution of activities. Furthermore, by recording which groups of vertebrae are commonly found in articulation, we can extract some information about the butchering to which the fish were subject (Barrett 1997). Any articulations encountered during excavation are therefore noted, plotted, and bagged separately from other bones from the same stratigraphic unit (Figure 9.4a).

An articulation might, of course, be a complete skeleton. Sometimes that will be quite obvious: the well-preserved articulated skeleton of a complete horse is difficult to miss (Figure 9.4b). Nonetheless, most animal bone specialists will have encountered bone assemblages amongst which there is clearly most of the skeleton of one animal, mixed with disarticulated bones from numerous others, with no numbering or separate bagging to show that the individual skeleton was recognized on site. That is more understandable with the smaller or less familiar classes of vertebrate: you cannot reasonably expect excavators to recognize the one complete frog lurking amongst a dense scatter of other small bones. An articulated skeleton might become displaced and difficult to recognize if the sediment undergoes disturbance or displacement. A good example is Driver's (1999) recognition of two originally complete raven (*Corvus corax*) skeletons in early Holocene deposits at Charlie Lake Cave, British Columbia. Neither skeleton was at all complete, and one was considerably dispersed by post-depositional movement of the deposit. Given the potential difficulties, it would be a counsel of perfection to require that all articulated skeletons must be recognized, separately bagged, and labeled on site. However, it is far better to conclude during the recording of a bone

(a)

(b)

Figure 9.4 (a) Articulated fish vertebrae. (b) A horse burial.

TERRY O'CONNOR AND JAMES BARRETT

Figure 9.5 A pig mandible *in situ* at Flixborough, UK.

assemblage that an alleged articulated skeleton was a coincidental association of parts of three different species than it is to be unable to confirm that a number of bones in the assemblage were originally an *in situ* skeleton.

Apart from the spatial distribution of bones, their appearance and condition may be informative. It is not unusual for the upper surface of a stratigraphic unit to be defined by a former ground surface; for example, when we are excavating superimposed floor deposits within a structure, or the surface of a buried paleosoil. In such cases, bones that lie in the surface of the deposit may show markedly different preservation and erosion on the upper and lower surfaces of the same bone. If a bone has lain in the upper centimeter or so of a deposit on which the sun has shone and people have walked, the upper surface may show the effects of subaerial weathering and trampling, from which the lower surface will have been protected (Figure 9.5). It takes little time to recognize and to note such a condition, yet it may be an important observation, contributing to the interpretation of site formation. Of course, the bone will show the same contrasting surfaces after excavation, and we might justifiably speculate as to the reasons, but it is obviously far better to make such an observation on site.

The point is that some intelligent observation on site can greatly enhance the quality of information obtained from animal bones, in part by indicating the effects of post-depositional processes, and in part by elucidating the spatial distribution of the bones. This could seem to be an argument in favor of the three-dimensional plotting of animal bones. On some sites, and given some research questions, plotting might be appropriate, if time-consuming. If the spatial relationship of individual specimens is likely to contribute to the research, then detailed plotting may be justifiable. In many cases, artifacts and other categories of material will be systematically plotted, so adding bones to that record might not represent a great amount of additional work. More often, the bone fragments are just clasts within a sediment, so their individual location is not significant, and the collection of material within excavation or sample units is sufficiently precise. That distinction might only be apparent on site, which is why it is important to look – and think – before you dig.

Bagging and Tagging   Having thought, looked, noted, sampled, sieved, and dried, we finally have a recognizable assemblage of bones ready to be packed for later study. The aim is to allow the eventual retrieval from store of intact containers of clearly labeled material that is secure from breakage or degradation. There should be no ambiguity or uncertainty in cross-referencing the labeling on the containers to the excavation records, and no difficulty in locating all the specimens recovered from a particular excavation unit, even if they are distributed among several containers. And, finally, it should be absolutely clear how the bones in a particular container were recovered from the excavated deposit.

To state the obvious, albeit frequently ignored, the aim of packaging is to give the bones adequate protection against fragmentation during handling of the containers, to prevent specimens from different stratigraphic units or sediment samples from becoming mixed, and to allow the contents of each container to be quickly and confidently identified. Prior to bagging, bones from some sites are directly labeled, by writing a site and context identifier on each specimen. This is generally accomplished using waterproof ink and a fine-tipped pen, and the labeling is often given a coat of clear varnish as protection. The labeling of individual specimens in this way obviously guards against the misplacement of specimens, and allows bone assemblages from a site to be recombined in various ways during the analysis without losing their contextual integrity. That said, it is a very time-consuming process, and not every project will be willing or able to spare the person–hours to allow all specimens to be labeled. Furthermore, the labeling has to be done with care, to rule out errors, and with a degree of thought and discretion. Labeling must not obscure important anatomical details or cut-marks, or other significant surface modifications, and should not be visually intrusive. For some projects, it may be a fine judgment whether or not to label bones individually. Good laboratory procedures can prevent the misplacement of unlabeled specimens, and bones can always be labeled at some later stage in the analysis if it becomes apparent, for example, that it is essential temporarily to combine bones from two or three different samples.

Labeled or not, the bones need to be packaged. All the bones from one stratigraphic unit or sediment sample are placed together in a labeled bag – several bags if the assemblage is large. Thick paper bags, of the sort used at

TERRY O'CONNOR AND JAMES BARRETT

some grocery stores, were formerly the packaging of choice. The advantage of paper bags is that they can be written on with ease, provide a permeable vapor barrier, and are relatively cheap. Their disadvantage is that if storage conditions are poor, they are susceptible to damp, or to attack by organisms ranging from insects to rats. The contextual information provided by storage in individual paper bags is easily lost when they disintegrate. Self-sealing polythene bags are now more generally used, and certainly give better protection from damp. However, they have the disadvantages that exterior labeling is less reliable and condensation may form on the inside of the bags (the latter can be reduced by perforating the bags with a pin). The ideal would probably be to use bags in a material that combines the advantages of both paper and polythene: nonwoven heavy-duty polypropylene fabric, perhaps. Realistically, the choice is likely to be between paper and polythene.

Above all, avoid overfilling bags. Whether paper, polythene, or finest cotton fabric, bags should not be filled more than about half-full, to allow the top to be folded over, tied, or sealed as appropriate, and to give some space – but not too much – for the bones to move around as the bags are packed into boxes or crates. The outside of the bag should be labeled with the site code and stratigraphic unit identifier, and a label bearing the same information should be placed inside the bag as well. Obviously, waterproof, nonfading ink should be used for any such labeling, and the labels should be of some indestructible material (i.e., not paper). Spun-bonded polythene is particularly effective, though offcuts of drawing film can make quite effective tough labels. Drawing film makes a good surface for labeling in hard pencil (4H or 6H), and is both water-resistant and relatively lightproof.

Bags of bones are likely to be collected into boxes or crates. The principles to follow are obvious, though frequently overlooked on site when time is short. As with bags, do not overfill boxes, and interleave layers of bags with some packaging material to give protection during transport. Closed-cell polyether foam is very effective, as is the more readily available "bubble-wrap." Even crumpled newspaper will be effective (and can be an interesting distraction years later when rediscovered in the museum store!). Boxes should be of a design that resists crushing, as it is inevitable that they will be stacked higher than originally intended.

The labeling on the exterior of the box should match that on the bags within it. If a particularly large assemblage fills more than one box, package it so that one assemblage comprises the whole contents of several boxes, rather than the whole of, say, two overfilled boxes, plus a small bag tucked into a third box with bags from several other contexts. Bones in storage are like a herd of deer: bags that become isolated from the herd are more likely to be prey to misplacement.

Good packaging is a form of passive conservation, and the whole process from washing, through drying, to packaging and labeling should be seen in those terms. Active conservation will only rarely be necessary, and ought to be the preserve of the trained conservator that any responsible project director will want to have on site. Realistically, it will occasionally be necessary to deal with fragmented specimens so as to keep the fragments together. Any conservation procedure should be reversible, or at least removable. It is particularly important that on-site first-aid treatments do not compromise any subsequent conservation or analyses of the bones that might be required, and that they are fully documented at the time. Fragmented bones that seem likely to fall apart during storage and handling can be wrapped in a couple of layers of aluminum foil. The foil will keep the fragments together without affecting any subsequent treatment of the bone. If it is necessary to stick broken specimens, then a reversible adhesive, soluble in a readily available solvent such as acetone, should be used. Adhesives such as epoxy resins and cyanoacrylate "superglues" cause more problems than they solve, and should be avoided. Keep a record of any reconstruction and repair work that is undertaken. That record should be made available to the zooarchaeologist who eventually records the bones.

To return to site, briefly, *in situ* consolidation of fragmented bone will only rarely be necessary or justifiable, and the advice of a suitably experienced conservator should be sought and followed. The advent of satellite phones and the Internet have successfully killed off the old excuse that "There was no conservator for hundreds of miles . . ." During the preparation of this chapter, one of our colleagues emailed from the depths of the Arabian Desert, seeking conservation advice for a Miocene elephant tusk. A conservator in rain-swept Yorkshire was able to view detailed photographs of the specimen and to email detailed recommendations back to colleagues. Those recommendations were adapted in the light of local expertise and logistical practicalities, and the tusk was successfully lifted and transported to specialist facilities in Abu Dhabi.

Storage protocols will depend upon the location and "house rules" of the store concerned, but a few obvious points can save time and blood pressure at a later stage. Do not stack boxes higher than is absolutely necessary: even if they do not crush or topple over, the box that you need will always be at the bottom. Stack and shelve boxes with the external labeling the right way up and facing outward. If at all possible, stack or shelve so that context identifiers are in numerical (or alphabetical) order. If a particularly large assemblage spans more than one box, ensure that all of those boxes are kept together. In such a case, a discrete note on the box, such as "1 of 3" or "2 of 3," can be very helpful when material is retrieved from storage. All of this is very simple and yet, in the authors' experience, each of these elementary precautions, and sometimes all of them at once, have been ignored on projects.

Remember that the aim is to allow the retrieval from store of intact containers of clearly labeled material that is secure from breakage or degradation. There should be no ambiguity in cross-referencing the labeling on the bone boxes to the excavation records, and no difficulty in locating all the specimens

TERRY O'CONNOR AND JAMES BARRETT

from a particular excavation unit, even if they are distributed amongst several containers. Finally, documentation that shows what material is stored in which boxes will greatly facilitate efficient work in the laboratory.

What facilities make for a satisfactory "bone laboratory"? Comparative collections are the heart of a zooarchaeology laboratory (although it is best to avoid letting them become an end in themselves). As a general point, a collection should be sufficiently extensive to allow confident identification of the great majority of the specimens likely to be found in the geographical region concerned. Most projects will generate a modest number of specimens for which the identity cannot be confirmed by the laboratory comparative collection, necessitating either a visit to the appropriate museum or the help of a colleague to whom the specimens can be sent. Once again, the Internet is proving to be a valuable adjunct, allowing images of a "mystery" specimen to be sent to colleagues around the world. Bone "atlases" and keys are also useful, not least as a means of ruling out some species not represented in the comparative collection (e.g., Olsen 1960; Scarlett 1972; Schmid 1972; Walker 1985; Cannon 1987; Amorosi 1989; Vigne 1995; Cohen & Serjeantson 1996; Watt et al. 1997). However, an identification made on the basis of an atlas description or illustration should be regarded as provisional until confirmed by comparison with reference specimens. Reference collections can be organized by taxon, by element, or (if sufficiently large) by both. They should ideally include a range of ages and both males and females from each relevant species. Methods of preparing reference skeletons are varied, but useful advice is provided by Wheeler and Jones (1989) and Davis and Payne (1992).

The Laboratory

Perhaps the next most important requirements are for sufficient space and good-quality light. Although bones may be recorded one by one, it will be necessary to lay out each sample, in order to sort the numerous fragments, and in order to gain an overview of the assemblage as a whole. If space is constrained, sorting can be seriously compromised, although it is equally true that zooarchaeology will expand to fill the available space, however much that is. A folding trestle table can be a good means of providing extra working space when necessary. Whatever the source of ambient light, some form of desk lamp, to give bright, oblique lighting, will be necessary, as will a good-quality, low-magnification binocular microscope. Unless you will be engaged in specialized thin-section work (to access seasonality through incremental growth structures, for example – see Liebermann 1994; Van Neer et al. 1999) or bone chemistry (to study bone preservation – see Nicholson 1996), your laboratory will otherwise need only a selection of calipers (digital ones are the most efficient), an electronic balance (from several kilograms to 0.1 g for most mammals, and from about 0.5 kg to 0.01 g for fish), and a computer for data entry. Access to X-ray and scanning electron microscope (SEM) facilities is also useful.

Making the Record

Turning to data recording, we must begin with a consideration of your goals. As discussed above, these will entail both project-specific objectives and the needs of the wider zooarchaeological community. The potential issues that can be addressed using zooarchaeological data are limited only by the imagination of the analyst and the quality of the data collected. They might range from paleoenvironmental reconstruction (e.g., Vigne & Valladas 1996), to food sharing among hunter–gatherers (e.g., Marshall 1994), to the construction of group identity in multicultural states (e.g., Stewart-Abernathy & Ruff 1987). Questions of these kinds are the *ultimate* goals of zooarchaeology, but what are its *proximate* goals (which allow you to achieve these broader aims)? In other words, what do you actually attempt to measure or do when collecting zooarchaeological data? Six basic goals unite most zooarchaeological work:

- to estimate the relative abundance of different animals or parts of animals in a given assemblage
- to estimate the relative potential meat yield of different animals or parts of animals
- to reconstruct age at death profiles of different taxa (which can yield information regarding – for example – hunting strategies, stock management practices, the exploitation of secondary products such as milk or wool, and seasonality)
- to measure changes in the size or shape of animals (which may have implications regarding – for example – domestication, selective breeding, and trade)
- to identify surface modifications (such as butchery marks and burning)
- to assess biases introduced by taphonomy (including bone transport, preservation, and recovery).

The data that most zooarchaeologists collect to address these proximate goals are also relatively well established. Each specimen is typically identified in terms of its origin on site, its biological taxonomy and anatomy, its age and sex (insofar as this is possible), its phenotype (including size, shape, and nonmetric traits), its pathologies, and its taphonomic history. The typical data fields during laboratory recording can thus be summarized as follows:

- site identifier
- specimen number (optional)
- stratigraphic unit identifier(s)
- recovery method used
- skeletal element
- body side
- part of element (i.e., distal epiphysis; ischial tuberosity, often as a coded *diagnostic zone*) and any other measures of fragmentation
- taxon
- butchery marks

- other surface modifications (e.g., carnivore gnawing, burning)
- bone tissue preservation (sometimes described as texture or weathering)
- bone weight
- age indicators (e.g., epiphysial fusion and tooth wear)
- phenotype indicators (measurements and nonmetric traits)
- pathologies.

The *site identifier* should be identical to that used elsewhere in the project records. It is not unknown for excavation records to be made for a site named, for example, Lowell 1317A, whilst the bone records are listed under Milly's Trench, by which sobriquet the site was informally known. A *specimen number* is sometimes useful in order to identify individual bones for curatorial purposes, and can serve as a link within a relational database (in which case it may be automatically appended). You will find it most efficient to write this number only on specimens that you are particularly intent on relocating (those with butchery marks, pathologies, or uncertain identifications, for example).

The *stratigraphic identifier* will generally be the context number or its equivalent. Again, this should be identical to the identifier used in excavation records. You may also include a sample number if the project has used a separate sequence for screened material. Given the discussion above, *recovery method* will also be a critical variable. *Skeletal element* is fairly simple, and follows the anatomical terminology appropriate to the Class of vertebrate concerned. Where nomenclature varies – for example, in the naming of fish bones (see Wheeler & Jones 1989) – most zooarchaeology laboratories will adopt a published system, quoting it in reports. Although it is important that the anatomical terminology should be unambiguous and used with precision, it does not need to be precious – "2nd phalanx" is just as satisfactory as *"phalanx secundus."*

Body side is simple enough: either left or right, unsided, or unknown. The last two categories (sometimes recorded together) distinguish elements that are not paired in the body, such as vertebrae, from damaged specimens for which the body side can no longer be identified. *Part of element* poses more of a challenge, as it requires us to describe briefly but exactly which parts of an element are represented in a fragment. Some zooarchaeologists have published systems that define "zones," based in part on anatomical landmarks and in part on experience of how different elements tend to break, and therefore what particular fragments tend to occur quite commonly (e.g., Watson 1979; Dobney & Reilly 1988; Cohen & Serjeantson 1996; Moreno-Garcia et al. 1996; Barrett & Oltmann 1997; Harland et al. 2003). A record of diagnostic zones facilitates the calculation of *minimum number of elements* (MNE) estimates, used for assessing butchery patterns and (by comparison with the bone density of each element) assemblage preservation (e.g., Lyman 1994; Marean & Cleghorn 2003). The number of zones per specimen can also serve as an indicator of fragmentation and thus of the taphonomic history of the specimen and assemblage (e.g., Serjeantson 1991; Morlan 1994). Fragmentation of this kind may also be recorded using a visual estimate of what percentage of a total element each specimen represents (e.g., Marean 1991; Barrett 1997; Zohar et al. 2001).

The determination of *Taxon* is one of the most fundamental, and often most difficult, challenges in zooarchaeology (cf., Gobalet 2001). The process of sorting out a pile of bone fragments in order to make identifications is rarely discussed in print. The first step should always be to sort by taxonomic Class, and then by body part or skeletal element. After all, if a specimen cannot be identified to a particular element of the vertebrate skeleton, then the chances that it can be identified to species are slim indeed. For a large assemblage, it may be best to make a rough sort (skull; teeth; legs; toes and podials; vertebrae, and so on), and then re-sort and identify each of those categories in turn. If space is limited, it may be necessary to record a large assemblage bag by bag. However, this makes it difficult to gain an overall impression of the bones recovered from that particular stratigraphic unit, and so to gain an impression of the state of preservation, variation in color, and other taphonomic parameters. The systematic, specimen-by-specimen, recording of bone modifications can reduce this problem, but there is no real substitute for seeing an assemblage "laid out" in whole or in part. Having sorted by skeletal element, size can be a useful criterion for mammal and bird bones, allowing a rapid separation of, for example, "cattle-sized" from "sheep-sized" limb bones. However, size is not a useful criterion for vertebrates that show indeterminate growth, such as fish. Fairly quickly, it becomes apparent that the same few taxa make up the majority of most of the assemblages that we are recording, and it becomes a simple matter to ensure that the necessary reference specimens are within easy reach (Figure 9.6).

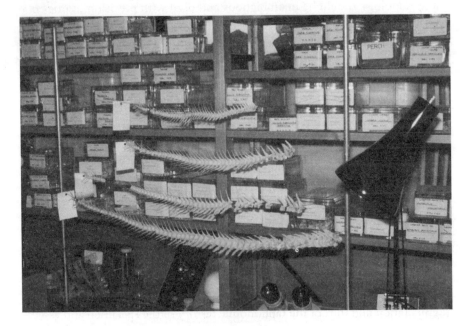

Figure 9.6   A fish reference collection set up for easy access.

TERRY O'CONNOR AND JAMES BARRETT

The level of taxonomic precision to which identifications are made should reflect the degree of confidence that the analyst has in those identifications. That confidence will be determined in part by the nature of the material, and in part by the experience of the analyst. Some vertebrate groups defy precise identification, however experienced the analyst and however comprehensive the comparative collection. A good example is the Old World hawks – the Family Accipitridae (Otto 1981). Although some elements of some species in this group may be identified to species, many simply cannot because the family is highly speciated, and the species are anatomically very similar. It is important to note that the increased confidence that comes with experience will often lead to *less* precise identifications being made, as the analyst has learned that hawks, or parrots, or macropods, or wrasse are a much more difficult group than appears to be the case at first acquaintance. Students undertaking their first zooarchaeological studies should not feel pressured into making more precise identifications than the specimens warrant. Note, too, that "experience" may not simply refer to years spent at the bench. Different zooarchaeologists will gain a particular familiarity with different Classes or Orders of vertebrate. One of us will claim to be "experienced" with mammals and birds, but not with fish, and the other vice versa. Given these observations, we must expect that different zooarchaeologists will often provide different identifications of the same specimen (Gobalet 2001). In some (hopefully few) cases, one or both will be simply incorrect. In most circumstances, however, it is the taxonomic precision of the identification that will vary. One advantage of modern database software is that it is easy to sort bone records at a number of taxonomic levels. By incorporating a look-up table which shows, for example, that the taxon *sheep* is included in the taxon *caprine*, which in turn is included in *bovid*, which is included in *ungulate*, it becomes possible to re-sort and re-quantify the data at several different taxonomic levels, chosen to be appropriate to the analysis in hand.

Not all identifications will be to Linnaean taxa, as there may be useful ways to describe and identify the specimens even when attribution to genus or species is beyond us. Taxa such as "bovid size 3," "large ungulate," "small larid" (i.e., seagulls), or "large macropod" (i.e., kangaroos and wallabies) appear quite frequently in published work. They are not an admission of defeat but, rather, a means of extracting further information from specimens for which precise Linnaean taxonomy is not appropriate or possible. Ultimately, some specimens will defy identification even to taxonomic Order. In samples recovered by screening on a 2 mm mesh, those specimens will be in the great majority. Depending on the project and its objectives, there may be some merit in recording as broadly as Class; for example, to separate the obvious, but nondescript, fish bone fragments from the mammals. Such material should be described with some care. There is a substantive difference between *unidentified* specimens (i.e., not identified in this particular research project by this analyst) and *unidentifiable* (i.e., not possible to identify by this analyst or any other).

At this stage, it is necessary to introduce the concept of diagnostic elements. Most zooarchaeologists focus their attention more on some anatomical elements than others (e.g., Davis 1987, 1992; Cohen & Serjeantson 1996; Harland et al. 2003). These elements are typically chosen for systematic identification because they are robust, easy to identify to species, and representative of most anatomical areas of a skeleton. Other elements may only be recorded if they exhibit informative modifications such as butchery marks. As long as one's methodology is explicit, this practice can increase the efficiency of recording without a meaningful loss of information.

Butchery marks and other *surface modifications*, such as abrasion, tooth marks, and evidence of burning, form evidence of the history of the specimen and possibly of the deposit from which it came. The recognition and significance of surface modifications have been discussed at length (e.g., Lyman 1994; Fisher 1995). Animal tooth marks on a bone may be isolated or grouped into dense patches. The size and cross-section of individual tooth marks will often give some indication of the species responsible for the damage. For tooth marks and cut marks from butchering, it is important to be able to examine the specimen under a fairly bright oblique light, turning the specimen over and around in order that the light shines across the bone at different angles. That need not require any special arrangements or equipment in the laboratory, but merely a small lamp, handily placed on the bench, which can be switched on or moved into position when needed. Given good lighting, even quite faint cut marks will show up clearly enough to be noticed with the naked eye, although a hand-lens or low-power microscope may be necessary to resolve the details and to differentiate "trowel trauma" or other surface modifications from ancient butchery (see Blumenshine et al. 1996). Rather like tooth marks, cut marks need to be recorded in terms of number, location, and, when possible, direction and implement. Metal and lithic tools generally produce cuts with quite a different cross-section when drawn across the surface of fresh bone: V-shaped for metal and square or W-shaped for lithics. The recognition of metal cut marks on prehistoric material from southeastern Europe has been used as evidence for early metalworking (Greenfield 1999). Cut marks are typically recorded on standard images of each element, often reproduced on file cards, and analyzed by means of composite drawings (e.g., Landon 1996).

The state of *preservation* of a specimen should be distinguished from the state of fragmentation of the original skeletal element, the latter of which was considered above. Preservation is generally assessed in terms of how closely the texture of the specimen resembles "fresh" bone on the one hand, or is cracked and crumbly on the other. It may be possible, therefore, to assess preservation in terms of a series of alternatives. Is the bone soft or hard; flaking or not; cracked or not? A number of published schemes exist, one classic example being the weathering stages defined by Behrensmeyer (1978). In the University of York zooarchaeology laboratories, we now use an ordinal

TERRY O'CONNOR AND JAMES BARRETT

scale of four texture categories (Harland et al. 2003). The recording of preservation is part of the documenting of the "history" of the specimen, and may help us to understand the preservation, or absence, of other materials in the same deposit.

Bone weight is a variable that has attracted some negative attention in the history of zooarchaeology, largely due to an ongoing misunderstanding of the curvilinear relationship between bone weight and animal weight (cf., Cook & Treganza 1956; Kubasiewicz 1956; Casteel 1978; Reitz et al. 1987; Jackson 1989; Mitchell 1990; Reitz & Wing 1999). Nevertheless, it remains useful as a broad measure of the relative potential meat yield of different taxa and is particularly suitable for inter-class comparisons (Barrett 1993; see also Glassow 2000).

The categories of information considered so far are the description of the specimen, and the evidence of its post-mortem history. The final three categories of data – age indicators, phenotype indicators, and pathologies – all pertain to the living animal represented by that specimen.

The age at death of hunted prey or domestic livestock is important for what it reveals about hunting and husbandry strategies. Hunters may target particular age/sex cohorts of their prey, perhaps at particular times of year. For large mammals that breed seasonally, such as bison, elk, and llama, the age at death also reflects the season of death. Thus, Carter (2001) has been able to infer seasonal hunting of red deer at the early Holocene site of Thatcham, UK, by a detailed analysis of the age distribution of deer mandibles from the site. Farmers and pastoralists will slaughter animals at particular ages depending on the intended product of the herd or flock, and the mortality due to disease or other "natural" causes. For example, Payne (1973) proposed optimal mortality profiles for Old World sheep and goat flocks for the production of meat, wool, and milk; work that has been influential in the interpretation of zooarchaeological material. In their study of pig remains from the Marquesas Islands, Rolett and Chiu (1994) demonstrated an age distribution consistent with the slaughtering of pigs for meat at the optimal point in their young growth. Age at death matters, therefore, but most bone specimens will reveal little about the *age* of the individual animal, apart, perhaps, from a general impression given by the size and robusticity of the specimen that it was adult or juvenile. More precise information on age at death is given by two main sources: the teeth, and the appendicular epiphyses.

This is not the place to go into the ontogeny of mammalian dentition in detail: the subject is usefully covered by Hillson (1986). For laboratory purposes, we need to record the state of eruption and attrition of the teeth at the time of death. This recording is normally based on the mandibles alone, for two reasons. First, in most mammals, the mandible is more robust than the maxillary bones, and so a greater proportion of mandible fragments is recovered with two or more teeth *in situ*. Secondly, if mandibles *and* maxillae are recorded, there is the risk that one individual animal will be recorded up to four times (both mandibles; both maxillae). Recording only the mandibles obviates this problem. It is relatively simple to review the records of a series of mandibles for obvious left/right pairs, but it is much less likely that mandible/maxilla pairs could be established with any degree of confidence. The ideal recording protocol will depend on the species concerned, although the predominance of bovids in zooarchaeological material from most parts of the world makes some generalizations possible. The record needs to note which teeth are present, obviously, and which tooth locations are represented by empty alveoli. Inspection of the alveoli will generally reveal which teeth have been lost post-mortem, and which ante-mortem. In the latter case, some "healing" of the alveolus will generally be apparent. The record format must be flexible enough to encode specimens in which only deciduous teeth, or only permanent teeth, or a mix of the two are present. The simplest means is to allocate one field for each tooth in the full adult dentition of the species concerned (i.e., six in bovids, for three premolars and three molars). For each field for each specimen, we note whether the tooth is absent ante- or post-mortem, or present, coding premolars to show whether the tooth is deciduous or permanent. If present, we note the eruption state, from un-erupted but detectable in the mandibular bone to fully erupted and in wear, or note the state of attrition. Attrition is generally described in terms of the increased exposure of dentine on the occlusal surface, as the enamel is worn away, first from the apices of the cusps then as the crown is progressively abraded. Published coding schemes, such as those proposed by Grant (1982) and Payne (1973) for the Old World domesticates, by Armitage (1997) for rats, or by Garniewicz (2001) for raccoons, allow a high degree of consistency between analysts, and their use is recommended.

However systematic we make our recording of tooth eruption and wear, we have to remember that animals vary, both in their genes and in their lifetime experience. Studies of tooth eruption and wear in "known age" samples show the extent to which the timing of eruption and rate of attrition can vary between individuals (e.g., see Moran & O'Connor 1994), and that variation limits the precision of our interpretation of those data (e.g., O'Connor 1998).

Epiphysial fusion is simpler than dental eruption and attrition to record, though more problematic in the analysis, not least because fusion is more subject than dental eruption to variation between individuals, and because the data will consist of fusion records from each of many different anatomical elements. Each mammalian appendicular epiphysis in the sample can be assessed as unfused, in the process of fusion, or fully fused at the time of death, and it is a simple matter to add a code to that effect to the identification record of that specimen. However, there is a danger that some articular ends will be recorded twice by this means; once as an unfused epiphysis, and once as the unfused diaphysis. There are two means of resolving this problem. One is to record only epiphyses, ignoring any unfused diaphyses. The down side of this procedure is that it will substantially reduce the sample size, and may differentially remove immature individuals from the record. The other option is to attempt matching of epiphyses and diaphyses. The undulating pattern characteristic of most epiphysial junctions varies considerably between individuals, and it is sometimes possible to reunite epiphyses and diaphyses with a high degree of confidence. Once reunited, those specimens could then be recorded as a single record of, for example, the distal diaphysis plus epiphysis of a cattle metatarsal, unfused. By whatever means the problem of double recording is overcome, it is important that any archived or published methods statement explains exactly how the epiphysial fusion data have been arrived at.

The phenotypic characteristics of a bone specimen are generally recorded by measurements, taken by means of calipers or similar precision measuring devices. At their most basic, the measurements of a mammalian limb bone will seek to describe and record:

- the length of the complete bone
- the medio-lateral width (breadth) of the articular surfaces
- the medio-lateral width of the diaphysis, usually at its minimum.

Some antero-posterior measurements are commonly taken on certain elements such as the bovid femur, for which the antero-posterior diameter of the femoral caput often stands in as a measure of the "size" of the proximal end of the bone. Clearly, it is essential that these measurements are consistently defined and the compendium published by Angela von den Driesch (1976) is widely used. This collation of biometric standards is oriented toward the common Old World taxa. Although capable of adaptation to skeletally similar taxa from other regions, it would not be applicable to, for example, pinnipeds or macropods. A good record of biometric data is generally a pragmatic compromise between following a standard such as von den Driesch and acquiring the data required by the specific research aims of the project. Bone measurements are usually reported to a precision of 0.1 mm, though for length measurements in excess of 150 mm, a precision of 1.0 mm is quite satisfactory. Measurements may occasionally play a role in species identification (e.g., MacDonald et al. 1993), but are typically used to assess variables such as sex and biological population or "breed" (e.g., Reitz & Ruff 1994; Albarella 1997; Davis 2000).

It may seem ambitious to include a brief account of bone pathology in a chapter intended to introduce the practical basics of zooarchaeology. The study and interpretation of animal paleopathology is a highly technical and specialized field. However, specimens with signs of disease or trauma do not only occur in assemblages studied by pathology specialists, and anyone who sets out to record a bone assemblage needs to know at the very least *what* to record about an abnormal specimen. There is a growing realization in zooarchaeology that the skeletal pathology of our samples can reveal information about the population health of wild mammals or the treatment and management of domestic livestock. The subject as a whole is reviewed by Baker and Brothwell (1980) and, more recently but much more briefly, by O'Connor (2000: 98–110). For laboratory purposes, we can propose the parameters that need to be recorded in order to give a description of the specimen from which a tentative diagnosis might be possible:

- *Location* – Whereabouts on the bone is the lesion located? This is best expressed in terms of anatomical landmarks rather than by measurements (e.g., "Around midshaft on the posterior aspect," rather than "3 cm below the proximal end . . .").
- *Extent* – How extensive is the lesion? Unlike location, this parameter is probably best expressed in dimensions ("About 5 × 10 mm"), rather than by terms such as "small" (compared to what?).
- *Nature* – What is the lesion? This is obviously the most difficult aspect on which to provide simple guidance. The key is to remember that the aim is to *describe*, so describe precisely what it is about the specimen that has led you to record it as pathologically abnormal. Is the whole bone distorted (twisted, bent, compressed) from its normal shape? Is there additional bone where it should not be, or a lack of bone where it should be? In the former case, what is the appearance of the new bone (dense, granular, finely or coarsely porous, woven)?
- *Activity* – Was the lesion active at the time of death, or is it evidence of an earlier event in the animal's life? Again, this may be quite difficult for the less experienced zooarchaeologist, but it is important if the significance of the pathology in contributing to the animal's death is to be understood. The vertebrate skeleton is quite adept at remodeling once the cause of a lesion has ceased. Thus recent fractures will be marked by the development of a substantial callus of bone around the fracture site, whilst old fractures may be almost undetectable when the broken ends have reunited and the large callus is no longer necessary. A site of infection, such as a dental abscess, may be associated with a proliferation of new bone around the infection site whilst it is active, much of that new bone being remodeled and removed if the infection ceases.

In short, recording pathology is not a simple matter, but if attention is focused on describing and recording the lesion, rather than attempting an on-the-spot differential diagnosis, a zooarchaeologist with little experience of paleopathology can produce a useful record.

Having considered each variable in turn, it is worth considering how you might physically record these data. Animal bones were once (and sometimes still are) recorded on paper, generally on some form of pro-forma (e.g., see Grigson 1978). This form of recording was fast, flexible, and portable, but not conducive to detailed quantitative analysis. The advent of computers, therefore, offered great opportunities for zooarchaeology, and numerous bone data recording systems were devised. Most early examples ran up against data

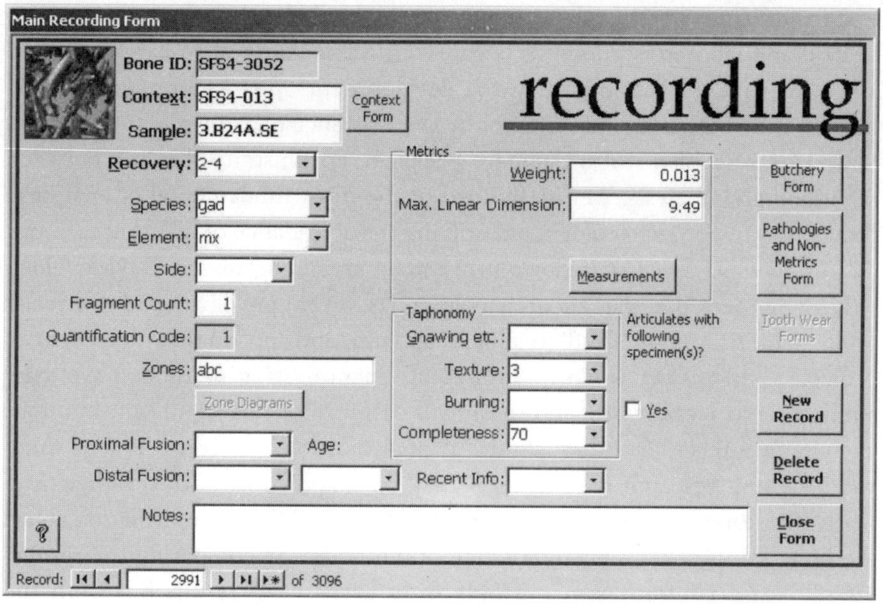

Figure 9.7 A specimen data-entry page for the York System.

storage limitations, and required highly abbreviated coding systems, which effectively made the bone records incomprehensible to any other user without the use of additional software to "translate" the coded data (e.g., Clutton-Brock 1975; Shaffer & Baker 1992). Early desktop and portable computers also had a tendency to overheat and break down, often causing their users to do the same. By the end of the millennium, computer technology had caught up with the aspirations of zooarchaeologists. It is now relatively simple to develop a recording system tailored to the needs of a particular project by constructing a "front end" for a relational database package. A fully relational database is preferable to a "flat" system such as a spreadsheet, because it allows different layers of data to be explored and combined more flexibly. Harland et al. (2003) describe the recording system used in York, which is based on a widely available relational database (Figure 9.7).

Computerized recording systems of this kind hold great promise for the future of data sharing and inter-analyst comparability. It is important, however, that their pre-programmed variables, tables, and reports are not used mechanistically. There is a danger that the very ease with which data summaries can be generated will lead to the production of tables and figures that do not address the research aims of your project. It is clearly important to think carefully about *what* needs to be recorded, tabulated, or graphed, and *why*.

A full account of the analysis and interpretation of zooarchaeological data lies beyond the remit of this chapter, and texts such as Chaix and Méniel (1996),

Using the Record – Quantification

Reitz and Wing (1999), and O'Connor (2000) should be consulted. Our outline of field and laboratory methods began with a discussion of research agendas, and ends with the reminder that the development of data summaries should be driven by research aims, and not by the existence of a convenient one-click option on one menu of a database package! To illustrate the link between recording and analysis, we briefly turn to the most fundamental of analytical procedures in zooarchaeology; quantifying the abundance of different taxa (for a digest of which, see O'Connor 2001b; and for greater detail, see Grayson 1984).

It might seem odd that zooarchaeology has not simply developed one really good quantification method, to general acclaim, and applied that method in all projects. The answer is twofold. First, all quantification methods have their strengths and weaknesses, and these will be more or less significant in different circumstances. In other words, a quantification procedure that is quite valid for one research investigation may be inappropriate for another. Secondly, the different procedures actually yield subtly different information about the bone sample. By applying a range of methods and comparing the results, we can extract information not only from each set of results but from the similarities and differences between them. Lyman et al. (2003) give a good example of this second point.

The strengths and weaknesses of various different forms of animal bone quantification may help to clarify the level of detail to which fragmentation, for example, needs to be recorded. For the present purposes, we consider three commonly used quantification procedures:

- *Number of Identified Specimens* (NISP) or *Total Number of Fragments* (TNF) procedures quantify each taxon by the number of specimens identified to that taxon. This procedure disregards the possibility that, for example, one dog femur that became fragmented in antiquity might be represented in the sample by three identifiable specimens (e.g., the proximal end, a substantial part of the shaft, and a small but identifiable fragment of the distal epiphysis). If there are fresh breaks on conjoining specimens, showing that they have broken during or after excavation, those specimens would normally be counted as a single specimen.
- *Minimum Number of Elements* (MNE) procedures attempt to adjust for fragmentation, quantifying each taxon by defining a list of discrete skeletal elements, then establishing the smallest number of, for example, dog distal femora or turkey coracoids that are represented by all the specimens identified to that part of that taxon. In the case of the dog femur above, the MNE count might be one, if "femur" is defined as one element, or two, if the proximal and distal ends are quantified as separate elements.
- *Minimum Number of Individuals* (MNI) procedures go one stage further, by seeking to estimate the smallest number of individual animals that could account for the specimens identified to each taxon. MNI estimation usually begins with a MNE estimation, separating paired elements into left and

right sides. The simplest estimate of MNI is then given by the most abundant nonreproducible element (i.e., if coracoids are the most abundant elements of turkey in the sample, and there are 17 left coracoids but only eight right coracoids, MNI must be 17 turkeys). More sophisticated calculations of MNI attempt to reconstruct left–right pairs in the sample, compiling MNI from the number of pairs, and the unpaired left and right elements. The procedure is widely and variously applied, despite having been subject to a range of criticisms, both practical and theoretical (not least by one of the present authors! – O'Connor 2001b).

It is quite clear that each of these procedures makes different demands of the data record. NISP methods require only that the same rigor in identification is applied to all of the taxa involved in the quantification. If, for example, shaft fragments have been identified and recorded for the carnivore taxa in a sample, but not for the bovids, then a simple NISP comparison of the relative abundance of hyena and gazelle will not be valid. The relative abundance of the two taxa expressed by NISP will be a distorted estimate of the relative abundance of those taxa in the original death assemblage. Such a recording bias may be hard to avoid if certain taxa can only be confidently identified on a limited range of elements – goat is an obvious example. In such a case, NISP data can be validly used to compare samples in which the recording bias is consistent, but cannot be taken to represent relative abundance in the original death assemblage. The analytical use that can be made of NISP data, therefore, depends very much on the consistency with which identification records have been made, and on the documentation of the identification and recording process.

MNE procedures actually make less stringent demands on the recording process than do NISP procedures. If the elements on which the quantification is based are defined in terms of, for example, articular ends of limb bones or hemimandible tooth rows, then differences between taxa in the recording of shaft fragments or loose teeth will not affect the quantification. It will be important to ensure that it is absolutely clear from the data record that a given specimen represents a specified element, and not a fragment of an element. That clarity can be achieved in a number of ways. Some analysts will choose only to record specimens that will be quantified as discrete elements (e.g., Davis 1987, 1992). For some samples, however, that might exclude the great majority of potentially identifiable specimens. Others will code each specimen (using diagnostic zones) to indicate whether or not it represents a "countable" element or just a fragment of that element. That procedure has the advantage of giving the clarity that MNE calculation requires, without being so reductive as to exclude NISP calculation.

MNI estimation is almost impossible to undertake satisfactorily from a data record, and is usually undertaken with the specimens arrayed across the bench. In order to facilitate a retrospective MNI estimation, the data set will require at the very least the same precision as the MNE data set. However, if left–right pairing is to be attempted, the data record would need to show, for example, that left mandible #3140 appears to pair with right mandible #3229, coding the record of each specimen accordingly. Note the word "appears," because left–right pairing of specimens is essentially an interpretation, open to experimental error and individual subjectivity. It is questionable, therefore, how far one analyst's MNI estimate *should* be encoded into the data record. The fastest route to developing a cynical view of MNI estimation is to ask several analysts to make such an estimate for the same sample of bones! However, what matters here is that we understand how the application of this quantification procedure will impose requirements on the data record.

We have touched on quantification only briefly, but with the aim of showing how the recording protocol may constrain the subsequent analysis of the data, and vice versa. This serves to underline the importance of planning the research methodology in some detail at the outset of the project, in order that recording procedures can be appropriately tailored, and the importance of properly curating recorded material, so that samples can be revisited as new analytical procedures require new data recording.

Conclusion   Bones matter: first, because all human and other hominin populations have closely interacted with those of other vertebrates in a bewildering range of processes and events that are reflected in the bone assemblages at archaeological sites; and, secondly, because bones are often amongst the most abundant "finds" at archaeological sites, and therefore command our attention.

We can choose to squeeze from them every last scrap of data, or choose to be selective, matching our data collection to specific research questions. Either approach will be valid in particular circumstances, but either can be seriously compromised by poor observation, handling, and recording between our first encounter with the excavated deposits and the data sets on which our eventual interpretations are based. The need to identify and record bones accurately and consistently is obvious enough, but the validity of that process relies on the quality of on-site records and recovery. A successful zooarchaeological study begins on site and requires cooperation and mutual understanding between the site excavator and the specialist who studies the bones.

Resources   Four journals carry much of the research development in zooarchaeology: *Journal of Archaeological Science*, *International Journal of Osteoarchaeology*, *Archaeozoologia*, and *Archaeofauna*. In addition, three others often carry papers that illustrate important applications of zooarchaeology: *Current Anthropology*, *American Antiquity*, and *Environmental Archaeology*.

Internet resources are more transient, and can vary in quality. Those that we have found to be useful include:

- International Council for ArchaeoZoology – www.nmnh.si.edu/icaz/
- *Journal of Taphonomy* – www.journaltaphonomy.com/
- Zooarchaeology Web – www.zooarchaeology.com/
- zooarchaeology discussion list – www.jiscmail.ac.uk/lists/zooarch.html

References

Albarella, U. 1997: Shape variation of cattle metapodials: age, sex or breed? Some examples from medieval and postmedieval sites. *Anthropozoologica*, 25–6, 37–47.

Amorosi, T. 1989: *A Postcranial Guide to Domestic Neo-Natal and Juvenile Mammals*. Oxford: BAR International Series, S533. Oxford: British Archaeological Reports.

Armitage, P. L. 1997: Provisional scheme for the identification and classification of wear stages in the upper molar teeth of *Rattus rattus* from archaeological contexts. *Journal of Zoology, London*, 241, 623–42.

Baker, J. R. and Brothwell, D. R. 1980: *Animal Diseases in Archaeology*. London: Academic Press.

Banning, E. B. 2002: *Archaeological Survey*. London: Kluwer.

Barrett, J. H. 1993: Bone weight, meat yield estimates and cod (*Gadus morhua*): a preliminary study of the weight method. *International Journal of Osteoarchaeology*, 3, 1–18.

—— 1997: Fish trade in Norse Orkney and Caithness: a zooarchaeological approach. *Antiquity*, 71, 616–38.

—— 2002: Quoygrew–Nether Trenabie. *Discovery and Excavation in Scotland* (New Series), 2, 73.

—— and Oltmann, J. 1997: Diagnostic elements and diagnostic zones for recording fish assemblages from northern Scotland. Paper presented at the Zooarchaeology Working Group workshop of the North Atlantic Biocultural Organization, New York.

——, Beukens, R. P. and Nicholson, R. A. 2001a: Diet and ethnicity during the Viking colonisation of northern Scotland: evidence from fish bones and stable carbon isotopes. *Antiquity*, 75, 145–54.

——, Nicholson, R. A. and Cerón-Carrasco, R. 1999: Archaeo-ichthyological evidence for long-term socioeconomic trends in northern Scotland: 3500 BC to AD 1500. *Journal of Archaeological Science*, 26, 353–88.

——, Simpson, I. and Davis, A. 1998: Cleat, Loch of Burness, Quoygrew–Nether Trenabie and Trenabie. *Discovery and Excavation in Scotland*, 1997, 61.

——, James, H., O'Connor, T. and Dobson, S. 2001b: Quoygrew–Nether Trenabie. *Discovery and Excavation in Scotland* (New Series), 1, 69–70.

Behrensmeyer, A. K. 1978: Taphonomic and ecologic information from bone weathering. *Paleobiology*, 4, 150–62.

Blumenschine, R. J., Marean, C. W. and Capaldo, S. D. 1996: Blind tests of inter-analyst correspondence and accuracy in the identification of cut-marks, percussion marks, and carnivore tooth marks on bone surfaces. *Journal of Archaeological Science*, 23, 493–507.

Cannon, D. Y. 1987: *Marine Fish Osteology: A Manual for Archaeologists*. Burnaby: Department of Archaeology, Simon Fraser University.

Carter, R. J. 2001: New evidence for seasonal human presence at the Early Mesolithic site of Thatcham, Berkshire, England. *Journal of Archaeological Science*, 28, 1055–60.

Casteel, R. W. 1978: Faunal assemblages and the "wiegemethode" or weight method. *Journal of Field Archaeology*, 5, 71–7.

Chaix, L. and Méniel, P. 1996: *Elements d'archaeozoologie*. Paris: Editions Errance.

Clason, A. T. and Prummel, W. 1977: Collecting, sieving and archaeozoological research. *Journal of Archaeological Science*, 4, 171–5.

Clutton-Brock, J. 1975: A system for the retrieval of data relating to animal remains from archaeological sites. In A. T. Clason (ed.), *Archaeozoological Studies*. Amsterdam: Elsevier, 21–34.

Cohen, A. and Serjeantson, D. 1996: *A Manual for the Identification of Bird Bones from Archaeological Sites*, 2nd edn. London: Birkbeck College.

Cook, S. F. and Treganza, A. E. 1956: The quantitative investigation of Indian mounds. In E. W. Gifford, A. L. Kroeber, R. H. Lowie, T. D. McCown, D. G. Mandelbaum and R. L. Olson (eds.), *University of California Publications in American Archaeology and Ethnology, Volume 40, 1942–1953*. Los Angeles: University of California Press, 223–59.

Davis, S. and Payne, S. 1992: 101 ways to deal with a dead hedgehog: notes on the preparation of disarticulated skeletons for zoo-archaeological use. *Circaea*, 8, 95–104.

Davis, S. J. M. 1987: *The Archaeology of Animals*. London: Batsford.

—— 1992: *A Rapid Method for Recording Information about Mammal Bones from Archaeological Sites*. Ancient Monuments Laboratory Report 19/92. London: English Heritage.

—— 2000: The effect of castration and age on the development of the Shetland sheep skeleton and a metric comparison between bones of males, females and castrates. *Journal of Archaeological Science*, 27, 373–90.

Dobney, K. M. and Reilly, K. 1988: A method for recording archaeological animal bones: the use of diagnostic zones. *Circaea*, 12(2), 79–96.

Driver, J. 1999: Raven skeletons from Paleoindian contexts, Charlie Lake Cave, British Columbia. *American Antiquity*, 64(2), 289–98.

Fisher, J. W. 1995: Bone surface modifications in zooarchaeology. *Journal of Archaeological Method and Theory*, 2(1), 7–68.

Garniewicz, R. C. 2001: Age and sex determination from the mandibular dentition of raccoons: techniques and applications. In A. Pike-Tay (ed.), *Innovations in Assessing Season of Capture, Age and Sex of Archaeofaunas*. Grenoble: Le Pensée Sauvage, 223–38.

Glassow, M. A. 2000: Weighing vs. counting shellfish remains: a comment on Mason, Peterson and Tiffany. *American Antiquity*, 65, 407–14.

Gobalet, K. W. 2001: A critique of faunal analysis: inconsistency among experts in blind tests. *Journal of Archaeological Science*, 28, 377–86.

Grant, A. 1982: The use of tooth wear as a guide to the age of domestic ungulates. In B. Wilson, C. Grigson and S. Payne (eds.), *Ageing and Sexing Animal Bones from Archaeological Sites*. BAR British Series, 109. Oxford: British Archaeological Reports, 91–108.

Grayson, D. K. 1984: *Quantitative Zooarchaeology*. London: Academic Press.

Greenfield, H. J. 1999: The origins of metallurgy: distinguishing stone from metal cut-marks on bones from archaeological sites. *Journal of Archaeological Science*, 26, 797–808.

Grigson, C. 1978: Towards a blueprint for animal bone reports in archaeology. In D. R. Brothwell, K. D. Thomas and J. Clutton-Brock (eds.), *Research Problems in Zooarchaeology*. Institute of Archaeology Occasional Publications, 3. London: Institute of Archaeology, 121–8.

Harland, J. F., Barrett, J. H., Carrott, J., Dobney, K. and Jaques, D. 2003: The York System: an integrated zooarchaeological database for research and teaching. *Internet Archaeology* 13. Electronic document: http://intarch.ac.uk/journal/issue13/harland_toc.html

Hillson, S. M. 1986: *Teeth*. Cambridge: Cambridge University Press.

Jackson, H. E. 1989: The trouble with transformations: effects of sample size and sample composition on weight estimates based on skeletal mass allometry. *Journal of Archaeological Science*, 16, 601–10.

Jones, A. K. G. 1983: A comparison of two on-site methods of wet-sieving large archae-ological soil samples. *Science and Archaeology*, 25, 9–12.

Kenward, H. K., Hall, A. R. and Jones, A. K. G. 1980: A tested set of techniques for the extraction of plant and animal macrofossils from waterlogged archaeological deposits. *Science and Archaeology*, 22, 3–15.

Kubasiewicz, M. 1956: O metodyce badan wykopaliskowych szczatkow kostnych zwierzecych. *Materialy Zachodnio-Pomorskie*, 2, 235–44.

Landon, D. A. 1996: Feeding colonial Boston: a zooarchaeological study. *Historical Archae-ology*, 30, 1–153.

Lauwerier, R. 2002: Animals as food for the soul. In K. Dobney and T. P. O'Connor (eds.), *Bones and the Man*. Oxford: Oxbow Books, 63–71.

Levitan, B. M. 1982: Excavations at West Hill Uley: 1979. The sieving and sampling programme. Western Archaeological Trust Occasional Papers, 10. Bristol: Western Archaeological Trust.

Lieberman, D. E. 1994: The biological basis for seasonal increments in dental cementum and their application to archaeological research. *Journal of Archaeological Science*, 21, 525–39.

Lyman, R. L. 1984: Bone density and differential survivorship of fossil bone classes. *Journal of Anthropological Archaeology*, 3, 259–99.

—— 1994: *Vertebrate Taphonomy*. Cambridge: Cambridge University Press.

——, Power, E. and Lyman, R. J. 2003: Quantification and sampling of faunal remains in owl pellets. *Journal of Taphonomy*, 1, 3–14.

MacDonald, R. H., MacDonald, K. C. and Ryan, K. 1993: Domestic geese from medieval Dublin. *Archaeofauna*, 2, 205–18.

Marean, C. W. 1991: Measuring the post-depositional destruction of bone in archaeological assemblages. *Journal of Archaeological Science*, 18, 677–94.

—— and Cleghorn, N. 2003: Large mammal skeletal element transport: applying foraging theory in a complex taphonomic system. *Journal of Taphonomy*, 1, 15–42.

Marshall, F. 1994: Food sharing and body part representation in Okiek faunal assemblages. *Journal of Archaeological Science*, 21, 65–77.

Mitchell, D. 1990: Coast Salish subsistence and a methodological barrier. *Northwest Anthro-pological Research Notes*, 24, 239–47.

Moran, N. C. and O'Connor, T. P. 1994: Age attribution in domestic sheep by skeletal and dental maturation: a pilot study of available sources. *International Journal of Osteoarchaeology*, 4, 267–85.

Moreno-García, M., Orton, C. and Rackham, J. 1996: A new statistical tool for comparing animal bone assemblages. *Journal of Archaeological Science*, 23, 437–53.

Morlan, R. E. 1994: Bison bone fragmentation and survivorship: a comparative method. *Journal of Archaeological Science*, 21, 797–808.

Nicholson, R. A. 1996: Bone degradation, burial medium and species representation: debunking the myths, an experiment-based approach. *Journal of Archaeological Science*, 23, 513–34.

O'Connor, T. P. 1991: *Bones from 46–54 Fishergate*. Archaeology of York 15/4. York: Council for British Archaeology.

—— 1998: On the difficulty of detecting seasonal slaughtering of sheep. *Environmental Archaeology*, 3, 5–11.

—— 2000: *The Archaeology of Animal Bones*. Stroud, UK: Sutton.

—— 2001a: Collecting, sieving, and zooarchaeological quantification. In H. Buitenhuis and W. Prummel (eds.), *Animals and Man in the Past*. Groningen: Rijksuniversiteit Groningen, 7–16.

—— 2001b: Animal bone quantification. In A. M. Pollard and D. R. Brothwell (eds.), *Introduction to Archaeological Science*. Chichester: John Wiley, 703–10.

Olsen, S. J. 1960: Post-cranial skeletal characters of *Bison* and *Bos*. *Papers of the Peabody Museum of Archaeology and Ethnology*, 35(4), 1–16 plus 24 figs. Cambridge: Peabody Museum of Archaeology and Ethnology.

Orton, C. 2000: *Sampling in Archaeology*. Cambridge: Cambridge University Press.

Otto, C. 1981: Vergleichend morphologische Untersuchungen an Einzelknochen in Zentraleuropa vorkommender mittelgrosser Accipitridae. Dissertation, University of Munich.

Payne, S. 1973: Kill-off patterns in sheep and goats. The mandibles from Asvan Kale. *Anatolian Studies*, 23, 281–303.

—— 1975: Partial recovery and sample bias. In A. T. Clason (ed.), *Archaeozoological Studies*. New York: Elsevier, 7–17.

Peacock, W. R. B. 1978: Probabilistic sampling in shell middens: a case-study from Oronsay, Inner Hebrides. In J. F. Cherry, C. Gamble and S. Shennan (eds.), *Sampling in Contemporary British Archaeology*. BAR International Series, 50. Oxford: British Archaeological Reports, 177–90.

Reitz, E. J. and Ruff, B. 1994: Morphometric data for cattle from North America and the Caribbean prior to the 1850s. *Journal of Archaeological Science*, 21, 699–713.

—— and Wing, E. A. 1999: *Zooarchaeology*. Cambridge: Cambridge University Press.

——, Quitmyer, I. R., Hale, H. S., Scudder, S. J. and Wing, E. S. 1987: Application of allometry to zooarchaeology. *American Antiquity*, 52, 304–17.

Rolett, B. V. and Chiu, M-y 1994: Age estimation of prehistoric pigs (*Sus scrofa*) by molar eruption and attrition. *Journal of Archaeological Science*, 21, 377–86.

Scarlett, R. J. 1972: *Bones for the New Zealand Archaeologist*. Canterbury Museum Bulletin, 4. Christchurch: Canterbury Museum.

Schmid, E. S. 1972: *Atlas of Animal Bones*. Amsterdam: Elsevier.

Serjeantson, D. 1991: "Rid Grasse of bones": a taphonomic study of the bones from midden deposits at the Neolithic and Bronze Age site of Runnymede, Surrey, England. *International Journal of Osteoarchaeology*, 1, 73–89.

Shaffer, B. S. and Baker, B. W. 1992: *A Vertebrate Faunal Analysis Coding System*. University of Michigan Museum of Anthropology Technical Report, 23. Ann Arbor: University of Michigan Museum of Anthropology.

—— and Sanchez, J. L. J. 1994: Comparison of 1/8" and 1/4" mesh recovery of controlled samples of small-to-medium sized mammals. *American Antiquity*, 59, 525–30.

Simpson, I. A., Perdikaris, S., Cook, G., Campbell, J. L. and Teesdale, W. J. 2000: Cultural sediment analyses and transitions in early fishing activity at Langenesværet, Vesterålen, northern Norway. *Geoarchaeology*, 15, 743–63.

Stewart, F. L. 1991: Floating for fauna: some methodological considerations using the Keffer site (AkGv-14) midden 57 faunal sample. *Canadian Journal of Archaeology*, 15, 97–116.

Stewart-Abernathy, L. C. and Ruff, B. L. 1987: A good man in Israel: zooarchaeology and assimilation in Antebellum Washington, Washington, Arkansas. *Historical Archaeology*, 23, 96–112.

Van Neer, W., Lougas, L. and Rijnsdorp, A. D. 1999: Reconstructing age distribution, season of capture and growth rate of fish from archaeological sites based on otoliths and vertebrae. *International Journal of Osteoarchaeology*, 9, 116–30.

Vigne, J.-D. 1995: Détermination ostéologique des principaux éléments du squelette appendiculaire d'Arvicola, d'Eliomys, de Glis et de Rattus. Juan-les-Pins: CNRS Fiches d'Osteologie Animale pour l'Archaeologie no. 6.

—— and Valladas, H. 1996: Small mammal fossil assemblages as indicators of environmental change in northern Corsica during the last 2500 years. *Journal of Archaeological Science*, 23, 199–215.

von den Driesch, A. 1976: *A Guide to the Measurement of Animal Bones from Archaeological Sites*. Peabody Museum of Archaeology and Ethnology Bulletin, 1. Cambridge: Peabody Museum of Archaeology and Ethnology.

Walker, R. J. 1985: *A Guide to the Post-Cranial Bones of East African Mammals*. Norwich: Hylochoerus Press.

Watson, J. P. N. 1979: The estimation of the relative frequencies of mammalian species: Khirokitia 1972. *Journal of Archaeological Science*, 6, 127–37.

Watt, J., Pierce, G. J. and Boyle, P. R. 1997: *A Guide to the Identification of North Sea Fish Using Premaxillae and Vertebrae*. Copenhagen: International Council for the Exploration of the Sea.

Wheeler, A. and Jones, A. K. G. 1989: *Fishes*. Cambridge: Cambridge University Press.

Williams, D. E. 1973: Flotation at Siraf. *Antiquity*, 47, 288–92.

Wing, E. S. and Quitmyer, I. R. 1985: Screen size for optimal data recovery: a case study. In W. H. Adam (ed.), *Aboriginal Subsistence and Settlement Archaeology of the Kings Bay Locality*, vol. 2: *Zooarchaeology*. Department of Anthropology, University of Florida, Reports of Investigation, 2. Gainesville: Department of Anthropology, University of Florida, 49–58.

Wolff, R. G. 1973: Hydrodynamic sorting and ecology of a Pleistocene mammal assemblage from California (USA). *Palaeogeography, Palaeoclimatology, Palaeoecology*, 13, 91–101.

Zohar, I., Dayan, T., Galili, E. and Spanier, E. 2001: Fish processing during the early Holocene: a taphonomic case study from coastal Israel. *Journal of Archaeological Science*, 28, 1041–53.

Wendy Beck

10
Plant Remains

Introduction: A Scene

> We are standing at the mouth of a sandstone rockshelter in the mountains
> of central New South Wales in Australia, having just climbed up from the creek
> below. The floor of the rockshelter is sunny and warm at this time of day. I turn
> to my archaeologist colleague: "I think this floor is gray because it contains
> organic material." He nods and peers at the sandy floor, which has a little
> mound at the side of the shelter: "There is a fossick hole here, I can see some
> kangaroo bone." We kneel down to look more closely, and sticking out of the
> surface we can see some knotted fibers and large seeds on the surface of the
> mounded deposit. "Are these plant remains? What are these seeds?" he asks.
> Because of my prior knowledge I recognized them as *Macrozamia* by their shape
> and size and the tiny holes in the ends. He says, "They are unusually well
> preserved, but I guess they are just on the surface and have blown in here, so
> there isn't much use in looking further. It would be too hard to use flotation
> anyway, as the creek is dry at the moment, and they wouldn't tell us anything
> much about the microlith industry around here anyway."

This scene illustrates the three main issues for the archaeological analysis
of plant remains. The first of these issues is the question of what plant
remains can contribute to archaeology as a whole; the second is the problems
associated with the identification and origin of plant remains; and the third
is the available methods that can be effectively used to retrieve and analyze
plant remains. I will return to the scene in a case study showing how we
addressed the issues at this rockshelter but, first, a general introduction to the
issues is needed.

Macroscopic Plant Remains
Macroscopic plant remains are those archaeological plant traces that are
large enough to be recognized without high-powered microscopy. These
kinds of plant traces include seeds, fruits, or wood fragments and are in contrast to microscopic plant remains such as pollen, phytoliths, starch grains,

residues, and so on (Hillman et al. 1993; Brown 2001; Bryant 2003). Microscopic plant remains are not covered in this chapter: however, analyzing both kinds of materials forms the most direct and readily observable evidence for interactions between humans and plants. Terms sometimes used for this type of archaeological study are *paleoethnobotany, archaeobotany, botanical archaeology*, or *phytoarchaeology* depending on the emphasis of the study and whether the investigator has a New or Old World background (Buurman & Pals 1994: 471). *Paleoethnobotany* is currently the most widely used term (Hastorf 1999: 56) with the most general meaning, although *archaeobotany* is also in common use.

Although plant remains are a very tangible link with the everyday life of the past, the analysis of macroscopic plant remains is somewhat neglected when compared with other kinds of macroscopic biological remains, such as bones. This is because it is often assumed that plant remains do not survive well, and their potential is unrecognized (Lepofsky et al. 2001; Losey et al. 2003). Often, archaeological macroscopic plant remains are those that are very resistant to decay (such as carbonized remains) or those that occur in unusual conditions (such as waterlogged or very dry sites). However, these conditions occur more widely than we might think at first glance (Clarke 1989). Studies of plant remains do not form part of the mainstream curriculum in many archaeological programs, but plant remains have an important place in archaeological field and laboratory studies. Macroscopic plant remains are contributing evidence for many archaeological questions (Hastorf 1999; Pearsall 2000).

The broad field of plant macroremains is large and diverse, so I have divided my review of the current state of knowledge in the study of archaeological plant remains into three categories:

- What can plant remains contribute to archaeology?
- What are the problems (and solutions) for identifying and determining the origin of macroscopic plant remains?
- What kinds of methods can be effectively used to retrieve and analyze plant remains?

I have used these questions as headings to structure this chapter and I will review each of these topics in turn with the following questions in mind: What is known about this topic? Why is it an important topic? What is unknown? Why are some things unknown? Why should the gaps be filled in?

The main message of this chapter is that some aspects of macroscopic plant analysis can be done by students with little botanical expertise, and can also contribute to the preparation of students for field and laboratory work in general archaeology. This chapter will not make anyone an expert paleoethnobotanist, but will alert you to the questions, methods, and approaches available and to the value of asking questions about plant remains.

There are several excellent manuals and papers about the techniques of recovering, analyzing, and interpreting macroscopic plant remains. I have listed some of these under "Further reading" below. In this chapter I have not provided an exhaustive literature review, but rather focused on literature that is accessible to students, and especially on literature of the past five years (1998–2003), as other recent manuals do not cover this.

What can Plant Remains Contribute to Archaeology?

The relationship between people and plants

The aim of archaeology is to learn about past human behavior through material evidence. From the study of archaeological plant remains and from other kinds of evidence, we can trace the use of plants by a range of past peoples, from early hominids (Sept 1994) to colonial settlers (Dudek et al. 1998; Gremillion 2002a). The origins of agriculture, environmental change, human/environmental influences, resource availability, resource use, stone tool function, long-term socioeconomic change, and staple foods are simply a few examples of the kinds of research to which the analysis of plant remains can contribute. The applications of paleoethnobotanical techniques continue to bring new ideas about how, when, and why changes in subsistence patterns occurred in the past. Macroscopic plant remains are important in archaeological debates about when prehistoric maize evolution occurred in the pre-Hispanic New World (Benz & Long 2000) and about the importance of plant foods in the diet of Pleistocene hunter–gatherers in both Paleolithic and Mesolithic Europe (Mason et al. 1994) and in Paleo-Indian contexts (Roosevelt et al. 1996).

Undoubtedly, the greatest amount of research worldwide has been directed at agricultural plants and their origins, rather than at how hunter–gatherers use plants (e.g., Renfrew 1973; Dimbleby 1978; Ford 1979; Crawford 1992; Hather 1992; Warnock 1998). This is partly due to the fact that there is often a greater visibility of evidence for agricultural plants, such as charred remains, house and crop processing sites, and the plant gardens themselves. Even within studies of hunter–gatherer plants, there has been greater emphasis on "incipient agriculture" rather than on other aspects of plant uses. The relationship between people and plants is of course always two-way, with both plants and people benefiting.

Although plants are used for a range of purposes (Cotton 1996), a dominant theme in the archaeological and ethnobotanical literature is that of plants and diet, especially staple plant foods (e.g., Cribb & Cribb 1981). Apart from their nutritional value in supplying carbohydrates, proteins, and vitamins, the concept of a staple as being a regularly collected, dependable resource is one that is applicable to archaeobotanical evidence. The difficulty for archaeologists is how to recognize this repeated pattern of resource use from the archaeological record. Which plant species present in an archaeobotanical assemblage could fulfill the role of a staple? How can regularly collected material gathered over years be identified archaeologically? How can dependability be identified from the archaeological record (Beck et al. 1989b; Clarke 1989)?

Until recent times, plants have provided most of the raw materials of human technology. The term "technology" is used here in the widest sense possible. It includes not only how material artifacts and tools are used to do things ("material technology") but also how the shared skills and knowledge of people facilitate activities ("nonmaterial" technology). In other words, *technology* may refer to the use of a grinding stone or the use of a sensitive nose or pair of hands. Technology is one way in which humans adapt to their environment and most past technologies were dependent on plants. For instance, most material culture before 1700 was constructed from plant materials. The properties of plants that make them suitable for technological uses are both their physical properties, such as the tensile strength of wood, the span of bark, and the flexibility of fibers (Nadel & Werker 1999), and their chemical properties, such as medicinal, nutritional, preservational, or combustible qualities, as well as symbolic, ritual, or aesthetic importance (Balick & Cox 1996; Boyd et al. 1996; Cotton 1996; Bearez 1998; Behre 1999; Serpico & White 2000; Vermeeren & van Haaster 2002; Zach 2002). Plants also occur in relatively fixed spatial and seasonal locations in the landscape, which makes them predictable raw materials.

This wide range of uses for plants means that it is difficult for archaeologists to predict or understand where and when technological plant remains may occur. Often, the technological uses of plants are studied less than their dietary uses and, just as often, the remains from technological uses may be waste products, such as wood shavings, or discarded leaves, rather than the artifacts themselves. This tends to makes them less visible to paleoethnobotanists.

Ecological analyses for the investigation of subsistence economies at the regional level commonly focus on vegetation resources in conjunction with macroscopic plant remains (Fairbairn et al. 2002). Although ecological reconstructions commonly use microscopic remains, such as phytoliths and pollen, this can also be done by using macroscopic plant remains such as charcoal pieces and seeds (Jeraj 2002). Many regional subsistence studies have now been completed, covering regions from the Himalayas (Knorzer 2000) to Old Prague (Benes et al. 2002) to British Columbia (Wollstonecroft 2002). The identification of potential site economies can be carried out by analyses of plant resources available within a catchment area (Sept 1994; Smith et al. 1995). Similarly, at a larger scale, vegetation mapping is often used to define seasonal or annual territorial ranges of communities. Quantitative data (such as fruit density by area) are required to indicate the small-scale variations in

Plants and technology

Plants and regional subsistence

the distribution and abundance of resources that may not be apparent to the casual observer (Walsh 1987; Sept 1994). Quantitative modeling based on macrobotanical remains has also been used to investigate regional changes in agricultural systems in Mesopotamia (McCorriston & Weisberg 2002).

Archaeological theories and plants

Many of the models that examine diachronic change in prehistory discuss changing roles for plant use, particularly as food but also as part of the technology. However, archaeologists – especially those studying hunter–gatherers – have, with few exceptions, mainly used stone tools and ethnographic data to construct their models. These models might change if plants were incorporated into them (Beck et al. 1989a; Mason et al. 1994; Gremillion 2002b). The relationship between plants and gender is also an important topic of recent research. Mid-range questions relating the archaeological record to human activity are the elements that are most often missing in studies of archaeobotany. Gendered activities can be investigated through the study of plant remains; for example, in terms of site functions (e.g., men's versus family activities) and stone tool functions (e.g., women's seed grinding stones). Plant preparation in most ethnographic small-scale societies is almost entirely carried out by women, and archaeological effort needs to be expended in trying to identify social variables such as the gender division of labor or social differentiation of other kinds (Hastorf 1991; Welch & Scarry 1995).

There are many types of archaeological reports of macroplant remains. These range from strictly empirical reporting of plant types found at site X, to articles about specific methods, to articles about the place of plant-based technology or plant processing in general archaeology. This indicates a healthy spread of research in the area of plant macroremains, particularly as publications in the new journal *Vegetation History and Archaeobotany*. Most of the literature could be placed under one of the headings used above. Some of the gaps where research has been lacking are indicated above: hunter–gatherer and hominid plant use are less well known archaeologically than agricultural uses; similarly, plants as technological items are less well known than food plants; and less is known about plant taphonomy than about other kinds of taphonomy. In order for plant macroremains to fully contribute to archaeology, this range of studies needs to continue and be expanded.

What are the Problems (and Solutions) for Identifying and Determining the Origin of Macroscopic Plant Remains?

Technical problems in analyzing macro-plants, and their solutions

The major problem of traditional paleoethnobotany is the survival of the evidence. All organic matter decays over time and much of the study of plant decay has focused on ecological recycling, rather than on the preservation of evidence. Both cultural and noncultural factors will contribute to the survival of plant remains, and much of the material surviving will be waste products that need to be clearly recognized (Beck 1989). The taphonomic study of plants – that is, the middle-range theory that allows for the translation of remains into interpretations of human behavior – is a relatively neglected area, with fewer publications than other research topics (Jones 1987; Gustafsson 2000; Charles et al. 2002; Wright 2003).

The various types of direct archaeological evidence for plant use should now be familiar. In summary, the kinds of macroscopic remains may be carbonized, waterlogged, dried, frozen, mineralized, or in coprolites and may consist of tubers, seeds, fruits, bark, wood, or leaves (Minnis 1989; Miller et al. 1998; Morcote-Rios & Bernal 2001). All of these types of materials have different taphonomic histories and will require different kinds of study.

Archaeological sources

Plant taphonomy is increasingly being studied, but much more remains to be done. The detailed analysis and interpretation of these remains requires multidisciplinary work, at different scales, some site-specific and local, as opposed to the regional and the continent-wide. Some techniques are more suited to small-scale rather than large-scale research. Often in the past, plant remains were ignored or went unrecognized, but greater attention to the role of plants in the past, and to the role of women in collecting, cooking, and processing plants has led to some changes in the relative importance of plant remains in archaeology in the past ten years or so (Hastorf 1999). However, the laboratory techniques required for paleoethnobotanical analyses remain labor intensive and are therefore expensive.

As well as direct archaeological evidence for plant remains, literature sources, and/or first-hand ethnographic observations are also important databases for archaeological research, and especially taphonomic research, but as with any ethnographic or historical materials, there are limitations associated with their use. A full account of ethnobotanical methods can be found in Cotton (1996), Gott (1989), and Meehan (1989); and interesting case studies in Shaw (1993) on gardens, Wandsnider (1997) on plant cooking technologies, and a recent ethnoarchaeological case study using the ecological attributes of weeds in current Spanish cereal plots (Charles et al. 2002) have interesting archaeological applications. These kinds of publications are a good source of research questions that subsequently can be answered through the analysis of macrobotanical remains, especially about the origin and likely use of plant materials.

Ethnobotany and ethnoarchaeology

When plants do survive, the technical problems associated with their interpretation extend to recovery and excavation techniques, identification, and preliminary analysis, all of which are needed to determine a plant's origin. These problems are starting to be overcome by the investigation of a wider range of plant remains such as waterlogged remains and carbonized remains (using techniques such as scanning electron microscopy), as well as traditional macroscopic remains, such as seeds, wood, and comparisons with micro-scopic remains (Miller et al. 1998; Zutter 1999). The contributions of history, ethnography, and ecology are also important here, particularly in places where the nature of archaeological sites means that remains are sparse and scattered.

What Kinds of Methods can be Effectively Used to Retrieve and Analyze Plant Remains? Recovery techniques need to be modified for the circumstances and condi-tions of archaeological recovery. Remains may include charcoal, wood, bark, leaves, seeds, fruits, or other plant parts. A reference collection is important for recognizing remains, especially for the identification of processed plants, such as cooked tubers, as well as for the identification of plants that have ended up in deposits by natural means (e.g., by blowing into a rockshelter from surrounding vegetation). Obviously sampling is an issue here, and it is usual to take some kind of bulk sample as well as sampling sieved material. The bulk sample can be a separate column sample or one taken during excava-tion. The bulk sample allows for comparisons of material and processes of recovery (for details of sampling techniques, see Lennstrom & Hastorf 1995; Hastorf 1999; Pearsall 2000). Flotation techniques are widely used on agricul-tural sites, but are not 100 percent successful. Wagner (1982) has measured the efficiencies of various techniques. Often, problems of breakage of fragile mater-ial in water and of successfully drying the material need to be overcome (Gott 1977) but this technique is still widely used (Mason et al. 1994; Weber 1999). Dry sieving is often the most effective method of recovery, but a minimum sieve size of about 1 mm needs to be used to recover small seeds and remains (Wasylikowa et al. 1997).

Systematic recovery methods are increasingly being used in a number of different kinds of archaeological contexts, ranging from Bronze Age cereal production (Chernoff & Paley 1998) in Israel, to Harappan seeds and agricul-ture (Weber 1999), to 40,000 years of plant remains from an Aboriginal site in Western Australia (McConnell & O'Connor 1997).

Preliminary analysis and quantification starts with sorting of the material. Some measure of optimal sample size is often necessary, because of the huge investment of time associated with sorting the material (see the case study in this chapter). Quantification is a big problem as well and there is a need to establish a standard measure of comparison. Minimum numbers of individuals or weight are often used. Quantification of plant remains is also complicated by the facts that plant remains usually occur in different densities across the site and that there is uneven preservation of different plant parts.

Laboratory work in the archaeology of plants requires familiarity with the "tools of the trade" – weighing and measuring, the use of chemicals, and the use of hand-lenses and stereomicroscopes. The use of microscopes effectively requires many hours of practice, but is a necessary skill for the identification and isolation of plant remains.

WENDY BECK

The classification of organisms into species should be familiar from other parts of archaeological study. Existing plant species are commonly identified with the use of dichotomous (i.e., two-branched) keys. There are many examples of these in basic botanical texts and in Pearsall (2000). You must have a grasp of botanical jargon to use botanical keys, although this gets easier with practice.

Basic plant classification

Most archaeological specimens are identified by reference to modern reference collections. Species identification and proper description is essential for setting up a modern plant reference collection, and it is also important to ensure that all the relevant information in regard to the plant (e.g., habitat, season, and abundance) is recorded for the specimen. For archaeological research, other information, such as the part of the plant utilized by humans and common usage of plant parts, is also useful. The definition of an "economic" plant assists in recognition of cultural and noncultural factors in plant deposition. While using actual specimens to check against archaeological ones is often better than a photograph, preservation of plants can alter their original appearance. For example, the flowers are crushed and lose their color, and the plants themselves are flattened and distorted.

The identification of archaeological plant remains is still an important area for new work, especially on the parts of plants other than seeds and nuts (Struzkova 2002), and on carbonized remains (Boyd 1988). For instance, tuber identification is a relatively new and important area (Ugent et al. 1987; Hather 1993). Detailed statistical analyses are also important for the identification of some macroremains (Lepofsky et al. 1998; Benz & Long 2000). However, new work on seed carbonization has suggested that distortions in the dimensions of wild and cultivated seeds may occur, which suggests that caution may be needed in applying this method (Wright 2003).

Fruits and seeds are some of the most useful botanical structures for the identification of archaeological plant remains, both wild and cultivated (e.g., Jacquat & Martinoli 1999; Rivera et al. 2002). They can often be recognized by nonbotanists, and illustrated manuals exist for the United States and Europe (e.g., Martin & Barkley 1961). Unfortunately, there are no comparable manuals for Australia and some other parts of the world. There are various techniques for separating seed and fruit remains from excavations of archaeological deposits. The commonest methods employed are hand sorting, flotation in fresh water, and flotation in other liquids (for details of flotation methods, see Pearsall 2000).

Archaeological retrieval and identification of seeds and fruits

Wood and charcoal from archaeological sites can be used as paleoenvironmental indicators and for dating, as well as for identifying economic resources (Smith et al. 1995; Nadel & Werker 1999; Asouti & Hather 2001). Wood structure and function are the parts of the plants that are most distinctive for identification.

Wood and charcoal

Carbonized wood is also one of the most enduring types of macroscopic plant remains in archaeological sites, and in large quantities is most often assumed to be of human origin (Hansen 2001). The use of carbonized material in AMS dating of New World agricultural systems has become a recent focus of attention, for both beans and maize (Kaplan & Lynch 1999).

Knowledge and skills in basic botanical identification are essential for this work, which requires many hours of practice. Without identification at least to Family level, there may be little that can be concluded from the macroscopic remains. However, there are many areas of the world where comprehensive and useful reference collections do not exist, and so there are gaps in our knowledge and ability to identify macroremains. The nature of the remains themselves, often without the reproductive plant parts that botanists use to identify plants, means that the archaeological analyst must develop special skills and techniques in identification.

More problems in the analysis of plant remains

A recent analysis of a large database of carbonized cereal seeds from the Indus civilization (Weber 1999; Fuller 2001) brings out some of the longstanding problems in macroscopic plant analyses – which can be divided into two categories. The first category is about the data themselves and the second is about the interpretation of the data. In the first category are problems of lack of detailed descriptions of the seeds, debated species identification, and whether some of the observed variation could be explained taphonomically by changes in plant processing rather than changes in plant cultivation. In the second category are questions about generalization in explanation. Is it possible to generalize from changes at one site to another site 1,000 miles away? In other words, how are regional trends differentiated from local ones? These are all issues that can be related back to the three basic questions with which we began.

The sources of information about plant use are often the archaeological remains themselves, but in order to fully investigate these remains, other sources of information may be needed, such as ethnobotanical information from historical sources or interviews, or written sources. New kinds of analyses are also being developed; for example, the tracing of thermal histories of seeds (maize kernels) using electron spin resonance (Schurr et al. 2001), and new ways of using physiological information about cereals in modeling prehistoric yields (Araus et al. 2003). However, the most satisfying studies of plant remains will be those that employ a range of kinds of evidence in support of the conclusions. Plants can contribute to a wider range of archaeological issues than perhaps is generally recognized, so they need to be incorporated more generally into theoretical studies.

Plant Remains from Kawambarai Cave, near Coonabarabran, Eastern Australia (by Wendy Beck and Dee Murphy)

Plant remains have been sadly neglected in archaeological analyses worldwide. Part of the reason for this is the lack of archaeological deposits containing well-preserved material (Beck et al. 1989b). This case study reports on the analysis of macroscopic plant remains from a sandstone rockshelter, Kawambarai Cave, that lies on the eastern slopes of the Warrumbungle Mountains in central New South Wales, eastern Australia. Kawambarai Cave (KACA) is a small rockshelter (Figure 10.1) about 12 m long by 6 m wide, situated in a sandstone cliff about 20 m above a small creek. The surrounding natural vegetation is predominantly shrub woodland, with a dense and diverse shrub and ground layer. The potential for good organic preservation in these rockshelters was recognized when archaeologists first visited Kawambarai Cave in 1986. Several pieces of knotted cordage and fiber were found on the surface in the spoil from fossickers' holes, together with large amounts of cycad (*Macrozamia* sp.) seed remains, and charcoal.

Excavations in the shelter began in 1987, as part of an ongoing regional archaeological project, and the initial aims of these excavations were to provide a chronological framework for understanding past Aboriginal settlement in the area and for the utilization of organic materials. The goals of the macroscopic plant analyses at this site were (in part) to: (1) increase our understanding of pre-contact plant use in eastern Australia, especially for the toxic seeds of *Macrozamia*; (2) to contribute information about the pre-contact plant environment in eastern Australia; and (3) to investigate the natural and cultural site formation processes at these sites. In this case study, we will focus on the first two objectives.

The excavations

A total of 14 squares, each 0.5 × 0.5 m, were excavated. The position of square J19 is illustrated in Figure 10.1. The deposits consisted of sandy layers, with many ashy inclusions, and charcoal-filled pits, with some layers featuring well-preserved plant material. A date of 630 ± 100 BP was obtained for charcoal 48 mm below the surface of KACA and a date of 1,980 BP was obtained for charcoal near its base, at about 500 mm below surface. All dates are uncalibrated.

Excavation was mainly with arbitrary spits of equal volume (1 spit = 40 liters per m²) using sieves of 5 and 1.6 mm mesh size and by sampling the smallest sieve residue fraction. Layers that could be discerned by eye were drawn in the section, and these were grouped together to form units, which were differentiated on the basis of Munsell color,

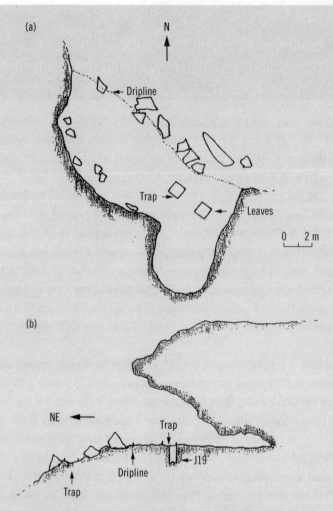

Figure 10.1 The floor plan (a) and profile (b) of KACA (drawings by Dee Murphy).

pH, and inclusions. The excavated material from each unit was weighed in the field and then the unit was divided in half. One half was bagged and labeled and taken unprocessed back to the laboratory. The other half was sorted in the field into carbonized and uncarbonized material, and the seeds of *Macrozamia* were separated out.

Recovery techniques

Dee Murphy, a student with botany and archaeology training, completed a research project on some of the material from KACA, entitled "Plant taphonomy in rockshelters: a study of plant material in sandstone rockshelters near Coonabarabran, NSW," and her analysis forms the basis of what follows. The excavated material used in this analysis comprompised the unprocessed half of three units from KACA J19, specifically a continuous column from the surface to a depth of about 10 cm, and formed part of a larger comparative study on the taphonomy of plant remains using data collected from field traps in nonarchaeological rockshelters.

An archaeobotanical reference set was compiled for the area, including a field herbarium, a seed reference collection, reproductive structures in various stages of decomposition, some processed fibers, a wood collection (blocks and microtome slides), and replicate carbonized samples of many of these collections. This reference collection was used to identify the plant remains recovered from the collections.

The samples were dry sieved using 5, 1.6, and 1 mm sieves. The material contained by the 5 mm and 1.6 mm sieves was sorted into components, by anatomical parts of species where identifiable, and this material was counted and/or weighed. The 1 mm fraction was scanned, and only recognizable plant material removed for identification.

A magnifying lamp (×10) and hand lens (×10) were used for the plant species and parts identification, and a dissecting microscope (×30) was used when identification difficulties arose. As much detail as possible was recorded about the types, sizes, weights, numbers, and features of the anatomical parts of the plant species and taxa identified. Constant reference to identified herbarium specimens enabled identification of most components. The certainty of the identification was noted on the record sheets, and questionable identifications were reviewed. For each separate collection, all part-groups were bagged separately in clip-seal bags containing labels stating relevant information about sites, dates, and identification details.

The other components of the collections were also sorted into types and weighed. These included components such as charcoal, animal remains (feces, bones, feathers, shells, and hair), stone (gravel, sandstone and stone artifacts), and "residue," which included the less than 1.6 mm fraction and the nondiagnostic material from the 1.6 mm sieve.

The entire collection of macroremains was sorted, identified, weighed, bagged, and recorded, although this took long periods of time. On average, to fully sort and record a collection took about 10 hours per 100 g of material, and the laboratory analyses took about 600 hours in total.

The recorded data were utilized in various stages of the analysis. These levels of analysis range from gross weights to morphological characteristics (anatomical parts, and lifeforms of the species from which the parts derive), and then to taxonomic groupings.

Quantification methods

The archaeobotanical analyses compiled a number of different quantitative measures of plant presence: percentages of each plant part type of the total plant weight in each excavation unit (Figure 10.2); the average weight and size of the excavated components; the density of components in the excavated material; comparison ratios in the excavated material (woody/nonwoody, fleshy reproductive/woody, carbonized/uncarbonized); and

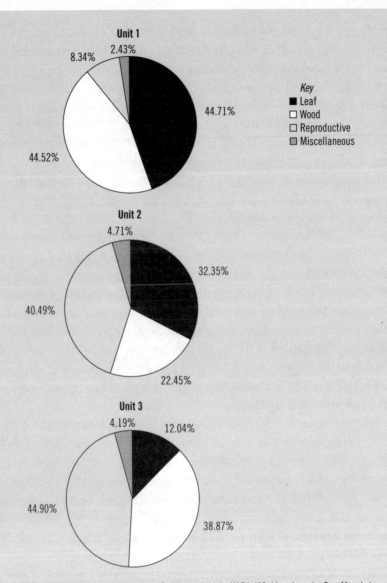

Figure 10.2 Plant parts as percentages of plant weight in KACA J19 (drawings by Dee Murphy).

the plant species found in the excavated material. The numbers of species identified in the various collections were compared by estimating the total species number per plant weight.

Case study results

The dry and protected nature of the site deposits has resulted in high densities of organic material. In KACA, these range from 85 g of plant material and 5 g of bone per kilogram of excavated sediment in one spit to 13 g of plant and 2 g of bone in a spit higher in the deposit. The archaeobotanical material includes a mixture of detached plant parts, some presumably deposited by cultural activities and some deposited by noncultural agencies such as wind and animals. Frequently occurring plant material includes charcoal, wood, leaves, bark, and reproductive remains, many of which could be identified by comparison with the reference collection. Woody remains of shrub "fruits" are well preserved. The majority of plant material could have been derived from species currently growing within 50 m of the rockshelters. Many of the plant species identified from the excavated material comprise very small amounts by weight and number (e.g., one or two seeds). In the upper portions of the excavations, there were usually more than 20 plant species identified per unit, and the majority of these species were potentially nonculturally deposited by wind or animals, and comprised very small amounts of detached parts of plant species growing within the adjacent vegetation. Leaves from eucalypts/angophoras were in high densities in the upper units.

The plant remains that are most likely to have been deposited as the results of human activities include large amounts of charcoal, wood, and cycad seed remains (these show no evidence of animal teeth marks). These remains occur in high densities, in some cases comprising more than 5 percent of the sediment weight per excavation unit. Processed fibers are also present, including several types of "string," ranging from a relatively unprocessed *Dianella revoluta* leaf tied in a knot to small fragments of fibers "spun" into string (fiber/hair type unidentified). Seed pods, and remains of the edible seeds, of *Brachychiton populneus* (Kurrajong) are found in the upper units of KACA, and their disappearance with depth may be due to the poor preservation potential of these remains.

Case study conclusions

Returning to the questions posed at the beginning of this chapter, the case study has demonstrated the following key points. First, *what can plant remains continue to archaeology*? The material from Kawambarai Shelter has shown that plants were being used as food (*Macrozamia* sp., *Brachychiton* sp., and various heath seeds), as fiber plants (such as *Dianella revoluta*) and as fuel (*Banksia* sp.) during the Holocene period. The *Macrozamia* remains are particularly interesting, as they are present throughout the sequence. Cycad seeds require complex and lengthy processing in order to make them safe to eat and this has implications for other aspects of the hunter–gatherer subsistence system in operation. These seed remains are quite fragmented and some are burnt, but they do not show evidence of animal gnaw marks (see illustrations in Beck 1989). Therefore they are likely to be the result of cultural deposition.

Secondly, *what are the problems (and solutions) for identifying and determining the origin of macroscopic plant remains*? The identification of the plant remains from

Kawambarai was time consuming and required the collection of a specific reference collection from the area, which contained herbarium material, seeds, woody tissue, and carbonized and uncarbonized material. It would not have been possible to work on this site without a site-specific reference collection. The origins of the material were investigated by experimental collections of material from natural wind-blown sediment traps inside and outside the rockshelters, and it was found that both cultural and natural factors contributed to the archaeological deposits.

Thirdly, *what methods can be used to recover and analyze plants?* The recovery methods were adapted to the field conditions, using readily available local materials (such as fly-screen from the local store for the 1.6 mm sieve). These methods were quite successful at recovering material, using unskilled field labor for sieving and initial sorting, so the recovery of plant remains is certainly a good possibility in many other field situations.

Conclusion

There are three important things about learning macroscopic plant analysis. First, you need to understand which kinds of plant remains can be observed macroscopically, and you need to study recent examples of archaeological analyses of these kinds of remains to understand how plant studies contribute to archaeology. Secondly, a basic introduction to the laboratory skills is required, and you need to recognize the need for specialized practice in this area. Thirdly, you need to keep up with recent work in the field and new techniques. Many plant remains analyses can be done by people with little botanical expertise.

In archaeology, the limitations of research into macroscopic plant remains have remained the same over recent decades. The lack of sites with well-preserved macroremains is a major factor, together with the relatively short period of serious archaeological research into the full range of plant remains. These factors are less important in countries with longer traditions of systematic archaeobotanical research, such as the United States, the United Kingdom, and Australia. The rise of multi- and interdisciplinary research projects is also encouraging (Hastorf 1999; Pearsall 2000). There is a greater appreciation of the range of issues to which plants can now contribute, such as important questions of socioeconomic change, rather than just who ate what, and when.

In the archaeology of plant macroscopic evidence, there still remain three levels of analysis where progress is needed (Beck et al. 1989a). First, there is a need for a continuation of middle-range research, such as ethnobotany, ecology, and actualistic studies, that contributes to the interpretation and analysis of plant remains – especially about the cultural and noncultural sources of plant remains. Secondly, there is a continuing need for technical knowledge about recovery, excavation, and plant identification techniques. There is a common need worldwide for local plant reference collections, with all the relevant plant parts in the relevant forms. Although some specialist training may be required, other kinds of specialist skills are often learnt by archaeologists. Thirdly, the use of a range of other kinds of plant remains, including residues, microscopic remains, DNA and biochemical characteristics will be needed to bring out the full potential of macroscopic plant remains. Multidisciplinary approaches will need to be developed even further than at present. The analysis of plant remains has had a relatively short history in archaeology, but it continues to be a new and productive avenue of evidence, which is becoming increasingly systematic.

For a very detailed examination of all the techniques for recovering, identifying, and interpreting plant remains in archaeological contexts, the standard reference for macroplant analysis in archaeology is D. M. Pearsall's *Paleoethnobotany: A Handbook of Procedures* (2nd edn, 2000). **Further reading**

For a recent review of paleoethnobotanical literature, see C. Hastorf's "Recent research in paleoethnobotany" (1999). For chapters by individual specialists that cover the major methods for analyzing microscopic and macroscopic plant remains, and that include Australian case studies, see W. Beck, A. Clarke and L. Head's *Plants in Australian Archaeology* (1989b).

For useful compilations of case studies of paleoethnobotanical work, see Gremillion (1997), Johannessen and Hastorf (1994), Harris and Hillman (1989), Hastorf and Popper (1988), Renfrew (1973, 1992), Van Zeist and Casparie (1984), and Van Zeist et al. (1991).

There are also several specialist journals that have arisen in the past few years, the major relevant one being *Vegetation History and Archaeobotany* – others are the *Journal of Ethnobiology* and *Geoarchaeology*.

References

Araus, J. L., Slafer, G. A., Buxo, R. and Romagosa, I. 2003: Productivity in prehistoric agriculture: physiological models for the quantification of cereal yields as an alternative to traditional approaches. *Journal of Archaeological Science*, 30, 681–93.

Asouti, E. and Hather, J. 2001: Charcoal analysis and the reconstruction of ancient woodland vegetation in the Konya Basin, south-central Anatolia, Turkey: results from the Neolithic site of Çatalhöyük east. *Vegetation History and Archaeobotany*, 10, 23–32.

Balick, M. J.,and Cox, P. A. 1996: *Plants, People and Culture: The Science of Ethnobotany*. New York: Scientific American Library.

Bearez, P. 1998: FOCUS: first archaeological indication of fishing by poison in a sea environment by the Engoroy population at Salango (Manabi, Ecuador). *Journal of Archaeological Science*, 25(10), 943–8.

Beck, W. 1989: The taphonomy of plants. In W. Beck, A. Clarke and L. Head (eds.), *Plants in Australian Archaeology*. Tempus, 1. St Lucia: Anthropology Museum, University of Queensland, 31–49.

——, Clarke, A. and Head, L. 1989a: Plants in hunter–gatherer archaeology. In W. Beck, A. Clarke and L. Head (eds.), *Plants in Australian Archaeology*. Tempus, 1. St Lucia: Anthropology Museum, University of Queensland, 1–10.

——, —— and —— (eds.) 1989b: *Plants in Australian Archaeology*. Tempus, 1. St Lucia: Anthropology Museum, University of Queensland.

Behre, K. E. 1999: The history of beer additives in Europe: a review. *Vegetation History and Archaeobotany*, 8(1–2), 35–48.

Benes, J., Kastovsky, J., Kocarova, R. et al. 2002: Archaeobotany of the Old Prague Town defence system, Czech Republic: archaeology, macro-remains, pollen and diatoms. *Vegetation History and Archaeobotany*, 11(1–2), 107–19.

Benz, B. B. and Long, A. 2000: Prehistoric maize evolution in the Tehuacan Valley. *Current Anthropology*, 41, 459–63.

Boyd, C., Dering, E. and Philip, J. 1996: Medicinal and hallucinogenic plants identified in the sediments and pictographs of the Lower Pecos, Texas Archaic. *Antiquity*, 70, 256–69.

Boyd, W. E. 1988: Methodological problems in the analysis of fossil non-artifactual wood assemblages from archaeological sites. *Journal of Archaeological Science*, 15, 603–15.

Brown, K. 2001: New trips through the back alleys of agriculture. *Science*, 292, 631–3.

Bryant, V. M. 2003: Invisible clues to new world plant domestication. *Science*, 299, 1029–34.

Buurman, J. and Pals, J. P. 1994: Palaeoethnobotany: what's in a name? *Antiquity*, 68, 471–3.

Clarke, A. 1989: Macroscopic plant remains. In W. Beck, A. Clarke and L. Head (eds.), *Plants in Australian Archaeology*. Tempus, 1. St Lucia: Anthropology Museum, University of Queensland, 54–89.

Charles, M., Bogaard, A., Jones, G., Hodgson, J. and Halstead, P. 2002: Towards the archaeobotanical identification of intensive cereal cultivation: present-day ecological investigation in the mountains of Asturias, northwest Spain. *Vegetation History and Archaeobotany*, 11, 133–42.

Chernoff, M. C. and Paley, S. M. 1998: Dynamics of cereal production at Tell el Ifshar, Israel during the Middle Bronze Age. *Journal of Field Archaeology*, 25, 397–417.

Cotton, C. M. 1996: *Ethnobotany: Principles and Applications*. New York: John Wiley.

Crawford, G. 1992: Prehistoric plant domestication in East Asia. In C. W. Cowan and P. J. Watson (eds.), *The Origins of Agriculture: An International Perspective*. Washington, DC: Smithsonian Institution Press, 7–38.

Cribb, A. B. and Cribb, J. W. 1981: *Useful Wild Plants in Australia*. Sydney: Collins.

Dimbleby, G. 1978: *Plants and Archaeology*. London: John Barker.

Dudek, M. G., Kaplan, L. and Mansfield King, M. 1998: Botanical remains from a seventeenth-century privy at the Cross Street back lot site. *Historical Archaeology*, 32(3), 63–72.

Fairbairn, A., Asouti, E., Near, J. and Marinoli, D. 2002: Macrobotanical evidence for plant use at Neolithic Çatalhöyük, south-central Anatolia, Turkey. *Vegetation History and Archaeobotany*, 11(1–2), 41–54.

Ford, R. I. 1979: Palaeoethnobotany in American archaeology. *Advances in Archaeological Method and Theory*, 2, 285–336.

Fuller, D. Q. 2001: Harappan seeds and agriculture: some considerations. *Antiquity*, 75, 410.

Gott, B. 1977: *On the Use of Seed Flotation Apparatus*. Report no. 12. Melbourne: Victorian Archaeological Survey.

Gott, B. 1989: The uses of ethnohistory and ecology. In Beck, W., A. Clarke and L. Head (eds.), *Plants in Australian Archaeology*. Tempus, 1. St Lucia: Anthropology Museum, University of Queensland, 197–210.

Gremillion, K. J. (ed.) 1997: *People, Plants and Landscapes*. Tuscaloosa: University of Alabama Press.

—— 2002a: Archaeobotany at Old Mobile. *Historical Archaeology*, 36(1), 117–29.

—— 2002b: Foraging theory and hypothesis testing in archaeology: an exploration of methodological problems and solutions. *Journal of Anthropological Archaeology*, 21, 142–64.

Gustafsson, S. 2000: Carbonized cereal grains and weed seeds in prehistoric houses – an experimental perspective. *Journal of Archaeological Science*, 27, 65–70.

Hansen, J. 2001: Macroscopic plant remains from Mediterranean caves and rockshelters: avenues of interpretation. *Geoarchaeology: An International Journal*, 16(4), 401–32.

Harris, D. R. and Hillman, G. C. (eds.) 1989: *Foraging and Farming: The Evolution of Plant Exploitation*. London: Unwin Hyman.

Hastorf, C. 1991: Gender, space, and food in prehistory. In J. Gero and M. Conkey (eds.), *Engendering Archaeology: Women and Prehistory*. Oxford: Blackwell, 132–59.

—— 1999: Recent research in paleoethnobotany. *Journal of Archaeological Research*, 7(1), 55–103.

—— and Popper, V. S. (eds.) 1988: *Current Palaeoethnobotany: Analytical Methods and Cultural Interpretations of Archaeological Plant Remains*. Chicago: University of Chicago Press.

Hather, J. G. 1992: The archaeobotany of subsistence in the Pacific. *World Archaeology*, 24, 70–82.

—— 1993: *An Archaeobotanical Guide to Root and Tuber Identification*, vol. 1: *Europe and South West Asia*. Oxbow Monograph, 28. Oxford: Oxbow Books.

Hillman, G., Wales, S., McLaren, F., Evans, J. and Butler, A. 1993: Identifying problematic remains of ancient plant foods: a comparison of the role of chemical, histological and morphological criteria. *World Archaeology*, 25, 94–109.

Jacquat, C. and Martinoli, D. 1999: *Vitis vinifera* L: wild or cultivated? Study of the grape pips found at Petra, Jordan; 150 B.C.–A.D. 40. *Vegetation History and Archaeobotany*, 8, 25–30.

Jeraj, M. 2002: Archaeobotanical evidence for early agriculture at Ljubjansko barje (Ljubljana Moor), central Slovenia. *Vegetation History and Archaeobotany*, 11(4), 277–87.

Johannessen, S. and Hastorf, C. (eds.) 1994: *Corn and Culture in the Prehistoric New World*. Boulder, CO: Westview Press.

Jones, G. 1987: Interpretation of archaeological plant remains: ethnographic models from Greece. In W. van Zeist and W. A. Casparie (eds.), *Plants and Ancient Man: Studies in Palaeoethnobotany*. Rotterdam: Balkema, 43–62.

Kaplan, L. and Lynch, T. F. 1999: *Phaseolus* (Fabaceae) in archaeology: AMS radiocarbon dates and their significance for pre-Columbian agriculture. *Economic Botany*, 53, 261–72.

Knorzer, K. H. 2000: 3000 years of agriculture in a valley of the High Himalayas. *Vegetation History and Archaeobotany*, 9(4), 219–22.

Lennstrom, H. and Hastorf, C. A. 1995: Interpretation in its context: sampling and analysis in palaeoethnobotany. *American Antiquity*, 60, 701–21.

Lepofsky, D., Kirch, P. V. and Lertzman, K. P. 1998: Metric analyses of prehistoric morphological change in cultivated fruits and nuts: an example from Island Melanesia. *Journal of Archaeological Science*, 28, 787–94.

——, Moss, M. L. and Lyons, N. 2001: The unrealized potential of palaeoethnobotany in the archaeology of northwestern North America: perspectives from Cape Addington, Alaska. *Arctic Anthropology*, 38(1), 48–59.

Losey, R. J., Stenholm, N., Whereat-Phillips, P. and Valliantos, H. 2003: Exploring the use of red elderberry (*Sambucus racemosa*) fruit on the southern Northwest Coast of North America. *Journal of Archaeological Science*, 30, 695–707.

McConnell, K. and O'Connor, S. 1997: 40,000 year record of food plants in the southern Kimberley Ranges. *Australian Archaeology*, 45, 20–31.

McCorriston, J. and Weisberg, S. 2002: Spatial and temporal variation in Mesopotamian agricultural practices in the Khabur Basin, Syrian Jazira. *Journal of Archaeological Science*, 29(5), 485–98.

Martin, A. C. and Barkley, W. B. 1961: *Seed Identification Manual*. Berkeley: University of California Press.

Mason, S. L. R., Hather, J. G. and Hillman, G. C. 1994: Preliminary investigation of the plant macro-remains from Dolni Vestonice II, and its implications for the role of plant foods in Palaeolithic and Mesolithic Europe. *Antiquity*, 68, 48–69.

Meehan, B. 1989: Plant use in a contemporary Aboriginal community and prehistoric implications. In W. Beck, A. Clarke and L. Head (eds.), *Plants in Australian Archaeology*. Tempus, 1. St Lucia: Anthropology Museum, University of Queensland, 14–28.

Miller, J. J., Dickson, J. H. and Dixon, T. N. 1998: Unusual food plants from Oakbank Crannog, Loch Tay, Scottish Highlands: cloudberry, opium poppy and spelt wheat. *Antiquity*, 72, 805–12.

Minnis, P. E. 1989: Prehistoric diet in the northern Southwest: macroplant remains from Four Corners feces. *American Antiquity*, 54, 543.

Morcote-Rios, G. and Bernal, R. 2001: Remains of palms (Palmae) at archaeological sites in the new world: a review. *The Botanical Review*, 67, 309–51.

Nadel, D. and Werker, E. 1999: The oldest ever brush hut plant remains from Ohalo II, JordanValley, Israel (19,000 BP). *Antiquity*, 73, 755–89.

Pearsall, D. M. 2000: *Paleoethnobotany: A Handbook of Procedures*, 2nd edn. San Diego: Academic Press.

Renfrew, J. 1973: *Palaeoethnobotany*. New York: Columbia University Press.

—— (ed.) 1992: *New Light on Early Farming: Recent Developments in Palaeoethnobotany*. Edinburgh: Edinburgh University Press.

Rivera, D., Inocencio, C., Obon, D., Carreno, E., Reales, A. and Alcaraz, F. 2002: Archaeobotany of capers (Capparis) (Capparaceae). *Vegetation History and Archaeobotany*, 11, 295–313.

Roosevelt, A. C., Lima da Costa, M., Lopes Machado, C. et al. 1996: Paleoindian cave dwellers in the Amazon: the peopling of the Americas. *Science*, 272, 373–85.

Schurr, M. R., Hayes, R. and Bush, L. L. 2001: The thermal history of maize kernels determined by electron spin resonance. *Archaeometry*, 43, 407–19.

Sept, J. 1994: Beyond bones: archaeological sites, early hominid subsistence, and the costs and benefits of exploiting wild plant foods in east African riverine landscapes. *Journal of Human Evolution*, 27, 295–320.

Serpico, M. and White, R. 2000: The botanical identity and transport of incense during the Egyptian New Kingdom. *Antiquity*, 74, 884–6.

Shaw, M. C. 1993: The Aegean garden. *American Journal of Archaeology*, 97, 661–5.

Smith, M. A., Vellens, L. and Pask, J. 1995: Vegetation history from archaeological charcoals in central Australia: the later Quaternary record from Puritjarra rock shelter. *Vegetation History and Archaeobotany*, 4, 171–7.

Struzkova, D. 2002: Cuticular analysis – a method to distinguish the leaves of *Pinus sylvestris* L (Scots pine) from those of *Pinus mugo* Turrs s. str. (dwarf mountain pine). *Vegetation History and Archaeobotany*, 11, 241–6.

Ugent, D., Dillebay, F. and Ranirez, C. 1987: Potato remains from a late Pleistocene settlement in southcentral Chile. *Economic Botany*, 38, 417–32.

Van Zeist, W. and Casparie, W. A. (eds.) 1984: *Plants and Ancient Man: Studies in Palaeoethnobotany*. Rotterdam: Balkema.

——, Wasylikowa, K. and Behre, K. (eds.) 1991: *Progress in Old World Palaeoethnobotany: A Retrospective View on the Occasion of 20 Years of the International Work Group for Palaeoethnobotany*. Rotterdam: Balkema.

Vermeeren, C. and van Haaster, H. 2002: The embalming of the ancestors of the Dutch royal family. *Vegetation History and Archaeobotany*, 11(1–2), 121–6.

Wagner, G. 1982: Testing flotation recovery rates. *American Antiquity*, 47, 127–32.

Walsh, F. 1987: The influence of the spatial and temporal distribution of plant food resources on traditional Martujara subsistence strategies. *Australian Archaeology*, 25, 88–101.

Wandsnider, L. 1997: The roasted and the boiled: food composition and heat treatment with special emphasis on pit-hearth cooking. *Journal of Anthropological Archaeology*, 16, 1–48.

Warnock, P. 1998: From plant domestication to phytolith interpretation: the history of paleoethnobotany in the Near East. *Near Eastern Archaeology*, 1, 238–9.

Wasylikowa, K., Mitka, J., Wendorf, F. and Schild, R. 1997: Exploitation of wild plants by the early Neolithic hunter–gatherers of the Western Desert, Egypt: Nabta Playa as a case-study. *Antiquity*, 71, 932–42.

Weber, S. 1999: Seeds of urbanism; palaeoethnobotany and the Indus civilisation. *Antiquity*, 73, 813–26.

Welch, P. D. and Scarry, C. M. 1995: Status-related variation in foodways in the Moundville chiefdom. *American Antiquity*, 60, 397–408.

Wollstonecroft, M. E. 2002: The fruit of their labour: plants and plant processing at EeRb 140 (860 ± 60 uncal BP to 160 ± 50 uncal BP) a late prehistoric hunter–gatherer–fisher site on the southern Interior Plateau, British Columbia, Canada. *Vegetation History and Archaeobotany*, 11(1–2), 61–70.

Wright, P. 2003: Preservation or destruction of plant remains by carbonization? *Journal of Archaeological Science*, 30, 577–83.

Zach, B. 2002: Vegetable offerings on the Roman sacrificial site in Mainz, Germany – short report on the first results. *Vegetation History and Archaeobotany*, 11(1–2), 101–6.

Zutter, C. 1999: Congruence or concordance in archaeobotany: assessing micro- and macro-botanical data sets from Icelandic middens. *Journal of Archaeological Science*, 26(7), 833–44.

11
Mollusks and Other Shells

Introduction

Shell middens are a kind of archeological site that is variously defined, and may be considered to be of two sorts. The first is a deposit containing shells occurring somewhere in the open, near a beach or estuary or rocky shoreline, or an inland lake or river. Sometimes these form large mounds that are visually distinctive in the landscape, or they may be a buried deposit that is only evident from close surface inspection. Sometimes only a surface scatter of shell, and usually other cultural material, is found, which may or may not be due to erosion of a more consolidated deposit. The second sort of midden is a deposit containing shells occurring within a cave or rockshelter, but also usually near one of the aquatic molluskan habitats mentioned. Middens differ from other prehistoric sites in that the deposit is dominated by a class of faunal remains: the shells of marine or freshwater mollusks. One definition is that a midden deposit contains 50 percent or more by weight of shellfish remains (Bowdler 1983: 35). Another is that a midden is "a cultural deposit of which the principal visible constituent is shell" (Waselkov 1987: 95). Claassen restricts the term "shell midden" to sites where "food refuse disposal is the known purpose of a shell deposit," and otherwise prefers the terms "shell-bearing site" or "shell matrix site" (Claassen 1998: 11). In this chapter, I use the term "shell midden" more loosely, although in general the discussion relates to sites formed by hunter–gatherers.

Middens present both an advantage and a problem. The advantage is that such sites preserve an abundance of dietary remains, which have the potential to tell us a great deal. The problem is that these remains are so very abundant; in most cases, it is simply not logistically feasible to keep all the shells that you excavate. We are accordingly faced with a *sampling problem*.

The main thrust of this chapter is to describe the usual techniques of, first, acquiring adequate samples from middens in the field, and secondly, analyzing these samples in the laboratory (see Figure 11.1). On the whole, only simple methodologies are described; more complex procedures are alluded to but not discussed in detail. Before discussing actual analytical procedures, a brief

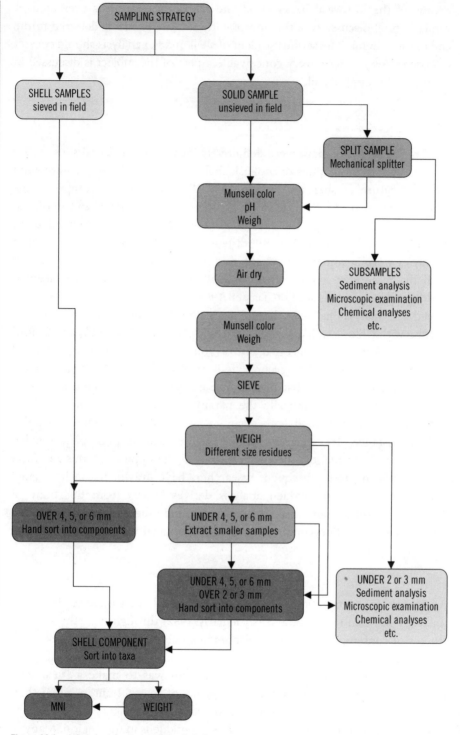

Figure 11.1 A flowchart for the analysis of shells.

review of the historical background and relevant literature is presented. A similarly brief discussion of the interpretation of the results is deferred to the end of the chapter. The serious student of shell midden analysis should consult Claassen (1998), where every conceivable aspect of the subject is discussed in lucid and thorough detail.

Background Shell middens in Denmark were definitively identified as cultural sites, rather than natural accumulations of mollusk shells, by a Royal Society commission into the nature of shell mounds in 1848. The commission comprised the archaeologist J. J. A. Worsae with geologist Forchhammer and zoologist Steenstrup. They defined the sites as *kjøkkenmøddinger*, or kitchen middens, a word that still has currency (Klindt-Jensen 1975: 72). Similar sites in other countries were also identified in the mid-nineteenth century, but it was not until the twentieth century that the shells in such deposits were deemed worthy of independent study (Claassen 1998: 2–5).

Midden analysis as such began with the so-called California school, starting with Uhle (1907), and continuing with Nelson (1909, 1910) and Gifford (1916). Thereafter, it burgeoned into a voluminous literature, summarized by Heizer (1960) and to a certain extent by Ambrose (1967). Its aims have varied considerably over that period. There has, however, been a consistent concern to establish empirically the parameters of the assumptions made, especially those concerned with accuracy of sampling procedures. To this end, for instance, Treganza and Cook (1948) excavated a complete midden mound to directly quantify the error limits of small samples. It is this empirical basis on which most subsequent researchers have drawn. It can be argued that the main line of midden analysis derives largely from this body of work. Numerous references, particularly unpublished ones, are omitted from this version. They may be found in the original version of this chapter (Bowdler 1983).

The Creation of Middens An important contribution to the study of coastal shell middens has been made by Meehan (1977a,b, and particularly 1982) through her ethnographic studies of contemporary Aboriginal hunter–gatherers. She spent a year with the Anbarra people, who live on the Arnhem Land coast of northern Australia and lead a largely traditional lifestyle. Her aim was to make a "year long quantitative record of the total diet of a group of coastal hunters and gatherers" (Meehan 1977b: 493). This work provides unique insights into all aspects of shellfish gathering and the creation of shell middens in this region. Many of her salient points are perhaps more pertinent to the interpretation of midden data than to its recovery and analysis, but this work should be considered as mandatory reading before such excavation is undertaken.

SANDRA BOWDLER

Further ethnographic information on the subject of midden formation may be found in Waselkov (1987), and see also Claassen (1998: 9) for further references. A particularly interesting study is presented by Moss (1993).

Middens may be confused with natural shell beds, and also with shell accumulations created by other species. Middens may also have suffered disturbance by natural forces, and thus not be suitable for analysis. Criteria for distinguishing shell middens from natural shell beds have been advanced by Gill (1951) and Coutts (1966), and these have been summarized by Hughes and Sullivan (1974) as follows: **The Identification of Middens**

1   Middens contain charcoal, burnt wood, blackened shells, artifacts, and hearth stones; these are absent from marine shell beds.
2   Middens are unstratified or roughly stratified; shell beds are generally well stratified and show sedimentary features of water-laid deposits.
3   Middens contain shells of edible species and sizes; shell beds contain shells of varied species and sizes, both edible and nonedible.
4   Middens do not contain shell worn due to transport in the offshore or beach zone; marine shell beds often do contain such shell.
5   Middens contain the bones of mammals used for food; shell beds do not.
6   Middens do not contain forms of marine life not used by people, such as corals and tube worms; marine shell beds do.

Attenbrow (1992), working in Sydney Harbor in an estuarine rather than fully marine context, and where the landscape had been extensively modified in recent times, found that these criteria needed some modification, and accordingly developed her own. It can be noted, however, that the criteria advocated by Hughes and Sullivan can usually be ascertained from an inspection of sites in question, whereas some of Attenbrow's depend on collection and/or excavation and analysis.

Two sets of observations derive from small islands on either side of the Bass Strait, which divides mainland Australia from Tasmania, the island state of Australia. Horton (1978) visited a fur seal colony on Seal Rocks, near Phillip Island, Victoria, and observed that the colony was littered with debris recalling a midden: seal bones, fish bones, and even swallowed sandstone pebbles, corroded by seal stomach acids into unusual shapes hinting at human activity; various nearby nesting seabirds had contributed to the debris. Horton also quotes the earlier observations of Teichert and Serventy (1947) to the effect that Pacific gulls drop quite large shellfish onto rocks to break them, and often do so repeatedly in the same locality, forming gull "middens" (their word). Such a "gull midden" is described by Jones and Allen (1978) from Steep Heads Island in the Hunter Group in northwest Tasmania. It will be seen that such seabird or fur seal "middens" may in fact conform to criteria 2–6 for human middens. Criterion 1, however, should provide a clue; clearly, seal/bird middens are unlikely to contain charcoal and artifacts, as Horton, and Jones and Allen, indeed point out. It is true, however, that small human middens may not contain these either; in this case, clearly, the burden of proof is at least positive, and the presence of charcoal and artifacts should be a sufficient guarantee of anthropogenesis. However, Horton additionally warns that "bone accumulation is likely to continue even in the absence of humans." These specific problems only arise, of course, where fur seals or Pacific gulls might be reasonably expected to have been, but other species no doubt can create similar misleading situations.

A recent debate has centered on the role of megapode birds (scrub fowl, mallee fowl, and brush turkey) in creating midden-like deposits in northern Australia. It has been argued that archaeologists were deceived by these birds into thinking that some of their mounded nests, which can incorporate shell and even stone artifacts, were cultural midden sites. It now seems clear that such nests may indeed incorporate midden material, but that they are easily distinguished from genuine middens. The argument is tidily summarized by Bailey (1993). He notes that a further cause of confusion lies with the natural shell formations known as cheniers, which may also be incorporated in megapode nests. There are thus three kinds of shell deposit in northern Australia that need to be distinguished: middens, cheniers, and megapode nests, which may incorporate shell material from either of the first two sources. There are of course other natural sources of shell accumulations in different parts of the world (Claassen 1998: 73). As Bailey points out, however, the use of the criteria discussed above will usually enable middens to be clearly identified

Having confidently ascribed a midden to a human origin by the presence within it of artifacts, charcoal, and so on, it should be determined whether the midden has been reworked by climatic events, particularly if it is located close to a shoreline. Hughes and Sullivan (1974) suggest that many apparently undisturbed middens have in fact been reworked and redeposited by storm waves or fluctuating lake levels. They offer the following inclusions as demonstrating this:

- shells of species and sizes not thought to have been eaten by people
- marine shell grit
- water-worn shells
- rounded pebbles
- pumice.

A detailed discussion of the effects of cyclones on coastal middens in relevant areas can be found in Przywolnik (2002).

Other sources of shell midden disturbance, and their consequences, are discussed by Ceci (1984), Stein (1992), and Claassen (1998: 78–85).

This chapter is not a treatise on excavation techniques, but some consideration of these is important. Insofar as shell middens can be considered as special kinds of sites, some tailoring of normal field techniques ought to be considered. Middens are among the largest pre-agricultural sites with spatially continuous archaeological deposits, and this fact alone poses special problems. The shell mounds at Weipa in Cape York (Australia) are particularly large; they were first investigated by Wright in 1963, with the help of a bulldozer (Wright 1971), and subsequently Bailey (1977) excavated a single square meter of one of them. Some intermediate strategy might be seen to be called for in such cases.

This immediately raises the nature of the problem: What scale of excavation is desirable? As in other situations, the answer must depend on the nature of the site, and the nature of the problem being investigated. To simply establish the chronological parameters of a site requires only a small cutting to obtain controlled charcoal samples. To answer questions about diet and economy, nature of occupation, seasonality, social issues, and so on requires a more rigorous and extensive sampling strategy. Homogeneity of content and structure can only be assumed, as ascertaining whether or not a site is homogeneous would require as much excavation as if you were assuming it to be not homogeneous. To excavate an entire site, as Treganza and Cook did in 1948, and as Ranson (1978) did more recently, is often precluded by lack of time or finances, or by the sheer size of the site. There are, of course, reasons that may be advanced for not excavating a complete site, in that a nonrenewable resource is thus destroyed and made inaccessible to future, improved techniques, and this may be enforced by the statutory authority.

Two approaches to a large open site are possible. One is a large continuous cutting or trench, which exposes the maximum possible horizontal stretch of stratigraphy across the maximum amount of the site possible. The other is a series of discrete cuttings, which reveal the stratigraphy of the site over a comparable area, but not continuously. The extent and location of your excavations within the site constitute a familiar archaeological sampling problem, but are only the first of many such decisions that need to be made in excavating shell middens. The procedure adopted will depend on the one hand on the questions being investigated, and on the other by the extent of your time and finances.

The fundamental problem is how to obtain an acceptable sample of the objects (shells) that constitute a major part of the deposit. There are two reasons why this is a problem. The first is, again, the question of homogeneity. Unless the site is assumed to be, or can in some way be demonstrated to be, homogeneous, as many samples as there are heterogeneities need to be obtained. Secondly, the other kinds of objects usually sought (stone artifacts, animal bones) occur in less abundance; if large areas are excavated to obtain large samples of these objects, it would usually be logistically impossible to retain all the shell from such areas. This means that you must choose how much to discard.

Moving from one extreme to the other, the choices are as follows. In the course of excavation, everything is retained, unsieved. That is, all the deposit is taken home; this is rarely done. The next possibility is that the deposit is sieved and everything retained by the sieve or sieves is taken home. This is often done in sites where the density of shell is not high; it does, however, require the selection of some small samples if unsieved deposit is to be examined at all. Where the density of shell is high and the scale of the excavation at all large, then only selected classes of objects will be retained from the sieves, and the remainder, usually shells, will be represented only in small samples, either unsieved, or a combination of sieved and unsieved. The other extreme, of course, is where these objects are not sampled at all; only in certain very special circumstances, such as rescue operations, can this be envisaged as being in any way justified.

When small samples are collected, it is desirable that as many as possible be unsieved. These are solid samples, as against small samples that are retained after sieving and that are often referred to as shell samples. Solid samples allow a close inspection of the composition of the deposit, in terms of the relative importance of constituents (or components), and also provide a useful specimen of deposit suitable for various sorts of soil tests and chemical tests, potential material for flotation of plant remains, and sources for pollen analysis.

The next decision, therefore, is how best to obtain the small samples. In general, three approaches may be outlined. One is the column sample (Claassen 1998: 101–3). This is a small column of deposit removed from the side or sides of a trench after excavation in vertical samples that conform to the stratigraphy as established by the larger excavation, and/or the spits removed in the course of the larger excavation. The same principle, but in negative, as it were, is where a pedestal of deposit is left in the corner of the larger excavation and removed later as a series of small samples.

Another technique involves acquiring small samples in the course of the excavation (Claassen 1998: 101–3). This may be done with varying degrees of randomness. The excavator may assess the deposit in terms of its representativeness and direct small samples to be bagged up accordingly. This is done so as to acquire at least one small sample per excavated unit. Some sort of pattern might be established, on the other hand, whereby every first (or fourth or fifteenth, etc.) bucketful might provide a small sample. Or a given area of the excavation might be bagged up as a small sample within every excavated unit – 20 × 20 cm in the northwest corner, for instance; this is the same principle as the pedestal, except that it is removed as the larger excavation proceeds, not afterwards. Similar to the column sample approach is one in which small samples are acquired from the sections after the larger excavation is completed. This involves subjective assessment by the excavator as to whence the small samples will be taken.

Alternatively, genuine randomness in the mathematical sense might be applied by using computer-generated random numbers or dice, or some such randomizing device. Peacock (1978) discusses the use of probabilistic sampling in the specific case of a shell midden on one of the western Scottish islands, where it was combined with a wide-area excavation.

It will be seen that there are many permutations and that many techniques are variants of others. The column sample approach, for instance, involves a subjective assessment of where the column will be located, but involves no further judgment selection. These different mechanical operations involve three different theoretical approaches: fixed-in-space samples, where an initial subjective decision is made but there is no further decision by the excavator; subjectively "random" samples, which are really arbitrary and embody what the excavator considers to be typical; and mathematically random or probabilistic selections. A combination of the previous two approaches is probably to be preferred in most situations. It is safest to start with the assumption that the site is not homogeneous but that it will contain some regularities that will be detected during excavation, and that will serve to make a sampling strategy feasible. As Peacock (1978: 188) observes, "all sampling is a compromise."

While not wishing to be overly prescriptive, since each site, and each project, has its own special problems, the following guidelines may be found to be of use:

1 For a large open midden site, as much of its area should be excavated as possible. Theoretically, excavation of the entire site will fulfill this, but there are arguments against such a procedure. The extent of your resources usually determines the scale of your excavation. Where possible, long continuous trenches sectioning as much of the site as possible are desirable; otherwise, a discrete series of cuttings that cover the same area discontinuously may be made.

2 Where all the shell (or other small abundant remains) is not retained during excavation, small samples need to be acquired. These may be solid samples, which are unsieved, or shell samples, which have been sieved in the field.

3 It is best to have two sets of small samples, one set being acquired during excavation and the other set being obtained after any cutting is completed.

4 In the first instance, a small sample should be retained of each excavated unit (spit or layer); this might be done arbitrarily, based on no particular criteria, or on the basis of some routine, such as every fifth bucketful from the same horizontal position within the square, or because of its representativeness. If there is any marked horizontal variation within units, then more than one sample should be acquired.

5 Similarly with samples obtained after excavation, some may be arbitrary – simply extracted from the sections where the excavator thinks they look typical or illustrate particular nontypical features – or they can be more systematically acquired. The most convenient way of doing this is by column sampling. Where a trench of some size has been excavated, column samples should be obtained from regularly spaced intervals along

it. Where discrete trenches have been excavated, at least one column per trench is in order. Again, there are situations of overlap between the two approaches; Lampert (1971: 59) used the column sample method at Currarong (Australia), with individual check samples taken from other sections within the same cutting.

It is impossible to give a precise answer to the question "How many samples should be obtained?" However, adherence to the above guidelines should ensure that sufficient numbers of small samples are acquired. The problem of how many are solid (unsieved) samples and how many are shell (sieved) samples is less straightforward.

The logistics of the particular site will ultimately dictate the answer; ideally, all small samples should be unsieved. This brings up two further problems:

1   How big should the samples be?
2   What size of mesh should shell samples be sieved through?

Treganza and Cook (1948: 292–3), on the basis of their exercise involving the excavation of a complete Californian midden, suggested that small samples of 1–5 pounds weight (~ 500–2,250 g) should be suitable for components that occur in large quantity and in a reasonably fine state of subdivision. Greenwood (1961), also analyzing a Californian midden, found little variation between samples of 1,110 g weight (representing total shell per level) and samples of 500 g. Empirical evidence suggests that this is not necessarily a function of absolute sample size, but that it is the proportion of the analytical unit that the sample represents that is critical, and that increasing this proportion should increase the accuracy of the sample.

In the field it is usually more convenient to estimate volumes rather than weights, particularly with column samples. I have found in practice that a sample of about 2,000 cm^3 weighs about 2,000 g, and that this is a convenient size that satisfies most empirical and theoretical requirements for accuracy. Claassen (1998: 100), however, quite properly advises that "there is no specifiable amount of matrix that can be deemed statistically adequate for world-wide application, nor can there be a fixed size of sample useful world-wide."

The question of sieve size is discussed in more detail in connection with laboratory procedures, but if shell samples are to be collected it needs to be considered before fieldwork is begun. There is always the possibility that fieldwork circumstances may alter prearranged plans and you will be forced to obtain shell samples when this has not been anticipated. In that case the size of mesh used will simply be that used for the larger excavation, and may not be entirely compatible with later laboratory analyses. The best rule of thumb is probably to use the finest mesh available. Most commonly used is probably a mesh size of 5 mm; this is really the largest mesh that should be used for small samples, but a mesh of 2 mm is probably best.

Perhaps the most important aspect of field procedure is simply to have a clear idea of why you are doing it. No amount of fancy methodology is going to compensate for lack of thought, and you may arrive back in the laboratory with a pantechnicon of small samples and no clear purpose in mind. There is no surer outcome than that if a hypothesis subsequently presents itself, the samples will not be adequate to answer it.

This topic is discussed elsewhere in this book (Chapter 5), and the usual principles and procedures of dating archaeological sites apply. However, marine shell is generally regarded as an excellent material for radiocarbon dating, while freshwater shell is regarded as more problematic. A more detailed discussion can be found in Claassen (1998: 93–5). **Dating Middens**

The following procedure for the analysis of small samples is one that has been found to be particularly useful. It has the advantage of flexibility in that, although it is set out here as for solid samples, the overall system can be tapped into at any point, and it provides for shell samples in its later stages. It also takes into account the need for yet smaller samples for different kinds of analysis, and the fact that some samples might need to serve several different purposes. **Laboratory Procedures**

The major problem with all small sample analysis resides in the matter of choice of mesh sizes through which the samples are to be sieved. It is common for archaeologists in the field to use nested sieves of 5 mm and 3 mm mesh. In the laboratory, a sieve of 10 or 12 mm may be added for dealing with solid samples. On the other hand, if a sedimentary analysis is also wanted, in conformity with Folk (1968), the mesh sizes of 2, 4, 8, 16 mm, and so on, representing $-1\ \phi$, $-4\ \phi$, $-3\ \phi$, $-4\ \phi$, might be desirable. Since sets of sieves in the ϕ scale are readily available, compatible with standardized sediment analyses, and are on a logarithmic scale that seems to reflect many kinds of natural scaling, perhaps this is the most convenient set of sizes.

If samples are too large, they should only be split with a mechanical sample splitter, which ensures that artificial sorting does not take place. Before proceeding, any subsamples should be extracted, for oven drying, for instance, or for inspection for pollen. The color of the deposit should be checked against a Munsell chart. Tests for pH might be carried out, but these are better done in the field before the sediments are bagged up. Bulk sediment samples that have been sealed for some time may produce bacterial and/or chemical activities that could alter the original pH values. Sediments are not necessarily inert. **Mechanical Sorting**

The sample to be tested is weighed, and then air dried in a drying cabinet for 18–24 hours at about 40°C (104°F). The main reason for this is to ensure that comparisons based on weight are not biased by variations in moisture content between samples. It also makes the samples considerably easier to process, and the results are often of interest. After drying, the sample is again weighed and the Munsell color checked again.

Initially, the sample should be passed through the larger sieve sizes (say, 2 mm and over) by hand, as the use of a mechanical sieve shaker may be damaging to shells, bones, small artifacts, and so on. The remaining sample can now be passed through the nest of sieves chosen. Ideally, this should be done by using Endicott sieves or similar and placing them in a mechanical sieve shaker for a consistent length of time and rapidity. The material retained by each mesh and the residue are then weighed, and the weights computed as percentages of the whole.

Hand Sorting into Components

After drying and mechanical sorting, the next step is to sort the samples by hand into their components: shell, stone, bone, charcoal, and so on. This should be done within the size ranges established by sieving, but a convenient "cutoff" size needs to be established: 2, 3, or 5 mm is normally selected as the critical screen size for mechanical sorting. For component analysis, it is best that all material over 3 mm is sorted. Using the ϕ series of sieves it is, in fact, possible to subdivide all material over 2 mm (-1 ϕ; the gravels). If there are large amounts of material between 5 mm (or 6 mm) and 3 mm, on the one hand, or between 4 mm and 2 mm, on the other, subsamples may be processed. This simply entails taking a small amount of the relevant material, weighing it, sorting it, weighing the resulting components, and calculating the percentages of these. The overall numerical relationship of the subsample to the overall sample can be easily calculated. Such a procedure can be justified on the grounds that the smaller and more finely divided the component, the smaller is the sample needed to assess its relative abundance.

The residue of deposit smaller than 3 mm, or 2 mm, as the case may be, can be stored after weighing, or subjected to further analysis. It can be inspected microscopically, tested for organic carbon by loss-on-ignition, tested for calcium carbonate by chemical means (e.g., Cook & Heizer 1965; Bauer et al. 1972), tested for phosphate, and so on. It can be further mechanically sorted to ascertain the proportions of silts and sands present or subjected to hydrometer or pipette analysis if a large number of fines (silts and clays) appear to be present (see Folk 1968). For a discussion of sediment analysis generally, see Huckleberry (Chapter 12 of this book); and for midden sites specifically, see Stein (1992).

This mechanical and hand sorting into particle sizes and components fulfills several functions. It is informative as to the degree of sorting of large particles (technically gravels), and the exact composition of them. It may serve to define living floors, with a lower percentage of gravels, as against refuse dumps, with a large percentage of gravels. It is a useful check on field recovery rates and enables comparison of the different sieve mesh sizes as to their efficacy in recovering different components. It also enables the recovery of small components that are usually overlooked or otherwise discarded in the field.

After separating all components above a certain mesh size, say, 3 mm or 2 mm, the usual procedure is to take the shell component above this size and sort the whole lot into species, as far as practicable, weigh the resulting species (or other taxa) groups, and calculate percentages. Minimum numbers of individuals within taxa may also be calculated in the usual way, by counting parts of the shell that are identifiable, representative of a single individual (nonrepetitive elements or NRE), and most commonly occurring; but this is not always done. There has been considerable debate about whether the weight method or the minimum numbers (MNI) estimation is preferable, and not just with respect to shellfish remains (Waselkov 1987: 157–63; Claassen, 1998: 106; Mason et al. 1998; Claassen 2000; Glassow 2000).

One of the usual objections to calculating MNI is that the way in which identifiable elements of an individual animal can be spread over a wide area or even between stratigraphic units can lead to an overestimation, but this really only applies to large animals. In the case of shellfish (and also fish), the animals are so small, and the NRE usually so limited, that calculations can confidently be made within a small area. Another objection is that MNI is just that, the estimation of a minimum number, and that that usually constitutes an *under-estimation*. This has been addressed by Koike (1979), who provides a correct-ive formula (but note Claassen 1998: 106).

The main justification for using the "weight method" rather than the "indi-vidual method" seems to be that minimum numbers disguise the significant differences of size of species, and of individuals. For instance, one abalone is considerably larger than one mussel, and this fact will be reflected in the weight of the relevant fragments but not in the minimum number estimates. On the other hand, people are not fazed by this fact when dealing with other faunal remains, such as bones; even though kangaroos are considerably larger than rats, minimum number estimates are felt to be the most appropriate mode of analysis. Size differences between species can be allowed for in sub-sequent calculations. Shellfish, however, may vary considerably in size within species, so it is obviously useful to provide measurements of some sort.

If time is at a premium, it is probably most efficient to estimate minimum numbers, and use the weight method in addition, if time is available. The weight method, where all of your material (over a certain size) is sorted into groups, is prodigal of time and effort, yet can be argued to provide less accurate information than the individual method. For estimating minimum numbers, the shell component only needs to be sorted into species on the basis of easily recognizable parts of the shell that are potentially useful for the minimum number estimates. Parts of the shell that are not unique to the individual – that is, small fragments that might be recognizable but are of no use for estimating the minimum numbers – are ignored. The saving in time to the researcher should be obvious. Ultimately, it should depend on the hypotheses being tested by the analysis, and in most cases a combination of the two procedures will be most beneficial.

Identification of Shellfish and Other Species

It would be inappropriate here to attempt to provide an extensive guide to the identification of shellfish species found in archaeological sites. The researcher should acquire some appropriate work; there are many such available, although some are more useful than others and some regions are better provided for than others. In Australia, for instance, McMichael (1960) provides an Australia-wide coverage of commonly occurring mollusks; Dakin et al. (1952 and later editions) are informative about many aspects of the New South Wales littoral, including shellfish; Macpherson and Gabriel (1962) is indispensable for Victoria, and also applicable to Tasmania; Cotton (1957) is useful for South Australia; Wells and Bryce (1986) for Western Australia; and so on.

In general, however, the following comments may be found useful (see also Claassen 1998: 16–52). Gastropods, mollusks with a single shell and a

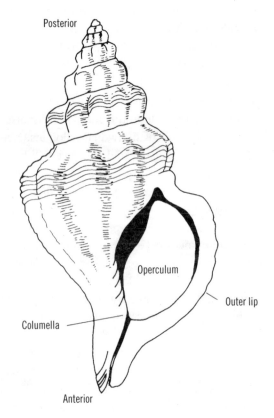

Figure 11.2 Gastropod parts.

SANDRA BOWDLER

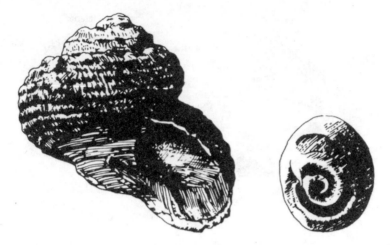

Figure 11.3 A Turbinidae shell and operculum (note that the sculpture on the latter varies from species to species).

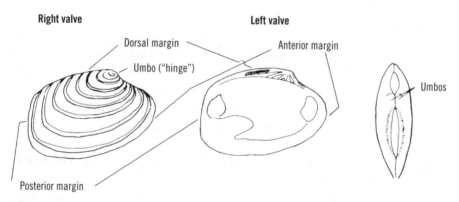

Figure 11.4 Bivalve parts.

"stomach-foot," are best identified by their posteriors, or "tops"; anteriors, or "bottoms"; or columellas, the central axis forming the inner lip of the mouth opening at the anterior end of the shell (Figure 11.2; see also Macpherson & Gabriel 1962: 26, 27).

Some gastropods, notably the Turbinidae (which include *Turbo (Ninella) torquata* of New South Wales and the warrener, or lightning turban *Subninella undulata* of New South Wales, Victoria, and Tasmania) have a characteristic that is exceptionally useful to the archaeologist. This is the operculum (*pl.* opercula), a calcareous plug attached to the posterior dorsal surface of the animal's body; it is quite separate (in life and death) from the rest of the shell, and singularly diagnostic (Figure 11.3). Some gastropods have a horny, rather than calcareous, operculum, which may or may not survive archaeologically.

Bivalves (Pelecypoda), animals with two separate, often symmetrical, shells, are best identified by pieces with the hinge or umbo intact. These can usually be identified as left or right shells (Figure 11.4). Chitons, or coat-of-mail shells,

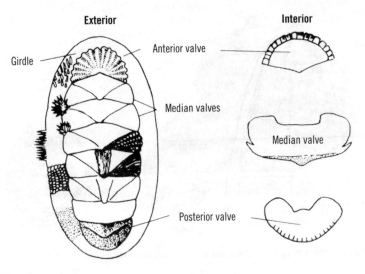

Figure 11.5 Chiton valves.

have eight separate shells, or valves, per animal, of which the posterior and anterior valves are readily distinguishable from each other, and from the six median valves (Figure 11.5). The phylum Molluska also includes the class Cephalopoda, or many-armed mollusks. It is not unknown for bits of cuttlefish gladius (shell) to turn up in middens (Figure 11.6). Anyone who has ever given cuttlebone to a pet bird should recognize these by their texture, which is light and cellular.

Some species of crustaceans may be represented in middens. The tips of crab claws are sufficiently calcareous to survive in the average midden, and are usually recognizable as such. Specific identification usually needs to be done by a specialist. In southern sites especially, crayfish (spiny lobsters) may be recognized by their mandibles (Figure 11.7). A detailed account of New Zealand examples may be found in Leach and Anderson (1979).

Echinodermata may also turn up in the form of sea urchin test fragments, spine fragments, or "teeth" – eight of the latter make up the jaw apparatus called "Aristotle's lantern" (Figure 11.8).

It is useful for the fieldworker to attempt to make a reference collection for the area in which he or she is working. Ideally, live animals should be collected, and a range of individuals within each species at different times of the year. Weight of shell to weight of flesh ratios may be calculated, and so forth. More ambitious surveys of the "standing crop" might be attempted (e.g., Shawcross 1967; Terrell 1967). In less than ideal conditions, simply having one example each of the most commonly occurring local mollusks, crabs, sea urchins, and so on, is helpful.

Inland middens bordering freshwater sources contain mollusks, usually bivalves, and may also yield freshwater crustacean fragments. The most common part preserved is the gastrolith or "stomach stone," which actually has

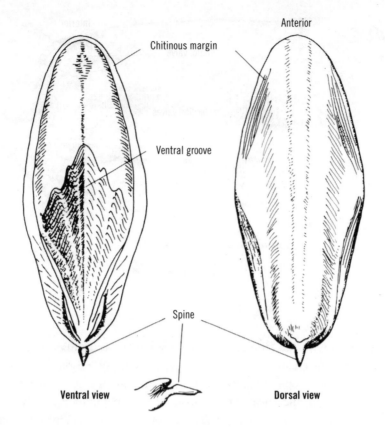

Figure 11.6   A cuttlefish gladius.

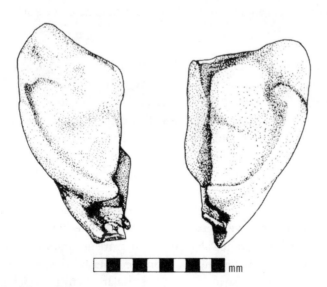

Figure 11.7   Crayfish mandibles.

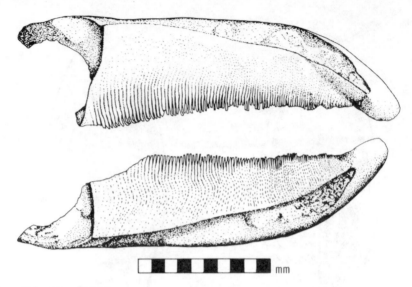

Figure 11.8 Sea urchin teeth.

nothing to do with the stomach, but represents an accumulation of calcium carbonate that the crustacea use to secrete a new shell after molting. Gastroliths are round button-shaped objects, 10–15 mm in diameter. It is possible to calculate live weight and meat weight from the diameter of the fully formed gastrolith. Gastroliths may not be used as seasonal indicators; in inland Australia, for instance, gastrolith growth may occur during any season when food is available to the crustacean. Other crustacea fragments commonly found include fragments of carapace and claws, which indicate genus, but not much more.

Further Analysis This chapter has so far outlined some basic procedures in sampling shell middens and analyzing the samples in such a way as to provide fairly low order, but essential, information about the density of shells within the sites and the relative importance of different species. There are many further analyses that might then be carried out, but these are on the whole beyond the scope of this chapter. Students should consult Claassen (1998) for detailed discussions.

The simplest and most obvious procedure which might be mentioned is that of measuring whole shells, or shells which are complete in some dimension such as width, height, length of operculum, and so on. Shell measurements may be informative in two ways. On the one hand, they mean that relative meat weights can be calculated with more accuracy than from simple minimum number estimates only. And on the other hand, shell measurements may also suggest the age structure of the populations from which the archaeological samples have been extracted, from which, in turn, inferences may be drawn about the nature and duration of the human predation (e.g., Swadling 1976, 1977a,b). Some shells may have other characteristics besides size that

SANDRA BOWDLER

indicate their age at death (for Papuan and New Zealand species, see Swadling 1976, 1977a). Growth ring analysis may be used to establish seasonality of shell fishing, amongst other things, but there are several traps for the unwary (see Claassen 1998: 146–74). If possible, oxygen isotope (^{18}O) analysis is the best technique for seasonality and other environmental information (Claassen 1998: 149–52). In all these cases, the ultimate limiting factor is the confidence that you can have in your sample. They will not work unless "death assemblages" of the species in question can be identified (Claassen 1998: 173–4).

The most common aim in analyzing a shell midden has probably been, over time, some notion of "dietary reconstruction." Much has been written about the drawbacks of such an aim, and there are many obvious problems. There is the question, of course, of sampling, and how much your sample represents the whole site, the problem of differential survival of the evidence, the issue of where the site may sit in the context of the seasonal round, how many people used the site how often, how much food was consumed off site, and so on. Claassen indeed concludes that the whole enterprise is "hopeless" and "futile" (1998: 191, 195). She suggests that, on the one hand, such information is better extracted by chemical analysis of human skeletal remains (Claassen 1998: 191–4) and, on the other, that there are still more interesting questions to be dealt with in the realm of social organization (Claassen 1998: 220–35).

Shell Artifacts

Objects that may occur in middens (and also in other sites) are artifacts made by modifying molluskan shell. Again, this is a matter beyond the scope of this chapter, but it should always be borne in mind when excavating and analyzing midden sites (see Claassen 1998: 196–219). These objects might include utilitarian artifacts, such as baler shells modified for use as containers or *Tridacna* clamshell formed into adzes, or decorative objects, such as pearlshell pendants. One of the oldest examples known is an assemblage of shell beads (possibly a shell necklace) from Northwest Cape, Western Australia, dated to ~ 34,000 BP (Morse 1993).

Fish Remains

Fish bones and otoliths should generally be treated in the same way as other vertebrate remains (see Chapter 9). I mention them here as they are a common and important component in marine and inland middens, as of course are other kinds of faunal remains.

Interpretation

This is, again, hardly the place for the detailed exposition of how to interpret the results of midden sampling and analysis. The reader is referred to the bibliography, particularly Claassen 1998), for an understanding of how to make reasonably sophisticated interpretations of their results. Again, some brief points are mentioned.

Some interpretation is clearly called for if similar sites contain different species, or proportions of species, of shellfish, or if such differences are observable in the same site or sites through time. Initially, such differences should be shown to be statistically significant through the use of appropriate tests. There is no reason to assume that shellfish numbers in archaeological sites, or in nature, are in any way normally distributed, so nonparametric tests should be used. Once these differences have been established, the kinds of explanation tend to fall into one of the following categories: taphonomic, environmental/ecological, or economic/behavioral. In the first instance, the differential survival values of different species might be considered; in the second, a change of habitat might bring about a change of availability of species (e.g., Coutts 1970: 90); in the third, a change in gathering habits brought about by some purely cultural factor might be suggested (e.g., Bowdler 1976). Clearly, other sorts of evidence must be taken into account; it is simply not proper to interpret one class of archaeological evidence while ignoring all the others.

In the end, your interpretation is only as good as your analysis, which is only as good as your sample. In the case of midden analysis, we are usually analyzing small samples of the larger excavation, itself a sample of a site, itself a sample of a set of sites. Each stage of the sampling process should involve the same amount of consideration; each stage of the analysis should involve the same amount of thought and care. Ultimately, of course, the analysis will be no better than the consideration given to the reasons for doing it. A methodological exercise will only really serve to answer methodological questions; if archaeology is to have any benefit for anyone other than archaeologists, wider issues should be addressed. At the very least, you should be addressing the question: What were *people* doing at this site?

Acknowledgments   In the original version of this chapter (Bowdler 1983), I needed to acknowledge the practical and theoretical help of many people; in particular Ron Lampert, Carmel Schrire, Rhys Jones, Phil Hughes, Hilary Sullivan, Marjorie Sullivan, Julia Coleman (Clark), and Harry Lourandos. Doug Hobbs drew the illustrations. For this version, I must thank the editors, my highly esteemed colleagues Jane Balme and Alistair Paterson, not least for their forbearance. I would also like to acknowledge Cheryl Claassen for providing such an exceptional resource as her book *Shells*.

Resources   Many archaeology journals refer to studies with a shellfish component: particularly the *Journal of Archaeological Science*, *American Antiquity*, *Australian Archaeology*, and *Archaeology in Oceania*.

References   Ambrose, W. R. 1967: Archaeology and shell middens. *Archaeology and Physical Anthropology in Oceania*, 2, 169–87.

Attenbrow, V. 1992: Shell bed or shell midden. *Australian Archaeology*, 34, 3–21.

Bailey, G. N. 1977: Shell mounds, shell middens and raised beaches in the Cape York Peninsula. *Mankind*, 11, 132–43.

—— 1993: Shell mounds in 1972 and 1992: reflections on recent controversies at Ballina and Weipa. *Australian Archaeology*, 37, 1–18.

Bauer, H. P., Beckett, P. H. T. and Bie, S. W. 1972: A rapid gravimetric method for estimating calcium carbonate for soils. *Plant and Soil*, 37, 689–90.

Bowdler, S. 1976: Hook, line and dillybag: an interpretation of an Australian coastal shell midden. *Mankind*, 10, 248–58.

—— 1983: Sieving seashells: midden analysis in Australian archaeology. In G. E. Connah (ed.), *Australian Archaeology: A Guide to Field Techniques*, 5th edn. Canberra: Australian Institute of Aboriginal Studies, 135–44.

Ceci, L. 1984: Shell midden deposits as coastal resources. *World Archaeology*, 16, 62–74.

Claassen, C. 1998: *Shells*. Cambridge Manuals in Archaeology. Cambridge: Cambridge University Press.

—— 2000: Quantifying shell: comments on Mason, Peterson and Tiffany. *American Antiquity*, 65, 415–18.

Cook, S. F. and Heizer, R. F. 1965: *Studies on the Chemical Analysis of Archaeological Sites*. University of California Publications in Anthropology, vol. 2. Berkeley and Los Angeles: University of California Press.

Cotton, B. C. 1957: *South Australian Shells*. Adelaide: South Australian Museum.

Coutts, P. J. F. 1966: Features of prehistoric campsites in Australia. *Mankind*, 6, 338–46.

—— 1970: *The Archaeology of Wilson's Promontory*. Canberra: Australian Institute of Aboriginal Studies.

Dakin, W. J., Bennett, I. and Pope, E. 1952: *Australian Seashores*. Sydney: Angus and Robertson.

Folk, R. L. 1968: *Petrology of Sedimentary Rocks*. Austin: Hemphills.

Gifford, E. W. 1916: *Composition of California Shellmounds*. University of California Publications in American Archaeology and Ethnology, 12, 1–29.

Gill, E. D. 1951: Aboriginal kitchen middens and marine shell beds. *Mankind*, 4, 249–54.

Glassow, M. A. 2000: Weighing vs. counting shellfish remains: a comment on Mason, Peterson and Tiffany. *American Antiquity*, 65, 407–14.

Greenwood, R. 1961: Quantitative analysis of shells from a site in Goleta, California. *American Antiquity*, 26, 416–20.

Heizer, R. F. 1960: Physical analysis of habitation residues. In R. F. Heizer and S. F. Cook (eds.), *The Application of Quantitative Methods in Archaeology*. Viking Fund Publications in Anthropology, 28. Chicago: Quadrangle Books, 93–124.

Horton, D. R. 1978: Preliminary notes on the analysis of Australian coastal middens. *Australian Institute of Aboriginal Studies Newsletter*, 10, 30–3.

Hughes, P. J. and Sullivan, M. E. 1974: The re-deposition of midden material by storm waves. *Journal and Proceedings, Royal Society of New South Wales*, 107, 6–10.

Jones, R. and Allen, J. 1978: Caveat Excavator: a sea bird midden on Steep Head Island, north west Tasmania. *Australian Archaeology*, 8, 142–5.

Klindt-Jensen, O. 1975: *A History of Scandinavian Archaeology*, trans. P. Russell. London: Thames and Hudson.

Koike, H. 1979: Seasonal dating and the valve-pairing technique in shell-midden analysis. *Journal of Archaeological Science*, 6, 63–74.

Lampert, R. J. 1971: *Burrill Lake and Currarong*. Canberra: Department of Prehistory, Research School of Pacific Studies, Australian National University.

Leach, B. F. and Anderson, A. J. 1979: Prehistoric exploitation of crayfish in New Zealand. In A. J. Anderson (ed.), *Birds of a Feather: Osteological and Archaeological Papers from the South Pacific in Honour of R. J. Scarlett*. New Zealand Archaeological Association Monograph II. BAR International Series, 62. Oxford: British Archaeological Reports, 141–64.

McMichael, D. F. 1960: *Shells of the Australian Sea-Shore*. Milton, Queensland: Jacaranda Press.

Macpherson, J. H. and Gabriel, C. J. 1962: *Marine Molluscs of Victoria*. Melbourne: Melbourne University Press and the National Museum of Victoria.

Mason, R. D., Peterson, M. L. and Tiffany, J. A. 1998: Weighing vs. counting: measurement reliability and the California school of midden analysis. *American Antiquity*, 63, 303–24.

Meehan, B. 1977a: Hunters by the seashore. *Journal of Human Evolution*, 6, 363–70.

—— 1977b: Man does not live by calories alone: the role of shellfish in a coastal cuisine. In J. Allen, J. Golson and R. Jones (eds.), *Sunda and Sahul*. London: Academic Press, 493–531.

—— 1982: *Shell Bed to Shell Midden*. Canberra: Australian Institute of Aboriginal Studies.

Morse, K. 1993: Shell beads from Mandu Mandu Creek rock-shelter, Cape Range peninsula, Western Australia, dated before 30,000 b.p. *Antiquity*, 67, 877–83.

Moss, M. L. 1993: Shellfish, gender and status on the Northwest coast: reconciling archaeological, ethnographic, and ethnohistorical records of the Tlingit. *American Anthropologist*, 95, 631–52.

Nelson, N. C. 1909: Shellmounds of the San Francisco Bay region. *University of California Publications in American Archaeology and Ethnology*, 7, 309–56.

—— 1910: *The Ellis Landing Shellmound*. University of California Publications in American Archaeology and Ethnology, 7, 357–426.

Peacock, W. R. B. 1978: Probabilistic sampling in shell middens: a case-study from Oronsay, Inner Hebrides. In J. F. Cherry, C. Gamble and S. Shennan (eds.), *Sampling in Contemporary British Archaeology*. BAR British Series, 50. Oxford: British Archaeological Reports, 177–90.

Przywolnik, K. 2002: Coastal sites and severe weather in Cape Range peninsula, northwest Australia. *Archaeology in Oceania*, 37, 137–52.

Ranson, D. 1978: A preliminary examination of prehistoric coastal settlement at Nelson Bay, west coast of Tasmania. *Australian Archaeology*, 8, 149–58.

Shawcross, W. 1967: An evaluation of the theoretical capacity of a New Zealand harbour to carry a human population. *Tane* (Journal of the Auckland University Fieldclub), 13, 3–11.

Stein, J. (ed.) 1992: *Deciphering a Shell Midden*. New York: Academic Press.

Swadling, P. 1976: Changes induced by human exploitation in prehistoric shellfish populations. *Mankind*, 10, 156–62.

—— 1977a: Central Province shellfish resources and their utilization in the prehistoric past of Papua New Guinea. *The Veliger*, 19, 293–302.

—— 1977b: The implications of shellfish exploitation for New Zealand prehistory. *Mankind*, 11, 11–18.

Teichert, C. and Serventy, D. L. 1947: Deposits of shells transported by birds. *American Journal of Science*, 245, 322–8.

Terrell, J. E. 1967: Galatea Bay – the excavation of a beach-stream midden site on Ponui Island in the Hauraloi Gulf, New Zealand. *Transactions of the Royal Society of New Zealand*, 2, 31–70.

Treganza, A. E. and Cook, S. F. 1948: The quantitative investigation of Aboriginal sites: complete excavation with physical and archaeological analysis of a single mound. *American Antiquity*, 13, 287–97.

Uhle, M. 1907: *The Emeryville Shellmound*. University of California Publications in American Archaeology and Ethnology, 7, 1–107.

Waselkov, G. A. 1987: Shellfish gathering and shell midden archaeology. *Advances in Archaeological Method and Theory*, 10, 93–210.

Wells, F. E. and Bryce, C. W. 1986: *Seashells of Western Australia*. Perth: Western Australian Museum.

Wright, R. V. S. 1971: Prehistory in the Cape York Peninsula. In D. J. Mulvaney and J. Golson (eds.), *Aboriginal Man and Environment in Australia*. Canberra: Australian National University Press, 133–40.

Gary Huckleberry

12
Sediments

Introduction

Archaeology and other historical sciences have the daunting task of reconstructing past phenomena from present material evidence. Artifacts and sediments are the primary material evidence that archaeologists have for reconstructing past human events and behavior. As a geoarchaeologist trained in soils and geomorphology, much of my work is focused on archaeological sediments and stratigraphy, and how they can provide a wealth of information regarding past natural and cultural processes. Although the focus in archaeology is material culture, it is the sedimentary matrix containing the material culture that provides key contextual information such as chronology, site formation, and paleoenvironments (Hassan 1978; Butzer 1982; Stein & Farrand 1985, 2001; Waters 1992) essential for fully understanding human behavior. Consequently, archaeologists need to understand the basics of sedimentology and soil formation as it pertains to the history of cultural deposits. This includes defining sediment origin, mode of transport and deposition, and any post-depositional processes (e.g., soil formation) that influence the nature of the archaeological record. To analyze cultural evidence without reference to its biophysical context can lead to incomplete if not incorrect inferences of the archaeological record.

For the past nine years, I have taught a graduate course titled "Sediments and Geoarchaeology" that aims to teach archaeologists with little to no training in Earth science some of the basic principles of sedimentology, stratigraphy, and soil formation, and their archaeological relevance. The course is a mixture of lectures, laboratory exercises, and field trips, the latter two components emphasizing hands-on learning. Whereas field trips to exposures of natural and cultural deposits are designed to develop skills in describing and sampling sediments and stratigraphy, the laboratory component gives students opportunities to learn common laboratory methods employed in geoarchaeology. In addition to learning the basics of measuring the physical and chemical attributes of sediments, students develop an ability to critically assess the potential applications of laboratory data, as well as their limits and uncertainties. At a minimum, laboratory analyses of archaeological sediments can provide objective documentation and supplement field descriptions. However, students learn that there is greater potential in using laboratory data in conjunction with rigorous field observations to construct and/or test hypotheses regarding archaeological site formation and function.

There are many laboratory methods for investigating archaeological sediments, and any one physical or chemical attribute can be usually assessed by multiple techniques (Holliday & Stein 1989). Most of these techniques are derived from the disciplines of geology and soil science, and have applications as diverse as from assessing nutrient availability to modeling water flow in porous media. A discussion of the full panoply of laboratory methods potentially relevant to archaeological research is well beyond the scope of this chapter (for a more extensive review, see Herz & Garrison 1998). Suffice it to say that most geoarchaeological laboratories emphasizing sediments tend to focus on physical and chemical properties such as mineralogy, micromorphology, granulometry, pH, organic matter, calcium carbonate, and phosphorus (Table 12.1). The types of analyses performed will depend on the nature of the samples, the research questions at hand, and – of course – cost. In this chapter, I focus on the laboratory tests performed in my "Sediments and Geoarchaeology" course with which most archaeologists should become familiar: granulometry, pH, organic matter, and phosphorus. I conclude with two personal case studies where such sediment analyses were applied to archaeological research.

Table 12.1 Common sedimentological analysis and methods employed in archaeological studies.

Type of analysis	Methods	References
Mineralogy	Petrography X-ray diffraction	Whittig and Allardice (1986) Mackenzie and Adams (1994)
Micromorphology		Brewer (1964), Bullock et al. (1985), Courty et al. (1990)
Granulometry	Sieve Settling (hydrometer and pipette) Laser diffraction	Krumbein and Pettijohn (1938) Bouyocous (1962) Gee and Bauder (1986), Janitzky (1986a)
Organic matter	Walkley–Black LOI	Walkley and Black (1934) Ball (1964), Janitzky (1986b)
Calcium carbonate	Acid-neutralization method Chittick	US Salinity Laboratory (1954) Machette (1986)
pH	Colorimetric Electrometric	McClean (1982)
Phosphorus	Spot or ring chromatography Visible light spectrometry	Olsen and Sommers (1982) Eidt (1985), Meixner (1986)

Granulometry The texture of sedimentary deposits refers to the percentages of different grain sizes, such as gravels, sand, silt, and clay. *Particle-size analysis* or *granulometry* is performed to determine texture and characterize the population of different grain sizes within a deposit. Particle-size analysis is routinely performed in disciplines such as hydrology, geomorphology, pedology, soil physics, and engineering. Likewise, in geoarchaeology, the applications of particle-size analysis are many (Table 12.2). Because texture is a fundamental physical property of deposits, granulometry serves the basic purpose of objectively characterizing archaeological sediments. This not only helps to document stratigraphy but also provides a basis for correlating deposits between spatially discrete areas. Beyond description, granulometry provides a basis for testing hypotheses regarding sediment origin and mode of deposition. Seemingly simple depositional settings may have sediments derived from several possible sources. For example, rockshelters and caves are generally protected from the elements and yet can contain deposits that are geogenic, biogenic, and anthrogenic, with each origin containing a multitude of different depositional

Table 12.2 Some applications of particle-size analysis in reconstructing sedimentary history and paleoenvironments.

Sediment origin
Identify sediment source areas (*in situ* versus exogenic)
Correlate deposits and stratigraphy between and within sites

Mode of deposition
Distinguishing alluvial, eolian, colluvial, and glacial sediment transport
Distinguish natural and cultural deposition
Distinguish discrete depositional events (e.g., graded bedding as markers of discrete events)

Depositional environment
Estimate depositional energy regimes
Distinguish geologic from pedogenic processes
Estimate surface roughness (for hydraulic reconstructions)
Estimate particle-entrainment requirements

Post-depositional processes and environments
Characterize soil properties
Determine precise soil classification
Distinguish pedogenic from geologic processes
Assess duration of surface stability and soil formation
Assess slope stability
Assess soil erosion potential
Assess bioturbation, cryoturbation, soft-sediment deformation, and other mixing processes

Other
Assess potential for paleomagnetism studies
Assess potential for microbotanical preservation
Assess potential for reworking of archaeological materials
Estimate soil productivity (fertility)

GARY HUCKLEBERRY

mechanisms (Farrand 1985, 2001). Granulometry can be a tool for distinguishing these different sources and mechanisms, as each is likely to produce different grain-size populations (e.g., rockfall versus eolian sedimentation).

Likewise, exposed archaeological sites can be buried by a variety of mechanisms, depending on the geomorphic context. For example, sites located in floodplains could be naturally buried by a combination of alluvial (waterborne), colluvial (movement of material down a slope), or eolian (wind-borne) mechanisms, each with their own implications regarding the preservation of cultural deposits and the ability to reconstruct archaeological systemic context (Waters 1992). Archaeological sites are commonly located on stream terraces along the margins of floodplains. In such locations, overbank deposits from the river commonly interfinger with colluvium and alluvium from hillslopes outside the floodplain, and potentially wind-reworked floodplain deposits. Ostensibly, you can expect that hillslope contributions of sediments on the margins of floodplains would have more variable grain sizes (depending on the nature of hillslope material available for transport) and be more poorly sorted than those formed by low-energy, backwater fluvial deposition or wind-reworked flood deposits. Statistical measures of grain-size distributions, such as particle-size mean, sorting, and skewness values (see Boggs 2001), used in conjunction with other stratigraphic and/or minerological information, can provide more rigorous data supporting interpretations of different sediment origins and modes of deposition.

Equally as important as using granulometry to infer depositional processes is its application for defining post-depositional processes and paleoenvironmental information (Mehringer & Wigand 1986). If a deposit remains at or near the surface for decades, centuries, or millennia, it will undergo a variety of transformations, translocations, and removals that are collectively referred to as *soil formation*, or *pedogenesis* (Holliday 1992; Birkeland 1999; Brady & Weill 1999). Identification of soils is important, as they represent surfaces of stability where past human activity is likely to be concentrated (Mandel & Bettis 2001). Soil formation involves a variety of biochemical processes and mass transfers, and changes to the original grain-size distribution of the parent material are only a small part of the process. Nonetheless, whether it is *in situ* formation of clay minerals or input of eolian dust, relatively coarse-textured deposits become finer textured with time, and the distribution of silt and clay related to pedogenesis should follow a pattern that is recognizable in particle-size data. This pattern is usually a zone of sediment that is low in silt and clay content (e.g., the "A" and "E" horizons of soil) overlying a zone of sediment that is enriched in silt and clay (e.g., "B" horizon) (for an explanation of soil horizonation letters, see Birkeland 1999: 3–8). Hence, vertical changes in texture with depth can be used as an important line of evidence in defining pedogenesis and thus can help in reconstructing depositional history.

In general, post-depositional processes disrupt the systemic context of archaeological materials. Although the best evidence for post-depositional disturbances is field observation and documentation of disturbed strati-graphy, particle-size data can help to distinguish to what degree sediments have been mixed. Geologic processes such as wind and water tend to sort materials by grain size, whereas biotic activity (roots, insects, worms, humans) tends to mix and make deposits less sorted. Sometimes, the type of disturb-ance process results in particular particle-size patterns. For example, bioturba-tion by rodents, insects, and roots, particularly in tropical and subtropical environments, often results in a mixed, poorly sorted "biomantle" overlaying a distinct stone line (Johnson 2002). In contrast, sedimentary deposits located in arctic or alpine environments prone to intense freeze–thaw conditions tend to experience the lifting of clasts toward the surface (Wood & Johnson 1978; Waters 1992: 292–9). Each process results in distinctly different vertical grain-size distributions with depth, and granulometry can be used to help elucidate which biomechanical process is likely to have modified the archaeological deposit.

Methods employed in particle-size analysis depend on the sizes of geologic material encountered. In general, large clasts (> 5 cm) can be measured manu-ally with tape or calipers. However, it is more often the case that archaeolo-gists are dealing with deposits that contain a multitude of different grade sizes that are less than 5 cm. In such cases, you are not measuring individual grains but, rather, populations of different grains or soil texture. The overall texture of a deposit can be estimated in the field by adding water to a small sample and assessing plasticity, stickiness, and grittiness by hand (Thien 1979), but the more precise determinations necessary for statistical analyses are usually made in a sediments laboratory. There are several possible laboratory methods used in granulometry (Table 12.1), but all require two basic steps. The first is to pretreat the sediment sample in order to remove materials that might inter-fere with the measurement of actual mineral grains. The two most common contaminants are organic matter, which adds extraneous mass to the sample, and calcium carbonate, which contributes the calcium ion (Ca^{2+}) that flocculates clay and fine silt. These two contaminants can be removed relatively easily by adding hydrogen peroxide and dilute hydrochloric acid, respectively, and rinsing with distilled water.

The second step in particle-size analysis is to actually break apart and meas-ure the populations of different grain sizes. Traditional methods of measure-ment involve some combination of sieving and settling analysis (Krumbein & Pettijohn 1938; Janitzky 1986a). Sieving can be performed with dry sediments provided that the sediments are fully disaggregated, usually with a mortar and pestle. Alternatively, sediments can be wet sieved, which better ensures com-plete disaggregation of silts and clays, but requires drying and thus more process-ing time. Silt and clay fractions are usually determined by mixing in water and measuring their settling velocity, which can be related to grain size via Stokes' Law (Hillel 1982: 32–3). The two most common approaches for measuring settling velocity in a sediment suspension are the hydrometer and pipette methods (Table 12.1). These traditional methods have the benefit of requiring relatively inexpensive laboratory equipment and reagents, and both have withstood the test of time as reliable techniques for determining sediment texture and/or grain-size distributions. Other, more technologically advanced, methods of granulometry exist, including laser diffraction, where the grain size is related to the scattering of laser light in a sediment/water mixture. Laser diffraction has the benefit of automation (i.e., increased sample processing speed) and the ability to calculate particle-size distributions for small, fine-textured samples. However, the initial start-up costs are greater and traditional methods (e.g., pipette) provide comparable results (Konert & Vanderberghe 1997).

In performing granulometric analysis, you have to decide whether to divide the grain-size population into many precise grades or lump it into fewer, larger grades. The precision – that is, the number of size grades measured – depends on the objectives of the study. If the purpose is simply to define soil texture and objectify field descriptions, then fewer size grades are probably adequate (e.g., gravel, sand, silt, and clay). If the purpose is to deduce and contrast different environments of sediment transport and deposition, and some basic statistical parameters (e.g., particle size mean, sorting, and skewness) are desired (Boggs 2001), then more particle-size grades are necessary. Grain-size distributions can then be presented as relative frequency curves and histograms, cumulative frequency curves, or in tabular format. In most geoarchaeological applications, it is important to display granulometric and other sedimentological data in a way that best demonstrates changes with depth. In tabular format, the samples should be presented in stratigraphic sequence from top to bottom. In graphic format, it is useful to plot changes in values with depth. Because laws of stratigraphic superposition dictate that older deposits occur below younger deposits, vertical changes with depth can help you to reconstruct depositional sequences and identify potential pedogenic or mixing processes. When combined with other chemical data (e.g., pH, organic matter, and calcium carbonate), particle-size data can be a very useful tool for defining site formation processes.

pH

Soil pH is one of the most commonly measured properties of soils. This is because soil pH is a reflection of many important physical and chemical properties (e.g., solubility of metals, nutrient availability, and soil fertility), and is relatively easy to measure. The pH is a measure of hydrogen ion activity in a solution (written as $[H^+]$). Although activity and concentration are not the same, pH can be thought of as a measure of H^+ concentration or, more precisely, the negative logarithm of H^+ concentration expressed in moles per liter:

$$pH = -\log [H^+]$$

Soils in arid and semiarid environments tend to have basic pH values; that is, pH > 7. Soils that contain calcium carbonate almost always have a pH close to that of calcite or 8.0. In contrast, soils in humid environments tend to have more neutral to acidic pH values, especially near the surface where organic acids reside.

In geoarchaeology, pH may be used to help characterize a soil or assess its fertility, or to help test for cultural signatures. Theoretically, cultural sediments should have more organic material that decomposes into humic acids, thus lowering the soil pH. However, archaeological middens that contain abundant wood ash and charcoal may contain elevated pH values (Weide 1966). Agriculturally modified soils ostensibly should have different pH signatures than nearby soils that were never tilled and cultivated, although the direction of pH change will vary with local conditions. In all cases, it is important to note that soil pH is a highly ephemeral property of soil, one that can change relatively rapidly in response to changes in the soil environment. Factors that can affect soil pH include parent material, texture, climate, vegetation, and groundwater, as well as human activity.

Soil pH is usually measured either by colorimetric or electrometric methods (Table 12.1). The colorimetric method is based on the fact that certain organic materials change color at different pH values. Indicator solutions – for example, phenolpthalein and methyl orange – can be used to determine pH, as can strips of paper coated with such solutions (e.g., litmus paper). Colorimetric methods can be useful in the field, but are not as precise as electrometric methods.

The electrometric method is based on the fact that H^+ concentration is proportional to electrical potential (Bohn et al. 1985: 227–31). Hence, a pH meter is a modified voltmeter that converts electrical potential into pH. It is important to be aware that several factors influence the measured pH. These include (1) the nature of the material being measured – in other words, what is contributing the H^+ – (2) the soil/solution ratio, (3) the salt content of the soil and solution, (4) the carbon dioxide (CO_2) content, (5) the temperature of the soil solution, and (6) errors associated with equipment calibration (McClean 1982). Consequently, when reporting pH results, it is important to state the method and some of these parameters if known.

Organic Matter   Determination of organic matter content in sediments is a common and useful type of analysis in archaeology. For archaeological studies, recognition of soil organic matter is important because it may indicate former surfaces of stability that supported human activity, and cultural materials are more likely to be concentrated within such zones. There are two general pathways

GARY HUCKLEBERRY

for organic matter to occur in sediment: (1) organic matter that is formed elsewhere and deposited with nonorganic sediment, and (2) organic matter that forms *in situ* through *pedogenesis* (Stein 1992). Attempts to distinguish depositional and soil organic matter in an archaeological deposit may turn out to be difficult. Where different lines of evidence point toward pedogenesis (e.g., color change, structure, bioturbation features, or abrupt upper surface contact but gradual lower surface contact), an *in situ* origin is likely. *Humification* – that is, the *in situ* development of soil organic matter – is probably the most rapid pedogenic process (Birkeland 1999: 215), and incipient soils are often identified by increased soil organic matter. However, both processes are not mutually exclusive, and indeed alluvial and colluvial soils normally have both components.

Furthermore, if numerical age control is desired, organics in sediments can be ^{14}C dated (see Chapter 5), and interpretation of the result will depend heavily on whether the origin of the organic matter is depositional or pedogenic. If pedogenic, the ^{14}C age can be viewed as an apparent mean age of the organic matter formed during that period of surface stability (Taylor 1987; Wang et al. 1996). If depositional, then the resulting age will be older than the depositional event, with a greater apparent discrepancy between the apparent and true ages.

The identification of organic matter in sediments also has paleoenvironmental implications, especially if derived through pedogenesis, where A horizon development may reflect environmental change (Moody & Dort 1990; Reider 1990; Nordt 2001). In most paleoenvironmental studies, the focus is on changes through time in organic matter accumulation. However, in archaeological sites, it may also be useful to define vertical and horizontal variability in organic matter content. In archaeological contexts, irregular spatial patterning might relate to intra-site features such as storage pits, hearths, and middens, or human activity areas such as animal processing sites. Obviously, the sampling strategy for assessing organic matter content will be heavily influenced by whether the intended goal of the study is to identify surfaces of stability (paleosols) or human activity areas.

Organic matter consists mostly of carbon, hydrogen, and oxygen, with smaller amounts of nitrogen, phosphorus (discussed below), and sulfur. Obviously, there are different types of organic matter with different proportions of these elements. Organic matter content is commonly determined in a laboratory by measuring only the amount of organic carbon and then multiplying by an empirically derived value to estimate total organic matter. A traditional method for measuring total soil organic carbon has been to determine the weight loss of a soil sample after cooking at 500°C (932°F) in a furnace (commonly known as "loss on ignition" or LOI; Table 12.1). This method works best with sandy, well-drained, nonalkaline soils (Ball 1964). Alternatively, the Walkley–Black method can be used, whereby organic matter is oxidized with a chemical reagent (Walkley & Black 1934). The method works relatively well, although sources of error include incomplete oxidation of organic matter and problems with interference by other oxidizable material; for example, ferrous iron (Fe^{3+}) in magnetite. In the latter case, samples can be treated with a magnet prior to analysis to minimize the problem. In the Walkley–Black method, the resulting organic carbon content is multiplied by a conversion factor to arrive at an estimate of percent soil organic matter. Traditionally, a conversion factor of 1.72 is used (the Van Bemmelen factor), because it was assumed that organic matter contained 58 percent organic carbon. However, it is now known that the percentage of organic carbon in organic matter is variable, and thus any factor selected is only an approximation. Consequently, some soil scientists feel that the results obtained from the Walkley–Black method should be considered semiquantitative (Nelson & Sommers 1982). On the other hand, the method is still commonly employed in both geoarchaeological and geomorphological studies due to its relative simplicity and reasonably accurate results (Holliday & Stein 1989).

Phosphorus   Phosphorus analysis is commonly employed in archaeological studies as an indicator of previous human activity in soil. Like organic carbon, phosphorus is incorporated into soil through both soil formation and deposition of organic matter. Although it is a minor constituent of soil organic matter, unlike most of the other organic elements, phosphorus binds with other soil materials, resists leaching, and persists for a relatively long time. Hence, areas of cultural activity may have elevated phosphorus levels in soil whereas other chemical indicators are no longer present. In general, elevated phosphorus is a signature for cultural activity at archaeological sites, and it has been applied to locating past settlements, reconstruction of land use, and identification and explanation of human activity areas (Schuldenrein 1995; Vizcaino & Canabate 1999; Terry et al. 2000). In most cases, human activity is associated with elevated phosphorus levels in soil, presumably due to the disposal of organic wastes. However, prehistoric agricultural areas may actually be identified by reduced phosphorus levels (Sandor et al. 1986). Furthermore, Eidt (1977, 1985) believes that the ratios of different phosphorus fractions in soil can be used to provide relative ages for cultural deposits. Hence, phosphorus analysis has many potential applications in archaeology.

There are different ways to measure soil phosphorus. A simple, qualitative method is called the *spot* or *ring* test. This can be performed in the field by adding acid extractant and color reagents to a sediment sample and assessing color changes on filter paper. Although qualitative (or semiqualitative if diffusion of color on filter paper is measured; e.g., Dormaar & Beaudoin 1991), this method has been repeatedly used in archaeological survey to identify human-affected soils and occupation areas where overt evidence of human activity is absent. More accurate measures of phosphorus are performed in a laboratory and commonly employ elaborate extraction techniques and analysis (Olsen & Sommers 1982). In such cases, the researcher has to determine what type of phosphorus is to be measured. Phosphorus seldom occurs in its elemental form. Instead, it is usually bound with oxygen-forming phosphate ion (PO_4^{3-}), which in turn bonds with other materials such as iron oxyhydroxides, aluminosilicate clay minerals, and organic compounds (Bohn et al. 1985: 190–4). In general, phosphorus occurs in one of three forms in soil: fixed, soluble, and organic (Eidt 1985). Fixed inorganic phosphorus is tightly bound with iron and aluminum minerals in acidic soils and calcium minerals in alkaline soils. Soluble phosphorus is loosely bound or in solution (normally present in very small quantities), and organic phosphorus is that still incorporated within organic matter. All three phosphorus types can be measured as "total phosphorus," or individual fractions can be analyzed, the latter requiring greater laboratory work. Eidt (1977, 1985) is an advocate of analyzing different fractions that might yield more precise cultural and chronological information, whereas others are less certain of the results (see Bethell & Máté 1989). Spot or ring tests analyze only the amount of soluble or "available" phosphorus, which does not always correlate with inorganic or total phosphorus.

Once the type of phosphorus to be analyzed is determined, the first step is to extract it from sediment. Phosphorus extraction is performed using either an acid or alkali solution, depending how the phosphorus is bound: low-pH soils require an acid extraction, whereas high-pH soils require an alkali extraction (Olsen & Sommers 1982). Hence the pH should be determined first to help select the appropriate extraction method. Inorganic phosphorus is more tightly bound and requires more rigorous extraction methods than soluble phosphorus. Total phosphorus requires rigorous digestion or ignition of the soil sample in order to oxidize organic matter and mineralize the organic phosphorus. After PO_4^{3-} is extracted, it is ready to be analyzed. Commonly, a colorimetric method is used whereby PO_4^{3-} is complexed with a reagent (e.g., ammonia molybdate), yielding a colored solution. Spectrophotometry, which measures the absorbance and transmission of polarized light through a colored solution, can subsequently be performed on the samples of unknown phosphorus content and then compared to a set of control samples of known phosphorus concentration. If phosphorus is to be used as a discriminator of possible areas of past cultural activity, it is essential that analyses be performed on both sediments suspected to have been affected by human activity and nearby "nonimpacted sediments" for control, and such control samples should be from comparable pedogenic and geomorphic contexts.

Prehistoric Canals in the American Southwest

Despite the possible applications of the laboratory methods described above in regards to reconstructing site formation processes and paleoenvironmental context, whether or not these methods should be employed in an archaeological investigation depends in large part on the questions to be addressed. Clearly, it is best to have specific research questions in hand and an idea of how laboratory analyses will help to answer those questions prior to sampling sediments in the field. Whereas sedimentological analyses usually yield some type of information relevant to archaeological enquiry, especially where excavation is involved, the cost of a full set of laboratory tests may not be warranted. In some cases, only one type of analysis may be required, whereas in others, multiple types of sedimentological analyses would be beneficial. In the first case study presented here, granulometry was selected as the key laboratory method for a geoarchaeological study of prehistoric canals.

An exciting research domain in American Southwest archaeology is to define the development and expansion of agriculture over the past 4,000 years. Maize worked its way up from central Mexico into the arid and semiarid lands of the Southwest by 2000 BCE (Matson 1991; Huckell 1996). The impact that this new way of life had on previous Archaic peoples was tremendous in terms of population, mobility, and social–political organization (Hard & Roney 1998). It had long been thought that it took a couple of thousand years for food production to evolve from horticultural dry and floodwater farming to intensive canal irrigation. However, recent discoveries of prehistoric canals in Arizona and New Mexico, dating to c.1000 BCE (Mabry et al. 1997; Damp et al. 2002), indicate that indigenous farmers began engineering and controlling water for food production much earlier than previously realized. By CE 600, canal irrigation had become a major way of life for farmers living in the low deserts of Arizona. The Hohokam (CE 600–1450) constructed the largest pre-Columbian canal systems in North America, with over 500 km of canal alignments mapped in the Phoenix Basin alone (Masse 1981; Howard & Huckleberry 1991; Figure 12.1). For reasons that are not fully understood, the Hohokam began struggling to meet the dietary needs of their people in the 1300s (Abbott 2003), and by 1450 huge swaths of desert were abandoned, including areas that had been witness to over 1,500 years of canal irrigation.

To understand the ecology of the Hohokam is to understand their canal systems, the lifeblood to their society, around which they organized their communities and farms. Historical photographs and archaeological excavations indicate that the canals were hand-excavated and well designed in terms of their engineering properties, such as channel geometry and gradient. Canal channels were parabolic to trapezoidal in form, with widths ranging from 1 to 10 m; the largest canals supported up to 10 m^3 per second of flow. Main canals connected to a series of smaller distributary and field lateral channels through a series of stone and brush-constructed water control structures (Masse 1991). Unfortunately, historical agriculture followed by modern urbanization has effaced over 99 percent of the prehistoric canal systems over the past 150 years. Nonetheless, the middle to lower dimensions of these linear features remain intact beneath plowed fields and city streets in the Phoenix Basin. The city of Phoenix is currently the second fastest growing city in the United States, and development projects over the past 20 years have provided archaeologists an opportunity to study the subsurface remains of these relict canal systems. These irrigation features are unlike most archaeological features in that they are linear and usually extend beyond the borders of a given project area. Moreover, they are defined solely by sediments and are amenable for geoarchaeological analysis. An investigation of prehistoric canals is by default an analysis of sediments and stratigraphy.

A recurrent question regarding Hohokam canals is the degree to which they were resilient or susceptible to environmental fluctuations such as floods and droughts. Indeed, a combination of geologic data (Huckleberry 1995; Waters & Ravesloot 2001), and archival records of historic canals (Ackerly 1989; Huckleberry 1999a) suggests that Hohokam canal systems were vulnerable to frequent floodplain dynamics associated with large floods, resulting in headgate destruction and siltation within channels. These canals had to be maintained and rebuilt regularly, which required large pools of human labor. If periods of recurrent flood damage combined with alternating periods of drought, a probable outcome would be collapse of the canal systems and consequent food stress.

Dendrohydrological reconstructions of annual runoff on the major rivers supplying the canals suggest that increased runoff variability (i.e., flood and drought) coincided with the decline of the Hohokam, starting in the late 1300s (Nials et al. 1989; Gregory 1991). If the decline of the Hohokam was due in part to increased canal system instability caused by increased flood frequency and magnitude, then there should be recurrent sedimentological evidence for uncontrolled flooding within the fill of the abandoned canals. Such evidence should be manifested in the grain sizes of canal sediments and changes in mean grain size and sorting within a depositional sequence. Ostensibly, sediments deposited in canals through normal operation and controlled water flow should be dominated by silt and clay, and should be relatively well sorted. In contrast, flood-damaged canal headgates allow large, erosive volumes of water to penetrate the system, depositing coarser-textured sediments dominated by sand and possibly fine gravel.

Over 20 years, numerous archaeological investigations in the Phoenix area have resulted in the collection of granulometric data on many prehistoric canals. Whereas these sediments do provide insights into past canal operation and flow history, several limitations are recognized. One is that much, if not most, of the canal has been destroyed by historical plowing and more recent urban mixing, such that only the middle to lower dimensions are preserved. Also, short canal alignment segments far from the system headgate are usually sampled with little understanding of their specific context within the larger irrigation system. In general, only an approximate distance from the headgate can be estimated. It is important to know exact distances from headgates, because high-energy alluvium produced through flooding ostensibly decreases in mean grain size down the canal channel, and it is thus difficult to compare mean grain-size values between different channels without knowing where within each system the segments are located. Despite these limits, sediment samples collected during these investigations should allow you to estimate whether or not canal deposits are reflective of high-energy, flood-like conditions, or more controlled, lower-energy flow regimes.

To test for the presence of flood stratigraphy in prehistoric canals, I compiled 363 sediment samples from 45 Hohokam canal segments excavated in the Phoenix metropolitan area in the 1980s and 1990s for which granulometric data exist (Huckleberry 1999b). These canals are the vestiges of approximately 1,500 years of water diversions from the lower Salt River. In most cases, only percentages of sand, silt, and clay are available, thus precluding the ability to construct detailed cumulative frequency distributions and statistical measures of graphical mean and sorting. Instead, I focused on characterizing the general texture of individual deposits and how they change from the bottom to

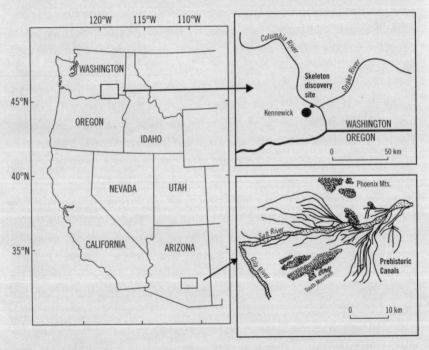

Figure 12.1 Two case study project areas in the western USA. Case study 1 is located in the Phoenix Basin of south-central Arizona. Case study 2 is located on the banks of the Columbia River in the town of Kennewick, Washington.

the top of the extant channels. I divided a simple ternary textural triangle into four areas and developed indices (e.g., clay-dominant = 1, silt dominant = 2, loamy sand = 3, and sand-dominant = 4). Each integer was used to assign an overall texture to each deposit and allowed for analysis of bedding sequences (e.g., coarsening versus fining upwards). Statistical calculations including Markov chain analysis indicated that no recurrent depositional cycle is evident, and that overall, most canal fill sequences are silt-dominant and relatively uniform, with a few exceptions. Some large, main canals located within the floodplain of the Salt River clearly contain high-energy, coarse-textured sediments in the upper part of the channel. On the basis of archival accounts of Anglo-European earthen canals from the late nineteenth and early twentieth centuries, uncontrolled floods would deposit sediment along most of the canal alignment. By reasonable hypothesis, the resulting depositional sequence should be relatively coarse (flood) sediment overlying relatively fine (canal operation) sediment, and such relative textural changes should be evident several kilometers from the headgate. However, the granulometric analysis of 45 Hohokam canals failed to identify this in more than just a few cases. Canal depositional sequences capped by relatively coarse-textured sediments are generally rare.

By itself, the paucity of flood-like sediments argues against floods reeking havoc on the Hohokam canals. Nonetheless, it is possible that canal flooding was a recurrent problem but did not produce the expected depositional sequence, or that the flood sequence is missing because only the middle to lower dimensions of the canals are preserved. Some sort of calibration was needed whereby relict canals known to have been flood damaged and abandoned could be sedimentologically analyzed and characterized. Toward that end, I performed granulometric analysis on sediments from abandoned main canal segments located along the Gila River (Figure 12.1), which are documented to have been destroyed by large floods in the early twentieth century (Huckleberry 1999a). In this case, I performed detailed granulometric analysis such that cumulative frequency curves and statistical measures could be calculated. The granulometric data confirmed that most flood-damaged, main canal segments located close to the system headgate do contain a coarsening-upward depositional sequence (Figure 12.2), but the overall textures are quite variable, ranging from silt to coarse sand. Gravel is generally not present. Moreover, because the canals may be partly filled with sediments from normal operation, flood sedimentation may be limited to the uppermost parts of the channel. In the case of most prehistoric canals, such sequences will have been removed by historical plowing. Thus flood damage to canals cannot be ruled out as a contributing factor to the collapse of the Hohokam, despite the paucity of flood-like stratigraphy. Flood deposits far removed from headgates might be dominated by relatively low-energy silt, or flood deposits may not be preserved. Sediment analysis of both partially preserved prehistoric and fully preserved historic canals thus provides insight into the depositional processes that form these features.

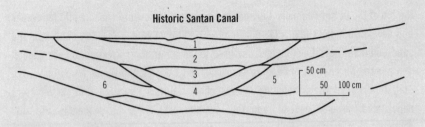

Historic Santan Canal

Stratum	Graphic mean (ϕ)	Graphic mean (mm)	Sorting (ϕ)	Skewness (ϕ)	Sand (%)	Silt (%)	Clay (%)
1	1.0	0.51	1.6	0.0	94	3	3
2	2.3	0.20	2.2	0.2	87	7	6
3	2.5	0.18	1.5	0.5	90	4	6
4	4.1	0.06	1.9	0.6	65	28	7
5	3.5	0.09	1.7	0.4	72	22	6
6	4.9	0.03	3.3	0.3	44	39	17

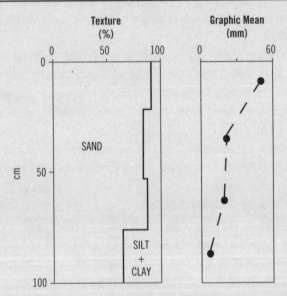

Figure 12.2 The profile and granulometric data for the relict canal located on the Gila River, south-central Arizona (canal profile reproduced from Huckleberry 1999b: fig. 4).

Sedimentological analysis has also contributed to resolving a much more contentious issue regarding the appropriate disposition of a 9,000-year-old set of human remains. In the summer of 1996 in the town of Kennewick, Washington (Figure 12.1), two young men found a human skull in shallow water along the shore of Lake Wallulla, a dammed segment of the Columbia River. Little did they know that this skull and associated bones represented the oldest well-preserved skeleton in the Pacific Northwest, or that its discovery would set in place a high-profile lawsuit pitting scientists against Native Americans and the US Federal Government (Downey 2000; Thomas 2000; Chatters 2001). A coalition of Native American tribes requested that the skeleton be returned to them for reburial, following their interpretation of a federal law known as the *Native American Graves Protection and Repatriation Act* (NAGPRA). This law has several statutory components, one of which states that all human remains and associated materials (e.g., funerary objects) recovered from public land that are found to be Native American are to be turned over to culturally affiliated tribes. However, many scientists and their supporters argue that these remains are too old to be culturally affiliated with modern tribes and, given their scientific importance, that they should be archived for future study. The conflict is multifaceted, involving components of science, religion, law, and politics, the details of which go far beyond the scope of this chapter (see "Resources" and also Chapter 2). Of interest here is how sediment analysis played a role in the investigation of the skeleton.

The skeleton had apparently eroded out of the stream bank in the spring of 1996 and lay in shallow water for several months. Over 90 percent of the skeleton was recovered along the shore (Chatters 2000), but it was unclear where in the stream bank the skeleton was originally contained. A preliminary, noninvasive geologic study of the shoreline was commissioned by the US Army Corps of Engineers, the agency in charge of the land where the skeleton was found. Performed in December 1997, this study, which was submitted to the US Army (Wakeley et al. 1998), provided important information regarding the general stratigraphic context of the skeleton as well as general geomorphic setting. Stratigraphic profiles, soil descriptions, and sediment samples were collected; sediment analysis included granulometry, petrography, and pH. In addition, several samples of organic sediment from the stream bank and subsurface vibracores were ^{14}C dated.

The stream bank marks the edge of an early Holocene Columbia River terrace and provides a less than 2 m exposure of deposits (Figure 12.3). The upper unit, Lithostratigraphic Unit I, is composed of loose to friable fine sand to very fine sand, and ranges from 25 cm to 80 cm in thickness. Many of the larger quartz sand grains are frosted, suggesting eolian transport. Mazama tephra, dated at 7,600 BP, is discontinuously

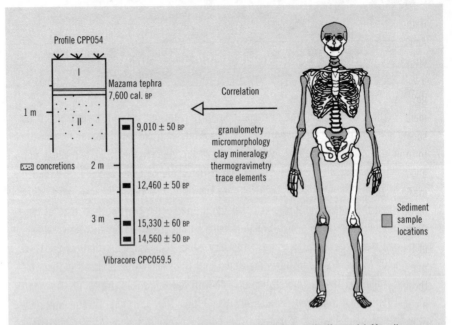

Figure 12.3 Skeleton sediment sample locations and geochronology at the Kennewick Man discovery locality. Physical and chemical tests of sediments were used to correlate the skeleton to the upper part of Lithostratigraphic Unit II, thus supporting the early Holocene age of the human remains (skeleton reproduced from Huckleberry et al. 2003: fig. 3).

preserved at or near the base of Unit I. The lower deposit, Lithostratigraphic Unit II, is exposed in the lower part of the terrace edge, although vibracores were used to provide additional subsurface information. Unit II is a finer-grained deposit, which is character-ized by weakly preserved, horizontally bedded, very fine sand and silt. In places, very fine, centimeter-scale graded bedding is evident in the upper deposit, but most of the primary bedding is not preserved in the upper 1 m due to bioturbation. Bedding becomes more distinct below 2 m and consists of several more distinct coarse-to-fine graded and cross-bedded sequences. The upper part of Unit II contains numerous calcitic concre-tions formed through soil formation, that match similarly described concretions on the exterior of post-cranial elements on Kennewick Man. This suggested that the skeleton likely came from the upper part of Unit II, which would match the ~ 9,000-year-old ^{14}C age of the skeleton (Taylor et al. 1998). Although scientists recommended that further testing be done (Wakeley et al. 1998), the US Army Corps of Engineers buried the site with tons of earth and rock debris, citing concerns of further erosive damage.

While the case was tied up in court, the federal government elected to perform a series of nondestructive tests on the skeleton in 1998, in order to better determine the applicability of federal law to these remains. Specifically, the federal government needed to confirm that these remains were "Native American" in order to fall under the jurisdic-tion of NAGPRA. They elected to use a chronological criterion for Native American status:

if the skeletal remains predate the year 1492, they are to be interpreted as "Native American." A single ^{14}C date indicated that the remains were approximately 9,000 years old, and the geologic study at the discovery site suggested that the remains predate a volcanic eruption dated at 7,600 BP. However, given the importance of this lawsuit, the government wanted additional chronological information, preferably without performing more ^{14}C dating, which would require additional destructive sampling of the skeleton, something opposed by most Native Americans. In an effort to better correlate the bones to the geologically dated levels at the discovery site, the government elected to perform a nondestructive analysis of sediments adhering to the skeleton. Although the preliminary geologic study of the site suggests that the skeleton came from the upper part of Unit II (confirming a pre-7,600 BP age), and an independent sediment analysis by Chatters (2000) correlated the skeleton to a more specific depth within the upper part of Unit II, the government wanted to test that hypothesis and affirm the early Holocene age of Kennewick Man. Interestingly, the requested sedimentological study is similar to those performed in forensic geology, whereby sediments are used to link a suspect to a crime scene (Murray & Tedrow 1992). In this case, the physical and chemical properties of sediments on the skeleton were to be compared to sediments from the stream cut in an effort to better define the provenance of the original skeleton. I was asked by the federal government to participate in the investigation. My colleagues and I selected laboratory tests including granulometry, thin-section and micromorphology analysis, X-ray diffraction (clay mineralogy), thermogravimetry (loss on ignition), and trace element analysis (Huckleberry et al. 2003). Unfortunately, detailed sampling at the discovery site for control was not possible because of its recent burial by the federal government. Consequently, sediments collected at the skeleton recovery site during the 1997 study were analyzed for comparison. These sediments were from stream bank profiles and a vibracore that sampled subsurface shoreline sediments (Figure 12.3). Granulometry data compiled by James Chatters (2000) during his original study of the site was also used in the analysis.

The main hypothesis to test was whether or not sediments located on the surface of post-cranial bones and within the cranium match those from the upper part of Lithostratigraphic Unit II (60–150 cm depth) containing the calcite concretions (Figure 12.3). Thermogravimetric analysis is a detailed measure of weight loss as a sediment sample is progressively heated to temperatures at which organic matter and calcite oxidize. It allows for an analysis of both components, and in this case demonstrated nicely that concretions from both the skeleton and Unit II are chemically similar (Table 12.3), further supporting a correlation. Another goal was to determine whether vertical changes in the physical and chemical properties of Unit II were sufficiently distinct to discern the depth of burial within a range of 20–30 cm. Chatters (2000) used granulometric data to indicate that sediments on the skeleton best match terrace sediments at depths of 80–85 cm and 135–140 cm. However, our analyses indicated that differences in grain size and sorting within Unit II are statistically insignificant, a likely result of bioturbation

Table 12.3 Organic matter and calcite data from (a) the Kennewick study site and (b) the skeleton (Huckleberry et al. 2003).

(a)

Location	Depth (cm)	Stratum	Organic matter (%)	CaCO₃ (%)
CPP054	10–20	I	2.2	2.8
CPP054	30–40	I	2.1	4.5
CPP054	50–60	I	1.7	6.7
CPP054	70–80	II	1.5	8.7
CPP054	80–90	II	1.0	48.7[a]
CPP054	95–135	II	1.8	5.0
CPC059.5	0–10	II	1.4	35.0[a]
CPC059.5	30–40	II	1.6	1.8
CPC059.5	60–66	II	1.7	1.8

[a] Analysis on concretion

(b)

Location	Element	Material	Organic matter (%)	CaCO₃ (%)
Ox coxea	97A.I.17a	Dark sediment	2.3	3.7
Metatarsals	97.L.24 (Mta + Mtb)	Concretion	1.8	18.5
Cranium	97.U.1a	Sediment	1.2	6.7
Unidentifiable fragment	97.I.25c	Concretion	1.2	51.5
Femur	97.R.18a	Sediment	1.3	18.4

(Huckleberry et al. 2003). Likewise, post-depositional processes and consequent homogenization of fluvial beds preclude any distinct matches in organic matter, calcium carbonate, mineralogy, or trace element chemistry at spatial scales of 10–20 cm. Instead, pedogenesis has mixed the originally stratified deposits such that the skeleton can only be correlated to a ~ 90 cm zone in the upper part of Unit II. We were, however, able to distinguish sediment derived from the original burial and darker sediment (e.g., element 97 A.I.17a, Table 12.3) that became attached to the skeleton after eroding out of the bank. We concluded that the skeleton is from a stratum located beneath the Mazama tephra and at an approximate level that ^{14}C dated to 9,010 ± 50 BP. Hence, the early Holocene age of the skeleton is further supported by these tests. Interestingly, the federal government, in an effort to be as certain as possible that Kennewick Man was indeed pre-Columbian in age, later elected to perform further ^{14}C tests of the skeleton, the results of which confirmed the age of approximately 9,000 years.

In sum, analysis performed on sediments attached to Kennewick Man and the original burial site was nondestructive to bone and further supported the hypothesis that the skeleton was derived from the upper part of a geologic unit that was approximately 9,000 years old. This added further credence to the original ^{14}C date on the skeleton, based on the geologic age of the deposits. It was not possible, however, to further distinguish the burial depth of the skeleton, due to insufficient variance of sediment chemistry, texture, and mineralogy with depth. It also remains to be proven whether or not the skeleton was interred in the ground by human hands or buried by flood sedimentation (Chatters 2001; Huckleberry et al. 2003). If the US Army Corps had not buried the site in 1998, more detailed sampling of control sections may have improved the precision of the analysis. Although questions remain regarding the burial context of Kennewick Man, these studies are a good example of how sedimentology can provide useful contextual information that otherwise might not be available for these controversial human remains.

The value of sediment analysis has long been recognized in archaeology, given that sediments and stratigraphy constitute an important environmental and chronological framework for interpreting the material record. To extract the maximum amount of information from archaeological sediments, you should be able to objectively and systematically observe and record sedimentological and stratigraphic features in the field. Indeed, this is probably the most essential skill in geoarchaeology, and one that I emphasize in my class. Beyond that, you need to turn to laboratory methods for confirming field observations and generating and/or testing hypotheses regarding site formation or contextual information for individual objects and features. There are a variety of laboratory methods for analyzing sediments, many of which do not require expensive, high-tech, or elaborate equipment. This chapter has reviewed some common laboratory methods for grain size, pH, organic matter, and phosphorus, and provided two examples where laboratory analyses of sediments helped to address archaeological questions. A proper combination of rigorous field descriptions and prudent laboratory testing can help to bolster interpretations and test hypotheses linking the physical evidence at archaeological sites to the ultimate goal of reconstructing human behavior.

Conclusion

For contrasting opinions on the Kennewick Man controversy, see www.cr.nps.gov/aad/kennewick/, www.saa.org/repatriation/index.html, www.umatilla.nsn.us/ancient.html, and www.friendsofpast.org

For a chronology of events related to the case, see www.kennewick-man.com/

Resources

Abbott, D. R. (ed.) 2003: *Centuries of Decline During the Hohokam Classic Period at Pueblo Grande*. Tucson: University of Arizona Press.

Ackerly, N. W. 1989: Paleohydrodynamic impacts on Hohokam irrigation systems. In N. W. Ackerly and K. Henderson (eds.), *Prehistoric Agricultural Activities on the Lehi-Mesa Terrace: Perspectives on Hohokam Irrigation Cycles*. Flagstaff: Northland Research, Inc., 46–83.

References

Ball, D. F. 1964: Loss on-ignition as an estimate of organic matter and organic carbon in non-calcareous soils. *Journal of Soil Science*, 15, 84–92.

Bethell, P. and Máté, I. 1989: The use of soil phosphate analysis in archaeology: a critique. In J. Henderson (ed.), *Scientific Analysis in Archaeology*. Los Angeles: UCLA Institute of Archaeology, 1–29.

Birkeland, P. W. 1999: *Soils and Geomorphology*, 3rd edn. New York: Oxford University.

Boggs, S. 2001: *Principles of Sedimentology and Stratigraphy*, 3rd edn. Upper Saddle River, NJ: Prentice-Hall.

Bohn, H., McNeal, B. and O'Connor, G. 1985: *Soil Chemistry*, 2nd edn. New York: John Wiley.

Bouyoucos, G. 1962: Hydrometer method improved for making particle size analysis of soils. *Agronomy Journal*, 54, 464–5.

Brady, N. C. and Weill, R. R. 1999: *Elements of the Nature and Properties of Soils*. Upper Saddle River, NJ: Prentice-Hall.

Brewer, R. 1964: *Fabric and Mineral Analysis of Soils*. New York: John Wiley.

Bullock, P., Fedoroff, N., Jongerius, A., Stoops, G. and Tursina, T. 1985: *Handbook for Soil Thin Section Description*. Wolverhampton: Waine Research.

Butzer, K. W. 1982: *Archaeology as Human Ecology*. Cambridge: Cambridge University Press.

Chatters, J. C. 2000: The recovery and first analysis of an early Holocene human skeleton from Kennewick, Washington. *American Antiquity*, 65, 291–316.

—— 2001: *Ancient Encounters: Kennewick Man and the First Americans*. New York: Simon and Schuster.

Courty, M., Goldberg, P. and Macphail, R. 1990: *Soils and Micromorphology in Archaeology*. New York: Cambridge University Press.

Damp, J. E., Hall, S. A. and Smith, S. J. 2002: Early irrigation on the Colorado Plateau near Zuni Pueblo, New Mexico. *American Antiquity*, 67, 665–76.

Dormaar, J. F. and Beaudoin, A. B. 1991: Application of soil chemistry to interpret cultural events at the Calderwood Buffalo Jump (DkPj-27), Southern Alberta, Canada. *Geoarchaeology: An International Journal*, 6, 85–98.

Downey, R. 2000: *Riddle of the Bones: Politics, Science, Race, and the Story of Kennewick Man*. New York: Springer-Verlag.

Eidt, R. C. 1977: Detection and examination of anthrosols by phosphate analysis. *Science*, 197, 1327–33.

—— 1985: Theoretical and practical considerations in the analysis of Anthrosols. In J. G. Rapp and J. A. Gifford (eds.), *Archaeological Geology*. New Haven: Yale University Press, 155–91.

Farrand, W. R. 1985: Rockshelter and cave sediments. In J. K. Stein and W. R. Farrand (eds.), *Archaeological Sediments in Context*. Orono, ME: Center for the Study of Early Man, 21–40.

—— 2001: Sediments and stratigraphy in rockshelters and caves: a personal perspective on principles and pragmatics. *Geoarchaeology: An International Journal*, 16, 537–58.

Gee, G. W. and Bauder, J. W. 1986: Particle-size analysis. In A. Klute (ed.), *Methods of Soil Analysis, Part 1: Physical and Mineralogical Methods*, 2nd edn. Madison, WI: Soil Science Society of America, 383–412.

Gregory, D. A. 1991: Form and variation in Hohokam settlement patterns. In P. L. Crown and W. J. Judge (eds.), *Chaco and Hohokam: Prehistoric Regional Systems in the American Southwest*. Santa Fe: School of American Research Press, 159–94.

Hard, R. J. and Roney, J. R. 1998: A massive terraced village complex in Chihuahua, Mexico, 3,000 years before present. *Science*, 279, 1661–4.

GARY HUCKLEBERRY

Hassan, F. A. 1978: Sediments in archaeology: methods and implications for paleoenvironmental and cultural analysis. *Journal of Field Archaeology*, 5, 197–213.

Herz, N. and Garrison, E. G. 1998: *Geological Methods in Archaeology*. New York: Oxford University Press.

Hillel, D. 1982: *Introduction to Soil Physics*. New York: Academic Press.

Holliday, V. T. (ed.) 1992: *Soils in Archaeology: Landscape Evolution and Human Occupation*. Washington, DC: Smithsonian Institution Press.

—— and Stein, J. K. 1989: Variability of laboratory procedures and results in geoarchaeology. *Geoarchaeology: An International Journal*, 4, 347–58.

Howard, J. B. and Huckleberry, G. 1991: *The Operation and Evolution of an Irrigation System: The East Papago Canal Study*. Phoenix: Soil Systems Publications in Archaeology, 18.

Huckell, B. B. 1996: The Archaic prehistory of the North American Southwest. *Journal of World Prehistory*, 10, 305–73.

Huckleberry, G. 1995: Archaeological implications of late-Holocene channel changes on the Middle Gila River. *Geoarchaeology: An International Journal*, 10, 159–82.

—— 1999a: Assessing Hohokam canal stability through stratigraphy. *Journal of Field Archaeology*, 26, 1–18.

—— 1999b: Stratigraphic identification of destructive floods in relict canals: a case study from the Middle Gila River. *Kiva*, 65, 7–33.

——, Stein, J. K. and Goldberg, P. 2003: Determining the provenience of Kennewick Man skeletal remains through sedimentological analyses. *Journal of Archaeological Science*, 30, 651–65.

Janitzky, P. 1986a: Particle size analysis. In M. J. Singer and P. Janitzky (eds.), *Field and Laboratory Procedures Used in a Soil Chronosequence Study*. Washington, DC: US Geological Survey Bulletin, 1648, 11–15.

—— 1986b: Organic carbon. In M. J. Singer and P. Janitzky (eds.), *Field and Laboratory Procedures Used in a Soil Chronosequence Study*. Washington, DC: US Geological Survey Bulletin, 1648, 34–6.

Johnson, D. L. 2002: Darwin would be proud: bioturbation, dynamic denudation, and the power of theory in science. *Geoarchaeology: An International Journal*, 17, 7–40.

Konert, M. and Vandenberghe, J. 1997: Comparison of laser grain size analysis with pipette and sieve analysis: a solution for the underestimation of the clay fraction. *Sedimentology*, 44, 523–34.

Krumbein, W. C. and Pettijohn, F. J. 1938: *Manual of Sedimentary Petrography*. New York: D. Appleton-Century Company.

Mabry, J. B., Swartz, D. L., Wocherl, H., Clark, J. J., Archer, G. H. and Lindeman, M. W. 1997: *Archaeological Investigations of Early Village Sites in the Middle Santa Cruz Valley*. Anthropological Paper No. 18. Tucson: Center for Desert Archaeology.

Machette, M. 1986: Calcium and magnesium carbonates. In M. J. Singer and P. Janitzky, P. (eds.), *Field and Laboratory Procedures Used in a Soil Chronosequence Study*. Washington, DC: US Geological Survey Bulletin, 1648, 30–2.

MacKenzie, W. S. and Adams, A. E. 1994: *A Colour Atlas of Rocks and Minerals*. London: Manson Publishing.

Mandel, R. and Bettis, E. A. III 2001: Use and analysis of soils by archaeologists and geoscientists: a North American perspective. In P. Goldberg, C. V. Holliday and C. R. Ferring (eds.), *Earth Sciences and Archaeology*. New York: Kluwer Academic/Plenum Press, 173–204.

Masse, W. B. 1981: Prehistoric irrigation systems in the Salt River Valley, Arizona. *Science*, 214, 408–15.

—— 1991: The quest for subsistence sufficiency and civilization in the Sonoran Desert. In P. L. Crown and W. J. Judge (eds.), *Chaco and Hohokam: Prehistoric Regional Systems in the American Southwest*. Albuquerque: University of New Mexico Press, 195–223.

Matson, R. G. 1991: *The Origins of Southwestern Agriculture*. Tucson: University of Arizona Press.

McClean, E. O. 1982: Soil pH and lime requirement. In A. L. Page (ed.), *Methods of Soil Analysis, Part 2, Chemical and Microbiological Properties*, 2nd edn. Madison, WI: Soil Science Society of America, 199–224.

Mehringer, P. J., Jr and Wigand, P. E. 1986: Holocene history of Skull Creek dunes, Catlow Valley, southeastern Oregon, USA. *Journal of Arid Environments*, 11, 117–38.

Meixner, R. 1986: Total phosphorus (extraction); phosphorus fractionation (extraction); phosphorus analysis. In M. J. Singer and P. Janitzky (eds.), *Field and Laboratory Procedures Used in a Soil Chronosequence Study*. Washington, DC: US Geological Survey Bulletin, 1648, 43–7.

Moody, U. and Dort, W. 1990: Microstratigraphic analysis of sediments and soils; Wasden archaeological site, eastern Snake River Plain, Idaho. In N. P. Lasca and J. Donahue (eds.), *Archaeological Geology of North America*. Boulder, CO: Geological Society of America, 361–82.

Murray, R. C. and Tedrow, J. C. F. 1992: *Forensic Geology*. Englewood Cliffs, NJ: Prentice-Hall.

Nelson, D. W. and Sommers, L. E. 1982: Total carbon, organic carbon, and organic matter. In A. L. Page (ed.), *Methods of Soil Analysis. Part 2: Chemical and Microbiological Properties*. Madison, WI: Soil Science Society of America, 539–80.

Nials, F., Gregory, D. and Graybill, D. 1989: Salt River streamflow and Hohokam irrigation systems. In D. G. Graybill, D. A. Gregory, F. L. Nials et al. (eds.), *The 1982–1984 Excavations at Las Colinas: Studies of Prehistoric Environment and Subsistence*. Archaeological Series 162, vol. 5. Tucson: Arizona State Museum, 59–78.

Nordt, L. C. 2001: Stable carbon and oxygen isotopes in soils: applications for archaeological research. In P. Goldberg, C. V. Holliday and C. R. Ferring (eds.), *Earth Sciences and Archaeology*. New York: Kluwer Academic/Plenum Press, 419–48.

Olsen, S. R. and Sommers, L. E. 1982: Phosphorus. In A. L. Page (ed.), *Methods of Soil Analysis Part 2: Chemical and Microbiological Properties*. Madison, WI: Soil Science Society of America, 403–30.

Reider, R. G. 1990: Late Pleistocene and Holocene pedogenic and environmental trends at archaeological sites in plains and mountain areas of Colorado and Wyoming. In N. P. Lasca and J. Donahue (eds.), *Archaeological Geology of North America*. Boulder, CO: Geological Society of America, 335–60.

Sandor, J. A., Gersper, P. L. and Hawley, J. 1986: Soils at prehistoric agricultural terracing sites, New Mexico III: phosphorus, selected micronutrient, and pH. *Soil Science Society of America Journal*, 50, 177–80.

Schuldenrein, J. 1995: Geochemistry, phosphate fractionation, and the detection of activity areas at prehistoric North American sites. In M. Collins, B. J. Carter, B. G. Gladfelter and R. J. Southard (eds.), *Pedological Perspectives in Archaeological Research*. Special Publication, 44. Madison, WI: Soil Science Society of America, 107–32.

Stein, J. K. 1992: Organic matter in archaeological contexts. In V. T. Holliday (ed.), *Soils in Archaeology*. Washington, DC: Smithsonian Institution Press, 193–216.

—— and Farrand, W. R. (eds.) 1985: *Archaeological Sediments in Context*. Orono, ME: Center for the Study of Early Man, University of Maine.

GARY HUCKLEBERRY

—— and —— (eds.) 2001: *Sediments in Archaeological Context*. Salt Lake City: University of Utah Press.

Taylor, R. E. 1987: *Radiocarbon Dating; An Archaeological Perspective*. New York: Academic Press.

——, Kirner, D. L., Southon, J. R. and Chatters, J. C. 1998: Radiocarbon dates of Kennewick Man. *Science*, 280, 1,171–2.

Terry, R. E., Hardin, P. J., Houston, S. D. et al. 2000: Quantitative phosphorous measurement: a field test procedure for archaeological site analysis at Piedras Negras, Guatemala. *Geoarchaeology: An International Journal*, 15, 151–67.

Thien, S. J. 1979: A flow diagram for teaching texture-by-feel analysis. *Journal of Agronomic Education*, 8, 54–5.

Thomas, D. H. 2000: *Skull Wars: Kennewick Man, Archaeology, and the Battle for Native American Identity*. New York: Basic Books.

US Salinity Laboratory 1954: *Diagnosis and Improvement of Saline and Alkali Soils*. Washington, DC: US Department of Agriculture Handbook, 60.

Vizcaino, A. S. and Canabate, M. L. 1999: Identification of activity areas by soil phosphorus and organic matter analysis in two rooms of the Iberian sanctuary "Cerro El Pajarillo." *Geoarchaeology: An International Journal*, 14, 47–62.

Wakeley, L. D., Murphy, W. L., Dunbar, J. B., Warne, A. G. and Briuer, F. L. 1998: *Geologic, Geoarchaeologic, and Historical Investigations of the Discovery Site of Ancient Remains in Columbia Park, Kennewick, Washington*. US Army Corps of Engineers Technical Report GL-98-13. Vicksburg: Waterways Experiment Station.

Walkley, A. and Black, I. A. 1934: An examination of the Degtjareff method for determining soil organic matter and a proposed modification of the chromic acid titration method. *Soil Science*, 37, 29–38.

Wang, Y., Amundson, R. and Trumbore, S. 1996: Radiocarbon dating of soil organic matter. *Quaternary Research*, 45, 282–8.

Waters, M. R. 1992: *Principles of Geoarchaeology: A North American Perspective*. Tucson: University of Arizona Press.

—— and Ravesloot, J. C. 2001: Landscape change and the cultural evolution of the Hohokam along the Middle Gila River and other river valleys in south-central Arizona. *American Antiquity*, 66, 285–99.

Weide, D. 1966: Soil pH as a guide to archaeological investigations. In *Archaeological Survey Annual Report*. Los Angeles: Department of Anthropology, University of California, 155–63.

Whittig, L. D. and Allardice, W. R. 1986: X-ray diffraction techniques. In A. Klute (ed.), *Methods of Soil Analysis, Part 1: Physical and Mineralogical Methods*, 2nd edn. Madison, WI: Soil Science Society of America, 331–62.

Wood, R. W. and Johnson, D. L. 1978: A survey of disturbance processes in archaeological site formation. In M. B. Schiffer (ed.), *Advances in Archaeological Method and Theory*. New York: Academic Press, 315–70.

Susan Lawrence

13
Artifacts of the Modern World

Introduction

One of the striking things about artifacts from sites of the recent past is their diversity. With the Industrial Revolution and the rise of mass consumption over the past 300 years and more, the archaeological record has extended far beyond the traditional materials of stone, bone, shell, and ceramics. At historical archaeological sites, it is common to find all of these as well as glass, many types of metal, plastic, and often textiles, leather, paper, and timber. What is more, each of these materials can be used in an endless variation of shapes and purposes. In his landmark text *A Guide to the Artifacts of Colonial America*, first published in 1969 (and reissued in 1991), archaeologist Ivor Noel Hume identified no fewer than 44 categories of objects, from "Armour" to "Wig curlers," and if it were to be extended to cover the nineteenth and twentieth centuries, the number would be even higher. Tracing this explosion of available goods and its implications is one of the themes pursued by historical archaeologists, but at the same time the abundance of objects also presents considerable challenges for artifact analysis. It is impossible to develop specialist skills in all types of historic artifacts, although many people will specialize in one material, such as pottery or glass. At the same time, any archaeologist working regularly on historic sites should attempt to achieve a basic familiarity with the most commonly found materials and, just as importantly, with the specialist resources available on the subject.

Of the plethora of goods that the modern world has increasingly made available, those of greatest relevance to archaeologists are generally those that preserve best in the soil or under water. Organic materials, including textiles and even paper, are probably more likely to be found at recent sites than at more ancient sites, but even so they are not terribly common. The most commonly found materials at historical archaeological sites are ceramics (Chapter 8), glass, metal (particularly iron), and bone (Chapter 9). Of these, ceramics, including clay tobacco pipes, and glass have received the greatest attention. Dietary bone has been studied by faunal analysts, but metals have been less studied. The reasons for this imbalance are many. In part, it is due to differences in preservation. Glass and ceramics are fragile while in daily use, but once in the archaeological record are relatively stable. In contrast, metal is durable in daily use but corrodes rapidly once in the ground or under water, and it can be very difficult to identify, let alone fully record, many metal artifacts. Another reason for the attention given to glass and ceramics is a perception about the way in which tablewares, bottles, buttons, clay tobacco pipes, trade beads, and so on encode information. Because of the way objects made from these materials are used in daily life, and because of their plasticity and amenability to decoration, they carry information about a wide range of subjects of interest to archaeologists, such as trade, status, gender, technological change, beliefs, and ideology.

Another aspect about most artifacts found at historical archaeological sites is that at some level there will be associated written documents. These documents might include things such as price lists, advertisements, patent information, or manufacturing instructions, that provide information about the companies or people who made the items, when and where they were made, how they were made, and how much they cost to make. Documents such as maps, title deeds, council rate books, census returns, and newspapers might also provide information about when the archaeological site was occupied and by whom. All of this information means that for an historical archaeologist it is often easier to identify artifacts, and to establish where and when they were made and how they were commonly used, than it would be for an archaeologist working on older sites. Historiographical studies of the relevant culture are another source of valuable information that assists historical archaeologists with analyzing and interpreting the artifacts that they find, and with testing hypotheses that the artifact patterns suggest. It is only because Diana diZerega Wall knew a great deal about the history of New York and of nineteenth-century families that she was able to interpret the ceramics that she studied as evidence of middle-class domestic ideology (Wall 1994). To adequately take advantage of this information the historical archaeologist must be familiar with its existence and where to find it, and must know its strengths and limitations. It is also necessary for someone to have already taken the time to study and synthesize the documentary information so that it is accessible to archaeologists. For example, even though many nineteenth-century ceramics have the manufacturer's name on the base, it would be very difficult and time-consuming for archaeologists to identify the age and origins of a dish without works such as Geoffrey Godden's *Encyclopaedia of British Pottery and Porcelain Marks* (Godden 1991).

There are several aims to this chapter. The first is to review some of the basic principles in cataloging historical artifacts. The second is to introduce some of the major categories of artifacts found at historical archaeological sites, so that initial identifications can be made. These categories include domestic ceramics and glass, building materials, and, more briefly, clay tobacco pipes, beads and buttons, glass tools, firearms, and metal containers. However, as this introduction can be no more than cursory, the third aim is to provide a guide to the most helpful literature on those categories, so that further guidance can be sought. A fourth aim is to introduce some of the methods used by historical archaeologists for quantifying and analyzing artifact information.

Cataloging Artifacts

The reporting of artifacts from an excavation is a multi-stage process, of which cataloging, or the description of the attributes of the individual artifacts, is only the first step. Subsequent stages of analysis and interpretation are of equal importance in the documentation process. The cataloging process is essentially a descriptive one, in which a series of observed variables are noted, identified, and recorded. The artifact catalog can be created on paper and later transferred to an electronic database, or it may be recorded electronically in the first instance. It will never be possible to envision or fully record all the variables that another archaeologist might want to analyze, but a good catalog will provide enough information to enable others to know what artifact is being described without having to have the actual artifact in front of them. All artifact cataloging depends on the ability to recognize and interpret artifacts and their attributes, and this comes only with training and experience.

An artifact catalog is a record of the attributes of an artifact relevant to the dimensions of space, form, and time. Space – or which site, and where on the site, the artifact came from – is the most crucial variable for archaeologists, and must be recorded both in the catalog and on the label accompanying the artifact. Form can be further broken down into attributes such as shape, size, weight, color, material, pattern, and manufacturing technique. Information about most of these attributes can be obtained by observation and measurement of the artifact. Time, or the age of the artifact, can often be determined with reference to the variable of form, because often one or more of the attributes will vary with time as technology or fashion changes. Finally, the quantity of artifact fragments should be recorded.

In addition to the formal attributes already discussed, historical artifacts are often classified according to functional attributes based on assumptions made about how they were used. It is common in most site reports, for example, to find artifacts grouped into categories such as *Domestic*, *Architectural*, and *Personal*, and these categories will include a range of material types. *Domestic* usually includes materials used in the home, such as glass bottles, ceramic tablewares, and bone and metal cutlery, for example; while *Architectural* items are used in constructing buildings and might include ceramic bricks, plaster, wallpaper, iron nails, and window glass. Most functional classification systems are based on the work of Stanley South, who advocated the use of functional classification in order to facilitate pattern recognition on sites (South 1977). This included the identification of site-specific activities and activity areas within sites, and the comparison of different sites. One problem with a rigid functional

SUSAN LAWRENCE

classification is that it assumes that artifacts were only used for one purpose, and that this was the purpose for which the item was originally manufactured. The reuse of a beer bottle to contain jam, or the use of buttons as gaming pieces, is difficult to accommodate in such a system. Functional analyses also tend to inhibit the recognition of temporal variability within an assemblage, compressing the entire occupation of a site into a single distribution (Orser 1989). Despite these limitations, functional classification is a valuable adjunct to formal classification, because it acknowledges that there is some degree of familiarity with the use of recent artifacts, and utilizes this familiarity to facilitate interpretation. An *Architectural* category that groups nails and bricks is often more meaningful than a *Ceramic* category that groups bricks and clay tobacco pipes, despite the potential for some misattributions. Most cataloging systems will use some combination of formal and functional attributes.

Domestic Ceramics

Pottery sherds are commonly found at historical sites. They can reveal information about chronology, diet, trade, status, ethnicity, and a variety of other aspects of the site and its occupants. For these reasons, there has been extensive research on historical ceramics by both archaeologists and collectors. Ware-type, decoration, and form are the attributes most frequently used by archaeologists to form the basis for analysis.

Until the end of the eighteenth century, there were three main ceramic bodies or ware-types: *earthenware, stoneware,* and *porcelain* (Miller 1980: 1). *Earthenware* was the most ubiquitous, manufactured by both local craftspeople and larger factory centers. It is comprised of clay that may be either coarse or refined, but that is fired at a comparatively low temperature, between 900 and 1,150°C (1,650–2,100°F). Clay does not vitrify at these temperatures and as a result unglazed earthenwares remain porous and permeable to liquids. If impermeability is required, some form of vitreous glaze must be applied to the vessel's surface before firing. Coarse earthenwares tend to be made from unrefined local clays, and have higher grit content and more variable grain size than do refined earthenwares. Refined earthenwares are made from finely sifted clay that may also contain a blend of clays from local and distant sources. Although many coarse earthenwares are red or ochre in color while refined earthenwares are generally paler or even white, color is not a good guide to determining whether or not the fabric is refined. In the post-medieval period, lead glazes in black, purple, green, and yellow were often used over fine red earthenware bodies, while tin produced an opaque white glaze known variously as *majolica, faience,* or *delftware.* Tin-glazed wares were often hand-painted in either blue or polychrome designs and were highly desirable because of their resemblance to fine porcelains.

A variety of earthenware called *colonoware* is sometimes found at sites in parts of the southern United States, where it appears to have been produced between the late seventeenth and nineteenth centuries. Colonoware was handmade using local clays, and was most commonly shaped into open forms such as bowls and jars. It was originally associated with Native Americans, but it is now clear that African-Americans also manufactured colonoware. Decorative motifs often feature African symbols and designs, and both design and associated foodways are increasingly the subject of study (Ferguson 1991; Mouer et al. 1999).

Stoneware bodies are the result of firing at higher temperatures, around 1,200–1,300°C (2,190–2,370°F), so that the clays are vitrified and impermeable to liquids without requiring a glaze. Many stoneware vessels are given a salt glaze, which produces a glossy transparent finish with a texture like that of an orange peel. Because of its superior strength and durability, stoneware has often been used for jugs and bottles to store and transport liquids such as gin and beer, and more recently for water and sewage pipes. During the second half of the eighteenth century, potteries in Staffordshire, England, also produced table- and tea-wares made from high-quality, white, salt-glazed stoneware.

Porcelain, which was first made in China between the second and third centuries AD, is the most refined and highly fired ceramic body. Porcelain is made of fine white ball clay or kaolin combined with feldspar, fired at 1,250–1,400°C (2,280–2,550°F), and may be glazed or unglazed. Commonly used for table- and tea-wares, porcelain is frequently decorated with either underglaze or overglaze hand-painted designs. When underglazed, the decoration is usually blue, because the cobalt ink is able to withstand the high firing temperature. Overglaze designs may be in other colors, and sometimes include gilding and enameling. Chinese export porcelain was made in China specifically for the export market, and although decorated with Asian designs was made in European forms. Other porcelain was made for domestic consumption within China and includes forms such as tea and rice bowls, sauce dishes, and spoons (Sando & Felton 1993). These may be decorated with underglaze patterns such as "Bamboo" or "Double Happiness," or in a solid mint-green called *Celadon*. Such wares were widely used by Chinese migrants to Australasia and North America in the nineteenth and twentieth centuries.

From the late eighteenth century, manufacturers in Staffordshire began to perfect the mass production of refined, light-bodied earthenwares that were able to successfully compete with export porcelain as well as to dominate the market for everyday wares (Miller 1980, 1991). The first of these was *creamware*, or "CC ware," so-called because of the pale color of the body, which needed only a transparent glaze. First marketed from the 1740s, it was initially very expensive but was later replaced in popularity by other wares, such as pearlware and then whiteware. Although the color of the body lightened gradually over time and was no longer cream colored, creamware continued to be made through the nineteenth century as inexpensive, undecorated table, kitchen, and hygienic wares. *Pearlware*, which was introduced in the 1770s, has a slightly lighter body and a bluer tinge to the glaze, and was made to deliberately imitate porcelain's blue-and-white colors. From the 1820s and 1830s, there was a gradual transition to whiteware as the blue tint in the glaze was reduced.

SUSAN LAWRENCE

Two introductions in the early nineteenth century were *ironstone* and *bone china*, both of which were European imitations of porcelain (Majewski & O'Brien 1987: 120–9). Ironstone is a further development of whiteware earthenware bodies, made of kaolin and flint but with a denser, more vitreous body than earthenware. Bone china is a soft-paste porcelain that was first made by British manufacturers from a combination of kaolin and ground animal bone. The result is a light vitreous body with a slightly creamy tint. Although both ironstone and bone china were first marketed around 1800, they achieved their greatest popularity in the second half of the nineteenth century.

All of these bodies could be decorated using a variety of techniques. While some archaeologists advocate classification of eighteenth- and nineteenth-century ceramics on the basis of technical analysis of the body (Majewski & O'Brien 1987: 106), others (Miller 1980: 80) argue that as the distinction between bodies becomes increasingly slight and subjective it is more useful to classify on the basis of decoration. Hand-painted designs can be applied either overglaze, as on the tin-glazed earthenwares, or underglaze, as on porcelains and later light-bodied earthenwares, where a clear glaze is used. Underglaze decoration must be done with colors that are able to withstand high firing temperatures, and for this reason cobalt blue was initially the most common underglaze color. Overglaze designs were able to make use of a wider range of colors, but can have a tendency to wear off through repeated use, although bright enameled colors can also be fired on overglaze.

Transfer-printing has been a popular form of decoration on light-bodied refined earthenwares, but is also used on ironstone and bone china. First introduced in the 1780s, it became widespread in the nineteenth century. Transfer-printing involves the production of an engraving on a copper plate, which is then inked and transferred to paper and thence to the once-fired vessel. The vessel is then given a clear glaze and fired a second time. Because of the versatility of the engraving process, highly detailed and complex designs could be reproduced quickly and accurately. Asian-inspired designs, of which "Blue Willow" is the best known, were popular in the early nineteenth century, while later motifs included floral, gothic, and classical themes (Samford 1997). Blue has always been the most popular color, but green, brown, and purple were introduced in the 1820s and 1830s and other colors followed (Miller 2000). *Flow blue* is a variation of transfer-printing in which ingredients are added to the clear glaze in order to make the transferred design blur and run. This was particularly popular in the 1830s and 1840s, but continued to be marketed until the end of the nineteenth century.

Manufacturers sometimes recorded their name and/or the name of the pattern in a separate transfer on the base of the vessel called a *maker's mark*, and this information can be used to identify the maker and when the item was made. From 1842, makers' marks often included a *registration diamond*, a shape that encoded patent information about the design. Geoffrey Godden (1991) has compiled extensive information on British makers' marks, while Coysh and Henrywood (1982, 1989), Samford (1997), and Sussman (1979) are among the most useful references for identifying transfer-printed patterns.

Industrial or factory-made slipware is the name given to a series of decorative techniques used on light-bodied refined earthenwares, especially pearlwares, that were most popular in the early nineteenth century (Sussman 1997). Once-fired vessels were dipped in colored slips (a liquid clay) to produce bands, or slips were applied to the surface using a variety of techniques that resulted in colorful abstract designs. One of the best known is "mocha," a leaf-like pattern achieved by placing a drop of colored acidic slip on a contrasting alkali band. This was the cheapest form of decoration available on hollow utilitarian vessels such as mugs, jugs, and bowls.

Molded decoration was popular on refined salt-glazed stoneware plates and from the 1850s on ironstone bodies, which were marketed specifically for the USA as "white granite" (Ewins 1997). In both of these cases, clear glazes were used and molding was the only decoration. While extremely popular in the USA, white granite never achieved the same success in other English-speaking countries (Lawrence 2003). By the end of the nineteenth century, decal decoration had become popular for ironstones, whitewares, and bone china. Similar to transfer-printing, this involved the application of a colored decal (a design printed on paper or film) over a glaze. These were available in bright colors and could be produced as polychrome designs. Gold or silver gilt, widely available from 1870, was used with decals or on its own on molded vessels of ironstone or bone china.

Clay Tobacco Pipes

Before ready-made cigarettes were popularized in the early twentieth century, tobacco was usually smoked in pipes made of unglazed fine white ball clay or kaolin. They were made in molds and were easily decorated with ornamental designs or political slogans, which were included in the molds. Manufacturers' marks were also sometimes stamped on the pipes, providing information on dating and trade networks. Clay pipes were also fragile and broke relatively easily, so they are frequently found at archaeological sites and are a valuable source of information for dating and about ethnic, political, and cultural affiliations. Most clay pipes found at New World and Australasian sites were imported from Great Britain, where there were important manufacturing centers in Bristol, Glasgow, Edinburgh, Liverpool, London, and elsewhere, but Holland and France also had industries that exported to the colonies (Walker 1977; Davey 1979–).

Tobacco smoking was introduced to Europe from the Americas in the late sixteenth century. The pipes used at that time were characterized by small, bulbous bowls with a large obtuse angle between stem and bowl, and a large bore diameter. Tobacco was rare and expensive at this time and was taken only in small amounts. The large bore diameter and the short stem allowed a large quantity of smoke to be swallowed in gulps, and pipes were said to be "drunk" rather than smoked. Over time, tobacco-growing in the USA became a major industry and tobacco itself became cheaper, so bowl sizes increased to accommodate a longer smoke. The size of the stem bore also diminished, further slowing the time taken to smoke a pipe of tobacco. Seventeenth-century pipes had little or no decoration with the exception of occasional makers' marks or rouletting around the rim.

In the eighteenth century, as the bowl increased in size and the bore diameter shrank, the angle between stem and bowl became more upright and less obtuse. Small spurs on the base of the bowl became more common, as did manufacturers' initials molded onto the bowl. Decoration became fuller and more elaborate in the nineteenth century and manufacturers often mold-impressed their initials or names in the stem. Manufacturers also began to dip mouthpieces in either a lead glaze or wax to provide a more comfortable grip.

Archaeologists were quick to recognize the dating potential of the changes in bowl shape and bore diameter, with Adrian Oswald publishing a guide to the former in 1961 (Oswald 1961). J. C. Harrington published a system for dating stem fragments by the bore diameter in 1954 (Harrington 1978), and in 1961 Lewis Binford refined this by devising a regression formula that could be used to calculate a mean date of occupation for the site by measuring an entire assemblage of stem fragments (Binford 1978). If the trend in decreasing size had continued, the bore would have disappeared altogether by the 1830s – instead, bore size reaches a minimum dimension by the late eighteenth century. For this reason, the Harrington/Binford method for dating assemblages is useful only on pre-1800 sites and is not used at all in Australia and New Zealand. Further, it applies only to pipes of English manufacture, and if Dutch or French pipes are also present in the assemblage the results can be misleading.

Aside from using pipes for dating purposes, patterns on the pipe bowls may provide insight into cultural or political affiliations of the smokers at a site. Masonic designs became popular motifs as the popularity of that organization increased, and Bradley notes that such designs at military sites reflect its place in British military life by the early 1800s (Bradley 2000: 113). Excavations at a former sailors' home in Sydney, Australia, produced a large assemblage of pipes with Irish motifs, which Gojak has attributed to the presence of Irish sailors during a period of intense sectarian violence in the 1860s and 1870s (Gojak 1995).

Usewear patterns can also be an important guide to behavior on the site (Bradley 2000). Some mouthpieces may have tooth marks that reflect the habits of the individual owner, such as holding the pipe upside-down in the mouth or twirling it around. Broken stems may also have tooth marks or show other signs of reworking that indicate that the pipe was reused after the stem broke. Some stems have score marks, suggesting that the stem may have been deliberately shortened. Reuse may be related to poverty, but may also be associated with limited access to new pipes, particularly at isolated rural sites (Gojak & Stuart 1999: 40). Gray or black staining on the interior of the bowl is evidence of the pipe having been smoked, with the intensity of the discoloration being directly related to the degree of smoking. However, such stains can be removed with washing, so care must be taken with post-excavation processing.

While most clay tobacco pipes are in this European tradition, there are two significant exceptions. The first is the opium pipe, which is usually associated with Overseas Chinese sites (Wylie & Fike 1993). These pipes, or more properly pipe bowls, are made from refined red clay that is unglazed but polished. The bowls are round and 2–3 cm in diameter, but flattened and almost fully enclosed, with only a small hole in the center of the top. They are often molded to resemble the head of a poppy. The clay bowl was fixed to the top of a wooden or bamboo stem, which had a brass mouthpiece, and the bowl had a hole on the base for attachment to the stem. The second non-European clay pipe is a style associated with African-Americans in the southern part of the USA, and particularly around the Chesapeake (Emerson 1999). These tobacco pipes are made of local orange and brown clays, and while either hand- or mold-made, exhibit great variety in form. They are decorated with representational and stylistic motifs, some showing African influences, which are incised, cut, or stamped into the clay.

Bottle Glass Glass is a combination of silica, soda or potash, and lime that has been melted at high temperature and then molded into a variety of shapes. It can be used in windows, to make beads, buttons, jewelry, figurines, tablewares, light fittings, and numerous other applications, but it is most commonly found on historical archaeological sites as bottle glass. Glass is very brittle and fragile, so that it breaks easily, but once in the ground it can be very durable. Over long periods of burial, it is susceptible to decay due to exposure to moisture in the soil or under water. This causes the surface of the glass to break down, first taking on an iridescent sheen known as *patination*, and then flaking off.

Glass can be made in a range of colors, from colorless to dark, nearly black, olive green (Jones et al. 1989: 13–14). This is the result of minerals and colorants present naturally in the silica source or added (or sometimes subtracted) from the mix. The most common color for bottle glass prior to the twentieth century was dark olive green, the result of iron impurities present in the silica. Colorless glass is made by refining the silica source and removing those impurities. Crystal is produced from ground flint or fine lead rather than sand. Some colorless glass takes on a purple tint when exposed to sunlight for long periods. This is because manganese was added to enhance the clarity of the glass. As this practice was followed only between 1890 and 1916, amethyst glass can be dated quite securely. Other colors were produced by adding other minerals: gold to make red or "cranberry" glass, cobalt to make blue glass, copper to make emerald green glass, carbon to make brown glass, and tin or zinc to make opaque white "milk" glass. Aqua-colored glass is partially refined

SUSAN LAWRENCE

and has had some, but not all, of the original impurities removed. It was particularly common in the nineteenth and early twentieth centuries.

Glass was first made in Mesopotamia around 1700 BC, and was initially used only for high-status goods such as jewelry, beads, and small vials. By 300 BC, the techniques of blowing glass bottles using a blowpipe had been developed in Syria, a technique that remained virtually unchanged until the seventeenth century. Until full mechanization of the manufacturing process, bottles were made by blowing the base and body first, then removing the blowpipe to form the neck and mouth. For this reason, the neck and mouth are commonly referred to as the *finish*. Free-blown bottles made in this way exhibit considerable variation in shape and size and will not be perfectly symmetrical. They were also expensive, because each was made entirely by hand by an individual craftsman. By the eighteenth century, many bottles were made by using a blowpipe to blow the glass into a mold. This made bottle manufacture more rapid and less expensive, and also had the effect of making the bottles more uniform in size and shape. Rapid changes in manufacturing technology through the nineteenth century, culminating in fully automated bottle production in the early twentieth century, mean that bottles from this period can be used effectively for dating purposes.

Different ways of manufacturing bottles leave distinctive markings on the bottles themselves. Familiarity with the common markings facilitates identification of the technology and thus the date range during which the bottle was made. All of these technologies were adopted gradually after their initial introduction, so there will be some time lag before all bottles can be confidently assumed to have been made in the new way. The standard texts on glass manufacture are those by Olive Jones and her colleagues at Parks Canada (Jones & Smith 1985; Jones 1986; Jones et al. 1989) and by James Boow in New South Wales (Boow 1992).

Free-blown bottles are asymmetrical and irregular in shape and size. Mold-blown bottles are more regular and usually have one or more seams from the molding process. Dip-molds are essentially cups that taper outward from the base to an open mouth, and they were used to form the base of the bottle. Dip-mold bottles will have a seam running horizontally around the shoulder of the bottle parallel to the top of the dip-mold. Some will also have two additional seams running vertically up the shoulders to the finish. These bottles were made in a three-piece dip-mold, a cup with two hinged sections attached to form the shoulders, and molds of this kind were used from around 1820 to 1920. Two-piece molds were hinged at the base and fit together around the sides of the bottle. Bottles made in two-piece molds have seams that run across the base and up each side of the bottle, essentially dividing it into two mirror-image halves. Both two-piece and three-piece molds could be used with a separate baseplate, a disk that fitted into the bottom of the mold and leaves an additional seam around the heel. Patented by the H. Ricketts Company in 1821, this baseplate could be stamped with lettering around the circumference. Whether made in a mold or free-blown, handmade bottles often have a kick-up or push-up on the base, where the center of the base has been pushed upward into the interior of the bottle. This was primarily to make the base more stable when the bottle was upright, and the different shapes and tools used to make them are discussed in Jones (1991) and Jones et al. (1989).

Not all mold-made bottles will have seams, as evidence of the seams could be removed by turning the bottle in the mold. Mold-made bottles sometimes display *whittle marks* as well as seams. Whittle marks are a dimpling of the glass surface that gives an orange-peel appearance. They are caused by the contact between the hot glass and the cold iron molds.

When the bottle was detached from the blowpipe, it was held with a *pontil rod* (Jones 1991). This was a solid iron rod that was usually fixed to the base of the bottle with a small glob of glass. When the bottle was completed the rod was snapped off, frequently leaving a patch of roughened glass or pontil scar on the base. In the 1840s, a new method of holding the bottles during finishing was developed and bottles made from that time on do not display pontil scars. The new method was called a *sabot* or *snap case*, an iron cradle that either held the bottle around the middle or supported the bottle from beneath.

While molds made bottle bases symmetrical and faster to produce, finishes were still done by hand and were irregular until the 1840s. Once the blowpipe was removed, the finish was formed by adding a ring of glass to the neck and shaping it to form a smooth rim that took a cork. A rough, irregular seam can usually be detected where the extra ring of glass was added to the neck. *Finishing tools*, developed in the 1840s, had a central rod that fitted into the bore and three attached sections that clamped down over the outside of the neck and rim, producing a smooth, regular finish. Bottles made with finishing tools will generally have striations around the circumference of the rim, due to rotation of the finishing tool around the bottle.

In 1903, Michael Owens patented a machine that completely automated bottle production (Miller & Sullivan 1984). It was also based on the use of molds, but made the finish of the bottle first and then the base. The seams left by this process are quite different to those on mold-blown bottles, and machine-made bottles are readily distinguishable. Two separate molds were used, one for the finish and one for the body and base. The second mold obscured the seams from the first mold, so that bottles will have a faint wavy *ghost seam* running parallel to the more obvious one. Because the finish is also made in a mold, the seams on a machine-made bottle run right up the neck and finish, rather than stopping at the neck as on mold-blown bottles. There will also be several horizontal seam lines on the finish, but no indication of extra glass being added.

Many different types of closures, or ways of sealing bottles, were also used in the nineteenth century and can similarly be used to date bottles. The most common kind was a simple cork, sometimes held down with wire or string. There are numerous variations to the shape of the ridge placed on the finish for the attachment of the wire, which are discussed most fully in Jones et al. (1989). Other types of closures were used primarily with the aerated soda waters and soft drinks that became increasingly popular in the second half of the century. Boow (1992: 117) provides a summary of when the different forms were in use in Australia. The first bottle designed specifically for aerated waters was the Hamilton patent of 1809, an egg-shaped bottle intended to be stored on its side so that the cork seal would not dry out, allowing the carbonation to escape. In 1845 this design was refined in the Maugham patent, in which the sides were flattened for more efficient packing and a rounded base was substituted for the pointed Hamilton base, resulting in a torpedo-shaped bottle. *Codd bottles* and their variations are common in Australasia and Britain. These bottles have a flat base and are sealed with a marble held against a rubber gasket by the pressure of the gas. A series of dimples around the neck, body, or base kept the marble from falling into the opening during pouring. Lightning stoppers, an externally fixed spring also used on jars, were invented in 1875. Internal screws were invented in 1880 and external screws in 1885. Crown seals, which effectively replaced most of these closures, were patented in 1892.

Glass bottles in different colors and shapes were intended to hold different kinds of liquids. The most commonly found bottles are the cylindrical olive green bottles intended for beer and wine. Glass of a similar color was used to make case bottles, also sometimes referred to as gin bottles because they were originally manufactured in the Low Countries (Europe) for bottling gin. The sides of case bottles have been flattened during manufacture, producing square bottles that fit more readily in packing cases. Soda water bottles are essentially cylindrical but have distinctive shapes and closures, as discussed above, and are usually made from thick aqua-colored glass. Medicine bottles and condiment bottles were also made from aqua or colorless glass, but this glass was much thinner. Condiment bottles are usually cylindrical, and those intended for olive oil, vinegar, and salad oil are only a few centimeters in diameter at the base and have long, narrow necks, sometimes with molded patterns on the sides. Bottles intended for sauces such as "HP Sauce" and tomato sauce, or ketchup, as well as those for pickles, may be round or square and have a larger-diameter base as well as wider mouths, and are also often decorated.

Bottles for proprietary or patent medicines and for chemists' preparations are usually rectangular and may have lettered panels on the sides or base (Fike 1987). They were frequently made in a two-piece mold and sealed with a glass stopper. In the late nineteenth century, patent medicines were popular curealls and a common, and less expensive, alternative to seeing a doctor. The concoctions often had high alcohol content and could include narcotics such as opium. They came under increased scrutiny in the twentieth century and were gradually banned. Well-known brands included "Parry Davis Vegetable Pain Killer," "Mrs. Winslow's Soothing Syrup," and "Dr. Morse's Indian Root Pills." Not all bottles were made of glass, however. As discussed in the preceding section on domestic ceramics, containers for some products, particularly aerated soft drinks, beer, ink, and blacking, were made from stoneware, while toothpaste and cosmetics were frequently packaged in porcelain jars.

Although distinctive shapes and colors are associated with particular products, it cannot be assumed that bottles were always used for the same purpose for which they were intended, and it is preferable to catalog bottles on the basis of form rather than function. Until the development of machine production, bottles were expensive commodities in their own right, and there is extensive evidence that they were reused and recycled many times before they were discarded (Busch 1987). The most straightforward reuse was when the bottles were collected, washed, and refilled with the original product, a practice that led to bottlers molding their names on the bottles and to complex networks of bottle collectors. Often, however, bottles were refilled with entirely different products. Empty bottles were imported into the Australian colonies to be filled with alcohol shipped in bulk (Morgan 1991), and even when wine and beer were imported in bottles, analysis of sealed bottles recovered from ship-wreck sites indicates that the contents were often quite different to what the shape of the bottle would suggest (Peters 1997). Beer and wine bottles were also collected by cordial makers for the bottling of their nonalcoholic products (Carney 1999). In addition to the potential for reuse, bottles were recycled in a variety of ways. A common practice in the early twentieth century was to remove the neck and finish of bottles and fill the base with home-made jams and preserves, sealing the top with wax (Stuart 1993). Bottles were used to line pathways, garden beds, and even cemetery plots (Burley 1995; Adams 2002), while people also used bottles as a source of raw material for the equivalent of stone tools (Allen 1973).

Glass Tools Bottle glass was virtually ubiquitous after European contact and made an excellent raw material for tool manufacture. It was readily available, broke easily, and produced a sharp edge. For Aboriginal and Native American people, it was used in addition to stone tools, while for African-Americans it replaced prohibitively expensive steel-bladed implements such as pocketknives and razor blades (Wilkie 1996: 45; Harrison 2000). Archaeologists have only recently begun to seriously investigate artifacts of this kind, and much work remains to be done. For example, the identification of deliberate fracture patterns has been complicated by the ease with which glass breaks accidentally. Problems such as this will only be resolved with the application of lithic analysis techniques, including residue and usewear analysis, and the testing of glass breakage patterns under a variety of controlled conditions.

When glass tools may be present, care should be taken in handling broken edges so that residues are not compromised. Recording should include information about the original form (e.g., bottle shape, color, manufacture, age, and lettering) and about the tool itself. The latter should include the portion of

SUSAN LAWRENCE

bottle used, the orientation of flaking on the bottle, platform preparation and flake scar size, and whether the worked surface was on the interior or exterior of the bottle.

Glass beads are found in a variety of archaeological contexts because they not only preserve well but also were used to adorn a variety of other objects, from clothing and jewelry to household items such as lace-making bobbins and lamp-shades, and to religious items such as rosaries. In North America they were an important part of trading systems between Europeans and Native Americans, and as a result considerable research has been done on trade beads in particular (Karklins & Sprague 1980; Sprague 2000). Although other materials, including clay, stone, bone, and shell, have been used to make beads, glass beads preserve best in the archaeological record. Glass beads are usually either blown or wound around a wire core, and can be monochrome or polychrome, clear, opaque, or patterned. Beads can be used to trace changes in trade patterns, costume, and religion. As some colors have specific meanings in different cultures, bead color can hint at symbolism and belief systems. Blue beads, for example, may have a special significance at African-American sites (Stine et al. 2000).

Beads and Buttons

Like beads, buttons too can be made from many materials, and used for many things, including clothing, footwear, and furniture. Bone, shell, wood, horn, metal, glass, ceramic, fabric, and, from the twentieth century, plastic, are the most common materials (Lindbergh 1999). Buttons are attached to the cloth either by sewing through the face of the button itself or via a loop or shank on the back of the button. Buttons made of bone, shell, wood, and horn were made by cutting out a circular disk, then drilling up to five holes through the surface, and then polishing. These buttons were often turned on a lathe, which may leave striations on the face, and buttons may also have a partially or completely drilled through central hole that was formed from the pin used to hold the button in place while the holes were being drilled. Glass, ceramic, and metal buttons were made in molds, while metal buttons could also be stamped. Some shanked buttons were covered with fabric, which occasionally survives in fragments around the edges. The diameter of buttons is measured in *lines*, from the French *ligne*, equivalent to 40 lines to 1 inch or 25 mm. Smaller buttons were used for undergarments and shirts, while larger ones were used for trousers and overcoats. Buttons are often recovered from cemetery excavations, where they can suggest the clothing of the deceased, and from areas where clothing was made or repaired. Glass and ceramic buttons were made in large quantities from the eighteenth and nineteenth centuries, while shell buttons were also mass-produced in the nineteenth century.

From the nineteenth century onward, many consumer goods were packaged in metal containers, including food and beverages, matches, tobacco, and kerosene.

Metal Containers

Although these do not generally survive well archaeologically, in arid or cold conditions archaeologists have found that tins too have much to reveal about the past. The process of preserving food by heating it in a sealed container was invented by Frenchman Nicholas Appert in 1812 (Farrer 1980: 33). Appert used glass jars, but this was soon superseded by the use of tin-plated iron or steel cans developed in England, and the British military was regularly using tinned foods by the second decade of the nineteenth century. The first commercial canning in the USA began in 1819 and glass was also used initially, with tin not adopted until 1839 (Busch 1981: 96). Tinned food was particularly popular among gold miners and others in remote locations, who needed to store provisions for long periods of time.

Changes in the technology of making and sealing metal food tins assist with dating. In the first tins, all edges overlapped and were soldered inside and out. Sometimes food was inserted before the lid was soldered on, but more commonly the lid was added first and the food inserted through a 1-inch hole. The cap used to seal the hole itself had a tiny hole through which steam escaped during processing, and which was then sealed with a drop of solder, giving the name *hole-in-cap* tin. The *sanitary can* had replaced this design by the end of the nineteenth century. Sanitary cans had locked end and side seams, which were soldered on the outside only, and the food was inserted before the ends were sealed. Steel replaced iron as the basis for tin plate from 1875.

Most food cans had paper labels, which seldom survive, but occasionally shape can be some guide to contents. Seafood was and is canned in shallow, oblong tins, while some meats are tinned in tapered containers so that the contents can be removed in one piece. The tins of nonfood products such as tobacco and matches frequently had lithographed or impressed labels, which may survive and provide additional dating information (Anson 1983).

Firearms   Archaeologists may encounter a variety of artifacts associated with firearms, including gun parts, ammunition, and gunflints. Flintlock guns, used in the eighteenth and early nineteenth centuries, held a stone, or flint, that was used to strike a spark. The spark then fell into and ignited gunpowder in a pan, which fired the shot (Noel Hume 1991: 212). Most gunflints used prior to 1800 are the honey-colored stones of French origin, while from 1790 the black flints of the Braddon, Suffolk, industry predominate (Kenmotsu 1991: 199). Both types are based on blade technology and the striking of blades from a prepared core. The heels of French flints have been retouched into a "d-shape," while English flints are unmodified. Flintlock guns generally fired round lead balls of various sizes, which could be purchased or made up by gun-owners, who cast lead in molds. Shot, molds, and the lead waste, or sprue, may all be found on site. From the 1870s, cartridges that combined powder and bullet within a single brass casing rendered flintlocks obsolete. Cartridges were usually mass-produced and sometimes have manufacturing information stamped on the base, which can assist with dating.

Using a combination of archaeology, forensics, and metal detecting, archaeologists Richard Fox and Douglas Scott (1991) had considerable success in analyzing troop movements at the site of General George Armstrong Custer's battle with the Sioux in Montana in 1876. Cartridges, bullets, and other metal objects were located using metal detectors, then mapped and recovered. Forensic specialist studied the distinctive marks left on the expended cartridges and were able to identify and track the movement of individual guns during the battle. Fox and Scott were able to demonstrate that the Sioux had both more and better weapons than the US Cavalry, which contributed to their victory.

The most common category of artifact on historical archaeological sites is generally that of building materials, which includes artifacts such as nails, door hardware, bricks, plaster, mortar, timber, building stone, corrugated iron sheeting, and window glass. While it is important to know something about these materials when processing finds from an excavation, some understanding of building materials is also invaluable when carrying out nonintrusive surveys of standing structures or ruins. Likewise, it is useful to understand something of the variety of building methods used (Lewis 1977). Common timber building methods include split slab, balloon frame, siding, and the horizontal laying of logs. Stone could be utilized as uncut cobbles laid with or without regular coursing, or as cut ashlar blocks. Mud bricks (*adobe*), rammed earth (*pisé*), cut sods, and wattle-and-daub are all common techniques using earth. The materials could be used in combination as well, such as in the infilling of timber frames with stone, brick, earth, sheet iron, canvas, or even fur.

The kind of material chosen and the methods used are often part of vernacular traditions, and can be very sensitive to geography and the ethnicity of the builders. In much of eastern North America timber construction predominates, while in the Southwest and on the prairies, where trees were rare, sod and adobe were used. In colonial Australia bricks were often used, because clay soils were widespread and bricks could often be made at the construction site. Although methods of manufacturing bricks remained unchanged for centuries, the development of mechanical production in the late nineteenth century means that bricks can often be used to distinguish more recently built structures from earlier ones. Traditionally, bricks were made by hand, by shaping a mixture of wet clay and sand or grit in individual wooden molds (Gemmell 1986: 18–20). The bricks were then stacked in rows or hacks and allowed to dry. Once dry, the bricks were fired in clamps, earth-covered mounds of brick and fuel. The entire process was carried on in the open air, which meant that it was vulnerable to weather conditions, as rain at the wrong time could ruin bricks in hacks or during firing. At permanent brickworks, hacks were usually built within open-sided sheds while enclosed kilns were built for firing.

Building Materials

Handmade or sandstock bricks have a number of distinctive characteristics. The matrix of the brick itself will often include a range of grain sizes and even small pebbles, due to the use of unrefined clay and grit sources. Sand or grit in the mold can leave striations on the surface of the brick, and thumb- or fingerprints may also occasionally be seen. The brick-maker deliberately added these as tally-marks so that the day's production could be more easily counted. Initials or simple shapes such as hearts or diamonds may be impressed on the face of the brick. Called "frogs," these marks could identify the manufacturer or the owner of the building and were produced by carving a special insert for the base of the mold. Paw-prints on the bricks were accidental additions when animals or birds walked across the drying hacks. Two parallel lines on the narrow or stretcher face of the bricks are the impressions left by other bricks stacked on top in the hacks. Finally, clamp-firing can also leave its mark. Bricks that did not receive sufficient heat, called "doughboys," will be lighter in color and more powdery in texture. Clinker bricks are at the opposite extreme and have had too much heat. They are dark in color and have a shiny, almost glassy surface.

By the 1870s, new technology was introduced that mechanized both the molding and firing processes (Gemmell 1986: 18–25). Steam-driven molding machines extruded long columns of clay that were cut into individual bricks. The extruder and the wire cutters can both leave striations on the brick surface that allow this process to be identified. Although much faster than hand-molding, the high moisture content required to make the clay sufficiently plastic caused problems during firing. Dry presses that relied on extremely high pressure to compress the dry clay were introduced in the 1890s. In this case, the lack of moisture in the bricks meant that steam had to be injected before firing. When it failed to penetrate completely, the result was a sugary, poorly consolidated interior in the bricks. Dry-pressed bricks generally are much denser and heavier than extruded or handmade bricks. Firing was improved with the introduction of Hoffman kilns, patented in Germany in 1859 and in use in Australia and the USA by the 1870s. These were multi-chambered kilns that were continuously fired. Previously, firing took many days to complete as the kiln had to be loaded, then heated up and fired, then cooled down, and then unloaded. In Hoffman kilns, the heat source was directed in turn through several adjacent chambers as the flame moved in a continuous circuit around the kiln. As one chamber was being fired, another could be loaded and a third unloaded. Automatic firing does not leave identifying marks on the bricks, but as it was so much more efficient it quickly dominated the market.

Whereas bricks will normally be recorded and sampled on excavations, nails often form a large part of the artifact assemblage, particularly if the site includes demolition deposits. However, depending on preservation conditions, the iron will often have corroded badly, making detailed identification and recording impossible. Copper nails, used in boat-building, survive much better in the

SUSAN LAWRENCE

archaeological record and are more readily analyzed (McCarthy 1983). The earliest iron nails were wrought nails made by hand. From the sixteenth century, British iron foundries produced nail rods, squared lengths of iron the diameter of the nail, These were cut by hand into the desired length, and tips and heads shaped to form the finished nails (Bodey 1983: 14). By the eighteenth century, shaping nails from the precut rods was a cottage industry that employed whole families. As the process was relatively simple and required only a small forge and anvil, the rods could be shaped into nails virtually anywhere, and both nails and rods were exported overseas (Varman 1980: 2). Wrought nails are generally square in section, with either a wedge-shaped or pyramidal pointed tip and a rose head. Nails known as "Eubanks" are wrought nails in which the cutting, heading, and pointing were done by machine. They have wedge-shaped tips and sharp edges along the shaft where the rods have been sliced.

Cut-nail technology was developed in the USA in the late eighteenth century (Wells 1998: 85). In this process, foundries produced flat sheets of iron, rather than rods, and the nails were sheared off the face of the sheet with the head and tip already shaped. This resulted in nails that were almost two-dimensional in appearance. Wrought nails, particularly Eubanks, were most common in Australia, while cut nails were more common in the USA. Wire nails began to replace both by the second half of the nineteenth century. Like wrought nails, wire nails are cut in lengths from a length of iron, but in this case the iron is circular rather than square in section, and pointing and heading was always done by machine as the length of nail was cut off. Wire nails were available from the 1850s, and some were imported into Australia at this time, but it was not until technology for cheaply producing wire was developed in the 1860s that wire nails were readily produced. By the 1870s they had effectively replaced the wrought nail in Australia, but although they began to be produced in the USA in the 1880s, cut nails continued to be widely used there until the end of the century (Varman 1980: 4; Wells 1998: 86–96).

Window glass is the final building material to be considered here. Flat glass for windows was originally made by the Crown process, in which a lump of molten glass was twirled on the end of an iron rod until it formed a flat disk (Boow 1992: 100–11). The disk was then cut into squares for windowpanes, but the size and shape of each pane was severely restricted by the circumference of the circular disk. Panes made in this fashion were seldom greater than 16 inches (400 mm) in size, and were also very thin, usually between 2 and 3 mm in thickness. This was the most common window glass in Britain and its colonies until the 1830s. In that decade, British manufacturers developed a means for producing window glass by flattening glass blown in a cylinder. This glass was both thicker (3.0–4.2 mm) and permitted the cutting of larger panes, either 30 × 25 inches (755 × 635 mm) or 36 × 22 inches (915 × 560 mm). By the 1860s, it had largely replaced Crown glass for windows. Plate glass was made by pouring molten glass onto a metal table and then grinding and polishing it. Although greater-sized panes could be achieved in this way, the labor-intensive process added considerably to its price and it was primarily used for mirrors, and later for frosted glass. Plate glass is generally thicker (approximately 4–5 mm) than either Crown or flattened glass.

Cemeteries and Gravestones

In the 1960s James Deetz realized that gravestones were in many ways the perfect artifact for archaeological analysis, providing "a laboratory situation in which to measure cultural change in time and space and relate such measurements to the main body of archaeological method" (Deetz & Dethlefson 1967: 29). Gravestones are fixed in space, in the cemetery; exhibit variation in form, including shape, decoration, type of stone, and the wording used in the inscription; and are neatly dated with the death of the deceased. After recording a number of cemeteries in the eastern USA, Deetz and his colleagues were able to demonstrate the movement of individual carvers, the evolution of certain designs, and shifts in the beliefs and customs about death. At the same time, Deetz tested archaeological hypotheses about seriation on a set of readily dateable artifacts. Since then, both gravestones and cemeteries have been popular subjects for archaeological study.

Artifact Analysis

Analysis is the process of synthesizing the raw data of the catalog in order to identify patterns and describe the assemblage as a whole, and it requires that data be quantified and summarized in some form. Two methods of analysis routinely used by historical archaeologists are the calculation of minimum vessel counts (MNV) for ceramics and glass, and the calculation of the mean start and end dates when a deposit was formed.

Minimum vessel counts, like Minimum Number of Individual counts in faunal analysis, use the number of representative parts as the basis for extrapolating the number of complete objects represented in the assemblage. Sherd counts and sherd weights are important measures for analyzing the relative proportion of artifacts on a site and their distribution across it, which in turn shed light on site use and taphonomy. However, vessel numbers, whether of plates, teacups, wine bottles, or clay pipes, are more meaningful measures for analyzing how objects were used before they were lost or discarded (Miller 1986; Sussman 2000). There are several steps in determining MNV counts. The first is to make sure that all of the artifacts to be counted have been given a catalog number. Then a typology will need to be established on the basis of ware-type, decoration, vessel size and shape, and any other relevant attributes; for example, 8-inch whiteware blue-willow transfer-print plates, 10-inch whiteware blue-willow transfer-print plates, or 6-inch whiteware blue-willow transfer-print teacups.

Once all the artifacts have been sorted, diagnostic elements in each group should be identified. These will vary according to the shape of the vessel – for glass containers bases and finishes are considered diagnostic, while for clay tobacco pipes Bradley (2000: 126) suggests the use of the stem/bowl junction and the mouthpiece. Ceramics can be more difficult, but generally the total rim diameter of all sherds in a type is calculated as a percentage of a complete plate. A measure of 80 percent of a rim would be the equivalent of a minimum of one plate, while 140 percent would be the equivalent of a minimum of two plates. Any type that is represented by a single fragment, such as the only piece of cobalt blue glass on a site, is counted as one individual regardless of size or whether or not it is a diagnostic element. Once these elements have been counted, the highest number for any given type is taken as the minimum number of objects represented by that type. Where there are 18 black case bottle finishes and 13 black case bottle bases, the minimum number of case bottles present cannot be less than 18.

The calculation of mean beginning and end dates for the formation of a deposit is based on the mean ceramic date formula developed by Stanley South (1977). As Harrington and Binford had done with clay pipes, South realized that pooling information about the manufacturing period of all the ceramics on a site would yield valuable insights into the site's age. By testing his formula on sites of known age, he was able to demonstrate that it could be reliably used on sites where there was less documentary evidence. The mean ceramic date is an average of the midpoint, or median, in the manufacturing ranges of all the datable ceramics on the site, weighted according to the frequency of each type of artifact. One problem with this method is that it lumps together all phases of a site's occupation, while another is that by emphasizing the midpoint of each manufacturing range it can be skewed by artifacts that were made for long periods of time (Adams 2003). A variation of South's approach that is more sensitive to temporal variation is to use the start and end dates for each manufacturing range. This will give an average beginning and ending date for when the deposit was created, which is more informative than simply knowing the midpoint, because it can reveal whether a deposit was created quickly or over a long period of time. On sites with a single phase of occupation, it can be done for the entire assemblage at once. On sites occupied for longer periods, particularly when stratigraphic units of different phases can be identified, it is more useful to calculate the mean beginning and end dates for each phase. Some archaeologists have also extended the technique to include all datable artifacts in the assemblage, not just ceramics. Glass, plastics, clay tobacco pipes, coins, ammunition, and lighting devices are just some of the other artifacts that have been used. The formula is:

$$y = \frac{\Sigma x(f)}{\Sigma f}$$

where y is the mean date, x is the date (start, end, or median) for each item, and f is the frequency, or number of times that item appears in the assemblage.

To use the formula, the datable items are listed together with their quantities and the start and end dates of their manufacture (Tables 13.1 and 13.2).

Table 13.1 Data for calculating mean artifact dates.

	f	TPQ	TAQ	fTPQ	fTAQ
Button	1	1830	1894	1,830	1,894
Plate	7	1780	1850	12,460	12,950
Plate	10	1780	1850	17,800	18,500
Cup	5	1830	1850	9,150	9,250
Cup	3	1830	1850	5,490	5,550
Plate	5	1805	1840	9,025	9,200
Plate	1	1820	1870	1,820	1,870
Bone handle	2	1780	1860	3,560	3,720
Cartridge	1	1916	1917	1,916	1,917
Gunflint	2	1790	1880	3,580	3,760
Clay pipe	2	1839	1902	3,678	3,804
Clay pipe	3	1828	1844	5,484	5,532
Clay pipe	1	1830	1861	1,830	1,861
Bottle (pickle)	2	1835	1910	3,670	3,820
Bottle (beer)	9	1820	1840	16,380	16,560
Bottle (beer)	10	1800	1920	18,000	19,200
Sum	64			115,673	119,388

Table 13.2 Mean artifact dates for whole assemblage and separate components.

	f	ΣfTPQ	ΣfTAQ	Mean TPQ	Mean TAQ
Assemblage	64	115,673	119,388	1807	1865
Ceramics	31	55,745	57,320	1798	1849
Clay pipes	6	10,992	11,197	1832	1866
Glass	21	38,050	39,580	1811	1884

Minimum vessel counts should always be used for this calculation, although in the past some researchers used sherd counts. To calculate mean start dates, the quantity of each item (f) is multiplied by the start date (x) for that item (referred to as *terminus ante quem*, or TAQ, in the tables), then the multiples of all start dates are added together and the total divided by the total quantity of items found. To calculate mean end dates the same process is used, replacing start date in the formula with end date (referred to as *terminus post quem*, or TPQ, in the tables). To calculate a mean median date, the midpoint of each manufacturing range is first calculated for each item and then this date used in the formula. This technique depends on accurate identification of the types and knowledge of the precise production dates. However, it has the advantage of providing information that can be used to analyze many aspects of the assemblage. These include potential time lag in the creation of the deposit – if, for example, the dates obtained from the artifacts are significantly later than known dates of occupation. This technique can also reveal whether all parts of the site were occupied simultaneously or whether they were occupied sequentially. The dates for ceramic and glass assemblages can be worked out separately, and compared to see whether containers are more likely to be discarded sooner than tablewares.

SUSAN LAWRENCE

Case Study

Kelly and Lucas's Whaling Station, Adventure Bay, Tasmania, Australia

Kelly and Lucas's station was the winter base for 20–30 men hunting whales along the Tasmanian coast (Figure 13.1). It was occupied for a few months each year from the 1820s until the 1840s. Surviving features indicate that the camp consisted of three or

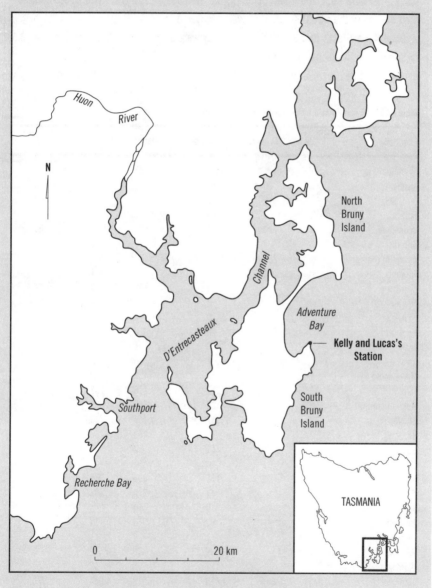

Figure 13.1   The location of the case study, Tasmania, Australia.

four bark huts, a large stone building, a stone storehouse, a tryworks for rendering the whale blubber, and two or three open-sided sheds. Although there are many histories of deep-sea whaling, little is known about shore-based whaling, and in 1997 the site was excavated in order to learn more about the way of life there (Lawrence 2001). Specific questions concerned what the men were eating, what kind of household and personal goods they had, and the construction methods used to build the structures. More general questions included the nature of status and power on the site, gender and the construction of masculine identities, colonial trade networks, and processes of abandonment and reuse. Two bark huts, the stone building, the storehouse, and the tryworks were excavated and more than 25,000 artifacts were recovered.

Once the artifacts had been cataloged, they were arranged into functional categories for analysis and discussion (Table 13.3). Within each category, minimum object counts and mean dates were calculated where appropriate. Variation in the distribution of

Table 13.3   Quantities of artifact fragments at Adventure Bay, Tasmania.

Function	Crew A	Crew B	Stone house	Midden	Storehouse	Tryworks
Aboriginal tool			17	24	23	
Alcohol bottle	12	20	623	1,792	703	5
Bird bone			23	75	4	4
Button		2	15	61	6	
Cooperage	110	20	173	645	672	109
Currency			0	0	1	
Domestic mammal	23	222	715	3,482	1,363	670
Firearms		1	7	17	4	
Fish bone	1		58	702	29	
Fishing			0	1		
Footwear			0	2		
Hardware			0	2		
Lock			0	1		
Medicine		1	1	6	2	
Metal scrap	1	7	95	452	12	19
Nail	16	26	1,311	116	103	32
Native mammal	2		22	95	63	14
Shellfish	83		2,357	4,204	533	93
Smoking	22	34	76	482	36	5
Souvenir			11	2		
Stationery			0	1		
Storage container	3	2	116	436	235	5
Tableware			44	270	231	
Toiletry			0	14	·	
Unidentified			0	3	11	
Utensil			1	2		
Whaling	1		9	30	2	3
Window	1		171	95	12	
Total	275	335	5,845	13,012	4,034	970

artifacts between the bark huts and the stone building indicated that crew members had probably lived in the bark huts, while the stone building was occupied by someone of higher status, probably the headsman or station manager. Very few artifacts were found at the bark huts, suggesting that fewer activities took place there and that the occupants probably had fewer goods to lose or throw away. More than 19 kg of bottle glass was found at Adventure Bay, almost 20 percent of the nonbone component of the assemblage, and apparently confirming the whalers' reputation for hard drinking. However, calculation of the minimum number of glass bottles indicates that only 16 alcohol bottles from the whaling period were represented. Alcohol might have been stored in bulk in wooden casks as well, but certainly 16 bottles is not much among 20–30 men over nearly 20 years. No European women lived at the camp, but some artifacts point to different versions of masculinity. While whalers had the reputation for being tough, violent, and living in rough conditions, the artifacts included stemmed wine glasses and delicate transfer-printed tea-wares that were probably used by the headsmen in more genteel, middle-class style. Artifacts also indicated that more than 50 years after the whalers abandoned the camp, local people started to visit it. Spent ammunition and broken bottle glass dating to the first two decades of the twentieth century suggest casual visits by hunting parties and those on fishing boats.

Resources

The following journals specialize in historical archaeology: *Australasian Historical*, *Historical Archaeology*, *Industrial Archaeology*, the *International Journal of Historical Archaeology*, and *Post-Medieval Archaeology*.

Further reading

Some key texts for this subject are as follows:

Barber, R. 1994: *Doing Historical Archaeology: Exercises Using Documentary, Oral and Material Evidence*. Englewood Cliffs, NJ: Prentice-Hall.

Birmingham, J. and Bairstow, D. 1987: *Papers in Australian Historical Archaeology*. Sydney: Australian Society for Historical Archaeology.

Brauner, D. (ed.) 2000: *Approaches to Material Culture Research for Historical Archaeologists*. Uniontown, PA: Society for Historical Archaeology and Parks Canada.

Brooks, A. 2005: *An Archaeological Guide to British Ceramics in Australia 1788–1901*. Melbourne: The Australasian Society for Historical Archaeology, Sydney, and the La Trobe University Archaeology Program.

Davey, P. (ed.) 1979–: *The Archaeology of the Clay Tobacco Pipe*, vols 1–16. BAR British Series. Oxford: British Archaeological Reports.

Karklins, K. (ed.) 2000: *Studies in Material Culture Research*. Uniontown, PA: Society for Historical Archaeology and Parks Canada.

Noel Hume, I. 1991: *A Guide to the Artifacts of Colonial America*. New York: Vintage Books.

Upton, D. and Vlach, J. M. (eds.) 1986: *Common Places: Readings in American Vernacular Architecture*. Macon, GA: University of Georgia Press.

References

Adams, W. H. 2002: Recycling bottles as building materials in the Pacific islands. *Historical Archaeology*, 36, 50–7.

—— 2003: Dating historical sites: The importance of understanding timelag in the acquisition, curation, use and disposal of artefacts. *Historical Archaeology*, 37, 38–64.

Allen, J. 1973: The archaeology of nineteenth century British imperialism – an Australian case study. *World Archaeology*, 5, 44–60.

Anson, D. 1983: Typology and seriation of wax vesta tin matchboxes from central Otago: a new method of dating historic sites in New Zealand. *New Zealand Journal of Archaeology*, 5, 115–38.

Binford, L. 1978: A new method of calculating dates from kaolin pipe stem samples. In R. Schuyler (ed.), *Historical Archaeology: A Guide to Substantive and Theoretical Contributions*. Farmingdale, New York: Baywood, 66–7.

Bodey, H. 1983: *Nailmaking*. Princes Risborough, Buckinghamshire: Shire Publications.

Boow, J. 1992: *Early Australian Commercial Glass: Manufacturing Processes*. Sydney: Department of Planning, New South Wales.

Bradley, C. 2000: Smoking pipes for the archaeologist. In K. Karklins (ed.), *Studies in Material Culture Research*. Uniontown, PA: Society for Historical Archaeology and Parks Canada, 104–33.

Burley, D. 1995: Contexts of meaning: beer bottles and cans in contemporary burial practices in the Polynesian kingdom of Tonga. *Historical Archaeology*, 29, 75–83.

Busch, J. 1981: An introduction to the tin can. *Historical Archaeology*, 15, 95–104.

—— 1987: Second time around: a look at bottle reuse. *Historical Archaeology*, 21, 67–80.

Carney, M. 1999: A cordial factory at Parramatta, New South Wales. *Australasian Historical Archaeology*, 16, 80–93.

Coysh, A. W. and Henrywood, R. 1982: *The Dictionary of Blue and White Printed Pottery 1780–1880*, vol. I. Woodbridge, Suffolk: The Antique Collector's Club.

—— and —— 1989: *The Dictionary of Blue and White Printed Pottery 1780–1880*, vol. II. Woodbridge, Suffolk: The Antique Collector's Club.

Davey, P. (ed.) 1979–: *The Archaeology of the Clay Tobacco Pipe*, vols 1–16. BAR British Series. Oxford: British Archaeological Reports.

Deetz, J. and Dethlefsen, E. 1967: Death's head, cherub, urn and willow. *Natural History*, 76, 29–37.

Emerson, M. 1999: African inspirations in a New World art and artifact: decorated pipes from the Chesapeake. In T. Singleton (ed.), *I, Too, Am America: Archaeological Studies of African-American Life*. Charlottesville: University of Virginia Press, 47–82.

Ewins, N. 1997: *"Supplying the Present Wants of Our Yankee Cousins": Staffordshire Ceramics and the American Market 1775–1880*. Stoke-on-Trent: City Museum and Art Gallery.

Farrer, K. T. H. 1980: *A Settlement Amply Supplied: Food Technology in Nineteenth Century Australia*. Melbourne: Melbourne University Press.

Ferguson, L. 1991: Struggling with pots in South Carolina. In R. McGuire and R. Paynter (eds.), *The Archaeology of Inequality*. Cambridge, MA: Blackwell, 28–39.

Fike, R. 1987: *The Bottle Book: A Comprehensive Guide to Historic Embossed Medicine Bottles*. Salt Lake City: Peregrine Smith Books.

Fox, R. and Scott, D. 1991: The post-Civil War battlefield pattern: an example from the Custer Battlefield. *Historical Archaeology*, 25, 92–103.

Gemmell, W. 1986: *And So We Graft from Six to Six*. Sydney: Angus and Robertson.

Godden, G. 1991: *Encyclopaedia of British Pottery and Porcelain Marks*. London: Barrie and Jenkins.

Gojak, D. 1995: Clay tobacco pipes from Cadman's Cottage, Sydney, Australia. *Society for Clay Pipe Research Newsletter*, 48, 11–19.

—— and Stuart, I. 1999: The potential for the archaeological study of clay tobacco pipes from Australian sites. *Australasian Historical Archaeology*, 17, 38–49.

Harrington, J. C. 1978: Dating stem fragments of seventeenth and eighteenth century clay tobacco pipes. In R. Schuyler (ed.), *Historical Archaeology: A Guide to Substantive and Theoretical Contributions*. Farmingdale, New York: Baywood, 63–5.

Harrison, R. 2000: "Nowadays with glass": regional variation in Aboriginal bottle glass artifacts from Western Australia. *Archaeology in Oceania*, 35, 34–47.

Jones, O. 1986: *Cylindrical English Wine and Beer Bottles 1735–1850*. Ottawa: Parks Canada.

—— 1991: Glass bottle push-ups and pontil marks. In G. Miller, O. Jones, L. Ross and T. Majewski (eds.), *Approaches to Material Culture Research for Historical Archaeologists*. Uniontown, PA: Society for Historical Archaeology, 87–98.

—— and Smith, E. A. 1985: *Glass of the British Military ca. 1755–1820*. Ottawa: National Historic Parks and Sites Branch, Parks Canada.

——, Sullivan, C., Miller, G., Smith, E. A. and Harris, J. 1989: *The Parks Canada Glass Glossary for the Description of Containers, Tableware, Flat Glass, and Closures*. Ottawa: Studies in Archaeology, Architecture and History, Parks Canada.

Karklins, K. and Sprague, R. 1980: *A Bibliography of Glass Trade Beads in North America*. Moscow, ID: North Fork Press.

Kenmotsu, N. 1991: Gunflints: a study. In G. L. Miller, O. R. Jones, L. A. Ross and T. Majewski (eds.), *Approaches to Material Culture Research for Historical Archaeologists*. Uniontown, PA: Society for Historical Archaeology, 197–222.

Lawrence, S. 2001: Foodways on two colonial whaling stations: archaeological and historical evidence for diet in nineteenth century Tasmania. *Journal of the Royal Australian Historical Society*, 87, 209–29.

—— 2003: Archaeology and the nineteenth century British Empire. *Historical Archaeology*, 37, 20–33.

Lewis, M. 1977: *Victorian Primitive*. Carlton: Greenhouse.

Lindbergh, J. 1999: Buttoning down archaeology. *Australasian Historical Archaeology*, 17, 50–7.

Majewski, T. and O'Brien, M. 1987: The use and misuse of nineteenth-century English and American ceramics in archaeological analysis. *Advances in Archaeological Method and Theory*, 11, 97–209.

McCarthy, M. 1983: Ships' fastenings: a preliminary study. *Bulletin of the Australian Institute for Maritime Archaeology*, 7, 1–24.

Miller, G. 1980: Classification and economic scaling of nineteenth century ceramics. *Historical Archaeology*, 14, 1–40.

—— 1986: Of fish and sherds: a model for estimating vessel populations from minimal vessel counts. *Historical Archaeology*, 20, 59–85.

—— 1991: A revised set of CC index values for classification and economic scaling of English ceramics from 1787 to 1880. *Historical Archaeology*, 25, 1–25.

—— 2000: Telling time for archaeologists. *Northeastern Historical Archaeology*, 29, 1–22.

—— and Sullivan, C. 1984: Machine-made glass containers and the end of production for mouth-blown bottles. *Historical Archaeology*, 18, 83–96.

Morgan, P. 1991: Glass bottles from the *William Salthouse*. BA Honors thesis, Archaeology, La Trobe University, Melbourne.

Mouer, L. D., Hodges, M. E., Potter, S. et al. 1999: Colonoware pottery, Chesapeake pipes, and "uncritical assumptions." In T. Singleton (ed.), *I, Too, Am America:*

Archaeological Studies of African-American Life. Charlottesville: University Press of Virginia, 83–115.

Noel Hume, I. 1991: *A Guide to the Artifacts of Colonial America*. New York: Vintage Books.

Orser, C. 1989: On plantations and patterns. *Historical Archaeology*, 23, 28–40.

Oswald, A. 1961: The evolution and chronology of English clay tobacco pipes. *Archaeological Newsletter*, 7, 55–62.

Peters, S. J. 1997: Archaeological wines: analysis and interpretation of a collection of wines recovered from the *William Salthouse* shipwreck (1841). *Australasian Historical Archaeology*, 14, 63–8.

Samford, P. 1997: Response to a market: dating English underglaze transfer-printed wares. *Historical Archaeology*, 31, 1–30.

Sando, R. and Felton, D. 1993: Inventory records of ceramics and opium from a nineteenth century Chinese store in California. In P. Wegars (ed.), *Hidden Heritage: Historical Archaeology of the Overseas Chinese*. Amityville, New York: Baywood Publishing, 151–76.

South, S. 1997: *Method and Theory in Historical Archaeology*. New York: Academic Press.

Sprague, R. 2000: Glass trade beads: a progress report. In D. Brauner (ed.), *Approaches to Material Culture Research for Historical Archaeologists*. Uniontown, PA: Society for Historical Archaeology, 202–20.

Stine, L. F., Cabak, M. and Groover, M. 2000: Blue beads as African-American cultural symbols. In D. Brauner (ed.), *Approaches to Material Culture Research for Historical Archaeologists*. Uniontown, PA: Society for Historical Archaeology, 221–47.

Stuart, I. 1993: Bottles for jam? An example of recycling from a post-contact archaeological site. *Australian Archaeology*, 36, 17–21.

Sussman, L. 1979: *Spode/Copeland Transfer-Printed Patterns Found at 20 Hudson's Bay Company Sites*. Ottawa: Parks Canada.

—— 1997: *Mocha, Banded, Cat's Eye, and Other Factory-Made Slipware*. Boston, MA: Council for North East Historical Archaeology.

—— 2000: Objects vs. sherds: a statistical evaluation. In K. Karklins (ed.), *Studies in Material Culture Research*. Uniontown, PA: The Society for Historical Archaeology, 96–103.

Varman, R. 1980: The nail as a criterion for the dating of building and building sites (late 18th century to 1900). In J. Birmingham and D. Bairstow (eds.), *Papers in Australian Historical Archaeology*. Sydney: The Australian Society for Historical Archaeology, 104–12.

Walker, I. 1977: *Clay Tobacco-Pipes, with Particular Reference to the Bristol Industry*. Ottawa: Parks Canada.

Wall, D. d. 1994: *The Archaeology of Gender: Separating the Spheres in America*. New York: Plenum Press.

Wells, T. 1998: Nail chronology: the use of technologically derived features. *Historical Archaeology*, 32, 78–99.

Wilkie, L. 1996: Glass-knapping at a Louisiana plantation: African-American tools? *Historical Archaeology*, 30, 37–49.

Wylie, J. and Fike, R. 1993: Chinese opium smoking techniques and paraphernalia. In P. Wegars (ed.), *Hidden Heritage: Historical Archaeology of the Overseas Chinese*. Amityville, New York: Baywood Publishing, 255–306.

Barbara Little

14
Historical Sources

Introduction

For the archaeologist, historical sources must go far beyond pottery records assigning a range of manufacturing dates for a type of ware, or a land deed confirming the sale date for an urban house lot. The integration of archaeological and documentary sources is a creative enterprise. Archaeologists find it less daunting (but no less challenging) as they come to understand that history exists only through interpretation, and that the interpretation of documents is no less fraught with uncertainties and judgments than the interpretation of archaeological resources (see Figure 14.1).

Details without context often are meaningless and there is a particular temptation to an archaeologist who may want to simply spice up a site report with some documentary authority and therefore search for a quote or a fact that appears to fit and bolster whatever point is being made. I caution against such raiding of historical sources, as it simply begs the question of when the fruitful integration of disciplines will begin.

By way of introduction to the historian's craft, I offer the following lengthy quote by historian Robin Winks (1970: xviii–xix) because it illustrates some of the breadth and hints at some of the difficulties of historical research:

> Clearly, then, the historian needs to assess evidence against a reasonably well-informed background. Is one writing of the Pullman Strike of 1894? One must, obviously, know quite a bit about general labor conditions, about business management, about employment opportunities and the nature of the economy, about Chicago and its environs, and about the railroad industry. But since many of the strikers were Welshmen, one needs also to know something of contrasting work conditions in that part of Wales from which the workmen came. Since the strike was compounded by inept police and militia work, one needs to know about the nature of such work in Illinois and, comparatively, elsewhere. One needs to investigate the judicial system, the role of President Grover Cleveland, the powers open to Governor John P. Altgeld, the ideas of Eugene V. Debs, and the effects of the [1893] Chicago World's Fair, which brought hundreds of drifters into the metropolitan area to contribute to the violence associated with the

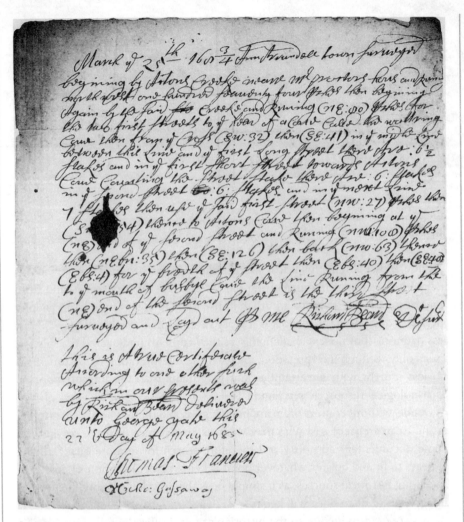

Figure 14.1 This handwritten document, which illustrates the difficulty of deciphering handwriting, is Beard's Survey of Anne Arundel Town, 1683/4. Annapolis Mayor, Alderman and Councilmen (Land Record Papers). Accession Number: [11200 1-22-3-23].

strike. Since the strike disrupted mail service throughout the nation, forcing letters north onto Canadian tracks, one needs to investigate at least briefly the Canadian rail network, the relationship with railwaymen elsewhere, and the applicability of the secondary boycott. One needs to know much of the general climate of opinion at the time to assess the meaning of the strike. One needs to look at company, city, union, judicial, militia, post-office, Presidential, legal, and gubernatorial records; at the private papers of Cleveland, Altgeld, Pullman, Debs; at the papers of the judges, magistrates, and strikers, if they can be found and, when found, if one can gain access to them. Much that one learns on such journeys will never appear in the final book, but every nuance, every sentence, will be better informed, closer to the truth, more protected against one's own biases (which can never be totally blocked out, and no responsible historian claims that they can be), than if such journeys were not taken at all.

BARBARA LITTLE

> At the end of a guide to archaeological analyses, I need not counter with a similar description of what you must know to analyze the archaeological record. Both disciplines can be tedious, enthralling, and all-consuming.

Begin by establishing and keeping a research journal in which you record topics, repositories and sources consulted or ignored (and why), permissions granted or denied, impressions, and notes to yourself about the research process. I cannot emphasize the value of such metadata enough. Although such a record often seems extraneous to beginning researchers, its absence may be costly in terms of time: it is far too easy to flounder or give up after finding that you are reexamining sources that have already been consulted. A research journal is a good place to keep track of the reasons for choosing particular topics and sources, as well as leads for further research.

Define a research domain and then work to define it more carefully. It is typical to begin with a very large question, which then needs to be refined into manageable pieces. You may be inspired, for example, to know how life changed for the convicts that England transported to her colonies. Start asking yourself questions about this interest: Is it the material conditions of London's poor that interests you or the financial gains of a specific colonial family during the nineteenth century? What is your own point of view about your research topic? What are your preconceptions and biases? As you do your research, try to be aware of how your own attitudes affect your work. Make those notes in your research journal.

Decide on the boundaries of your research in space and time. Your research is likely to be influenced directly by the archaeological project with which you are working. Recognize, however, that there are many possible avenues for historical research, even if you are working on a particular site. Define your purpose in terms of topic, results, and the time available for research, analysis, writing, further research, and production of the results. Think in advance what you plan the result to be: A chapter in a report, an article, a dissertation? Also plan for the final location of your notes. If you original research is to be of use to other researchers in the future, you need to organize it in such a way that anyone (including you) can go back to it and use it.

Create a plan, but be flexible. Be realistic about the time you need to spend. Too often, inadequate time is budgeted for documentary research. Both archaeological and documentary research are time-consuming pursuits that require organization, attention to detail, dedication, persistence, and a high tolerance for ambiguity.

You will need to do background research to learn about your topic before you narrow your focus and start your research with historical sources. This may sound redundant, but it is important to realize that reading secondary material is preliminary to research with primary sources; it cannot substitute, although depending on your needs, it may be adequate. Find out what is already available. You'll need to judge whether it is trustworthy and determine the authors' points of view. Read scholarly texts with an analytical and critical eye. Try to identify the strengths and weaknesses of the work. You will be influenced by what you read and how carefully you think about it. Write your impressions in your research journal.

Read analytically. Assess the effectiveness of secondary sources to judge how convincing the argument is. What are the author's goals? How well are the goals met? What is not addressed? Consider that the silences may be revealing or, in some cases, suggestive of research that should be done. Consider what sources the author has consulted and how. Is the methodology explained? Is it valid? Where does the evidence fit into the argument? Does the author carefully analyze data to build an interpretation, or does the author begin with an idea and then go in search of evidence to support it?

Read critically to find the underlying assumptions or motives of the author. How does the author present his or her theoretical viewpoints or biases? Are they hidden or revealed? How does the author characterize society? Is it driven by consensus or conflict? Are people active players or are they at the mercy of social and economic forces? Does the author make judgmental remarks that are not supported by evidence? Are there unspoken assumptions that underlie conclusions?

Develop and practice critical thinking skills. Clearly define ideas and concepts and challenge assumptions and biases – both others' and your own. Be willing to challenge tentative conclusions, even after you've spent a good deal of energy developing them. Support your judgments with reason and evidence.

Critical thinking requires the following six elements; these are adapted from the Franklin D. Roosevelt library and museum research guide (www.fdrlibrary.marist.edu/resear38.html):

- *Asking questions.* Be willing to challenge whatever evidence you are confronted with. This challenge stems not from a sense of hostility, but from a realization that there is always more to be learned about a subject or topic.
- *Carefully defining the problem.* Determine the key issues at the heart of the topic you are examining. What is at stake? Why is it important? What do you hope to discover or learn?
- *Examining the evidence.* Consider the source and the nature of the evidence being presented. Is it reliable? Is it valid? Is it pertinent? Are the arguments being put forth based on opinion or are they fully supported by "facts"? How broad was the scope of the research that produced these facts? How deep was the research?
- *Considering biases and examining the premise.* What biases does the presenter of the evidence hold? What agenda – seen or hidden – might they be trying to advance? Upon what premise do they base their claims? Is it fair and

BARBARA LITTLE

valid? What biases do you hold that may color or cloud your examination of the evidence? How might you overcome these biases?

- *Recognizing that there are likely to be other worthy interpretations.* It may be wise to consider other interpretations of the evidence before you settle on your own understanding. Be especially careful in considering the relationship between cause and effect.
- *Embracing uncertainty.* Recognize that your conclusions should be viewed as guiding principles in your understanding of the topic. New evidence should be considered and continually incorporated into a better and more meaningful understanding. Keep in mind that the "facts" of today often turn into the fallacies of yesterday. Critical thinking requires keeping an open mind.

Get organized. Create a citation system that is logical, easy to use, clear, and complete. Find out how primary documents are to be cited before you start so that you don't have to go back. Keep your notes neat and organized and fully cited, and back up both electronic files and paper files (photocopy and file a second copy in a location different from that of the originals). Assume that you will need a backup (for example, never pack the only copy of your research notes into checked airline baggage)!

Have a firm idea of your starting and ending dates, but be flexible, as you may find that there are some important earlier sources that provide important details for your time period of interest. Be somewhat firm with yourself as well, however, as it is tempting to get lost in the simple joy of finding things out and very easy to get side-tracked from your purpose.

Keep track of what you know. You may want to make a time line with basic information to help you keep events in order as you do your research. The use of a time line can help to suggest cause and effect relationships between the items that you record. It is most helpful in an historical archaeological project to include known archaeological dates (or ranges of dates) so that you can more easily integrate all of your data sources. It will also be helpful to keep a chronological record of your sources, so that you can quickly identify trends and gaps.

Categorizing sources by their sponsors, authors, or curators points to various locations of historical documents and suggests the range of sources that may be available. This categorization below, adapted from Pitt (1972), is also useful because it emphasizes the influence of origin on a document's intention, tone, and coverage. The expectation, for example, that private papers will embody different opinions and priorities than government documents should affect the way such documents are used to aid archaeological interpretation. Your research purpose is likely to affect your selection of sources from the ten main categories that follow. Ask the research staff in libraries and archives for any research guides or finding aids for your topic. These guides will be invaluable to your research:

Identifying sources

- *Public and official archives* include government documents such as minutes, journals, official papers, political records, policy documents, court records, and statistics such as census, taxes, and production figures. Also included are officially sponsored explorers' and travelers' accounts and government-sponsored research. Many businesses, institutions, schools, social organizations, and political groups donate their archives to governmental archives.
- *Mission and Church sources* include letters, journals, parish and other records, and other related papers. Congregations often keep archives and produce their own histories.
- *Business and company sources* include all pertinent records including, but not limited to, account books, personnel records, union records, and insurance files.
- *Scholarly institutions and repositories* hold acquired collections and unpublished notes. Historical societies and local libraries are often important resources. Secondary sources may be used as leads to primary documents. Archaeologists need to recognize how secondary sources – as interpretive works in history, anthropology, geography, social science philosophy, and other subjects – impact our questions, assumptions, and interpretations.
- *Letters, diaries, and private papers* may include other items such as photograph albums and memorabilia. In the United States, start by consulting the *National Union Catalog of Manuscript Collections*, an index of collections held throughout the country.
- *Literature* includes travel literature by outsiders and locals, as well as fiction, novels, short stories, plays, and poetry.
- *Transient documents* are items such as newspapers, pamphlets, brochures, broadsheets, directories, catalogs, or any other mass media with a limited circulation or life span. Such ephemera are often housed at state archives, but could be found in many locations.
- *Oral history, oral tradition, and local sources* are types of direct reporting by local or otherwise affiliated people. In document form, such reporting may be found, for example, in testimony in court records. Researchers may need to consult the transcripts or tapes of oral history interviews or may need to conduct such interviews themselves. Oral history includes the memories of individuals who experienced the time about which they speak. Oral tradition extends beyond living memory and is regarded as accurate by its narrator.
- *Maps, pictorial, and sound and electronic archives* also include architectural drawings, plans, and photographs.

Decide what sources would be relevant and useful. Think broadly. What is the relation of the topic to public record keeping and to other kinds of sources that are available? What kind of documents do you need? Begin with online searches, but expect research to involve a good deal of time in libraries and archives or in other repositories. Into the foreseeable future, online guides will include only small fractions of what archives have in their holdings. Be aware that topics concerning the modern world may often require consulting documents in other countries. For example, there are sources in the National Archives of Ireland that are relevant for research into the transportation of Irish convicts to Australia. You may have to make the trip, but plan it carefully first and contact the repository in advance to plan your visit and schedule assistance. An important assistant in the task of figuring out what resources are available and where to find them is the research librarian or archivist. Be clear about what you are researching and he or she will be able to help you identify and find relevant resources. In your research journal, record the names of people who help you, as it is customary to acknowledge their assistance.

Consider the full range of media that might exist: in addition to paper documents that are handwritten or typed, there may be maps, photographs, film, and audio recordings. Do not underestimate the value of finding pictures (see Figure 14.2). It may not, however, be easy to find these. You'll need to look for pictures in period books, newspapers, magazines, printed material such as postcards, art museum collections, travelers' accounts (sketch books), trade books, and depictions of various trades (D'Agostino 1995).

Archaeologist Mary Ellin D'Agostino (1995: 119) provides a preview of what the researcher might expect:

> Documents are not easy to use – they are obscure and are biased in both content and survival; they are difficult to read, to locate and to interpret . . . Documents are a biased, consciously composed record that needs to be carefully treated for intentional bias in a way that is not typical of the archaeological material record. In addition, access can be problematic. There is no guarantee that the relevant documents survive or are located in an accessible collection. Documents are often not completely catalogued or are not catalogued in a way useful for the kinds of questions archaeologists or anthropologists want to ask of them . . . Once located the documents still need to be read, interpreted, and analyzed. A variety of problems in reading and low-level interpretation include: working from hard to read microfilms, untranscribed documents where the handwriting and scripts require knowledge of paleography, and heavily edited transcriptions that are not always reliable . . . Also, published collections of official documents often include only a selection of the available material of interest to the transcriber, author, or publisher with little or no notation as to the quantity or type of documents left out.

Recognize that using an archives and archival material is different from using a library. Many libraries are self-service and you can browse through the shelves on your own, but most archives are not. Find out before your visit what the rules are for using the collections.

Follow conservation ethics. You should do everything you can to protect and preserve original documents that are entrusted to you for your research. Such care includes the obvious, such as handling documents as little as possible and keeping your hands clean. Don't eat, drink, or smoke around documents,

Figure 14.2 This drawing, which illustrates costume and material culture, is Alexander Hamilton's drawing of "The Tobacco-Pipe Procession," from his history of the Tuesday Club, a social club that he established in Annapolis in 1745. Jonas Green was a prominent member of the club (courtesy of the John Work Garrett Collection, Johns Hopkins University, Baltimore, MD).

even if you're in a repository that has low curatorial standards. Keep material in the order in which it is presented to you to maintain the filing system that is in place. Always ask permission prior to photocopying or taking photographs. Be careful to not damage bindings or pages if you are allowed to photocopy. Acquire necessary permissions for making and publishing copies of pictorial or other documents.

Verify, evaluate, and discriminate

Credible research judges the credibility of its sources. Evaluate evidence in terms of its reliability, relevance, and significance. Ask basic questions: What? Who? When? Where? How? Why?

What is it? What type of source is this? Is it authentic – are there anachronisms, improbabilities, and inexplicable portions? Is it complete? Is it competently translated? Is it properly transcribed? If it's a photograph, how is it cropped? Has it been censored, purposefully or not? Were, for example, certain types of information edited out of a published version of a famous person's papers for "patriotic" or prudish reasons? What is the content? Are there other likely sources with similar content?

Who created it? How close in time was the author to the event that is recorded? Is the author dependable? Is the author in a good position to provide reliable information? What social or political considerations might have influenced the author?

When was it created? How close in time to the event that is recorded?

Where was the source created and where has it been? How close is it to the event that is recorded? Where has the source been kept? Has it been safe? Has it been affected by poor conditions? Has it been subject to alteration?

How was it created and how has it been kept? How was the source made? How was it copied, stored, altered, or edited for publication or distribution?

Why was it created? Who was the intended audience? What was its use? What was the propaganda value? What was the social setting? What did it mean to contemporaries?

It is worth reminding yourself that you cannot necessarily trust something simply because it has been published, printed, or written down. Remember that the record of history reflects the personal, social, economic, and political points of view of the recorder. Also remember that the creation of history involves the personal, social, economic, and political views of the researcher.

Case Study

The Use of Documents at Annapolis

This case study is adapted from *Scales of Historical Anthropology: An Archaeology of Colonial Anglo-America* (Little & Shackel 1989) to demonstrate using broad scales of history and to show that researchers rarely start from scratch. Archaeologists draw upon previous research and interpretations. Both history and archaeology are incremental, additive practices.

Archaeologists also use other researchers' ideas to develop methods, theory, and organizational frameworks. For example, in this case the work of Fernand Braudel influenced the research framework. Braudel (1980 [1949]) organized his monumental work on the Mediterranean world with three scales of history that he calls "individual time," "social time," and "geographical time." Individual time, or the history of the event, encompasses the shortest time span and includes events and individual actions. Social time is concerned with groups over longer time spans of perhaps 10, 20, or 50 years. Geographical time is long-term history, the *Annales* school's "*longue durée*," which might be measured in centuries and millennia. Structure is key to understanding inter-actions among the scales of time. Structures are the underlying organizational schemes for ordering the world and may be geographical, technological, biological, spiritual, or social. Braudel's scales of history are useful archaeologically in providing an organiza-tional framework for considering relationships through time among actions and ideas and material culture.

In an effort to understand the meanings and uses of ceramic assemblages from both archaeological and documentary sources, we (Little & Shackel 1989) placed items within short- and long-term contexts. The structures of social time in the context of urban Annapolis are created by relationships among wealth groups. Other structures, such as those created by ethnicity and gender, are not considered in this particular analysis.

We chose to focus on the development of etiquette and changing personal discipline related to dining, because many of its accoutrements are well represented archaeologic-ally. Ceramic dining items are ubiquitous in eighteenth-century American sites. Dining is an arena of everyday life that is a ritual, socializing action that plays important roles in social strategies. Using documentary and archaeological sources, we discuss the long-term history of dining etiquette in Anglo culture, the social history of etiquette in eighteenth-century Annapolis, Maryland, and the history of particular actions by the Green family in that city.

Long-term history

For this scale of history, our documents included secondary sources analyzing etiquette (e.g., Elias 1978 [1939]), which led to published etiquette books, and published contem-porary commentary, such as the letters of Lord Chesterfield. For a thorough description, see Shackel (1993). Our long-term archaeological context is that developed by James Deetz for seventeenth- and eighteenth-century New England Deetz (1972, 1977, 1983).

The institution of courtesy during medieval times was a developing structure used to create and direct inequalities in society. Within it, an emphasis on table conduct developed, as dining was one of the few social rituals at which people would gather and interact daily. The first courtesy books were originally published in Latin as early as the twelfth century and English translations appeared in the fifteenth century. Through the next several centuries, the meanings, actions, and material culture involved with dining became increasingly complex and disciplined. Meanings associated with dining etiquette produced inequalities through the development of a naturalizing ideology that legitimated social exclusion. Of course, "[n]othing in table manners is self-evident or the product, as it were, or a 'natural' feeling of delicacy . . . Each custom in the changing ritual, however minute, establishes itself infinitely slowly, even forms of behaviour that to us seem quite elementary or simply 'reasonable', such as the custom of taking liquids only with the spoon" (Elias 1978 [1939]).

By the middle of the eighteenth century, when George III was king, England had become the center of high decorum. Lord Chesterfield's letters to his son (1901 [1776]) emphasize the roots of a modern etiquette, driven by time discipline, with segmentation of most daily activities. The idea of mechanical balance and individuality replaced the older order of organic asymmetry and corporateness both in Britain and its American colonies. James Deetz's influential analysis of this long-term cultural change was based on decades of field research in New England.

Using Deetz's observations on long-term change in ceramic use in New England, we expected to see, by the second half of the eighteenth century, a great increase in the absolute numbers and in the varieties of ceramic forms as they were used for more specific functions. We looked for reasons for the change in assemblages in terms of changing structures within social time.

Social time

Our analysis of the middle scale of history focused on changing social structures within the city of Annapolis, in the Chesapeake region of the mid-Atlantic USA. Documents provided the information that allowed us to suggest links between dining etiquette and wealth group. Archaeological data provided the specifics of ceramic choice that were not otherwise available.

Probate records are a rich source for studying material culture, as the probate inventory of an estate undertaken at death (for an individual without a will) lists goods and chattels and their perceived market value. Accounts of administration are sometimes available as part of the probate record of an estate. These accounts list debtors and creditors as an estate is administered and are useful for assessing wealth. The probates that we used are available at the Maryland State Archives in Annapolis, which is the state capital. For this study, Paul Shackel read and coded a total of 255 inventories dating from 1688 to 1777.

No less essential for our purposes than the primary documents is the well-published work of and personal consultation with historians who have carefully analyzed the economic history of the Chesapeake region (e.g., Carr & Walsh 1980; Russo 1983). The probate data can be controlled tightly for wealth. Economic historians have divided Chesapeake probates into four wealth groups on the basis of their assessed estate values in pounds sterling: £0–£49, £50–£225, £225–£490, and over £490 (e.g., Carr &

Walsh 1980). We controlled all probate values for inflation by using Carr and Walsh's (1980) commodities price index, which deflates all seventeenth- and eighteenth-century estate values to the pound sterling as of 1700.

In general, there is very little difference between the kinds of material (aside from real estate and slaves) owned by rich and poor in the late seventeenth and early eighteenth centuries. The clearest difference is that the rich owned more of everything. That relationship changed later in the eighteenth century.

Our analysis looked at the presence of sets of plates and of cups and saucers as well as the artifacts of formal and segmented dining (salad dishes, tureens, dish covers, fruit dishes, custard cups, castors, butter boats, and wine glasses). In the probate inventories, dining items are listed with sufficient detail frequently enough to allow a presence/absence count of particular items. However, inventory takers often lumped all ceramics together, which results in relatively low overall percentages of ownership of particular items. That is, you cannot count butter boats or sets of plates if an inventory lists only a "parcel of China." We made the assumption that the presence of these items in inventories indicated that their owners were structuring their meals in a segmented way, following rules of discipline and etiquette prescribed in the guidebooks. We based this assumption partly on the fact that the etiquette books are found in probate inventories among the elite, first appearing in 1720. It seemed reasonable to suggest as well that the specialized dining items would not appear unless purchasers were aware of rules for their use.

We were able to find various sizes of plates and see more clearly segmentation at the dinner table in the archaeological record than in the probate data. Data regarding both standardization of ceramic type and the variety of dish sizes, signifying the division of the meal, are important archaeological contributions that show that the rules of modernizing etiquette are being followed, not only prescribed. To compare segmentation associated with a changing etiquette, we analyzed ceramics from four sites from the middle and upper wealth groups from the mid-eighteenth to the mid-nineteenth centuries.

The archaeological finding of an increasing variation of plate sizes suggested that there was greater segmentation at the table. From the data collected, it appeared that the residents of all four sites were increasingly segmenting their actions at the table. An increasing variety of dish sizes and types of wares indicated the developing segmentation at the table and at least a partial acceptance of the new discipline. This new form of dining served both as a training ground for a segmented life and as a reinforcement of it.

Individual time

At the scale of individual action, we observe material culture remains of a household to assess what fine dining items were owned and by whom, and when they were acquired, passed down, or discarded. Within this scale of history, our focus is on relationships between structures and individuals or households. Questions of who, what, and when may be constructed. Addressing the "why" requires that we refer to both social structure and to long-term history, each themselves comprised of the results of innumerable events and actions.

Again, probate records were the documents used in this particular study, although we also referred to a tax assessment. For our work in Annapolis, we consulted a greater range of documents, including maps and plats, deeds, court records, militia records, newspapers, and even printers' poetry. Although I spent a great deal of time with the newspaper that the family printed for a century, I found the probate inventories to be the most directly useful for aiding archaeological analysis (e.g., Little 1994). Both probate data and the archaeological record allowed us to assess events associated with dining activity in two generations of the Green family of Annapolis. Jonas Green was a printer, who came to the city in 1738 to answer a call for official printer to the province. He and his wife Anne Catherine had six surviving children, three of whom worked with the family printing business. Anne Catherine became the official provincial printer after Jonas died in 1767, and Frederick Green inherited the business in 1775 on the death of his mother. Frederick and his brother Samuel printed together until both died in 1811.

Using adjusted probate estate values and wealth groups according to Carr and Walsh (1980), we placed Jonas Green in the second wealthiest group. For Jonas, there is no available account of administration. The account for Anne Catherine placed her in the highest wealth category, although the inventory alone would place her in the second lowest group. The accidental survival of that document thus influences and perhaps skews our impression of the family's wealth. Frederick Green's inventory and the tax assessment of 1783 placed him firmly in the wealthiest group.

Jonas and Anne Catherine owned no formal dining items. Jonas owned one "set of China." Anne Catherine's inventory lists much of her kitchen and tableware simply as "a parcel of delph, china, glass & stoneware." Frederick owned six of the eight formal dining items, many of which are represented by several pieces in silver plate as well as ceramic. Frederick also owned other specialized dining items, such as pudding dishes and sugar dishes. "Sets" of plates are not specified, but the "11 dozen" plates are almost certainly in sets. Thirty-two unspecified cups and saucers and 18 coffee cups also are listed.

The first generation of Greens did not own the kind of dining items associated with the display of the new, fashionable etiquette. Instead, the archaeological assemblage indicates that they owned display items that were "old-fashioned," which marked wealth but not the particular social knowledge implied by the new etiquette. This generation followed old rules; the next generation exhibited nearly all the proper dining possessions for the new discipline.

What are the Relationships between Documents and Archaeological Evidence?	Documentary and archaeological data may be thought of as interdependent and complementary or as independent and contradictory. Oddly enough, both of these views are viable; the adoption of one or the other depends on the questions that you are asking and the point of view of the interpretation. There are roughly six ways to characterize the interplay, some of which are closely related. The specific uses to which documents may be put to aid interpretation range from the identification of objects and their functions to the explication of a culture's worldview. In practice, researchers using several types of sources will find that they come across all these relationships between their sources.
Identification	Identification includes such familiar activities as identifying artifact functions, dating specific forms or makers' marks, and naming objects according to contemporary typologies. Archaeologists should recognize how much of this sort of analysis is done almost automatically and often noncritically. Our tendency is to take the first plausible, documented answer. Resist, if you are able, substituting typology for explanation. Be willing to question even this lowest level of interplay between documents and artifacts.

Elizabeth Scott (1997) notes that typologies drawn from potteries and store day books give us the names for various utensils and vessels, and that our own experience colors our perceptions of the ways in which things were – or ought to have been – used. Her reading of British colonial and Anglo-American cookbooks from 1770 to 1850 revealed unanticipated, multiple uses of ceramic, glass, metal, and wooden items in the kitchen. She cautions against interpretations of function that are too restrictive and are thereby misleading.

Identification also includes the use of documents to identify the location and identity of sites. When we think of primary historical sources relevant to finding historical archaeological sites, we normally think of contemporary sources such as maps and other landscape descriptions. But because the traces of settlements may persist above ground, it is important to consult subsequent maps, photographs, and aerial photographs when they are available. Oral history and tradition, folklore, and place names may also provide important clues to site locations.

An example of using maps and aerial photographs is the work done by Annalies Corbin to identify the locations of steamboats that sank in the Missouri River from 1819 to the 1920s (Corbin 1998). After 1860, river surveys by the Army Corps of Engineers produced maps and field notes that Corbin used to track some of the shifts of this turbulent, meandering river and to predict the locations of wrecks in the modern topography.

Complement	Archaeologists may seek complementarily of documentary and archaeological resources and may create their interpretations by blending documentary and

BARBARA LITTLE

archaeological information and using each source to fill in where the other fails. A common goal is to document the everyday lives of poorly documented people, or poorly documented aspects of life of those who are well documented.

For example, Joanne Bowen (1988) has used farm account books for their information on individuals and their use of livestock, animal husbandry, and exchange of meat within a community. The use of these documents from eighteenth-century Suffield, Connecticut, required that Bowen understand the nature of such records, including who kept them and why, and the economic system in which they were written. She also drew upon a historian's analysis of land records, wills, probates, tax lists, and maps in her study of seasonal variability in the slaughter of livestock. In her continuing research, Bowen (1994) has developed a method for analyzing faunal remains in a broad context of interregional comparisons. She raises basic questions about subsistence strategies, including the role of the marketplace and the relationships between rural producers and urban consumers. By analyzing herding systems and comparing the New England and Chesapeake regions through the seventeenth and eighteenth centuries, Bowen demonstrates how these two English settlements developed different strategies related to herding. Bowen uses the documentary record to reconstruct the outlines of the herding systems in these two regions.

One rule of hypothesis testing is that documentary and archaeological data are kept distinct to avoid circular arguments as one is tested against the other. In a recent forum in the journal *Historical Archaeology*, Chuck Cleland argues for such testing. His methodological suggestion is that artifacts and documents be used in "empirical opposition" (2001: 6); that is, assume that neither is correct, but test propositions formed from the documentary record with archaeological data and vice versa. Lower-level questions are those related to particular facts or events; middle-level questions are "why" questions; and higher-level questions are often asked at multi-site, regional, or broader scales. These broad question, he proposes, generally derive from documentary data. *Hypothesis formation and testing*

In the application of Middle Range Theory, documents and artifacts are seen as independent sources of data that can be played off against one another. Researchers look for an appropriate matching of documentary information to the archaeological question, but the matching is not intended to "fill in the gaps." It is intended to identify anomalies that will lead to further questions. In some cases, seeming contradictions between sources forcefully demonstrate that interpretation is the essence of history. *Contradiction*

In a middle range approach, historical archaeologists create "descriptive grids" from the documentary record "against which to array the archaeological record, and uses the deviations from the expectations . . . as the basis for a new set of questions about the archaeological record and about the documentary record as well" (Leone & Potter 1988: 14).

Patrick Kirch and Marshall Sahlins have joined to create an integrated historical anthropology of the Anahulu Valley on O'ahu Island in Hawaii from late prehistory to 1852 (Kirch & Sahlins 1992). They link landscape features such as walls, irrigation terraces, and habitation platforms to documentary record through land records and surveys. Archaeological evidence required a reevaluation of the accepted interpretation of the social effects of the conquest of O'ahu based on archival sources. The conquest period cannot be understood unless archival sources are evaluated in the light of the archaeological record of land use. The reverse is also true: archaeological remains from the period 1812–30 can be interpreted more accurately in light of archival evidence of demographic decline.

Confronting myths

The use of archaeology to confront historical myths is a special case of contradiction, as myths have a particularly tenacious hold on perceptions of the past. Such cases involve more than simple corrections of historical "fact." They raise and address the issue of authority, not only of documentary versus archaeological resources, but also of the political and social authorities that help to create and uphold historical myths. Archaeology may be able to suggest a more complex and dynamic past when social preconceptions are reexamined. This confrontation is particularly important for ethnocentrically motivated myths. Archaeology may raise questions about the purposes of history and the selective writing of the past, both to simplify and to gloss over social tensions.

Archaeology has been able to challenge historical accounts. McDonald et al. (1991) describe an archaeological project commissioned by the Northern Cheyenne to document escape routes taken during the outbreak from Fort Robinson, Nebraska, in 1879. Archaeological results successfully challenged official Army-based accounts of the escape by providing data that bolstered Cheyenne oral tradition. Oral history and archaeology thus may be mutually supportive in providing data and perspectives that contribute to a more accurate history in which biases and the politics of knowledge are acknowledged.

Creating context

Chuck Cleland expresses his exasperation that historical archaeology has become infatuated with particular events that are often presented without social context and are therefore meaningless. He observes that archaeologists are often misled into thinking that they understand the culture and society of the past if they speak the same language and recognize the artifacts. Cleland (2001: 5) writes, "It should be the goal of each piece of research in historical archaeology to address larger problems and to seek conclusions which advance our knowledge of the cultural practices which are involved in the formation of

BARBARA LITTLE

sites. There is a way to make the remains of a nineteenth-century Wisconsin farmhouse relevant to broader problems but it must be contextualized as part of a cultural system."

The call for an ethnographic, contextual historical archaeology is widespread. Archaeologists, however, may differ on the best methods to create such rich history, but they will need to use a range of documents to create interpretive contexts.

Historian Rhys Isaac describes the method he used to research his influential book, *The Transformation of Virginia, 1740–1790* (1982: 323–57). He has been successful in blending the methods of history and anthropology to evoke the changing world of Chesapeake society and culture in the eighteenth century. His method recognizes that both disciplines have in common the observation of the things that people do and translation of behavior into something understandable by outsiders (in place or time). Culture "comprises gesture, demeanor, dress, architecture, and all the codes by which those who share in the culture convey meanings and significance to each other" (1982: 325). The goal of ethnographic history, he writes, is a *"pervasive reconstruction of the experiences of past actors"* (1982: 357). Isaac analyses evidence of interactions in terms of scenarios, which he analyzes as dramatic interactions to explore ritual, power, and meaning in eighteenth-century Virginia. Although he is not an archaeologist, his use of material culture effectively informs the anthropological history that he creates.

Many historical archaeologists caution against the tendency to privilege the documentary record, to believe the results of documentary research or long-accepted historical conclusions more readily than archaeological research. As researchers learn their craft, they come to appreciate that history, whether pursued through documents or material culture, exists through interpretation. There are some circumstances in which an archaeologist relies on documents more than others, but there should never be a time when interpretations are not open to question.

Making an archaeological contribution to history

Regardless of the contribution that archaeology could make to historical understanding, in many situations historical archaeologists will face a major problem in the dominance of the historical record. Innocent Pikirayi and Gilbert Pwiti (1999: 86) highlight the situation in one African country: "In Zimbabwe, the program of historical archaeology appears to have been set by history and the historical perception of the past. Not only are the materially based studies of archaeology regularly subordinated to those of the literary record but the entire conceptual framework of questions and evidence has been limited by historical concerns."

Archaeologists must bear some responsibility for this widespread privileging of documentary data, as we are not necessarily providing new and significant insights through historical archaeology. In a 1988 article in the influential journal, *Science*, James Deetz protests that instead of integrating archaeological and documentary sources, researchers often start with the documents and look for reflections in the archaeology, or start with the artifacts and look for reflections in the documents. Both approaches fall short of the potential of historical archaeology by guaranteeing that nothing significant will be contributed by archaeology.

He goes on to demonstrate an effective synthesis of data. His analysis moves between the data sources, raising questions and searching for relevant answers in a broad context. Based upon dating sites with pipe stem data, he identifies three periods of occupation among 30 sites on Flowerdew Hundred on the James River in Virginia, dating to between 1620 and 1750. Having established a clear pattern in the archaeological record, Deetz consults the historical record to look for explanations. The historical record indicates changes in the tobacco economy and the institutionalization of slavery, which suggests further questions for the material remains. Archaeologically, colonoware dating to the third period (1710–50) is found at the sites, which raises the question of why there is no colonoware earlier. Deetz returns to the historical record to see what is different about these sites or this time period. History indicates changes in house size and settlement plan, and changes in the housing of servants and slaves and in the relationships between masters and slaves. Finding a correlation between architecture and colonoware raises questions about archaeologically observed differences in the forms of colonoware in Virginia and South Carolina. This leads to new insights and questions about racial relationships and the experience of enslaved workers in the two colonies.

My summary here is brief and made to illustrate the cyclical approach that alternates between sources, rather than to explain the historical discoveries. I urge you to read the original article and reflect on the potential of using careful methodology. Deetz's method combines elements of each kind of source interplay identified above.

Resources Many archaeology and historical journals present research involving the use of historical documents; however, there are rarely discussions of critical documentary methods. Despite this, the following sources may be useful. For North America: *Historical Methods, Historical Archaeology*, the *Journal of Anthropological Archaeology*, the *Journal of Archaeological Method and Theory*, the *Journal of Anthropological Archaeology, Archaeology, American Antiquity*, and *Industrial Archaeology*. For Oceania: *Australasian Historical Archaeology* (published until 1993 as the *Australian Journal of Historical Archaeology*), the *Journal of the Royal Australian Historical Society, Australian Archaeology, Archaeology in Oceania*, the *Australian Institute for Maritime Archaeology Bulletin*, the *New Zealand Journal of Archaeology*, and the *New Zealand Archaeological Association Newsletter*. General: *Antiquity*, the *International Journal of Historical Archaeology*, and the *International Journal of Nautical Archaeology*.

BARBARA LITTLE

- Archives Library Information Center (ALIC) of the US National Archives and Records Administration: www.archives.gov/research_room/alic/reference_at_your_desk.html
- International Oral History Association: www.filo.uba.ar/Institutos/ravigni/historal/Ioha.htm
- Internet History Sourcebooks Project, which is dedicated to making original primary sources available on the Internet: www.fordham.edu/halsall/
- National Archives of Australia: www.naa.gov.au/
- National Library of Canada and National Archives of Canada: www.archives.ca
- National Archives of India: http://nationalarchives.nic.in/landing.html
- National Archives of Ireland: www.nationalarchives.ie/transp1.html (see the useful page of links from the National Archives of Ireland to other archives around the world: www.nationalarchives.ie/otherscountries.html)
- Archives New Zealand Te Whare Tohu Tuhituhinga o Aotearoa: www.archives.govt.nz
- Public Record Office, the National Archives of England, Wales, and the United Kingdom: www.pro.gov.uk/
- US Library of Congress: www.loc.gov
- US National Archives and Records Administration (NARA): www.nara.gov
- The University of Berkeley's Finding Aids to Archival Collection: www.oac.cdlib.org

American Library Association 1990: *A Consumer's Guide to Research Guides for Historical Literature: Antiquity, the Middle Ages, Modern Europe, the United States, and Latin America*, prepared by Bibliography and Indexes Committee, History Section, Reference and Adult Services Division, American Library Association. Chicago: The Association.

Andren, A. 1998: *Between Artifacts and Texts: Historical Archaeology in Global Perspective*. New York: Plenum Press.

Beaudry, M. C. (ed.) 1988: *Documentary Archaeology in the New World*. Cambridge: Cambridge University Press.

Davidson, J. W. and Lytle, M. H. 2000: *After the Fact: The Art of Historical Detection*, 4th edn. Boston: McGraw-Hill.

Duke, P. and Saitta, D. J. 1998: An Emancipatory Archaeology for the Working Class. Assemblage 4. Electronic document: www.shef.ac.uk/assem/4/4duk_sai.html

Echo-Hawk, R. C. 2000: Ancient history in the New World: integrating oral traditions and the archaeological record. *American Antiquity*, 65, 267–90.

Gilbert, L. A., Driscoll, W. P. and Sutherland, A., 1974: *History Around Us: An Enquiry Approach to Local History*. Sydney: Hicks Smith.

Green, J. 2000: *Taking History to Heart: The Power of the Past in Building Social Movements*. Amherst, MA: The University of Massachusetts Press.

Harvey, C. and Press, J. 1996: *Databases in Historical Research: Theory, Methods, and Applications*. New York: St Martin's Press.

Howell, M. C. and Prevenier, W. 2001: *From Reliable Sources: An Introduction to Historical Methods*. Ithaca, NY: Cornell University Press.

Knapp, A. B. (ed.) 1992: *Archaeology, Annales, and Ethnohistory*. Cambridge: Cambridge University Press.

Little, B. J. (ed.) 1992: *Text-Aided Archaeology*. Boca Raton, FL: CRC Press.

Mason, R. J. 2000: Archaeology and Native American oral traditions. *American Antiquity*, 65, 239–66.

Phillips, C. 2000: *Waihou Journeys: The Archaeology of 400 Years of Maori Settlement*. Auckland: Auckland University Press.

Praetzellis, A. and Praetzellis, M. (eds.) 1998: Archaeologists as storytellers. *Historical Archaeology*, 32(1), 94–6.

Reagan, P. D. 2002: *History and the Internet: A Guide*. Boston: McGraw-Hill.

Stahl, A. B. 2001: *Making History in Banda: Anthropological Visions of Africa's Past*. Cambridge: Cambridge University Press.

Topolski, J. (ed.) 1994: *Historiography between Modernism and Postmodernism: Contributions to the Methodology of the Historical Research*. Atlanta, GA: Rodopi.

Vansina, J. 1985: *Oral Tradition as History*. London: James Currey.

Whitley, P. M. 2002: Archaeology and oral tradition: the scientific importance of dialogue. *American Antiquity*, 67, 405–15.

References   Bowen, J. 1988: Seasonality: an agricultural construct. In M. C. Beaudry (ed.), *Documentary Archaeology*. Cambridge: Cambridge University Press, 161–71.

—— 1994: A comparative analysis of the New England and Chesapeake herding systems. In P. A. Shackel and B. J. Little (eds.), *Historical Archaeology of the Chesapeake*. Washington, DC: Smithsonian Institution Press, 155–68.

Braudel, F. 1980 [1949]: Preface. In *La Mediterranee et le monde mediterraneen a l'epoque de Phillippe II*, trans. S. Matthews. Chicago: University of Chicago.

Carr, L. G. and Walsh, L. S. 1980: Inventories and the analysis of wealth and consumption patterns in St. Mary's County, Maryland, 1658–1777. *Historical Methods*, 13, 81–104.

Chesterfield, P. D. S. 1901 [1776]: *Letters To His Son*, ed. L. M. W. Dunne. London: Leigh M. Walter Dunne.

Cleland, C. E. 2001: Historical archaeology adrift? *Historical Archaeology*, 35, 1–8.

Corbin, A. 1998: Shifting sand and muddy water: historic cartography and river migration as factors in locating steamboat wrecks on the far Upper Missouri River. *Historical Archaeology*, 32(4), 86–96.

D'Agostino, M. E. 1995: A full complement: employing diverse sources in historical anthropology. In M. E. D'Agostino, E. Prine, E. Casella et al. (eds.), *The Written and the Wrought: Complementary Sources in Historical Archaeology*. Kroeber Anthropological Papers, 79, 116–36. Berkeley, CA: Kroeber Anthropological Society.

Deetz, J. 1972: Ceramics from Plymouth, 1635–1835. In M. G. Quimby (ed.), *Ceramics in America*, I. Charlottesville: University of Virginia, 15–40.

—— 1977: *In Small Things Forgotten: The Archaeology of Early American Life*. New York: Doubleday.

—— 1988: American historical archaeology: methods and results. *Science*, 239, 362–7.

—— 1983: Scientific humanism and humanistic science: a plea for paradigmatic pluralism. *Geoscience and Man*, 23, 27–34.

Elias, N. 1978 [1939]: *The History of Manners: The Civilizing Process* 1, trans. E. Jephcott. New York: Pantheon.

Isaac, R. 1982: *The Transformation of Virginia, 1740–1790*. Chapel Hill, NC: University of North Carolina.

Kirch, P. and Sahlins, M. 1992: *Anahulu: The Anthropology of History in the Kingdom of Hawaii* (2 vols). Chicago: University of Hawaii Press.

Leone, M. P. and Potter, P. B. Jr 1988: Introduction: issues in historical archaeology. In M. P. Leone and P. B. Potter, Jr (eds.), *The Recovery of Meaning*. Washington, DC: Smithsonian Institution Press, 1–22.

Little, B. J. 1994: "She was . . . an example to her sex": possibilities for a feminist historical archaeology. In P. A. Shackel and B. J. Little (eds.), *The Historical Archaeology of the Chesapeake*. Washington, DC: Smithsonian Institution Press, 189–204.

—— and Shackel, P. A. 1989: Scales of historical anthropology: an archaeology of colonial Anglo-America. *Antiquity*, 63, 495–509.

McDonald, J. D., Zimmerman, L. J., McDonald, A. L. et al. 1991: The Northern Cheyenne outbreak of 1879: using oral history and archaeology as tools of resistance. In R. H. McGuire and R. Paynter (eds.), *The Archaeology of Inequality*. Oxford: Blackwell, 64–78.

Pikirayi, I. and Pwiti, G. 1999: States, traders, and colonists: historical archaeology in Zimbabwe. *Historical Archaeology*, 33(2), 73–89.

Pitt, D. C. 1972: *Using Historical Sources in Anthropology and Sociology*. New York: Holt, Rinehart, and Winston.

Russo, J. 1983: Economy of Anne Arundel County. In L. Walsh (ed.), *Annapolis and Anne Arundel County, Maryland: A Study of Urban Development in a Tobacco Economy: 1649–1776*. On file at Maryland Hall of Records. NEH Grant RS-20199-81-1955.

Scott, E. M. 1997: A little gravy in the dish and onions in a tea cup: what cookbooks reveal about material culture. *International Journal of Historical Archaeology*, 1, 131–55.

Shackel, P. A. 1993: *Personal Discipline and Material Culture: An Archaeology Annapolis, Maryland 1695–1870*. Knoxville: University of Tennessee Press.

Winks, R. W. (ed.) 1970: *The Historian as Detective: Essays on Evidence*. New York: Harper Colophon Books.

Peter White

15

Producing the Record

A discovery dates only from the time of the record of it, and not from the time of its being found in the soil.

Pitt Rivers (1898: 28)

Introduction

I recently received a book catalog entitled *Archaeology: Method, Theory and Practice*. Among the four pages of books on method, there were books about survey, sampling, excavation, dating, GIS, electronic databases, and other things. Elsewhere, there were books on interpretations, public outreach, museum presentation, and working with communities. But there wasn't a single book on the nuts and bolts of writing anywhere in the 24-page catalog.

I found this surprising. Most of the end results of archaeological research, its reporting, reasoning, and interpretation, are produced as writing, either in hard copy or electronically. It is by our written work that the public, our teachers, and our peers evaluate us. So we should be paying attention to how we write and how we present our findings and results.

The purpose of this chapter is to help you move from field, laboratory, and library research and analysis to a written account of aspects or all of it. It presents some simple guidelines concerning organizing the structure of written works and using effective language.

This chapter is about how to think about and present the content of your work. It is not about the philosophy of archaeology, how to interpret your material, or the technology of publishing. I have tried to focus on what will be useful to the most likely readers of this chapter, namely undergraduate and postgraduate students. But even senior professors need to think about the organization and language of their writing, so I hope some of them will also read this.

Before starting to write, ask yourself:

1 What is the purpose of this writing? What do I want to write about?
2 Who am I writing for? Who is my audience?

The answers to these questions will determine what goes into the piece – and what gets left out.

In most student contexts, what you are writing about will be determined by the question or topic set for you. So the first rule is *read the question*! Read it and make sure that your planned paper covers what is being asked. **What do I want to write about?**

In other situations, you will have more scope to define your own topic. It may be a report on an excavation or survey, an analysis of data, or an interpretation of a period, place, or phenomenon. But you need to start out by deciding what you are writing about. Unless you are simply reporting what you did on a day-to-day basis, every piece of writing needs a *point*. What is the *basic* message you are trying to communicate? Is it that this site covers a certain period, that one argument about this pottery type is right and another wrong, or that you favor a religious rather than an economic interpretation of this city layout?

To anyone who has been working on a problem or data set, this advice may seem rather curious. You have been slaving away looking for sites, measuring artifacts, constructing a philosophical position, counting bones, reviewing the origins of agriculture or whatever, so of course you know what you're going to write about. But if you just start writing it is actually surprisingly easy to stray away from your topic. There are sidelines that you find interesting, or you perceive the need to qualify or explain some aspect that is not really central to your theme. Novelists say that they are often surprised by how some minor character develops importance as a story proceeds; the same can be true in archaeological writing. Conversely, it is not difficult to forget aspects of the topic that are really relevant to a full understanding of the data or argument. So answer this question first. Write out a plan of what this piece of writing must contain.

Deciding who you are writing for is particularly important for determining both the length of the piece and the style of your language, but to some extent it also affects the content. You should consider the *genre* within which you should write. An essay or thesis will need to be written in academic language, explaining your methods fully, using technical terms as appropriate, and documenting your statements with full referencing. A report to a local community that has given you permission to work with them or on their land will need to be in plain English, with technical terms avoided or explained. Reporting the **Who is my audience?**

results of contracted research to a local authority or private developer will require clearly spelled out recommendations for (in)action, which you can justify on the basis of the research. In each case, the approach and language will be different and you should decide how you are going to write before you begin.

What readers get out of your text is, of course, only partly within your control. Every reader brings his or her own knowledge, attitude, and viewpoint to any text. This conditions what a reader makes of your work and how they use it. But by thinking about your intended audience, you can try to make it user-friendly for them and less liable to misinterpretation of what you want to tell them.

Structure   Half a century ago, the famous English archaeologist Sir Mortimer Wheeler wrote that "Plain and effective writing requires a plain and effective structure" (1956: 215). He was writing about excavation reports, but the structure that he advocates for these has been used widely by academics, especially most scientists, for much of the past century and is advocated by all the main writing gurus. While this formula is most applicable to scientific writing, it can be modified and simplified for almost any kind of archaeological writing, since it embodies a basically narrative structure (see, e.g., Pluciennik 1999).

The formula is as follows:

*   introduction (aims)
*   background
*   methods
*   results
*   discussion and conclusions.

This basic formula clearly separates actions from thoughts, discoveries from deductions. It organizes the material logically so that a reader can understand how the work proceeded. On the other hand, it lets a reader who doesn't necessarily want to read the whole piece use it to satisfy his or her particular requirements.

Using this formula effectively implies that you should divide your work into appropriate sections, each with a heading. For long pieces, you may also need subsections. Don't be afraid of these. Section and subsection headings help to guide readers through your text, showing where they have reached the end of one topic and are embarking on another.

I will now discuss each part of the structural formula. This discussion is oriented toward report writing, but the basic structure can be adapted to almost anything more organized than stream of consciousness. The most usual modification among archaeologists will be to say little about methods and to combine results, discussion, and conclusions. This might be expected in a paper on the origin of language or problems of ontology in archaeology. You are not discarding the formula but modifying it to suit your needs.

PETER WHITE

This should tell the reader broadly what this piece of writing is about: what problem was being researched, what you are aiming to demonstrate, and what conclusions were reached. The introduction is the most difficult part to write and will usually need to be totally rewritten after you have finished a first draft of the whole work. This is because what you thought you were going to say when you started often isn't quite what you end up saying.

Introduction

Here, you review the theoretical and/or practical situation when you began the work. If a bulldozer had dug up part of a skeleton, which you then excavated, what had happened before your arrival? If your study is about seasonality in shell middens in Sydney, or California or the Orkney Islands, what did we know about the general problem and work in the specific area when you began? For a piece on archaeological ethics, you might need to outline the ethical code of the World Archaeological Congress and refer to codes of other disciplines. The point of this section is to identify the *relevant* context for your research. It is *not* to display the full extent of your knowledge about the topic. Ask yourself: What does a reader need to know to understand the context in which I am working? Stick to the answer!

Background

What goes in here should be obvious: say what you did and how you did it. Where did you survey? How much did you dig? What recovery methods were used? What analyses were undertaken, using what protocols? In a scientific report, this section is where you demonstrate that you knew what you were doing; or, in a public report, it is where you explain how and why you went about it the way you did. This is the section that anyone who doubts your results or conclusions will read to check that your methods were appropriate and correctly used.

Methods

What did you find out? This section will need clear descriptive prose, as well as tables and figures, so that the correctness, strength, and importance of your results can be readily assessed. This is where other people will look for material for their research, to see whether what you found is consistent with what is already known and with what they found. You therefore need to be very careful to say what you actually mean. You also need to ensure that your story is consistent. Working on manuscripts as editor of an archaeological journal, I regularly find that numbers given in the text and tables don't agree, distances or positions stated are not what the map shows, stratigraphies don't match, tables are inconsistent in totals or units and, only too often, that people just can't add up! Errors of these kinds may be simple slips of the keyboard, but they don't inspire confidence among readers in your research.

Results

Conclusions	This part of the document will depend a great deal on the overall purpose and audience. An essay, thesis, or archaeological paper will require your opinion about what has been achieved. This may include considerable discussion about what you understand by the results and their implications (Where do we go from here?). A mitigation (contract) report will include a series of recommendations for action, phrased in plain English.

Attached to the basic structure there are usually three add-ons – an abstract, references, and acknowledgments. |
| The abstract | An abstract summarizes the text. It is for readers who don't have access to, or time to read, your text. An abstract is a short version of the paper, not a description of it – so avoid phrases such as "We describe . . ." or "We then analyzed . . ." It answers several questions: Why did you start? What did you do? What did you find? What do the findings mean? (O'Connor 1991: 70). It should do all this in 100–200 words, as in the following example from a paper entitled "Japanese Jomon sherds in artifact collections from Mele Plain on Efate in Vanuatu" (Dickinson et al. 1999: 15): |

> Fourteen cord-marked sherds collected from the surface of yam gardens on Mele Plain near Port Vila on the island of Efate in Vanuatu are unlike any known prehistoric wares from Pacific islands. Based on typological analysis, comparative petrographic study of sand tempers supplemented by microprobe analysis of characteristic microperlite sand grains and thermoluminescence dating of key examples, we believe these sherds were made during the Early Jomon period in Aomori Prefecture near the north tip of Honshu. Although we are unable to specify the time or means of their introduction into Vanuatu, the sherds cannot represent indigenous pottery and are not part of the Oceanian ceramic legacy.

References	Unless something different is specified, a list of references (bibliography) should contain *all and only* those works included in your paper. Although there are now various computer programs for organizing these and presenting them in a consistent manner, the "GIGO" maxim still operates. If you put Garbage In, you will get Garbage Out. In other words, you are responsible for the original accuracy of the citations. Getting references right is not easy. You should check the accuracy of every reference – even your own publications. The reference that is wrong or left out in someone else's work is always the one you want! Don't do this to your readers.
Acknowledgments	Thank those organizations and individuals who gave you substantial or timely help in the form of permissions, grants, materials, or advice. Especially in archaeology, it is highly unlikely you have worked all on your own and people like to be acknowledged, while institutions often require it.

PETER WHITE

It is not easy to write simple and clear English. Texts that are easy to read have usually been difficult to write and are the product of several drafts. Most writers who are known for their good writing, whether academics or novelists, tell of rewriting each paragraph many times – although, as with many skills, ability often improves with practice. It also helps if you have decided what you want to say and who you are writing for.

There are a number of steps in the actual production of good written work:

1   Start by writing an outline of what you want to say. A one-page summary of your aims, methods, results, and conclusions will help you to work out what to write.

2   Next, just write it. Start at the beginning and write according to the plan. Don't agonize over each word and sentence – you can do that next time round. Try to get down what you think is a reasonably complete draft. But perhaps you, like many writers (including myself) sometimes get a "threshold complex," when you just can't start – when no sentence seems right. If so, start in the middle with the easy bits, which are usually the methods and results. You know how you went about your work and what you found, so write about those topics. Once that's in hand, the discussion and conclusions should follow. Then you can go back and write your introduction.

3   Having got some words down, look at the *structure* of what you have created. Does it follow the plan you made? Does the introduction cover the whole paper? Are the methods and results in logical order? Does the discussion mirror the results? Shuffle sections, paragraphs, and sentences until the structure and content are clear. Make a note on the text of what is missing at that place.

4   Rewrite. In this second draft, pay particular attention to the first section – the aims. This is where readers will start, so it needs to encourage them to persist. It is also, in my experience, often the worst part of any piece, loaded with generalities, irrelevancies, references, and inappropriate personal detail. The first section should map out the ground ahead and the goal to be reached.

5   When you think you have written something reasonable, put it away, if you have time, for at least a week or longer. Do something else. Then re-read it. You will be surprised at how it has changed! What you thought was organized and elegant will have become badly structured and poorly expressed. Rewrite it again. Be ruthless!

6   This time, after rewriting, don't bury it, but give it to several friends to read. Try to choose a range of people – a colleague who knows what you're talking about, your mother who doesn't, or a friend who you think

writes well. Choose people who you can expect to be honest with you, and who you know will be prepared to put some time into reading your work carefully and critically. But be prepared for shocks. Your friends will almost certainly find faults. Your reaction is likely to be hostile, to defend your writing right down to every comma. *Don't.* Swallow your pride and listen to your friends. It is quite likely that they will be right.

When you think you have a moderately decent draft, there are three aspects that you need to consider specifically. These are your spelling and grammar, which I consider together, your use of quotations, and your documentation or referencing.

First, now that most people use a word processor with spelling and grammar checkers, the number of errors in a piece of written work might be expected to have fallen. But I am not sure it has.

It is clear that many writers, especially students, are very casual about their spelling and know little about grammar. This is sometimes justified by arguing for "free expression." But poor presentation in these matters suggests that you are illiterate – and thus probably also incompetent. I suggest that you should *never* let any of your work escape into the hands of others until you have checked it for spelling and grammatical errors. If you know that you are weak in this area, get help from someone who is better trained.

You should also realize that no spelling or grammar checkers can check for improperly used words. "For" and "four" are both correctly spelled, but have quite different meanings; the same is true of "today" and "toady," "grave" and "gravy," and many other words. You actually need to read your work before letting it loose on the world. This is often best done with a friend, one of you reading it aloud to the other. Boring and slow it may be, but it can save you a lot of embarrassment, especially if your typing or grammar is not perfect.

Secondly, consider your use of quotations from the work of others. The use of long chunks taken directly from other authors, even with acknowledgment, should be avoided except in quite specific circumstances. Many students use lengthy quotes in the belief that "experts" have said it better than they can, but the point of student essays, theses, and academic papers is to demonstrate that *you* are sufficiently on top of a topic to write about it yourself. Of course you will have to draw on data and even opinions of other workers in the field, but what readers will want to know is *your* contribution and how *you* make use of work already done.

These thoughts about quotations lead directly to the third topic, referencing. When you use information that originally appeared in other works, this needs to be acknowledged. Failure to do so can be seen as plagiarism – in other words, stealing. Among students and academics, referencing is necessary to avoid any suggestion of plagiarism as well as to show what you have considered in producing your work. There are various systems of referencing, and examples of the three common ones are given in the Appendix. The choice of system that you use may be dictated by your lecturer, department, or journal, but whichever it is, successful use of it should aim for clarity, accuracy, and consistency.

This chapter cannot cover the writing of good English – to do that would need the whole of this book. What I can do here is point out a few simple, obvious do's and don'ts:

Language

1 Does each sentence say what you intend?

> One clue [to the disappearance of Neanderthal peoples] is that they lived chiefly during hard winters when death rates must have been high. (Pfeiffer 1969: 194)

This is simple and direct, but nonsense.

> This powder was then placed into an 0.5 mm capillary which was sealed. (Blau et al. 2002: 814)

How did they place the powder into a sealed tube?

2 Is each sentence simple and clear?

> None of these [the distributions of archaeological remains] can be understood, however, without taking into account the ecological nature of the habitat exploited by the toolmakers and it is especially important for the prehistorian to know what main plant and animal resources were present and so available for use by the hunting/gathering populations during the Pleistocene when the biomes may often have differed significantly from those of the present day in response to fluctuations in humidity and temperature. (Clark 1975: 606)

Why not:

> None of these [the distributions of archaeological remains], however, can be understood without taking account of the toolmakers' habitats. It is especially important to know what main plant and animal resources were available to Pleistocene hunters/gatherers. These resources may often have differed significantly from those now present, since biomes respond to fluctuations in humidity and temperature.

3 Are you taking responsibility for your work by using the first person and the active voice?

- "During the excavation it was noted that the stratigraphy of layers 7 and 8 was dissected in places by several pits" is a complicated way of saying "While excavating, I noted several pits which cut through layers 7 and 8." Similarly, I could rewrite Blau et al. (2002: 814) quoted above: "We sealed the powder into an 0.5 mm capillary."

- Using "It was done" instead of "I did" is not more objective. Rather, it's a cop-out – a way of saying "No, it wasn't me – I'm not responsible. What I did was dictated by some higher authority."

4   Is each sentence complete?

- "Whereas the second sample of points came from layers 6 and 7" is not a complete sentence, because "whereas" shows that it requires the previous sentence to understand the contrast being made.
- When you read each sentence it should make sense on its own, without requiring any reference to previous or following sentences.

5   Are you using the right words?

- I have been faced with people's "rolls" (instead of "roles") in "sedimentary," rather than "sedentary," communities, which were "effected," rather than "affected," by drought. If long words bother you, use a dictionary.
- The *Oxford English Dictionary, Merriam–Webster's Collegiate Dictionary*, and the *Macquarie Dictionary* are among some of the online dictionaries (see www.oed.com, www.m-w.com, and www.macquariedictionary.com.au).

Examples similar to the above problems can be found in many reports. You will usually find that it is readers of your work, not you, who notice your bad writing. Having others read your work for you is the best way of avoiding these problems.

Writing for Publication   Much of what I have outlined above about structure and approach applies to papers written for publication as well as to term papers or theses. But there are several specific aspects to submitting works for publication that are often overlooked or ignored, to which I shall now turn.

Target carefully   In this case, deciding who you are going to write for involves the journal or publisher as well as the audience. Study the form, structure, and content of the papers in the journal in which you want to publish, or of the books produced by the publisher you are thinking of approaching. Is what you want to write compatible with their current output? If not, can you rewrite it to be compatible or would you be better off approaching someone else? Look around. Different venues work in different genres and you should consider your options within these genres.

If you are trying to write an archaeological paper based on a thesis or report, don't think that you can just paste together chunks extracted from the previous work, or even necessarily follow its format. Put your previous work away and start again. Write it out of your head, following the steps suggested above. There will be time enough to get the data right afterwards, when you can go back to the original. But if you want a paper to be clear and convincing, it *must* be written as a separate piece of work.

Start afresh

Read, mark, digest, and *use* the Instructions to Authors of the journal or publisher you have chosen. These will cover such matters as acceptable length of article, form of submission (e.g., disk or hard copy), bibliographic style, the acceptable number, size, and style of illustrations, presentation of radiocarbon dates, and so on. If you have a problem, look at recent issues of the journal, or consult the editor. Instructions to Authors can be very precise – those for *American Antiquity* cover 22 pages – but failure to follow them will put you immediately offside with the editor, who may simply return your manuscript, unread.

Follow instructions

Plan pictures, tables, and graphs while you are writing. These will be rough drafts, but doing this concurrently will help you to decide what goes in them and what goes in the text. You need to decide what is the function of each illustration. Is it to present an impression or provide a large amount of information? Answering this will help you to decide how to structure it. Illustrations should not duplicate the text, but should vividly elucidate it or amplify the data. Students, in particular, often put pictures into their essays, but then don't refer to them or use them. This is a nonsense – the pictures become just irrelevant decoration. As Moser (1998) points out, pictures are persuasive in their own right, so you need to ensure that they interact with the text, each adding to the other. Use them or lose them.

Think about illustrations and tables

As with the text, *don't even think* that you can just pluck illustrations out of a previous work. Most graphics drawn up for theses or reports are on A4 paper and nearly always include very large amounts of unused space. Very few journals or books will allow you to be this wasteful: look at the illustrations that they publish. What you need to produce are graphs and tables that fit well onto a page or into a column of the publication. You can get a sense of this by photo-reducing your intended illustrations to the likely final size. This will also tell you whether your lettering is too small (the usual problem) or you have tried to put too much in. Your aim should be to produce graphs and tables that *communicate*. O'Connor (1991, chs 3 & 4) has useful advice about preparing tables and figures (see Figure 15.1). However, for really elegant graphic and map presentations that avoid "chart junk" and maximize the data–ink ratio, Tufte (2001) reigns supreme. Many computer-drawn graphics are

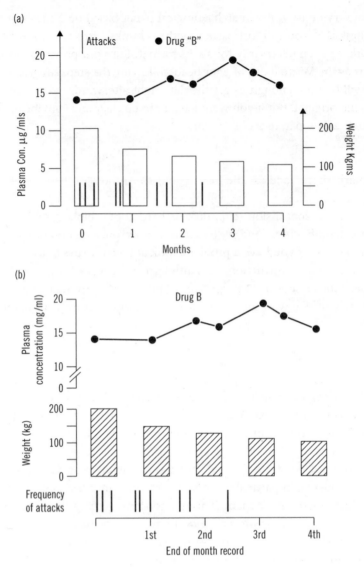

Figure 15.1 Obscure and clear data presentation. (a) Several sets of data have been superimposed to save space; data are measured in unrelated units, unit labels are wrong, and arrows are unnecessary. (b) The same data, separated into three components and using no more space. (Reprinted from O'Connor, 1991, *Writing Successfully in Science*, HarperCollins Academic, with permission.)

clumsy and inelegant, sometimes even obscuring the data (Figure 15.2). Remember KISS – Keep It Simple, Stupid – to help you to choose the best way of presenting your data consistent with your aims in presenting them.

Illustrations such as maps and photographs should be essential to the paper. Use them to make basic or key points clearer, especially those that are hard to describe in words. Excellent examples are descriptions of making stone tools or pottery, where a set of clear pictures can replace mounds of hard-to-read text. Similarly, a paper discussing the difference between shell mounds, middens,

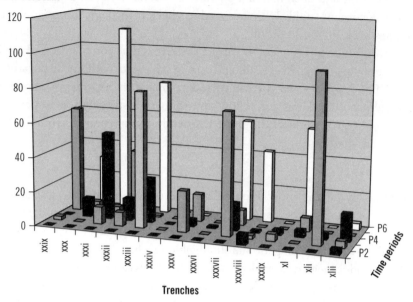

Figure 15.2 This is probably one of the world's ugliest and most misleading graph forms. I suggest that you should never use it. It crams in a great deal of data, but note how hard it is to work out the actual value of a particular count. For example, the gray column in xxxiii/P3 is actually a higher count than the white column in xxxiii/P6, while the tall black column xxxiii/P4 is of lower value than the gray column xxxv/P3. It is also easy for tall columns in front rows to obscure shorter columns in the rear rows (created in Microsoft® Excel by Trudy Doelman).

and cheniers will usefully use a photograph and/or drawing of each, which will bring out their differences. In the case of maps, consider what the reader *needs to know*: For instance, are all the contours or stream courses really necessary? Once again, KISS is a good guide.

Reference efficiently

Your bibliography should contain all and only those items referred to in your paper. Present them in the *precise* style chosen by the publisher. Journals and book publishers are often quite fussy about this. If their style is not the same as the one used by your bibliographic computer program, well, tough: you will have to change, for they won't (see Appendix: Referencing).

Read the proofs carefully

Proof reading is critically important in publication. A work will come to the editor or publisher on floppy disk, CD, or by email. Translating it onto paper, and especially formatting into a journal or book, allows errors to occur. This is notably the case with symbols such as Greek letters or unusual abbreviations. But lines or blocks of text can be lost or transposed, captions wrongly placed, apostrophes re-symbolled, and so on. The reason is, of course, not "computer error," but human error. It is people who use the formatting programs, decide on the layout, and push bits of a document around. So even if you send off a perfect document (unlikely!), you need to check it through thoroughly when it comes back to you in proof.

By proof stage it is too late to correct the errors that you overlooked earlier, unless they are very small-scale and can be changed without disturbing the layout. But at proof stage you can correct technical errors, and you should use standard proof markings and follow any editorial instructions as to pen color and so on. I give some of the most frequently used proofing symbols at the end of this chapter.

Conclusion Writing is by far the most frequent method of communicating archaeology. Even if your final output is a talk or lecture, video, CD, or TV program, the structure and organization will have involved writing. Clear, logical writing is the pathway to an intelligent and intelligible result.

The development of a well-written piece involves understanding the steps to be taken. First, you must know what the point of the piece is – what you want to get across. At the same time, you need to think about your readership and how to make your writing suitable for them.

Next, plan the structure. Aims, background, methods, results, and conclusions is a well tested formula, although it can be modified to suit your particular circumstances. Be clear to yourself why you are modifying it.

Then write, rewrite, rest, try out on your friends, and rewrite. Check your logic and language, your grammar and spelling, and your references for clarity, accuracy, and consistency. Plan your tables as you go along, so that they illuminate your text: a picture or graph may be worth a thousand words, but you have to use it to make it so.

If you are writing for publication, follow the instructions – because all else fails.

Finally, as with any sport or skill, good writing requires practice, as well as help from trainers and courage to admit that you can do better. No pain, no gain.

Acknowledgments I thank the editors for inviting me to write this chapter, of which this is the third version (amended, with thanks to the editors); thanks also to Robin Torrence for helpful comments (second draft) and Trudy Doelman for graphs.

Appendix: getting things right

SI units

Most of the world now uses SI units. Even where this is not so, most academics and many businesspeople work with them. The three base SI units are the meter (m), the kilogram (kg), and the second (s). Often, multiples of these, such as the millimeter (mm) and the gram (g), are more appropriate working units. Units should be used consistently within any piece of work – don't jump between meters and millimeters, or between grams and kilograms. Decide which is best for your work and use it.

The symbols for these units are set by the International Organization for Standardization and should be used in the proper way, such as "kg" rather than "Kg," and "g" rather than "gm" or "gms." Symbols never take a plural ("gms" is wrong) but names do ("grams" is fine).

There is no absolute international standard for the presentation of radiocarbon (^{14}C) dates, but leading international journals such as *Antiquity* and *American Antiquity* largely agree on the information needed and the form in which this should be given. These forms are derived from the resolutions of the International Radiocarbon Conference and they should be what we all use. A common format will allow accuracy to be checked and improvements in the radiocarbon dating process incorporated. Full and accurate presentation of known information is especially important when dealing with dates produced over past decades, since these have different levels of precision and accuracy, and may well need revision. **Radiocarbon dates**

Start with the uncalibrated age supplied by the laboratory. Give the laboratory abbreviation and sample number, the age in years BP, the one sigma (symbol = σ) standard error, and the material dated. The abbreviation "BP" means "before present": international agreements set this date at AD 1950 and this is what the laboratory will use. *Never* change the BP date supplied by the laboratory.

Calibrated dates should now always be used for interpretation and discussion, except for ages older than 24,000 years (Stuiver et al. 1998). Calibrated dates are determined by using a calibration program that gives results in terms of date ranges along with associated probabilities. Calibrated dates are solar years and must therefore always be presented as cal BC/cal AD (cal BCE/cal CE is also acceptable). The calibration program used (e.g., CALIB 4), the probability for each date range, and the material dated (if not already stated) should be given, along with any necessary corrections made, such as the Southern Hemisphere offset.

- *The author–date (Harvard) system.* "Russell's (1990) analysis and my fieldwork (White 1993, 1994) have shown that the data are incomplete." The references are given in alphabetical order of author, as in this book, although the format used here is closer to the Vancouver standard form. **Referencing**
- *The documentary-note system.* "Russell's[1] analysis and my[2] fieldwork have shown that the data are incomplete." In this case, each numbered reference will contain as many publications as necessary (and may contain explanatory notes).
- *The Vancouver system.* "Russell's[1] analysis and my[2,3] fieldwork have shown that the data are incomplete." The reference list will give each publication in numerical order.

Proofing symbols

Symbol	Meaning	What to do
(add text symbol)	Add text here	Write the symbol at the location in the text; write the text to be added in the margin with the symbol
(delete symbol)	Delete text	Put a horizontal line through the text to be deleted; put the symbol in the margin
/	Change letters or text	Put a slash through the letters to be changed; write the changes followed by "/" in the margin
(triple underline)	Change to capitals	Underline the letters to be changed; write "caps" in the margin
(lower case symbol)	Change to lower case	Put a slash through the letters; write the symbol in the margin
(transpose symbol)	Transpose letters or words	Use the symbol looped under and over letters or words to be exchanged; put the symbol in the margin
(close up symbol)	Close up	Write the symbol at the space to be eliminated and in the margin
(colon symbol)	Change punctuation to this	Put a slash through the incorrect punctuation in the text; write the correct punctuation encircled in the margin (in the example, the new punctuation is a colon)

The complete range of proofing symbols is given in the *Style Manual for Authors, Editors and Publishers* (2002) and the *Chicago Manual of Style* (1993) (see below).

Further reading You will find a range of books about writing in any large library or bookstore. There are books on writing science and popular science, writing in psychology, the humanities, or fiction, and on how to write a report or a term paper. I think that the most useful, basic, general account is O'Connor (1991). What she has to say is applicable to any kind of scientific writing and most archaeological writing. There is, however, a developing range of forms of writing archaeology that I have not discussed here at all. Approaches such as multiple stories in multiple voices and narration in fragments are enlivening the field considerably, as Joyce (2002) demonstrates. An excellent example is Schrire (1995). However, you will notice that such writing still needs structure, clarity, and precision.

For much more detailed and precise advice on technical aspects of writing (especially books), from when to use parentheses to proof reading, the *Chicago Manual of Style* (1993), now in its fourteenth edition, continues to be the basic guide, especially for readers in the United States:

- *Chicago Manual of Style*, 14th edn. Chicago: The University of Chicago Press, 1993.

PETER WHITE

The *Chicago Manual* is rivaled in clarity and comprehensiveness by the *Style Manual for Authors, Editors and Publishers* (2002). While its chapter on the legalities of publishing is directed to Australian conditions, in all other aspects it is internationally applicable. It is also elegant and easy to use:

- *Style Manual for Authors, Editors and Publishers*, 6th edn. Sydney: John Wiley, 2002.

References

Blau, S., Kennedy, B. J. and Kim, J. Y. 2002: An investigation of possible fluorosis in human dentition using synchrotron radiation. *Journal of Archaeological Science*, 29, 811–18.

Clark, J. D. 1975: A comparison of the Late Acheulean industries of Africa and the Middle East. In K. W. Butzer and G. L. Isaac (eds.), *After the Australopithecines*. The Hague: Mouton, 605–60.

Dickinson, W. R., Sinoto, Y. H., Shutler, R. Jr et al. 1999: Japanese Jomon sherds in artifact collections from Mele Plain on Efate in Vanuatu. *Archaeology in Oceania*, 34, 15–24.

Joyce, R. A. 2002: *The Languages of Archaeology*. Oxford: Blackwell.

Moser, S. 1998: *Ancestral Images: The Iconography of Human Origins*. Ithaca, NY: Cornell University Press.

O'Connor, M. 1991: *Writing Successfully in Science*. London: HarperCollins Academic.

Pfeiffer, J. 1969: *The Emergence of Man*. New York: Harper and Row.

Pitt Rivers, Lieutenant-General 1898: Address to the Archaeological Institute of Great Britain and Ireland. In *Excavations at Cranborne Chase, near Rushmore, on the borders of Dorset and Wilts*, vol. IV. Privately printed, 5–30.

Pluciennik, M. 1999: Archaeological narratives and other ways of telling. *Current Anthropology*, 40, 653–78.

Schrire, C. 1995: *Digging through Darkness*. Johannesburg: Witwatersrand University Press.

Stuiver, M., Reimer, P. J., Bard, E. et al., 1998: INTERCAL98 radiocarbon age calibration, 24,000 – 0 cal B.P. *Radiocarbon*, 40, 1041–84.

Tufte, E. R. 2001: *The Visual Display of Quantitative Information*, 2nd edn. Cheshire, CT: Graphics Press.

Wheeler, M. 1956: *Archaeology from the Earth*. Harmondsworth: Penguin.

Index